MW00619787

The Biography
Marcel Lefebvre

BERNARD TISSIER DE MALLERAIS

Translated from the French by Brian Sudlow, M.A.,
with additional material from Rev. Fr. Sebastian Wall
of the Society of Saint Pius X

Angelus
Press

PO Box 217 | Saint Marys, Kansas 66536

Library of Congress Cataloging-in-Publication Data

Tissier de Mallerais, Bernard, 1945-
  [Marcel Lefebvre. English]
  Marcel Lefebvre / Bernard Tissier de Mallerais ; translated from the French by
Brian Sudlow.
    p. cm.
  Originally published: Clovis, 2002.
  Includes bibliographical references and index.
  ISBN 1-892331-24-1 (alk. paper)
  1. Lefebvre, Marcel, 1905- 2. Catholic Traditionalist movement--History.
  3. Catholic Church--France--Bishops--Biography. I. Title.

  BX4705.L474T5713 2004
  282'.092--dc22

                                                              2004000120

Originally published as *Marcel Lefebvre*
© Clovis 2002

©2004 by Angelus Press

ANGELUS PRESS

PO Box 217
Saint Marys, Kansas 66536

Phone: 816-753-3150
FAX: 816-753-3557
Order Line: 1-800-966-7337

www.angeluspress.org

ISBN 978-1-892331-24-3
FIRST PRINTING—April 2004
FOURTH PRINTING—October 2020
Printed in the United States of America

CONTENTS

PART I
THE HEIR

PART II

THE MISSIONARY

PART III

THE COMBATANT

PART IV
THE RESTORER

PART I

THE HEIR

CHAPTER I

THE FAMILY SANCTUARY

I. ORIGINS

A LONG LINEAGE IN THE WOOL TRADE

As far back as records go, there seem always to have been Lefebvres in Tourcoing. When the merchant-manufacturer Henri Lefebvre married Isabeau Desrumeaux[1] on October 13, 1644, Tourcoing was a flourishing town completely dominated by its wool industry and numbering some fifteen thousand souls. Lille, nearby, was a major trading center for textiles, whilst Roubaix was still only a small borough. Walloon Flanders, which extended from Lys to Douai, was the southern region of the Spanish Low Countries until the armies of Louis XIV seized Lille and its dependencies for France in 1668. After the Spanish War of Succession (1701–1713), the Treaty of Utrecht fixed the border where it still lies today. This meant that when Jacques-Antoine Lefebvre, the son of Pierre-Allard Lefebvre, married Catherine Dumortier, on October 5, 1738, in Wasquehal, he was well and truly French. Their merchant son, Jean-Baptiste, had two sons of his own: Louis, from whom Joseph Cardinal Lefebvre, Archbishop of Bourges, was descended, and Jacques, who in 1799 married the daughter of a cloth merchant in Tourcoing.

Jacques Lefebvre was a merchant-manufacturer in Tourcoing. He would buy sheep, have them sheared, and the fresh fleeces would then be sent to his factory. The raw wool was combed, degreased and dried, and taken away to be spun. The combing and spinning was done by professional combers and spinners in their own homes. Then, the merchant-manufacturer sold the wool in Lille or sent it to buyers elsewhere.[2] Tourcoing was still surrounded by green fields, but its appearance began to change with the advent of steam-driven weaving looms powered by coal: as in Roubaix and Lille, factory chimneys sprang up everywhere, and the three towns were henceforth cloaked in a smoky mist.

The wool merchant Charles Lefebvre, known as Carlos, had a son called Eugène. He was a wool spinner in Tourcoing, and in 1878 in Lomme he married Marie Théry, the daughter of Henri-Théodore (from a

---

[1] Genealogy manuscript, Ecône Archives.
[2] Paul Delsalle, *Lille, Roubaix, Tourcoing: Histoire et traditions* (Éd. Charles Corlet, 1991), 84.

family of Lille lawyers) and Hortense van Rullen. Hortense and her daughter Marie, both heads of the Franciscan Tertiaries in their respective towns of Lille and Tourcoing, were devoted to the apostolate. Everyone called Marie "good Madame Lefebvre."[3]

Eugène Lefebvre, a hardworking businessman who enjoyed good relations with his workforce, successfully ran the wool spinning business of Vermersch-Lefebvre. Without being very religious he was nonetheless a man of his word: His wife, who died a holy death on October 8, 1917, asked him to say his rosary every day; he kept his promise and said the rosary every evening with the cook, Adelaide.[4] He died on February 8, 1926. He had two children: René, who was born on February 23, 1879, and Marguerite, who married the Roubaix industrialist Alphonse Lemaire.

René Lefebvre, the future father of Archbishop Lefebvre, had been a boarder at an rigorous school run by the Jesuits at Boulogne-sur-Mer.[5] His father spared no efforts to make a successful industrialist out of him; he spoke good English and German, and had been to Germany to study working practices. However, he was an only son with a delicate and sensitive temperament. He was also a little timid, very pious, and rather given to solitary reflection, whence his aspirations to the consecrated life, in particular as a Benedictine.[6] He was thinking about this when he met a young woman from Roubaix, Gabrielle Watine.

GABRIELLE LEFEBVRE-WATINE

The Watine family was a good example of leading northern stock who had been successful in industry. Louis Watine (1814–1883), the son of Philippe Watine-Meurisse, was a manufacturer in Roubaix. He married Elise Wattine from Tourcoing, the granddaughter of Pierre Wattines-Dewavrin (1719–1812), who was an architect and in 1800 mayor of Tourcoing. Their second son, Louis Watine (1848–1919), was a cloth manufacturer and vice president of the savings bank.[7] His wife Gabrielle Lorthiois, whom he married June 27, 1874, looked to him for clear guidance and constant support.

The Lorthiois family were noted for their militant Catholic faith and an optimism that got things done. By 1940 there were 1,200 descendants of Louis Lorthiois-Duquennoy (1764–1810) of whom sixty had become

3   Joseph Valynseele and Denis Grando, *A la recherche de leurs racines: Généalogies de 85 célébrités*, 1st series, *L'intermédiaire des chercheurs et des curieux* (Paris: 1988); Rev. Louis Le Crom et al., *Un père et une mère: brève biographie de M. et Mme Lefebvre, parents de S. Exc. Mgr. Marcel Lefebvre* (Bulle, Switzerland: Controverses, 1993), 22.
4   Joseph Lefebvre, Letter of June 1997.
5   Pierre Pouchain, *Les maîtres du Nord du XIXe siècle à nos jours* (Perrin, 1998), 251.
6   Le Crom, *Un père et une mère*, 21.
7   Valynseele, *A la recherche de leurs racines*, 126.

priests, monks, or nuns and scattered across the globe. It was from this lineage blessed by God that Gabrielle Lorthiois was born in 1855, the twelfth of thirteen children. Her father, Floris Lorthiois, who was a carpet maker in Tourcoing, had married Marie van Dooren, who was twenty years his junior. Two of Gabrielle Lorthiois's sisters became nuns; if she herself did not receive a calling she was consoled by the fact that thirteen of her grandchildren were consecrated to our Lord. The Roubaix Franciscan Third Order of which she was the president could not give her enough to do. She walked quickly through the streets of the town getting help and work for numerous religious communities.

From the busy and productive home of Louis Watine and Gabrielle Lorthiois, God raised up an elite soul: Archbishop Lefebvre's mother, Gabrielle Watine. If it is true that "the soul of a priest is formed on his mother's lap" then seeking to know Gabrielle Watine will help us understand Archbishop Lefebvre more fully. Gabrielle Watine was born in Roubaix on July 4, 1880, the fourth of seven children. As a schoolgirl she was plainly drawn to piety. Her conduct complemented her prayers, and she was a good influence on her companions; in a word, she was a child of duty. Family life was marked by faith, prayer, and a spirit of sacrifice, and zeal for relieving the sufferings of others.

Gabrielle Watine clearly inherited her mother's energetic spirit and was a good example to others. She accompanied her mother on visits to working families and the poor under the aegis of the St. Vincent de Paul Society; seeing the weeping sores and pale faces of the anaemic[8] was a valuable experience. At sixteen, Gabrielle was sent to the boarding school of the Bernadine Ladies of Esquermes in Lille, where her aunt, Sister Marie-Clothilde (Clara Lorthiois), was a nun. There she showed "a balanced temperament, smiling energy, a pleasant manner, modesty and gentleness."[9] Her personality came out in the discussions of ideas in which she participated energetically, never wanting to give way out of weakness. When she had finished her education, Gabrielle Watine was uncertain about her future. Should she become a nun? After much prayer and reflection, and having discussed the matter with Mgr. Fichaux, her spiritual director, she decided she should marry.[10]

---

[8] Letter of Sister Marie-Louise to Sister Marie-Christiane Lefebvre, June 20, 1947; Le Crom, *Un père et une mere*, 15,17.

[9] Letter of Sister Saint John to Sister M.-Christiane, Oct. 28, 1947.

[10] Pouchain, *Les maîtres du Nord*, 145; Le Crom, *Un père et une mère*, 21.

6 MARCEL LEFEBVRE

II. THE FAMILY HOME

MARRIAGE—HONEYMOON—SETTLING IN

On what criteria were the young woman and her parents to select a husband? The big factories in the North depended on family relations and alliances, although one could not say that marriages, which require natural affection, were solely determined by self-interest. The daily life of the textile factory owners united family and business concerns. However, the moral and religious criteria were no less important.[11] A curate from Our Lady of Tourcoing vouched for René Lefebvre's moral character, and introduced him to the family. The young man was eighteen months older than Gabrielle. He was slim and rather tall, with brown hair, soft blue-green eyes, a straight nose, and a small moustache; he soon won the hearts of Mr. and Mrs. Watine as well as Gabrielle.

René Lefebvre and Gabrielle Watine were married on April 16, 1902, in St. Martin's Church in Roubaix by the Dean, Fr. Berteaux. The young couple went on honeymoon to visit the Virgin of the Grotto in Lourdes since René had been a helper for the sick since 1897. They then went to Rome where they received the blessing of Pope Leo XIII.[12] On their return to Tourcoing, the young couple moved into a small house on Rue Leverrier, a quiet street of sober red brick façades and impeccably aligned windows. It was a model of the ordered urban life of the region.[13]

THE FAMILY SANCTUARY

The first child was born on January 22, 1903, and was given his father's Christian name, René. He was followed by Jeanne in 1904. Marcel arrived on Wednesday, November 29, 1905, too late to be baptized that day. The following day on the feast of the crucified apostle, St. Andrew, lover of our Lord's Cross, the child's uncle Louis Watine-Duthoit and his aunt Marguerite Lemaire-Lefebvre took the boy to the baptistery in the Church of Our Lady and named him Marcel François Marie Joseph: Marie and Joseph were included by every northern Catholic family among their children's names; they chose François because of the family association with the Franciscan Tertiaries, and Marcel in reparation for the disgraceful incarceration of Pope St. Marcel, whose stable-cell in Rome had so touched Mrs. Lefebvre.[14] The Archbishop's mother never waited to be back on her feet before having the children baptized; the family went to

---

[11] Pouchain, *Les maîtres du Nord*, 92; *Biographie de M. François Flipo, 1869-1941* (n.p., n.d.), quoted by Pouchain, 82.
[12] Mrs. Lefebvre, Letter to Sister M.-Clothilde, May 17, 1902.
[13] Le Crom, *Un père et une mère*, 22.
[14] Mother Marie-Christiane, *Mon frère, Monseigneur Marcel* (manuscript, 1991), 1.

the church without her and it was only after the ceremony that she was happy to hold the baby, born again to the divine life and resplendent with sanctifying grace. When Louise, the maid, gave her Marcel to kiss, Mrs. Lefebvre received one of those intuitions which she often had: "He will have an important role in the Church close to the Pope."[15]

Convinced that the future of a Catholic homeland depends on fruitful Christian marriages, the Lefebvre-Watines wanted to surround themselves with many children, and so in 1907 Bernadette was born. Her mother said of her that she would be "a sign of contradiction," which is what the future Sister Marie-Gabriel would in fact become when she, together with her brother, founded the Congregation of the Sisters of the Society of Saint Pius X. In 1908 came Christiane, the last of the five older children. Mrs. Lefebvre predicted that she would become a Carmelite, which was indeed the case; moreover she re-established the traditional Carmelites. The last additions to the family were Joseph, born in 1914, Michel in 1920, and Marie-Thérèse in 1925.

As a mother Mrs. Lefebvre was profoundly spiritual and extremely apostolic; we must bear in mind these characteristics of her moral physiognomy since Marcel was to inherit them. She was a qualified Red Cross nurse and devoted one and a half days a week to the care of the sick in a clinic, seeking out the tasks which others preferred to avoid. She and her husband were also members of the St. Vincent de Paul Society, but her most important apostolate was with the Franciscan Tertiaries. Under the guidance of Mrs. Lefebvre, who became president of the chapter in Tourcoing, the number of Third Order "sisters" reached eight hundred. The novice mistresses were chosen by her, and they had their own retreats.

Her spiritual director, Fr. Huré, was a Montfortian priest. Her soul attained a state of constant union with Jesus Christ, and she meditated and did spiritual reading. She was courageous and magnanimous, and practiced mortification and self-sacrifice. In 1917, she took a vow always to do the more perfect thing (which she renewed at each confession). She lived by faith, referring everything to God and His holy will, and the most abiding characteristic of her soul was gratitude to Divine Providence. Moreover, she was an excellent educator. Her husband set high standards for his children, but tended to be excessively severe in his demands. She, on the other hand, was more balanced; she preferred to guide the family by establishing an atmosphere of trust that never crushed the children's spontaneity, but stimulated their generosity by good example.[16]

---

[15] Fr. Jean-Jacques Marziac, *Monseigneur Lefebvre, soleil levant ou couchant?* (Paris: NEL, 1979), 55.

[16] Le Crom, *Un père et une mère*, 28; Interview with Mother Marie-Christiane, May 18, 1996; Joseph Lefebvre, Letter of June 1997.

The Lefebvres' home was a sanctuary with its own liturgy. Whilst Father went to Mass with Louise at 6:15 A.M. and served for the Dean, Mother woke the children, made the sign of the cross on their foreheads, and made sure they made their morning offering. Then she went to Mass at 7:00 A.M. with the children who were old enough to walk. When they were older, they went to Mass at boarding school.[17] Every evening, family prayers gave them the opportunity to put right any disagreements that might have occurred throughout the day, and to unite their hearts in God's love. The children never went to bed without receiving their parents' blessing. Christiane later said: "In May we would make a pilgrimage to La Marlière on the outskirts of Tourcoing near the Belgian border. We tried to make a novena of pilgrimages during the month. We had to get up at 5:00 A.M. and walk for three quarters of an hour (fasting), hear Mass at 6:00, then come back in time for classes."[18]

FIRST COMMUNION

In January 1908, the family moved to a larger house, 131 (later 151) Rue Nationale. The two elder children went to school; René at the Sacred Heart School and Jeanne at Convent of the Immaculate Conception. The convent stood at 7, Place Notre Dame and had been built by the Sainte-Union Sisters.[19] The secularized Ursulines took over from them in 1905.[20] The school accepted boys in the lower primary classes and Marcel was among them. A postcard from 1911 shows some of the children sitting on the grass at the garden entrance in front of the statue of our Lady; Marcel can be recognized from the long fringe that hangs just above his solemn and attentive eyes.

After a preparatory retreat and having been to confession–one of the first, if not the first, times he received the sacrament of penance–Marcel made his first Holy Communion on December 25, 1911, at the Convent of the Immaculate Conception. Since he was already six, there was no special permission needed to receive communion; the kindly Fr. Varasse willingly applied the decree of St. Pius X which had been issued the previous year. The Pope's decision met some resistance here and there, and St. Pius X once complained to Bishop Chesnelong of Valence: "In France my decree allowing small children to receive Communion is bitterly criticized. Well, We say that there will be saints from among those children, you'll

[17] Interview with Mother Marie-Christiane, May 18, 1996; Letter of Joseph Lefebvre to the author, June 1997.
[18] Mother Marie-Christiane Lefebvre, *Mon frère, Monseigneur Marcel*, 4-5.
[19] Congregation of teaching sisters founded in 1826 in Douai by Fr. Jean-Baptist Debrabant. It spread throughout Europe, America, and Cameroon. (*Annuaire des missions catholiques d'Afrique, délégation apostolique de Dakar* [1959], 52).
[20] *Historique de l'Immaculée*, Mrs. Fidélio Henri-Rousseau, 3 pages typed.

see!" As indeed we have! During the Midnight Mass, celebrated at 7:00 A.M. by Fr. Varrasse, Marcel had his first intimate conversation with the Eucharistic Lord. He was the youngest of the fifteen communicants;[21] later, at home he took his finest pen and wrote to the Pope to thank him for the decree which enabled him to receive Holy Communion at the age of six. From now on he was able to receive Communion every day. His enlightened soul went straight to God with the greatest simplicity, as his sister Christiane observed: "Without realizing it," she said, "he radiated God, peace, and a sense of duty."[22] But the child was not cut off from the events which affected his family: his father's business and very soon the war.

III. A NORTHERN CATHOLIC FACTORY OWNER AT WORK

THE BUSINESS

Marcel Lefebvre was very much influenced by the atmosphere of work that prevailed in the North. It was a part of the country, he said, where one worked and where work decided everything. From half past five in the morning one could hear the factories starting up. The worker would get to work at six and would stay until the sound of the bell, and that, six days out of seven. This monotonous life ticked away beneath a grey sky that encouraged work rather than lazing about. The people liked working and they would have been unhappy if they could not have gone to work; such was their life.[23] For a long time the factory owners and their families used to live on the work premises, like the Lefebvres' grandfather, Floris Lorthiois (1793–1872). Their dwelling would be adjacent to the factory.[24] Many owners would get to work before their workers, have a short break at lunch time with their wife, and then come back to work until nine or ten at night.[25]

René Lefebvre had been trained by his father in this hard school of work, and although he liked his job he also wanted to sanctify each day by Mass and Communion in the morning. Then, after a good cup of black coffee, he would walk the ten minutes it took to get from his home to the family factory at 18 (later 10), Rue du Bus. He kept the wool industry tradition of his family in making yarns for the popular balls of wool sold under the brand name "Sphinx."[26]

---

[21] *Cahier de l'abbé Varrasse*, First Communion register kept by him.

[22] Mother Marie-Christiane Lefebvre, *Mon frère, Monseigneur Marcel*, 1.

[23] Cf. *Petite histoire de ma longue histoire*, autobiography of Archbishop Marcel Lefebvre told to the Society Sisters (Corlet, 1999), 10-12. [Published in English as *The Little Story of My Long Life*, by the Sisters of the Society of Saint Pius X (Browerville, 2002).]

[24] Pouchain, *Les maîtres du Nord*, 94.

[25] Cf. *Georges Motte, Industriel, 1846-1904* (n.p., n.d.), quoted by Pouchain, 95.

[26] Stationery heading of the business.

JUSTICE AND SOCIAL WORKS OF CHARITY—THE CORPORATIONS

With regard to his workers, René Lefebvre was good and kind but he was also bound by economic necessities and could not abdicate his responsibilities. In the nineteenth century the prevailing liberalism propagated a false idea of a just wage as simply a portion of the cost price. In order to make up for low wages factory owners in the North developed charitable institutions: through charity they gave freely what they did not believe themselves obliged to give in justice. In opposition to this compromise, René de La Tour du Pin's[27] social theories claimed that the worker's salary should take into account all his needs and those of his family. Leo XIII's encyclical *Rerum Novarum* (May 15, 1891) approved this idea to some extent.

However, the Northern factory owners did not limit themselves to charitable works such as providing workers with free lodging and insurance. They created true works of social justice such as savings banks, and notably real negotiating bodies. In 1884 under Camille Féron-Vrau in Lille and Fr. Fichaux in Tourcoing, thirty-six of them founded the Catholic Association of Northern Factory Owners (ACPN).[28] This body created corporations or unions for both workers and owners, bringing them together through their business interests and professions, rather than dividing them on the grounds of class. The Northern factory owners were applying the principles laid down by Pius XI in *Quadragesimo Anno* (1931): social justice can never be so perfect that there is no need of charity to make good what is lacking. Even if social justice manages to suppress all the causes of injustice, it still cannot bring about the union of hearts–a task which belongs to charity alone.[29]

Along with the corporations the ACPN also founded in 1888 "Our Lady's Factory Confraternities." There were four thousand members and they were based on the worker's apostolate among his peers, for example, through the owners' nominating "dizeniers": exemplary workers. The confraternities had their own ceremonies and public processions. Thanks to the binary structure of corporation-confraternity, a complete Christian social order flourished. René Lefebvre, who believed in the principles of order and hierarchy, was an ardent defender of the system of corporations

---

[27] [René de la Tour du Pin (Arrancy, 1834–Lausanne, 1924). An associate of Albert de Mun, he was a champion of the Church and the working classes. He collaborated in the foundation of *Cercles Catholiques d'Ouvriers* (1871), denounced liberalism in his monthly magazine, *L'Association Catholique* (1874-1891), and promoted corporatism as the ideal Catholic economic policy. Trans.]

[28] René Talmy, *L'Association catholique des Patrons du Nord* (Lille: Fac. Catholiques, 1962).

[29] *A.A.S.* 23 (1931), 223; (Bonne Presse), VII, 167-8; cf. Calvet and Perrin, *L'Eglise et société économique* (Aubier, 1959), 226-227.

because by their very nature they were counter-revolutionary, hindered class warfare, and promoted the sort of charity that brings the classes together.[30]

---

[30] Talmy, *L'Association des Patrons du Nord*, 51-56.

CHAPTER 2

VOCATION

I. THE TRIALS OF THE GREAT WAR

The Great War began. Marcel Lefebvre's childhood was deeply marked by these events, and he described them as he had experienced them: almost overnight, all the men were mobilized and the women were left alone at home with their children. In schools only old or medically unfit teachers remained, and in parishes the curates were gone: where there had been five or six priests there were now only one or two. Then came the battles. News arrived from the front and the wounded who were brought back told their own tales. There were many deaths, and large numbers of prisoners were taken.

RENÉ AND GABRIELLE LEFEBVRE, TWO HEROES WHO FOUGHT FOR THEIR COUNTRY[1]

As a father of six children, René Lefebvre was exempt from conscription, but he offered his services to the Society for the Relief of Wounded Soldiers in Tourcoing; he went by car through the German control points to look for wounded French soldiers. The enemy troops very quickly invaded Lille on September 2, 1914, and by October the suburbs were also occupied. The entry of Bavarian troops into Lille on October 13 was preceded by an intense bombardment of the city. From Tourcoing, Marcel Lefebvre could see the flames and the following day he watched as the hussars and uhlans (or mounted lancers) rode by.

Once Tourcoing had been occupied, René Lefebvre looked after the wounded French prisoners and took advantage of his position to help English prisoners escape. From January 1915, feeling himself watched, he carefully hid his stock of wool, and went into Holland using documents from Belgian Intelligence and thence to England, where he undertook missions to Belgium on behalf of the Intelligence Service. Returning to France he was a courier for the S.S.B.M radiological bureau at the front, and then administrator of Hospital 60 in Paris.

---

[1] Lefebvre, *Petite histoire*, 13, 15; Le Crom, *Un père et une mère*, 24-25, 88-89; Mother Marie-Christiane Lefebvre, *Mon frère, Monseigneur Marcel*, 9.

Mrs. Lefebvre was left alone to look after the house and the factory. More than once Marcel was struck by her strength of soul. The people were more or less starving; Marcel later recalled the soup kitchens which were set up in the Town Hall, the American chickens which were rotting by the time they arrived, the bread that was black and sticky beneath the crust... The Germans requisitioned the factory stocks in 1915 and discovered any hiding places...then they took away or destroyed the machines in order to inflict a lasting handicap on any dangerous competition. Finally, they demanded collaboration with the Reich's war effort. The factory owners made their *non possumus*–their refusal. Whereupon they were imprisoned the same day and soon 131 inhabitants of Roubaix were deported to Güstow in Mecklenburg, amongst them Felix Watine, Mrs. Lefebvre's brother.[2]

The valiant Christian woman and patriot turned to *agere contra*, the counter attack. She redoubled her efforts in the clinic where she contracted scabies. The sister who treated her using a scrub brush declared in admiration to the children: "Your mother is a saint!"[3] In the school infirmary she even looked after the wounded Germans, but when German deaconesses were billeted with the family, the living rooms on the ground floor were out of bounds to them, and she only offered basic rooms on the third floor to visiting troops. When she pushed the German occupiers too far, she was locked up for several days in the cellars of Tourcoing Town Hall.

HARD TRIALS—RENÉ'S VOCATION

They remained close to the front which moved from Belgium to Ypres, and then to the infamous Mount Kemmel. Marcel Lefebvre could recall the evenings and nights when exploding shells constantly lit up the horizon; all the sky seemed ablaze and there was an incessant thunder of artillery. The following day the convoys of German wounded would arrive at the improvised hospital opposite the Lefebvres' house.

On Good Friday 1916[4] the Germans announced the mobilization of all girls aged seventeen and over to work in their munitions factories. The order was given for them to be ready and waiting on the sidewalk. Behind the curtains the Lefebvre children watched the foray. The continual worry, and now the cruel abductions, made an impression on their souls. Archbishop Lefebvre would say later: "It changed us. Even if you're only nine, ten, or eleven years old, you can't help it...War is really a terrible thing....Obviously it affected us, the older children. We five, we were

---

[2]   Pouchain, *Les maîtres du Nord*, 195-198; 200-201.
[3]   Sister Marie-Christiane, Letter of Sept. 9, 1996.
[4]   Bishop H. Masquelier, *Madame Paul Féron-Vrau* (Paris: Bonne Presse, 1931), 193; Lefebvre, *Petite histoire*, 11.

scarred by those events, and I think that in part at least we owe our vocation to them. We saw that human life was insignificant and that one has to know how to suffer."[5]

In 1917, the war would bring another separation for Mrs. Lefebvre that would play a providential role in Marcel's future life. René, his elder brother, was now fourteen years old; to avoid the obligatory work service imposed by the Germans he escaped, taking a Red Cross train via Switzerland and finally rejoining his father in April 1917 in Versailles. He stayed there for two years to finish his studies in the minor seminary of Grandchamp, not because he had already told anyone that he felt called to the missions, but because he was made welcome there as being from an occupied area.

Finally the armistice was declared on November 11, 1918, bringing peace to the ruins of Europe. Mr. Lefebvre could finally go home. On December 2, all the family went to Lourdes to thank the Blessed Virgin; then they went to Versailles for a month to be with René. The excellent priest Fr. Henri Collin, who was René's philosophy teacher, prepared little Joseph for his first Communion at the age of five and even gave almost daily lessons to Marcel![6] Fr. Collin was very keen on Rome and much attached to Rome's French Seminary where he had studied from 1910 to 1914. When he heard about René's vocation he said to Mr. Lefebvre: "You must send your son to Rome!" And since René was still hesitant, his father decided for him: "I'm determined for you to go to Rome!"[7] At Easter 1919, René, the sixteen-year-old minor seminarian, received the cassock. He came home for the summer and left for Rome on October 24;[8] he would be Marcel's forerunner.

II. AT THE SACRED HEART SCHOOL

BEFORE THE WAR: 1912-14

Marcel Lefebvre attended the Ursuline school until November 19, 1912.[9] It was a grey winter day when he was taken by his elder brother for the first time to the Sacred Heart School which he attended as a day boy. Founded in 1666 by the Récollet Fathers, the original St. Bonaventure's School had had to close in 1790. In 1802 Tourcoing Council opened a secondary school on the property which was soon handed over to be run by the diocesan clergy (the diocese was Cambrai). In 1853 the school

---

5 *Ibid.,* 19-20.
6 Letter of Mrs. Lefebvre to Sister Marie-Clothilde, Jan. 23, 1919.
7 Letter of René Lefebvre (father) to René, Feb. 13, 1931.
8 Letter of Mrs. Lefebvre to Sister M.-Clotilde, Nov. 12, 1919.
9 Letter of Mrs. Fidélio Henri-Rousseau, 1998.

moved to a disused factory on Rue de Lille and in 1871 the Superior, Fr. Lecomte, rededicated it to the Sacred Heart.[10]

The school's life was centered on the vast chapel where the students' minds were directed towards the sanctuary. Hundreds of pupils came to daily morning Mass and assisted at the retreats at the start of the school year or the recollections in preparation for Confirmation and their Solemn Communion.[11] Every morning Marcel would look at the rose window above the high altar. It was an image of the Presentation of the Blessed Virgin and showed a young, determined Mary climbing the steps of the sanctuary to offer herself to the Lord. This picture of generosity could only imprint itself on his soul.[12]

Marcel went into Fr. Beaudier's fourth grade class where he met Robert Lepoutre, who was to become a great friend. The superior at that time was Fr. Achille Leleu. The school was five minutes' walk from home. Every morning the two boys went to Mass or at least received Holy Communion at Notre Dame Church, and later their mothers or one of the two servants packed them off to school for the first class at 8 o' clock. There were classes until 10 o'clock, then private study from ten till midday when the pupils could either eat at school or go home if it was not too far. The afternoon began at 1:30 P.M. with private study for half an hour followed by classes until 4 o'clock when there was a short recreation. Then there was study until 6:30 P.M. and a spiritual talk before the school day finished at 7 o' clock.

Marcel had to put up with his elder brother's friends making fun of him: "Teeny, weeny, titchy!" He governed his tongue and never answered, knowing full well that they would soon get tired of it if he pretended not to hear. But things were quite different when one day he saw a small boy being turned into a punching bag. As soon as they were out of sight of the school his companions fell upon the boy, but Marcel immediately came to his aid and sent the other boys packing with bruised pride.[13]

In 1913 he went up to fifth grade under Fr. Patoor; he maintained a high score average and gained five certificates of merit.[14]

---

[10] Sacred Heart School prospectus, 1989.
[11] [The French still have the custom of two "first" Holy Communions. The "private Communion" takes place when the child is six or seven in accordance with the custom of the Church since St. Pius X. The "Solemn Communion" takes place when the child is around twelve years of age. It used to mark not only the first reception of Holy Communion but also the child's elevation to a more adult status. From then on, children were allowed to sit at table with their parents to eat, serve themselves at mealtimes, and enjoy other privileges. Thus historically the "Solemn Communion" marked an important social step as well as a sacramental one. Trans.]
[12] Interview with Paul Loridant, May 29, 1997, ms. II, 23, 59.
[13] Mother Marie-Christiane Lefebvre, *Mon frère, Monseigneur Marcel*, 5.
[14] Prize lists of July 1914, Archives of Sacred Heart School.

THE WAR YEARS 1914-18: MARCEL'S VOCATION

In 1914 the college lost many teachers, sometimes the best ones, who were conscripted as chaplains to the army. Any replacement priest is unfortunately bound to be somewhat lost. There was complete chaos in the classroom and Marcel was so indignant about it that his mother had to go and complain to the superiors. Christiane who reported the incident concluded: "Unfairness whether in games or the way things were run really made him hopping mad."[15] Marcel went into sixth grade-A1 in 1915 and kept up an impressive standard; he received twelve nominations for prizes in July 1916. That year he joined the Congregation of the Holy Angels, a piety group organized for pupils of his age, and he made the act of consecration to the Holy Angels with his friends Jacques Dumortier, Christian Leurent, and Georges Donze.[16]

The school year from 1916-1917 was disrupted by the partial, and later, total requisitioning of the school by the German Army (with the exception of the chapel). Classes took place in temporary classrooms. Some patriotic pupils who were arrested for misdeeds against the German Army were freed thanks to the intervention of Fr. Maurice Lehembre, the German teacher: his case for the defense delivered in polished German impressed the judges, and they let the children off.[17]

The school year from 1917-1918 was decisive in Marcel's spiritual, moral, and intellectual development (classes were still being held in temporary accommodation). He showed his courage and piety by going each day before the lifting of the curfew to serve the Mass of his confessor, Fr. Desmarchelier. One morning he just managed to escape the clutches of a German patrol that seemed to be lying in wait for him and could easily have manhandled him. In these conditions would he be able to carry on serving Mass? Father simply advised him to go via the street on the other side, Rue de l'Abattoir. Was that safer? Marcel made an act of faith and courage each morning for which God could only bless him.

Whenever Mother Marie Christiane was asked her opinion as to when her brother Marcel received his vocation, she would reply: "I think he always had it!"[18] One day when they were both studying at opposite ends of the table in the dining room, she asked him straight out: "What are you thinking of doing when you grow up? What are you going to become?" But straightaway I realized that he would let nothing slip and would just tease me. So I carried on: "Are you thinking of becoming a priest?"

"Oh, more than that!"

---

[15]   Mother Marie-Christiane Lefebvre, *Mon frère, Monseigneur Marcel*, 5.
[16]   Sacred Heart School Archives, 25 Z 16, book 35.
[17]   Sacred Heart School, Commemorative Album, 1865-1965, 31-32.
[18]   Interview with the author, May 18, 1996.

"You're not supposed to want to be a bishop!"

"Why not, St. Paul said you could."

"So, you want to be a bishop!"

"Oh, more than that!"

"At any rate, you can't become Pope because these days only Italians become Pope."

"O.k. then, almost Pope!"

"But he was just teasing me, so I got huffy and shut up. Funnily enough, without meaning to, wasn't he predicting what would happen later on in life?"[19]

The gifted Fr. Louis Desmarchelier helped reveal the boy's vocation, especially in the eighth grade when he was their main teacher (1917-1918). The whole class looked up to him, and he turned them into a model class. "Did Marcel have a part to play in this?" Christiane wondered. Probably, if his results are anything to go by: first prize for overall effort and for Greek (a new subject), second prize for classical recitation and a dozen merit certificates, the second of which was for Religious Education.[20] At the end of the school year the whole class got together and successfully petitioned the superior to be allowed to keep their teacher for another year. He was spiritual director to most of the pupils and proved to be a choice instrument of divine grace. Of the ten or twelve former pupils who spent two years with Fr. Desmarchelier, only two got married and all the others entered the religious life.[21]

In October 1918 Tourcoing had the great joy of being liberated a few weeks before the armistice. For the new school year the pupils could at last return to their classrooms. Marcel was in the ninth grade with his beloved Fr. Desmarchelier. 1919 was his best year and in the school prize ceremony he was nominated for fourteen awards in total: he won first prize for overall effort and Latin and Greek composition, and second prize for mathematics. He joined the school's Congregation of the Blessed Virgin. Reading carefully through the records of the meetings shows how truly zealous this group was in teaching the Catholic Faith and devotion to the Blessed Virgin, for example, as shown in the explanations of the meaning of the Marian feasts. Marcel was a keen member of this congregation, becoming a "member" in 1918-19, "counsellor" in 1920, and finally "prefect" in 1922-23. He similarly became a member of the Eucharistic Crusade in 1920 and proudly wore its badge. "Prayer, communion, sacrifice, and apostolate" is the demanding motto of the Crusade, and Marcel practiced it generously both at school and at home.

---

[19]   Mother Marie-Christiane Lefebvre, *Mon frère, Monseigneur Marcel*, 6-7.

[20]   Prize list, the war years 1917-1918.

[21]   Mother Marie-Christiane Lefebvre, *Mon frère, Monseigneur Marcel*, 6.

III. GROWING UP (1920-23)

FR. BELLE'S PUPIL

After a modest tenth grade, in 1920–21 Marcel Lefebvre went into the "rhetoric" class, *i.e.,* junior year, in the literary stream run by Fr. Belle. The class photograph, taken by Tourte and Petitin,[22] shows a young man in school uniform seated with his arms crossed. His face is pale and calm and bears a thoughtful, slightly mischievous look. There is nothing to show the difficulties that Marcel was going through at that time in his studies as indicated by his mediocre results. Nonetheless, Fr. Maurice Belle, the rhetoric teacher, drove his pupils: "He thinks, he captivates; he seizes his listeners, leading them to think and be captivated with him. He was a good psychologist too; to a pupil who tended to be over-romantic–not Marcel Lefebvre–he wrote: "You must toughen up, look at things with more simplicity, love action...."[23]

Action was certainly something that Marcel, a member of several organizations, did not lack. How then are we to explain his difficulties with school work? Was it an adolescent crisis? Probably not, considering his zeal in attending meetings and his constant willingness to help. Doubtless that year when he turned fifteen Marcel was growing too fast and he was working too hard. He was also especially troubled by his mother's illness–she had Pott's disease. From April 1920 to May 1921 she had to stay prostrate, encased in a corset of plaster of Paris, sleepless, tortured, living like Jesus on the Cross, although her face was nonetheless radiant and her soul united to God. What an example of Christian suffering for Marcel! But he was very painfully aware of his mother's inability to look after her children.[24] On July 1, however, he sat the first part of his baccalaureate,[25] which he seems to have failed.[26] At any rate he had to retake his eleventh grade. His second year in 1921-22 must have been a considerable consolation to his parents, for his certificate contains nine prizes including a second prize for excellence; a third prize for mathematics indicates that he was good at scientific as well as literary subjects.

As "counsellor" he took the chair for the meetings of the Congregation of the Blessed Virgin. The notes taken by Georges Donze reveal that a wind of reform was shaking the congregation! On February 13, 1922, Georges Donze asked: "What is a member of our congregation?" He continued by "saying what he is not: first of all he is not a snitch, nor a public

---

[22] Souvenir Album 1920-1921.
[23] Commemorative Album, 41.
[24] Le Crom, *Un père et une mère*, 25.
[25] Letter of Mrs. Lefebvre to Sister M.-Clotilde, June 20, 1921.
[26] Prize list from 1921, where Marcel's name is not on the list of people who passed in July, nor on the list of those who sat the examination.

censor. He is first of all a pupil who stands by his fellow pupils." Marcel Lefebvre was not influenced by this feeble logic. He took issue with it at the meeting of June 12. The secretary's report begins with these words: "Marcel Lefebvre forgot to read the title of his submission. It seems he talked about the necessity of informing authority." The young orator talked about "three ways of stopping evil, especially in bad conversations: 1) by not approving of it–not smiling nor agreeing, 2) by protesting, 3) by telling the necessary authority...and doing similarly in the case of bad books."[27] This was an adolescent who had not mastered the art of presenting a speech, but who would not tolerate the chaos caused by bad example, and who was conscientious in helping authority.

A ROBUST PHILOSOPHER

In October 1922, Marcel went into the philosophy class. Fr. Joseph Deconinck, his teacher, had been a pupil of Fr. Lagrange, O.P., in Jerusalem. In 1912, he was writing a thesis on Sacred Scripture but when he realized it would put him in the camp opposed by the authorities in the Church–who at that stage were trying to eradicate modernism[28]–Fr. Deconinck burned his work.[29] But would this admirable act of submission make the priest fit to train young minds? According to his pupils, he was trying rather to "train their hearts."[30] To this end he took his philosophy pupils two years in a row to Verdun to show them where he had distinguished himself as a chaplain to a Zouave regiment. "I want to make you understand what these men went through at Douaumont in the trenches with bayonets," he said. The young men were impressed by the long march past the shell holes looking for the bones of old soldiers to take to the ossuary...

The young students really took to the "scientific philosophy" taught by Fr. Deconinck, but what Marcel really excelled in was "psychology and metaphysics," receiving the first prize ahead of his friend Jacques Dumortier. He received other prizes, and notably–and this might surprise some readers–first prize for physical education! He had a good physique that was well filled out; isn't that just what is needed for the hard life of a missionary? But the young athlete seems to have been keen on acting, too, if we are to believe the testimony of his sister Bernadette: "Sunday afternoon at four, Dad, Christiane, and I are going to see *Polyeucte*. We've got very good seats....It's amazing how many people are going. Marcel will be the bish-

27 Sacred Heart School Archives (minutes of the meetings of the Congregation of the Blessed Virgin).
28 Motu proprio *Sacrorum Antistitum*, Sept. 1, 1910 (Bonne Presse), V, 146.
29 According to a written note on Canon Deconinck, by Bishop Georges Leclercq, 1975.
30 Interview with Dr. Henri Dessonets, May 16, 1997, ms. II, 15, 50-51.

op: he has to pour water over Polyeucte. He doesn't have any lines. Someone else in the wings will sing for him. He just has to pretend he is singing." And there he was, Marcel Lefebvre the bishop, "baptizing" Christian Leurant, while Robert Lepoutre played Felix and Hippolyte Scalabre was Pauline.[31]

"Fr. Deco's Old Boys"

In Marcel Lefebvre's last two years of high school there were many striking personalities. Besides Georges Donze whom we have already mentioned, who became a priest and later rector of the major seminary in Lille, and who died in the battle for Boulogne on May 26, 1940, there was Georges Leclercq, the future rector of the Catholic University of Lille, and Henri Duprez, an industrialist and active member of *"Bourgeoisie Chrétienne."* He founded the Roubaix-Tourcoing Factory Owners Union[32] to which Jacques Dumortier was secretary. The philosophy pupils Fr. Deconinck taught during his two years in Tourcoing (1921–22 and 1922–23) decided to keep in touch with their former teacher and each other. This developed into an association called "Fr. Deco's Old Boys"; they had an annual meeting from then on and also produced a newsletter.[33]

In 1945 there were fifty-five members on the role of whom thirteen were dead. Of those fifty-five there were twenty-eight priests or religious including four missionaries, one Trappist, two Dominicans, and a Jesuit. Such were the tremendous achievements of a school which, while it respected each pupil's freedom, nonetheless managed to bear the same fruits as a minor seminary (as Archbishop Lefebvre later remarked[34]). It also succeeded in forming laymen for life in the world. We could add that this school in Tourcoing had thirty-five teaching priests at the time.[35]

Looking After the Poor

During his last year (philosophy) at school, Marcel belonged to the school's St. Vincent de Paul Society, founded with the intention of "providing material help for the poor whilst at the same time engendering and fostering true bonds of fraternal charity among the members."[36] When Fr. Deconinck was appointed to teach at the school, he added to the SVP a

---

[31] Letter of Bernadette to Jeanne, February 10, 1922, and letter of Mrs. Lefebvre to Jeanne, February 12, 1922; the play took place at the school on February 11, 1922.

[32] Pouchain, *Les maîtres du Nord*, 269.

[33] *Les Anciens du Père Deco*, Sacred Heart School Archives, 25 Z 42; address of Fr. Jean Lecomte, Dec. 31, 1945, at the end of the Reunion Mass of "Fr. Deco's Old Boys"; Interview with Paul Loridant-Motte, May 29, 1997, ms. II, 24, 53-65.

[34] Marcel Lefebvre, *Spiritual Conferences at Ecône*, 24 B, Nov. 27, 1975.

[35] *Ibid.*

[36] Commemorative Album, 25.

study group called the "Ozanam Circle" which he chaired. The young Marcel became a member during his philosophy year. Many of the minutes from these meetings are priceless; taken by a pupil they show that the various members interacted with great freedom of spirit and a healthy sense of humor. Marcel Lefebvre, the temporary secretary on November 16, 1922, took the notes on a talk given by his friend Albert Strée on the causes of social conflicts; there had in fact been a general strike in Tourcoing in the previous September and October.[37] At the end of the talk Fr. Deconinck remarked that the source of these disagreements was "bad nineteenth-century organization which itself was caused by the disintegration of older professional associations." When the discussion came to the remedies, however, it was simply a case of "following public opinion and finding a benign mediator between the two parties" (owners and workers), instead of coming to the logical conclusion that it was necessary to re-establish professional associations and adapt them to modern circumstances. Can we not detect here a lack of faith in the effectiveness of principles?

Marcel had a practical mind and did not confine his activities to the Ozanam circle. He felt more at home with the poor and in 1921 began actually working with them. In 1922–23 he became vice president of the St. Vincent de Paul Society and in this capacity called upon the generosity of his comrades in the pages of *Chez Nous* [At our place], the school's magazine; donations on Sunday, second hand clothes, shoes that had become too tight–anything that could be useful to families going through hard times. Similarly he found time to visit the poor, asking the priest where he could find the neediest individuals and then assigning visits to his various associates. One poor man, paralyzed from the waist down, was depressed and unemployed. Marcel visited him, tidied up his lodgings, found him work, and gave him back a taste for life.[38] Marcel never boasted about what he was doing. In Lourdes where he sometimes went on pilgrimage with his family he found it perfectly natural to offer his services as a brancardier[39] to Count Beauchamp who was in charge of the *Hospitalité*.[40] His charity was effective but discreet, like his temperament.

---

[37] Pouchain, *Les maîtres du Nord*, 229.
[38] Cf. Mother Marie-Christiane Lefebvre, *Mon frère, Monseigneur Marcel*, 1-2; Marziac, *Monseigneur Lefebvre, soleil levant*, 64.
[39] [Literally a stretcher bearer. In Lourdes, *brancardiers* are male volunteer workers who help transport the sick on pilgrimage. They are distinguished by special brace-like shoulder straps which nowadays are merely decorative but which were used originally to help the *brancardier* support the weight of the stretcher he was carrying. Trans.]
[40] Interview with Mrs. André Cagnon, Feb. 22, 1997.

A Varied but Balanced Temperament

Christiane gives an excellent account[41] of the character of Marcel as an adolescent. "The good Lord gave Marcel a very balanced temperament, very calm but with a strength of character quite out of the ordinary." With his brother René he was the live wire of the "gang of five." "Mom remarked that she rarely had to organize games for the five older children: they could manage very well on their own. We were full of enthusiasm and happiness, and of course it was especially our two brothers the [future] missionaries who led the little gang."

René had initiative whilst Marcel knew how to get things organized. In the summer of 1920 he arranged a day trip for his brothers and sisters from Bagnoles-de-l'Orne to Mont St. Michel. The young man also had a gift for picking up local accents, for example that of the factory caretaker who enjoyed Marcel's little visits. On the latter's return home he would give a good rendition of the "Ch'timi" patois.[42]

There was a difference between Marcel and his elder sister Jeanne, who was a perfectionist but easily fell into moralizing. "Marcel was a perfectionist," says Christiane, "but in a more relaxed way. He radiated a certain peace and just seeing him made you feel happy; he had a laid back way of gently teasing that made everyone laugh."

Practical Sense and Remarkable Judgment

Marcel's willingness to help was unanimously praised in his family. At home he tried to make the servants' work as easy as possible;[43] at meal times he was quite happy to read a passage from the life of a saint while his elder brother would try to get out of it. In 1917, the young man liked to visit his grandfather Eugène to keep him company. His grandfather said that he had a soft spot for Marcel because he could guess where a wine came from just by the bouquet. However, although he would not admit it, the old man was especially touched by the adolescent's simple but real charity.

These qualities of heart were matched by a mind that was open to all knowledge. Although he constantly applied himself, he was nonetheless more at home with practical matters. After the war in 1919 Marcel decided that it was time to do away with the big oil lamps that provided lighting for the bedrooms. Thus on his days off he could be seen studying a huge book on electricity; then with his friend and neighbor Robert Lepoutre he

[41] Mother Marie-Christiane Lefebvre, *Mon frère, Monseigneur Marcel*, 1, 9, 11-12.
[42] "Ch'timi" is the Northern French dialect.
[43] Mother Marie-Christiane Lefebvre, *Mon frère, Monseigneur Marcel*, 2; Letter of Sister M.-Christiane, May 20, 1993; Letter of Joseph Lefebvre, June 1997; Interview with Michel Lefebvre, ms. II, 5, 22-27.

set about installing electricity on the first and second floor of the house: he thought of everything. When they had finished, they installed electricity in his friend's house, holding huge ladders steady for one another as they worked in the stairwells, and sorting through all the technical problems.[44]

He was good with his hands, and when he was about sixteen, he loved carving various things out of wood; for example, he made a pedestal for a statue of the Virgin Mary and finished it off with delicate carvings.[45] Neither did he lack a good head for business: with the help of a servant, he took charge of the hens and rabbits, and charged his mother for the eggs. He used the profits to buy himself a bicycle which meant he could run errands when asked, and of course visit the poor. Christiane stated:

> Of the two brothers, René who was easily top of the class had a lively mind. Marcel, who was usually a few places down the class ranking, stood out more for having clear judgment. So, when he had to leave for seminary, Mom made this remark to me: "How is the house going to manage without Marcel?" His departure was certainly one of the hardest sacrifices they had to make.[46]

IV. THE BIG DECISION

A CAREFULLY WEIGHED DECISION

Mrs. Lefebvre felt she knew what Marcel's future held for him but she was careful not to influence him in his choice. It was probably in the summer of 1919, when his elder brother's appearance in cassock impressed the family and was the topic of much discussion, that Marcel felt compelled to declare his vocation to his parents: "I would like to be a priest."[47] Barely three weeks after beginning his studies at the French Seminary in Rome, René wrote Marcel, full of enthusiasm: "I only wish one thing for you: that you join me here three years from now. You will experience a joy that you will find nowhere else, neither in the world nor in any other seminary in France, I think. Rome and the French Seminary are two graces you should ask God for."[48]

Marcel felt the desire to be a priest growing within him. During his last year at school when the Easter holidays were approaching, he heard Fr. Deconinck warn his pupils, "Think carefully! During these holidays, you will have to make a decision about your future." But Marcel was rather confused. How was he to make such a serious decision on his own? His

---

[44] Mother Marie-Christiane Lefebvre, *Mon frère, Monseigneur Marcel*, 3; Letter of Mrs. Lefebvre to Sister M.-Clotilde, Jan. 4, 1920.

[45] Interview with Michel Lefebvre, Apr. 28, 1997, ms. II, 8, 44-48.

[46] Mother Marie-Christiane Lefebvre, *Mon frère, Monseigneur Marcel*, 2.

[47] Lefebvre, *Petite histoire*, 23.

[48] Letter of Mrs. Lefebvre to Sister M.-Clotilde, Nov. 12, 1919.

spiritual director, Fr. Desmarchelier, wanted his *dirigés* to feel the call directly in their souls without any guidance from him.[49] Marcel on the other hand was awaiting the Holy Ghost's inspiration in the promptings of his director, but nothing at all was forthcoming from that quarter. During the holidays he spoke to his younger sister Christiane about his doubts: "So, I don't think I'm going to be a priest. It's madness to decide for yourself that you can be a priest. So, I'm going to do what St. Francis did: I want to be a saint, I will become a brother but I can't think of becoming a priest."

"You can't carry on without making some sort of decision," replied his sister. "Why don't you do a retreat for a few days?"

There were times when he felt himself drawn towards the austere life of the Trappists. Near St. Omer was the Benedictine abbey of Wisques which his father had often visited all those years ago when he was boarding in Boulogne.

"Go to Wisques, then!" advised his parents. "Fr. Guestmaster looks after the retreatants and will help you to see what to do."

Marcel went to Wisques and when he got back the whole family had the same question for him: "Well, what did Fr. Guestmaster say?"

"He thinks that I'm not called to be a Benedictine because I'm attracted towards the apostolate." But that wasn't enough for the young man, he needed a positive indication. At Poperinghe in Belgium there was a Trappist monastery where one of his father's uncles, Alban Théry, was a lay brother. "I went to see him and found that way of life very attractive. I would even have liked to enter as a brother. I found those brothers so marvelous, and so close to God. In their simplicity, in their candor, they were a reflection of heavenly happiness." Obviously he would have to think more about it…But in this abbey there was a monk famous for his holiness and his gift of prophecy, Fr. Alphonse.[50]

"I feel like going to Poperinghe," said Marcel, "to speak to Fr. Alphonse." So, he took his bicycle and went to the monastery, said hello to his Uncle Alban, and asked to speak to Fr. Alphonse. As soon as he came into the parlor, even before Marcel had the chance to ask him anything he said: "You will be a priest…You must be a priest."[51]

---

[49] Mother Marie-Christiane Lefebvre, *Mon frère, Monseigneur Marcel*, 7; Marziac, *Monseigneur Lefebvre, soleil levant*, 65.

[50] Julius Garmijn (1861-1926); ordained in Bruges in 1884, curate at Armentières for Flemish speakers. Enters the Scheutists in 1888 and goes as a missionary to the Belgian Congo with his elder brother. In 1904, becomes a Trappist at Westvleteren where he preached retreats and gave spiritual advice to retreatants. He was affable, modest, and practiced all the religious virtues. He was an "indomitable supporter of St. Thomas Aquinas." In 1918 he spent nine months at the Trappist monastery of Sept-Fonts where he met Dom Chautard [author of *The Soul of the Apostolate*. Trans.] (Saint Sixtus Obituary Register).

This time there was nothing for it! All that was left was to decide which seminary...

YOU'RE GOING TO ROME!

"I couldn't see myself going to Rome at all," Archbishop Lefebvre would say later. "I wasn't a great intellectual and you had to do your studies in Latin... Going there, the Gregorian University, the tough exams...I would have preferred, like the seminarians of my own diocese, to go to Lille and to become the parish priest of a country parish. Looking after the faith in a parish: I saw myself as a Father, the spiritual Father of people to whom I could become attached and in whom I could inculcate faith and Christian morals. That was my ideal."

"I would like to stay in the diocese," Marcel told his father. "Since I want to work in the diocese there's no point going to Rome."

"No, no, no, no! You must go and join your brother! Your brother is in Rome, you must also go to Rome; there's nothing for it, you can't stay here in the diocese, after all, the diocese..." He paused a little and then continued, "No, no, Rome will be better."[52]

Archbishop Lefebvre later remarked: "And that's how I was led by Providence; God used the war. If there hadn't been a war, obviously my brother would never have gone to study in Versailles. He would have joined a missionary order straightaway because he had a missionary vocation. But in Versailles Fr. Collin advised him to go to Rome...Otherwise, I would have gone to the seminary in Lille and I would not have gone to Rome; that would have completely changed my life—in all respects."[53]

"You will go to Rome!" Mr. Lefebvre's determination had won the day. Marcel did not try arguing, for his father's authority was respected and feared at home. Mr. Lefebvre was the head of the family, a head who thought, a man of principles, and he saw clearly the liberalism that had infected a number of seminaries in France. He was determined to put his son into the reliable hands of Fr. Le Floch, provided the bishop of Lille, Bishop Hector Quilliet, gave his consent.[54]

HOW TO DISMANTLE A BASTION

Lille had always been a bastion of Roman Catholicism. When in 1875, the Lille weaver Philibert Vrau showed Pius IX his plans for a Cath-

---

[51] Mother Marie-Christiane Lefebvre, *Mon frère, Monseigneur Marcel*, 7, 8; *Fideliter*, no. 59 (1987): 7.

[52] Lefebvre, *Petite histoire*, 23; talk in Montreal, 1982; *Fideliter*, no. 85: 3.

[53] Cf. Lefebvre, *Petite histoire*, 21, 24.

[54] Msgr. J.-A. Chollet, Archbishop of Cambrai, *Pages choisies* (Cambrai: H. Mallez, 1936), xxi-xxii.

olic University in Lille he explained to the sovereign Pontiff: "Our sole aim is to create an establishment which, inspired by the healthy doctrines of the Church and particularly the teachings given by Your Holiness in the Syllabus, will apply the true principles of the Faith in all the subjects taught there."[55] During the reign of Leo XIII, business leaders in the North–Catholics and monarchists–supported by the *Croix du Nord* (Northern Cross) and Canon Delassus's *Semaine Religieuse de Cambrai* (Cambrai's religious weekly) fought against the Democrat priests Lemire, Six and Bataille–this latter founded the first Christian workers' union in Lille in 1893. But these priests were soon boosted by the "*Ralliement*"[56] to the Republic that the Pope had asked for. Marc Sangnier's *Sillon* movement recruited its members among the clergy who had followed the Pope's call and also in the Catholic universities where the winds of change were blowing (for example, Eugène Duthoit, Fr. Thellier de Poncheville).

The arrival of St. Pius X cleared the air. Compromise was consigned to oblivion. The *Sillon* was condemned in 1910, and, partly to continue the anti-liberal fight, Lille was made a bishopric by dismantling the diocese of Cambrai on October 25, 1913. Addressing his clergy, Bishop Charost greeted "the city of Lille which shines with the sun of pure truth and rejects with all the might that God has given our Flemish race the mirage of false and seductive liberalism."[57] But with the advent of Benedict XV the deleterious influences returned; Canon Delassus retired and Fr. Six[58] and Eugène Duthoit were rehabilitated,[59] the former being put in charge of the diocese's social projects and the latter taking over the social services across the North. And in 1919, Bishop Charost authorized a parish priest in Roubaix, Fr. Debussche, to relaunch the Christian trade unions: they could not think of any other way of counteracting the revolutionary work of the CGT.[60]

René Lefebvre hated this new, liberal orientation; he remained attached to the corporative principle and was a sympathiser of Action Fran-

---

[55] Pouchain, *Les maîtres du Nord*, 123.

[56] [The *Ralliement* was the name given to Leo XIII's call to French Catholics to participate in the democratic system under the Third Republic. Trans.]

[57] Pierre Pierrard, *Histoire des diocèses de Cambrai et Lille* (Beauchesne, 1978), 289-296.

[58] Already in 1916, Bishop Charost had lifted the interdict which he had imposed on Fr. Lemire.

[59] Certain socialist theses of his *Semaines Sociales* had been censured by Rome: Pierrard, *Histoire des diocèses de Cambrai et Lille*, 296; Letter of Cardinal Merry del Val to Albert de Mun, Jan. 3, 1913, *A.A.S.* 5 (1913), 18-19; Bonne Presse VIII, 114-115; *Courrier de Rome*, II, 491-492.

[60] [CGT is the "Confédération Générale du Travail," a major French trade union associated with hard-line socialism. In 1922 in the wake of the split between Communists and Socialists at the Congress of Tours (1920), the Communist CGTU (Confédération Générale du Travail Unitaire) was formed. Both organizations still exist. Trans.]

çaise, which mainly recruited from amongst Catholics. He did not, however, belong to the Textile Industry Consortium, which had taken over from the ACPN, and neither did he agree with the method of brutal salary reduction which between 1919 and 1921 provoked strikes of an almost insurrectionary nature, especially in the factories in Tourcoing. Eugène Mathon, president of the Consortium, was ready to lodge a complaint in Rome against the Christian trades unions which he accused of "taking part in the class struggle."[61] René Lefebvre was also of this opinion but stayed out of this thorny debate in which both sides were in the wrong. Similarly he wanted to keep his younger son out of the liberal atmosphere that had even seeped into the diocesan seminaries, preferring to put him into the climate of peace and doctrinal certainty which his elder brother was already benefiting from in Rome. Bishop Quillet, who was trying to keep the diocese faithful to the Magisterium as of old, granted the industrialist's desire. He could only recommend that Marcel Lefebvre become truly Roman.

---

[61] Pouchain, *Les maîtres du Nord*, 229; Pierrard, *Histoire des diocèses de Cambrai et Lille*, 304.

CHAPTER 3

ROMAN SEMINARIAN

I. WITH THE HOLY GHOST
AND THE IMMACULATE HEART OF MARY

ARRIVAL AT SANTA CHIARA (OCTOBER 25, 1923)

In spite of his brother's absence–he had to do his military service–and Robert Lepoutre's having gone to the seminary at Annapes, Marcel Lefebvre was happy to travel to Rome with his fellow pupils from school, André Frys and Georges Leclercq. As they approached the city they all stood at the windows of the train trying to spot the dome of St. Peter's. "There it is!" Did Marcel realize at that moment that he himself was to write a page– a small page but what a page!–in the history of this city which, like God, is called eternal?[62]

Just inside the seminary's entrance on the Via Santa Chiara, the new students, who were welcomed by their "guardian angel" Henri Fockedey, noticed a marble statue of the Blessed Virgin smiling down on them: *Tutela domus*. Following the example of Fockedey, Marcel knelt down somewhat nervously in front of this Lady whom he would soon get to know better: no-one ever entered or left the college without paying their respects with a short hello–which the Virgin always returned with her smile. Then Marcel, preceded by his mentor, went off to find his room. "His room" is going a little too far since there were two students to each one: the rooms had been converted into twin accommodation[63] to house some 220 seminarians from various countries and religious "battalions": diocesan seminarians, "scholastics" from the Holy Ghost Fathers, "canons" from St. Maurice-en-Valais, *etc.* Marcel was to share his room with Georges Picquenard, who was one year his senior and came from the diocese of Laval.

Marcel paced around the four storeys of the beautifully constructed quadrangle starting from the terrace, known as the loggia—from where he learned to find his bearings amongst the city's forest of cupolas—and coming down to the shady cloister surrounded by a beautiful pink granite colonnade which enclosed a cool interior courtyard that danced with colors: in its center stood a statue of the Sacred Heart above a bubbling fountain:

---

[62] Raymond Dulac, *La maison de Sainte Claire*, memories of the French Seminary.
[63] *Échos de Santa Chiara*, no. 112: 29-30.

In die illa erit fons patens.[64] Nearby, the chapel, the heart of the seminary, would welcome the seminarians who had to cram into their narrow pews close to the simple white marble altar and the statue of the Immaculate Heart of Mary, refuge of sinners.[65]

AT THE HEART OF THE ETERNAL CITY

The following day, October 26, was completely taken up with getting to know the city. One after the other the seminarians went to St. Peter's where they found a veritable treatise *"de Romano Pontifice"* in the very majesty of the buildings, the ornamentation and works of art, and in the important inscriptions which decorated the gilded frieze in the nave and cupola. The relics of the popes and martyrs, the most eloquent voices of Tradition, invited them with St. Cyprian to love ever more "this See of Peter and this principal Church whence springs the unity of the priesthood."[66] On their way back they wandered in the streets close to the seminary discovering that the great ecclesiastical universities were all only five minutes away from Santa Chiara. What an ideal location for the French Seminary! Its purpose was to form young men in Roman doctrine, according to the will of Pius IX, who suggested and, later in 1853, gave his permission for the new establishment to be placed under the care of the Holy Ghost Fathers. But why them?

THE CONGREGATION OF THE HOLY GHOST

The Congregation of the Holy Ghost had been founded as it were twice.[67] Around 1700 a young Breton, Claude-François Poullart des Places, had come to Paris to prepare for the priesthood, choosing the Jesuit college in preference to the Sorbonne, which was infected with Jansenism. He was struck by the poverty of certain fellow pupils, and on Whitsunday, May 27, 1703, the twenty-four year old cleric founded a "community and seminary consecrated to the Holy Ghost under the patronage of the Holy Virgin conceived without sin."[68] Ordained priest in 1707, he died in 1709 at the age of thirty, leaving behind him the touching example of a humble, poor, and pious priest who was well versed in doctrine.

---

[64] "In that day there shall be a fountain open to [the house of David]" (Zach. 13:1).
[65] Among the "seniors" who were preparing for their doctorate in Theology were the future Bishops Lebrun, Ancel, and Guerry, and the future Vicars General Michel and Layotte; Finet, future chaplain of the Foyers de Charité, and Robert Prévost, future curate of Our Lady of the Angels in Tourcoing. *Mélanges de Science Religieuse* 54 (1997), no. 3: 41-47; Robert Prévost, *Dieu n'échoue pas*, 3 vols. (Téqui, 1983); *Échos de Santa Chiara*, no. 115: 44.
[66] St. Cyprian, bk. 59, ch. 14, n. 1; quoted by Pius XII, allocution during an audience with the French seminary, April 16, 1953.
[67] Cf. Rev. V.-A. Berto, *Pour la sainte Eglise romaine* (Paris: Cèdre, 1976), 122-124.

Claude Poullart's "poor clerics" were to be "educated in the soundest doctrinal principles of the Roman Catholic Church."[69] The young founder liked to repeat his favorite maxim, "a pious cleric without knowledge is blind in his zeal, and a learned cleric without piety risks becoming a heretic and a rebel in the Church."[70] The priests formed in this doctrinal piety fostered at the Holy Ghost Seminary returned to their dioceses or joined Grignion de Montfort's Company of Mary; but soon some of them left for the foreign missions in Canada (1732), Cochin China, and Senegal (1770-1790). After the Revolution, the community, which had been recognized as a congregation by the Holy See, provided excellent priests for nine colonial territories including the West Indies and Senegal. The seminary became a center for Roman Catholic thought where Rohrbacher the historian, Bouix the canonist, Migne the patrologist, and Dom Pitra the palaeographer came to stay. Other famous figures such as Dom Guéranger, Bishop Parisis, Cardinal Gousset, and Louis Veuillot also came to speak about contemporary problems in the light of Rome's teachings.[71]

In 1847, however, the congregation ran into difficulties. Providence then injected some new blood by grafting onto Poullart des Places's old stock the young shoot of the Venerable Libermann.

FATHER LIBERMANN, THE IMMACULATE HEART OF MARY, AND THE HOUSE OF ST. CLAIRE

Born on April 11, 1802, Jacob Libermann, son of the Rabbi in Saverne, received the grace of baptism on Christmas Eve 1826, taking the Christian names François, Marie, Paul: "As the sacred waters flowed over my Jewish head," he said, "Mary, whom I had previously hated, became my love."[72] Having been to the Saint Sulpice seminaries in Paris and then Issy, he acquired a large group of disciples who were soon enthusiastic about his idea of launching an entire army of apostles[73] on Africa "amongst

---

[68] Joseph Michel, *Claude-François Poullart des Places* (Paris: Éd. St. Paul, 1962); *L'influence de l'AA, association secrète de piété, sur Cl.-F. Poullart des Places* (Paris: Beauchesne, 1962); H. Koren, C.S.Sp., *Les Spiritains, trois siècles d'histoire religieuse et missionnaire* (Beauchesne, 1982), 18. Cl. Poullart learnt his devotion to the Holy Ghost from the missionary Jesuits in Brittany, disciples of Fr. Lallement: Rigoleuc, Huby, Legrand, Maunoir, and Champion; Michel, *Claude-François Poullart des Places*, 147-157; Koren, *Les Spiritains*, 18-19.

[69] Grandet P.S.S., *Vie de Messire Louis-Marie Grignion de Montfort* (Nantes, 1724), 563, quoted by Michel, *Poullart des Places*, 204-205.

[70] "*Vir clericus divinarum rerum studiosus sed expers scientia, caecum habet zelum, et clericus doctus sine pietate prope est ut fiat haereticus et Ecclesia rebellis.*" *Gallia Christiana*, vol. VII, col. 1043; Henri Le Floch, *Cinquante ans de sacerdoce* (Aix-en-Provence, 1937), 371; Michel, *Poullart des Places,* 205; Koren, *Les Spiritains*, 28.

[71] Michel, *Poullart des Places,* 321; Koren, *Les Spiritains*, 151.

[72] Notes and documents on Ven. Libermann, I, 98-99, note 1.

[73] Koren, *Les Spiritains*, 185-192.

ROME

THE DELLA PIGNA QUARTER AND THE FRENCH SEMINARY

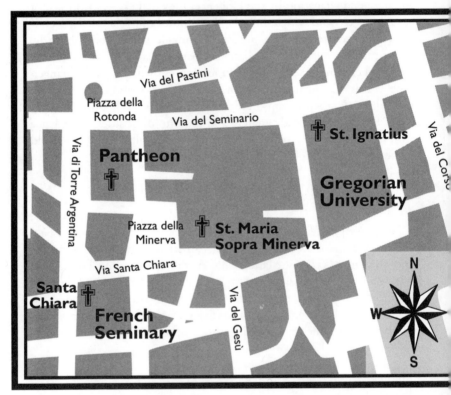

On the right, the Gregorian University and the Church of St.Ignatius; on the left, the Pantheon (today, Our Lady of Martyrs); in the center, Our Lady of Minerva; at the bottom, the French Seminary.

the most disadvantaged blacks." Encouraged by Rome and miraculously cured of epilepsy, he was ordained priest in 1841 and sent his first "missionaries of the Immaculate Heart" to Senegal and Gabon. The presence of the Holy Ghost Fathers in certain lands gave him food for thought. In 1848, the amalgamation of his institute with that of the Holy Ghost came about under the name of the "Congregation of the Holy Ghost under the patronage of the Holy and Immaculate Heart of Mary."[74] He died four years later on February 2, 1852. The following year, in response to the wishes and appeal of Pope Pius IX, the Congregation founded the French Seminary in Rome. In 1854 it moved to the old convent of St. Claire and became a busy hive of intellectual and spiritual activity: *pietas cum scientia*. In 1902 Leo XIII gave it the title of Pontifical Seminary, something quite rare at that time. Then in 1904, the tired hands of Fr. Alphonse Eschbach passed on the flaming torch of Roman doctrinal thinking to Fr. Le Floch.[75]

II. FR. LE FLOCH, THE POPES, AND THE CRUSADE

HENRI LE FLOCH

On the evening of October 26, 1923, the Father Superior gathered the seminarians together to give them their first spiritual talk of the year.[76] At sixty-one, Fr. Henri Le Floch was on the downward slope as regards his age but not as regards his intellectual faculties. According to Fr. Berto,[77] one of his pupils from 1921 to 1926, he was a Breton oak in all the magnificence of full maturity. He was quite tall and exuded confidence. He had a ruddy complexion and a broad face in which his prominent eyebrows contrasted with the fine nose and lips. He carried himself with noble dignity, and his blue-grey eyes had a look of firmness although his natural seriousness was lightened by an air of goodness and a smile which was discreet but readily displayed. He made his mark without any affectation—he was dignity and affability itself. Besides that, there was a mixture of extreme self-assurance and total self-forgetfulness: he was but a servant of the Church, a man of truth and Catholic doctrine, obviously a theologian, but intuitive and impatient, his spirit reaching the heights without having to go through all the levels of theological argument. It was not that he looked down on theology as a rational science, but ultimately he hardly ever used it in that way. His

---

[74] *Ibid.*, 224, 227. The majority of the Holy Ghost "novices" (priests in the colonies or seminarians in Postes street) resigned rather than accept this demand. *Ibid.*, 228.

[75] Cf. Yves Chiron, *St. Pius X: Reformer of the Church* (in French) (*Courrier de Rome*, 1999), 176, quoting a letter from Bishop Turinaz to Cardinal Merry del Val, April 25, 1904.

[76] *Échos de Santa Chiara*, no. 115, chronicle.

[77] Berto, *Pour la sainte Eglise romaine*, 113, 141.

firmness in the Faith was matched by his profound grasp of the most fruitful theological concepts.[78]

THE SPIRIT OF CLAUDE POULLART DES PLACES
—ROMAN DOCTRINE AND DOCTRINAL PIETY

Fr. Le Floch used the documents of the Holy Ghost Fathers' 1848
"amalgamation" to give a memorable talk in Chevilly in 1902.[79] In his address, he showed that even if the Venerable Libermann had been the re-
storer of the Congregation and the author of its missionary religious spirit,
nonetheless its founder had been the Servant of God, Poullart des Places.
The Community of the Holy Ghost, approved as a French association by
royal decree in 1734,[80] did not cease to exist in 1848 as Bishop Le Roy, the
Superior General, had just proven to the State (thus saving the congregation from the "expulsions" of August 1901). Consequently, Claude Poullart's original intentions continued to be fulfilled, and the French Seminary in Rome was the heir of the glorious Seminary of the Holy Ghost,
although it trained clergy not only for the colonies.[81]

The tradition of attachment to sound Roman doctrine and a profound piety based on this doctrine was what Fr. Le Floch had found when
he came to Santa Chiara. He played his part in developing and restoring it,
making it part of the seminary rule. He also reinforced it by the readings in
the refectory; once every three years the life of Fr. J.-B. Aubry would be
read.[82] He was a graduate of the French Seminary and had received within
its confines his enthusiasm for the study of theology and a taste for theological piety:

> Another ruse of the anti-theological school is to separate piety from
> doctrine in the priesthood: theirs is a sentimental school which, under the
> pretext of piety, ruins true piety! Doctrine without spirituality and spiri-
> tuality without doctrine go together—dry doctrine together with dull, in-
> consistent, unhealthy spirituality that is mere sentimentality, and
> therefore short-lived. It is a school which denies the need for a true priest,
> the spiritual and apostolic man, to acquire the deepest possible sense of
> dogmatic theology.

And it is wrong, continues Fr. Aubry, that certain people limit their
studies to moral theology, separating it from the dogmatic theology which
they consider to be useless! By doing this they remove from their studies

---

[78] Cf. *ibid*, 129.
[79] *Bulletin Général de la Congrégation du Saint-Esprit*, 630: 366-367; hereafter, *General Bulletin*.
[80] Koren, *Les Spiritains*, 35-36; texts in *General Bulletin*, 520: 468-497.
[81] The "colonial seminary" stayed in Paris in the motherhouse's buildings, Rue Lhomond.
[82] J.-B. Aubry, missionary and theologian.

"everything which helps to make the young theologian into a priestly soul with a theological sense, a man of principles and doctrine, with a strong mind and an elevated spirit."[83]

"SENTIRE CUM ECCLESIA"—THINK WITH THE CHURCH

Faith in the principles and in the practical effectiveness of the truth–of Catholic truth–was what Fr. Le Floch tried to inculcate into his students. At his golden priestly jubilee in 1936 his former students wrote to him of their gratitude for the formation they had received at his hands.[84] "I have the enthusiasm of an eighteen year old," wrote Canon J. Taillade, superior of the major seminary of Perpignan, "which I owe to you and to Santa Chiara where I received the principles which make my life so happy." Fr. Roger Johan, professor at the minor seminary of Sées and future bishop, wrote: "What joy to have been formed to live fully on principles!" And Dom Albert de Saint-Avid, a monk of Solesmes, reminded him, "You taught us to worship the whole truth and have a horror of mitigated truths....I remember your 'fatherliness' which was so perfect that it inspired our respect and won our affection."

Fr. Johan also described "the sense of the value of charity, the need for theology, and divinely perfected philosophy." Fr. Victor-Alain Berto asked, "Can one define [this] spirit? Basically it is *Sentire cum Ecclesia*, not understood in a rigid sense, obviously, nor mathematically nor in a narrow-minded way!"[85] "*Sentire cum Ecclesia*": judge as the Church judges, in the light of the teaching of the Councils and the Popes, in the light of St. Thomas Aquinas, leaving aside all personal ideas in order to embrace the mind of the Church. Such was the spirit of the Father Superior.

A REVELATION

In his sermons or spiritual talks, the Archbishop often expressed gratitude, veneration, and affection towards his Roman superior. In his jubilee sermon on September 23, 1979, he was happy to recall "the superior guidance of dear Fr. Le Floch, a well-beloved Father, a Father who taught us to see contemporary events clearly by commenting on the encyclicals of the Popes."[86] "I will never thank God enough for allowing me to know that truly extraordinary man." Archbishop Lefebvre remarked that Fr. Le Floch's teaching was a "revelation" for him:

---

[83] Fr. Augustin Aubry, *Vie sacerdotale, conseils pratiques tirés des oeuvres du Père J.-B. Aubry* (Ghent, 1928), 45, 48-49.

[84] Henri Le Floch, *Cinquante ans de sacerdoce*, 201-214

[85] Fr. Berto, Letter of Nov. 21, 1936, in Le Floch, *Cinquante ans de sacerdoce*, 207

[86] *Fideliter*, no. 12 (1979): 6.

He was the one who taught us what the popes were to the world and the Church, what they had taught for a century and a half–against liberalism, modernism, and Communism, and the whole doctrine of the Church on these topics. He really made us understand and share in this battle of the popes to preserve the world and the Church from these scourges which plague us today. That was a revelation for me.

What did this revelation consist of? The former pupil of Tourcoing school gave this clear explanation: "During my studies I had never really grasped how much was at stake in this fight of the Church for the Church and Christianity."[87] "I remember...coming to seminary with incorrect ideas which I modified during my studies. For example, I thought that it was excellent that the State was separated from the Church. Oh yes! I was a liberal!" Obviously this confession made the seminarians who heard it at Ecône burst into laughter: Archbishop Lefebvre had been a liberal! What had brought about his intellectual conversion? Quite simply,

> I listened to what the older students were talking about. I listened to their reactions and especially to what my professors and the Superior had taught me. And I realized that in fact I had quite a few wrong ideas....I was very pleased to learn the truth, happy to learn that I had been wrong, that I had to change my way of thinking about certain things, especially in studying the encyclicals of the popes, which showed us all the modern errors, those magnificent encyclicals of all the popes up to St. Pius X and Pius XI.[88]

> ...For me it was a complete revelation. And that was how the desire was quietly born in us to conform our judgment to that of the popes. We used to say to ourselves: but how did the popes judge these events, ideas, men, things, and times? And Fr. Le Floch showed us clearly[89] what the main ideas of these various popes were: always the same thing, exactly the same in their encyclicals. That showed us...how we should look at history...and consequently it stayed with us.[90]

"How the popes had judged things": Archbishop Lefebvre's constant concern was to align himself with the judgments of the popes and to have no personal ideas, but rather to be simply faithful to the "truth of the Church and what she had always taught."[91]

WE ARE ON A CONTINUAL CRUSADE

As she taught, the Church was always poised for battle. According to Archbishop Lefebvre, "Fr. Le Floch made us enter into and live the history

---

[87]   *Fideliter*, no. 59 (1987): 32.
[88]   *Spiritual Conferences at Ecône*, 36 A, Nov. 30, 1976.
[89]   In his spiritual talks from 7:05 to 7:30 P.M. alternating with other spiritual directors from the seminary.
[90]   Lefebvre, *Petite histoire*, 26.
[91]   *Spiritual Conferences at Econe*, 36 A, Nov. 30, 1976.

of the Church, this fight that the perverse powers take to our Lord. *We were mobilized against this dreadful liberalism,* against the Revolution and the forces of evil which were trying to overcome the Church, the reign of our Lord, the Catholic States, and the whole of Christianity." Most of the seminarians took up this fight and the others left, explained Archbishop Lefebvre. "We had to choose: we had to leave the seminary if we didn't agree, or else join in the fight."[92] But taking up the fight meant taking it up for one's whole life: "I think that our whole life as priests—or as bishops—has been marked by this fight against liberalism."[93] This liberalism was practiced by liberal Catholics, "two-faced people" who called themselves Catholics but who "couldn't bear hearing the whole truth and who didn't want to condemn error or the Church's enemies, or who could not bear to live with being always on crusade."

As Archbishop Lefebvre concluded: "That was it, we're on a crusade, in a state of continual struggle" and this crusade, he pointed out, might also require martyrdom.[94]

UNDER THE BANNER OF CHRIST THE KING AND PRIEST

According to Denis Fahey,[95] the seminarians had to read or had read to them in the refectory, the writings of Godefroid Kurth[96] to make them consider how "the mystical Body of Christ transformed the pagan society of imperial Rome and prepared the growing movement that recognized the plans for society of Our Lord Jesus Christ, Priest and King"; the seminarians also learned through the writings of Fr. Deschamps[97] that "revolutions caused the exclusion of Christ the King from government with the final goal of eliminating the Mass and the supernatural life of Christ the sovereign High Priest." Fr. (later Cardinal) Billot, S.J.'s *De Ecclesia* made them grasp "the sense of the royalty of Christ and the horror of liberalism." Through the works of Cardinal Pie they learned "the full meaning of 'thy kingdom come,' *i.e.,* that Our Lord's kingdom must come not only in individual souls and in heaven, but also on earth by the submission of States and nations to His rule. The dethroning of God on earth is a crime to which we must never resign ourselves."

"Pius IX's Syllabus and the encyclicals of the last four Popes," said Fahey, "have been the principal object of my meditations on the royalty of

---

[92] Cf. Prévost, *Dieu n'échoue pas,* I, 165-166.
[93] *Fideliter,* no. 59: 32.
[94] Lefebvre, *Petite histoire,* 28.
[95] Fr. Fahey, C.S.Sp., a disciple of Fr. Le Floch at Santa Chiara from 1908 to 1912. He wrote the lines quoted here in the *Apologia pro Vita Mea* around 1950. Cf. *Catholic Family News* (USA), April and May, 1997.
[96] *Origines de la civilisation moderne,* 2 vols. (Brussels: Albert Dewitt, 1912).
[97] In his book *Les Sociétés secrètes et la société.*

Christ and its relation to the priesthood." The same was true of Marcel Lefebvre. In St. Peter's, when he visited the basilica, Fahey stopped at the "Confession" and there promised the first Pope "to teach the truth about his master in the same way that he and his successors, the Roman Pontiffs, would want it to be taught."[98] The truth about Christ the King and Priest in the light of the popes' teachings, in the fight against the enemies of this truth: that was the sacred deposit which Marcel Lefebvre was determined to pass on in his turn.

III. A CONTEMPLATIVE PHILOSOPHER

THE GOOD OLD GREGORIAN!

But before passing it on he had to be trained in its ways. On November 5, the Gregorian University opened its doors for the *lectio brevis* with a picturesque and multicolored bustle of seven hundred young clerics who piled out from the neighboring streets each morning: the Germans in red wool, the Spanish in blue and black, and religious in all kinds of different habits. Of this inaugural lesson given in sonorous, fluent Latin by Fr. Lazzarini, Marcel only understood a few snatches. He was somewhat discouraged, but he would soon get the hang of it.[99]

He joined the Philosophy faculty in the "second year"[100] course whose daily program comprised two or three hours of lessons in the morning and the same in the afternoon. It took three minutes to cross the Piazza della Minerva and reach the via del Seminario and the main entrance of the Palazzo Borromeo, which had housed the Gregorian University since the confiscation of the Collegio Romano in 1870. Its original name had been given by its founder, St. Ignatius: the Roman College.[101] Within its walls, Louis Billot, as *Divus Thomas redivivus*,[102] had taught Thomism and the fight against modernism and liberalism which he described as being "perfectly and absolutely incoherent due to the opposition which its followers created between principles and praxis; the principles that they claimed to hold were simply practical rules of action, which is precisely what they refused to admit." Made a cardinal by St. Pius X in November 1911, he had to give up teaching but was still there in 1923, a model professor, venerated by the Fathers and seminarians of Santa Chiara.

---

[98] Fahey, *Apologia pro Vita Mea.*

[99] *Échos de Santa Chiara* (Jan. 1956): 33; 115, 165; Prévost, *Dieu n'échoue pas*, I, 131-132. Marcel received the cassock on November 1.

[100] Enrollment record for philosophy faculty, matriculation no. 04112. His year of philosophy in Tourcoing counted as one year's study.

[101] Cf. *Échos de Santa Chiara*, 117: 61; 131: 150.

[102] Expression used by the Cardinal Vicar of Leo XIII, cf. Billot, *De Ecclesia*, vol. II, q. 17, a. 2 §3; Le Floch, *Cinquante ans de sacerdoce*, 57-58.

DRY METAPHYSICS AND HARD POLITICAL TRUTHS

Gingerly the young student took his first sips of "the only true philosophy of good sense and reality"[103] as taught by Fr. Charles Boyer in his logic and general metaphysics courses. These classes delighted minds more speculative than Marcel's. He passed his July 2 examination with a "*bene probatus.*" He didn't enjoy "having to study pure philosophy without any relation to the Faith"; the Christian paths that led from the philosophical principles were missing. Marcel thought "philosophy is not outside Our Lord's universal kingdom, it is the handmaid of theology" and is "assumed by grace in the same way that Our Lord's human nature was assumed by His divine nature."[104]

Marcel was greatly interested in the politics taught by Fr. Lorenzo Giammusso in his ethics course. It was full of hard truths about the revolutionary myths of the "will of the people" and the "harmony of personal freedoms"; and it concluded that civil society, conceived by the Author of nature, must honor God with public worship. Philosophy thus becomes the throne of Christ the King.

TALKS ON ST. THOMAS

In seminary, in honor of the Angelic Doctor, there were the "St. Thomas Lectures" designed to stimulate the philosophy and theology students' taste for studying contemporary questions in the light of St. Thomas and the Popes. On December 2, in the presence of Archbishop Chollet of Cambrai, Georges Michel put the Declaration of the Rights of Man on trial. This talk was to acquire a certain fame and it was Archbishop Chollet who added this epilogue to the young theologian's exposé: "God alone is a pure right...originally we have nothing but debts; we have rights precisely to help us pay our dues."[105] This beautifully expressed the objective nature of rights and reaffirmed the primacy of the common good—both of which were ideas ignored by the liberal individualism of the Revolution.

In later lectures Pierre de La Chanonie refuted the liberties of thought, conscience, and religion; Robert Prévost, who was considered to be something of a "democrat"—an opinion tolerated by the Father Superior, but cursed by Fr. Voegtli—expounded the origins of secularism.[106] Some of these talks were printed as pamphlets for limited distribution whilst Fr. Roul was to publish his work *The Catholic Church and Common Law* in 1931.[107]

---

[103] Archbishop Lefebvre, panegyric at Fr. Berto's funeral, Pontcalec, Dec. 21, 1968, in *Notre Dame de Joie*, 330.
[104] Retreats given at Ecône, Sept. 8, 1982, 3 o'clock talk.
[105] *Échos de Santa Chiara*, 116: 15.
[106] Prévost, *Dieu n'échoue pas*, I, 134, 173, 179.

TWO NOVICES IN THE FAMILY

Marcel Lefebvre absorbed to the depths of his soul these teachings that paved, as it were, the very streets he walked on. After Christmas, in a New Year greeting card to his parents, his main wish for them was "to advance in perfection."[108] The desire for perfection by which he lived was shared by his elder siblings: at Easter 1924 he learned from his mother, who wrote to him regularly, that his sister Jeanne had joined the novitiate of Marie-Réparatrice in Tournai. As for his brother René, he finished his military service with the 15th R.A.C. in Douai. In August the two brothers in their cassocks went to Saint-Savin in the Pyrenées[109] with their two sisters. Christiane tells how René had not quite reacquired his ecclesiastical air. He even hummed Alhambra songs in her presence, bringing forth this reproach from Marcel: "René, surely you're not going to teach your sister barrack-room songs!"[110] But René had hidden depths, and since he was determined to follow his missionary vocation without further ado, he entered the Holy Ghost Fathers' novitiate in Orly on October 5, 1924.[111]

PHILOSOPHY AND CONTEMPLATION

Marcel Lefebvre returned to Rome October 20, 1924, determined to come to grips with his "third year" of philosophy. Among the new seminarians, he met a young Irish priest, John Charles McQuaid, the future Archbishop of Dublin. It was the beginning of the Holy Year. In November, Marcel assisted at a Mass said with "touching devotion" by Cardinal Merry del Val. He wrote of his feelings to his parents, and his mother noted: "Marcel writes us letters that speak of nothing but Rome. He is really enjoying all the ceremonies which they're having there for the Holy Year, and is ever happier to belong to the Church."[112]

At the Gregorian, the young student's favorite course was Fr. Attilio Munzi's theodicy. Finally, at the summit of philosophy he could breathe some pure air; despite its weakness, human reason can learn something about the existence of God and contemplate His infinite perfections. But Fr. Munzi's finer points and those of his master, Cajetan, the great commentator of St. Thomas, "almost made easy things difficult" but increased thereby the students' joy of discovery and the development of their minds

---

[107] *Échos de Santa Chiara*, 122: 112, 118; 123 (from 1925 to March 1926); Éd. Doctrine et Vérité, lib. Casterman.

[108] Letter of Mrs. Lefebvre to Sister Marie-Clotilde, Jan. 1, 1924.

[109] Sister Marie Christiane, handwritten family journal.

[110] Mother Marie Christiane Lefebvre, *Mon frère, Monseigneur Marcel*, typed supplement, 1.

[111] Family journal.

[112] Letter of Mrs. Lefebvre to Sister Marie-Clotilde, Dec. 30, 1924.

"because we only love and understand the things that we grasp with difficulty."[113]

When things got "too difficult to grasp," the young Marcel went to consult Santa Chiara's "student mentor" for philosophy, Fr. Joseph Le Rohellec.[114] Seminarians queued in front of his door but he always had the right answers. It was amazing to see him pull down a huge volume of St. Thomas, read a text, then, with a quickness which showed just how well he knew the holy Doctor, put together parallel passages, comparing them, using them complementarily and then drawing out the Master's doctrine... And then a huge smile would light up his face.[115]

For, of course, at Santa Chiara, with the tacit but well-known approval of Fr. Le Floch, the very texts of St. Thomas were studied: for example, the text of the *Summa Theologica* as St. Pius X had prescribed in his *Motu Proprio Doctoris Angelici* of June 29, 1914. A veritable Thomist fever raged at the seminary as we learn from Fr. Berto: "Five years under that regime was meant to make us Thomists. In truth nothing in our training led anywhere else and everything went in that direction; certainly it was not meant to make us Thomist theologians–a ridiculous pretension–but at least Thomists in theology, and Thomists by conviction and method."[116]

During the public "revision classes" which Fr. Le Rohellec held, Marcel liked "the way the professor always went back to the principles and through them solved all problems; he had a way of reducing everything to the unity of being which gave some idea of the sublime harmony in Creation."[117] The young seminarian set out in search of the central unifying principle and wrote this little note to the Father Librarian, "Father, I would like the *Revue des sciences philosophiques et théologiques*, April 1909 by Fr. Del Prado; *De veritate fundamentali philosophiae christianae*. Marcel Lefebvre."[118] The principle which he found there was simple enough: "In created things there is a real distinction between essence and existence." The immediate corollary is that God alone is being: unshared and not received from another. God is *a se*, He exists by Himself; we are *ab alio*, we exist through another. This self-existent being is moreover the definition which God gave of Himself to Moses, "I am who am."[119] It follows that we

[113] Dulac, *Cette bonne vieille Grégrorienne* (n.p., n.d.), 33.
[114] Fr. Le Rohellec, C.S.Sp., from the diocese of Vannes, was at Santa Chiara from 1904; an accomplished Thomist and author of two fine Marian studies: *Marie et le sacerdoce* (Mary and the priesthood) and *Marie dispensatrice des graces divines* (Mary dispenser of divine graces).
[115] *General Bulletin*, 484: 969; cf. Prévost, *Dieu n'échoue pas*, I, 131.
[116] Berto, *Pour la sainte Eglise romaine*, 79-80.
[117] *General Bulletin*, 484: 967-972.
[118] Lefebvre Archives at Ecône, notebook "Creation, Theodicy, Ontology." Cf. *Revue Thomiste*, March and May, 1910.
[119] Ex. 3:14.

do not have being of ourselves. Then, the seminarian meditated on this truth: "I am nothing, I am nothing without God, I have everything from Him. Everything I have, therefore, is from our Lord Jesus Christ who is God." This truth became "his fundamental disposition: recognition of our nothingness before God and our continual dependence on God in our existence and in whatever we do."[120]

That was how Marcel Lefebvre came to drink deeply at the fountain of philosophy.

HOLIDAYS IN UMBRIA—A VOCATION PUT TO THE TEST

Tired minds looked forward to the short holidays, especially the Easter ones. The summer house of San Valentino welcomed a whole host of apprentice mountaineers. The year before, Marcel had joined the Italian mountaineering club[121] and had climbed Pizzutto.[122] But this year he preferred, it seems, to follow the footsteps of the pilgrims of old and share in their merits by walking with his staff in hand, rucksack on his back, asking for modest lodgings in the old Franciscan convents or in the presbyteries of the small towns of Umbria.[123]

> We spent the night in these small villages where we were amazed to see how important the local priest was. He was everything: judge, mayor, he knew everyone; he was welcomed joyfully by all the families. Nothing was done without the priest and he did everything with zeal and devotion, living in great poverty. Coming from France where the spirit of secularisation had seeped so far into society that the priest was considered almost like a stranger in the village…all that made a great difference for me.[124]

The young student prayed fervently at the tomb of his second patron saint in Assisi. Strengthened in all sorts of ways from his pilgrimage, he made the final push during the third term and on June 27, 1925, gained his doctorate in philosophy with a *"feliciter."*[125]

Summer gave him the opportunity for a change of scene by helping[126] a parish priest in a parish boys' club. There he was stupefied, he says, to see amongst certain priests "vehement discussions that were harsh and unpleasant, causing bad moods and almost rifts. I must admit that that was very hard for me, so much so that I had doubts about my vocation during seminary. I said to myself; if you have to live like that in a presbytery where

---

[120] *Spiritual Conferences at Ecône*, Dec. 13, 1984; in *Cor Unum*, 100.
[121] Registration form in the Roman section of the Italian Mountaineering club, not dated.
[122] This is at the very least probable.
[123] *Échos de Santa Chiara*, 131: 129.
[124] *Spiritual Conferences at Ecône*, 27 A, Feb. 12, 1976.
[125] Student record, 1925-26.
[126] We conjecture that it was that summer, for Marcel only had his short holidays with the family at the end of October (family journal).

you have such arguments, it's terrible." Marcel Lefebvre learned that lesson for the rest of his life: "We must make the firm resolution to do everything necessary not to be a subject of scandal."[127]

INTEREST IN THE TREATISE ON THE CHURCH

Marcel Lefebvre went into the "major course" of theology at the Gregorian November 2, 1925.[128] During Fr. Fabro's course of fundamental theology he remarked that "non-Catholics are not part of the Church since for them–the adults–the social link of the unity of faith is hindered even by material heresy." The course stressed the existence of a visible, living magisterium (in opposition to the *Sola Scriptura* of Luther), the infallibility of the pope speaking *ex cathedra*, and that of ecumenical councils "which share in the ordinary infallibility of the Sovereign Pontiff."[129] This theology of the Church was, as Fr. Berto put it so well, "the theology of Romanity" or "theological Romanity": not just a theology learnt in Rome but a "formally Roman theology." And the first thesis of this theology, he continued, is precisely that "the Roman Pontiff is not only the infallible Doctor of Christian dogma, but the first theologian in the theologian Church."[130]

What blessed times! Pius XI's encyclicals continued to illuminate fully the Church with this Roman theology that filled the pages of *Denzinger*! The seminary's Roman fervor[131] meant total devotion to the pronouncements of the successor of Peter. Marcel Lefebvre shared in this fervor. For him referring to the magisterium or the Roman authorities was enough to end any discussion and correct any deviation.

THE PRIESTHOOD AND ROYALTY OF OUR LORD JESUS CHRIST

The young student blossomed as he encountered these first theological treatises, but his soul was more at home in the seminary than at the Gregorian! At Santa Chiara, Fr. Voegtli continued his thrilling series of talks on the person of Our Lord Jesus Christ, that year[132] giving a commentary on the Encyclical *Quas Primas* of December 11, 1925. A former superior of the minor Scholastic faculty of the Holy Ghost Fathers in Cellule (Puy-de-Dôme), Fr. Marc Voegtli had been the "Spiritual Director" at Santa Chiara since 1909, with the task of giving spiritual talks and spiritu-

---

[127] *Retreats and Instructions at Ecône*, Sept. 21, 1979.
[128] Student record for the theology faculty; enrolment form (*schedula*) for the year 1925-26.
[129] Ecône Archives, Archbishop Lefebvre, handwritten summaries; cf. Hermann van Laar, *Institutiones theol. Fund., Repetitorium*, (*Sola Scriptura*: The Bible Only Theory).
[130] Berto, *Pour la sainte Eglise romaine*, 80, 82.
[131] *Ibid.* ("Henri Le Floch, a Man of Truth"), 120.
[132] *Échos de Santa Chiara*, 125: 40.

al direction to the majority of the seminarians, including Marcel. The gravity of his voice and spirit of faith made him an impressive figure: "He captivated his audience, even when expressing paradoxical ideas that were often knowingly extreme and hinted at the absolute, for he was an advocate of the Thomist Theses."[133] But "what inexpressible gentleness," and what "a magnificent gift he had for teaching us about Wisdom and for making us grasp the spirit…of Jesus and of His Church."[134]

"His teaching was simple, he spoke only of Our Lord Jesus Christ the King.…He taught the integrity of the priesthood, the priesthood taken to its logical conclusion: the sacrifice of the priest for the reign of Our Lord Jesus Christ. Everything was judged in that light."[135] "My dear friends," the Father would say, "I beg you to love Our Lord Jesus Christ!" or "My dear friends, you must preach Our Lord Jesus Christ with all your heart!"[136] A collective testimony signed by twelve seminarians, including Henri Barré, Emile Laurent, and Joseph Trochu, declares: "Through him we learned to see our Lord Jesus Christ, the King, as the center of everything, the answer to all questions, our food, our thought, our life, everything.…That is what he wanted to impress upon us: that will remain!"[137]

Fifty years later, one of his rare faithful disciples, Marcel Lefebvre, also bore witness to the indelible impression produced by his "talks, which were very simple, taking the words of Scripture, showing who Our Lord Jesus Christ was.…That remained with us for life!" It even became the subject of the seminarian's meditation:

> "We shall never have sufficiently meditated on, or sought to understand, what Our Lord Jesus Christ is.…He should rule our thinking, He makes us holy. He is also our Creator since nothing whatsoever was made without the Word, and therefore without Our Lord Jesus Christ who is the Word. So we must only think about and contemplate Our Lord Jesus Christ. And that transforms one's life!"[138]

He was lost for words to express his experience as a seminarian when the mystical words of Fr. Voegtli awakened in him the spirit of Wisdom and Understanding and helped him to grasp the depths of the mystery of Christ. They gave him at the same time a supernatural perspective on things and made him want to do something practical for the reign of Our Lord Jesus Christ.

---

[133] Death notice, *General Bulletin*, 476: 618; *Échos de Santa Chiara*, 125: 41; 141, 149.
[134] Berto, *Notre Dame de Joie*, 72.
[135] Testimony of Fr. Roger Johan in 1927, in Henri Le Floch, *Les événements du Séminaire français de mars à juillet 1927* (photocopy, supplements), 29.
[136] Berto, *Notre Dame de Joie*, 72.
[137] Le Floch, *Les événements du Séminaire français*, 29, 34.
[138] *Spiritual Conferences at Ecône*, 9 B, Oct. 5, 1974.

IN THE SACRED SERVICE

The Holy Year was when the young Marcel took his first steps in the clerical state. On December 19, in the Roman Seminary's church in the Lateran, he was tonsured by Archbishop Giuseppe Palica, the Cardinal Vicar's deputy. From then on he was "devoted to the divine mysteries" (can. 108, §1), set apart, "*clerus*" by a divine calling to participate in the hierarchy of order and jurisdiction which by divine institution is separate from the lay state (can. 107). On *Sitientes* Saturday, March 20, 1926, in the Basilica of St. John Lateran he received the first two minor orders of Porter and Lector from the hands of the Cardinal Vicar, Cardinal Pompilj. Finally after a pre-Easter retreat on the topics of the priesthood and royalty of Christ preached at the seminary by Fr. de La Taille, S.J., he received the last two minor orders of Exorcist and Acolyte from Archbishop Palica in the church of the Roman Seminary on Holy Saturday, April 3.[139]

At the same time, a similarly long ceremony of ordinations to major orders was taking place in the neighboring basilica of St. John Lateran: the Cardinal Vicar was ordaining many of Marcel's older colleagues and friends including Paul Nau, a future Benedictine at Solesmes and a theologian specializing in the ordinary papal magisterium,[140] Alphonse Roul, of whom we have already spoken, Raymond Dulac, future canonist from Versailles and Roman correspondent for the *Courrier de Rome* during and after Vatican II; and also Victor-Alain Berto,[141] a favorite of Fr. Le Floch, who was an impassioned and convinced Roman, founder of the Our Lady of Joy Residence and aggregator of the Institute of the Dominicans of the Holy Ghost belonging to the Order of St. Dominic. This priest, who was knee high to a grasshopper, was steeped in the metaphysics of St. Thomas. Above all "*pius cum doctrina,*" he was to be Archbishop Lefebvre's theologian at the Council.

SOLDIER-SEMINARIAN (1926-27)

The cassock in which Marcel Lefebvre appeared at the Valenciennes conscription office meant he was treated with consideration and respect, as it had done for his brother in 1923. He had just passed his first theology exams on April 22 and 23, 1926, and was sorry to have to interrupt his studies, but like his brother, he was convinced that "one can do a lot of good in the army."[142] Since his companions knew he was a seminarian they

---

[139] Le Floch, *Les événements du Séminaire français,* 122, 119; 123, 147; Holy Ghost Fathers' record; ordination letters.

[140] Cf. *Une source doctrinale, les encycliques* (Paris: Cèdre, 1952); "Le magistère pontifical ordinaire au premier concile du Vatican" in *Revue Thomiste,* no. 3 (1962); "Le magistère pontifical ordinaire lieu théologique" in *Verbe,* no. 136 (1962).

[141] *Échos de Santa Chiara,* 123; Berto, *Notre Dame de Joie,* 17.

shared their confidences with him. In order to serve better and to enjoy a relative freedom, he chose to train as a reserve officer; [143] thus he joined the 4th company of the 508th Tank Regiment at Mourmelon Camp. In the mornings he would trudge through the mud or snow, and in the afternoon there were lessons. Apparently the soldier-seminarian was not too zealous since he had only reached the rank of sergeant when stationed at Valenciennes in December with the 509th Light Tank Regiment.

Working "behind a desk," he had a certain degree of freedom and could receive Holy Communion almost every day. The young soldier was not overly concerned with military regulations: he surprised his family by visiting them on Christmas Eve…without leave! He felt a bit lonely sometimes since he had nobody to talk to; so he kept himself busy by teaching people to read and write in the evenings and tried to give them a few catechism classes, which they seemed to enjoy.[144] In October he was working for the Third Order of St. Francis–was he in fact a member? It is possible–and he ordered five hundred information leaflets for thirteen Francs!

RENÉ THE SUBDEACON AND BERNADETTE THE NOVICE

On April 17, 1927, Marcel went with his family to René's ordination to the subdiaconate in Chevilly.[145] On November 5, a "certificate of good conduct" signed by Colonel Lemar testified that Sergeant Marcel Lefebvre had "continually served with honor and loyalty."[146] Thus he was able to go as a cleric to René's priestly ordination on November 15 in Chevilly,[147] and there he saw his sister Bernadette, who was now a postulant with the Missionary Sisters of the Holy Ghost. Founded in Lorraine on January 6, 1921, by Eugénie Caps and Bishop le Roy,[148] this institute was established to "work for the salvation of abandoned souls, especially unbelievers of black origin in the missions run by the Holy Ghost Fathers." This young female congregation had produced its first fruits in 1924 with the profession of twenty-three sisters.[149] Of these, eight had left for Cameroon the same year. Bernadette took the veil on January 20, 1928, at Jouy-aux-Arches,[150] taking the name in religion of Sister Marie-Gabriel. She was professed at Béthisy on March 25, 1930.[151] She finally left for the missions

---

[142] Mrs. Lefebvre, Letter to Sister M.-C., May 18, 1923 and April 2, 1926.
[143] Holiday addresses, column "absent friends."
[144] Mrs. Lefebvre, Letter to Sister M.-C., Dec. 26, 1926; Mother Marie-Christiane Lefebvre, *Mon frère, Monseigneur Marcel*, 11.
[145] Letter of Mr. René Lefebvre to Bernadette and Christiane, Paris, April 16, 1927; Mrs. Lefebvre to the same, the same day.
[146] Photo Archives at Ecône ; Ph. Héduy, *Mgr. Lefebvre et la Fraternité* (Éd. *Fideliter*, 1991), 10.
[147] Letter of Mrs. Lefebvre to Sister M.-Cl., Nov. 15, 1927.
[148] Superior General, C.S.Sp.
[149] *Mémoire Spiritaine*, no. 1 (1995): 30-31, 40; *General Bulletin*, 468: 249.

in November 1933, "giving herself up to the workings of grace and divine omnipotence," leaving her parents "at peace."[152]

Returning to Rome on November 17, Marcel Lefebvre found the seminary had quite changed. Caught up in spite of himself in the condemnation of Action Française, the venerable Fr. Le Floch had been removed.

IV. THE CONDEMNATION OF ACTION FRANÇAISE

Founded in 1899 in reaction to the combined forces of Freemasonry, Liberalism, *etc.*, which together formed an "anti-France," Action Française became a source of analysis and political action, "a workshop of nationalist studies." "Actually," said Charles Maurras (1868-1952), the head of this movement, "there are political truths which are not thought up, rather they are simply there; let us test them!" What he realized was that the Revolution and democracy were destroying France. A "traditional, hereditary, anti-parliamentary, decentralized monarchy" was what suited the country, and moreover was what had to be restored.[153] Thus far, there was nothing really to say against such healthy political realism. Indeed, Maurras's pertinent criticism of liberalism and the Revolution was approved of by Cardinal Billot,[154] and represented a force for common sense. Through Maurras's movement, an entire French elite abandoned false liberal dogmas and underwent an intellectual and moral conversion: some unbelievers even found their way to the Faith.[155]

Unfortunately–paradoxically even–Maurras was an agnostic: "I was unfortunate enough to lose the faith," he said. "But I am not an atheist, as some have falsely accused me. I have never been one."[156] Whilst for the Catholic Church he professed "admiration, respect, and love towards this bastion of intellectual and moral order,"[157] it was, in the beginning, more because of its Roman character. With this "Romanity" he believed the Church had harnessed the Hebrew Gospel, otherwise a source of anarchy that broke free through Protestantism.[158] This idiosyncratic attitude was unfortunate and spoiled many of the author's pre-1914 writings. Similarly,

---

[150] Family journal. But the date of March 20 seems more likely. Cf. Letter of Mrs. Lefebvre to Sister M.-Cl., April 1, 1928.

[151] Letter of Mrs. Lefebvre to Sister Marie-Clotilde, Jan. 1, 1930.

[152] Letter of Mrs. Lefebvre to her missionary sons, Nov. 5, 1933.

[153] Cf. Charles Maurras, *Enquête sur la monarchie* (1900).

[154] Cf. Louis Billot, *De Ecclesia* (Rome, 1922), II, 31-33.

[155] Charles Maurras, *La Démocratie religieuse* (NLN, 1931), 548-549; Canon Egret, "Charles Maurras à la recherche de Dieu," in *Cahiers Charles Maurras*, no. 43: 30-31.

[156] Canon A. Cornter, *Mes entretiens de prêtre avec Charles Maurras* (NEL, 1970), 23.

[157] Charles Maurras, "*L'Action Française* from Dec. 25, 1905," in *La politique religieuse* (1912); in *La démocratie religieuse* (NEL, 1978), 291.

[158] Cf. Adrien Dansette, *Histoire religieuse de la France contemporaine* (Flammarion, 1952), II, 565.

some of his maxims (such as "Politics first!"[159] and "Politics isn't morality"[160]) which "in context"[161] were full of unassuming wisdom were certainly open to being tendentiously interpreted with disastrous consequences. Nonetheless, St. Pius X refused to condemn the writings of the head of Action Française; "They are doing too much good," he said, "they defend the principle of authority, they defend order."[162]

Twelve years later, Action Française's influence had reached its zenith amongst Catholics and a militant episcopate. However, it was a stumbling block to the religious politics of Pius XI, who was anxious to develop good relations with the Republican government.[163] Moreover, the influence of the head of Action Française made him fear for the youth in Catholic Action. Without the lights of faith and supernatural prudence, might not this master's opinions, which were listened to so intently, twist young people's judgment and lead his disciples to act reprehensibly?[164] The Pope decided that a French Cardinal should publish a warning, which he would then approve. But Cardinal Andrieu, Archbishop of Bordeaux, wrote such a clumsy admonition[165] that the Pope's approval[166] of it seemed unreasonable. This "most unfortunate affair"[167] finished up with the Catholic leaders of Action Française resisting Rome's heavy sanctions against the impenitent readers of their newspaper that had now been placed on the Index.[168] For example, the mortal remains of Count Dugon were refused Church burial due to his "sinful adherence to Action Française." The body was finally blessed by his son Fr. Robert Dugon in front of the closed doors of

---

[159] Charles Maurras, *Mes idées politiques* (Fayard, 1937), 95; (reprint 1973), 155

[160] Charles Maurras, *Romantisme et Révolution* (Versailles, 1928), preface to final edition, 20; *Mes idées politiques* (1937), 125; (1973), 179.

[161] Jean Madiran, "Pius Maurras," in *Maurras* (NEL, 1992), 132.

[162] Audience of Pius X with Archbishop Charost, bishop of Lille, July 1914. Cf. Charles Maurras, *Le bienheureux Pie X, sauveur de la France* (Plon, 1953), 72; Lucien Thomas, *L'Action Française devant l'Eglise* (NEL, 1965), 83.

[163] Cf. Philippe Prévost, *La condemnation de l'Action Française vue à travers les archives du ministère des aff. Étrangères* (Paris: La Librairie Canadienne, 1996), 76-78.

[164] Rev. Marie-Réginald Garrigou-Lagrange, O.P., "Les exigences de la fin dernière en matière politique," in *La Vie Spirituelle*, (March 1937): 754; Henri Massis, *Maurras et notre temps* (Paris-Geneva: La Palatine, 1951), II, 101; Dansette, *Histoire religieuse*, II, 576; Fr. V.-A. Berto, "Une opinion sur l'AF," in *Itinéraires*, no. 122: 22; Georges Jarlot, *Pie XI, doctrine et action* (Rome: Univ. Greg., 1976), 113; Thomas, *L'Action Française*, 366; Jean Daujat, *Pie XI, le pape de l'action catholique* (Téqui, 1995), 92.

[165] *L'Aquitaine*, Bordeaux religious weekly, August 27, 1926; Thomas, *L'Action Française*, 109-113.

[166] Pius XI, Letter to Cardinal Andrieu, Sept. 8, 1926, *A.A.S.* 18 (1926), 382-385; (Bonne Presse), III, 255-256.

[167] According to Cardinal Billot's expression.

[168] *A.A.S.* 18 (1926), 517-520, 529-530; 19 (1927), 158; (Bonne Presse) III, 290-296; IV, 221-224; Thomas, *L'Action Française*, 166-172, 175-176, 338-340; *General Bulletin*, 437: 1-2.

the church. With the permission of the Archbishop of Besançon, the young priest joined…the Holy Ghost Fathers.[169] More seriously, the condemnation of Action Française meant the triumph of its enemies: the Christian democrats and the liberal Catholics. "It is sadly very true," wrote Fr. Berto, "that Action Française was the only solid anti-liberal force in France: there was no 'third force.' Once Action Française had been forbidden to Catholics, the liberals were left to rule the roost, and they have stayed in power ever since."[170] The condemnation of Action Française was a turning point in the history of the Church; from then on the bishoprics were given to left-wing clerics whilst all opposition to liberalism was falsely tarred with the same brush as Action Française. Fr. Le Floch was branded in this way, as was Archbishop Lefebvre later on.

MARCEL LEFEBVRE'S SILENCE

In fact, the soldier-seminarian was very upset by the condemnation. In Action Française he saw the fight for Christian order which he supported. He later said: "Oh, it was not a Catholic movement, but it was a movement against the disorder sown by the Freemasons in the country, in France: [it was] a healthy reaction, a determination to re-establish order and discipline, a return to morality and to Christian morality." "The fact that the Holy Father condemned it undermined order and effectively clipped the wings of the Counter-Revolution."[171]

That is what he saw or feared as a young man without ever having read Maurras or having belonged to Action Française. Besides, since prior to his military service in the beginning, he "had wanted to avoid talking politics" says his sister Christiane.[172] His brother René did not have the same reticence; thus during his novitiate he became friends with Henri de Maupeou. It was 1924-25 and they both took out their fellow student Alexis Riaud for a walk. Riaud later related: "They wanted me to get to know Action Française. They took me out for a walk, just the three of us, but they saw that I wouldn't take the bait…."[173] After the condemnation, Marcel personally avoided talking politics all the more. During one of the two visits he made to his brother in Chevilly in 1927, the latter, according to Christiane,[174] "kept on trying to lead the conversation [onto the hot topic of Action Française] and seeing that he wasn't getting anywhere, I can still hear him saying, 'You couldn't care less!' But that most certainly wasn't the case." It wasn't indifference but a deliberate decision: one of his seminary

---

[169] Ms. II, 53.
[170] Letter of Oct. 15, 1961, *Itinéraires*, no. 132 (April 1969): 27.
[171] Lefebvre, *Petite histoire*, 32; *Spiritual Conferences at Ecône*, Jan. 8, 1974.
[172] Mother Marie Christiane Lefebvre, *Mon frère, Monseigneur Marcel*, 10.
[173] Interview with Fr. Alexis Riaud, C.S.Sp., Nov. 8, 1997, ms. II, 43-45.
[174] Mother Marie Christiane Lefebvre, *Mon frère, Monseigneur Marcel*, 10.

confreres reports: "Among friends we spoke about Action Française but I never heard Marcel talk about that. One of his mottoes was: Rome has spoken, the matter is at an end."[175]

Moreover, as painful as it was, the ban on Action Française was nothing to Marcel Lefebvre compared with the departure of the venerable Fr. Le Floch.

THE FRENCH SEMINARY IN THE CHAMBER OF DEPUTIES[176]

On January 25, 1925, the lunchtime recreation at Santa Chiara was lively. A group had formed around a priest who was reading the newspaper: the President of the Council, Edouard Herriot, set out to undermine the Vatican embassy by standing up in the Palais Bourbon and attacking the French Seminary where, he said, "political ideas which go against the laws of the Republic are flourishing."[177] Meanwhile, on March 10, the Cardinals and Archbishops of France issued a declaration on the injustice of the secular laws and the "steps to be taken against them."[178] Its publication irritated the Pope beyond measure, anxious as he was for some sort of entente.

In fact, on March 20, in the Chamber of Deputies, Herriot attacked the bishops' declaration and denounced where he thought it came from: "It comes directly from the French Seminary in Rome."[179] And Herriot quoted extracts from a talk given by Fr. Georges Michel[180] during one of the St. Thomas Lectures: "The State has the duty to recognize the Catholic religion as the sole true form of divine worship...(cries from the Left and extreme Left) and to profess it publicly" and to protect it "if necessary with the armed forces" (same reactions). A talk by Fr. Lucien Lefèvre was also singled out: "The State has no rights over education" (same reactions). Henri Michel shouted out, "That is the respect they have for the secular laws!"[181]

On April 30, Aristide Briand, the Minister for Foreign Affairs, wrote to his ambassador at the Holy See, Jean Doulcet, suggesting that the Secre-

---

[175] Letter from Fr. Jean de Dieu Vadi to J.-M. Savioz, Feb. 19, 1993, in Fr. Jean-Marie Savioz, *Essai historique sur la fondation de la FSSPX par Mgr. Lefebvre* (Univ. of Fribourg, 1995), app.3.

[176] [The equivalent of the House of Representatives. Their debates are held at the Palais Bourbon. Trans.]

[177] Cf. J.-B. Frey, *Le Séminaire français de Rome à la chambre des députés* (Rome: Sem. Fr., 1925), 27; *Échos de Santa Chiara*, 121: 65.

[178] Le Floch, *Les événements du Séminaire français de Rome de mars à juillet 1927*, 14; Dansette, *Histoire religieuse*, 741; Prévost, *La condamnation de l'Action Française*, 77.

[179] *Journal Officiel* (publication of the French government), 1755-1756; Le Floch, *Les événements du Séminaire français*, 14.

[180] On the rights of man. Published, like the other talks by Fr. Frey.

[181] *Journal Officiel*, 1756; Frey, *Le Séminaire français*, 36-37, 52-53.

tary of State, Cardinal Gasparri, "watch over the influence which those in charge of the French Seminary in Rome are having on the episcopate; let him find out what sort of spirit is reigning in this establishment and consider the influence enjoyed there by the leaders of Action Française" if he "really wants to do something to pour oil on troubled waters."[182] There he touched on something close to Pius XI's heart, since pouring oil on troubled waters was precisely the task he had set himself in his inaugural encyclical, *Ubi Arcano.*[183] Soon, on July 5, 1925, the Sacred Congregation of the Consistory, of which Fr. Le Floch was an influential consultant, lost its power to appoint bishops to the Sacred Congregation for Extraordinary Ecclesiastical Matters and the Secretariat of State. Pius XI wanted less belligerent bishops who were more open to his politics of "détente and reconciliation."[184]

Looking back on the crisis, Archbishop Lefebvre took a rather dim view of Pius XI's religious politics: "On the doctrinal level" (*e.g.* the social reign of Christ) "Pius XI was not a liberal."[185] But he was "weak, very weak in the practical sphere," "he was rather inclined to compromise with the world."[186]Moreover, like Leo XIII, Pope Pius XI "was anxious to deal with the *de facto* governments, whether they were Masonic or revolutionary," and he gave "by his example the wrong impression" to those with whom he dealt.[187]

FR. LE FLOCH AND ACTION FRANÇAISE

Teaching a divinely revealed Faith and serving the divinely assisted Roman magisterium, Fr. Le Floch was entirely opposed to the positive and empirical school of Action Française. The only common ground the Father Superior could find with Action Française was that "we are fighting against liberalism, laicism, and the principles of the French Revolution from a doctrinal point of view. Action Française is fighting against the same errors but from a political point of view."[188] He was nonetheless careful to tell his seminarians as they left in July 1926: the Seminary "is neither for nor against Action Française. Not for, since it is a political organiza-

---

[182] Prévost, *La condemnation de l'Action Française,* 72-73.
[183] Encyclical of Dec. 23, 1922 (Bonne Presse), I, 154.
[184] Terms used by Cardinal Gasparri to Jean Doulcet. Prévost, *La condemnation de l'Action Française,* 73.
[185] Pius XI had said to Fr. de La Brière on Nov. 1, 1926, "When he fights liberalism, Maurras is right a hundred times over." Prévost, *La condemnation de l'Action Française,* 88.
[186] Talk in Montreal, 1982, *Fideliter,* no. 86: 6; Lefebvre, *Petite histoire,* 30-31.
[187] Reflexions on a thesis on *Gaudium et Spes,* Dec. 8, 1990.
[188] Le Floch, *Les événements du Séminaire français,* appendix 35; Letter of Fr. Le Floch to Lucien Corchepot, editor-in-chief of *Gaulois,* published in *Le Gaulois* on Dec. 4, 1927 and by *Le Figaro* the same day.

tion, and not against, for the same reason. As far as some of Maurras's works are concerned, we condemn in them what Catholic doctrine condemns."[189]

FR. LE FLOCH'S SUBMISSION—SUBVERSIVE MANOEUVRES

The Secretary of State, Cardinal Gasparri, seemed to be closely, though indirectly, informed of the internal situation of the Seminary: thus whilst he reproached Fr. Le Floch for his "non-committal attitude,"[190] the latter replied that he had always "recommended the most perfect docility amongst his beloved pupils" to the Pope's letter to Cardinal Andrieu.[191] And on the day following the consistorial allocution condemning Action Française, December 20, 1926, the Father Superior wrote to Pius XI to thank him for his "clear line of conduct," and assured him of the Seminary's obedience.[192] He summoned each seminarian individually and obtained their submission, and gave the necessary explanations in the staff meetings and to the seminarians during the evening talks.

But the "enemy of all good" incited a group of seminarians who were studying the anti-liberal spirit of the house to spy on their fellow students' conversations and then to tell certain professors... One of them, Fr. Eugène Keller, sent a report to the Pope denouncing the impenitent Action Française mentality at Santa Chiara and accusing Fr. Le Floch of not doing his duty, of being an "anti-liberal" and "another Lamennais."[193] This denunciation, which came from a malicious or unbalanced interpretation, unfortunately had a disastrous effect on the Pontiff. In an allocution given to the assembled seminary on March 25, 1927, Pius XI denounced those who united "declarations of submission" to "disobedience and revolt," and then went on that "there was precious little use in coming to Rome and doing one's studies in Rome" if it was only to imitate "Lamennais's post-Roman activities."[194]

When Bishop Le Hunsec, the Superior General, came to Rome during the Easter holidays,[195] he saw Pius XI, who spoke categorically: "In spite of his great work in the past, Fr. Le Floch is no longer right for the French Seminary." And when the bishop did his best to defend the Rector, even

[189] Le Floch, *Les événements du Séminaire français*, 22.
[190] Letter of Cardinal Gasparri to Fr. Le Floch, *ibid.*, app.7, 15.
[191] Letter from Fr. Le Floch, Nov. 18, 1926, *ibid.*, app.12.
[192] Letter of Fr. Le Floch to Pius XI, Dec. 21, 1926, *ibid.*, app.12
[193] Le Floch, *ibid.*, p.40; Letter of several spiritual directors to Pius XI, April 1927, protesting about the allegations in the "report": *ibid.*, app.17, 40.
[194] *L'Osservatore Romano*, March 27, 1927; Le Floch, *Les événements du Séminaire français, 1926-27*, 121-127; *General Bulletin*, 630: 378.
[195] Rather than "the following day" as Koren says, *Les Spiritains*, 452: *Les événements du Séminaire français*, 14; so between April 18 and 24.

daring with the forcefulness and inexperience of a young bishop to ask his Holiness to receive Fr. Le Floch in audience, he received this answer: "I don't want another Lamennais coming to visit me!"[196] And he added: "Father has asked for a canonical visit and he shall have one."

ENQUIRY, COUNTER ENQUIRY, AND FR. LE FLOCH'S DISMISSAL

The enquiry undertaken from April 26 to May 6 by Dom Ildefonse Schuster, Abbot of St. Paul Outside the Walls–later Cardinal of Milan and beatified–showed that "it was all just a *montatura*,"[197] as he wrote to the Pope. He even went as far as to say to some seminarians that "for some who don't agree with the spirit of the Seminary...this Action Française business has been just an excuse to try and salvage already old doctrinal tendencies."[198] But it was to no avail, the Sacred Congregation of Seminaries and Universities received new complaints and then tried to find something wrong with the Rector. In desperation, it invoked Canon 505–wrongly–and asked for Fr. Le Floch to be replaced.

Bishop Le Hunsec who had come to Rome was ordered by Pius XI: "You must dismiss Fr. Le Floch immediately." When the Superior General refused to accept the responsibility for this,[199] the Pontiff banged his fist on the table: "I am the Pope!" And he started talking about Action Française and anti-liberalism.[200] Faced with the iron will of Pius XI, Bishop Le Hunsec asked if Fr. Le Floch could be allowed to offer his resignation to the Pope. "He's a rebel," said the Pontiff, "he won't obey."

"Most Holy Father, I might make so bold as to guarantee his obedience, I beseech Your Holiness at least to let me try."

"As you wish" said Pius XI finally, "but you will see, I tell you he's a rebel, he won't listen."

Of course the Rector "listened" to his superior and immediately handed in his resignation. Bishop Le Hunsec also obtained permission to put into practice the decision of the General Counsel of the Congregation and moved Fr. Keller, threatening to resign himself as Superior General if it wasn't done.[201] Fr. Le Floch left Rome three days later.[202] Giving his opin-

---

[196] *General Bulletin*, 630: 378; Koren, *Les Spiritains*, 453.

[197] Le Floch, *Les événements du Séminaire français*, 45.

[198] *Ibid.*, app.23, 48.

[199] *Ibid.*, 55-56; Koren, *Les Spiritains*, 453-454.

[200] Le Floch, *Les événements du Séminaire français*, 56; *General Bulletin*, 630: 379, claims that Pius XI actually said, "Le Floch is a supporter of Action Française," which seems false.

[201] Koren, *Les Spiritains*, 454, who omits mentioning the dismissal of Fr. Keller.

[202] René Lefebvre, father of the two seminarians, sent a letter of sympathy to Fr. Le Floch: my two sons, he said, "appreciated your guidance and the truth of your advice so much." Jacques Prévotat, *Les Catholiques et l'Action Française, histoire d'une condemnation, 1899-1939* (Fayard, 2001), 480.

ion later, Bishop Le Hunsec said to Fr. Berto: "Now they can do what they want to me; there's nothing worse that can happen to me. I can take anything now."[203]

An Italian priest, Mgr. Pucci, who knew well what had gone on would soon write (we summarize): "Pius XI had decided that Fr. Le Floch, having served for twenty years under a different political dispensation, was not apt to serve under his or to teach its implementation." As if an "implementation"[204] of this kind had anything to do with studies at seminary.

V. FACING THE LIBERAL STORM

THE MALICE OF THE LIBERALS

In his first floor office, the new Rector, Fr. César Berthet, received Marcel warmly; but Marcel's heart remained cold remembering the Rector he had loved! The seminarian learned from his fellow students the "scandalous" circumstances of the plots of the preceding spring; he was indignant, as he would say later, it was a providential lesson for him in the malice of the liberals:

> I was always very suspicious later on, especially when I was a bishop, of all those people who wanted to compromise the Church with modern errors. It taught me to be very vigilant and to keep my eyes open when priests visited me or when I visited dioceses and heard reports of this or that; straight away I thought: Aha! They may be opposed to one another because of the liberals.[205]

From time to time still, some seminarians had to pack their bags because, according to the Father Superior, "the Roman climate didn't suit them."[206] They were called "pro Action Française" whereas in fact they were unable to put up with the departure of Fr. Le Floch and the new atmosphere. Georges Frénaud seems to have been one of them and he was welcomed by Solesmes, where the Novice Master had a special understanding for such black sheep. Marcel Lefebvre stayed at Santa Chiara, but as his sister Christiane remarked, he hated the "secret maneuvering and spying on Fr. Le Floch's supporters that went on."[207] "It spoiled the atmosphere of peace that had been there before" she said.

---

[203] "Une opinion sur l'Action Française," in *Itinéraires*, no. 122: 85.

[204] *La Nouvelle Europe*, Oct. 8, 1927, in Le Floch, *Les événements du Séminaire français*, 61; Fr. Berto, Letter to Bishop Eugène Le Bellec, Feb. 27, 1951, in *N.-D. de Joie*, 191; *Les événements du Séminaire français*, 56.

[205] *Échos de Santa Chiara*, 129: 33; Lefebvre, *Petite histoire*, 34.

[206] Rev. Jerome Criqui, Letter of March 4, 1997 to Fr. J.-M. L.

[207] Mother Marie Christiane Lefebvre, *Mon frère, Monseigneur Marcel*, 10.

AN ENTIRELY THEOLOGICAL STRENGTH

To cope with the strain that the seminary's new regime imposed upon him, the young seminarian was very much helped by his new spiritual director who had arrived in 1927, Fr. Louis Liagre, C.S.Sp. Born in Tourcoing in 1859, Marcel's fellow Northerner had been a professor and spiritual director all his life. He was a faithful disciple of the venerable Father Libermann, and encouraged souls to submit themselves totally to the divine will through generously renouncing themselves. On this basis could be built true humility, peace, and a life of continual prayer towards which Fr. Liagre directed those in his care. However, he wanted this renouncement to be joyful, loving, and filial.[208] Adopting this attitude, Marcel Lefebvre attained peace.

On January 2, 1928, Fr. Liagre began a series of talks: *Charity according to St. John and St. Paul.*[209] God is charity, says St. John, and the law of God, like that of creatures, is charity: leaving yourself behind, going out to one's neighbor, sacrificing oneself for him as far as possible. One must enter into this network of charity and recognize the "charity that God has for us" and to "believe" in it: "*Credidimus caritati.*"[210] Fr. Liagre wrote to a correspondent: "Theology is the knowledge of God! *Deus caritas est*! May this sublime summary of 'theology' according to St. John mean more and more to you than the concepts and formulae of metaphysics."[211] Well suited to a seminary that had had its trials, this teaching took hold of Marcel and carried him to God. He made it his doctrine and his life; later he would adopt it as his episcopal motto.

Fr. Liagre exhorted his pupils to free themselves from a particular method of meditation in order to meditate properly.[212] His beloved little St. Theresa, whom Pius XI had just canonized on May 17, 1925, wanted people to embrace charity towards God at the start of the spiritual life and not just at the end, *i.e.,* to make it the basis for the spiritual fight and not something to be attained by it: "She caused the soul to be filled from the beginning with confidence and the desire to love: she inspired joy and courage, she made the soul brave and strong."[213]

Focusing on God through the contemplation of Divine Love, Marcel did not let himself be overcome by sadness. He was not ruled by his moods, nor overwhelmed by recalling his hurt feelings. That was the atti-

---

[208] *General Bulletin*, 552: 656.
[209] *Échos de Santa Chiara*, 130.
[210] I Jn. 4:16.
[211] *General Bulletin*, 552: 649.
[212] Rev. Louis Liagre, *En retraite avec sainte Thérèse de l'Enfant-Jésus* (Office central de Lisieux, 1991), 75.
[213] *Ibid.*, 7.

tude that he would later recommend at Ecône, having adopted it himself at Santa Chiara in 1927-28:

> I hope that all through your seminary life, you love God and are so close to Him that your love and attachment to Him remain balanced, peaceful, solid, and constant. In this way, all difficulties and all the things that you have to put up with during your life will no longer be able to take away your love of the Good Lord.[214]

Armed with this completely theological strength, Marcel silenced his regrets and overcame his repugnance. He decided to do all he could to achieve union and peace in order to make Fr. Berthet's tricky job easier and to maintain the right attitude. No wonder then that some of his fellow students called him the "Angel" of the seminary, while another of his contemporaries said, "his piety, spirit of obedience, and his hardworking attitude were impressive."[215]

Having entered the second year of major theology at the Gregorian, Marcel Lefebvre began his studies of Canon Law with Fr. Felix-Maria Cappello, whose confessional in St. Ignatius was always under siege and who died *"un uomo santo"* after thirty-eight years as a teacher. Consulted by everyone, he drew the pastoral wisdom and resolute certainty of his answers from the highest principles.[216] He made Marcel love the maternal and ordered spirit of the Church expressed in her laws. In Frs. Heinrich Lennerz and Lazzarini's dogmatic theology courses, Marcel had difficulty learning theses, preferring instead the beneficial *ordo disciplinae* of St. Thomas's *Summa Theologica*. Finally, passing the examinations on June 27 and July 2, he received his bachelor's degree in theology.[217]

A CRITICAL JUDGMENT ON THE LIBERAL WAY OF THINKING

But hard work and a spirit of obedience did not hinder our seminarian's clear-sightedness. Inevitably, the new superior changed the seminary's way of thinking. Archbishop Lefebvre was to keep this realist impression of Fr. Berthet who was "a two-faced man, appearing traditional but who was at the same time very eager to please. There was no longer any question of condemning or fighting against error. Let's leave that aside and be sensible."[218] This clear departure from Fr. Le Floch's anti-liberalism was dictated to Fr. Berthet by the Pope himself. The new rector wrote in the *Echos of Santa Chiara*: "The direction to follow...the excesses to forestall,

---

[214] *Spiritual Conferences at Ecône*, 16 A, Jan. 27, 1975.

[215] Fr. Jerome Criqui, Letter of March 4, 1997; Marziac, *Monseigneur Lefebvre, soleil levant*, 82.

[216] Student record, 1927-28; *Échos de Santa Chiara* (July 1962): 39-40.

[217] Student record and booklet.

[218] Lefebvre, *Petite histoire*, 35.

and the pitfalls to avoid have been clearly pointed out to me by the Holy Father to whom I spoke for almost an hour, and His Eminence, the Cardinal Prefect for the Congregation of Universities and Seminaries with whom I have had several meetings." In another private audience given to Fr. Berthet on April 22, 1928, then in an audience which was granted on June 16, 1928, to the French Seminary, Pius XI congratulated the Rector for having "interpreted the Holy Father's intentions so well in the running of the seminary."[219]

Marcel Lefebvre heard these words. Did he understand that Pius XI was at the root of the change in direction in the seminary? Did he realize that the Pope himself had asked for *détente* instead of *crusade*? Probably not since his devotion to Pius XI remained intact, and he did not attach any blame to the Pope when he talked about the years under Fr. Berthet. Then he admitted: "Well, those last years in the seminary were a bit unpleasant because of that."

In order to understand the reality of the change in thinking, one only has to read the very clear description of the situation found in the General Bulletin of the Holy Ghost Fathers in 1932 by Fr. Dhellemmes: "The practical formation of the pupils with a view to the work they will one day have to undertake has been carried out with some discernment. According to the desire which the Holy Father has expressed several times the most important thing is to teach seminarians how to evaluate the conditions in which principles must be adapted to the necessities of real life." Obviously, Marcel Lefebvre had learned from Fr. Le Floch that principles are made to change things: not themselves to be changed by the way things are. Behind this hoo-ha there was more than just a disagreement over words. Fr. Dhellemmes continued: "The tendency in youth is to extremism: in their opinion principles must be applied entirely and absolutely. Their excessive intellectualism lays a charge of timidity, weakness, or ignorance on any conduct which is not in conformity with their rigorous deductions, even if this conduct is nothing more than a rational and legitimate adaptation of the directives established by means of reasoning."[220]

This was the death of the healthy enthusiasm which Fr. Le Floch had enkindled in his pupils' minds: a denial of "living vigorously by principles" which had been the joy of their life. Marcel Lefebvre was too much a Thomist to say that you can never depart from the principles. With St. Thomas, he well knew that when a principle cannot be applied due to some unfortunate circumstance, another principle, higher and more general needs to be applied.[221] But one never gives up principles as such. Having said

---

[219] *Échos de Santa Chiara*, 129: 5-7; *General Bulletin*, 454: 668; 455: 680.
[220] *General Bulletin*, 498: 531.
[221] *Summa Theologica* II II, q. 51, a. 4; Pius XII, alloc. *Ci Riesce*, Dec. 6, 1953 (*P.I.N.* 3040).

this, for him the first principles, especially if they come from the natural or divine law, never lose their rights and must never be abandoned in despair.[222] Similarly any act based on these principles, no matter how much they have been adapted to the circumstances, can never be praised without reservation. Fr. Dhellemmes finished by saying: "This explains the suspicion some people feel with regard to all our social organizations, professional or international, which seem to them to be run contrary to the principles of order and authority." Marcel Lefebvre had chosen to be justifiably suspicious, rather than imprudently accept all and sundry.

Similarly the talks given at the seminary by Bishop Pic on the *Ralliement,* by Fr. Arnou on the Geneva Institution,[223] and by Bishop Liénart on unionism[224] called for the seminarian's critical judgment, especially when the bishop of Lille began his talk by speaking of the clergy: "We are the leaven which makes the dough rise and we must mix our doctrine and our faith with contemporary ideas." Moreover, he finished with these words: "Christian unions will form minds and hearts; they will bring the faith into every aspect of social life."[225]

VI. THOMIST AND ROMAN

A MAN WHO TOOK LIFE SERIOUSLY

More than ever Marcel was interested in what was essential–the faith of St. Peter and the Martyrs. During Easter Week 1928 he organized a pilgrimage for his mother and his sister Christiane in no time at all. At the catacombs of St. Callistus the pilgrims went down sixty steps, and in the dark on an altar lit only by two candles, their priest-friend Marcel Collomb said Mass.

In the summer holidays he met René and Christiane in Saint-Savin. Christiane was going into the Carmel in Tourcoing on September 24, and René was setting out for Gabon on November 18. So, one after the other, Jeanne, René, Bernadette, and Christiane embraced the religious life. Would Marcel remain the only secular? With this question still in his mind he returned to Rome; was he still attracted to the Benedictine life? He was still going happily every Sunday to join his voice to those of the Benedictine Monks at their conventual Mass at St. Anselm on the Aventine.

---

[222] Even if the circumstances *hic et nunc* (the hypothesis) suggest that one must abandon the ideal order which comes from the entire application of the initial principles (the thesis), Fr. Le Floch wants us not to give up trying to establish this order, *i.e.,* the Social Reign of Christ King.

[223] The future League of Nations and later the United Nations.

[224] *General Bulletin,* 498: 532.

[225] *Échos de Santa Chiara,* 137: 220, talk given at Santa Chiara on April 11, 1929, summarized by someone in attendance.

At the beginning of the school year in 1928, Father Superior appointed him "guardian angel" to two new seminarians–there would soon be four of them–who were Swiss German. One of them, Alois Amrein, wrote his impressions in the pages of his personal journal: "Of course we sized him up, and he fixed his eye on us. He wasn't a run of the mill person. His features were those of someone who took life seriously. My companions told me, 'He knows what he wants and he knows how to get it.' He made a very good impression on me, I found him impressive."[226]

ALREADY A GOOD ADMINISTRATOR

On October 22, a Monday, Alois wrote: "Marcel left us to our own devices. Catechism has been forbidden in schools for sixty years…the youth is thus abandoned (that was the case until February 1929 he added). So Marcel went into the streets and gathered together the poor children." These were the young boys whom the seminarians, under the guidance of a senior student, catechized in Italian, preparing them for their First Confession and Communion: but just try preparing a thirteen or fourteen year old for his First Communion when he still cannot read! Out of one hundred who had put their names down, sixty came quite regularly to the chapel where classes were held on the Via dei Cestari. It was called the "St. Catherine Parish Project" after the saint whose body lay under the altar in the nearby church of Santa Maria Sopra Minerva. The parish project gave the boys a Christmas tree complete with presents, a prize giving ceremony, and the opportunity to make a retreat at Ponte Rotto, *etc.*

Marcel Lefebvre therefore got to know Italian as spoken by his "ragazzoni." That year, Pierre Bonnichon was kept in charge of the parish project by Fr. Larnicol whilst Henri Fockedey took over from Just Liger-Bélair organizing the catechism.[227] Marcel Lefebvre's practical gifts meant he was responsible for looking for materials. Helped by two confreres, including Jerome Criqui, he ran the bookshop selling new and secondhand books. "Marcel Lefebvre was very good at that, he knew literature, he looked after the accounts and did it very well," says Jerome.[228] On the side they sold secondhand things, collars, and hats: and they trimmed tonsures. All the profits went to St. Catherine's.[229] And thanks to Marcel Lefebvre every seminarian could build up his own library; he only sold "good stuff" starting with papal documents.

---

[226] Fr. Aloïs Amrein, Diary, 1, 2, 5.
[227] *Échos de Santa Chiara*, 120: 20-24; 137, 228; Prévost, *Dieu n'échoue pas*, I, 154-157.
[228] Fr. Jerome Criqui (1927-1934), interview with Fr. J.-M. L., April 1, 1997.
[229] *Échos de Santa Chiara*, 147: 158-160.

AN OBSTINATE THOMIST FERVOR

In the year that Marcel Lefebvre was to be ordained he worked flat out to get his theology licentiate. At the Gregorian there were courses on God, Creation, Grace with Fr. Lennerz, and the Old and New Testament complemented with Biblical Greek. He passed his licentiate or *"polytatus"* on June 22, 1929.

At the seminary his fellow students admired his hardworking attitude: "He had a deep mind," said Jerome Criqui, "he applied himself and worked hard. In the evenings we had an optional recreation but he preferred to work in his room."[230] "He was always ready to help if we didn't understand something," another seminarian remembers: "He had a very high level of philosophical and theological understanding."[231] "Nonetheless," said one clear-sighted confrere, "I didn't get the impression that he was an intellectual, he was more a man of action."[232] Notwithstanding the admirable mental discipline of the scholastic *disputatio* in which he was skilled, he preferred, like Fr. Le Floch, to contemplate the central ideas of theology and to meditate on the sayings of his beloved St. Thomas in order to nourish his spiritual life and form his apostolic zeal.

During the weekly revision classes in theology, reports another fellow student: "The able dogma teacher, Fr. Larnicol, went through what we had covered at the Gregorian, making it understandable and very often developing what we had learned. At these classes Marcel was a very active participant. During the discussions there were usually diverse opinions. In those cases Marcel would only accept what St. Thomas had taught. Sometimes it would be to such an extent that the other theology students called him the 'petrified dogmatician.' He kept the name and rather enjoyed it! He always stayed very faithful to St. Thomas!"[233]

Sometimes the phrase "healthy petrified doctrine" was used—*sana doctina petrificata*.[234] Fossilized his doctrine most certainly was not, since for him it was the immediate source of wisdom for the Christian and apostolic life. But it is true that Marcel Lefebvre liked to hold tried and trusted positions and defend these positions tenaciously. Behind this attitude lurked the mischievousness of a clever man who enjoys teasing others, and this was a trait of his character which many of his fellow students were to re-

---

[230] Fr. Jerome Criqui, Letter of Feb. 25, 1997.
[231] Letter of Canon Joseph Giry (1925-1932), July 7, 1997.
[232] Fr. Alexis Riaud, interview in Chevilly, Feb. 1, 1997.
[233] Amrein, Diary.
[234] Canon Edmund de Preux (1926-1928), interview with Fr. Jean Anzevui, his notes, Anzévui family archives, in Savioz, *Essai historique*, app.4, 1.

member later: "He seemed a bit stubborn already in seminary,"[235] said one of them. And another declared:

> Admirable and formidable–that's how the figure of Marcel Lefebvre appeared to us after so many years. We admired his care for the truth such as it appeared to him, according to St. Thomas Aquinas. But he was formidable: he took no account of the opinions of those who do not agree with him! His faith put to flight those who loved theological distinctions. It was not in his nature to be "conciliatory." That's how the Lord made him![236]

And that's how Marcel Lefebvre was. But his Thomist enthusiasm had a very deep root. In St. Thomas he found what can never be found in the manuals: "They all take their inspiration from St. Thomas," he explained, "but they don't have the same spirit, the Holy Spirit, which is to be found in St. Thomas. True, St. Thomas is quite dry to read but there are often one or two well turned sentences that summarize the spiritual aspect of the teaching and open up extraordinary horizons."[237] Like Pius XI, Marcel "found in the Angelic Doctor a perfect union of doctrine, piety, knowledge, virtue, truth, and charity" that was also highly recommended at Santa Chiara; and like the Pope he admired in his beloved Doctor "what St. Paul calls 'the word of wisdom' and that union of acquired and infused wisdom that go so well together with humility, a spirit of prayer and the love of God."[238]

THE PRIEST, RELIGIOUS OF GOD THE FATHER

Listening to the spiritual talks of Fr. Frey, Marcel especially learnt the importance of mental prayer. This energetic, stocky Alsatian with spiked hair was to stay at Santa Chiara uninterruptedly from 1906 until his death in 1939. He was Fr. Le Floch's right hand man and took over from Fr. Berthet in 1933. From 1925 he was secretary of the Biblical Commission, where he sometimes had to condemn erroneous tendencies.[239]

> His spiritual discourses looked at the virtue of religion according to St. Thomas: Religion, he said, is not something we do to make God happy nor yet a service we do Him: it is a duty that we owe Him in justice. Since we have everything from God we must give everything back to Him. "The spiritual creature," he says, "is by definition religious, otherwise it would be denatured. Is it possible to imagine a priest who didn't have this spirit

---

[235] Bishop Jean de Canbourg (1926-1934), bishop emeritus of Valence, Letter of Dec. 3, 1996.

[236] Fr. Joseph de Tinguy, of the Oratory (1928-1934), Letter of Sept. 11, 1997.

[237] *Retreats given at Ecône*, priestly retreat, Sept. 8, 1982, 3 P.M. talk.

[238] Pius XI, *Studiorum Ducem*, June, 29, 1923 (Bonne Presse), I, 244.

[239] *General Bulletin*, 589: 154-158; *Échos de Santa Chiara*, year 1953.

of religion, the continual presence of God, and who did not adore God in his soul?"[240]

Marcel Lefebvre was to become imbued with this spirit, and suffused with religion. He loved the liturgical gestures which expressed the internal adoration of God as well as the respect for those who share His authority or who are by grace the temples of the Holy Ghost.[241] He learned that the Christian civilization is the civilization of respect. Its religion is centered on our Lord Jesus Christ and its "great prayer" is the Holy Sacrifice of the Mass.

For Marcel, the best practical school of the virtue of religion was run by Fr. Joseph Haegy, the Prefect of Liturgy in the Seminary. This tiny man had a strong Alsatian accent and walked with small, hurried steps. He made jerky, symmetrical movements with his hands when he had something to say. With the help of his Masters of Ceremony, including Marcel, he oversaw the frequent rehearsals he demanded. He required precision and attention to detail: "The piety of a priest," he would say, "is not to be measured by how long he pauses at the *Memento* but by the degree of his obedience to the rubrics." Marcel would write in 1931: "His care for perfection showed us the great faith he had in the presence of the divine Victim. He knew by experience that traditional rites are so often replaced by arbitrary practices."[242] When the seminary was invited to the city, either for a Pontifical Mass or Exposition in the presence of a Cardinal, Father chose the best servers because "the honor of the seminary was at stake" and accompanied them there well in advance "leaving nothing to chance."

Marcel was Head M.C. from 1927 until 1930, having for his predecessors Alfred Ancel and Lucien Lebrun, future bishops.[243] He was Fr. Haegy's last Head M.C.; the priest's health was failing and he left more and more to Marcel, who later said: "I had to go and give a report after every ceremony to make sure everything had been all right, if the celebrant didn't 'make a mess of it'... He made us laugh"[244] with his funny ways, but in fact he gave his pupils excellent principles. The most important of these was to know the rubrics well in order to be anonymous before the Church's rules. In this way the personality of the priest is put aside and the action of Christ and the Church shines through.

---

[240] *General Bulletin*, 589: 154-158; *Échos de Santa Chiara*, year 1953; Archbishop Lefebvre, talk in Fribourg, Nov. 20, 1969; *Spiritual Conferences at Ecône*, 25 A, Nov. 28, 1975, and 25 B, Dec. 2, 1975; *Sermons given at Ecône*, 39 A1, May 28, 1987.

[241] Archbishop Marcel Lefebvre, *Lettres pastorales et écrits* (Escurolles: Éditions *Fideliter*, 1989), 221; *Cor Unum*, 56.

[242] *Échos de Santa Chiara*, 145: 105; 149: 13.

[243] Sermon, Paris, Sept. 23, 1979, *Fideliter*, no. 12: 6.

[244] *Spiritual Conferences at Ecône*, 64 B, Oct. 28, 1978.

The little slips of paper on which Marcel described what each minister was to do at a solemn or Pontifical Mass are wonders of precision. His rehearsals were done with the same care and "he performed the functions of M.C. with a great dignity and great confidence," either at the seminary or, very often, outside: "He did that to perfection."[245] Archbishop Lefebvre would say in the sermon of his golden jubilee of priesthood: "We loved preparing the altar and getting the ceremonies ready; and we were always excited the day before a big feast or ceremony. Already as young seminarians we learned to love the altar."[246]

His fellow students remembered him as a "very pious seminarian with a great devotion to the Virgin"; he was a member of the Association of the Blessed Virgin to which belonged those seminarians who "wanted to commit themselves to loving, and making others love, the Blessed Virgin."[247] They met regularly in the choir loft. Moreover, "with the Head Sacristan, Louis Ferrand, Marcel formed a partnership which enjoyed the trust of the authorities."[248] Mother Marie Christiane relates: "It was very edifying to see that there was never any argument between the M.C. and the Sacristan whenever they were put in joint charge of anything. It was unheard of."[249]

THE POPE, ROMANITY, AND THE HOLY CITY

This trust was such that Marcel was able to visit Cardinal Billot in his retirement. It is known that the Cardinal, sorry that he was unable to dissuade Pius XI from condemning Action Française, had resigned the Roman Purple in September of 1927.[250] Obedience sent "Fr. Billot" to the Novitiate in Galloro on the shore of Lake Nemi in the country. Marcel "was very pleased" to go and see him, said Alois Amrein, who went with him.[251] Marcel wanted to pay homage to a fearless and irreproachable man of the Church and cheer up an exile. But his companion knew that "he respected and venerated Pius XI" as well. Archbishop Lefebvre expressed his veneration for Pius XI to the seminarians at Ecône: "We in the French Seminary had the joy every year of being received by the Holy Father....God knows we learned to love the Pope, the Vicar of Christ!"[252] In the audience of December 3, 1927, Pius XI, a former Roman student, confided in the seminarians that he himself considered it "one of the

---

[245] Fr. Jerome Criqui, Letter of March 4, 1997; interview April 1, 1997.
[246] *Fideliter*, no. 12: 6.
[247] *General Bulletin*, 552: 648-649.
[248] Canon Paul Boinot (1926-1936), Letter to Fr. J.-M. L., August 20, 1997.
[249] Mother Marie Christiane Lefebvre, *Mon frère, Monseigneur Marcel*, supplement.
[250] Dansette, *Histoire religieuse*, II, 601-602; Prevotat, *Les Catholiques et l'Action Française*, passim.
[251] Amrein, Diary, 7-8.
[252] *Spiritual Conferences in Ecône*, 55 B, Jan. 17, 1978.

choicest graces God could grant to be able to breathe for a while this atmosphere so full of faith and the Catholic spirit, this 'Romanity' which is the soul of the Catholic Faith itself."[253]

Marcel Lefebvre drank deeply from this spring of Romanity then and during his whole life. "In Rome," he would say later, "we were convinced we were in a school of Faith: the Stations in Lent, the sanctuaries of the Apostles and Martyrs...." In St. Marcel, the church of his holy patron, he used to like to venerate the miraculous crucifix that was carried in procession on important occasions. The church is run by the Servites, who are devoted to the Cross and the Compassion of our Lady, a double devotion which became dear to him.[254] There were also audiences with the Pope and canonizations at St. Peter's.[255] "I had," he said, "the joy of taking part in the canonizations of St. Theresa of the Child Jesus and the Curé of Ars. They were magnificent ceremonies. It took our breath away. Anyone who has stayed in Rome without increasing the vigor and fervor of his Catholic Faith has understood nothing of the city of Rome."[256]

The young seminarian wanted his family to share in his Roman fervor and even arranged papal audiences for them. Around Easter 1929, Mr. René Lefebvre with his wife and his sister, Marguerite Lemaire-Lefebvre, and one of her daughters,[257] were privileged to be with a group of pilgrims who had a private audience. The Pope came into the room, then sat down to address a few words to the visitors who were standing in front of him in a semi circle. Then rising, he slowly went round, congratulating some and blessing them. Marcel, who was also there, whispered to the M.C.: "Could you please tell His Holiness that I would be very grateful if he could bless my dear parents who have five children consecrated to God?" The Holy Father approached, the Lefebvres kissed his ring, then Marcel did so; the Pope put his two hands on the young seminarian's head saying aloud: "You have done a lot of good for the Church."[258] These words were obviously addressed to the parents but because they came at the same time that he blessed their son, they seemed a curious sign of divine providence for the future life of the young subdeacon.

Marcel had in fact been a subdeacon since Holy Saturday, March 30, 1929. The eight-day retreat that preceded the reception of the first of the

---

[253] *General Bulletin*, 449: 463-465; Fr. Frey, *Le Saint-Siège et le Séminaire français* (Rome: Lib. Vatican, 1935); Fr. Didier Bonneterre, "On ne peut être catholique sans être romain," in *Fideliter*, no. 99 (May-June 1994): 8.

[254] Retreats given at Ecône, 63 A, Easter retreat 1984.

[255] *Fideliter, loc. cit.*

[256] *Spiritual Conferences given at Ecône*, 55 B, Jan. 17, 1978.

[257] Claire Lemaire. Cf. Letter of Mrs. Lefebvre to her son René, Feb. 8, 1929. St. Pius X had simplified the ceremony for audiences.

[258] Marziac, *Monseigneur Lefebvre, soleil levant*, 82, according to an account by Mrs. Paul Toulemonde-Poissonnier.

major orders—to which is joined the implicit vow of perfect chastity—reminded them of the necessity of the virtue of chastity in the subdeacon.
He later recalled:

> It is absolutely certain that the whole tradition of the Church teaches us that the nearer one gets to God the more one has to practice the virtue of chastity and virginity following the example of those whom He chose to be close to Him while He was on earth: the Blessed Virgin, St. Joseph, the Apostle St. John who accompanied him to Calvary. Our Lord chose virginal souls; so it is normal that as one gets closer to God one becomes more spiritual and less carnal, because God is spirit.[259]

The ordination took place at the Lateran seminary and was performed by Archbishop Carlo Raffaele Rossi, Assessor of the Consistory; seventeen students from Santa Chiara received the same order; amongst them the Swiss, Henri Bonvin, from Valais with whom Marcel had struck up a friendship. Marcel liked the Swiss a lot but also liked to tease them, if Alois Amrein's naïve disdain for Marcel's supposed love of the Avignon Papacy is anything to go by![260] No, dear Alois, your friend Marcel preferred to see the Pope—spiritual Sovereign of Christendom and temporal ruler of Rome and the Papal states—in Rome. On February 11, 1929, during the celebrations of the Lateran Treaty between the Holy See and Italy, Amrein wrote: "Everyone rushed out of the seminary to buy the newspapers…even *Action Française* though it was strictly forbidden.…In the seminary, the mood was rather depressed, especially in Marcel's case. I felt that the Roman question had been resolved quite otherwise than he had hoped, he looked upset."[261] Marcel obviously regretted that the Lateran Treaty approved[262] of the secularization of the Eternal City, even if the Concordat[263] reaffirmed its "sacred character." Marcel would say:

> By locking Catholic Rome in the Vatican State, Masonry wanted to destroy the strength of the Catholic Faith which is rooted in its Romanity. Rome, recognized in the agreement as the "Capital of the Italian State" was soon to be invaded by Masonic lodges, brothels, and flea-pit cinemas [which would cause] the infiltration of liberalism and modernism within the Vatican.[264]

---

[259] Sermons given at Ecône, 3 B2, subdiaconate, Ecône, March 15, 1975.
[260] Amrein, Diary, 7; *Échos de Santa Chiara*, 135.
[261] Amrein, Diary, 8.
[262] Lateran Treaty, *A.A.S.* 21 (1929), 210.
[263] Between the Holy See and Italy, *A.A.S.* 21 (1929), 276.
[264] *Spiritual Journey* (Ecône, 1990), supplementary notes; *Spiritual Conferences*, 87 B, Sept. 18, 1981; 109 A, March 15, 1984.

VII. PRIEST AND DOCTOR IN ROME

PRIESTLY ORDINATION

But his coming priestly ordination was enough to keep Marcel busy. Already on May 25, he had been ordained deacon at St. John Lateran by Cardinal Pompilj[265] and thus was numbered among the levites who, like the Church, "are always ready to take up arms and fight tirelessly against the enemy."[266] Having passed his licentiate in theology on June 22, 1929, he was encouraged by the Fathers of Santa Chiara to crown his studies by a doctorate in theology. Without wanting to "climb the career ladder" Marcel was ready to serve the Church better. But having finished the courses necessary for the priesthood he could already be ordained. That is what the Lille diocese decided: he would be ordained by his bishop before returning to Rome for a year.

The new bishop, Achille Liénart, from a rather liberal Lille family of cloth merchants, was at forty-four the youngest bishop in France. As parish priest of St. Christopher's in Tourcoing he had shown himself to be bold and very open to new ways. Consecrated as bishop of Lille on December 8, 1928, replacing Bishop Quilliet who had retired, he was considered a man "with a sense of reality, a shrewd appreciation of possibilities, and the calm courage of duty."[267] What a pity that this man of action got deeply involved in "possibilities" and was not rather a man of principles! His unreserved approval of the J.O.C. was typical, whereas Cardinal Mercier had been very reticent[268] about this apostolate of young Catholic workers among their peers because its aims were ambiguous (eternal salvation and social reform) and it gave priority to action rather than to studying the principles of social doctrine.

During Bishop Liénart's episcopacy Rome published its reply to Eugène Mathon's complaint[269] accusing the Christian Trades Unions of participating in the class struggle. Rome reaffirmed the legitimacy of the unions provided that they were exclusively Catholic and "absolutely rejected the class struggle," although it said mixed boards of arbitration should be set up.[270] Marcel accepted Rome's decision. He was loath to condemn what Rome allowed and what could achieve a certain good. Even if the separated unions contradicted the philosophical principles of La Tour du

---

[265] Personal notebook: Amrein, Diary, *passim*; *Échos de Santa Chiara*, 137; Ordination letters. The *General Bulletin* 466 mistakenly gives Archbishop Palica as the ordaining bishop.

[266] Roman Pontifical, Ordination of Deacons, admonition.

[267] *Almanach*, 64.

[268] Marguerite Fievez and Jacques Meert, *Cardijn* (Brussels: EVO, 1978), 72-75.

[269] President of the consortium of the textile factory owners of Roubaix-Tourcoing; complaint lodged in Rome on Aug. 26, 1924.

Pin, he was too practical–we could easily say pragmatic–to condemn in the name of philosophy something that was not opposed to either theology or the natural law. Similarly, following Popes Leo XIII, Pius X, and Pius XI, he accepted separate unions as long as they were Catholic.[271]

René Lefebvre was certainly no great friend of his new bishop but he never showed any hostility towards him as some would have liked.[272] In 1935 he decided to enter local politics and was a candidate in the council elections in Tourcoing representing a list of candidates defending the ideas of corporation and family. "My list received 1,200 votes," he wrote to his son, René. "It had been a list drawn up at the last minute and with no advertising or money….At home it was battle stations: everything was getting muddled up: corporation, family, and Action Française. At last your mother gave her approval and supported me."[273] Such was the true Christian social struggle of this courageous factory owner.

Marcel Lefebvre spent the whole summer preparing for his priestly ordination. Without being obliged,[274] he went on retreat to one of his favorite Benedictine monasteries, Maredsous Abbey, where he wanted to soak up the teachings of Dom Marmion. The famous Abbot had died six years previously in the odor of sanctity but his spiritual treasures,[275] it seemed to him, were being forgotten. Following Dom Marmion and Dom Chautard, whose marvelous book *The Soul of the Apostolate*[276] he reread, he was determined to seek a contemplative union with the Sacrifice of the Cross, the source of fruitfulness in his future apostolate.[277]

Finally the great day came. His father had just suffered the collapse of some of his business ventures in Falaise (Normandy), Saint-Parres-aux-Tertres (near Troyes), and Audruicq (near Calais). But thankfully an acceptable solution had been found for the Rue du Bus:[278] for the family it was a ray of sunlight in a dark sky. Then his two great friends, Marcel Col-

---

[270] Reply of June 5, 1928 (Calvei and Perrin, *L'Eglise et société économique*, 479, note 20) and made public on Aug. 28, 1929, post-dated to June 5, 1929. By his personal intervention Cardinal Liénart succeeded in averting a social crisis: *Mémoires de Science Religieuse* 54 (Univ. Cath. de Lille, 1997), no. 3: 16.

[271] Cf. Robert Talmy, *Aux sources du catholicisme social, l'école de La Tour du Pin* (Tournai: Desclée, 1963); Xavier Vallat, *La Croix, les lys et la peine des hommes* (Aubenas, 1973); St. Pius X, *Singulari Quadam* to the German bishops, Sept. 24, 1912 (Bonne Presse) VII, 275-277; *Courrier de Rome*, II, 473-474.

[272] *Rita Rosen* (monthly in memory of St. Rita of Cassia), no. 11 (March, 1978): 2, quoting the *Anzeiger für die Kath. Geistlichkeit* (Herder, Nov. 1977), 379.

[273] René Lefebvre, Letter to René, May 12 and June 13, 1935.

[274] His last retreat, preparing for the diaconate had been less than six months previously (cf. Can. 1001, §2).

[275] Retreats given at Ecône 85, Easter retreat 1988.

[276] 1912 *Imprimatur*. The author, the Abbot of the Trappists at Sept-Fons, recommended the meditation of his book to everyone who was being ordained.

[277] *Cor Unum*, Jan. 14, 1982, 61.

[278] Letter of Mrs. Lefebvre to René, Sept. 25, 1929.

lomb from Versailles and Louis Ferrand from Tours came to the house to help Marcel celebrate.

The ordination ceremony performed by Bishop Liénart took place on Saturday, September 21, 1929, in the chapel of the Sisters of the Sacred Heart in Rue Royale, Lille. The bishop ordained five priests, some subdeacons, and some minor clerics. The long Mass of the Ember Day, with its four readings from the Old Testament punctuated by the successive ordinations, showed the liturgy at its most splendid. Marcel and his fellow ordinands lay prostrate in the sanctuary after which came the laying on of hands by the bishop followed by all the other priests present. Then the bishop sang the consecratory preface: "Grant, Almighty God, to pour out on thy servants the dignity of the priesthood, renew in their hearts the spirit of sanctity...." It was done: Marcel Lefebvre was a priest for ever.

After the Pontifical Mass, the young priest, full of emotion, went out into the courtyard to give his parents and the rest of his family and friends from Rome and the College his first blessing, letting them each kiss the palms of his hands consecrated by the sacred chrism. Then came the visit to the Carmel in Tourcoing to the great joy of the young novice Christiane. The next day, the Eighteenth Sunday after Whitsun, the family parish church, Our Lady of Tourcoing, was the setting for the first Mass with forty-two altar boys and thirty priests present. The whole liturgy glorified the priesthood and the sacrifice. The Offertory described Moses "consecrating an altar to the Lord and offering on it holocausts and celebrating the evening oblation as an odor of sweetness for the Lord God in the presence of the sons of Israel."[279] It was easy enough for Fr. Robert Prévost to extol the power of the priest and the propitiatory sacrifice at the sermon; but the Secret in its recollected whisper plumbed even further the depths of the Eucharistic mystery: "Oh God, who makest us participate in thy unique and sovereign divinity by the marvellous transformation wrought in this sacrifice...." Then what adoration, what interior oblation in the heart of the priest when for the first time the Eucharistic Lord came down into his hands!

The mother of the young priest, however, felt herself transported. "For my part," she said, "the alleluia at the end during the procession suddenly moved me in a way I cannot describe: I thought of a triumphal entrance into Paradise and I can promise you," she wrote to René, "everything else disappeared."[280]

[279] Ex. 24:4-5.
[280] Letter of Mrs. Lefebvre to René, Sept. 25, 1929.

ROMAN DOCTORATE IN THEOLOGY

After celebrating two other First Masses in the convents of his two other sisters, Jeanne's in Tournai and Bernadette's in Jouy-aux-Arches, the young priest returned to Rome as a priest-seminarian to live in the "palazzo" joined to Santa Chiara, in order to study for his doctorate. As a "student in the fourth year theology course"[281] at the Gregorian, he studied in even greater depth the sublime Treatises of the Incarnate Word and Grace, and in Moral Theology he studied the virtues. In ever increasing detail, he learnt about the mystery of our Lord Jesus Christ and His divine-human psychology; from his study of Grace he took the great principles for his pastoral action: the consequences of the wounds of Original Sin, the double role of divine grace, healing and perfecting–*gratia sanans* and *gratia elevans*. He studied the radical incapacity of natural means to produce the least degree of supernatural life. He was to live from these key principles of moral theology for the whole of his life. For the final three months, every evening before the *Ave*, Marcel and his best friend, Louis Ferrand, recited the curriculum's hundred theses of theology to each other,[282] defining and arguing in Latin through the tiny streets of the Pincio quarter which took them to the church of the saint or the Station of the day.[283]

Already a Doctor of Philosophy, Fr. Lefebvre became Doctor of Theology on July 2, 1930. From then on he was no longer obliged to "take the biretta by the peak opposite the side which has none"[284] as Fr. Haegy had explained in his picturesque language. That of course was only a very small part of it....The most important part of the Roman doctorate lay in acquiring an overview of all theology, as well as a profound and complete knowledge of its formal principles.[285] However, Fr. Marcel didn't neglect his duties in the seminary. He came back as Head M.C. to prepare the ceremonies for the reception of two new Cardinals: Pacelli (on January 26, 1930) and Liénart (on June 17). Three days later he went to see Pope Pius XI, who granted an audience to the seminarians about to leave Rome.[286]

Before considering his departure from the Eternal City, let us try to describe the physiognomy of the young priest. Contemplative rather than intellectual, he was nevertheless active and methodical. The contrast was only too obvious: because it unites us to God, supernatural wisdom tends to order everything and everyone to the Sovereign Master. Marcel was pious without ostentation; as a friend said "he was very simple, self-effacing,

---

[281] Student record for that year.
[282] Letter of Bishop Louis Ferrand, Christmas 1996; interview with Bishop Ferrand, June 7, 1997, ms. II, 26, 38-41.
[283] Cf. Fr. Robert Prévost, *Dieu n'échoue pas*, I, 177.
[284] Cf. *General Bulletin*, 493: 336-341, note on Fr. Joseph Haegy.
[285] Berto, *Notre Dame de Joie*, 147.
[286] *Échos de Santa Chiara*, 140: 103; 142: 161, 173-174.

hidden, he didn't make any noise at all."[287] He filled his ordinary actions with a religious spirit and his manner of saying daily Mass was exemplary in gesture. The only tangible display of his piety: when on November 21, 1929, Bishop Suhard came to unveil the statue of St. Theresa of the Child Jesus at the seminary, it was Marcel Lefebvre who in the name of the community recited a prayer which he had written himself.[288] Otherwise he was already "a strong personality with very set and firm convictions"[289] which he showed whenever *sana doctrina* was at stake. Finally he was a "marvelously kind" seminarian: he had an "undeniable aura,"[290] and was devout and devoted. "He was always an example for us," said another witness, "always smiling, always friendly; and good Fr. Berthet introduced him to us as such."[291]

To this collection of rather contrasting but well balanced traits and qualities, we can add an habitual calm and the ability to get things organized; on top of everything he also had sound judgment, a well-assimilated knowledge of principles: in fine, a good head. One has to say he was a first-rate example of a priest capable of giving the very best service to the Church.

MISSIONARY VOCATION

So Fr. Marcel went into the service of his diocese. But his soul was elsewhere. For several years he had been looking for something more. On his return to seminary in 1928 his uncertainty about the direction of his vocation had returned. Speaking about her younger son to her Bernadine aunt, Mrs. Lefebvre wrote: "I would ask you to say a special prayer for him, my dear Aunt, for he seems at the moment not to know exactly what to do."[292] The example of his four brothers and sisters who were religious had provoked a desire in him to make an even more perfect gift of himself. Moreover, in the seminary, Fr. Berthet had undertaken a missionary drive. Fr. Pédron came on April 21, 1929, to talk about the missionary work in Africa and covered just about everything: the languages, the catechists, the small number of missionaries, the threat of Islam, and he finished by saying: "Be missionaries, either by your prayers or your alms."[293] Bishop Shanahan, the great bishop from Nigeria, came on January 21, 1930, to talk about the missionary success of his Catholic schools. Moreover, Marcel's elder brother's letters were insistent: "What are you going to do in Lille?

---

[287] Fr. Alexis Riaud, C.S.Sp.(1925-1929), ms. I, 37, 22.
[288] *Annales de Sainte-Thérèse de Lisieux* (Jan. 1930): 20.
[289] Fr. Jerome Criqui (1927-1934), Letter of Jan. 25, 1997.
[290] Canon Paul Boinot (1929-1936), Letter to Fr. J.-M. L. of Aug. 20, 1997.
[291] Bishop Paul Carrière (1929-1931), Letter of Jan. 7, 1997.
[292] Letter to Sister M.-Cl., Nov. 18, 1928, 6.
[293] *Échos de Santa Chiara*, 137; *General Bulletin*, 498: 532.

Come and join me in Gabon!" It was a more pressing and demanding field of apostolate.

On March 23, 1930, Marcel Lefebvre gave a talk for the St. Thomas Lectures on "No salvation outside the Church."[294] Often meditating on St. John (I Jn. 5:12) and St. Paul (Rom. 10:14-15), he asked himself, "How many will have the faith and after that eternal life? Who among the pagans will be saved?" And he would confide in his seminarians later: "That is the question which to a great extent explains our vocation."[295] Was he not revealing here the origin of his own vocation? For he added: "That must give us a missionary spirit, just asking ourselves that question!"

He didn't wait to leave Rome to make the big decision and after mature consideration and fervent prayer, he wrote to his bishop. This is what Mr. René Lefebvre wrote to Fr. René on 13 July:

> I don't want to let Marcel's decision pass without talking to you. Dear Marcel has left Rome and I can understand how sorry he must have felt in doing so. He told us he had asked permission from Cardinal Liénart to enter the Holy Ghost Fathers. We were very surprised because we didn't think he had a missionary vocation. If that is the will of God we are very happy about it. *Deo gratias*! At any rate I couldn't really see him in the secular clergy. I thank God for this great grace. It's a very important step for us! We now know what it is to be separated! But we must know that everything that we have is in our Lady's hands.[296]

So, Marcel had written to Cardinal Liénart. The bishop was not a man to oppose missionary vocations, rather the opposite.[297] But when a seminarian asked to go on the missions the general custom in France was to keep him for a year in the diocese. That was the answer that Marcel got back from the diocesan curia; he understood it all the better since his was not the only request that had been received! His mother explained to Fr. René: "Marcel is still the same: calm, peaceful, it does one good to see him like that! His Eminence is keeping him for a year in the diocese, near Lille, he said, and not in the ministry. His departure and that of two others who want to do the same would be a bit difficult....Marcel followed the advice he had been given and didn't insist."[298]

Did the bishop intend to make him a teacher in a boarding school?[299] Did Marcel tell him how he did not really like teaching? The fact remains that at the end of summer he received his appointment as curate to Marais-

---

[294] *Échos de Santa Chiara*, 141: 131.

[295] Archbishop Lefebvre, talk at Fribourg, Nov. 21, 1969.

[296] René Lefebvre, Letter to Fr. René Lefebvre, July, 13, 1930.

[297] Roger Desreuneaux, "Les missionnaires au diocèse de Lille," in *Mémoires de Science Religieuse*, (1997): 54, 59.

[298] Mrs. Lefebvre, Letter to René, July 7, 1930.

[299] Like his fellow student André Frys, sent to a school at Marcq-en-Baroeul (*Échos de Santa Chiara*, 144: 38).

de-Lomme. He would therefore do his "year of penance"–as the seminarians somewhat disrespectfully called it–in a parish; it would remain to be
seen if he found it a penance...

CHAPTER 4

CURATE IN A WORKING CLASS PARISH (1930-31)

LOMME

For a long time the economy of Lomme, a small suburb to the west of Lille, was dominated by the bleaching factories in the "Marais"; there were thirty-eight of them in 1930. They were built next to the canal system and poured the water they used back into the Deule Canal. But the reason for the town's growth was the opening of the Verstraete Textile Factory at La Maladrerie[1] in 1857, and later the Delesalle (1905) and Paul Leurent (1912) factories in the Marais. Finally in 1921, with the laying of the electric tramway from La Délivrance, Lomme became a blue-collar town with many railroad workers, which made it an appealing location for the metal industry and increased the population from 2,465 in 1856 to 9,000 in 1900 and 20,684 in 1931. At that time, Lomme had three parishes: Lomme-Bourg (including La Délivrance), Mont-à-Camp, and Le Marais. The latter was the most populated, and many of its 7,700 inhabitants[2] who lived in endless neat rows of identical houses came from the Boulogne area, which was blighted with unemployment.

The Cardinal in his wisdom sent Marcel Lefebvre to this simple but lively working-class parish, thinking that for a young bourgeois, the son of a factory owner, an apostolate among the most humble would be a better introduction to the apostolate than teaching the youth of a social elite from which he himself came. Our Lady of Lourdes, Le Marais's charming parish church, was built in a stark neo-Romanesque style in imitation of the Marian basilica in Lourdes. Beside it stood the presbytery, a pretty little detached house on the square next to the church, which had a large garden adjacent to the town park. It was at the door of this house that Fr. Lefebvre presented himself in August or September 1930.

"Here I am," he said in his quiet, calm voice.

The parish priest was summoned to the door by one of his nieces who kept house for him and had a good look at the stranger. The young priest calmly repeated: "Here I am…what are you going to do with me?"

---

[1] Pouchain, *Les Maîtres du Nord*, 53, 139, 142; Delsalle, *Lille, Roubaix, Tourcoing*, 159.
[2] *La Croix du Nord*, May 3, 1931.

The parish priest was of course aware that the bishop had sent him another curate; however, he couldn't help himself making the following little reflection, amusing in itself because he said it very tongue in cheek.

"Oh, you know, I didn't ask for a second curate, I don't really need one. I found that one was enough!"

"Oh, I see."

"Yes, for a parish like ours, I don't really see the necessity of having a second curate."

"Oh!" said the new arrival with a disarming simplicity, "I'll try and find something to do nonetheless!"

Won over, the parish priest replied: "No, of course, you're very welcome here, come in and make yourself at home. We'll give you a room." [3]

Was it really such an easy thing to find a room in such a small house? Nonetheless, Marcel Lefebvre would say later: "The parish priest ended up giving me a room." [4]

They got on very well together. The parish priest, Fr. Delahaye, was a good priest who was both cultivated and fatherly. He was about sixty and very active; he was also a good pastor and much loved by his parishioners. The first curate, Fr. Paul Deschamps, was as old as Marcel, and like him was a former pupil of Tourcoing's Sacred Heart School[5] and one of "Fr. Deco's old boys."

PARISH ACTIVITIES

In truth there were all sorts of things that needed doing in the parish, including most importantly the liturgical ceremonies. On the First Fridays of the month the Sacred Heart was honored in a special way: at 6:00 A.M. exposition of the Blessed Sacrament followed by Mass; at 7:15 Mass with Communion for the children. In the afternoon, there was adoration of the Blessed Sacrament from 3 to 5 P.M., and in the evening from 7 to 8. At 8 P.M. prayers of reparation to the Sacred Heart were recited. On Sundays there was a low Mass at 6, 8, and 9 A.M. The 9 o'clock Mass was set aside for the catechism children; the main Mass was at 10 o'clock, with Vespers and Benediction in the afternoon at 3 o'clock followed by post-confirmation catechism. Each month one Sunday was dedicated to a "General Communion" either for children or young ladies, or for men and youths.

Liturgical rehearsals for major feasts were organized by the young curate Fr. Lefebvre. The choir sang polyphonic Masses—like the Gounod Mass—for important occasions. There were meetings for Catholic mothers, the St. John's Society, and the National Catholic Federation, founded by

---

3   Lefebvre, *Petite histoire*, 36-38.
4   *Retreat given at Ecône*, Sept. 8, 1982.
5   Lefebvre, *Petite histoire*, 38.

General de Castelnau. There were three groups: men who met at Place Ronde, and young men and children whose activities took place on Thursdays and Sunday afternoons at the St. Joseph Building at 23, Rue Kuhlmann.[6]

Fr. Lefebvre looked after the young men's group; he later praised such initiatives: "The young men's groups, organized by a curate, were very useful. They've now broken up…which is a pity. The contacts the youngsters had with the curate meant moreover that they could go and confide in a priest whom they knew."[7] In Le Marais, the young men's group organized recreational activities and sometimes put on respectable and edifying plays. The young curate had to supervise the rehearsals. He also organized group trips to the cinema to watch Charlie Chaplin films. Later he recognized that at the beginning of his priesthood his "zeal had been a little too naturalistic" and that he had not made enough use of supernatural means that make souls fervent and apostolic without the need for technical "gimmicks." As for the "Circle," there was one of young men from thirteen to twenty-one, and another for adults who met each Sunday after Mass until 1 o'clock and played cards. The curate Fr. Lefebvre used to call in: "He always had time," said one, "he never just came and left."[8] The first curate was in charge of the parish JOC[9] group; Marcel was not directly involved.

Catechism (First Communion, Solemn Communion, and post-Confirmation groups) were given by the three priests; Marcel had to prepare the first communicants for the "private" communion which took place at the 7 o'clock Mass on Christmas day. What care he took explaining to the children the great truths of salvation in order to engrave in their hearts the truths that the good Lord loved them and that they ought to love Him in return! He was not one of those priests who all too easily ask a few reliable parishioners to give the lessons saying, "you can give catechism just as well as I."[10] No, because of the affinity of the priest with the love of Jesus, Victim and Bread of Life, it seemed important to him that a priestly soul should educate the impressionable souls of the little ones in such mysteries. Moreover, remembering the devotion, advice, and piety of a good priest can create the flame that enkindles the fire of a vocation or sheds the light that dissipates the doubts of adolescence.

Fr. Lefebvre was a beginner when it came to sermons; he preached calmly without notes from the pulpit especially commenting on the Gos-

---

6   *Bulletin du Marais de Lomme*, parish monthly newsletter.
7   Archbishop Lefebvre, spiritual talk, Fribourg, Nov. 25, 1969.
8   Maurice Lannoy, interview Aug. 1998.
9   [The JOC (Young Catholic Workers), an organization for extended Catholic Action for young Belgian and French men and women workers, was begun by the Belgian priest Canon Joseph Cardijn in 1924. It was brought to France by Fr. Georges Guérin in 1928. Trans.]
10 *Spiritual Conferences given at Ecône*, 96 A, Feb. 11, 1983.

pel, but his sermons were quite long.[11] At the beginning, he found it difficult to bring his theology down to a level his parishioners could understand.[12] He liked quoting St. Thomas, for example, when he preached
about the love of neighbor: "We must love our neighbor that he may be in
God and because of what there is of God in him."[13] Applying this principle in his sermons on marriage he said, "We may not love in our spouses
that which is opposed to God, or which leads away from God. Therefore,
we can't be indulgent with regard to their weaknesses."[14]

In his relations with parishioners, Fr. Lefebvre was gentle with children whilst at the same time knowing how to be strict when it was necessary. "Rather open and relaxed with men and youngsters he was never distant but always smiling.[15] He was careful not to be unedifying. It was even
one of his pastoral rules for he knew that

> parishioners judge religion according to the priest. "Well, well," they will
> say, "look at the new curate who's just arrived"; they soon know what sort
> of man they're dealing with. What is it that convinces people of the truth
> of the Church? It is sanctity: that is obvious. The faithful must know that
> their priest is a man of God and not someone who is run of the mill, over-
> sophisticated, or someone who takes his holidays like everyone else, a man
> with "a good job" and nothing more.[16]

Marcel seemed to have been given the apostolate at the "Family
House" run by the Sisters of the Sacred Heart where young female workers
from the Delesalle factory lodged. The women and girls of Lomme remember a priest who was "quite friendly and knew how to make conversation" but who was also a little reserved: "He was serious. Something distinguished him from the other clergy–his priestly dignity: he was a bit
distant,"[17] reports Marie-Catherine Gomber, who was the same age as he.

He was not "overly dignified," but in addition to remaining a little
shy, he was careful not to become too familiar with women. The other
curate, Fr. Deschamps, was not so restrained. It was a sore point with the
parish priest that he had a gift for attracting young ladies to his confessional, although it is true that he sent many of them to the convent.[18] Fr. Lefebvre wisely preferred to be a little reserved. He kept a happy medium in
the virtue of modesty. This helped his zeal develop in a more supernatural
way.

---

[11] Maurice Lannoy and Marie-Catherine Gomber, interview Aug. 1998.
[12] Spiritual talk, Fribourg, Nov. 24, 1969.
[13] St. Thomas, II II, q. 25, a. 1, corpus and ad 1.
[14] *Spiritual Conférences at Ecône*, 83 A, April 6, 1981.
[15] Maurice Lannoy, interview cited.
[16] Spiritual talk, Fribourg, Nov. 25, 1969.
[17] M.-Cath. Gomber, interview Aug. 1998.
[18] *Retreats given at Ecône*, 100, 3 A, ordination retreat, 1989.

At the presbytery, Fr. Lefebvre was hospitality itself, aware that "if the priest shuts the door in someone's face saying, 'I haven't got time right now, come again later,' that he's lost them and they'll never come back."[19] But through his childhood and at Santa Chiara, Marcel had learned to be always ready to speak to people, which nowadays can make the difference in someone's salvation.

APOSTOLIC VISITS AND CONVERSIONS

Besides the core of two thousand fervent, regular parishioners, there were five thousand "lost sheep." He had to get to know them by going and visiting them. The zealous and practical parish priest had divided the parish up between himself and his curates. So, Fr. Lefebvre went off visiting, knocking on people's doors at an hour when the man would be home from work. Generally he was well received but sometimes they shut the door in his face. Then he went next door.

"What's up with your neighbor? Why's he like that?"

"You know, he's a communist, so he didn't want to speak to you. But he's not a bad man, I'll try and talk to him, and he'll end up talking to you."[20]

And in fact the next time he actually crossed the threshold. In this regard Fr. Delahaye told Mr. René Lefebvre how "after [the family] of a sick man had made one or two attempts to get a priest to visit, the man had asked for 'the new curate'; he went to see him, heard his confession and gave him the other sacraments, and the following day the man died peacefully."[21]

These visits did a lot of good; they meant that the irregular marriages could be rectified and the children could be encouraged to go to catechism; they were an opportunity for the people who were basically not bad to get to know the parish and the priests. Then they could return to the practice of their religion. Marcel Lefebvre therefore had the joy of baptizing numerous children, as the baptismal register shows. He was always very careful to explain the miracle of grace that is the birth of a soul into the divine life, encouraging the parents to have their children baptized as soon as possible: "We don't have the right to deprive a child of supernatural life, no more than a mother has the right to deprive her child of her milk." Later he would say the same thing to those priests who wanted to

---

[19] *Spiritual Conferences given at Ecône*, 96 A, Feb. 11, 1983.

[20] Lefebvre, *Petite histoire*, 36, 38-39.

[21] Mrs. Lefebvre, Letter to Sister M.-Cl., Dec. 26-28, 1930; José Hanu, *Non, Entretiens de José Hanu avec Mgr. Lefebvre* (Stock, 1977), 61; Marziac, *Monseigneur Lefebvre, soleil levant*, 90.

wait until children were old enough to "make up their own minds": "make up their own minds if they want spiritual life or death!"[22]

Thus, the young curate also took his turn in the confessional to give back to souls this divine life when they had lost it through sin or else to patch up the wounds of others. There he learned to identify fervent souls and give them direction: "In a parish, there are souls who are destined for a more elevated spiritual life. One discovers them on retreat or during confession; then one can form them into an elite of the parish. That's where one gets vocations."[23]

> The ministry of directing souls is one of the best means the priest has to sanctify himself....One realizes suddenly that there are souls who are considerably in advance of oneself. One is amazed to see souls who are very simple and who haven't studied a great deal, but who have reached a degree of sanctity, humility, and simplicity of which there can be no doubt.[24]

PROCESSIONS AND SHOWS OF STRENGTH

During the liturgical year at Lomme there were many public manifestations of the faith. The national feast of St. Joan of Arc was marked by a torchlight procession, and people would decorate their houses with candles. Every first Sunday of the month, after the High Mass, there was exposition of the Blessed Sacrament followed by a procession round the church square or inside the church while men and youngsters carried torches. In the afternoon, after Vespers and Rosary, there was a procession of Our Lady of Lourdes, also in the church. They did not go out into the streets if the procession was strictly religious. Five years previously in 1926 the Socialist mayor had forbidden the Corpus Christi procession. But under pressure from the young men of ACJF and Action Française, he retracted his prohibition at the eleventh hour so that the processions could take place in the parishes of Mont-à-Camp and Bourg on June 13. However, in Le Marais the rabid Socialists and the Communists blocked the church entrances, although the faithful were protected by a line of policemen at the door.

In the end the militant members of Action Française,[25] the "commissars," rescued the faithful by breaking through the enemy lines. The besieged parishioners streamed out of the church and greeted their liberators

---

[22] Marcel Lefebvre in collaboration with Marc Dem, *Lettre ouverte aux catholiques perplexes* (Albin Michel, 1985), 55. [English version published as *Open Letter to Confused Catholics*, tr. Rev. Michael Crowdy *et al.* (London: SSPX, 1986; reprint, Angelus Press, 1987).]

[23] Spiritual talk, Fribourg, Nov. 24, 1969.

[24] *Retreats given at Ecône*, Sept. 18, 1979.

[25] Action Française's devotion was criticized as a mix of religion and politics.

with cheers, but it was too late to begin the procession. The parish priest at least gave the benediction of the Blessed Sacrament outside the church, and then cheering began once again. It was a moment of true joy, all the Catholics united together, aware of their rights, and knowing that they had the muscle to exercise them freely.[26]

But for reasons of prudence, Fr. Delahaye shortened the routes of the two Corpus Christi processions in the following years. However, together with the first curate, Fr. Lefebvre, zealous for the honor of Jesus Victim, undertook to convince the parish priest to hold a large procession.[27] Thus for the solemnity of Corpus Christi on the Sunday following the feast, Christ the King in the sacred Host was carried by the parish priest (or rather, He carried the parish priest) in triumph through the town. However, at one point there was the sound of a shot. The parish priest jumped, murmuring to Fr. Marcel who was on his left, "See, I told you so!" But the procession continued through the streets seemingly without hindrance: Rue de l'Eglise, Rue Kuhlmann, Rue Jean-Baptiste Dumas and Rue Victor Hugo. They stopped at the altar which had been put up at Hermitage House where the parish priest learned to his relief that the bang had only been the noise of a firework thrown by an enthusiastic but noisy parishioner! The following Sunday the parish priest and his Divine King led an equally glorious procession to an altar erected next to the Brasserie de l'Etoile. *Christus vincit! Christus regnat! Christus imperat!*

MISSIONARY VOCATION—PART TWO

Although he was completely absorbed by his duties as a pastor of souls, Fr. Lefebvre did not neglect his own soul; thus he found time to spend some days on retreat at the end of November 1930 at Wisques Abbey.[28] He did not forget his family, and came every Monday for the midday meal at home; his good humor and the tales of his apostolate helped his parents rise above their hard financial trials. They were guided by his counsel regarding the education of the youngest of his brothers and sisters, and his conciliatory comments even tamed the excessive severity of René Lefebvre and had an almost physical effect on him.[29]

Thanks to his parents, Marcel was able to read the monthly "letter" of their missionary in Gabon. In July 1930 then in February 1931, Fr. Defranould, one of René's colleagues in Gabon, paid a visit to Rue du Docteur Dewyn,[30] giving the latest news from the mission. Marcel was all ears. The

[26] Albert Marty, *L'Action Française racontée par elle-même* (NEL, 1968), 239-240.
[27] Marziac, *Monseigneur Lefebvre, soleil levant*, 90; *Retreats given at Ecône*, 22 B, Sept. 22, 1978.
[28] Mrs. Lefebvre, Letter to René, Nov. 28, 1930.
[29] Michel Lefebvre, interview April 28, 1997, ms. II, 5-6.
[30] René Lefebvre, Letter to his son René, July 13, 1930.

call of Africa probably prevented the young curate from getting too attached to his ministry during his "year of penance." Mrs. Lefebvre saw the obstacle: "There will still certainly be," she wrote, "a degree of detachment to be acquired by the end of the year, I suppose....Oh well, God is guiding him; for my part I am happy just to pray."[31] She confided to René: "Marcel is putting his heart and soul into it, even though he knows he must leave it all finally."[32]

He really did feel at ease and was very happy with his parishioners: "I saw myself as a parish priest, zealously looking after my little flock. The missions didn't appeal to me: running around a jungle or a desert in order to find how many people? I would have much preferred to keep the faith going in a village."[33] So he enjoyed his apostolate but wanted above all to do the will of God. He felt himself drawn towards a priestly life, if not more elevated, then at least harder, probably more useful, and certainly with more self-sacrifice.

In the spring of 1931, his mother described the state of her son's soul as she perceived it: "Marcel gets lots of requests (though he doesn't tell us) to stay on and moreover he is greatly attached to his ministry. If he leaves he will gain much merit; I think the religious life will be the main reason." But Mrs. Lefebvre was wrong; the only reason Marcel was becoming a religious was to be a missionary. His mother was right, however, when she added: "He seeks to do what is best, but he has dreamed of a parish: to be a parish priest without the responsibilities—he says that he will never be so happy."[34] Fr. Lefebvre sought to do "what was best"; he had already taken the first step in this direction the previous year when he wrote to his bishop, but it was not clear what this "best" was. His mother wrote again to René: "The will of God is clear for you! Every day I ask Him to make it as clear for Marcel as if it were written down...or spoken, it makes no difference."[35]

The will of God became, nonetheless, more and more tangible when Fr. René got involved. He had often invited his brother to Gabon, but in 1930-31 his letters became more urgent:

> My brother bombards me with letters, saying "Come and help us, we can't cope with all the work here; there are far too many of you in the diocese." It was quite true, really; since the parish priest had said I was a spare part, I felt it was really the case! Logically I left.[36]

---

[31] Mrs. Lefebvre, Letter to Sister M.-Cl., Dec. 26-28, 1930.
[32] Mrs. Lefebvre, Letter to René, March 12, 1931.
[33] *Retreats given at Ecône*, Sept. 8, 1962, 5:00 P.M.
[34] Mrs. Lefebvre, Letter to René, April 21, 1931.
[35] Mrs. Lefebvre, Letter to René, April 26, 1931.
[36] *Retreats given at Ecône*, Sept. 8, 1982, 5:00 P.M.

Both reason and faith spoke eloquently in the elder brother's letters; there was nothing for it but to obey and offer up the sacrifice—because, indeed, that is what it was. He would never regret it. Archbishop Lefebvre would later share the secret of his missionary vocation with his dear Carmelites in Dakar; we quote from their diary:

15 September 1952. Visit from Bishop Lefebvre. He told us his joy at being a missionary, for in France one does not give so much of oneself. He admitted not understanding this in his youth, thinking that working in France was just as good as working in a missionary country. It was his brother who brought him to the missions.

Giving more of himself: that was the impulse of divine charity which pushed rather than drew Marcel Lefebvre to the missionary life. So, after one year of apostolate, Fr. Lefebvre took up his pen to remind his bishop of his desire to join the Holy Ghost Fathers. The reply, dated July 13, signed by Fr. Duthoit, came back straight away: "H.E. the Cardinal Bishop of Lille has ordered me to inform you that he gives his permission for you to leave the parish of Marais-de-Lomme on July 20. Your replacement will be decided on at the next diocesan council meeting." Having received this confirmation of the divine will, Fr. Lefebvre wrote to the motherhouse of the congregation in Rue Lhomond, Paris, asking to be admitted to the Holy Ghost Fathers' novitiate.

CHAPTER 5

NOVICE-PRIEST (1931-32)

IF HE IS REALLY LOOKING FOR GOD...

The fortunate influx of missionary vocations to the Holy Ghost Fathers–120 alone in the novitiate of future priests in 1929–had forced the French Holy Ghost Fathers to split their novitiate in two. There was now one at Orly and another Neufgrange in Alsace.[1] Fr. Marcel Lefebvre entered the novitiate at Orly on September 1, 1931. Located at 126, Rue de Grignon in Orly, south of Paris, the property consisted of two buildings set at right angles, of which the main building had a ground floor, a first floor, and an attic converted into sleeping accommodation. There were also various minor buildings and a huge, beautiful Gothic chapel. The whole nave of this building was taken up by four rows of stalls facing each other and in the choir loft there was an organ.[2] The interior courtyard, a small garden, and a few vegetable plots left hardly any space for exercise or meditative strolls, and the adjoining fields were only used for relaxation on days when the community went on a long walk. Such was the austere welcome waiting for the young novice. The name Orly obviously brings to mind the airport, but "the present airport didn't exist at that time," remembers a novice from 1934-35, "just an air base; the 'gyros,' the forerunners of the helicopter, used to fly about above our heads."[3]

On that first day of September 1931, Fr. Marcel Lefebvre, accompanied by his young brother Joseph, who wanted to try his vocation with the Holy Ghost Fathers–but was not to persevere on that road–arrived in the evening at the door of "Grignon." His attention was attracted by a group of young men sitting on the opposite side of the street who were looking at him wryly. Marcel walked over to them:

"Good evening...what are you doing here? Are we supposed to ring the bell?"

"Not worth it! They don't answer!"

"So, you're just waiting?"

"Yes, we're waiting."

"And what are you waiting for?"

---

[1] *General Bulletin*, 469: 284.
[2] The Holy Ghost Fathers built the house and the chapel. The latter was blessed on
     September 8, 1887, by the Very Rev. Fr. Superior General. *General Bulletin*, 568: 329.
[3] Fr. Louis Carron, interview Oct. 11, 1997, ms. II, 30, 35-36.

"Huh, for them to open the door!"

"But why don't they answer?

"They're doing it to test us: closed doors!"[4]

"Oh," said Marcel, "I see; it's like in the Rule of St. Benedict: 'Do not grant newcomers to the monastic life an easy entry.'"[5]

Only, Saint Benedict said that you must persevere in knocking... And Fr. Marcel went to ring the bell with long, persistent rings...but to no avail.

"As long as they don't keep us hanging about 'for four or five days' as St. Benedict says!"

Finally, by dint of waiting, but nevertheless before nightfall, the postulants saw a small door open. But this cold shower of a welcome had given them an appetite; and so, even though they ate in silence, the hot soup warmed their hearts and they were ready to undergo any other difficulties. The novitiate, after all, is, according to an old, venerable saying, "the time during which the candidate to the religious life tests his strength and his character to see if the community suits him, and a time for the novice master to study and test the novice to see if he suits the community."[6]

Marcel had read and reread the chapter in St. Benedict which he had quoted just now: "A senior monk chosen for his skill in attracting souls should be appointed to look after the new arrivals with careful attention. His concern must be whether the novice truly seeks God and whether he shows eagerness for the Work of God, for obedience and for trials...." Yes, Marcel came here for no other reason than "to seek God." As far as obedience and trials were concerned, he wanted those too since they came with the territory!

Among the sixty novices from all over the world–Canada, Poland, Trinidad, Mauritius[7]–there was a good proportion of seminarians who had heard the call of the Pope on behalf of the missions. This call to "the better way" had similarly drawn three of Marcel's fellow students from Santa Chiara,[8] including two priests. The first, Jean Wolff, had just spent two years as a curate in Saint-Maixent and would later become the bishop of Diego-Suarez in Madagascar. The second was Emile Laurent, who had entered Santa Chiara in 1923 with Marcel and had been the youngest student; he had done an extra year of study in Rome. With him Fr. Lefebvre "renewed a deeper friendship."[9] Other novices included Jean Mouquet, nephew of the Dean of Our Lady of Tourcoing and a future "Gabonese,"

4   Fr. Alexis Riaud, interview Nov. 8, 1997, ms. II, 42, 26-27.
5   St. Benedict, *Rule*, ch. 58, "How to Receive Brothers."
6   Rev. Paul Connauche, *Fr. Edouard Epinette, Missionary* (Paris: Éd. Dillen, 1936), 40.
7   *General Bulletin*, 502: 709; 506: 883-884: forty-four were professed.
8   *General Bulletin*, 498: 532.
9   *Échos de Santa Chiara*, 59; Lefebvre, *Petite histoire*, 43.

and Joseph Michel, the ninth of a good Breton family of twelve who gave seven consecrated souls to the Church! In December Gilles Sillard, another future "Gabonese" and Gerard de Milleville, future archbishop of Conakry, joined the little group, while Robert Dugon, whose travels we have already chronicled, finished his novitiate on December 8.[10]

HOLY TEACHINGS OF THE SPIRITUAL LIFE

The Superior of the house, Fr. Joseph Oster, the oldest member of the congregation, had been Apostolic Prefect of St. Peter and Miquelon. But the priest who was in constant contact with the young recruits was Fr. Noel Faure, the novice master, who had been recalled from Guadalupe in 1929 to succeed Fr. Henri Nique in the post.[11] He was austere but kind, and as a sharp psychologist he invited the novices to lay bare their souls totally. He was also a good teacher, and he gave an interesting course on the spiritual and religious life that also dealt with the constitutions.[12]

Fr. Gaston Cossé, deputy novice master, had come from Loango (Congo) and was trying to get over sleeping sickness; he gave courses on the missions. Fr. Charles Desmats was the novitiate's confessor. Although he suffered from eye trouble, he gave the course in "regular law,"[13] a detailed examination of the religious state, stressing the vow of obedience, "the holocaust of the will and strength of the religious body."

To help Fr. Desmats, Marcel was given a course to teach.[14] The carefully kept notebook on Sacred Scripture can only be the novice teacher's lesson notes. In it he wrote reflections on the Gospel, the Acts, and the Epistles, crowning everything with the Beatitudes which sum up the spirit of Jesus Christ.

The course on the spiritual life given by Fr. Faure was the novice's favorite. He had really missed a course like that in Rome, regretting that his numerous classes did not allow him time to follow the lessons in spiritual theology by Fr. Joseph de Guibert, S.J., at the Gregorian: "We really missed this year of reflection," he would later say, "of prayer, and studying what the interior life and the life of perfection really are." We are "hearts made to live an intense interior life in union with our Lord, trying to acquire the virtues needed to make us like our Lord." When he was a curate in Lomme, Fr. Lefebvre had similarly felt he lacked something by not having done a course in spiritual doctrine since he wanted to "communicate his knowledge by bringing it down to the level of those faithful who were

---

[10] *Mémoire Spiritaine*, no. 4: 52, 87.
[11] *General Bulletin*, 442 "Our Deans"; 502, 711; 471; 381.
[12] Ms. II, 30, 8-10; 40, 30-33.
[13] Ms. II, 40, 66-68; 42, 34-38.
[14] Marziac, *Monseigneur Lefebvre, soleil levant*, 91; Héduy, *Mgr. Lefebvre et la Fraternité*, 7.

aspiring to the interior life."[15] Fr. Faure used Tanquerey's classic *Précis de théologie ascétique et mystique* that was complemented perfectly by three important retreats: the "conversion retreat," the prayer retreat, and the profession retreat.[16]

THE SPIRIT OF THE VENERABLE LIBERMANN

The "conversion retreat" or major retreat, took place from November 25 to December 4, 1931; it followed the plan of the "first week" of St. Ignatius's Spiritual Exercises, which confronts the soul with sin, "the great evil, one might say the only evil," in order to uproot it. This helps the soul make "real and deep progress," as long as it does not stay at the level of servile fear but develops filial fear instead.[17]

This was achieved more solidly during the "prayer retreat" given in spring according to the spiritual teaching of the Venerable Libermann. Marcel took notes on the three movements of this demanding but peaceable spirituality: "renouncement, peace, union with God." Little by little divine grace gave him this union in an almost habitual way, through simply considering the mystery which since Rome had captivated his soul: the mystery of our Lord Jesus Christ and His Cross, "the deep mystery of God's love for us." How can we not respond to this gift by a reciprocal love for God: "*Sic nos amantem, quis non redamaret!*"[18]

Marcel Lefebvre did not experience the hiatus that some do between prayer and action: "The life of the Holy Ghost Fathers," he said, "must be contemplation put into action. As far as is possible we must bridge the gap between prayer and work. We do not leave God to give ourselves to our brothers."[19]

SPIRITUAL CURRICULUM AND PURIFICATION

The foundation of the life of union with God, according to Libermann, lies in the perfect and universal renouncement of all things including oneself,[20] which was precisely the object of the novitiate's spiritual curriculum. The way the time was allotted so that there was never more than three quarters of an hour without a change of activity, the impromptu jobs, *etc.*, were designed to encourage readiness and the sacrificing of one's own opinion. Every week, at the chapter of faults, everyone was picked out

---

[15] *Spiritual Conferences given at Ecône*, 59 A, May 16, 1978; 80 A, Nov. 3, 1980; Anrein, *passim.*
[16] Ms. II, 40, 35-37.
[17] *Retreats given at Ecône*, Sept. 18, 1979.
[18] *Ibid.*; *Spiritual Conferences given at Ecône*, 80 B, 4 Nov. 1980.
[19] Notes taken at Orly.
[20] *Lettres spirituelles*, I, 205-206 (letter 38).

by one vigilant fellow novice or another for something which he had done wrong. "For a triviality you had to go down on your knees and kiss the floor. It was common sense not to take it too much to heart." But Marcel did carry out these acts of humility seriously; being a priest he had to give a good example.

Similarly, he did not try to get out of taking the discipline. This penitential practice, common at Orly, was among his resolutions at the end of his novitiate. But he didn't keep it up; moreover, Fr. Libermann considered that a missionary has lots of other mortifications, if only the heat... But it was the cold that tested our novice: "It was a cold year, my goodness, it was cold! How is it possible to put novices through that sort of thing? Unbelievable!" Only the community room was heated; water taken from the tap at the end of a corridor would freeze in the wash basins; at night "you could put on four, five, or six blankets, which were quite heavy but it made no difference, you couldn't get warm. We were always cold. Oh, it was terrible! I don't know how I managed not to die of cold!" "And on top of that, we had to read this book by Fr. Rodriguez (*Christian Perfection*) walking one behind the other in the courtyard outside! It was icy cold! After a while you couldn't feel your fingers holding the book."[21]

After the cold came a testing illness. From the end of 1931 he suffered from terrible headaches; after a respite, he suffered from serious mental exhaustion in June, 1932. His Carmelite sister relates: "His novitiate was done with the greatest faithfulness in order to be nothing other than an ascent to God; all his letters have this savor and he gained more experience. But his health failed to such an extent that he had to rest in the garden for hours....What a humiliation!" He accepted this "in all simplicity," she added, for "he knew how to turn every trial into an act of thanksgiving."[22]

Reading Dom Vital Lehodey's *Saint abandon* (Holy Abandonment) helped him accept the will of the divine pleasure, but since resting in the garden didn't help "ventilate his brain" the novice was sent to breathe the air of his home region, or at least that of a country house where he had his mother's company. She wrote: "Marcel spent a fortnight with us–as much time as he could spend outside the postulancy [novitiate]....I thank God for this short time I was able to spend with him, a bit of paradise...to the point of wondering whether his stay was not brought about by a delicate touch of divine Providence!"[23]

---

21 Fr. Louis Carron C.S.Sp., ms. II, 30, 23-27; Bishop de Milleville, ms. II, 40, 19-20 and 41-43; Lefebvre, *Petite histoire*, 44.
22 Mère Marie Christiane Lefebvre, *Mon frère, Monseigneur Marcel*, 3, 10.
23 Mrs. Lefebvre, Letter to the six children, June 23, 1932.

CONSECRATION TO THE APOSTOLATE

These trials strengthened the future missionary and made him practice the much needed virtue of fortitude, which above all consists in patience and constancy. Fr. Faure taught them:

> To be an apostle, you have to have fortitude and goodness. *"Conforta te et esto vir!"* Be strengthened and be a man! Apostolic fortitude consists in a holy boldness. Timidity and human respect are similarly obstacles to this fortitude. Goodness comes from being kind, forgiving and flexible, and being able adapt oneself to others, whether instinctively or by learning to do so.[24]

These ideas of apostolic virtue were complemented by the rather lively talks given by visiting missionaries; those given by the Superior General of the White Fathers and the Superior of the Lyons African Missionaries were impressive, but it was quite an experience to listen to Bishop Tardy vividly describing the progress of his mission in the jungle amongst the wild animals in Gabon! Photographs were passed around showing a "sleeper" in a trance or of a good Christian family revealing "the profound effect of baptism on man." "When a soul becomes Christian," the bishop went on, "one sees a complete transformation in the face, the bearing, the expression and attitude."[25]

Like all the novices, Marcel was curious to know where he would be sent. Would he be with his elder brother? It was a dream! Besides, that was a secret only revealed on the day of the "consecration to the apostolate." So, he was rather surprised when Bishop Tardy drew him aside in the corridor and said straight out to him:

"You're coming to us, you know?"

The novice's heart skipped a beat, but, forcing himself to remain calm, he replied: "Oh, I don't know, it depends on the Superior General."

"Oh yes, yes," the bishop went on, "I'm sure of it. Whatever you do, don't refuse! Your brother is there, you must join your brother."

Marcel once again signaled his desire to obey his superiors: "If the Superior General wants me to, I'll come and join you."

But Bishop Tardy continued, revealing what he had in mind: "And since you did your studies in Rome, you will be a professor in the seminary!"[26]

"Oh, that," Archbishop Lefebvre would say in retrospect, "that was what scared me the most. Oh no! It was too dreadful! I liked pastoral work,

---

[24] Notes taken in Orly; *General Bulletin*, 526, Monthly Letter by Bishop Le Roy.
[25] *General Bulletin*, 502: 710; *Échos de Santa Chiara*, Dec. 1931-Jan. 1932, 61-62. Bishop Tardy had given the same talk in Santa Chiara.
[26] Lefebvre, *Petite histoire*, 45.

the ministry; I felt that was what I was made for. But a professor, oh, no, no, no; professor in a seminary, no way!

He replied to the bishop, "You know, I'm no better for that job than anyone else! Don't think that because I went to Rome I would be a better professor."

"But of course you would, of course," the bishop replied.[27]

There was nothing for it but to agree; after all it was still in Africa. However, the end of the year was approaching. The novice was still feeling tired; but he told himself simply that "it will all change with the change of lifestyle."[28]

The preparatory retreat for religious profession explained the duality of the Holy Ghost Fathers' "religious and apostolic life" in a unifying principle. Marcel wrote:

"As professed missionaries, our personal end is our apostolic end. The one depends on the other. The love of God and of neighbor go together. Often priests look for their own sanctification and neglect souls. Others, on the other hand, using the pretext of zeal for souls, do more evil than the first group."[29]

The fruits of these nine days of retreat were summarized by Marcel in very original synoptic tables of the spiritual life under two headings. The first: "*Et nos cognovimus et credidimus caritati*" (we have known and believed in charity–I Jn. 4:16), joined to the words "*caritas Deus*" (God is love) and "*Sapientia a Deo*" (wisdom is from God), with the word "*Caritas*" (charity) written by the novice on a hand-drawn picture of the Immaculate Heart of Mary. The second heading, worthy of a faithful disciple of Fr. Le Floch, concerned preaching: "The word–of faith–the truth: clear, pure, whole, simple and strong. No compromise where the truth is concerned." Does that not sum up the future of the Archbishop?

Finally the 8th of September came. The novices, already dressed this past year in their cassocks with hidden buttons and the Holy Ghost Congregation's rope cincture, were gathered around the altar in the presence of Bishop Le Hunsec. They made their engagement in the religious and apostolic life of the Congregation, and then took the three vows of poverty, chastity, and obedience for three years. Then, with his two fellow priests, Fr. Marcel Lefebvre made his consecration to the apostolate before the Blessed Sacrament exposed:

> Farewell, then, to my homeland where I leave so many memories, childhood friends, beloved parents!...Farewell!...For the love of God who created, redeemed, and sanctified me, in the presence of our Lord Jesus Christ...I consecrate myself solemnly to the apostolate of the Congrega-

---

[27] *Ibid.*, 46.
[28] Mrs. Lefebvre, Letter to Bernadette, Aug. 17, 1932.
[29] Notes from Orly.

tion of the Holy Ghost and the Immaculate Heart of Mary, and I give myself as a servant of abandoned souls for ever...."[30]

Fr. Marcel's parents and the two priests who had come for the occasion, the Dean of Our Lady's and the good old parish priest of Marais-de-Lomme, hid neither their tears nor their evident emotion.[31] The Superior General had already told the three about to leave where Providence was sending them: Emile Laurent was off to the minor seminary of Yaoundé, Marcel Lefebvre was going to the seminary in Libreville, and Jean Wolff was assigned to Diego Suarez.

FAREWELLS AND DEPARTURES

Before leaving, Marcel Lefebvre had a short holiday with his family which he spent traveling throughout the diocese giving talks on the missions and showing a film made by Fr. Nique, the French Provincial; he preached, therefore, in numerous parishes,[32] and gave two retreats for children at Our Lady's and St. James's in Tourcoing.[33] Sunday, October 2, 1932, was the day he said goodbye to the parish at Lomme. "Sermon from Marcel at the High Mass," wrote Mrs. Lefebvre, "dinner with the family, including Granny, at the parish priest's house,[34] film shown in the afternoon, came back at nine. Marcel was received in a very touching way, they really loved him; it was a sort of triumph. As soon as he came into the room everyone wanted to shake his hand."[35] Someone who was there remembers: "I can see him now, he had a little beard, he was a good looking man, a handsome chap. We had a little party in the room on Rue Kuhlmann. We sang 'Ce n'est qu'un au revoir' [We'll meet again]. He wept! I was small but I remember. He had grown fond of the parish."[36]

Having learnt that Marcel was being sent to the seminary in Libreville, Fr. René admitted that he "hadn't even dreamt that Marcel would come to Libreville." He added, "There can be no more beautiful role in the missions than the one he has been given."[37] Mrs. Lefebvre was still anxious that Marcel's headaches would come back when he started teaching in the seminary,[38] but she also had a supernatural view of things: "Marcel is coming to join you," she wrote to René, "he will be very happy to see you

[30] *General Bulletin*, 504: 801-804.
[31] Mrs. Lefebvre, Letter to Bernadette, Sept. 24, 1932.
[32] In Roubaix, Tourcoing, Linselles, Estaires, Valenciennes, Lannoy, Cambrai, Florennes, and Lomme.
[33] Mrs. Lefebvre, Letter to René, Sept. 29, 1932.
[34] A few photographs were taken on this occasion.
[35] Mrs. Lefebvre, Letter to Bernadette, Oct. 5, 1932.
[36] Léonie Vanreye-Vauchelle, interview, Aug. 1998.
[37] Cf. Mrs. Lefebvre, Letter to René, Sept. 1, 1932.
[38] Mère Marie Christiane Lefebvre, *Mon frère, Monseigneur Marcel*, 3.

again, though he only desires to be obedient....That's precisely why you'll both be happy being with one another; you could wish for nothing better."[39] Finally, with his father's blessing and that of his Superior General Fr. Marcel left for Bourdeaux. He stopped off at "Our Lady of Embaloge," at Mirande (Gers), said goodbye to his sister Bernadette (Sr. Marie Gabriel) and left Bourdeaux on November 12, 1932, on "The Foucault," a new steamer of the Chargeurs Réunis Company, which since 1930 had been in service on the route of the East African Coast.[40]

---

[39] Mrs. Lefebvre, Letter to René, Sept. 29, 1932.
[40] Mrs. Lefebvre, Letter to Bernadette, Oct. 31, 1932; *General Bulletin*, 508: 975; 471: 358.

PART II

THE MISSIONARY

CHAPTER 6

THE BUSHMAN OF GABON

I. THE SONS OF THE VENERABLE LIBERMANN IN AFRICA

THE JUNGLE AND ITS INHABITANTS

Gabon is situated on the basin of the immense Ogooué and its neighboring rivers. Their waters pour into estuaries broken into a maze of lakes and sinuous inlets; navigable down stream, their forbidding upper reaches are torrents boasting dangerous or impassable rapids. As far as the eye can see the equatorial forest extends over a hilly terrain. The climate, which is continually warm and humid, is only made worse by eight months of torrential rains every year. This attracts numerous unpleasant insects that cause malaria, sleeping sickness, bilious hematoma, *etc.*, all of which are far more dangerous than the agile panthers and the voracious crocodiles. Apart from a few indigenous pygmies, the population, for whose salvation the missionaries risk their health and indeed their lives, consists of twenty five semi-nomadic (due to the exhaustion of the soil) Bantu tribes who grew independent and settled down with their own customs and dialect;[1] Fr. Marcel knew particularly the intelligent and commercially minded Pongoués along the estuary, their cousins the Galoas or Myénés of the lower Ogooué, and the Fans or Pahouins, the warlike and vengeful inhabitants of the North who had invaded the whole estuary.

It helped the ministry that all these natives lived in villages of from twenty to a hundred huts scattered along the river. Sometimes they dwelt inland alongside paths which snaked over the hills of the endless bush. They lived in families extended to include all the descendants of one progenitor with uncles, aunts, and cousins, either descended from the first wife or from the others wives, so long as they had been bought. The missionaries, who disagreed with such polygamy, were nonetheless careful to respect the hierarchy of the tribe which found its *raison d'être* in the protective unity that baptism turned into charity. The natives believed fundamentally in a personal God who created them, and in the immortality of the soul. However, their worship included the rites of their ancestors and a belief in the protecting powers of demons. The witch doctors used these spirits through lots or divination and thus fostered constant fear, long-held

---

[1] C.S.Sp. *General Bulletin*, 498: 521.

hatreds, murder, and, most of all, ignorance of the true God and sole Sa
ior.[2]

It was to this place that Fr. Marcel Lefebvre came in the footsteps
his predecessors determined to make the charity of God flourish: *Credi*
mus caritati!

THE EVANGELIZATION OF GABON
– BISHOP BESSIEUX AND HIS SUCCESSORS

Thanks to missionaries the evangelization of equatorial Africa was b
gun by the Portuguese in 1491, and quite soon indigenous priests from tl
islands and the continent helped out. The Church established herself
the kingdoms of Benin and the Lower Congo. Her hour of glory can
when, on May 8, 1518, Henry, the son of Pedro III, the king of the Co
go, who studied at Coimbra [Portugal], was consecrated bishop by Po
Leo X. In 1596 the See of Angola and Congo was established. Gabo
where Duarte Lopez landed at the Cape which now bears his name, pos:
bly experienced successive waves of missionaries: Augustinians, Jesui
and Capuchins. At any rate, there was no trace of their work by the nin
teenth century.[3]

Through the providential intervention of Fr. Desgenettes, pari:
priest of Our Lady of Victories in Paris, the Venerable Libermann can
into contact with Bishop Edward Barron, an American prelate recently a
pointed Apostolic Delegate of the "Two Guineas," an immense regic
stretching from the River Senegal to the River Orange in the South. U
fortunately, the first expedition of Libermann's sons to the Cape of Paln
in Liberia ended in tragedy when six of the seven missionaries died fro
African fevers. The survivor, Fr. Jean-Rémy Bessieux (1803-1876), wl
was thought dead, ended up where he had not been sent—Gabon—o
September 28, 1844. He settled close to the Fort Aumale built by tl
French Navy four years previously. In 1848 a group of blacks freed from
slave ship were given quarters near the station on a little plateau which fc
that reason was called Libreville. Bessieux and his first companions bega
to instruct them in the catechism. In 1849 the first Sisters of the Immacu
late Conception arrived from Castres[4] and after his episcopal consecratio

---

[2] *Échos de Santa Chiara*, Dec. 1931–Jan. 1932; *General Bulletin*, 498: 521. Fr. Marcel
Lefebvre, notes for a talk on the mission in Gabon, 1945–1946; *Spiritual Conference:*
at Ecône, 81 A, Nov. 6, 1980; *Retreats at Ecône*, Sept. 8, 1982, 3 P.M.

[3] M. J. Bane, S.M.A., *Catholic Pioneers in West Africa* (Dublin: Clunmore and Reynold
1955), 34; Rev. A. Boulanger, *General History of the Church*, part 3, VII, 588; G.G.
Beslier, *The Apostle of the Congo: Msgr. Augouard* (Paris: Éd. de la vraie France, 1926)
94; Koren, *Les Spiritains*, 198; *French Bulletin*, 86 : 296; 109: 371.

[4] Founded in 1835 by St. Emilie de Villeneuve, they were also called the "White
Sisters." They were the preferred helpers of the Holy Ghost Fathers in Gabon and
elsewhere.

in Europe, Bishop Bessieux came back to Gabon as Vicar Apostolic of the Two Guineas.

In 1860 he founded the Libreville parish of St. Peter's for the conversion of the Pongoués. His successors went further inland traveling by river—the Komo, the Ogooué and its tributaries, and the Ngounié—founding around a dozen stations, the last being Oyem, established in 1929 by Bishop Tardy thanks to an army of 120 catechists who were drafted in from the existing stations. These "great measures" bore fruit: one year later Oyem already had 7,000 catechumens. Bishop Louis Tardy had been a missionary in Ndjolé from 1904 to 1918. Returning as a bishop in 1926 he had twenty-five Holy Ghost Fathers, six native priests, sixteen Holy Ghost brothers, three St. Gabriel brothers teaching at the Montfort school at St. Mary's, Libreville, and thirty-three Immaculata Sisters teaching the girls. Bishop Tardy's genius was to develop the native Congregation of Little Sisters of St. Mary in Gabon, founded in 1911. The congregation was the master stroke of his fight for the dignity of women. It soon had fifty religious trained by the Blue Sisters and became independent in 1949. The bishop's second stroke of genius was the systematic training of catechists, the indispensable helpers of the priests, who were spread out in the villages under the responsibility of regional head catechists. Thanks to this growing army, Christianity in Gabon made amazing progress as the following table should make clear:

Year[5]	1925	1931	1938
Catechists	152	700	1,451
Baptized Catholics	18,660	30,000	69,684
Catechumens	3,400	35,000	43,130

Thus in accordance with the Holy See's instructions, the Catholic Church truly began to "occupy" the country.

II. ST. JOHN'S SEMINARY IN LIBREVILLE (1932-38)

TOWARDS A NATIVE CLERGY AND A NATIVE SEMINARY

From the beginning, in the fifteenth century, the Holy See had had this objective for the mission: a local Church sufficiently developed to

---

[5] *General Bulletin*, 432: 743; 555: 749; 498: 522; 581: 21ff.

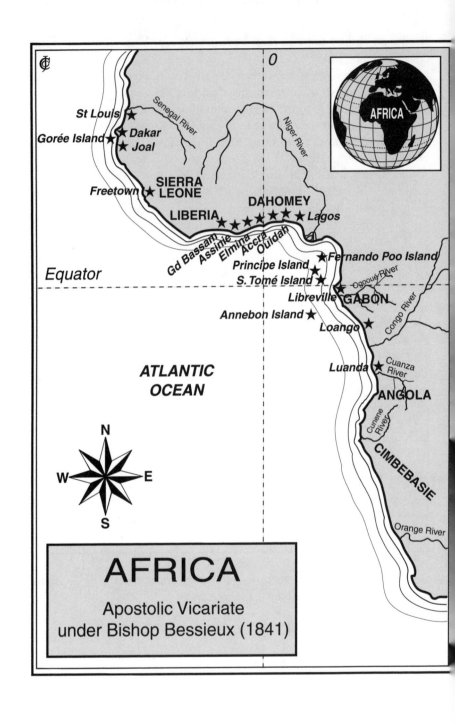

AFRICA

Apostolic Vicariate
under Bishop Bessieux (1841)

continue under the direction of its own clergy.[6] Training an indigenous clergy was similarly Fr. Libermann's own concern; but with his knowledge of Africa that would come to be recognized by the Church, he wanted to train African priests in Africa itself.[7] Thus in 1847 in Dakar and 1861 in Libreville, the sons of Libermann opened their first minor seminaries.

ST. JOHN'S SEMINARY IN LIBREVILLE

At first, studies would begin in Africa and be finished in Paris. The major seminary opened in 1874, but it was only in 1899 that the first Gabonese priest, Fr. Andrew Raponda-Walker, was ordained. He was a specialist in the local flora and fauna,[8] and Fr. Marcel knew him. What prevented seminarians persevering was the weak intellectual cultures in families and the attraction of lucrative positions that ex-seminarians could obtain due to their studies. By 1929, Bishop Tardy had ten native priests, and the seminary under the rectorship of Fr. Charles Rémy had thirty pupils: twenty-two in the minor seminary, looked after by Fr. Fauret, and eight in the major seminary.[9]

The following year, following the suggestion made by the Sacred Congregation for the Propagation of the Faith on January 31, 1926, St. John's Seminary in Libreville became intervicarial, taking students from Gabon, Congo-Loango (the future Pointe-Noire vicariate), and Congo-Brazzaville. Fr. Fauret was appointed Rector and Fr. René Lefebvre his assistant in 1931. The latter had previously been posted in Ndjolé, Sindara, and Port Gentil, and was awaiting the arrival of Fr. Marcel so that he could take up a post as curate of St. Peter's in Libreville.

At that beginning of December 1932, Fr. Marcel Lefebvre, his brother, and the Vicar General Fr. Paul Defranould, a sturdy native of the Vosges, clambered up the steep little hill from the port to St. Mary's Mission. From the hill they had a magnificent view: behind, the whole estuary stretching up to Pointe Denis, and before them the modest cathedral[10] brilliantly white in the sunshine where Fr. Marcel offered a short prayer in the dark of its paneled vault and frescoes. To the right the path led to the Blue Sisters, their school of 350 girls, and to the novitiate for the native sisters and the Pahouine[11] women's project. Beyond, the immense court-

---

[6]   Koren, *Les Spiritains*, 527; Instruction of the S.C. of Propaganda, 1659; Pius XI, encyclical *Rerum Ecclesiae*, Feb. 28, 1926.

[7]   *Collectanea S. C. de Propaganda fide* (Rome: Polyglot Press, 1893), no. 228, 84; *General Bulletin*, 425: 457; *French Bulletin* 86: 290.

[8]   Koren, *Les Spiritains*, 528; *General Bulletin*, 516: 308; detailed index of missionaries, National Archive of Gabon, IE 187.

[9]   *General Bulletin*, 423: 392; 432: 749.

[10] As apostolic delegate Archbishop Lefebvre blessed the first stone of the second cathedral on June 28, 1959; *General Bulletin*, 686: 164.

yard was bordered on the far side by Fr. Jean Kerjean's school with its hundred apprentices, and on the left by the brothers' house and the printing shop built by Fr. Joseph Petitprez. Further on the left, the seminary buildings comprised a fine house of good solid brown stone from the coast and a perpendicular building, built on a lower level, with its two stories built entirely of a lighter material. There was also the Montfort school which moved to St. Peter's in 1930 and left its buildings to St. John's, which had great need of them.

Fr. Marcel was welcomed by Bishop Tardy at the fine presbytery that was surrounded by cool, airy cloisters and was where the Apostolic Vicar also lived. It had been decided that Fr. Marcel would work with Fr. Fauret in that supreme art of the Church and missionary pursuit *par excellence:* the training of a local clergy. Born in 1902 in Arrens-en-Bigorre to a family of farmers, Jean-Baptiste Fauret hid an enterprising and ardent heart beneath an austere, bony face, with its broken nose, fine d'Artagnan moustache, and wispy pointed beard.[12] Obediently and zealously, the young Fr. Marcel set about teaching, and shared all the courses at the minor and major seminary with Fr. Fauret. Amongst other subjects Fr. Marcel taught dogmatic theology and Sacred Scripture, delivering a cyclical curriculum so as to have all the students in the one class. Noticing his skills as a mechanic, Fr. Defranould used him as the mission driver and soon he was also in charge of the seminary's finances.[13]

The food included bread but was based on produce from the mission plantation: manioc and bananas especially, yams and sweet potatoes as delicacies, accompanied by fish or more rarely pork prepared in coconut or pistachio oil with pepper. The missionary-professor's father Mr. René Lefebvre wrote to René and rather idealized his younger son's life: "We are following Marcel's progress in his monastery which is ideal according to what we've heard about the atmosphere, piety, the quiet and beauty of the surroundings, and the vegetation."[14] Marcel obviously kept quiet about the exhausting heat and humidity that left him constantly covered in sweat and having to make a constant effort to study and prepare his lessons. But as a man of iron will, Fr. Lefebvre managed to remain in good health and even to sleep through the humid nights.

He got on well with Fr. Fauret who nonetheless was "rather difficult." Fr. Fauret liked to tease Fr. Marcel at the dinner table but he soon realized that he would not have the last laugh, since the answers he got back were calm but unanswerable—to the great amusement of Bishop Tardy. The

---

[11] Young girls waiting to be married or young women married polygamously who had taken refuge at the mission. *General Bulletin*, 432: 748.

[12] *General Bulletin*, 446: 350; biographical note, June 1994.

[13] Lefebvre, *Petite Histoire*, 47-48; Marziac, *Monseigneur Lefebvre, soleil levant*, 91-92.

[14] René Lefebvre, Letter to Fr. René, March 29, 1933.

friendship between the stubborn northerner and the proud southerner grew stronger.

When the holidays came, Fr. Marcel and his brother went with the seminarians for a trip into the bush. The second year of teaching strengthened the good relations betweens the priests and their bishop, who wrote of his satisfaction to the Lefebvre family, giving them "heartfelt gratitude."[15] According to Fr. Fauret, Fr. Marcel was very flexible and pleasant, smiling, firm in his principles, very popular with his pupils, and appreciated by the priests. From the beginning of his missionary life, he showed an inclination and a particular talent for training priests.[16] Marcel, wrote Mrs. Lefebvre, was "very happy but he had no illusions about the work to be done in order to enlighten the weak minds and strengthen the wills of those whom he had been put in charge of....Only grace," she said, "could work this miracle."[17]

RECTOR OF THE SEMINARY—PRAYER AND ORGANIZATION

In 1934, Bishop Tardy made Fr. Fauret the superior of the mission in Lambaréné and due to Fr. Marcel's qualities of tact with the Africans and his sense of order, the bishop considered him capable of taking over the seminary. The young Fr. Augustin Berger, who had arrived in October, became his assistant.

Since he had to look after fifty-seven seminarians, both major and minor, as well as the novitiate for the indigenous brothers, Fr. Marcel urgently asked for his family's prayers. For greater efficiency he reorganized the layout and the rule. For the novice brothers he wrote "Reminders for the Native Brother" and a very detailed rule. In December he introduced separate seating for the laity and seminarians during services and began to build a much larger chapel. He threw himself into the work and at times felt very tired.[18] He was able to rest during the short holidays at the estuary with the seminarians: Cape Esterias and Owendo Point[19] were excellent places for fishing.

The Rector constantly kept a close eye on everyone, even during recreation, and did not hesitate to get rid of people who did not have the required dispositions or who were not making progress in the necessary virtues. It has since become legend what Fr. Marcel did during one of these

---

[15] Biographical note on Fr. Fauret; Mother Marie-Christiane, *Mon frère, Monseigneur Marcel*, 10; Mrs. Lefebvre, Letter to the five older children, Oct. 7 and Dec. 24, 1933.

[16] Marziac, *Monseigneur Lefebvre, soleil levant*, 92.

[17] Mrs. Lefebvre, Letter to Bernadette, May 20, 1934. Cf. Fr. Jean Criaud, *La geste des spiritains, histoire de l'Eglise au Cameroun 1916-1990* (Centenary Publications Mvolyé-Yaounde, 1990), 150.

[18] Mrs. Lefebvre, Letter to Bernadette, Nov. 18 and Dec. 16, 1934.

[19] Fr. Marcel Lefebvre, Letter to the Administrator, March 14, 1937.

holidays with the seminarians. He discovered that he hadn't brought any bread so he ate manioc like everyone else. So one of the students, Ange Mba, began to make fun of him, saying to his fellow:

"Look, a white man eating manioc!"

Fr. Marcel interrupted the jester: "What are you laughing at, Ange? Are you making fun of your Father Superior?"

"Yes, Father, because I can see you eating manioc!"

"Ange," he replied, "Ange, I see that the seminary is not the place for you."

Ange's seminary career finished that afternoon. Of course, later he was to become the father of Casimir Oye Mba, a future Prime Minister of Gabon.[20]

"There is a good atmosphere here," wrote Fr. Marcel in 1935, and he hoped that the improvements he had made would soon provide good training.[21] Fr. René admired the order which Marcel brought to the seminary: "First the interior life, the chapel, regular confessions, retreats."[22] Plans for retreats take up a lot of the Rector's papers: retreats for the new academic year, Easter retreats, ordination retreats. In them he put across "God's charity," the source of the apostolic spirit, and he underlined the wound of ignorance and its remedy, supernatural wisdom: "I belong to God, I am here for God—poor sinner that I am—'God is everything, man is nothing' (Libermann)."

He also did much for St. Mary's Mission: at the end of 1934 he installed the first electric generator, providing all the connections needed to distribute the power. He took advantage of the occasion to give a class on electricity and Catholic scientists, and as a *finale* he threw the switch and to everyone's amazement there was light.[23] In 1935, he installed the first battery-powered long wave radio. He also repaired a print machine which became profitable and even lucrative.[24] Bishop Tardy admired his collaborator's wide-ranging qualities and the good fruits borne by grace when supported by organization and good order. The Bishop went to France to raise money for his schools and during summer 1936 he visited Tourcoing. There he told Mr. and Mrs. Lefebvre how much he valued Fr. Marcel: "Everything he does is perfect. I can rest easy, even if I know he has to take decisions in my absence."[25]

In everyone's opinion, Fr. Lefebvre was an excellent seminary rector, "firm, moderate, considerate in his judgments and decisions, and remark-

[20] Ms. III, 19, 25-37.
[21] Mrs. Lefebvre, Letter to Bernadette, May 26, 1935.
[22] René Lefebvre, Letter to Fr. René, June 13, 1935.
[23] Fr. Patrick Groche, Interview, Nov. 1997, 3.
[24] Marziac, *Monseigneur Lefebvre, soleil levant,* 92.
[25] Mother Marie Christiane, *Mon frère, Monseigneur Marcel,* 10.

able at organizing and arranging practical matters."[26] The trust that the nearby Vicar Apostolics had in the Seminary of St. John meant that at the start of the new school year 1935 they had many students...too many, as Bishop Tardy feared. For a while he thought about sending the major seminarians to Yaoundé. But by separating the minor and major seminarians,[27] Fr. Marcel organized things in such a way as to avoid this costly and risky measure. To Gabon's honor, St. John's would remain St. John's.

APPRENTICE EXPLORER—EFOK

On September 28, 1935, in the presence of Fr. Defranould, Fr. Marcel Lefebvre made his perpetual vows. However, since his responsibilities as Rector had weighed heavily on him in 1935-1936, and to give him a change of air, he was granted permission to visit the bush and to go and see Sister Marie Gabriel in Efok, Cameroon. He left the port of Owendo on October 12, 1936, and went to Donguila where he began traveling up the Komo. When he reached the first impassable rapids, he continued on foot traveling along muddy paths that were sometimes churned up by elephants. He climbed the Crystal Peaks ascending the slopes by pulling at branches and roots, and made his way through overgrown former plantations and vast pastures. He crossed rivers on floating bridges or in native boats. He visited all the villages and paid his respects to the regional chiefs and catechists, offering Mass, hearing confessions, and once helping to dress the wounds of a leper.[28] At night he sometimes suffered from stomach ache or severe toothache and at times in his visitor's hut he was obliged to beat a retreat before the waves of implacable red ants.

In the mission stations everywhere, Fr. Marcel was welcomed with open arms by his colleagues, and sometimes one or other of them would accompany him to the next mission. On November 11 at Bitam where Fr. Page was posted, he noted: "I feel he is alone without any precise guidance, 'running every which way' trying to help the lapsed Catholics, turning in circles with no idea of where to go." Yes, the solitude of the missionary is always a difficult situation.

On November 12, he crossed the Ntem and went into Cameroon. At Alono where he arrived on the 15th, Fr. Lefebvre visited the minor seminary. It had been founded in 1924 and there were already 102 pupils with four Holy Ghost Fathers and an African priest. Fr. Marcel remarked: "There doesn't seem to be an atmosphere of trust here." However, many of the students persevered.

---

[26] Testimony of Fr. Berger, in Marziac, *Monseigneur Lefebvre, soleil levant*, 91.
[27] Mrs. Lefebvre, Letter to Bernadette, Oct. 13, 1935.
[28] Fr. Marcel Lefebvre, travel diary, Oct.-Dec. 1936.

On November 15, Fr. Marcel was at Yaoundé and climbed up to the small Mvolyé plateau where the old mission was located. The Vicar Apostolic who lived there, Bishop Vogt, welcomed our traveler who noted: "He really seems to have an air of goodness and holiness." Marcel admired the religious regularity of the community and the apostolic initiatives of Fr. Pierre Bonneau: "There are three confraternities: one for young men, one for young women, and one for young married couples. This last group promise not to accept payment for their daughters." Marcel did not note down his views on such radicalism.

He also visited the major seminary located at Mvolyé. In 1927, Fr. Eugène Keller, who came from Rome in circumstances we have already related, had really taken this Cameroon seminary in hand and earned the trust of his pupils. Unfortunately, his successors, the Swiss Benedictines of Engelbert,[29] had been less successful. The tension Fr. Marcel had noticed in Akono was greater still at Mvolyé. However, Marcel did not get bogged down in these negative impressions. Besides, on November 16, he was delighted finally to come to the end of his voyage and see Sister Marie Gabriel—his sister Bernadette—at Efok.

On June 11, 1928, the Holy Ghost Sisters had come to take charge of the postulants' house of the Cameroon sisters—the Daughters of Mary of Yaoundé—who had been moved from Mvolyé to Efok. Sister Marie Gabriel had arrived in November 1933 having spent the summer of 1932 at the Holy Ghost Fathers' Villa Notre Dame in Montana, Switzerland. In September she moved to Mirande in the region of Gers before going on to the novitiate at Béthisy in 1933.[30] At Efok, she was appointed as a nurse in the crèche that had been set up to care for newborn babies and orphans under eighteen months.[31] Sister Marie Gabriel had the consolation of being able to baptize numerous newborn children who were in danger of death. With pride she took her brother to visit her apostolate.

Dining with Fr. Ritter, Fr. Marcel was able to meet Louis Ajoulat (1910-1973). Ajoulat had been a medical student at the Catholic University of Lille where the chaplain was Fr. Robert Prévost. He founded the lay Catholic Missionary association called *Ad Lucem*. The students in the association took a promise to put their skills at the disposition of the missions. Dr. Ajoulat was soon invited to Cameroon[32] by Bishop Graffin, auxiliary to Bishop Vogt, and when Fr. Marcel arrived, Ajoulat had just

---

[29] Criaud, *La geste des Spiritains*, 156-162. The Benedictines arrived in 1932 as teaching staff, but in 1933 they asked for Fr. Keller to be moved so that they would be free to run the seminary as they saw fit.

[30] Mrs. Lefebvre, Letter to Bernadette, July 29, 1932, Sep. 24, 1932, Sep. 10, 1933, Nov. 6 and 19, 1933.

[31] Criaud, *La geste des Spiritains*, 177.

[32] *Ibid.*, 216; Jean-Pierre Ribaut, "Le Cardinal Liénart et *Ad Lucem*," in *Mémoire de Science Religieuse* 54, no. 3 (1997): 38-54.

established a brand new hospital in Efok where Sister Marie Gabriel was working. Later Fr. Bonneau, who became chaplain to the doctors at the hospital, launched a special Catholic Action project in liaison with the diocese of Lille.

THE FRUITS

At the end of 1936 Fr. Lefebvre returned to Libreville by boat from Douala and got down again to the difficult work of priestly training. Student numbers remained constant, fluctuating between forty and fifty. Two group photographs taken in 1936 show six theology students in white cassocks and black cord missionary cinctures: Reverends Augusta Nkonkou from Brazzaville, François Ndong from Gabon, Denis from Mid-Congo, Jean Marie (probably Jean-Marie Efène from Ndjolé), Eugène Nkwaku from Brazzaville, and Thomas Mba from Gabon. Fr. Lefebvre's comments on François Ndong's examination in Fundamental Theology were: "Too short. The Roman Church is the only true Church." And his remark on Auguste Nkonkou's was: "You ought to have given more importance to the thesis of [the Pope's] primacy." As for the thirty philosophy students dressed in shirt uniforms, the eldest were Aloyse Eyéna, Théodore Obundu, Ange Mba, and an unknown fourth. Finally in front there were seven junior seminarians from Gabon among whom can be seen the young Félicien Makouaka.[33]

Three future bishops—François Ndong (auxiliary at Libreville and then bishop of Oyem, who was consecrated by Archbishop Lefebvre on July 2, 1961), Cyriaque Obamba (Bishop of Mouila), and Félicien Makouaka (Bishop of Franceville)—were, therefore, pupils of Fr. Lefebvre. "You have to accept that they were not lacking in ability," he said soberly.[34] Ministers such as Valentin Obame and Vincent Nyonda and future heads of state such as Léon Mba (Gabon) were also pupils at St. John's but after Fr. Marcel's time.

Fr. René Lefebvre became parish priest of the growing parish of St. Peter's in January 1938.[35] In preparation for Easter of that year,[36] Fr. Marcel Lefebvre preached a retreat to the eldest theology students (including François Ndong) in preparation for their ordination to the priesthood on April 17. His views were summarized in a few well thought out principles:
1. "True zeal does not exist without obedience."
2. "You must love the truth above all things, and really see in it the salvation of souls."

---

[33] Photo Archives, Ecône.
[34] *Spiritual Conferences at Ecône*, 45 B, Sep. 20, 1977.
[35] *General Bulletin*, 647: 29.
[36] Mrs. Lefebvre, Letter to Bernadette, Apr. 27, 1938.

3. "Always see our faithful from the perspective of justification" *i.e.*, the state of grace.
4. "Have no personal principles but rather the principles of our Lord and the Church." "This is true charity and not the charity of modernists and liberals." "Charity is truth in action!"
5. "The Pope is the successor of Peter, Christ on earth, the unshakable rock, the light of the world."
6. "When the Bishop visits the mission, let us speak to him of our projects and ask him for advice."

With these very clear counsels, Fr. Marcel drew to a close his ministry among these future priests. In fact he was suffering from malaria[37] and liver trouble. One night around 2 A.M. he could stand it no longer and woke up Fr. Berger: "I think I am really ill, one never knows. Perhaps I am going to die. Hear my confession!" The priest heard his confession, calmed him down, made him an herbal tea, and sent him back to bed. He later said: "I was practically half-dead and I couldn't go on working. I had no strength left. I was really at the end of my tether."[38] Then Bishop Tardy sent him "to get a rest in the bush" and after hesitating for a while[39] decided to appoint him no less a post than interim superior in Ndjolé. The seminary carried on under the guidance of Fr. Berger. In 1944 there were five theology students, seven philosophy students, and twenty junior seminarians. In 1947 St. John's became a junior seminary and sent its older students to the major regional "Libermann" seminary set up some time before by Fr. Emile Laurent.[40]

THE HOLY DEATH OF MRS. LEFEBVRE

In August 1938, Fr. Marcel received the news of his mother's death, which had occurred on July 12. She felt seriously ill but she had worked until the end in the factory office. She was hospitalized on the 7th and on the 11th was given Extreme Unction. She admitted: "I could not have imagined that it was possible to suffer like this." On the 12th she received Communion and made a large sign of the cross to bless from afar her five eldest children who could not be there. Then she said to her three youngest: "I am not St. Theresa of the Child Jesus, but I will obtain for you whatever you ask me." And then turning towards her husband: "You too, René," she said. That morning she had said to her brother Félix: "You

[37] He was still suffering from the effects in Dakar. Cf. Diary of the Carmel of Sébikotane.
[38] Archbishop Lefebvre, *Petite histoire*, 50-51; Marziac, *Monseigneur Lefebvre, soleil levant*, 92.
[39] The bishop hesitated between sending him to Fernan-Vaz, Mitzic, or Lambaréné. Mrs. Lefebvre, Letter to Bernadette, April 27, 1938; Letter to his missionaries, June 13, 1938.
[40] *General Bulletin*, 604-605: 223.

know, I'm going to heaven." And when he looked at her speechless, she added: "I am called to Paradise." In the evening around 5 P.M., she gave her last piece of advice to her children: "Put the good Lord above everything on earth"; and after the prayers for the dying recited by the family, she had "this amazing look on her face as if she were seeing something impossible to describe and towards which she felt drawn, because she seemed to be trying to prop herself up in bed"[41] and then she breathed her last.

Convinced of the holiness of their mother, the Lefebvre children did not hesitate to invoke her intercession. Fr. Le Crom's[42] study of the soul of Mrs. Lefebvre reveals her continual renouncement and constant union with God in thanksgiving—a mark that shows that the fundamental gift of wisdom has been active.

III. INTERIM SUPERIOR OF ST. MICHEL DE NDJOLÉ (MAY 1938-AUGUST 1939)

A PRETTY MISSION

Ndjolé was formerly a very densely populated town. When the mission was founded in 1898, there were an estimated fifty thousand Pahouins living in the area. This figure dropped dramatically, especially when the trade in wood emptied entire villages, whose inhabitants then relocated on the coast and the Lower Ogooué. However, Ndjolé's geography remained of interest: it was a terminus for steam-driven boats navigating up the Ogooué, and the road for Mitzic, Oyem, and Cameroon started there. St. Michael's Mission was perched high on a hill above the Left Bank[43] a little upstream from the center of Ndjolé, which was on the opposite side of the river. It sat between the broad River Ogooué, which could be crossed by ferry at the village of St. Benoît, and two tributaries which joined the larger river behind the Ile Samory up stream and down.

The massive house of the Holy Ghost Fathers was built on two levels and flanked with cool galleries that opened out onto a beautiful terrace from where one could look out over the river. The first church built close by in European pinewood had had to be abandoned. The brothers and apprentices built the second church of St. Michael's, working in brick and creating a visible, ornate framework and bell tower. The imposing structure could accommodate one thousand faithful. It had just been finished

---

[41] René Lefebvre, Letter to Fr. René, July 23 and 28, 1938.
[42] Rev. Le Crom, *Une mère de famille, 1880-1938: Mme René Lefebvre* (1938); reprinted, *Un père et une mère* (1993). [Published in English as *The Life of Gabrielle Lefebvre: The Mother of Archbishop Lefebvre* (Kansas City, Mo.: Angelus Press, 1994).]
[43] [The French consider the Left Bank to be the left side of a river as one faces down stream. Trans.]

by Fr. Joseph Petitprez who, having become exhausted, went to Paris and died in 1931.[44] Also near the Fathers' accommodation was a boarding house[45] for boys and a primary school; close to the sisters' residence was a boarding house for girls and the stables. There was also a health clinic run by the sisters which had been founded by Fr. Grémeau, a peripatetic missionary doctor.

Apart from the daily work and looking after the crops—palm trees, manioc, banana trees, pineapples, oranges, sugar cane, and plantations of coffee, cocoa, and vanilla which enabled the mission to live and kept the pupil workforce[46] busy—there was work to be done at the mission's brick factory and in the carpenter's workshop.

DOING THE ROUNDS IN THE BUSH

Leaving behind him the books that had followed him from Rome, the ex-Professor arrived at Ndjolé in May, 1938, bringing no baggage other than his breviary, catechism, rosary, a watch, and personal linen; that was the rule.[47] He was only standing in for the superior, Fr. Henri Neyrand, his former fellow student at Santa Chiara (1925-1928), who was away on holiday. Leaving the boys' boarding house in the care of his curate who was none other than his pupil Fr. François Ndong, Fr. Marcel began visiting his immense district. Some of the catechism posts were an eight days' journey away. He went north to Lara, and to the west as far as Abanga and Samkita, traveling by river in a dugout canoe or on foot via rough paths. The eldest pupils carried the baggage: food and traveling Mass kit. In the villages "the Catholics loved him for his gentleness, for he was like an angel, he did not speak much, he made the people laugh."

However, he needed patience. One day he saw a messenger arriving at Ndjolé from a far off village: "Father," said the man, "come quickly to N. Old man So-and-so is at death's door!" Was this for real? The village was four hours away. Nonetheless, without saying a word Fr. Marcel soon prepared his things and set off in the dugout canoe. He rapidly covered the distance and arrived at the village: "Where is old man So-and-so who is at death's door?" Then the supposedly dying man came out: "Here I am, Father, but I am not ill; I just wanted to see you." Fr. Marcel didn't turn a hair, but he was only able to offer this gentle reproach in his usual calm voice: "Albert! So, it's not serious..."[48]

---

44 *General Bulletin*, 495: 412.
45 In 1930, there was even a "seminary school" (formerly at Lambaréné) that sorted out the candidates sending them either to the seminary or the brothers' novitiate. *General Bulletin*, 484: 958.
46 *General Bulletin*, 433: 774.
47 "Relations between Rome and Ecône," Ecône, Sep. 8, 1982, 5 P.M.
48 Ms. III, 19; *Spiritual Conferences at Ecône*, 108 B.

The Pahouins were still relatively nomadic and their movements had to be followed carefully so that the catechism posts could be varied accordingly. Fr. Marcel improved his command of the Fang language and spoke it so well that "he was as Fang as a Fang." To help the catechists in their bitter fight[49] against the Protestants who had arrived before the Catholic missionaries and set themselves up along the banks of the Ogooué, he distributed a pamphlet entitled *Ollé Lang*, which in Fang meant "Everyone can read it." It explained that "Luther had stolen the Bible" and had "gone off to make his own personal church."[50] Sometimes when Catholics and Protestants passed in their dugout canoes there would be shouts of "Heretics! Heretics!" But as Fr. Marcel said: "At least ours know they are Catholics!"[51]

CATECHISTS AND COUNCILS

Every village where there were Catholics had a catechist. The Fathers would choose a man who was in a position to leave his village, or his region (together with his family if he were married), to go and evangelize other villages, knowing perfectly well that he was risking his life. Archbishop Lefebvre later said: "I knew catechists who were poisoned and died, all because of their missionary spirit."[52]

Each district had a head catechist. The civil authorities considered some of these educated natives to be "evolved" (their term), an idea created to give French citizenship to certain indigenous people until in June, 1946, all natives were granted citizenship status. Fr. Lefebvre took an extremely dim view of these measures that were discriminatory and completely demagogical. Besides, the idea of an "evolved" person that the missionary had in mind was quite different; for Fr. Marcel this notion presupposed a complete Christian transformation in the soul. "Although they had acquired Christian convictions and received the grace of God, there were hardly any who could remain in that condition without the help of the missionary, and even then…! There was Paul Ossima and some others, perhaps, but on the topic of women and justice they kept to pagan principles."[53] Paul Ossima was one of the head catechists transformed by the grace of the Holy Mass,[54] and Fr. Marcel trusted him. His job was to train and supervise the group of catechists in the district of Ndjolé itself. He was dynamic but rather full of his own authority; no matter could be

---

[49] *General Bulletin*, 433: 775.
[50] According to Alphonse Mbome-Ekomy, 1-2, and Marc Obiang-Meye, 5, 8, 10, 11, 17.
[51] *Retreats at Ecône*, 66 A, Sep. 2, 1984, priestly retreat.
[52] *Homelies at Ecône*, 6 B, Jan. 11, 1976.
[53] Talk given at Mortain in 1945-1947.
[54] Archbishop Lefebvre, jubilee, Paris, Sep. 25, 1979, *Fideliter*, no. 12.

settled without him, and he pointed out to the missionaries certain moral disorders so that the priests might hand out punishment.[55]

Working with these catechists, who were experienced in spite of their almost incorrigible faults, Marcel Lefebvre furthered his own experience and refined his judgment. He understood that he had to "work astutely, with prudence, patience, and order, *i.e.,* respecting the work of his predecessors even if it meant changing [his] way of doing things a little. [He] listened to the advice of the blacks and the catechists, always surely with a few doubts on [his] mind, which often later disappeared when it was shown that their advice was well thought out."[56]

During his rounds, Fr. Lefebvre often had to arbitrate at village councils. The matter, having already been batted about by the head Christian and leaders of the village, would be brought in public before the priest. All the parties to the dispute would be present as well as the witnesses. The first day the missionary would not see things clearly but quickly he would seize where the truth of the dispute lay. Then in a final plenary session, the priest would pass judgment and impose a penance if necessary. Generally those in the wrong mended their ways and peace would be restored.[57]

When he had to deal with a Catholic who had two wives, Fr. Marcel was sometimes obliged to use force. With a few stout young men who were delighted to lend their assistance, he would come and take away the first wife who would shout, fight, or even throw herself into the water to pretend not to be co-operating—although she knew very well what was going on—and they would lock her up at the girls' boarding house. In this way the man would come to the mission and protest. However, he would have to promise to send away his second wife and give her dowry back to her parents. Only then could he get his first wife back. And if their marriage had only been performed in a tribal ceremony, a Christian marriage would be celebrated.[58]

But even this was not without its risks, as was shown when a bigamist unfortunately murdered Fr. Henri de Maupeou in Cameroon in 1932.[59] Moreover, by doing this the missionary could get in trouble with local authorities because the law recognized tribal marriage and polygamy but not monogamous marriage (not even among Catholics).

---

[55] Marc Obiang, 12.
[56] Another talk at Mortain.
[57] Marziac, *Monseigneur Lefebvre, soleil levant,* 18.
[58] Marc Obiang, 10; Archbishop Lefebvre often told this story.
[59] *General Bulletin,* 501: 665.

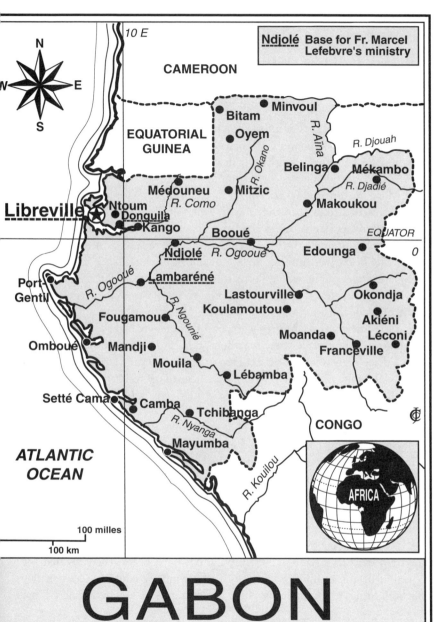

Ndjolé Base for Fr. Marcel Lefebvre's ministry

N
W · E
S

10 E

CAMEROON

EQUATORIAL GUINEA

Minvoul
Bitam
Oyem
R. Aïna
R. Djouah
Belinga
Mékambo
R. Djadié
Médouneu
Mitzic
R. Okano
R. Como
Makoukou
Ntoum
Donguila
Kango
Boqué
Libreville
Ndjolé
R. Ogooué
Edounga
EQUATOR
0
Lambaréné
Port-Gentil
R. Ogooué
Lastourville
Koulamoutou
Okondja
Fougamou
R. Ngounié
Akiéni
Léconi
Moanda
Franceville
Omboué
Mandji
Mouila
Lébamba
Setté Cama
Camba
Tchibanga
CONGO
R. Nyanga
Mayumba
R. Kouilou

AFRICA

ATLANTIC OCEAN

100 milles
100 km

GABON

GOOD ORDER AND IMPROVEMENTS

When he returned from his visits, Fr. Lefebvre made a note in the sacramental registers of the sacraments he had conferred and filled out the *status animarum* ("state of souls": file on individual parishioners) cards. He then saw Fr. Ndong to ask how things were going at the mission. Later he would go and have a joke with the brothers: Brother Honoré[60] was in charge of plantations and food stocks, and Brother Jean-Marie, a native, worked in the carpenter's' shop with the apprentices. Then Fr. Marcel would go and give a spiritual talk to the Immaculata Sisters[61] (Mother Valérie, Sister Delphine[62]—sacristan) and the Sisters of the Sacred Heart of Mary (Sister Andréa[63] of mixed race, and Sister Monica). (At times he also preached retreats to the sixty-five girls in the boarding house.) Then he went to see what progress was being made with the works to expand the mission,[64] and finally he would visit the boys' boarding house to check on how the priest was running things for the eighty boarders.[65] Every morning a few day pupils would come to the school as well. Pierre Nzoghé recalled: "I was eleven years old. We used to swim across the river to get to the mission and we loved it. The course of the river between the mission and the brickyard wasn't very wide, and Fr. Lefebvre had made a very solid bridge over it." In fact, there is a photograph showing a brother (Jérôme[66]) and three men working on enormous wooden beams stretched between very solid piles made out of large stones heaped up and hemmed in by wire mesh. "[The bridge] lasted for years," said Pierre, "and we used to dive off it."

During the dry season, the children used to go and fish at Lake Nghéné on the Abanga. They would spear their catch from a canoe or draw nets from the edge of the lake. They smoked enormous quantities of fish (carp, macheron, threadfins, silurids) after they were caught. Then the fishermen would burn a few dead banana leaves inside a barrel, put the fish inside, and seal the lids with okoumé resin. The fish would keep for up to two or three years without spoiling.[67]

To encourage the children to learn such skills, Fr. Marcel established a system of "fish payments": they weighed the fish and then divided the weight by the number of fishermen. This money could be used to buy school things and loincloths. (Like Fr. Neyrand, Fr. Lefebvre ordered ma-

---

[60]   Gaspard Boissière, born in 1889, arrived in French Equatorial Africa in 1913.
[61]   Interview with Pierre Nzoghé, July 17, 1998, 9; Marc Obiang, 4.
[62]   Eugénie Lorber, born in 1889 in Orschwiller.
[63]   Cécile Walker-Zékouwé, born in 1896 at Libreville.
[64]   Sister Gabrielle-Marie, July 20, 1998, 4 and 7; Obiang, 4.
[65]   Lefebvre, *Petite histoire*, 51.
[66]   Accoring to Marziac, *Monseigneur Lefebvre, soleil levant*, 65.
[67]   Pierre Nzoghé, 5, 6, 8; Marc Obiang, 2.

terial from France to dress the children in loincloths.) He had the idea of creating an "office" on the ground floor of the Fathers' house where visitors could be received and from where comings and goings to the house could be seen.

Every Thursday evening he gave all the children a talk or catechism lesson.[68] From time to time Ndjolé sent students to the minor seminary.[69] Fr. Marcel sent Charles Aboghé[70] there; one or two years later Jean-Pierre Elélaghe followed him (as a priest he served in Cameroon).[71] On the other hand, the young girls who desired to enter the religious life were sent as postulants to Sindara at the Trois Epis Mission.

The locals recalled the improvements that Fr. Lefebvre made to the mission. They remembered him as a "gentle man who did not raise his voice but spoke kindly and calmly" and who, moreover, was "welcoming and never showed himself irritated by anyone."[72] Thus they were sorry to see him leave. Fr. Neyrand returned to the mission and Fr. Marcel was able to go on his planned holiday to France on August 11, 1939.[73]

IV. Holiday—Declaration of War—The Draft

Eventful Holidays Cut Short[74]

Marcel had only just boarded the ship that took him home when to his surprise he met a colleague and childhood friend, Fr. Emile Verhille. This priest was a missionary in Congo-Brazzaville,[75] and he too was going home on holiday. Rumors of war were growing louder. They were just approaching Sierra Leone when the ship's captain warned the two priests: "I have just received an urgent order status number 3: 'Report immediately to the nearest friendly port.'" So, they docked in Freetown. In fact, on September 1, the German forces had invaded Poland, and on the 3rd England and France kept their word to Poland and declared war on Germany.

When the boat was appropriately camouflaged it was able to set sail for Dakar, but when they disembarked the two priests received notice that they were being drafted.

---

[68]   Marc Obiang, 2, 3, 7, 9.
[69]   Cf. Vincent de Paul Nyonda, *Autobiographie d'un Gabonais* (Paris : L'Harmattan, 1994), 25-26.
[70]   Priest in Booué in 1998.
[71]   Marc Obiang, 12.
[72]   Pierre Nzoghe, 7.
[73]   Fr. Honoré, Letter to Fr. Marcel, Nov. 5, 1939.
[74]   Lefebvre, *Petite histoire*, 52-53; *Spiritual Conferences at Ecône*, Dec. 23, 1981.
[75]   *General Bulletin*, 471: 377. Born on Jan. 22, 1903, at Orchies, he was nearly three years older than Marcel.

"Drafted in Dakar? Oh no!" said Fr. Marcel to himself. "Staying in the desert here? No way! At least let's go to France. If we have to go to war, we'll go to war, but not in Dakar!"
"What do we do then?" said Fr. Verhille.
"Let's take off. Whatever we do we're going to be drafted but let's not be drafted here!" And the two friends went back on board. What the sergeant does not see, the soldier gets away with!

A convoy of five or six passenger boats was formed and escorted by a few warships. The journey was not without danger, for some boats had already been sunk off the coast of Mauritania, but at last they arrived in Bordeaux. Straightaway Marcel was drafted and he remained there for a month. This was the period of the "drôle de guerre" (the phony war) when France waited for Germany to deign to attack. In France they did not believe in the war that had been declared, and the General Headquarters had no concerted plan of attack.

When Marcel arrived at the motherhouse where he was to stay for a while, it was a relief to learn about the ministerial instructions stating that Frenchmen (and therefore missionaries) who were resident in the colonies would be drafted there.[76] Marcel made an application so that he could go back to Gabon.[77] In mid-October[78] his pink colonial draft card came through. Then he was able to spend a month with his family, and see his father for the last time before returning to Bordeaux to take a boat with nine other priests and the Holy Ghost Sister, Sister Josepha.[79] Thus the boat took Fr. Marcel back to Gabon after an uneventful three-month holiday that was cut short.

V. SUPERIOR OF THE MISSION OF ST. MARY OF LIBREVILLE

DECEMBER 1939-AUGUST 1940

In the French missions in 1939 recruits were lacking, but the missionaries on holiday could therefore be sent back to their mission. Most of those who were liable for the draft were able to stay where they were in the colonies,[80] and thus the situation in Gabon was not that bad. When Fr. Marcel returned, Bishop Tardy appointed him as interim superior of the Mission of St. Mary of Libreville where he temporarily replaced Fr. Defranould,[81] who had gone to Port Gentil. Fr. Defranould remained, nevertheless, Vicar General. The position of superior at St. Mary's was one of trust;

---

[76] Orders issued on Sept. 2, 5, and 22, 1939; *General Bulletin*, 586: 94.
[77] Request acknowledged by the Etat-Major in the Place de Paris on Oct. 4, 1939.
[78] Summoned to an appointment at the Hôtel des Invalides on Oct. 11.
[79] Marie-Thérèse Lefebvre, Letter to Marcel, Nov. 25, 1939.
[80] *General Bulletin*, 586 (Nov.-Dec. 1939): 94.
[81] Fr. Defranould, Letter to Fr. Marcel, Port-Gentil, Dec. 30, 1939.

on this occasion, so we believe, the bishop took Fr. Marcel as his confessor.[82] Bishop Tardy also shared his concerns[83] with Marcel since the Vicar General was absent and the religious superior,[84] Fr. Fauret, was some distance away at Lambaréné.

Fr. Marcel was the superior of the mission as much in matters temporal as spiritual. He had to run the fisheries and plantations of St. Mary's, manage the profits, keep the accounts, and also fill in for Fr. Defranould in the Gabon accounts department[85] which oversaw transactions between the colonial missions and France. Thus through his brother Michel, he ordered three electric motors for St. Mary's and other mission stations, as well as a motorbike[86] (Fr. Fauret had taken the one he used with him to Lambaréné).

As for more spiritual pursuits, Fr. Lefebvre took care of the little mission parish, visited the villages to the north of the town, and provided spiritual talks for the sisters and girls. He also gave talks on the priestly virtues, leading the priestly life, and the principles of pastoral theology to the fourth year theology students who would be ordained within the year. He preached many ordination retreats to the seminarians, retreats for the sisters, and even retreats for his fellow priests—one on the "Sublime Nature of Our Missionary Apostolate" focusing on their ideal as priests, and the other on "Our Lord and the World" for which he used that "wonderful little book" of Bishop Chollet, *The Psychology of Christ*.[87] His missionary experience in Ndjolé gave him more confidence, and later on he gently reproached some priests who in spite of their zeal were frightened at the thought of having to preach to fellow priests or nuns.

At the end of April 1940, Fr. Defranould came back from Port Gentil but soon went to fill in for Fr. Guillet in Donguila.[88] During the German offensive in May 1940, Fr. Marcel was drafted into the First Company of the Gabon Colonial Infantry, and on June 17 he was given his military kit by Lieutenant Gouval, commanding officer of the company.[89] But when the Armistice was signed on June 22, leaving the French Empire free and requiring the French Armed Forces to demobilize, Marcel found himself demobilized...but only for a short while as we shall see. In August, 1940, he was providentially appointed as the interim superior at the Mission of St. Paul in Donguila; thus he neither saw nor played a part in the fratricid-

---

[82] Marziac, *Monseigneur Lefebvre, soleil levant*, 92.
[83] Bishop Tardy, Letter to Fr. Marcel, Apr. 15, 1940.
[84] *General Bulletin*, 589: 143, Council meeting of March 19, 1940.
[85] Fr. Defranould, Letter to Fr. Marcel, Dec. 30, 1939.
[86] Michel Lefebvre, Letter to Fr. Marcel, Dec. 10 and 29, 1939.
[87] Paris: Lethielleux, 1903, 2 vols. Cf. Archbishop Lefebvre, *Le mystère de Jésus* (Clovis, 1995), Note to the Reader, 6-7.
[88] Bishop Tardy, Letter to Fr. Marcel, April 15, 1940.
[89] Note for personnel from military outfitters, June 17, 1940.

al battle that took place between General de Gaulle's "Free French" troops and those fighting for French unity embodied by Marshal Pétain.

VI. FRATRICIDAL CONFLICT

In Libreville on October 25, 1939, the 1st Battalion of the Gabon Colonial Infantry boarded ship[90] to go to the aid of France. One year later, it was France who seemed to be coming to attack and crush her African daughter. In fact, while the battle for France was still raging, General de Gaulle set himself up in London. He later rejected the armistice that Marshal Pétain asked the Germans for, and called for the war to be continued. On October 27, 1940, in the Sacred Heart at Roubaix, Cardinal Liénart would cry out: "The armistice! Those who signed it have the right to our respect because they came to our aid in a time of humiliation. They were not at all responsible for the defeat; they came to help us and to soothe our pains, and ever since they have worked with all their might to save what could be saved and build up our forces within. So that if France is allowed to live, she might again be able to hold her place in the world."

The same day, by a curious coincidence, General de Gaulle launched his own manifesto: "There is no longer a French government....So a new power must assume control to direct the French war effort...I will exercise my powers in the name of France." The armistice was his only chance and he knew how to seize it. He began his war in Africa on August 12, 1940, when his delegation under General Leclerc landed at Lagos in Nigeria. In two weeks and without any resistance, Leclerc managed to rally almost all of French Equatorial Africa to the cause of Free France. Only Gabon held back.

On August 29, Governor Masson sent a telegraph saying that he supported de Gaulle, but subsequently other high standing officials led by René Labat protested. On August 30, the submarine Poncelet dropped anchor off Libreville. She had been sent by Governor General Boisson and carried reinforcements from Dakar. She sailed under the command of two resolute leaders: Air Marshal Têtu and Colonel Claveau. Finally the views of Bishop Tardy were decisive: Gabon had to remain loyal to Marshal Pétain,[91] and Masson retracted his first telegram on September 1. Leclerc tried to "rally" Gabon from the outskirts of the country; in the North General Dio seized Oyem, and in the South General Parant took Mayumba by surprise. The Pétain loyalists paid dearly when Dio took Mitzic on October 27, and also when Parant came down the Ngounié and took Fougamou. There Brother Odilon acted as a mediator to avoid more deaths.

---

[90] Nyonda, *Autobiographie d'un Gabonais*, 49-51.
[91] *General Bulletin*, 629: 311.

Parant put Lambaréné to seige and the town surrendered on November 5 after a missionary, Fr. Samuel Talabardon, had been killed by mortar fire.[92] "The conquest of Gabon was dragging on";[93] shaken by the defeat of his forces outside Dakar on September 25, de Gaulle hesitated. Then Leclerc pushed him into ordering a surprise landing near Libreville, which happened overnight between November 8 and 9. Fratricidal fire-fights took place on the outskirts of the airport. The situation was still hanging in the balance when in the afternoon an escort vessel, the Bougainville, opened fire on the Gaullist ship Savorgnan de Brazza, which returned fire and sank her opponent. This loss led to Libreville's surrender on the night of November 9 and 10. The supply ship Cap de Palmas was transformed into a floating prison where Leclerc had the officers, Governor Masson, Fr. René Lefebvre, and the Bishop himself incarcerated.[94] Before being arrested, Bishop Tardy had had his red ribbon sewn on to his cassock, for he wished to be taken with his Legion of Honor[95] medal which he had just been given by General Weygand in recognition of his loyalty to French unity.[96] The clergy then refused to sing the *Te Deum* asked for by Leclerc, and a military chaplain led the thanksgiving service in an empty cathedral while General Koenig played the organ. It required all the diplomatic skills of Fr. Defranould to secure Bishop Tardy's release; the Bishop was placed under house arrest for six weeks in Lamabaréné. But the imprisonment of the Bishop after such bitter in-fighting left the Gabonese confused: "It wasn't a good example and it didn't help our ministry," Archbishop Lefebvre concluded soberly.[97]

Later, Parant allotted subsidies to the missions, while one of the priests became the chaplain to Leclerc's troops who crossed the Sahara to reach the border of Libya.[98]

VII. SUPERIOR AT DONGUILA

AUGUST 1940—APRIL 1943

Fr. Henri Guillet, superior of St. Paul's Mission in Donguila, had worked until he was exhausted, especially while overseeing the extension to the mission church. In January 1940, Bishop Tardy decided to give him a six-month sabbatical in France. To replace him for this period the Bishop

[92] *General Bulletin*, 590: 451.
[93] Letter of Captain Tutenges, in Général Jean Compagnon, *Leclerc Maréchal de France* (Flammarion, 1994), 169-70.
[94] Pierre Messmer, *Après tant de batailles* (Albin Michel, 1992), 40.
[95] Sr. Gabrielle-Marie, Interview in Lambaréné, July 20, 1998, 5.
[96] *General Bullletin*, 590: 441-442, 451.
[97] Gabrielle Chort-Rouergue, *Mémoires d'Outre-mer* (Alma, Mémoires Vivantes, n.d.), 35; Lefebvre, *Petite histoire*, 35.
[98] *General Bulletin*, 629: 311-312.

appointed Marcel, to whom Fr. Henri said: "There were no further objections I could make when he promised me you would be stepping into the breach." Marcel, however, had to wait until August, during which time Fr. Defranould filled in.[99]

The mission was situated on a promontory next to the estuary where the waters of the Komo meet the waves of the Atlantic. It served an old Pahouin Catholic community and had just celebrated its sixtieth jubilee. There was a charming wooden church with bell tower and transepts, and various other buildings that go to make up the classic Catholic mission. In 1930 Donguila was losing many of its inhabitants to Libreville due to the intense wood trade. Fortunately the priests' ministry also extended to the villages further inland towards the Crystal Peaks and right up to the frontier with Spanish Guinea.

CHASING A THIEF

The St. Paul's Mission depended on its immense plantations, and the harvests were transported by boat and sold at Libreville. The mission garden and food supplies were still managed by Brother Norbert Lorgeray (nicknamed "Brother Honor"), who had been born in 1878 and who came to Gabon in 1903.[100] One Sunday before the main Mass, he ran to find Fr. Marcel: "All the things from my storeroom have been stolen...there is nothing left, no pans, no salt, no loincloths!" From the pulpit Fr. Lefebvre threatened to suspend Sunday Mass, imposing a sort of "local interdict" until the thief was denounced. The chief catechist, Marcel Mebale, made a very rapid inquiry: "Father, the thief is such and such!" Fr. Lefebvre took a few men and in the fishing smack "Colette" they crossed the Komo estuary and arrived at Chinchoua. The local sheriff lent them two officers and they found the thief eating in his hut; he denied taking anything. The priest was about to leave when an old woman arrived: "All the things are hidden in the banana trees over there!" They found everything, but the thief had disappeared into the bush.[101]

At Donguila visitors[102] admired the carpenters' shop, which had palm olive-driven motorized tools linked to a generator nick-named "Saint Denis"; Brother Chanel and his apprentices were kept busy. Brother Marin was the mission's builder. According to Etienne Meviane, Fr. Marcel himself had a lime oven built, and thanks to a local quarry they were able to produce cement and cinder blocks.

---

[99] Bishop Tardy, Letter to Fr. Marcel Lefebvre, April 15, 1940; Interview with Etienne Meviane, Libreville, July 23, 1998, 1.

[100] Detailed index of Missionaries, 1923, National Archives of Gabon, 1E 187.

[101] Address given at Donguila, Jan. 21, 1985; *Spiritual Conferences at Ecône*, 108 B.

[102] *General Bulletin*, 484: 951; Etienne Meviane, 5.

RUNNING THE BOARDING HOUSE

At first Fr. Marcel was helped in Donguila by an African priest, Fr. Auguste. Moreover, Reverend Paul Lemaire, a seminarian and cousin of Fr. Lefebvre, lent a hand, hoping to be allowed to take orders. The African priest looked after the boarding house of 175 boys while the Immaculata Sisters and an indigenous nun looked after the boarding house for sixty-eight girls under the guiding hand of Mother Marie Elizabeth.[103] In the past the sisters had suffered greatly as a result of tropical diseases. The little mission cemetery reveals the sacrifices generously offered by those young religious for the evangelization of the area; there was Sister Canisius who died in 1908, aged 38, and Sister Maria Pia who was called to God in 1909, aged 24. On such foundations God continued His work providing baptism and a Catholic education for the Gabonese youth.

The village catechists and the priests on their rounds would recruit for the two "main schools" of the mission. They looked for the most talented children, who were first sent to "district schools" where they would prepare to go on to the schools at Donguila. Fr. Guillet had only given one directive to Fr. Marcel: "I hope that during your stay there you will visit our districts. As you know through your own experience, these visits are pleasant for the missionary priest and useful for the Catholics and catechumens. They are also less tiring and more productive than doing the rounds of the villages. The whole mission [his territory] is divided into eight district centers including Mfoua, which can rightly be called a district."[104]

Each of these centers had a head catechist, a hut chapel, and a district school affiliated to the school at Donguila where its students were destined to go. Besides Mfoua, there were district centers at Ekouk, Remboué, Ezène—which Fr. Marcel moved to Kango[105]—and at the "Consortium" HQ (a large foresting business), etc. The boys in the boarding houses were split into three-year groups: the most recent recruits called the "new boys"; those who were preparing for baptism and who were in their second year—the "old boys"; and finally the "Catholics," who had received Baptism, Communion, or even Confirmation. The latter group were getting ready to leave school after being clothed in the scapular. Naturally the "Catholics" were not slow to tease the "old boys," and the old boys in turn teased the "new boys." The priests put up with this situation, which built up the morale of their troops.

Valentin Obame, who was chosen from his village by Fr. Marcel, considered his schooling in the following way: "If I have gotten somewhere today, it is thanks to him. He helped me do something with my life!"[106]

---

[103] Numbers from 1945, which cannot have been that different from those in 1940.
[104] Fr. Guillet, Letter to Fr. Marcel, Jan. 1, 1940.
[105] Valentin Obame, interview at Kango June 22, 1995; Etienne Meviane, 6.

Fr. Marcel also improved the school curriculum. He thought that there were not enough classes and changed the timetable from two to four hours every day,[107] although he kept a period for manual labor in the cool of the early morning.

WAR—YELLOW FEVER—THE MISSION IN QUARANTINE

Up to that time, Donguila had not been directly affected by the war. But soon the mission heard the dreadful news of the fighting in Lambaréné and of the death of Fr. Talabardon. This priest had been Fr. Guillet's curate and worked very hard at Donguila. Thus, Fr. Marcel sent a priest and a delegation of ten pupils to the funeral.[108]

Some time later a detachment of Parant's troops landed unexpectedly one evening in Donguila. They arrived at Chinchoua and tried to come ashore by stepping onto a fishing smack which had canoes moored to its side. However, some of the Chadian veterans were caught unexpectedly by the swell, fell overboard, and drowned.[109] Seeing the lights of the village, the survivors landed but they were furious with their white officers and threatened to kill them. Fr. Marcel calmed them down and let them sleep in the school classrooms.

Several weeks later the children fell ill with temperatures of over 100 degrees. They had yellow fever. The Chadians had been carriers of the virus and their brief stay was enough for mosquitoes to transmit the illness (which was deadly for adults). Reverend Paul Lemaire, who devotedly looked after the sufferers, became the first victim: he died in the old priests' hut on March 2, 1941, closely followed to the tomb by Fr. Auguste. Everyone was distraught. The sisters also fell ill. The mission was put in quarantine and sulphur was burned in all the buildings beginning with the church; its beautiful chandeliers were ruined. Brother Honor's banana trees had to be cut down. It was quite a trial for Fr. Marcel![110]

MOBILIZED AGAINST THE ITALIANS—MISSIONARIES IN ISOLATION

Fr. Lefebvre was not a man who self-indulgently bemoaned his fate. Fr. Jérôme Mba-Békale replaced Fr. Auguste, and Donguila returned to normal. However, there was more disruption when Fr. Marcel was mobilized again, although this time against the Italians: "Apparently, they were coming from Libya, but we never saw hide nor hair of them!" On this

[106] Valentin Obame, Kango, June 22, 1995, 3, 7.
[107] Fr. Patrick Groche, in interview with Obame, *ibid.*, 2.
[108] Etienne Meviane, Interview in Libreville, July 23, 1998, 7.
[109] Cf. Nyonda, *Autobiographie d'un Gabonais*, 54.
[110] Msgr. Lefebvre, address in Donguila, Jan. 21, 1985; Etienne Meviane, Interview in Libreville, July 23, 1998.

occasion, Fr. Marcel was sent with the troops to Bangui.[111] There, rather than waiting in vain for the Italians, they were kept busy ridding the diocese's coffee trees of an infestation of ants. The bites of these little creatures were not at all pleasant. After that he was sent back to Gabon while his comrades were posted to Cameroon.[112]

Now in the hands of the Free French, Gabon found itself cut off from France, and young missionary recruits could not come to the colony.[113] Out of necessity as much as out of conviction, the motherhouse was loyal to Marshal Pétain. On December 8, 1942, Bishop Le Hunsec wrote to the Fathers: "With Bishop Grimault and Fr. Gay, I had an interesting meeting with Marshal Pétain. I admired his sprightliness, his clear-sightedness, and extraordinary presence of mind."[114] Bishop Tardy wrote on September 10, 1941, from Gabon to the motherhouse: "Do not worry about us; as for resources, the government[115] is helping and the missionaries are doing their utmost. Everyone's morale is 'more than praiseworthy.'" Fr. Fauret wrote: "Our work is continuing as normal and only one [of us] has been drafted. We have all the essentials; were it not for being separated, we would be living in relative peace."[116]

THE MISSIONARY BUILDER

Although he was only stand-in superior, Fr. Marcel could not but initiate some projects which were obviously needed by the mission. He was also responsible for building a church at Kango and a wharf at Donguila. Kango's population was growing because the village was close to where the Bakoué joined the Komo. Moreover, to follow the main road from Libreville to Lambaréné one needed to take a ferry across the river at Kango. Therefore, it became necessary not only to establish a district school but also to build a permanent church. Archbishop Lefebvre would later say:

> The goal of the priest is to draw everyone to church. So on the missions, the first thing to do in an area is to build a church so that the Mass can be celebrated and the people can be drawn there and given the sacraments. And the people ask for nothing more....You ought to have seen how the natives took pleasure in the beauty and grandeur of their churches, even people who were living in the greatest poverty![117]

---

[111] A battalion was stationed at Bangui in Sep.-Oct. 1941 (cf. de Gaulle, *Mémoires de guerre*, I, 624).

[112] *Spiritual Conferences at Ecône*, Dec. 23, 1981.

[113] Because of the British. Cf. *General Bulletin*, 590: 483, which speaks about the priests who were stopped and sent back at sea by the English in 1943 but who were able all the same to reach Dakar after passing via Gibraltar and Wahran (Algeria).

[114] *General Bulletin*, 590: 206, 238. [Pétain was 84 at the time of the 1940 armistice. Trans.]

[115] The government of French West Africa under the Free French administration.

[116] *General Bulletin*, 590: 463.

Fr. Marcel chose a site for the church and drew up the plans. The cinder blocks were made on site or brought from Donguila on barges. The timbers were got ready in the mission's carpenter shop and erected also on site. Thus the church of St. Marcel in Kango was built.

Something also had to be done about Donguila, where business was suffering due to the silting up of the estuary which prevented boats from docking at the jetty. One day, Bishop Tardy had fallen into the muddy water when as usual he was being transported from his boat to the bank in a dugout canoe with the assistance of a couple of burly students. So, Fr. Marcel decided to build a real wharf; it was to be a long peer that would go right out into the water and alongside which fishing smacks, barges, and boats could be moored. The brothers and their apprentices worked on the project. The piles were made ingeniously from barrels stacked on top of each other. At low tide concrete was poured into them and they were linked by beams covered with planks. Progress was slow: two piles a day following the rhythms of the tide. Fr. Marcel himself got involved and was seen wading in the muddy waters up to his waist[118] to make sure the barrels were correctly stacked. When the pier was finished it was three hundred meters long.[119] Much later a boat crashed into the wharf breaking it in two. They decided not to repair it, but for a long time the wharf was the pride of Donguila.

LAST WORDS OF ADVICE—LEAVING DONGUILA

At Christmas 1942, in the presence of more than seventy leaders from the villages in the districts surrounding Libreville, Kango, and Donguila, *The Proposal for Rectifying the Marriages of Fang Natives*[120] was given official recognition at Donguila. Fr. Marcel had had a hand in writing the documents. Instigated by Parant himself,[121] it required Catholics to recognize the demands of monogamy, outlawed the traffic of underage girls, and recognized the usefulness of a dowry. It ruled that "marriage without a dowry is reprehensible because it puts the husband and wife in a relationship which seems too much like slavery" (with respect to the father or guardian of the woman). However, it determined that the size of a dowry should be limited to one thousand francs. Some impediments to marriage were also established. Such a document illustrated the excellent relationship establish between the new government of Gabon and the Church.

---

[117] *Spiritual Conferences at Ecône*, Nov. 30, 1971.
[118] Fr. Patrick Groche, in interview with Valentin Obame, 4; interview with Etienne Meviane, 1-2.
[119] Approximately 1,000 feet long.
[120] Handwritten text by Fr. Marcel and typed text.
[121] Circular from the Governor of Gabon, Oct. 24, 1942.

On the day the eldest students left the boarding school, Fr. Lefebvre gave them a few final words of advice that were very practical and easily summed up: "You are going back home. You are going to remain poor. You must take up a trade."[122] However, soon it was Fr. Marcel's turn to say goodbye to Donguila. In fact, in March 1943 the exhausted Fr. Defranould had had to go to take some rest at Mouila, and Fr. Fauret was summoned by Bishop Tardy to Libreville to succeed Fr. Defranould as Vicar General.[123] Consequently the mission at Lambaréné needed a new superior. The unambitious Fr. Fauret was sad to leave his beloved bush and was not slow to put some respectful objections to Bishop Tardy: "Excellency, you know that I have no degree, and yourself when you were my superior at Chevilly told me off for not trying my best when it came to the books."[124]

"That is true, but I have chosen you anyway."

"But Excellency, why not choose Fr. Marcel Lefebvre? He studied in Rome and he has his degrees."

Then Bishop Tardy replied: "I am not going to choose someone to work with me when he is as stubborn as a mule!"[125]

However Fr. Fauret was hardly more accommodating. Nevertheless, he was a senior missionary to Fr. Marcel and therefore more worthy of being the Bishop's right-hand man. This was how Fr. Marcel came to be appointed to Lambaréné not as a stand-in but as the Father Superior. Therefore, he had to leave his beloved Donguila to which he had become attached through all his trials. He generously offered the sacrifice that was asked of him, and with his few meagre possessions, he set off for Lambaréné.

VIII. Superior of the Mission at Lambaréné

April 1943-October 1945

The mission of St. Francis Xavier was well situated geographically between the Myéné people of Ogooué, the Fangs in the North, and the Echira in the South. Its impressive brick buildings stood on a promontory between two arms of the river near where the Ngounié and the Komo meet. However, the mission was not a quiet place: there were three Protestant missions, one or two of which had been longer established. Two of them, Ngômo and Samkit, ran industrial and farming businesses. The "evangel-

---

[122] Etienne Meviane, interview July 23, 1998, Libreville, 8.

[123] *General Bulletin*, 590: 497; letter from Bishop Tardy to the motherhouse, March 23, 1943.

[124] Biographical note on Bishop Fauret, 15 pages, (n.p., n. d.), 6.

[125] Recollections of Bishop Fauret himself recounted to Fr. André Buttet, C.S.Sp., ms. I, 26, 8-15.

ical missions" no longer proselytized but the number of their faithful was not inconsiderable: out of a population of fourteen thousand, 3,800 were Catholics, 1,200 were catechumens, and 2,500 were Protestants. The "missionaries" spread a hateful attitude amongst the natives which the superior Fr. Le Bloch described in 1938 as "Hatred of Catholicism, the spirit of pride and freethinking, and indiscipline too."[126]

But what was this in comparison with the 6,500 pagans who needed to be converted to the grace of our Lord Jesus Christ? What could be done to push back the reign of Satan? The mission only had two priests, Fr. Lefebvre and Fr. Theodore Kwaou, to share the ministry. Fr. Marcel took care of administration and the priestly ministry, and the native priest looked after the 213 boys in the boarding school. The 161 girls who were also borders were looked after by nuns: Mother Marie Agnès (management, catechism, talks), Sister Gonzague (washing and linen), Sister Saint-Roger (nurse, sacristan, kindergarten), Sister Praxède (kitchen, henhouse) and the Gabonese Sister Julia (teaching, manual labor, plantations).[127]

The girls' school with the sisters was quite separate from the Fathers and boys' accommodation. The buildings were well constructed in large quadrangles which enclosed courtyards shaded by trees. The old, attractive chapel of the sisters contrasted with the priests' large, well-kept, Romanesque church. They added a brick bell tower soon after the departure of Fr. Lefebvre.

In addition to the work of the catechists (about seventy spread throughout five regions and managed by the head catechists such as Thomas Atondo Dyanoare, who ruled over Petite Rivière and Lake Onangué from 1936 to 1962), there was also the work of the schools, as Fr. Marcel saw very clearly: "[They are] the highway to the complete Christianization of the country. Without them we can no longer hope to preserve the considerable influence the Catholic missions presently have. This is crucial for us."[128]

A "DO-IT-ALL" SUPERIOR

When Fr. Marcel was at the mission, he took on the spiritual duties of the superior as he had done at Ndjolé, and alternated with the other priest preaching at Sunday Mass every other week. He recounted: "At Lambaréné, when I had a bit of time, I looked at the writings of St. John Chrysostom and was astounded to think that I could have translated them into the native language and given them as they were to the faithful! And the peo-

---

[126] *General Bulletin*, 484: 957.
[127] Annual Statistics of the Apostolic Vicariate of Gabon, Nov. 20, 1945; Anastasie Igala, 1.
[128] Handwritten plan for a talk on Gabon, 1945.

ple would have understood."[129] He also preached retreats for baptism and first Communion, took care of the oral examinations for the children about to receive the sacraments, and heard confessions when scheduled, taking his time to admonish and advise. "He was too...long," thought one of his former penitents. The penances were not much shorter: three decades or even five and "that was a little too much."[130]

He also took extreme unction or even the sacrament of baptism to the patients at Dr. Schweitzer's hospital. Every time, he was amused by the "village atmosphere" that reigned there. In fact, Albert Schweitzer, who had come to Lambaréné in March 1913, had wanted this kind of atmosphere in his hospital. He said: "You have to make the patients live as if they are in their normal habitat. So, invite relatives, and have pigs and chickens...this cheers a patient up. Moreover the relatives can pay in kind for medical care by doing jobs for the hospital: sweeping, cleaning, carrying water."

Fr. Lefebvre admired the doctor's practical sense, even if he did not share his philosophy, which tended towards pantheism: if everything is a little bit of God, one must even respect mosquitoes. "Do not kill zat mosquito," he said one day to the priest, "e az ze right to live." The Alsatian accent made the statement seem even more amusing! But the best of relations existed between the Catholic mission and Schweitzer the Protestant. Had not the mission helped in the construction of the hospital, lending the use of its boats and the help of the elder children to collect and carry stones? Thus the doctor even went to the mission to treat the priests who were ill. Dr. Schweitzer was also a good organist and came for major feasts to play the organ in the choir loft of St. Francis Xavier's.[131]

Fr. Marcel kept for himself the responsibility of running the liturgical rehearsals for the numerous altar boys. When they did not do things perfectly, he would say stubbornly, "No, let us start again!" "He taught us respect for the sanctuary,"[132] as one of his acolytes recalled. Since he was less musically gifted, the Father Superior left it to Fr. Kwaou to run the choir, and choose and train the soloists. The natives were very enthusiastic about Gregorian chant, and knew by heart their *Kyriale* and a good number of Masses for Sundays and feast days, thanks to their "Gaschy."[133] When one of the choir members managed to get a copy of this famous tome, he shouted for joy: "Now I have my 'Gaschy.' Well, I will go to heaven. I will be an eternal soloist in heaven!"

---

[129] *Retreats at Ecône*, Sep. 8, 1982, 5 P.M.

[130] Agathe Mouenkoula, 6, 10; Richard Rebela, 6.

[131] Nyonda, *Autobiographie d'un Gabonais*, 30. *Spiritual Conferences at Ecône*, 113 B, Feb. 22, 1985.

[132] Ms. III, 19, 44; Pierre-Paul Tsire-Mendome, 12.

[133] [A classic layman's missal containing also the melodies for the *Kyriale*, etc. Trans.]

Under the guidance of the nuns at the boarding school the eldest girls learnt household tasks. When they left, the sisters would find them young Catholic husbands or a catechumen.[134]

Fr. Lefebvre treated the boys of the boarding school with fatherly kindness and managed to get balls for their games or machetes for clearing undergrowth.[135] When he had to refuse permission for something, he said no: "Well, when he said no, it was no!" Fr. Théodore was responsible for discipline and punishment, and he readily armed himself with a stick that was called *Azougamé*: "Don't quibble with me, don't upset me." His stick and his strap of twisted hippopotamus hide hurt, although they were completely safe. They were nothing in comparison with the unreasonable punishments inflicted by parents in the village, such as putting hot pepper in the eyes or under the armpits. The mission fostered a sense of justice and provided educational work. It was rare that Fr. Marcel had to hand out punishments himself and "he hit you very timidly because he was too used to forgiving people." "He always had a smile on his face," recalled his former pupils. One of them said: "He was very kind. All the children were happy with him. And even the villagers called him 'the good Father,' 'it's the good Father.' "[136]

Fr. Lefebvre provided new liturgical accoutrements for the sacristy,[137] and, as at Ndjolé, he renovated a reception room on the ground floor underneath his bedroom. Before, the priests did not receive visits after High Mass but the faithful would come anyway, climbing over the gates at the front of the presbytery. Sometimes to drive the people away, the pupils would spray them with water: "Leave, on your way, off you go!" But Fr. Lefebvre would not allow this chaos to continue. He wanted people to be welcomed, so they could sit down and be heard accordingly. With this new reception room everybody could take a turn.[138]

A REAL BUSINESS FOR THE SAKE OF SOULS

To undertake such renovations in the house, the brothers' practical knowledge was priceless. Firstly there was Brother Roch. Already advanced in age, he looked after the gardens and taught the children how to grow crops.[139] He was also in charge of the sheep and the stable (the sisters had kids). He arrived in Gabon in 1899 and stayed there sixty years until his death in Lambaréné on February 1, 1959. He was skilled as a mason, joiner, and carpenter, and he had become a true master builder able to con-

---

[134] Anastasie Igala, 1.
[135] Pierre-Paul, 4; Antoine Bastien, 4.
[136] Antoine Bastien, 9; Pierre-Paul, 9; Richard Rébéla, 1.
[137] Antoine Bastien, 4, 6.
[138] Pierre-Paul, 4-5.
[139] Marc Obiang, 19; Richard Rébéla, 4.

struct a building, finish it, and furnish it. He liked to see work well done. This excellent man, Brother Roch, was very much loved in Libreville. He was sometimes mistaken for the bishop, and in Lambaréné many thought he was the superior. He was an exemplary and regular religious who was very often first in chapel. His gentle, witty teasing made him popular and he was appreciated by his colleagues—things he shared in common with Fr. Marcel. Above all, all he was loved because he was very charitable.[140]

The large carpentry workshop was built on land between the road and the Ogooué. There Brother Arcade (brother of Fr. Talabardon, who was killed in the war) was helped by Brothers Marcien and Barthélemy and also by some apprentices. They went into the bush to cut down and chop up wood. They would bring back the materials and from them make all kinds of frames, hulls for dugout canoes, fishing smacks, trawlers, and barges, all of which were used to bring essential resources to the mission. The budget drawn up by Fr. Lefebvre bears witness to this. These figures are calculated in French francs at their value in 1945.

EXPENSES	FUNDS RECEIVED
Mission staff .... 85,000 Mission and district School........................ 125,000 Buildings and training for the apprentices .... 45,000 Catechism and ministry ... 65,000	Grants from the Propagation of the Faith..................... 40,000 Government grant to the schools 80,000 Mass stipends .... 10,000 Gifts from Europeans .... 30,000 Gifts from the locals .... 20,000 Mission workshop 140,000
Total 320,000	Total............................... 320,000

The work of training apprentices was meant to prepare young men—catechumens or Catholics—to practice some trade and thus put them in a position to found Catholic families. Practical training in the workshops was complemented by classes in more general training, professional courses, spiritual talks, and daily catechism. Secondarily, the apprentices helped to look after and maintain the mission. If we bear in mind the college for training primary school teachers and the health clinic of the sisters, which cared for sixty patients daily, we will have just a small idea of the spiritual and temporal ventures that Fr. Marcel was to manage for two years.

Finally, for the great feast days of the year—Sts. Peter and Paul (end of the school year), St. Michael (beginning of the school year), Christmas,

---

[140] *French Bulletin*, 104: 223-224.

and Easter, the river was full of multicolored dugout canoes, many of them built at the mission itself, which brought families from the farthest flung villages to experience the liturgical festivals at the "village of the Catholics" within this little Christendom.

IMPROVING THE YIELD...FIGHTING THE DEVIL

A missionary's life is woven from matters material, spiritual, temporal, and eternal: it is this specific vocation that makes it appealing. Fr. Marcel was in his element. The Kingdom of Heaven was making progress with more than 450 baptisms a year at Lambaréné. From 1932 to 1945, the number of Gabonese Catholics went from 33,800 to 85,471 with, however, a decline in the rate of growth beginning in 1940. But at St. Francis Xavier this Kingdom also had to be reflected in the daily round of affairs. And for that Fr. Lefebvre was a "leader" who excelled in getting the most out of the mission.[141]

Primum vivere, first of all live. War is tough and one must be organized. In the dry season as soon as classes were over, the boys would get the nets ready. Then they would set themselves up for the fishing season on the banks of mission-owned Lake Niogo to the north. As at Ndjolé, they dried the fish and put it into barrels. The girls went to Lake Zilé in the east and worked on the nearby plantation that belonged to the mission. The stocks that they did not need themselves would be sold and the profits used to buy manioc and rice (which the children went crazy about). They said of their kind Father: "We have got the man of God! There he is!"

Moreover, Fr. Lefebvre sent away for a rifle, and found a hunter and also a fisherman to provide fresh meat and fish for the children. They ate large carp from Lake Zilé.

"So, children," Marcel asked with a smile, "are you eating well?"

"Yes, Father, we have eaten well ever since you came! We eat very well!"

Not content with improving the meals, the Father Superior wanted to have the best manufacturing resources. An old brick oven situated next to the cemetery was replaced by a larger one outside the village. Similarly, he ordered a generator and an emergency generator. The whole mission was given lighting, and the carpentry shop circuit was connected to the emergency generator. "There," said the people, "there is the man of Lambaréné. He is the one who brought us light." Then Fr. Marcel improved the road that led from the town to the mission, making it suitable for all vehicles. One day a kapok tree, a large tree, was blown down and fell across the road. They had difficulties in chopping it up where it lay.[142] A similar inci-

---

[141] Antoine Bastien, 7.
[142] Antoine Bastien, 2, 3, 4, 8, 9.

The father, a leading industrialist and deported Resistant.

The mother, a dynamic mystic.

As a four-year-old,
determined and tenacious.

As a nine-year-old,
suffering the trials of war.

1914: The Lefebvre Family. On the left, Marcel as
calm as ever, and at the back, the mischievous René.

1919: Marcel in the
Eucharistic Crusade.

1921: High
School Sophomore.

1921: The eldest brother, René, sets an
example for the next four children.

Fr. Le Floch

Fr. Libermann

Marcel (second row, at left). At the
French Seminary with Fr. Le Floch.

The Seminarian: "He knows what he wants."

1931: Curate at Lomme with the
parish's Catholic Action group.

Driver and mechanic of the only car in the diocese.
Fr. Marcel Lefebvre on the Nomba ferry.

1947: The young Apostolic Vicar of
Senegal is enthroned in the cathedral at Dakar.

1945: The collegiate church in Mortain.
A sign of hope amid the ruins.

At White Abbey: Members of the community
gathered around their loving and beloved father.

September 18, 1947: Episcopal consecration in Tourcoing. From left to right: Bishop Le Hunsec, Cardinal Liénart, Bishops Bonneau, Ancel, Lefebvre, Fauret and Dutoit and Canon Deconinck.

1952: Consecration of the Senegalese
Bishop Dodds in Saint-Louis.

Pope Pius XII with "the best of [my] apostolic delegates."

1951: Surrounded by his parishioners of the mission on the island of Gorée, of the Diocese of Dakar, Senegal.

1956: The leader of the Church in French West Africa. Cardi Liénart (left) has just enthroned Archbishop Lefebvre.

1951: With his missionary brother and sister (Cameroon).

1957: A meeting of archbishops. Archbishops Sartre, Leclerc, Strebler, Milleville, Lefebvre, Graffin, Parisot, Socquet, Boivin, Bernard, and Cucherousset.

1961: Cardinal Agagianian and the insistent Archbishop.

1962: A celebration in Sierra Leone in gratitude for the arrival of the missionaries. The Superior General of the Holy Ghost Fathers, Archbishop Lefebvre, is welcomed.

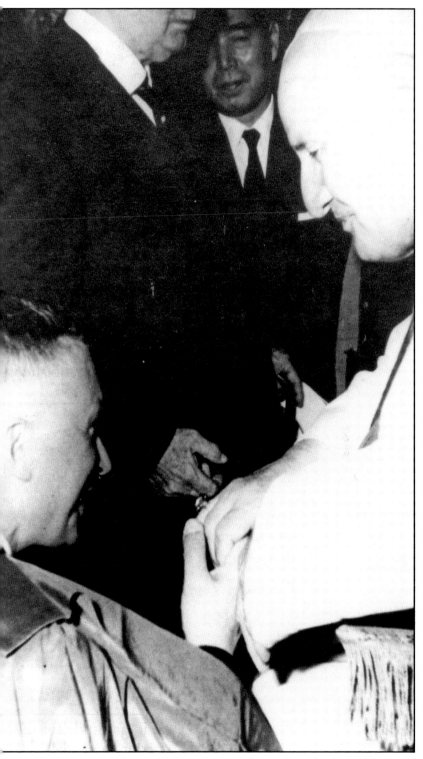

With Pope John XXIII: the Faith versus diplomacy.

1962: Tulle's welcome for its bishop.

At the Prefect's side, placing a wreath at the monument
for the Martyrs and Dead of the Resistance.

dent was photographed:[143] it shows Fr. Lefebvre standing next to a brand-new truck he bought and drove himself, discussing with two brothers and one of the locals in front of the tree trunk.

He also replaced the Fathers' old car with another that was an older model but ran well. How in the middle of the war was he able to find and buy all these machines? This was the question that his colleagues asked themselves, although they were very happy with the improvements.

And that was not all. Fr. Lefebvre came up with the plan to build a bell tower and personally plumbed running water into the Fathers' bedrooms.

Finally, foreseeing the development of the Isaac district on the other side of the river, he set off one fine day with his servant Pierre Paul, compass and machete in hand, so as to mark out the site he had secured for the new Chapel of Our Lady of Ogooué. They adapted the plans to accommodate the metallic framework provided by a plane hanger donated by the Aubertin building company.[144] A catechist took up residence there.

We must mention that this district was sometimes visited by the Bwitists. In fact the head of the Isaac family in Lambaréné, Jean-Marie Isaac, was one of the few Europeans initiated in this sect. On some nights tom-toms and other deep drums beat out a diabolical rhythm, and the men who gorged themselves on warthog and palm wine held their secret meetings, their faces covered with masks, and then began to dance in the flickering light, contorting their bodies and leaping over the fire, as their wide-eyed audience grew in number.[145] Now, this was something Fr. Marcel did not like; once, flanked by a few burly apprentices, he went to try to disperse these people who were "washing the Bwity," as it is said. Behind the façade of these shady and unhealthy traditions that were sometimes frankly lewd, he saw the power of the devil too clearly to have the least desire to start "dialoguing."

Certainly he did not directly attack the fetishists, but if he learned that a Catholic or a catechumen had fallen back into fetishism, he would not put up with it. Once he was seen going to the hut of such an individual who looked on with frightened eyes as the priest took his machete to a well-crafted fetish.

Fr. Marcel was very aware of fetishism's corruption of religion. This was especially the case for sacrifices the Africans offered, not as a sign of submission to God but as a means of driving away the evil spirits surrounding them (and which were sometimes very real). Thus, Archbishop Lefebvre would later explain: "They believe in the devils but live in fear and their sacrifices are warped from the beginning. They even go as far as to offer human sacrifice. This is religion being turned away from its true

---

[143] Héduy, *Monseigneur Lefebvre et la Fraternité*, 17.
[144] Pierre-Paul, 9, 6, 13; Ant. Bastien, 4, 6, 8.
[145] Dedet, *La mémoire du fleuve*, 456, 185-186.

end. In the true religion the oblation of the victim or offering is a sign of our interior oblation."[146]

THE HEROIC DEATH OF MR. RENÉ LEFEBVRE

Periodically news of the war reached the missionaries and filled their hearts with hope or anguish. On November 8, 1940, the Allied landings in North Africa raised their hopes. On January 30, 1944, the future of Black Africa was sketched out at the Brazzaville Conference. Soon the Normandy landings started the push for the liberation of France. One week later the *Nord Libre* announced the death of Mr. René Lefebvre, father of our missionary. As soon as war was declared, he had begun again working for Belgian Intelligence. He was able to pass on information and hide escaped soldiers or civilians who wished to enlist in England: he gave the help needed for them to reach their destination. He was arrested by the Gestapo on April 21, 1941, and thrown into prison. His last letter to family and friends on September 9, 1941, said: "You know that I die as a French Catholic and monarchist. For me it is through the establishment of Christian monarchies in Europe that the world can find stability and real peace."

He was condemned to death in Berlin on May 28, 1942, for "conniving with the enemy and recruiting young men capable of carrying arms against the German Reich," and he was finally interned in the prison at Sonnenburg. He was forced to make straw shoes, a process which made his fingers bleed and stripped the skin off his hands. Nevertheless, he contrived to botch his work: he remained ever a patriot. The cold, the dampness, and boils from which he suffered could not conquer his piety—he prayed his rosary ceaselessly—or his confidence in the victory of his homeland. He died in February 1944 after becoming paralyzed down one side and falling into a fainting fit for which the guard rained blows on him. He was a true resistance fighter and one of the heroic pioneers of France's reconquered freedom.[147]

DOING THE ROUNDS OF THE LAKES

During his visits in the bush to the villages and forest worksites, Fr. Marcel brought Christian liberation from the slavery of sin. Traveling aboard a motorboat called *Madouaka*, he visited the industrial sites on Lake Gomé to the west. As in the mines, the state of the workers was pitiable: "The manner of recruitment is hateful and shameful. It really is slavery. The working conditions, wages, and dwellings are deplorable, espe-

---

[146] *Spiritual Conferences at Ecône*, Jan. 11, 1972.
[147] Le Crom, *Un père et une mère*, 89-107; *Fideliter*, no. 11: 17-19.

cially in the mines. The natives are able to do good work as long as they have the support and ambiance of the village and the religious help they desire."[148]

Fr. Lefebvre never failed to mention these things to management when he got permission to bring the workers together for Mass or confession. Sometimes to reach the furthest sites, he had to "trudge along and trudge along"; he carried his own briefcase, and his servant Pierre Paul carried his small suitcase. One day taking the paths they covered thirty kilometers.[149] According to his companion, Fr. Lefebvre "was up for a hike and the way he walked was surprising. He seemed to walk very lightly on his feet and he was very supple." He walked this way around the mission leaning forward onto the balls of his feet: it frightened the children a little and they gave him the nickname of "Kodo Kodo."[150]

One evening, however, when he was coming back from a drawn out visit, he got lost. Night was falling. He imagined that he would die there alone with God. At this thought his soul was filled with joy: to die there, lost, alone with God![151] Fortunately his guardian angel helped him find the path and his visits continued.

Doing the rounds in the lake region to the South made for a charming excursion. The glistening waters of the Ogouué took him to Omponwona ("cheerfulness") where he had founded a district boarding school with fifty boys. Saving for the return journey the Orombo-Mounédjoué[152] ("Pelican River") where they would also see hippopotamuses, Fr. Lefebvre then took the Wombolié ("the great river"). But it is not always wise to be sailing at the end of the afternoon when a storm breaks. For a few hours before, the highly charged atmosphere becomes unbreathable. Darkness falls and stretches from one side of the leaden sky to the other. Flashes come one after the other at increasingly brief intervals. Heavy rolls of thunder crash against the banks and echo back and forth; the new sound waves seem to collide with older, ceaseless rumblings. The rain soon begins lashing down on the river, making the surface boil and bubble. Visibility is practically at zero even within the boat. Water must be bailed out of the hull and the boat moored as quickly as possible.[153]

They would spend the night at Nombedouma and, the following day, enter the immense Lake Onangué. Fr. Marcel drew a map of its islands, promontories, and inlets which wander away into uncharted archipelagos.

---

[148] Talk on working conditions, Mortain; cf. Dedet, *La mémoire du fleuve*, 121-157.

[149] [Approximately nineteen miles. Trans.]

[150] Pierre-Paul, 15; Olivier Akilémy, Libreville, 1998, 3.

[151] Recollections of a discussion with Archbishop Lefebvre in a parlor at the Carmel of Sébikotane.

[152] Agouma on the map.

[153] Cf. Dedet, *La mémoire du fleuve*, 124, 128-130.

The wind lashed their faces, and the waves would batter the craft. On the edge of Lake Oghémoué, they moored at Inigo opposite the Petite Savanne. On another day, Fr. Marcel was at Oguéwa ("Waves breaking on the shore"—is it possible to say so many things in so small an expression?). This was where the seminarian Cyriaque Obamba came from, and also where the head catechist Thomas Atondo-Dyano lived. Father would inspect the district school and its boarding houses to see they were being run well.[154]

How impatiently the people waited for the visit of the priest! His arrival would be announced in advance and the chapel hut got ready. Fr. Marcel would go in and listen to innumerable confessions, for he knew that if the graces of the Eucharistic Sacrifice and Communion were essential—since they sanctify men's efforts and strengthen the commitments undertaken in marriage—the other sacraments are nevertheless needed to dispose souls to receive them. He was extremely careful to apply this first principle of pastoral theology! It was a great joy to see the gradual transformation of souls through the grace of the Holy Mass for which they had been well prepared. The village itself was transformed spiritually but also "physically, socially, and politically."[155]

The last visit in this region was at Lake Ezenga, and the return journey would take them past the pelicans' colony where they saw the birds soaring over the trees along the river bank. And then the boat would again reach the Ogouué. There one day in October 1945, the children who were with him said: "Father, a canoe is coming!"

"So it is!"

"Oh, Father! It is a canoe from the mission."

"From the mission? Why? What is up? Why are they coming here? Is there some news?"

"Oh! Yes, for sure. It is a canoe from the mission for sure!"

In fact the canoe was coming closer and closer towards them, and finally it drew up alongside them: "Father," said the messenger, "urgent orders have arrived for you. Here they are."

The letter was from Paris and the envelope was made out in the handwriting of the Superior General. He opened it and read: he was being recalled to France!

---

[154] Pierre-Paul, 14; Richard Rébéla, Oguéwa, 3.
[155] Jubilee Sermon, 1979, *Fideliter*, no. 12 (1979): 6-7.

RECALLED TO FRANCE[156]

The very brief letter from Bishop Le Hunsec bore a delicately phrased message: "The Superior General of the Holy Ghost Fathers...wishes Fr. Lefebvre to return to France. He means to send him to our philosophy scholasticate." Marcel Lefebvre would later say, "That little letter broke my heart. At that moment there were tears in my eyes. The natives noticed but not too much, I think." Only a missionary can understand this kind of heartbreak: toiling with might and main to save souls in a far-off land, becoming a Fang with the Fangs and a Galoa with the Galoas, and then having to leave and go home to France when one no longer wished to do so. It is hard...very hard indeed.

But Fr. Marcel pulled himself together straight away and offered up his *fiat*.[157] The Superior General was only expressing a wish, but Bishop Tardy would confirm that it was a written order: at the next Council meeting, Fr. Lefebvre would be named "superior of the community and philosophy scholasticate"[158] at Mortain. His acceptance was required and he obeyed. He would later say:

> Obedience is always a good thing. I came back with the happy thought that I was only doing my duty. I had taken the resolution never to try to learn why my superiors were sending me here or there...or wherever, and to get back down to work without forming a complex and without lamenting the loss of the post I had just left. Besides, there is the grace of God! You live with your temperament and character, and according to your training, and the Good Lord gives you graces of state to do your job. We are working under the watchful eyes of God,...not to have a successful career but to save souls and do good.[159]

He passed some advice on to his successor, Fr. Neyrand, and gave his rifle to the catechist Henry Ngome, and some clothes to his servant Pierre Paul. Then he went to bid farewell to the mission and the girls' school. The children wept, and all he could say was "My God" in Galoa. The faithful stood there in tears and did not want to let him to leave. They pooled their money so that they could send a telegram to Libreville: "Let us keep Fr. Marcel. Let Lambaréné be his last post, and if he dies we will bury him at Lambaréné." Bishop Tardy simply replied that even if Lambaréné needed Fr. Lefebvre, the Church needed him for more important things.[160]

---

[156] Marziac, *Monseigneur Lefebvre, soleil levant*, 105; Lefebvre, *Petite histoire*, 54-55; E. Olivier Akilemy, 3.

[157] [*Fiat voluntas tua*: Be it done according to Thy word. Trans.]

[158] *General Bulletin*, 590: 301. Congregation Council meeting on Oct. 16, 1945.

[159] *Spiritual Conferences at Ecône*, 109 B, May 24, 1984.

[160] Marie-Agathe Mouenkoula, Interview at Lambaréné, July 20, 1998, 1; Antoine Bastien, 4; Pierre-Paul, 2-3.

The riverboat took Fr. Marcel to Port Gentil where he waited at the mission run by Fr. Henri Clément until he could catch the next Libreville boat.[161] At St. Mary's Mission he said goodbye to the bishop and his brother Fr. René, and boarded one of the military airplanes that usually repatriated old or infirm Europeans. It was a small plane which stopped at Douala, Kano in northern Nigeria, and then at Algiers. In Paris Bishop Le Hunsec gave him a warm welcome at Rue Lhomond, and then sent him to the Father Provincial: "Go and see Fr. Laurent," he said to him. "He did it! He's the one that wanted you!"[162]

---

[161] Sr. Gabrielle-Marie, 4-5.
[162] Cf. Lefebvre, *Petite histoire*, 55; ms. I, 26, 16-17; 40, 4-8.

CHAPTER 7

THE BATTLE OF MORTAIN

In accordance with the decision of the 1938 General Chapter, the headquarters of the Holy Ghost Fathers' French province was moved in 1943 from the congregation's motherhouse in Rue Lhomond to 393, Rue des Pyrénées, in the north of Paris. On June 6, 1944, the day of the Normandy landings, Fr. Emile Laurent took up residence there, succeeding Fr. Aman who was worn out by his ministry.[1] A new man was there to face a new situation. Emile Laurent, who had been a friend and companion of Marcel Lefebvre at seminary and in the novitiate, was first a teacher at the junior seminary in Cameroon, and later became student mentor at Santa Chiara. On October 8, 1940, after France had been divided into two zones, he was made director of the scholasticate at Cellule, Puy-de Dôme, that catered for some fifty students who either had not been called up, or who had been released by the Germans.[2]

The scholasticates of Chevilly and Mortain had been requisitioned in 1939. Although Chevilly's theology students were able to return to their seminary in June 1944, the philosophy students from Mortain, who had fled to Langonnet in Brittany, remained there until the end of the war. Despite working with a skeleton staff, these seminaries were able to continue their work and trained more than a hundred young missionary priests.[3] With the liberation of France, the students in the scholasticates were joined by demobilized soldiers, liberated prisoners, and newly professed students from the novitiates. This welcome rise in numbers had to be dealt with. In France, Mortain had suffered the most from the ravages of the war. To deal with these problems, Fr. Laurent chose his friend Fr. Marcel Lefebvre as the key man and sound organizer who was also solid in doctrine. Fr. Laurent asked Bishop Tardy to release him "at all costs,"[4] and his repeated requests were finally granted. Thus Fr. Marcel Lefebvre was given the difficult post of rector of the scholasticate that had just returned to White Abbey at Mortain.

---

[1] *General Bulletin*, 71; 590: 304; 590: 300.
[2] *Ibid.*, 507: 941; XXXVIII, 202; 590: 298, 479.
[3] *Ibid.*, 591: 9.
[4] Marcel Lefebvre, *Petite histoire*, 55.

I. NOTRE DAME LA BLANCHE IN THE BATTLE OF NORMANDY

WHITE ABBEY

White Abbey was founded at Savigny[5] in 1112 by Adeline, sister of Vital the Hermit, and was rebuilt in 1151 in a pure Cistercian style. After the Revolution, it became a junior seminary. Later there were added two high and narrow buildings in grey granite which together with the existing abbey church and cloister formed a grand, interior courtyard. The 1906 Law of Separation deprived the abbey of its students, but in 1923 it was finally given over to the Holy Ghost Fathers, who turned it into a philosophy scholasticate. The future missionaries who had finished their novitiate and were ready to begin their priestly training, were organized into two streams, one lasting two years and the other lasting three.[6] The abbey became a military hospital in 1939, but it was occupied in summer 1940 by the German army after all its students had gone.

THE BATTLE OF MORTAIN (AUGUST 1-14, 1944)

On June 7, 1944, the day after the Allied landings, the Abbey was converted into a field hospital, and from June 8 onwards the Germans who had been wounded in the initial battles began to arrive. Immense red crosses painted on the roofs of the Abbey and other hospitals seemed to plead to heaven for the protection for the town.[7] While Patton advanced towards Avranches, the American 1st Army marched east towards Mortain. On August 3, the Germans left the town, and in the early hours its inhabitants thought they could at last breathe a sigh of relief. Unfortunately, the Germans had only retreated beyond position 314 to the east to organize the counteroffensive ordered by the Führer. It began on August 5 at 11 P.M. with an aerial bombardment, and as Mortain went up in flames the people fled. The following night General Hausser's Panzer divisions charged west in an attempt to cut off Patton from his rearguard. The Germans reoccupied Mortain.

On the morning of the 7th, Typhoon squadrons of the RAF made low level attacks on the German positions, and with astonishing accuracy destroyed a third of the German armored vehicles. In the area around White Abbey the Americans stood their ground under fire from small arms,

---

[5] Savigny-le-Vieux, to the south of Mortain, *Lexikon für Theologie und Kirche* [hereafter *LThK*] 9, 352.

[6] Three years for students who had not studied philosophy at school and who needed to do so before beginning scholastic philosophy.

[7] Michel Coupard and Jack Lecoq, *Le Mortainais, Mortain et Juvigny-le-Tertre* (Éd. Alan Sutton, 1997), 16-17; *General Bulletin*, 590: 189; Dr. Gilles Buisson, *Mortain 44* (Coutances: Éd. OCEP, 1997), 13. In these works the events of the battle are recounted in detail.

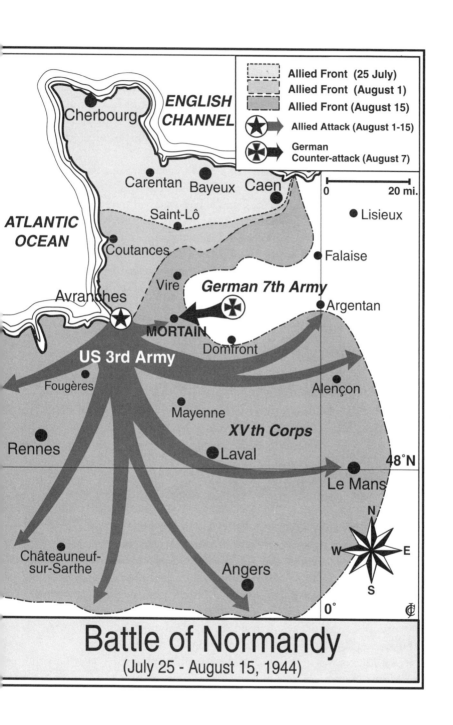

Battle of Normandy
(July 25 - August 15, 1944)

tanks, and artillery. The Panzers' momentum was lost. Fierce fighting ensued but on the 11th the Germans came close to being trapped between Falaise and Alençon by a masterfully executed pincer movement: Marshal Von Kluge gave the order to retreat. Eighty percent of Mortain had been flattened, but above the ruins could be seen the silhouette of the collegiate church of St. Evroult with its tower intact, a sign of hope, as it were, standing above the devastation.

The Holy Ghost Fathers attributed the safety of their own buildings to the same divine protection: from the park above the abbey where her statue stands, Notre Dame La Blanche had watched over her abbey and kept it safe. Nonetheless, between August 3 and 12, the Abbey had taken eighteen mortar blasts, more than a hundred shells, and two large bombs: there was no glass left in the windows but the priests and brothers were unharmed. White Abbey welcomed numerous refugees from the town, in addition to the sick and elderly of the hospice which had been destroyed.[8] These were still being housed in a wing called the "hospice" when Fr. Lefebvre arrived.

II. REBUILDING AND ORGANIZING

"WE TOOK HIM TO OUR HEARTS BECAUSE OF HIS SIMPLICITY"

It was a cool, late autumn morning on November 1, 1945, when the new rector of the scholasticate arrived at Mortain. He had been able to spend a month's vacation with his family at Tourcoing where he stayed with his brother Michel. "In any case," Fr. Laurent had said to him, "your predecessor Fr. Riaud won't be there to meet you because the Superior General has asked him to take up his new posting in Canada as soon as possible. Fr. Macher will take the helm until you arrive."

Fr. Marcel traveled from Paris to Mortain[9] by car with Fr. Laurent, and listened somewhat apprehensively as during the journey his superior and friend explained to him the sensitive nature of his new position. That morning of All Saints' Day, the car passed through the heart-breaking ruins of the flattened town, entered the abbey through the front gate that was still off its hinges, and stopped before the grim looking building. When the priests learned of their arrival they gathered together in the courtyard, and Fr. Macher came towards them saying, "Welcome, Father."[10]

Fr. Marcel was introduced to the assembled priests: "This is Fr. François from Normandy, our bursar; this is Fr. Félix-Simon, a former naval

---

[8]   Coupard, *Le Mortainais,* 71; Buisson, *Mortain 44,* 119-125; *General Bulletin,* 590: 515-524.

[9]   Marcel Lefebvre, Letter to Michel Lefebvre, Nov. 1, 1945; ms. I, 26, 26; 40, 10-12; ms. II, 44, 10.

[10] Marziac, *Monseigneur Lefebvre, soleil levant,* 105.

officer [he had the bearing] who teaches philosophy; Fr. Marcel Diebold [who looked very severe] who teaches philosophy to students preparing for the baccalaureate; Fr. Videlo, your fellow student in Rome, who teaches scholastic philosophy [whose delivery in class was mumbled]; Fr. Jean Rozo from Brittany who teaches history [eloquent and cultured]; Fr. Jenvrin, who is retired; and Fr. Muller, who teaches post-baccalaureate philosophy."[11]

Then he was introduced to the seminarians. Fr. Emmanuel Barras, who was among them, later recalled: "I can still see him, his arms outstretched in greeting, simply saying to us, 'Here I am!' We took him to our hearts because of his simplicity."[12]

Finally the brothers, who formed their own separate community, were introduced to the new superior. The notes of Fr. Lefebvre, which have saved so many details from oblivion, provide us with the names of these religious: Brothers Robert, Nicolas, Longin, Roger, Guy, Bernard, Marin, Pierre, and also Brother Alphonse, who built the church at Akono and who dreamt up the idea of having a spiral staircase leading to the gallery (it was constructed without blueprints but nevertheless finished at the right spot). There was Brother Mélaine who would die in 1948 and be buried in the little community graveyard in the abbey park. There was also Brother Eudes, the farmer, who spent so much time with his animals that the others joked: "The cows smell of Brother!" All trades were practiced among these men: there was a gardener, a carpenter, a blacksmith, a cobbler, a tailor, and a barber. There was also a lay helper who looked after reception.

A community of Holy Ghost Sisters, numbering twelve in 1932, washed, sewed, and cooked[13] for the scholasticate. Fr. Marcel was very attentive to their needs and the sisters would say, "At last we have a father!"[14] However, most of his time was given over to the students. "You will have no teaching to do," Fr. Laurent reassured him, "but you will take the rector's conference on Saturday and the daily spiritual conferences."

Throughout that All Saints' Day, they made a fuss over their new superior whose arrival they had joyously awaited, and the following evening Fr. Lefebvre summoned the students to the lecture room. He introduced himself very simply; to his friends in Tourcoing, he had described himself as "an African bushman trying to rebuild his life in France." With the same humble irony, he won over the seminarians, and asked them to use their study-time well, "You owe every minute to the souls who await your min-

---

[11] Ms. II, 44, 1-15; 49, 1-57.
[12] Ms. I, 50, 25-27.
[13] Notes of Fr. Marcel Lefebvre, Mortain. For the rest of this chapter, all quotations without references are taken from these notes. *General Bulletin*, 501: 682.
[14] Mother Marie Christiane Lefebvre, *Mon frère Monseigneur Marcel*, 10.

istry." He concluded: "As for me, whatever I can give you, I will give you."[15]

ACHIEVING UNITY IN DIVERSITY

Even if Fr. Lefebvre arrived surrounded with the glory of his Gabonese apostolate, especially with his work at Lambaréné where he rubbed shoulders with the famous Schweitzer, it was still a challenge to govern and unite more than a hundred young men who came from a variety of backgrounds.[16] Besides the twenty-four students who had returned from Langonnet with Fr. Riaud[17] on July 16, and the forty or so newly professed brothers fresh from the novitiate at Recoubeau, there were others from the nearby novitiate of Piré in Ile-et-Vilaine, and yet more from the novitiate far away in Blonay, Switzerland. In addition, the Rector had to handle older students who had spent up to four years in prison camps, and others who had done two years military service prior to that. He also had to cope with students who had fought throughout the Battle of France in De Lattre's Army or in Leclerc's 2nd Tank Division, and who six months earlier had been in combat on the German front. While some seminarians had fought in the Resistance, others were returning from the Eastern front, having been among those Alsatians who were drafted into the Wehrmacht...[18]

Fr. André Buttet, then a student, explained how Fr. Lefebvre coped with these problems: "The superior had countless psychological tactics to discipline kindly the restlessness of these young men whose attitude to regimentation was sometimes colored by bitter memories. Without raising his voice or brandishing the rulebook, he transformed a very disparate group into a family that was united around him."[19]

Maurice Fourmond and Roland Barq, two very young seminarians whose gifts Fr. Lefebvre nevertheless noted, were appointed as "go-betweens," one for the first year of scholastic philosophy, the other for the second year: they were the link between the students and their superior. Far from being a liberal concession to the spirit of the times, this bold measure was meant to establish and control discipline in order to ensure that obedience was more perfectly observed. "Fr. Lefebvre knew how to manoeuvre cleverly," one former student said, "so, he decided not to tick off a few ex-servicemen who, it was known, would slink off to smoke the occasional cigarette." Not only was he tolerant, but one day when the manager

---

[15] *Les Anciens du Père Deco*, Annual Bulletin, 1945; C.S.Sp. French *Bulletin*, 37, 39.

[16] There were 73 students at the beginning of October but the numbers soon rose above a hundred.

[17] *General Bulletin*, 590: 547. Some of them had witnessed Patton's breakthrough at Piré.

[18] *Ibid.*, 590: 501, 514; ms. I, 25, 34; 54, 39-45; Vieira, *Sous le signe du laïcat*, 401.

[19] Buttet, *Le bâton et le rocher*, 100; Marziac, *Monseigneur Lefebvre, soleil levant*, 109.

of the hospice had given him a packet of cigarettes as a present–which happened rarely–he had them passed on to the veterans.[20]

The unity and sense of togetherness that Fr. Lefebvre brought about in the community resulted in no small part from his ability to deal with material problems, especially the issues of lodging and comfort. Patching the holes in the roof meant that both the students and the elderly of the town no longer had to live in a building that leaked. The gaping holes in the windows where the North Wind rushed in were all more or less covered temporarily with tarpaulin until Fr. Lefebvre was able to have all seven hundred panes replaced. They stoked the stoves not only with wood but even with sawdust in an effort to take the chill off the classrooms and dormitories. The sleeping accommodation was rather Spartan in fact, and the partitions between the beds were torn down perhaps to improve the circulation of heat.

The superior encouraged his seminarians: "Be patient; accept the conditions such as they are; soon there will be tables you can share to put your washing basins on, and everyone will have his own wardrobe."

Through his brother Michel, who owned a factory,[21] the Father Superior managed to persuade relatives and friends to sell him various basic materials and essential items at a reasonable price: a rheostat and electric motor for the sisters' ironing machine, a large quantity of socks and stockings, putty to install the windows which at last had arrived, large barrels of paint, a hundred blankets, *etc.* For the provincial bursar, Fr. Lefebvre drew up an estimate of the expenditure needed to put the seminary back on its feet:

ESTIMATION OF EXPENSES FOR RECONSTRUCTION	
Painting of seminary area (pending) 1,500,000	
Windows Entreprise Loret (was pending total payment of bill) .280,000	
Roof (being repaired, almost finished, already paid 30,000) 150,000	
Repairs to masonry (being done, almost finished). 30,000	
Plasterwork – Dormitories (pending) 40,000	
Plasterwork and painting of hospice	
(quotation[22]): painting, 400,000	
plasterwork, 1,000,000 [*sic*].............250,000	
Hospice staircase (pending) 30,000	

The entire bill, which came to 2,280,000 francs, was paid to the bafflement of the bursar: who would have believed money could be found in

---

[20] Ms. I, 25, 35-38; 32, 30-33; 54, 49-52; ms. II, 27, 53-54.
[21] Fr. Marcel, Letter to Michel Lefebvre, Nov. 1, 1945 - Oct. 4, 1946.
[22] No doubt they saved money on labor.

all that poverty? However, Fr. Lefebvre had already acquired the reputation of knowing how to spend money, a virtue which his beloved St. Thomas labeled as "munificence," and which left the provincial bursar short of breath as he tried to keep up with it.

"HE FED US!"

Fr. Lefebvre proved to be most zealous—and earned the boundless gratitude of the students—in feeding those hundred or so hungry mouths who had to endure food rationing and who needed more than could be provided by the Abbey's farm, henhouse, and garden. The ruined town was itself barely managing to survive: the countryside showed more evidence of the ravages of war than of livestock or agriculture. The burnt-out wrecks of German and American tanks could be seen dotted across the fields, and half-buried, unexploded mortar shells and mines made the farmers' work dangerous. Here and there fragments of bone would still be found in an old helmet or abandoned boot. Many farms had been destroyed by the duels between opposing artillery. Fr. Lefebvre's ingenuity in these circumstances was truly marvelous.

From his brother Michel he obtained one of the family cars that nobody used and converted it into a kind of pick-up. After morning Mass, he would climb behind the wheel of this unusual but sturdy vehicle and travel through the Normandy countryside going from farm to farm, and widening his search upon the advice of this or that farmer. Then, he would return to the seminary with piles of food: vegetables, potatoes, butter, camembert, and even bread. He even brought back large quarters of meat for which he had a cold-room built. "He really fed us," as one former Mortain student exclaimed: "He was the superior, but he managed the money....He was an organizer. We were cold but it wasn't his fault; we certainly didn't die of hunger, no indeed!"[23]

"When you are young, you are hungry," as another former student put it. "When you realize that the superior is spending time in his father's car—the car of his father, a factory owner, who was martyred and died after being deported—then you realize there is something special going on. He rolled up his sleeves. That was how he looked after us. We felt that he took care of us and that he loved us."[24]

---

[23] Ms. I, 25, 40; 25, 51-55; 50, 28-30; Buttet, *Le bâton et le rocher*, 101.
[24] Ms. I, 55, 8-15.

III. SOUND DOCTRINE AND REVOLUTION

THE FERMENTATION OF IDEAS[25]

Since he had come to give "whatever he could," Fr. Lefebvre also set about correcting the false ideas and destroying the unhealthy utopias that were widespread among the clergy. By condemning the Vichy regime, the liberation had both rejected the restoration of the Christian social order approved by Marshal Pétain, and brought back to France everything that the Marshal had gotten rid of. Thus the elections of October 23, 1945, resulted in the presence of Communists in the government of General de Gaulle. Besides, during the war some seminarians and priests had been in constant close contact with Communist militants: impressed by their zeal for the victory of the proletariat, they wondered whether this movement could not be Christianized, or at least redirected towards Christ.

Moreover, at Lisieux on October 5, 1942, the seminary for the Mission of France had been opened. Its rector, Fr. Louis Augros, P.S.S., a devotee of Jacques Maritain, claimed that since human society had grown into adulthood, it rejected all supervision including even that of the Church, and wished to be self-sufficient in its own affairs. In essence the work of missionaries had to be to seek to bring a Christian influence to the new civilization being built: they had to find "priests who are willing to baptize it and create a synthesis between Christianity and this new civilization, thus bringing about a new Christendom."[26]

Not only the apostolate but priestly life itself risked being corrupted by such thinking. October 1945 saw the return of former prisoners or victims of worker deportation schemes, full of their simplified, "brotherly" Masses and their pastoral experiments. They encouraged their superiors to simplify the liturgical rites and sacred vestments and to send seminarians for work experience in factories or to sessions organised by *Economie et Humanisme*. Founded in Marseilles in 1940 by Fr. Louis-Joseph Lebret, O.P., this center for sociological studies analyzed capitalist economics and even examined the parish apostolate. In place of the latter—now free of "rigid theories" and "outdated ideas"—the center proposed structural reforms such as the introduction of "priest-teams" operating in dechristianized rural areas (which was not a bad idea). By 1949 Lebret, who was anxious to salvage certain Communist values, denounced the "daft, simpleminded anti-Communism" of too many Catholics.

---

[25] Cf. Jean Paillard, *1940-1944, La révolution corporative spontanée* (Annonay: Éd. du Vivarais, 1979); Robert Wattebled, *Stratégies catholiques en monde ouvrier dans la France d'après-guerre* (Éd. Ouvrières, 1990), 150.

[26] Augros, *La Mission de France 1941* (1945), 22, 48 (cf. Jacques Maritain, *Humanisme intégral* [Aubier, 1936], 144).

These periods of work experience bore their own fruit: in May 1946 Louis Augros was dreaming of worker-priests and in June some seminarians asked permission to join the Communist Party: "We cannot open up Communism to Christ except from the inside....Our hopes and our struggles must be the same as theirs."[27]

ZEAL TO ENLIGHTEN WITH THE TEACHING OF THE POPES

At Mortain some seminarians were won over by this "new atmosphere"[28] and Fr. Lefebvre reacted. "Do not get worked up, and do not be divided," he recommended. "Study thoroughly the social doctrine of the Church. Be wary of basing your action on being 'for the poor' or on being 'for the rich.' Both exist and will always exist." The superior trusted his staff to teach social ethics but he was suspicious of the slippery, pretentious beliefs of syndicalism and of specialist Catholic Action:[29] as he told his students: "Although it is true that one should know a lot about these subjects, it is above all necessary to go to Africa with deep humility."

He allowed the participants of "study-circles" to have meetings on a Sunday morning provided they were studying doctrine. Fr. Lefebvre was quite open-minded in these matters and succeeded in affiliating Mortain to the Catholic Institute in Paris: thus, several gifted students were able to obtain baccalaureates in scholastic philosophy and continue their studies in Rome.[30]

In the library the students could find various doctrinal journals from *La Pensée Catholique*[31] to Action Populaire's review *Cahiers de l'Action Religieuse et Sociale*, alongside the *Revue Thomiste*. The superior saw it as his responsibility to oversee a healthy degree of freedom in the students' studies; in some students he had noticed "an ill-informed zeal, seeking self-satisfaction and excitement at the expense of charity and the hierarchical Church." The Father Superior tried hard to correct this unhealthy attitude without acting in such a way as to undermine the atmosphere of trust: He explained simply that "true joy and true freedom of mind come from the love of authority, of truth, and of one's confreres."

To help these young minds tempted by schemes that were ill-inspired, Fr. Lefebvre had official Church teachings read in the refectory: Leo XIII's

---

[27] Wattebled, *Stratégies catholiques en monde ouvrier*, 44-45, 119, 131-133, 174.

[28] *Fideliter*, no. 59: 51.

[29] The ACO and the JOC (two Catholic social movements) were vehemently opposed to Communism and the presence of priests in factories. Sadly, the clergy would corrupt these good instincts.

[30] *General Bulletin*, 723: 195.

[31] A theological review founded by former colleagues of Fr. Lefebvre from his student days in Rome, the Reverend Fathers Luc (Lucien) Lefèvre and Victor-Alain Berto.

letter to Cardinal Gibbons on Americanism, Pius X's encyclical *Pascendi* on modernism, and his letter on the *Sillon* concerning social modernism.

While Pius XII was recalling for the French "the marvelous gifts France received at her baptism at Rheims," and warning them against "the assaults of destructive forces which aim to tempt France and make her fall— which would be to her detriment and to the detriment of all nations and peoples,"[32] the Father Superior was reminding his young students of the missionary role of Catholic France, their role as the "salt of the earth," and their mission to enlighten others while "keeping the incorruptible deposit of the faith and the truth in its entirety." "The truth remains unchanged, it does not evolve. If the circumstances change the way one applies the truth, they change neither the way it is explained nor its content. Truth is eternal like God Himself." The danger was "to carry unconsciously in us the errors of the naturalism that surrounds us and to act in accordance with those errors. Would you like some examples? What do you think of freedom of conscience, freedom of religion, freedom of the press, secularization of the State, the 1789 Declaration of the Rights of Man?"[33]

"HE MADE US READ A BOOK OF ACTION FRANÇAISE!"

Fr. Lefebvre hit some raw nerves. Several of his listeners whose minds had become inadvertently secularized took offense at seeing their superior attack the sacrosanct dogmas of republicanism. "Listen to Pius IX," Fr. Lefebvre insisted: "Study the teachings of the popes!" To drive the lesson home, he had a certain little book read in the refectory…which, if we are to judge by the reaction of one of the students, challenged some stubborn prejudices: "I remember that at mealtimes they read a book of Action Française. I was young but I was a little taken aback. I said to myself, 'Hold on, how can this be…?'"[34]

The book that was read had nothing in fact to do with Action Française. It was called *La Révolution française, à propos du centenaire de 1789* and was written by Bishop Freppel, Bishop of Angers. Unlike Maurras, Freppel sought not to criticize the abolition of the monarchy but denounced the Revolution as a fruit of naturalism and for being contrary to the social reign of Jesus Christ. Faced with the surprise of certain students, and shocking them still more, Fr. Lefebvre drove the point home even more strongly:

> The astonishment that the reading of this book has caused to some of you hardly surprises me, especially since we live in a secular atmosphere created by the Revolution. It is unsurprising given the education you get

---

[32] Pie XII, Allocution to French Journalists, April 17, 1946.
[33] Lefebvre, Conference at Pentecost 1946, Mortain.
[34] Ms. I, 32, 22-23; 34, 40-52.

in schools where they follow curricula and textbooks that falsify the notions of Christian history. So, you have to ask yourself some questions: you must understand that there is a proper way to look at history, and it is taught by the Sovereign Pontiffs and the bishops who follow their teachings. You must judge history in the light of the Church. Has the Church been rejected by men? Every civilization [which rejects her] collapses and is doomed to anarchy and slavery.

Another similar objection went thus: "We are in a seminary and you want to give us an education in politics. But we are told a priest should not play at politics." Fr. Lefebvre gave a clear answer to this:

> You must understand this truth correctly: the priest should not be involved in politics, but let us make a distinction. If politics means the various acceptable ways of ruling and governing, then yes. If politics means the model of the body politic, its origin, constitution, and goal, then it falls under the moral law, and thus under the teaching of the Church. The priest must be able to say such and such a principle is wrong or significant. You must be guides who are able to enlighten others; you must be men of principle.

FR. LEFEBVRE AND POLITICS

Fr. Lefebvre could clearly see the implementation of these principles in France in 1945. Marshal Pétain was iniquitously condemned to death on August 15, the Feast of the Assumption of the Blessed Virgin, and was moved on November 15 to the Fort de la Pierre Levée on the Ile d'Yeu. Did Fr. Marcel make his strong feelings on the matter known at the time? In any case he did so later, explaining to his seminarians: "De Gaulle brought back everything that Marshal Pétain had driven out of France. Everything was once again ruined, and the movement for Catholic and Christian order was decapitated."[35]

On April 13, 1987, at the tomb of Marshal Pétain on the Ile d'Yeu, he paid tribute in the following words to the soldier who had heroically sacrificed himself for his country: "You saved France twice, and you not only saved it but you rebuilt it spiritually and morally by making it rediscover its deepest traditions of faith, work, and love of family....In this you showed so much exceptional heroism and virtue that you should have been given the title of Father of the Country."

On the other hand, some clergy spoke of collaborating with the Communists, but the priests in the know, the Communist infiltrators, understood like Lenin that "class struggle will lead Christian workers to socialism and atheism a hundred times better than a sermon on pure atheism."[36]

---

[35] Lefebvre, *Spiritual Conferences at Ecône*, Jan. 8, 1974.
[36] Lenin, *De la religion*, cited in Jean Madiran, *La vieillesse du monde* (DMM, 1975), 109.

Aware of the dangers, the Father Superior spoke out with Pius XI: "Communism is intrinsically wrong, and no one who would save Christian civilization may collaborate with it in any undertaking whatsoever."[37] And Fr. Lefebvre concluded, "*Roma locuta est, causa finita est*, Rome has spoken, the matter is closed." That was how he put it.[38]

Similarly, during the parliamentary elections of 1946, the superior did not hesitate to give the seminarians very explicit advice on voting: he advised them to vote for the PRL—a "solidly Right-wing party," as a former student said—because he was neither on the Left, nor a Radical, nor a Christian Democrat. During the referendum of October 1946 concerning the Constitution of the Fourth Republic, Fr. Lefebvre called upon his students to vote "No," although his reasons for a "No" vote were totally different from de Gaulle's. "In matters concerning education, marriage, property, *etc.*, God and the Church are excluded from the Constitution. The whole of morality is at stake."

The Father Superior was also "categorical when addressing the faithful who came to Mass." His approach amazed the other priests.[39] "Oh, Fr. Lefebvre, weren't you a little bit strong?" But their remarks were always met with a smile and the simple reply: "One has to say the truth."

How he thanked God for the love of truth in its entirety which he had learned at Santa Chiara! *Sentire cum Ecclesia* was his rule; to his seminarians he gave this counsel: "Never again think in a manner at odds with the truth of the Church."

IV. SOUND DOCTRINE, SPIRITUAL LIFE, MISSIONARY ZEAL

OUTSIDE THE CHURCH THERE IS NO SALVATION

The first "truth of the Church" is the need for every man to belong to the Church in order to be saved. The dogma "Outside the Church there is no salvation" was for Fr. Lefebvre "the *raison d'être* of the missionary apostolate," since according to God's Providence the baptism of water and explicit faith in Jesus Christ are ordinarily the door to the Church. He also attacked Fr. de Lubac for his *Le fondement théologique des missions*.[40] In this book the Jesuit underlined the importance of "the light of the Word which enlightens every man" and the "thousands of undetectable forms of grace." He concluded: "It is false to say that without the missionary the 'pagan' is inevitably destined for hell."

---

[37] *Divini Redemptoris*, March 19, 1937, §58.
[38] Ms. I, 50-51.
[39] Ms. I, 50, 43-54; 30, 1-4.
[40] Reviewed in *La Revue Thomiste*, Sept.-Dec., 1946, 575-602.

In answer, Fr. Lefebvre did not even touch upon the questionable orthodoxy of Fr. de Lubac's arguments as exposed by the Dominican Fathers Labourette and Nicholas in their own refutation of the Jesuit. He relied instead upon a realism derived from his African experiences: "The theories of Fr. de Lubac would sweep away all missionary zeal. It is a fact, and a fact that is seemingly borne out by experience, that even if some pagans are able to co-operate with grace in the beginning, it is quite difficult for them to persevere because of the societies in which they live." In Marcel Lefebvre, the bushman's wisdom went hand in hand with accurate, theological language. He stated that the supernatural order was not optional and saw in the Blessed Virgin "the shield of the faith, the pillar of the supernatural order." As he would say, the wound of ignorance, the most serious wound of original sin, deprives souls of the light: "Death sends to hell millions of souls that ignorance has drowned in a sea of vice or selfishness."

Fr. Lefebvre was keen to show the power of these principles, and invited missionaries visiting Mortain to relate their experiences to the seminarians. The evening of Easter Sunday, 1947, his own sister, Sister Marie-Gabriel, gave a conference to the seminarians about the hospitals, children's homes, and turbulent schools of Cameroon. Pentecost Tuesday, May 27, Bishop Pierre Bonneau, whom Fr. Lefebvre had not seen since they were in Mvolyé, and who had been consecrated bishop on February 16, by Cardinal Liénart, came to speak about the indigenous clergy.[41] Early the next day, Marcel left with Bishop Bonneau for Lourdes, where he would attend the episcopal consecration of his friend Jean-Baptiste Fauret, recently appointed Vicar Apostolic of Loango. "You know," Bonneau said during the journey, "there have been several vicariates to fill one after the other."

"Yes," said Fr. Lefebvre, "Bangui, and now Douala and Loango."

"Dakar too, Bishop Grimault has resigned."

"Yes, and Libreville since the death of Bishop Tardy on January 28."

"Yes...," said Bonneau, "they're thinking about you!"

It was clear that Bishop Bonneau was "testing the water." However, in his humility Fr. Marcel said to himself: "How can they think about me? Besides, have I not been taken out of the missionary field?" Ultimately he would do whatever the superiors wanted.[42]

"PHILOSOPHY PREPARES YOU FOR A LIFE OF UNION WITH GOD"

Some of his seminarians compared Mortain with its healthy liberty to the rough and tough training in the novitiate. "Here we are at last, far from the novitiate!" they would say. In this attitude Fr. Lefebvre detected a loss of fervor, or a loss of focus in spiritual training and in the pursuit of sanc-

[41] C.S.Sp. French *Bulletin*, 37, 38.
[42] Mother Marie-Christiane Lefebvre, *Mon frère, Monseigneur Marcel*, 10.

tity. The too exclusively intellectual approach adopted by the philosophy students was a serious pitfall. He warned them to beware:

It is not normal; the opposite ought to be the case. After the novitiate, your studies should provide food for your spiritual life and not lessen it. When all is said and done, philosophy, understood and loved, leads to God who is present everywhere, incomprehensible in so far as He exceeds our weak intelligences. Here is where the door of faith opens....Philosophy is a preparation to sanctity and to a life of union with God....True knowledge leads logically to humility: false knowledge which stops along the way, which is incomplete, leads to pride and self-importance.

The remedy was readily available: St. Thomas. The Father Superior went through the *Summa Theologica* in his spiritual conferences. He devised a "triptych of the spiritual life," which he planned to expound over three years and which he later spoke of at Ecône:

The first year was given over to the study of the "unjust man" with all the consequences of original sin. The second year covered the "just man" sanctified by grace with his virtues, the gifts of the Holy Ghost, and the beatitudes. In the third year—had I stayed for a third year—I would have explained the means by which man passes from the state of injustice to the state of justice: firstly our Lord himself [His work of redemption] then the means of sanctification that He instituted: the Mass, the sacraments, prayer, doing God's will, the means to fight against our failings and grow in virtue. I would have finished off with the four last things, and the fulfilment of justification.[43]

A former student recalled these conferences: "It was always St. Thomas, St. Thomas, St. Thomas! We had come from the novitiate where they did not refer much to St. Thomas....At [Mortain] we practically bathed in St. Thomas; as for me, I liked it."[44]

The Father Superior spoke in a calm voice and his Thomistic conferences sprinkled with recollections from Africa were delivered with little oratorical polish. "He wasn't an orator; it was a little painful listening to him," recalled one of his students who would have preferred a more "engaging style." According to another student, "He wasn't an orator, but we listened to him."[45]

V. AN UNDERSTANDING LEADER

The same seminarian said, "We valued him a lot. We really loved him because he was very simple and direct." Since he sang a little off key, Fr. Lefebvre asked one of the youngest seminarians who had a good voice to

---

[43] Lefebvre, *Petite histoire*, 57; Lefebvre, *Spiritual Conferences at Ecône*, 16 B, Jan. 28, 1975; 25 A, Nov. 28, 1975.
[44] Ms. I, 50, 37-38; 53, 21-36.
[45] Ms. I, 30, 50; 55, 46.

help him practice singing the Prefaces of the Mass. According to another student: "He was always happy to see seminarians in his office, to speak, to say something that needed saying, talking in his small, gentle voice."[46]

With the approach of the summer vacations in 1946, the Father Superior drew up the vacation plans for the students. Some would stay at the seminary; others would go to houses of the congregation or to help on summer camps. Normally the students were not allowed to go home to their families. However, "Fr. Lefebvre, who was very open-minded and even a little bit ahead of his time, said to himself, 'As most of them have been through the war, if they can go home to their families, that will do them some good.' He allowed many to go home." The Swiss students, who could not be said to have "been through the war," could not really hope for permission to go home on that basis. Fr. Lefebvre told them, "I'll have to see. Perhaps those whose health is not too strong might get permission."

One day two Swiss students, Emmanuel Barras and Auguste Fragnière, both in reasonably good health, waited before his door: "Auguste," said Emmanuel, "if anybody is staying for the vacation, it's us two!" Emmanuel entered, sat down, and heard Fr. Lefebvre say: "Barras, it seems to me that you are in need of some rest..." "But Father," said the zealous student, "all the same I feel quiet well!" "No, no, no, you have lost weight, you seem tired to me!" As Fr. Barras later said, "I could have given him a hug, I felt so grateful. He was a very understanding man, very understanding."[47]

During another vacation period, Fr. Lefebvre allowed the Swiss (them again!) to go on foot to Mont Saint Michel. André Buttet explained: "It was a novelty. He hooked us up with two French students, one of whom was François Morvan. We had a bike and a tent, and whoever was on the bike would go on ahead to try to find a farm. That kept us amused for a week." Colleagues visiting Mortain were surprised by the mutual trust between the priests and students, a trust that enabled the students to act often on their own initiative.[48] Such were the fruits of the leadership of an understanding Father Superior.

This was how Fr. Lefebvre conceived of the right relationship between authority and obedience. France after Liberation was suffering from a crisis of authority brought about by the crisis of obedience among the Free French. Restoring authority's real meaning meant showing its true face. The Father Superior led by example, and that was a language the seminarians could understand. One day he asked them to write an essay on authority, starting from a beautiful description of authority which he gave

[46] Ms. I, 50, 34-35; 35, 5-9, 39-41.
[47] Ms. I, 51, 8-20; 55, 17-22.
[48] Ms. I, 30, 19-24; II, 50, 44-49; C.S.Sp. French *Bulletin*, 37, 40.

them but providing their own examples to illustrate their arguments: "One can say that authority is totally divine in its origins, and sweet and powerful in its essence. And, if it is moved by the gift of counsel and supported by prudence, it is also amazingly fruitful, bringing order, prosperity, and peace."

He showed a practical example of this peace when dealing with German prisoners who were being held near the seminary. André Buttet recalled the situation: "Some worked in the park and could be recognized from their clothing. We would greet them with a '*Guten Tag.*' I remember one Christmas going to sing in their camp. Their chaplain, Fr. Diebold, had got permission from the French authorities and Fr. Lefebvre had said yes....even though his own father had died in Germany, worn out through suffering in a Nazi concentration camp! In certain circumstances loving your neighbor becomes heroic. So many memories forge bonds of friendship and respect." "I loved him," another former student of Mortain said.

His good nature did not stop the Father Superior being clear-sighted about his students. The day of his consecration he said to Bishop Le Hunsec: "In those dear students I found generosity, goodwill, and a love of truth and learning, all of which gave me genuine satisfaction....In them I found elite souls."[49] However, if we are to take into account the remarks of Fr. Côme Jaffré at Chevilly, sometimes his judgment on those going from Mortain to Chevilly was rather more severe, "If we took on board all of Fr. Lefebvre's views, we would kick out a lot of students."[50] Doubtless some students gave him cause for concern, all the more so because he knew Chevilly to be receptive to modern ideas. Ultimately what he was able to give, he gave: and the majority of his students responded to the efforts he made to transform them into men of principle.

Fifty years have gone by: the witnesses remember a father who was loving and beloved, without being able to grasp that the same source of inspiration made him so affable and yet so strong. It is true that Vatican II has since happened. The "small, gentle voice" of their superior did not seem to them to go with the commandment of "living by principles" which he inculcated in them. One of them says: "The memories I have of Fr. Lefebvre are very different. I remember a character with great spiritual and human capacity for warmth, organization, and intelligence. At the same time he was a man with a very strong vision in Church matters and in politics."[51]

Happy were they who understood how Marcel Lefebvre combined the most attentive, fatherly love with the greatest doctrinal firmness. *Fecit illud caritas*:[52] what brought this about was charity, a charity that was obeyed in

---

[49] Marziac, *Monseigneur Lefebvre, soleil levant*, 105.
[50] Ms. I, 53, 12; II, 50, 30-38.
[51] Ms. I, 35, 47-50.

all things. Dear former friends of Fr. Lefebvre, far from being impropriety or a lack of charity, the imperturbable faithfulness of your father to the "truth of the Church"—with all that it entails—was the sign of a greater love and a deeper charity.

VI. AN UNEXPECTED POSTING

Fr. Lefebvre would get the chance to test this *majorem caritatem*, this greater love. In mid-June 1947, he was thinking about the vacations during which he planned to make a retreat from July 20 to August 17 and to spend a few days jotting down an outline of his mother's biography "to make her saintly soul known a little more."[53] A telephone call upset these plans. On June 25, Fr. Macher, his vice-rector, knocked on his door and said to him very simply, "Father, you have been named as the Vicar Apostolic of Dakar!" Straight away Fr. Lefebvre called Bishop Le Hunsec in Paris.

"Hello?"

"Hello, Father, it was you I wanted. Steady yourself! You have been...you have been named as the Vicar Apostolic of Dakar! (Silence from Fr. Lefebvre.) Well then, Father?"

"Dakar! Oh my! Oh my goodness!" Fr. Lefebvre thought to himself: "I was expecting something, but before, they talked about Gabon. Now it's Dakar...in Muslim territory...where I know nobody."

Bishop Le Hunsec said: "You are a professed religious, you have to obey! You don't have the choice, you must say yes."

He had of course to say yes. There was no need to hide the news, so that evening at supper when the reader had finished the passage from the Gospel, there came a bell from the Fathers' table; Fr. Macher got to his feet and an air of anxiety descended on the room. His voice trembling with emotion, he said: "My dear friends, my dear friends. Let me announce some wonderful news, a great joy and a great honor: our dear Father Superior has been named Vicar Apostolic of Dakar!" Applause broke out. Fr. Lefebvre spoke with the same simple, fatherly tone that he had always had: certainly he was surprised by the posting to Dakar, and certainly he would not refuse to do his duty. But he added: "I recall those words of the Gospel: '*Duxerunt eum et crucifigerent.*'"[54] Faced with this task, he said what he said the day of his arrival at the scholasticate: "Whatever I can give, I will give!"[55]

---

[52] Bernard, *Sermo de duodecim stellis*, in fest. Septem Dol. B.M.V., lect. 6.

[53] Fr. Marcel Lefebvre, Letter to Sister Marie Christiane, June 16, 1947.

[54] "They took him away and crucified him" (Mt. 27:31).

[55] C.S.Sp. French *Bulletin*, 37, 38-39.

CHAPTER 8

ARCHBISHOP OF DAKAR

I. THE CONSECRATION

THE SACRED CONGREGATION'S GAME OF CHESS

As he drove to Paris, Fr. Lefebvre was beset by doubts: "Perhaps I ought to become a Trappist? Haven't they made a mistake in choosing me? Anyway, why Dakar? Didn't they talk about Gabon at first?"

True, when Bishop Tardy died at Chevilly in January 1947, the name of Marcel Lefebvre had been on the Libreville *terna*[1] to replace him. However, ever since December 1946, René Graffin, Vicar Apostolic of Yaoundé, had been mooted as a replacement for Bishop Grimault after the latter's resignation as Vicar Apostolic of Dakar.[2] Graffin was not well liked by his clergy, and a move to Dakar would have killed two birds with one stone. As for Graffin's diocese at Yaoundé—an area more densely populated than Gabon—Fr. Lefebvre seemed perfect for the job. And Fr. Jérôme Adam would do very well at Libreville. Then, however, Bishop Graffin refused to change posts. He stayed at Yaoundé, and in the Sacred Congregation's game of chess, Marcel Lefebvre finally ended up in Dakar.[3]

It is significant that Rome chose this forty-one year old ex-missionary for the capital of French West Africa,[4] whose diocesan structure was finally emerging.[5] We must conclude that they found "a job that was big enough"[6] for him, to use the words of Cardinal Liénart. In addition to the qualities listed in Canon 331, the future bishop also had a gift for organization and was a genius when it came to material and practical matters. His only fault was stubbornness. When this point was raised, it was noted

---

[1] A *terna* is a list of three candidates chosen according to a range of criteria and submitted to the Sacred Congregation for the Propagation of the Faith (for missionary countries) who then ask the pope to choose among them.

[2] *General Bulletin*, 598-599: 99, 111; *Ibid.*, 600-601: 143.

[3] *Ibid.*, 596-597: 69; Criaud, *La Geste des spiritains*, 233.

[4] Comprising eight colonies: Dakar, Senegal, French Guinea, Ivory Coast, Dahomey, French Sudan, Mauritania, and the Niger, numbering all together about 20 million people.

[5] The Apostolic Delegation of Africa was being dismantled, *A.A.S.* (1947): 39, 96.

[6] Toast proposed during the celebrations for the consecration of Msgr. Lefebvre, Marziac, *Monseigneur Lefebvre, soleil levant*, 108; Bull of Pius XII, June 12, 1947: "*Te, ad pastorale munus requisitis dotibus, ut Nobis relatum est, præditum.*"

that tenacity was a virtue (as seemed to be the case with Marcel Lefebvre) when sound doctrine was at stake.

In Paris the future bishop got a warm reception from Archbishop Le Hunsec, who put his doubts to rest and reminded him of St. John Bosco's motto: "Ask for nothing, refuse nothing." He gave him much encouragement, and presented him with a beautiful amethyst ring. Since Dakar was not a diocese with a resident bishop, the Vicar Apostolic's jurisdiction was only exercised in the name and under the orders of the Pope. Nevertheless, he actually had more power than a resident bishop in virtue of the unpredictable conditions prevailing in missionary countries.[7] He was to receive episcopal consecration according to Pius XII's bull *Dilecto Filio Marcello Lefebvre*,[8] dated June 12 but issued on July 23. He also received a bishopric *in partibus infidelium*, becoming titular bishop of Anthédon[9] (El Blakiyeh near Gaza in Palestine). This title had belonged to Bishop Charles-Louis Gay, Cardinal Pie's auxiliary in Poitiers from 1877-1880.

THE CONSECRATION

Since Cardinal Liénart was the bishop of his home diocese and a great supporter of the missions, Fr. Lefebvre asked him to perform the consecration. As co-consecrators he chose Bishop Alfred Ancel, auxiliary bishop of Lyons, who had been a few years ahead of him at Santa Chiara, as well as his friend Bishop Fauret. It was finally decided that the consecration would take place in his family's parish church in Tourcoing.

In Tourcoing, as in Mortain where the community had held a celebration for him on July 6, he began to notice the marks of respect now shown towards him and to feel the distance this created between him and his friends. According to his sister Christiane, however, he did not behave differently since he loved simplicity and good friendship too much. At Lophem-les-Bruges where he went for a few days on retreat at the monastery of his cousin, the famous liturgist Dom Gaspar Lefebvre, the monks insisted on seating him on a conspicuous throne. He objected:

"But I haven't yet been consecrated bishop!"

"On the contrary, you are a bishop-elect, and that is sufficient."

He fared better at Solesmes between September 7 and 9, where the monks respected his wishes.[10] He meditated on his favorite words from St. John which he had chosen for his episcopal device, "*Et nos credidimus car-*

---

[7]   1917 Code of Canon Law, can. 293 and commentary of Raoul Naz, *Traité de droit canonique*, I, 589-591.

[8]   Latin text in *General Bulletin*, 604-606: 202-203.

[9]   Brief of May 8, 1947, cf. *A.A.S.* 39 (1947): 639.

[10] Mother Marie Christiane Lefebvre, *Mon frère, Monseigneur Marcel*, 10; Fr. Vincent Artus, O.S.B., Letter to Msgr. Lefebvre, March 29, 1967; Dom Jean Prou, Letter to J.-M. L., June 24, 1999.

itati."[11] Yes, he said, we have believed in the great charity that God and that our Lord has for us.[12] This was an echo of the spirituality of the late Fr. Liagre and of St. Theresa of the Child Jesus, who based her sanctity on having faith in the infinite, merciful love of God.[13]

On the coat of arms of the elected bishop, the congregation's emblem appeared on the left above the "African memorial"–the future cathedral of Dakar–while on the right "on a gold background stands a red cross with a six-pointed star and four five-petal, azure flowers"–the arms of his great uncle Pierre Lefebvre, a burgher of Tournai, dating from 1690.[14] Be that as it may, the Archbishop also saw in these symbols our Lord's cross steeped in blood, the cross of the crusade for His reign which is based on the gold of God's charity and supported by the universal mediation of our Lady.

For the fifth time he took the anti-modernist oath with his hand on the Gospels, affirming with conviction, "I firmly hold, then, and shall hold to my dying breath the belief of the Fathers in the charism of truth, which certainly is, was, and always will be in the succession of the episcopacy from the apostles. The purpose of this is, then, not that dogma may be tailored according to what seems better and more suited to the culture of each age; rather, that the absolute and immutable truth preached by the apostles from the beginning may never be believed to be different, may never be understood in any other way."

He received the fullness of the priesthood on September 18, 1947, in the church of Our Lady of Tourcoing, in the presence of Archbishop Le Hunsec and six other missionary bishops; Bishop Dutoit, bishop of Arras; the parish priest of Mortain; and numerous priests from France, Senegal, and representatives of the French Seminary in Rome. Fr. René Lefebvre and Fr. Jean Watine, S.J., the brother and cousin respectively of the bishop-elect, were the deacon and sub-deacon of the Pontifical Mass of consecration.

During the reception at the Sacred Heart School, hosted by Cardinal Liénart, the young bishop very simply expressed his loyalty to the principles he had learned in Rome from Fr. Le Floch: "I thank him sincerely from the bottom of my heart because he showed us the path of truth."[15] Then, addressing himself to the representative of the Governor General of French West Africa, he clearly defined France's mission in Africa: "The Africans greatly love the Christian culture and civilization of France. There is something in France that one finds nowhere else; France, which is Catho-

---

[11] "We have believed in charity" (I Jn. 4:16).
[12] Marcel Lefebvre, *Retreats preached at Ecône*, March 26, 1975.
[13] Liagre, *Retraite avec sainte Thérèse de l'Enfant Jésus* (Lisieux, 1991), 13.
[14] General armorial of France, Flanders, Dept. of Lille, Tournai office.
[15] The cardinal listened without turning a hair but soon reported these amazing remarks to the Nuncio Msgr. Roncalli: Lefebvre, *Petite histoire*, 61.

lic almost in spite of herself, brings with her a charity and understanding for souls and a deep, psychological appreciation of the needs of neighbor, which she draws directly from her Catholicism."[16]

In view of his Senegalese apostolate, the bishop was given a Renault "4CV" which was quite rare at the time and which was gladly received.[17] A friend from Lille obtained for him a drawing board and all the equipment he would need for designing plans. The "building bishop" was on his way.

On October 5, Bishop Lefebvre went to Mortain to say his last good-byes. All his friends among the clergy were there, and in the evening, with his even voice and air of supernatural goodness, their beloved father reread the words of the Gospel from the night of the Last Supper, "My children, love one another."[18] A month later on November 11, ready at last, he boarded a plane for Dakar.

II. THE VICARIATE OF SENEGAL

The diocese that was placed in the care of the young bishop covered all of Senegal, apart from Casamance in the South, which was a distinct area under separate ecclesiastical jurisdiction. British Gambia had defined its territory, cutting off Casamance from Senegal, and Bishop Lefebvre was never in charge of it. The 199,000 square km. of Senegal's sandy terrain stretch east from the River Senegal to the Atlantic Ocean where Cape Verde reaches out into the sea, and runs south to the mountains of Fouta-Djalon on the borders of Guinea. How different it was from Gabon! Soon, however, the bishop grew attached to this countryside, to the semi-desert plains dotted with massive baobabs, palm trees, and thorny bushes. He came to like the sandy paths that wound their way through fields of millet and groundnuts, the ponds from which the wild ducks suddenly take flight, the "tanns" that the antelopes cross in a few gracious, agile leaps, and the quiet estuaries harboring tiny, picturesque islands on which nestle pretty little fishing villages.[19]

Among the 2,500,000 inhabitants of Senegal, from whom we must subtract the 300,000 in Casamance, there were only 55,000 Catholics—half Senegalese or Cape Verdians, half Europeans or Syro-Lebanese—surrounded by a world of 1,500,000 Muslims and 250,000 animists,[20] the latter themselves facing the all-conquering Islam.

[16] Marziac, *Monseigneur Lefebvre, soleil levant*, 104-105.
[17] Mother Marie Christiane Lefebvre, *Mon frère*, 11.
[18] *C.S.Sp. French Bulletin*, 37, 41.
[19] *Horizons Africains*, Jan. 1961, leader by Archbishop Lefebvre.
[20] *General Bulletin*, 617-618: 46-47.

ISLAM, THE SLAVE TRADE, AND THE CROSS[21]

The history of Senegal is in fact dominated by Islamic wars. The Moors of Lower Senegal who converted to Islam in the eighth century seized, in the course of the eleventh century, the Sarakole kingdom of Ghana which stretched from the Atlantic to the Niger. They later conquered Morocco and Spain. In the thirteenth century, Soundiata Keita, a cripple who could nevertheless stand, went off to subjugate the neighboring areas and found the Mandingue Empire of Mali: his legend, passed on through oral traditions, recalls the warrior virtues of the Malinkés, as well as their sense of honor and the antiquity of their civilization. However, Soundiata became Muslim, and drew Mali and soon after the neighboring Songhaï kingdom into Islam. In the sixteenth century the Songhaï and later the Peuls relaunched the holy war. The center of their dominance was Timbuktu, the urban and commercial capital of Islam.

However, in 1660 the animist Bambaras seized Timbuktu, and the states Mali had acquired slowly gained their independence. On the River Senegal the kingdom of Tékrour, the home of the Toucouleur race, lost its hold over the southern Wolof provinces, which then separated from each other. The Peuls continued spreading Islam through the Turup fraternities which created a cross between popular Islam and animism. Finally, in the eighteenth century the Guélowar princes from the North arrived in the Sine. They preferred exile to accepting Islam and were called the "Séré-abés," "those who had separated themselves," "the Sérènes."

Wherever the Muslims took over, they established the slave trade. They were aided in this by the Portuguese who discovered the mouth of the River Senegal in 1445, and later by the French who in 1663 founded the Cape Verde Commercial Enterprise after building Fort Saint Louis on the Island of Ndar.

Fr. Alexis, a Capuchin from Saint-Lô, established the first mission on the banks of the Rufisque in 1635. Then, the Holy Ghost Congregation was given responsibility for the Apostolic Prefecture of Senegal that Rome set up at Saint-Louis. However, evangelization was often interrupted by the Dutch in the seventeenth century and by the English in the eighteenth century. Christ's cross returned to Saint-Louis and Gorée with the Holy Ghost Fathers (1818) and the Sisters of Saint Joseph of Cluny, led by Mother Mary Javouhey (1820). She sent several young blacks to France,

---

[21] Annual of the Catholic Church in Africa (1960); Jacqueline Sorel, *Léopold Sédar Senghor* (Éd. Sépia, 1995), 20; Pierre Biarnes, *Les Français en Afrique noir de Richelieu à Mitterand* (Armand Colin, 1987), 16-97, 194, 253-256; Robert Dugon, "Dakar et ses premiers missionaires," in *L'Église catholique en Afrique, AOF Magazine*, no. 15 (August, 1956): 16-30.

three of whom became priests and later came back to their own country: Moussa, Fridoil, and Boilat.

In 1845, the Governor Bouet-Willaumez made an appeal to the Holy Ghost Fathers and the Ploërmel Brothers. Thus it was that after the disaster of Cap de Palmas, a second group of missionaries of the Holy Heart of Mary landed on the island of Gorée in June 1845. They knocked at the door of the presbytery, and Fr. Moussa appeared at a first-storey window:

"What is it you want, sirs?"

"We have been sent to make our foundation here," replied the irritated Fr. Arragon. His unfortunate turn of phrase made the native priest protest indignantly:

"Make your foundation! You can think again! Here everything depends on the Holy Ghost Seminary and the Apostolic Prefecture of Saint-Louis."

In the end all was well, and the sons of the Venerable Libermann set up their mission on the Cape Verde Peninsula.

THE MISSION AND ITS ADMINISTRATION[22]

Until 1854 the French occupied only the coastal areas, but then Faidherbe, the Governor of Senegal, undertook the territorial conquest of the rest of the country. In 1857 the navigator Protêt founded Dakar, and the port begun by Pinet-Laprade was opened in 1866. In 1876 the inhabitants of the "old coastal municipalities," who had intermarried with the French, were given French citizenship. An 1855 decree created French West Africa and made Dakar its capital. However, instead of advocating the law of Christ, the secular laws favored Islam with secular schooling, recognition of Islamic courts, and the imposition of Islamic leaders on animists.

The missionaries very soon clashed with an administration so aligned with Islam. Besides, Christian morality appeared difficult because it rejected polygamy, a custom that was however acceptable to Islam. Islamic Africa felt that it was part of an African spiritual family which was ancient, glorious, and powerful. The Muslim merchant Le Dioula was an untiring propagandist for his faith. The marabouts'[23] influence was also everywhere: they knew the Koran a little, organized prayers, and presided over the Koranic schools where the pupils repeated the sura in Arabic. They were also fetishists, using occult forces to cure the sick, bring rain, and conjure evil spirits.

---

[22] Biarnès, *Les Français en Afrique noir*, 91-97; Koren, *Les Spiritains*, 200, 213-219; Msgr. Bressolles, Conference in Paris on March 19, 1958, for the Alliance Jeanne d'Arc chaired by General Weygand, in *La Pensée Catholique*, no. 55: 37-50.

[23] [Marabouts are Muslim hermits or holy men. The term is North African. Trans.]

THE MOUTH OF THE LION

Due to Gambia's location, the map of Senegal looks like a lion's head with its nose at Cape Verde pointing towards the Atlantic. Casamance to the south is completely separate from Senegal, both ethnically and in terms of its hierarchy. The neighboring Guinea-Bissau is Portuguese speaking. Its last native ruler, Doctor Batica, was a friend of Archbishop Lefebvre.

In this land that was both physically and spiritually barren, the pioneers of evangelization understandably needed a deep faith. The first superior appointed by Libermann, Eugène Tisserant, who was one of his first two companions, never arrived in Dakar since he died in a shipwreck at Papin in 1846. In May 1847, Fr. Benoît Truffet, another of Libermann's disciples, arrived at the mission. He had been appointed Vicar Apostolic of both French Guinea and Guinea. His fate was hardly better: his taste for native food killed him within two years, and his suspicions concerning the "interference" of the civil authorities nearly killed off the mission.[24] His successor, Bishop Bessieux, moved to Gabon. However, in 1849, Bishop Aloyes Kobès (1820-1872), consecrated bishop after only three years of priesthood, was appointed as his auxiliary and took up residence at Dakar.

CONQUESTS OF THE CROSS[25]

Bishop Kobès's plan was to spread out into as many areas as possible, even at the risk of failure, in order to minister in the midst of the people who were open to the Gospel, i.e., the Sérènes animists of Sine, Gambia, and a few Wolof areas inland. Thus, at the request of the king of Sine, the missionaries set up a station on the coast at Joal. At Ngazobil ("the wells of stone") the Fathers asked Christian families to move near the mission with its plantations and schools, in order to make a truly Christian village. The missionaries went deeper into the country to Fatick and Kaolack between 1859 and 1861.

In 1874 a mission was founded on the island of Fadiout near the mouth of the River Sine. Despite the presence of some die-hard pagans, the island became a Christian bastion that numbered some 2,000 Catholics. Catholicism also reached Thiès and Popenguine, although these missions unfortunately had to be abandoned in 1914 after the priests were drafted. Subsequently, these areas were taken over by Islam in the wake of an aggressive propaganda campaign. When Bishop Jalabert died tragically at sea, Bishop Louis Le Hunsec became Vicar Apostolic of "Sénégambia," an area comprising Senegal and Gambia. He founded the mission at Kaolack and numerous others in Gambia and Casamance.

Following Bishop Le Hunsec's election as superior general of the congregation, Bishop Auguste Grimault was appointed Vicar Apostolic and also Administrator of the Apostolic Prefecture of Senegal (Saint-Louis). On March 31, 1929, he laid the foundation stone of the future cathedral known as the "African memorial," based on an idea of Governor General Merleau-Ponty for a monument to the African soldiers who had died for

---

[24] *General Bulletin*, 468: 254; Koren, *Les Spiritains*, 216-217.
[25] *General Bulletin*, 425: 405-479; 476; 604-605; 604-606, 204; 636, 96-100; 637, 133-137; *C.S.Sp. French Bulletin*, 86, 92; Sorel, *Léopold Sédar Senghor*, 32-33.

France. Fr. Daniel Brottier, the delegate of Bishop Jalabert, had begun fund-raising efforts in 1911 to pay for the cost of construction. The building was consecrated in March 1936 by the papal legate Cardinal Verdier.

The work of establishing Catholic schools—the indispensable means of protecting the faith of Catholic children, who were in danger of being influenced in secular schools by the large Muslim majority—was also a matter that drew attention. In addition to a few girls' schools, there was a primary school for boys in Dakar which, after the expulsion of the Ploërmel Brothers under the "*lois scélérates*"[26] (rogue laws), became the parish primary school. It later became a secondary school known as the Libermann Seminary-school, and from 1924 it accepted junior seminarians. Léopold Sédar Senghor was a pupil there from 1922 to 1926.

Just before World War II, Pius XI changed the name of the vicariate from "Sénégambia" to Dakar and the name of the prefecture from "Senegal" to "Saint-Louis of Senegal." Gambia became an apostolic prefecture, as did Casamance. The latter became known as the Apostolic Prefecture of Ziguinchor and was managed from 1939 onwards by the half-caste Holy Ghost Father Joseph Faye. He left in 1946 to become a Cistercian at Aiguebelle. His successor, appointed on June 13, 1947, was a native of Saint-Louis called Prosper Dodds, whose great-uncle General Dodds had conquered Dahomey.

Bishop Grimault, who had fostered the mission in Casamance, founded the mission of Diohine in Sine, Senegal, consecrated the magnificent church at Thiès in 1945, and created the second parish of Dakar at the cathedral by dividing the existing parish of the Sacred Heart in two. For lack of priests, he had to close Foundiougne and give up on founding a mission at Fatick. Worried by the lack of resources, he forbade any new initiatives that might put a strain on his budget. Seriously ill from 1940 to 1941, he was in de Gaulle's bad books by 1945.[27] He had to offer his resignation to the Apostolic Visitor and returned to France in 1946. A lot of important matters were left pending, and thus the clergy, faithful, and authorities awaited anxiously the arrival of their new bishop.

ARRIVAL—DIOCESAN VISITS—ACTION PLAN

Fr. Salomon, the stand-in Vicar Delegate, had organized a small welcoming ceremony. However, High Commissioner Barthes, the new Gov-

---

[26] [In this case, "*lois scélérates*" refers to the anti-clerical legislation that burgeoned in the strongly Republican French parliament during the 1880's. These laws included new rulings on secular education, the expulsion of some religious orders from France, the abolition of military chaplaincies, and permission for divorce. Trans.]

[27] In a pastoral letter of November 1942 written after the American landings in North Africa, he advised French West Africa not to join forces with the government of Algeria. Ms. III, 9, 49-70; 10, 1-25.

ernor General of French West Africa, wanted to show solemnly the cordiality of relations with the new bishop. Bishop Lefebvre was himself determined to take full advantage of the government's positive attitude towards the Church. Besides, as Fr. Libermann had recommended to his missionaries: "'Get along' with the authorities; God's will and the good of souls demand it."[28] The civil authorities might well have been Freemasons representing a weak-minded and liberal regime, but by maintaining personal, friendly relations with them, Bishop Lefebvre intended and succeeded in securing advantages that cold diplomatic relations would not have obtained. "Charity thinks no evil...it believeth all things, hopeth all things" (I Cor. 13:5-7).

On November 16, 1947, the young bishop entered his cathedral through a guard of honor provided by the Senegalese military, as the High Commissioner arrived at the cathedral flanked by the cavalry. The young bishop spoke with the charity of St. Paul, addressed himself firstly to the Commissioner whose presence, he said, was "especially significant," and then to the faithful, enjoining them to "contribute to the great work we all share that is entirely the work of charity, of charity with love, the gift of oneself." "I give myself to you," he said. "Give yourself to me, come to me."[29]

His voice was clear and even, and he spoke with a persuasiveness and gentle authority that impressed and conquered his listeners. For the French civil servants, this immediately confirmed the reputation that had already reached them of his being "an exceptional man" and a "first rate person."[30] For their part the clergy of Senegal saw the Church in Senegal for the first time in years governed by a pastor who had not been a missionary in the country.[31] The bishop overcame this handicap by undertaking a tour of the whole vicariate—to which as of January 9, 1948, was added the apostolic administration of the Prefecture of Saint-Louis—which allowed him to become acquainted with his forty-two priests, thirty-seven of whom were Holy Ghost Fathers.

Archbishop Lefebvre later made known his feelings on taking on these responsibilities: "One realizes that one is always destined to rule, to be in charge, with all those souls for whom one is responsible. It is terrifying because it will be like that until one dies; one wears a ring which is there to remind one....There is no way back."[32] Thus he resolved to forge ahead: *try*

---

[28]   Fr. Libermann, Letter of May 26, 1844.
[29]   Letter of Fr. Catlin, Oct. 12, 1947; *General Bulletin*, 609-610: 297; *Horizons Africains*, Dec. 1947.
[30]   Gérard Dubois-Burthe, interview, July, 1998, 3.
[31]   Fr. Jean-Jacques Marziac, *Des évêques français contre Mgr. Lefebvre* (Fideliter, 1989), 108.
[32]   *Fideliter*, no. 50: 16.

to be the best. He did this by throwing himself energetically into his work and using his gift for organization.

He weighed up immediately what needed to be done and drew up an action plan that catered for the long-term needs of the Church and country rather than offering knee-jerk reactions to short-term problems. He planned to set up a secondary school for boys and a teacher training school for primary teachers. He reorganized the arrangements for priestly training, envisaged the creation of new inner-city parishes, and co-ordinated Catholic Action. Lastly, he relaunched the campaign for evangelization in pagan areas. For each of his objectives, he chose the right man and, having put faith in him, found that he was not disappointed. But since his congregation was unable to send him enough missionaries, he decided to look elsewhere for additional priests, brothers, and religious.[33]

In February 1948, he returned to France and within a few weeks had managed to establish a network of benefactors. He also secured financial help from the Pontifical Missionary Works, whose secretary, Bishop Henri Chappoulie, became a good friend. Several religious congregations also agreed to work in the diocese in the coming years. Going to Rome for his *ad limina* visit to the successor of Peter, he was granted a fifteen-minute private audience with Pius XII on March 9. The Pope asked him about his training in Rome and said warmly, "Oh, dear Fr. Le Floch." Then the Pope told him of his own worries concerning the Communist persecutions. Marcel Lefebvre took this concern of the Holy Father very much to heart.[34]

III. HIS FAVORITE PROJECTS

Without shadow of a doubt, the works dearest to the heart of Archbishop Lefebvre were his school, seminary, and the African religious congregations.

SCHOOL OF SAINT MARY OF HANN

As soon as the new bishop arrived, Catholic parents began asking him to start a secondary school for boys.[35] In fact there were four such institutions for girls run by the Sisters of Saint Joseph of Cluny and the Sisters of the Immaculate Conception of Castres. However, there had been nothing

---

[33] *General Bulletin*, 617-618 (Statistics of the Vicariate of Dakar); 611-612, 314; Fr. Jean Delcourt, *Histoire religieuse du Sénégal* (Dakar: Éd. Clairafrique, 1976), 91.

[34] *General Bulletin*, 611-612: 326. On this occasion, Msgr. Lefebvre ordained 19 priests at Chevilly on February 15, 1948; *Horizons Africains*, no. 12 (March 1948): 1; interview with Fr. Ph. François, Jan. 24, 2000.

[35] Lefebvre, *Petite histoire*, 62.

for the boys ever since the "seminary-school" had become the "junior seminary."[36] Bishop Lefebvre was convinced that the training of a Catholic elite was essential for the future of Senegal and French West Africa, and that training such an elite would require the foundation of a secondary school for boys. He appealed to Archbishop Le Hunsec, who said he had nobody both qualified and available to become headmaster. The click as Archbishop Le Hunsec hung up convinced the Vicar Apostolic that he had to call upon other religious congregations. He spoke to the Marist Brothers, whose French Provincial, Fr. Thomas, lived at Brieuc. Courageously Fr. Thomas agreed to send Fr. Chièze, who, with the help of two other priests and a seminarian, began teaching classes for ten to thirteen year olds in the temporary accommodation provided by the Brothers of the Sacred Heart on Rue Malenfant. The bishop would have St. Michael's School built for them.[37]

Six kilometers from Dakar among the dunes of Hann, Bishop Lefebvre had already found the ideal site for the future school, an area of ground measuring five hectares. He designed a school to accomodate 700 pupils and 240 boarders. On January 14, 1950, he blessed the school in the presence of High Commissioner Paul Béchard, who then officially opened it: it was an excellent example of the good relations maintained by the bishop with the civil authorities.[38]

The school was open to both whites and blacks, and it was also fee-paying like the schools that Bishop Graffin and Bishop Bonneau built at the same time in Mvolyé and Douala. Muslims could be enrolled at the school up to a proportion of one in five, as was the practice in all the schools of the vicariate. Since they were in the minority the young Muslims agreed to learn the catechism. Sometimes one of them would be first in the class, and would cry on the day his classmates made their First Communion because, unlike them, he could not receive the Bread of Angels.[39]

The school lived up to all expectations. In 1960 there were five hundred pupils. Despite the government's refusal to subsidize the school and its ban on the addition of further grades,[40] Bishop Lefebvre—who immediately appointed a Director of Education—was able to develop Catholic education in the primary, secondary, and vocational sectors,[41] and the Catholic schools became more successful than the secular schools: in

---

[36] Schools of the Immaculate Conception, of Saint Joseph of Cluny (on the Médina), Notre-Dame Institute and the St. Joan of Arc Institute (LC 53, 32); *Horizons Africains*, Jan. 1961.

[37] *General Bulletin* 621-622: 535; 627: 172; *Horizons Africains*, 17, Sept. 1948, 13; 506 (June 1998): 96.

[38] *General Bulletin*, 629: 270; 636: 102-103; *Horizons Africains*, Feb.-March 1950, 30.

[39] Criaud, *La geste des spiritains*, 218-220, 236-237; Circular Letter 30 (1953): 3; 53 (1956): 14; 57 (1957): 10; Marcel Lefebvre, *Sermons at Ecône*, 38 B, April 19, 1987.

[40] Msgr. Lefebvre's report to O.P.F., Nov. 30, 1949; *Échos*, Jan. 1954.

1959, fifty percent of the eleven and twelve year old pupils graduated, and ninety percent passed the Certificate of Studies. Between 1947 and 1962, the numbers of children in primary education rose from two thousand pupils in nine schools to twelve thousand pupils in fifty-one schools. In 1947, there were only 150 pupils in four secondary schools whereas in 1962 there were 1,600 pupils in eleven schools. One out of every 5.6 pupils was studying in a Catholic school. Sixty-two schools might be said to be a modest number compared to Yaoundé's 325 or the 890 schools in Onitsha, Nigeria. Nonetheless, these sixty-two flowers in the desert were a greater miracle.

THE SEMINARY—THE APPLE OF HIS EYE

Bishop Lefebvre was able to build his seminaries securely on the foundations of such schools. St. Pius X's exhortation to the bishops was that "the chief part of your diligence will be directed to governing and ordering your seminaries aright....Regard your seminary as your heart's delight."[42] This is what Bishop Lefebvre did. Ever since the closure in 1930 of the Libermann Junior Seminary, young vocations had been sent to the apostolic school at Allex in France, and later to the junior seminary of Oussouye in Casamance, from where Bishop Grimault brought them back to Ngazobil. Since Bishop Lefebvre found Ngazobil's facilities poor, he decided in 1948 to send his eleven junior seminarians to join the other twenty-four Casamance seminarians at Oussouye, where they would be in the excellent care of Fr. Michel. According to the bishop's wishes, Ngazobil was converted into a college for candidates of the high-school certificate, trainee primary teachers and future seminarians. In 1950 there were altogether forty-one students.[43]

Later in 1952 the "Dakarians" came back to the vicariate from Oussouye. The lower secondary school classes moved to Ngazobil where new accommodation was built, while the upper classes went to study at Hann. There, thanks to a bishop from Fribourg, Bishop Delatena,[44] a boarding house was built and a Marist priest was put in charge. God blessed this arrangement since at the start of the new school year in 1961 there were eighty-six junior seminarians from Ziguinchor, Ngazobil, and Hann. The future of the major seminary was assured.[45]

---

[41] Circular Letter 24 (1952): 8-10; 38 (1954): 19-22; 53 (1956): 32; *General Bulletin*, 636: 103; Delcourt, *Histoire religieuse du Sénégal*, 95.

[42] *E Supremi Apostolatus*, Oct. 4, 1903, §11, in *Acta Pii X*, I, 9; [English version: Kansas City: Angelus Press, 1998].

[43] *General Bulletin*, 621-622: 535; 637: 137; Delcourt, *Histoire religieuse du Sénégal*, 93.

[44] Hubert Delatena, student at Santa Chiara (1896-99), on central council of Society of St. Peter the Apostle in Rome.

[45] Circular Letter 18 (1951): 7; 53 (1956): 19; 71 (1961): 16; *General Bulletin*, 700, 694.

THE DIOCESE OF SENEGAL (1962)

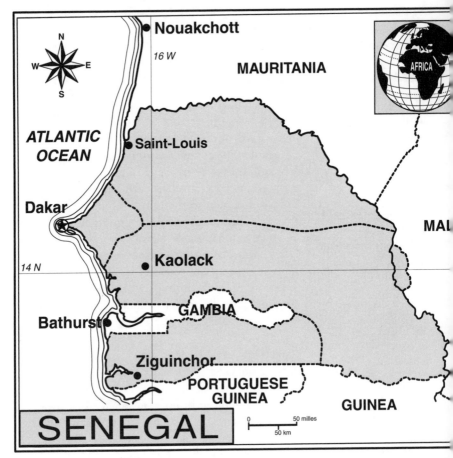

The creation of the diocese of Thiès in 1969 would again redu
in size the diocese of Dakar. The Apostolic Prefecture of
Tambacounda was founded in Kaolack in 1970. Nouakchot
would be made independent of Saint-Louis in 1965.

The major seminary had been established around 1857 when two young men who had finished their secondary school education with the "Lamennais Brothers" were considered for the major seminary and "took their first tottering steps" in philosophy. In 1864 Guillaume Jourga, the first priest trained exclusively in Black Africa, was ordained at Saint-Joseph of Ngazobil. He was the sixth Senegalese priest.

From 1869 to 1902 thirty-two ordination ceremonies would be performed in the same church on twenty-two different clerics, eight of whom reached the priesthood. Perseverance was rare: although there were seven students in 1921, there was only one by 1923.[46] The seminary opened its doors again in 1930 and now stood overlooking the sea in the clean mountain air of Popenguine. Ordinations began once more in 1940 with the tonsure of two theology students. Some other Senegalese who had gone to study in France entered the Holy Ghost Congregation: Frs. Faye, Ndiaye, Crétois, and Dodds.[47]

However, according to Bishop Kobès's initial wish that "a major seminary should be separated from every other educational foundation and be under the eyes of the bishop," Bishop Lefebvre wanted to move his seminary nearer to the capital to make it the apple of his eye.[48] He discovered an ideal, permanent location for this foundation at the "Château of Sambam," whose fairy-tale name belied a very real and inviting spot just over a mile from the village of Sébikotane on the road from Dakar to Thiès. The original buildings sat on the African hillside, surrounded by filaos, mango trees, and bougainvillea, and at the end of 1951, they became an oasis for philosophy and theology students from the jurisdictions of Dakar, Saint-Louis, Casamance, and French Guinea: the Libermann Seminary, now inter-vicariate, was reborn. Soon another building with accommodation and classrooms was constructed, and the chapel, blessed in 1957, was added. Later there were other extensions.[49]

Recruitment varied from region to region: among the vicariates, Fadiout was the best, followed by Dakar, Mont-Roland, Popenguine, and finally Palmarin and Thiès. At first the student numbers fluctuated: there were nine in 1946, ten in 1947, eight in 1948, four in 1950, three in 1954 and four in 1956, to which must be added the six or seven students that came from Casamance and Guinea. In 1959 the seminary doubled in number, going from twelve to twenty-four students, ten of whom were

---

[46] *Ibid.*, 425, 465-479.

[47] *Ibid.*, 113-114; *C.S.Sp. French Bulletin*, 86, 289-392; *AOF Magazine*, no. 15: 103; *Horizons Africains*, Jan. 1961.

[48] *General Bulletin*, 637: 138; *C.S.Sp. French Bulletin*, 86: 292; ms. II, 45, 51.

[49] *General Bulletin*, 673: 113; *C.S.Sp. French Bulletin*, 86: 292; Circular Letter, 53 (1956): 20.

from Casamance. The seminary was underway and truly became "Bishop Lefebvre's pearl."[50]

The former superiors and professors—Arthur d'Agrain until 1948 and Charles Catlin afterwards—were succeeded by young priests two of whom were from Mortain: François Morvan (1945-1946) and Maurice Fourmond (1946-1947) had been sent to Rome by the then Fr. Marcel for their theology studies, and were asked for by Bishop Lefebvre in Dakar. Other young professors came to work at the seminary under the direction of Fr. Morvan (from 1953 until 1962). The bishop "had perfect faith in the team of young 'Roman' professors whose average age in 1953 was below 31"[51] and who taught all the courses. In theology the bishop asked them to use a textbook, recommending that they follow as closely as possible the order of St. Thomas's *Summa*, the "only true synthesis of faith and morals,"[52] although his orders were no more prescriptive than that. Nevertheless, he kept his eye on discipline and did not like changes, although he did not indulge in fault-finding.[53]

His role as Apostolic Delegate often kept him away from Dakar. However, he never failed to chair the deliberations over the candidates for orders. Strict in essentials, he could be lenient on certain faults. Through too much kindness, he approved the ordination of an over-politicized candidate in 1953, and kicked himself for it:

"Oh," he said to Fr. Bourdelet, a former professor, "I shouldn't have approved his ordination."

"*Monseigneur*," the priest replied, "say your *mea culpa* because in his case I didn't agree with your assessment. And you approved his ordination knowing full well that I was going to oppose it."

"I shouldn't have," replied the then Archbishop, "it's true. I was wrong."

When he had made a mistake, he had the humility to recognize it. Besides, the veneration that the priests had for Archbishop Lefebvre did not stop them expressing their views freely. On another occasion in 1954, he approved the ordination of a seminarian who had not quite reached the intellectual level required. Basing his decision on the example of St. John Vianney, he suggested:

"What if I ordain him and put him as curate with Fr. Perraud who was a professor at Chevilly?"

[50] *Ibid.*, 19; *General Bulletin*, Annual Statistics; Delcourt, *Histoire religieuse du Sénégal*, 100; ms. II, 45, 27.
[51] *Horizons Africains* 20 (Jan. 1949): 11; ms. I, 32, 34-56; Msgr. F. Morvan, Letter, Oct. 29, 1997.
[52] Cf. Msgr. Lefebvre, reply to Cardinal Tardini, Feb. 26, 1960.
[53] Fr. Louis Carron, Fribourg, Interview, April 18, 1997, ms. I, 70, 12-29; Fr. G.-H. Thibault, Chevilly, Interview, Nov. 9, 1997, ms. II, 45, 49-55.

"Well," replied Fr. Bourdelet, "if you put him with Fr. Perraud, that will do the trick."

And it did indeed. Without realizing why he had been put in that particular parish, the young priest recognized the benefits of the appointment. "How lucky I am! Having a parish priest like Fr. Perraud is extraordinary. He explains everything to me."[54]

Through the work of the priests and the perseverance of the bishop, the seminary began yielding fruit. In Dakar cathedral on April 18, 1949, Archbishop Lefebvre ordained Fathers Hyacinthe Thiandoum (later his successor) and François-Xavier Dione (who became bishop of Thiès in 1969). They were the twenty-first and twenty-second priests of black origin in the vicariate. Archbishop Lefebvre and his ancillary ordained seven more, and other priests were ordained in Casamance and Guinea. When Archbishop Lefebvre arrived in Dakar, there were three native priests, one of whom one was a Holy Ghost Father. When he left, there were ten. Thanks also to the Libermann Major Seminary the number of native priests in Casamance rose from three in 1955 to seven in 1960.[55]

A RESCUE MISSION: THE DAUGHTERS OF THE HOLY HEART OF MARY

Another project dear to Archbishop Lefebvre was recruiting for his congregation among the Africans. In fact, one ought to say his "congregations" because in addition to the nuns of whom we shall speak, Senegal also had the Little Brothers of St. Joseph, whose novitiate was temporarily closed in 1956 and reopened in Fatick in 1960.[56] However, the bishop's constant, fatherly care was most apparent with regard to the Daughters of the Holy Heart of Mary. This native congregation had been founded in 1858 by Bishop Kobès, and was affiliated to the Sisters of St. Joseph of Cluny. The steady growth in numbers meant that the vicars apostolic could deploy the Daughters of the Holy Heart of Mary in clinics and small schools on the coast and in the missions inland. Msgr. Jalabert had tried to make them independent of the Sisters of Cluny, but this was not feasible since their growth had slowed.[57] Bishop Tardy in Gabon and Archbishop Graffin at Yaoundé both saw that the "Daughters of Mary" faced a serious challenge in attracting vocations: giving up the chance to be a mother and practicing obedience to women of the same age and race were things the Africans found difficult.[58]

---

[54] Fr. Jules Bourdelet, Vieux-Rouen, Interview, Dec. 4, 1998, ms. II, 55, 4-38, May 28, 1999, ms. II, 61-62.

[55] *General Bulletin*, 624; 625: 105; 673: 114; 691: 337; 694; Delcourt, *Histoire religieuse du Sénégal*, 95.

[56] *General Bulletin*, 700, 693-694.

[57] Notes on the history of the Congregation of the Daughters of the Holy Heart of Mary in Senegal.

The Daughters of Mary were founded in Cameroon in 1933. They came under the direction of the Missionary Sisters of the Holy Ghost, first under their Mother General Sister Joseph Bieth, then in 1945 under Sister Benoît. From 1948 to 1953 the Mother General was Sister Marie-Gabriel Lefebvre. When Archbishop Lefebvre visited Yaoundé in 1948 he spoke with his sister about the difficulties of his Senegalese congregation which had become independent under Archbishop Le Hunsec.[59] What could be done in the vicariate to attract vocations, reform the religious life and training according to canon law, and encourage fraternal charity?

The bishop was able to take three bold decisions. In 1949 he put the novitiate of the Sisters of Cluny under the care of Mother Marie of St. Anne, to whom he also gave the role of Visitor of Religious Communities.[60] He asked the female missionary congregations to delay opening their novitiates for a few years. On June 11, 1951, with the permission of the Sacred Congregation for the Propagation of Faith, he withdrew the mandate from the African Mother General and conferred it upon Mother Marie of St. Anne. Then the postulancy and novitiate were moved to Popenguine, which had been vacated by the seminary, and pre-postulancies were also created. The bishop's characteristically decisive action,[61] and the "strong, supernatural, and understanding support" he gave Mother Marie of St. Anne saved the Daughters of the Holy Heart of Mary, whose numbers had risen to fifty-nine by 1962.

IV. RELAUNCHING THE MISSION

Archbishop Lefebvre's great passion was to spread Christianity and "to establish the reign of our Lord in the animists' lands"; as he said himself, it was a desire that "caused him anguish."[62] Certainly there were strongholds of Catholicism in Senegal such as the Island of Fadiout, where the bishop admired the spiritual fervor and temporal Christian order that had been brought about by divine grace. In 1979 during the sermon from his priestly jubilee, he was probably thinking about Fadiout when he said: "There I saw, yes, I saw what the grace of holy Mass could do."[63]

However, such strongholds were not enough for him. "It must be said that to his credit he relaunched the mission in Senegal, a mission the congregation regarded as moribund," a former colleague said. At Christmas 1948, the bishop received a letter from a young priest who had arrived

---

[58] Criaud, *La geste des spiritains*, 187.
[59] On Nov. 18, 1929, Msgr. Grimault consulted with his advisers but they were against his proposal of reattaching the indigenous sisters to the Sisters of Cluny.
[60] Circular Letter 10 (Dec. 3, 1949) and 14 (May 1950).
[61] Letter of Feb. 14, 1962, to Msgr. Lefebvre.
[62] Circular Letter 38 (1954): 12; Msgr. Guibert, Interview, Jan. 18, 1997, ms. I, 22, 16.
[63] *Fideliter*, no. 12: 6; no. 59: 6-7.

barely a month before and who stayed for a short while in one of the missions. There had been no conversions in the last year and he felt there was no impulse to seek the conversion of the Sérères: "Your Excellency, this is the impression I have of your mission: it is like a routed army."

The Vicar Apostolic took no offense at this observation since he knew it to be more or less true. As the same priest said later, "Under Bishop Grimault, everything was static."[64] Had not the bishop one day dined with Marshal Pétain without even asking him for a contribution to the missions? Was not his favorite saying, "If the good Lord wanted, He could convert the world with His little finger," as if the grace of God could do away with the need for human co-operation?[65]

Archbishop Lefebvre's attitude was quite different, and he listened to the pagans' request for the missionaries to teach them the catechism and to set up schools. It was a request that was to be granted by setting up missions amongst them and by building chapels and schools. The pagans' appeals were all the more urgent, whether or not they felt the urgency themselves, because they were surrounded by Islam. One had to "get there first, otherwise the Church would lose its footing, and those villages which today are open and welcoming, tomorrow might shut out (for how many years or centuries?) the light and life of God."[66]

In Fatick two attempts to found a mission had failed. Moreover the King of Sine, Makékor Diouf, was opposed to the project. He said to the missionaries: "I don't even want you to cross the bridge. And on your side of the river you had better not construct any big buildings!" Only grass huts were tolerated, so the mission had been established at Diohine twenty-five kilometres away.

One fine day in 1949, the young Fr. Gravand decided with the permission of his superior to "cross the bridge." As he was thinking to himself, "I'm crossing the Rubicon like Caesar," he found himself face to face with the King of Sine who was coming in the opposite direction.

"Excellency, I was looking for you," said the priest respectfully to the sovereign, and he explained to him that he was going to three villages "to begin recruiting for the Church of the Catholics."

In an instant, the King consented. He replied, "Very well!" He gave orders to the African companion of the priest: "Go to see the Bour (king) of Pourtantok on my behalf and say to him, 'The Bour says to you, Gather together the elderly in the center of the village and give your children to the priest.'" Thus it was done.

---

[64] Ms. II, 72, 1-23.

[65] Ms. III, 9, 1-70.

[66] Fr. Louis Carron, ms. I, 61, 6-14; *General Bulletin*, 636: 98.

The Bour Sine (king of Sine) later explained: "The first day that I saw him (the missionary), he spoke to me as a son to his father. So I felt like a father to him, and whatever he asked me, I was going to say yes."[67]

Riding this wave of grace, Fr. Gravand had the happiness of enlisting his first hundred catechumens, and Archbishop Lefebvre soon took the decision to establish a mission at Fatick. Thus, with or without miracles, but with the help of many newly arrived missionaries, he was able to raise the number of independent mission stations from ten to twenty-five.[68] As Fr. Gervais remembered: "*Monseigneur* had an almost prophetic instinct about where to deploy missionaries and build mission stations. We were often surprised by his bold projects and decisions, but their wisdom was quickly seen as things developed, as much in Dakar as in the mission stations in the bush. He did not impose his opinions, but when he had said, 'In your place this is what I would do,' we knew that his plan was the best and that he would closely follow its implementation."[69]

On the second day of his visit to Diohine, Archbishop Lefebvre took Fr. Gravand with him to visit Fatick: "'We are going to Fatick, I'm going to show you where you must build the mission,' said *Monseigneur*. Then I saw how he founded a mission: meter by meter he paced out the area on which to build. He knew that so many square meters were necessary for the presbytery, such a spot for the church, at such a distance the school, a bit further the nuns, and many other things; I stood there watching....One felt that he had thought through this foundation, and that it had to be done as it was in his head."[70]

One day the bishop said to the parish priest of Bambey: "Look here, I have just received this gift from Switzerland. It's enough to build a health clinic at Ngaskop."

"At Ngaskop! That group of pagan villages twenty kilometers away in a totally inaccessible place! And what about the cinder blocks that I'll have to transport there? *Etc.*"

It was no good Fr. Bourdelet raising all these objections. The bishop was inflexible and replied each time, "But we have to do it at Ngaskop."

Finally surrendering, the priest exclaimed, "You're as stubborn as a mule!" As he explained later, "I could say that to Archbishop Lefebvre!"

The bishop had planned things well. The "Fogola" or "friends of the Christians" registered themselves as sympathizers of Christianity, making the resolution to resist Islam, and to have themselves baptized at least before death. Those villages of three thousand or four thousand animists

---

67 Henri Gravand, *Visage africain de l'Église* (Paris: Orante, 1961), 89-91; ms. II, 74-76.
68 *General Bulletin*, 628: 210; 637: 134-135; Circular Letter 38: 12; Delcourt, *Histoire religieuse du Sénégal*, 97.
69 Fr. Albert Gervais, Letter of March 27, 1998.
70 Fr. Gravand, Interview, Nov. 2000, ms. II, 74, 18-27.

were henceforth attached to the Church. Very soon there were baptisms and many catechumens, and large numbers of children were baptized. With a view to evangelizing these people, Archbishop Lefebvre wished first to preserve their villages from the threat of Islam, and he succeeded perfectly.[71]

V. URBAN PROBLEMS AND NEW PARISHES

Three years after arriving in Dakar, Archbishop Lefebvre had acquired such a sound knowledge of the country that he was able to write a noted pastoral letter on the social and economic problems of Senegal that was read publicly at the 1953 missionary convention at Lourdes.[72] We shall analyze later the bishop's thinking on doctrine, but for now let us examine the solutions to the social problems that he attempted to solve. Dakar's population increased rapidly with the arrival of managers and workers recruited in France, Lebanese and Syrian retailers, and the many natives leaving the bush. The Europeans established new quarters for themselves: the residential area of Fane, and the more reasonably priced area of "Point E" in Dakar. Meanwhile, the natives tended to crowd into quarters such as Médina, Reubeuss, and Pikine, that were far from the center and densely populated.

The gulf between the various ethnic communities only grew larger. Without wishing to do away with the differences, Msgr. Lefebvre tried hard to draw the classes and different ethnic groups closer together by inviting the European and African Catholic Action movements to collaborate and discuss common religious and social problems. "Thus," he said, "they will know each other better, appreciate each other, and overcome the prejudices that divide them." However, this spirit of mutual collaboration was only achieved by the Cité Catholique and the Explorer Scouts whose co-ordinator, François Lagneau, had to oppose his French bosses' racist policies against white colonialists.[73]

Taking account of the emergence of an urban proletariat, the bishop looked for solutions to the problems this posed. He made contact with French-based housing associations, such as the Roubaix-Tourcoing interprofessional housing committee.[74] He also sought to develop Catholic Action—an issue we shall return to—by creating new parishes.

This was why Archbishop Lefebvre decided to bring Fr. Fernand Bussard—an energetic giant of a man—from the Cape Verde Islands to Dakar, so that he could look after the Capeverdian Portuguese Creole speakers. In

---

[71] Circular Letter 57 (1957); Fr. Bourdelet, Interview, Dec. 4, 1998, ms. II, 55-56.
[72] C.S.Sp. *French Bulletin* 66 (Jan. 1954); *Lettres pastorales et écrits*, 27.
[73] Biarnès, *Les Français en Afrique*, 323 ; Bussard, ms. I, 8-9; F. Lagneau, Letter of Aug. 22, 1998.
[74] Correspondence of March 1950.

church on Sunday they surprisingly out-numbered the Europeans who also attended the 11:30 A.M. Mass. Archbishop Lefebvre would never allow a "Mass for the whites" and a "Mass for the blacks," but the custom was that no whites came to the 8 A.M. Mass or the High Mass at 10 o'clock, which were both attended by natives. For the Lebanese, the Archbishop secured from the Holy See the services of Fr. Augustin Sarkis, and in 1952 he blessed the foundation stone of the church of Our Lady of Lebanon, where the Maronite rite could be celebrated.[75]

The Church of the Sacred Heart, which was forty years old, was falling into disrepair. In January 1949, the bishop organized a parish festival, the first of many, to solicit the charity of the Catholics and raise some funds. The money only enabled them to buy an immense metal hangar, but some clever stonework gave it the appearance of a church, and it was blessed in December 1949. In Médina ever since 1945, a former stable had been used as a chapel. Later it moved to a cinema, and then to an American army camp. Archbishop Lefebvre had a church built, and in December 1949 he established the parish of St. Joseph of Médina. In 1959 an extension to the church was added in a beautiful Romanesque style, and the Archbishop oversaw the construction of a high clock tower, the sign of a Christian presence in what was a very Islamic quarter.[76]

Other churches, in other future parishes, were constantly being built: St. Theresa of the Child Jesus of Greater Dakar in "Point E" (1956), St. Christopher of Yoff (1956), Our Lady of Cape Verde at Pikine, St. Anne of Bel-Air—all of which were for a long time humble chapels—Our Lady of the Angels of Ouakam (1961), etc., not to mention St. Dominic's, an ugly blockhouse blessed by Bishop Maury in 1961. The bishop sought help from the architects Strobel at the mission in Yaoundé, and from Joseph Muller in Clomar. Mullar drew up plans for free.[77] As for the cathedral parish, which went from ten thousand souls in 1951 to fifteen thousand in 1960, the High Mass was broadcast each Sunday by Radio Dakar. The last parish priest appointed by Archbishop Lefebvre, on October 9, 1960, was Fr. Thiandoum.

When he arrived in Dakar the Archbishop found two parishes and three churches. He left his successor nine parishes and thirteen churches.[78]

---

[75] Bussard, ms. I, 9, 39-41; *Horizons Africains*, Dec. 1949, 12-13; *General Bulletin*, 644.
[76] Delcourt, *Histoire religieuse du Sénégal*, 92-103; *General Bulletin*, 636, 106-108.
[77] *Ibid.*, 644, 667, 369; Criaud, *La geste des spiritains*, 239.
[78] *General Bulletin*, 679: 383; 694: 464; *Horizons Africains*, 137 (March 1962): 8-9.

VI. A GREATER NUMBER OF WORKERS FOR THE GOSPEL

A REMARKABLE EXPANSION[79]

"Since there were not enough missionaries, and vocations were getting rarer, I took the initiative and appealed for help to other congregations. It seemed to me that one should not reserve this diocese for that congregation (Dakar for the Holy Ghost Fathers), but rather build on the deployment made by the Sacred Congregation for the Propagation of Faith. If one wanted to develop the apostolate, one had to find a greater number of workers for the harvest."[80]

First the Marists came to run the college at Hann, and in 1954-1955 Archbishop Lefebvre welcomed the Dominicans, who opened a cultural center. Then in 1955 came the Missionaries of the Sacred Heart of Issoudun, who were put in charge of the district of Kaolack. In 1954 Archbishop Lefebvre went to the Vendée to solicit the help of the Brothers of St. Gabriel, who came to Dakar to run the primary schools and the teacher training college. The Brothers of the Sacred Heart, who came from Canada in 1959, took charge of the cathedral primary school and later St. Michael's School, the latter having been extended to take junior high school pupils. From then on Senegal became their star province since they attracted many vocations there. Through their schools they exercised a considerable influence, and many of their former pupils came to hold important jobs in the country. As for catechists, thanks to the help of Msgr. Adrien Bressolles, director-general of the Mission of the Holy Childhood, Archbishop Lefebvre was able to provide them with training and a small gratuity, and raise their numbers from 147 to almost 400.

In 1947 there were five houses of the Senegal sisters, three houses for the sisters of Cluny, and four for the sisters of Castres. During his reign as archbishop, these congregations opened new houses: the Senegal sisters opened twelve, the sisters of Cluny one (the beautiful orphanage at Médina in 1950), and the sisters of Castres two. He managed to bring to Senegal no less than twenty-one other female congregations who between them founded forty religious houses.

The Franciscan Missionary Sisters of Mary arrived in 1948. They took up posts at two hospitals, and founded a kindergarten, a social-worker training college, and a pediatric clinic which was a model institution. Archbishop Lefebvre particularly liked their simplicity and their devotion to duty. Schools and health clinics were also run by the Sisters of St. Thomas of Villeneuve (1952), the Sisters of St. Charles of Angers, and the Sisters of Our Lady of the Apostles (1956), and the Missionary Sisters of

---

[79] Delcourt, *op. cit.*, *passim*; *General Bulletin*, 609-700; Bussard, ms. I, 11, 7-16.
[80] *Fideliter*, no. 59: 24-27.

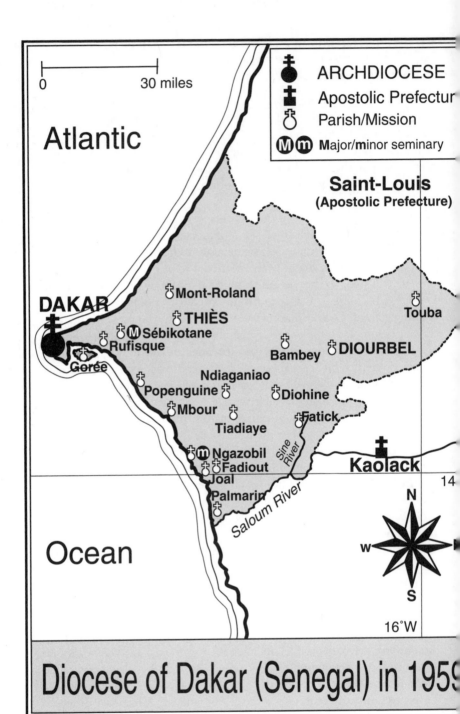

Diocese of Dakar (Senegal) in 1959

the Holy Ghost (school at Oukram in 1957). In 1955 the Sisters of St. Paul of Fribourg became the diocesan printers.

The statistics speak for themselves: during Archbishop Lefebvre's tenure (as archbishop), the number of priests went from forty-two (three of whom were African) to one hundred and ten (ten of whom were African), the number of brothers rose from fourteen (seven Africans) to thirty-three (eighteen Africans), and the number of sisters went from one hundred (forty Africans) to two hundred and fifty (sixty of whom were Africans). According to Archbishop Lefebvre, this growth created a magnificent vitality, and was a wonderful example for the other dioceses. "Why couldn't we do as much?" said the other bishops when they came to Dakar for meetings. Sometimes the Archbishop had to deal with the oversensitive "older" congregations who said: "The new congregations are looked after better than we are!"

The last to arrive were the Benedictines of Solesmes. In the early 1950's, Archbishop Lefebvre had asked the abbot, Dom Cozien, to found a monastery in Senegal. His successor, Dom Jean Prou, finally granted the request. In February 1961 he came to look at some prospective sites, and later in November he returned to oversee the laying of the foundations near Sébikotane in the hamlet of Keur-Moussa (Moses's house), from which the future monastery took its name.[81]

THE CARMEL OF SÉBIKOTANE, HEART OF THE DIOCESE

Numerous contemplative orders liked branching out in missionary countries. The Trappists of Aiguebelle went to Obout (Cameroon) in 1951, and the Benedictines of Pierre-qui-Vire went to Msgr. Fauret's diocese in 1957. In 1949 the Carmel of Tourcoing moved (with Sister Marie-Christiane Lefebvre) to Parkes in Australia. On Christmas Eve 1936, Msgr. Grimault went to the Carmel of Cholet to ask them to found a convent in Senegal. Although Cholet had made foundations in Bangalore in 1932, in Tokyo in 1933, and in Colombo in 1935, Mother Aimée of Mary who founded Cholet, was inclined to accept as soon as possible. In the refectory on the Feast of St. Martha, each sister was served a dish piled up in the shape of Mount Carmel on top of which was a flag that proudly read, "Rampart against Islam."[82] But then came the war...

Bishop Grimault told his successor about this project, and Archbishop Lefebvre went to Cholet on August 15, 1949. On November 25, 1950, the sisters who were sent to found a Carmel at Dakar arrived. They were greeted by the Archbishop, who thanked them for coming, inquired after their

---

[81] *Horizons Africains*, Nov. 1961, 12; Delcourt, *Histoire religieuse du Sénégal*, 103 ; *General Bulletin* 696: 544.
[82] Review *Scapulaire*, no. 4 (July-Aug. 1955), supplement to *Carmel*, 81-84.

health, closely inspected their temporary quarters, and soon began looking for a sewing machine for them. On January 15, 1951, during the cloistering ceremony, the Archbishop preached to the faithful: "Do not be surprised that the Carmelites are going to shut themselves away. God has created us to love Him. The sisters give witness to the primacy of this commandment. By loving God alone, they draw down graces upon souls."

One week later he invited the sisters to visit the convent buildings he had set aside for them at Sébikotane. A year later, the seminary would be established nearby, and there would also be a community of Daughters of the Holy Heart of Mary with three young boarders. However, on April 23, 1952, the bank refused to grant the loan needed for the construction of the convent: what could Archbishop Lefebvre do? He prayed, and obeying the order, "Seek ye first the kingdom of God" (Mt. 6:33), postponed the building of the Apostolic Delegation headquarters and gave the Carmelites two million francs to build their convent. However, he did admit to them: "The rain leaks through my ceiling and onto my bed…too bad! It happens so often in Senegal, and you know, it dries so quickly."[83]

Finally, on April 18, 1953, the Carmelites moved into their convent in Sébikotane. In 1958, Archbishop Lefebvre performed the veiling ceremony for the first Senegalese Carmelite. Thus, the Carmel put down its roots in African soil. As far as the eye could see, there was nothing but bush land, and behind a small hill one could just make out the roofs of the huts in a nearby village of Muslim Peuls. The wishes of the bishops of Dakar had been realized. On a shady hill that Archbishop Lefebvre called "the heart of the vicariate," stood the statue of the Blessed Virgin, "unshakable rampart of the Church," interceding for the people as the Mediatrix of all the graces of conversion.

VII. BELOVED LEADER AND ORGANIZER

ORGANIZING ACCOMMODATION—AN AUXILIARY BISHOP

All the diocesan project offices and staff were housed in cramped accommodation at the "Catholic mission" with the new Vicar Apostolic and his Vicar Delegate (successively Frs. Saloman, Alexis, Quenet, and Catlin), the archbishop's private secretary, Fr. André Duguy, and, three years later, the auxiliary bishop. There was also the priest responsible for diocesan purchases, the brothers from the diocesan supply office and print shop, the priest in charge of diocesan projects, and, of course, the cathedral parish priest and his curates.

---

[83] Diary of the Carmel, *passim* and June 10, 1952.

Bishop Grimault had put up with these conditions,[84] but Archbishop Lefebvre meant to put things in order. At the request of the parish priest, Fr. Bussard, the presbytery was separated from diocesan accommodation where the bishop had his private room and office. The latter was so small that he simply could not receive visitors there. Then the bishop had a new building constructed on the other side of the courtyard, which from 1949 housed a spacious and up-to-date print shop on the ground floor.[85]

In 1957 he had a new bishop's residence constructed near the cathedral presbytery which was situated on a plateau close to the colonial administrative offices. It was a pretty house that was small but functional. Next, the diocesan project office was relocated. First, it was moved to the basement of the print shop in July 1949, and then into a new building on the Rue Sandiniéry. In 1957-1958 a new building was constructed opposite the Church of the Sacred Heart to house the new office for diocesan supplies and Catholic education. There were also twelve guest rooms intended for visiting priests and religious.[86]

Although he was helped by the vicar delegate (Vicar General of the Vicar Apostolic), Archbishop Lefebvre could not do both jobs as a vicar apostolic and apostolic delegate alone. He asked Rome for an auxiliary bishop, as had been given to Yaoundé in 1931 when Bishop Vogt secured Bishop Graffin as his auxiliary. The Holy See granted this request, appointing Fr. Georges Guibert, C.S.Sp., who had spent four years in Senegal and was currently stationed at the Holy Ghost Fathers' headquarters in Paris. Bishop Guibert was appointed titular bishop of Dices, and was consecrated bishop on February 19, 1950, by Archbishop Lefebvre in the procathedral of the "African memorial" in the presence of High Commissioner Béchard. The ceremony made a great impression on the people, including the Muslims.[87]

Bishop Guibert, who was at that time the youngest French bishop, had been chosen because he was an excellent administrator. He was also very good-natured and devout, and more than ready to serve his missionaries. In 1954 after four years of close collaboration, Archbishop Lefebvre said that he was "very happy to be assisted with so much selfless devotion by His Excellency Bishop Guibert, our most beloved auxiliary."[88] The auxiliary bishop had administrative duties, and carried out parish visits and confirmations. However, despite his frequent absences as apostolic dele-

---

[84] *General Bulletin*, 636: 105; Bussard, ms. 29, 21-22.

[85] Opened by Msgr. Lefebvre on March 6; *Horizons Africains*, 1949; Delcourt, *Histoire religieuse du Sénégal*, 93.

[86] *Ibid.*, 93, 99; *General Bulletin* 679: 383; Bussard, ms. II, 28, 30-38.

[87] Criaud, *La geste des spiritains*, 159; *C.S.Sp. French Bulletin* 47: 197; *General Bulletin*, 628: 209; 629: 270; 636: 102.

[88] Circular Letter 14 (1950): 3; Circular Letter 38 (1954): 4.

gate, Archbishop Lefebvre made arrangements for an annual visit of all the mission stations to decide on the activities and objectives of his missionaries.

Before going away, he established with his auxiliary what needed to be done, although he made all the most important decisions himself. Even when he was in La Réunion, he would reply quickly to his mail with a friendly note, regardless of whether the issue was minor or somewhat more serious. He continued to rule his diocese, and in spite of distance he was "omnipresent."[89]

PRIESTLY LIFE—PRIESTLY VIRTUES

No bishop was as diligent as Archbishop Lefebvre in gathering his priests together in order to listen to them, sanctify them, and guide their apostolate. It is amazing to note the rise in the number of all kinds of priestly meetings during his reign as bishop. There were annual meetings for superiors (parish priests and superiors of mission stations), monthly meetings of the parish clergy, monthly meetings for charity projects (in each mission station), and days of recollection every three months (held in four retreat houses where the priests had to arrive the night before). There were also district meetings twice a year, meetings for the leaders of charity projects (in the towns), and meetings for headmasters and schoolteachers. There were also annual meetings for those in charge of charity projects, and deanery meetings from 1956 onwards (the *collationes* as determined by Canon 428), not to mention the Holy Ghost Father meetings or "chapters" to discuss matters related to the religious life.[90]

Archbishop Lefebvre himself preached numerous retreats: for the Carmelites, for the junior seminarians (Ngazobil, September 1960), and notably for the clergy to whom he gave a retreat in winter 1959 on "the adoration and knowledge of God" (it was a retreat he had already preached to the Portuguese Province of the Holy Ghost Fathers in September 1959). He also preached a retreat concerning "the inner life and social virtues of the Blessed Virgin Mary." For him the spiritual life was always rooted in faith and sound theology: "He asked his clergy to direct their life as priests, religious, and missionaries according to the mind of the Church as expressed in her laws: canon law, the liturgical books, the ritual" (AM 153).

His letter to fellow priests in 1958[91] concerning the priestly spirit gives a glimpse of his supernatural inspiration: "You are priests, and your priesthood is firstly one of prayer, praise, and adoration. Secondly, your priest-

---

[89] *Horizons Africains*, Nov. 1957; Bussard, ms. I, 10, 11-20; 11, 18-21; Bourdelet, ms. II, 57, 39-42.

[90] Circular Letter 14: 1-2; 18: 1-2; 24: 7-8; 38: 6.

[91] Quotations from *Lettres pastorales et écrits* (Éd. Fideliter, 1989).

hood makes you a sanctifier of souls, of your own soul, of your neighbor's soul, and especially of those to whom you are sent. Consequently, your priesthood is a priesthood of immolation and self-sacrifice" (ES 96).

He repeated incessantly that their apostolic zeal should come from their life of prayer: "Have that thirst and that haunting desire to live with God and to be inwardly united to our Lord, ...but do not forget that this union cannot be truly achieved if you neglect your pious exercises: prayer, the breviary, and especially the holy Mass.... What delusion to believe oneself capable of giving the life of God to others while neglecting to drink from the springs of that very life!" (RS 87).

He could have given himself as an example when he said to them: "Think about how edified the faithful are by a priest who prays and unites himself to God. Now more than ever, the people who see us and who meet us must be convinced that they are dealing with a man of God" (RS 87).

This life of union with God was to be aided by a regular community life, organized (CS 138) so as to allow for prayer (AU 93) in common. The rule would help the priests to avoid living according to their whims, getting lax or lukewarm, or forgetting the social virtues (ES 100-101). It would help them practice fraternal charity, co-operation (CS 138), and the counsels of religion. They could practice poverty by looking after the possessions of the community, particularly the four-wheel-drive jeeps that Archbishop Lefebvre had provided for each mission to cope with the sandy or muddy roads. Chastity would also be protected by the ruling that in each house the parlor should have a door with a window in it. The priests' bedrooms were to be on the first floor so they could take their siesta easily, and have one part of the house reserved strictly to them.[92]

Lastly and above all, Archbishop Lefebvre emphasized the virtue of priestly charity, firstly fraternal charity among the missionaries, and then true apostolic charity with an understanding for souls "and the ways in which they have fallen into error and sin." However, this charity was demanding: "True charity does not mean leaving minds in error and souls in sin." There was to be no liberalism in the apostolate! "It is easier never to contradict, and always to approve of people: to make oneself popular at the expense of truth, *i.e.*, at the expense of our Lord Himself" (CS 139).

THE APOSTOLATE: THE PRIMARY ROLE OF SUPERNATURAL MEANS

Since the apostolate is the continuation of the Incarnation and Redemption, it is "an essentially divine activity" (AP 130) which depends entirely on the free grace of God, and thus on prayer. The pagan searches in vain—and the missionary labors in vain—if the Holy Ghost, "soul and

---

[92] Circular Letter 18 (1951); Bussard, ms. I, 19, 4-12; Marziac, *Mgr. Lefebvre, soleil levant*, 111.

182   MARCEL LEFEBVRE

source of our apostolate," does not move souls from within: "Without me, you can do nothing" (*S. Th.*, I-II, q. 109, a. 6). However, God wishes to use human instruments in pouring out His graces on men: "I have chosen you so that you may bring forth fruit" (Jn. 15:16), whence the need for the apostle to have zeal in order to be the living instrument of Christ (AP 132).

The third principle is that "men receive divine grace each according to his measure," or as the Council of Trent teaches, "The sacraments are for men who are well disposed." Consequently, the entire apostolate consists of "disposing souls for grace and for grace in ever greater abundance, and creating the right environment: good families, Catholic schools, and works of charity in parishes" (AP 135). These truths must lead the missionary to think carefully about the main ways in which he can sanctify his parish.

These means are firstly supernatural. "Looking at what is expedient, at purely temporal means, and putting our confidence in rational and systematic organization" would be to "copy the Church's enemies" (AP 131). In his first pastoral letter written in 1948 "on religious ignorance," Archbishop Lefebvre said that the first essential means for the apostolate should be the teaching of Christian doctrine and the catechism. He argued: "Some Africans, even those with university qualifications, are incapable of distinguishing the true religion in which they were baptized from heresies or sects founded by men" (IR 1).

The bishop condemned the "naturalism" of those who, when evangelizing pagan children, wished not to speak about Jesus in the first instance, but only about natural truths concerning God and creation: they scorned the "infinite and mysterious power" of conversion in the name of Jesus. [93] He also condemned the error of those who think "that before converting underdeveloped people, one must first help with their development and civilize them," which is impossible without divine grace, given its capacity to raise and heal human nature from laziness and hatred, the wounds inflicted by original sin. [94]

For Archbishop Lefebvre, declining awareness of supernatural means lay at the root of the problems with Catholic Action and the deluded worker-priests movement whose members wanted "to be like the workers" instead of " being like priests" (VV 145). In his "Missionary Rules" written in 1954, the Archbishop recommended to his priests to read Pius X's encyclical *Acerbo Nimis*, Pius XII's *Menti Nostrae*, the Catechism of the

[93] Circular Letter 59 (1957): 3; Marcel Lefebvre, *Spiritual Conferences at Ecône* 9 A, Sept. 30, 1974, AF 42.
[94] Marcel Lefebvre, Spiritual Conference, Fribourg, May 20, 1970. Cf. Msgr. Lefebvre's intervention in Conciliar Central Preparatory Commission, *A. Doc.*, vol. 2, pt. 4, p. 559 (June 1962).

Council of Trent, and the first chapter of the ritual. "There you will find the sources of the authentic, apostolic spirit" (NM 53).

In a circular letter on priestly charity, he wrote: "The priest who does not perfectly reflect the thinking of the Church loses his *raison d'être*, and makes himself unworthy of his priesthood" (CS 139).

THE APOSTOLATE: METHODICAL ORGANIZATION

However, having faith in the power of grace does not excuse the priest from organizing his apostolate methodically. His 1952 circular letter "Towards an ever more fruitful apostolate" reveals the Vicar Apostolic's practical mind. Firstly,

> we should make a list of all the means at our disposal…health, our time, our spiritual faculties, all the gifts received from the Church,…even material means,…the help of our auxiliaries, the type of terrain, climate, and people we are dealing with.…All these things should be considered calmly and prudently. Have we ourselves taken the trouble to sit down and think about things? *Sedens computavit* (Lk. 14:28). Have we asked advice from our fellow workers? Have we divided up the responsibilities of our ministry correctly? (AF 39)

"Getting worked up, stumbling from one job to the next, running about to do the most important things without being organized: all these things cause confusion and the missionary ends up wearing himself out. They also tax the goodwill of our catechists and collaborators" (NM 60).

Archbishop Lefebvre's answer to all this was pragmatic: "There is a way of organizing our pastoral work like a business, an industry, or any secular activity. Why should we use less intelligence than worldly people to organize our ministry with the providential means that are given to us, seeking to make things grow in so far as Providence itself wishes to make them grow?" (AF 40). Above all, Archbishop Lefebvre wished the priests to give themselves to the priestly work while "avoiding being too absorbed by material considerations, and neglecting to prepare sermons, catechism lessons, or spiritual talks" (AM 153).

THE APOSTOLATE: INVENTIVE AND INGENIOUS ZEAL

In addition to being well organized, the Archbishop wished his priests to have "an inventive and ingenious zeal" (AP 134), since "our Lord means for us to blaze new trails and to avoid the immobility that comes through mere routine or the tendency to do slavishly what our predecessors did. In their own time they blazed new trails, and when we do the same thing we are continuing their work and imitating them" (NM 51). Bringing the methods of the apostolate up-to-date is necessary because of changes in material circumstances, and because of new dangers: "We are in the Senegal of the twentieth century in a given time and place, with the means of our time, and the errors and enemies of the Church of our time" (NM 52).

One of these initiatives of inventive zeal was the founding of the Fogola. One day Fr. Gravand said to Archbishop Lefebvre: "*Monseigneur*, many of our pagans cannot immediately receive baptism, for example, the polygamists or tribal chiefs. Couldn't we make an 'Old Testament' for them?"

"Tut, tut! What on earth are you talking about?"

"Failing baptism, give them something..."

"No baptism? Do you want them all to be Muslims? Muslims?"

"That's not what I mean, not at all!"

"Good, good: what exactly do you mean then?"

On Easter Tuesday at the annual meeting of the mission superiors, the creation of Fogola or "Friends of the Christians" was unanimously accepted and received the Archbishop's approval. The Fogola would receive a special identity card and be registered at a mission station. Without actually being Christians, they would belong sociologically to the Christian community, get to learn about Revelation, and could be baptized if the obstacle impeding their baptism were removed. Later, after independence, the fruits of this high-risk strategy were apparent when the "sociologically Christian masses," as Archbishop Lefebvre called them, were able to resist the Islamic wave that surged over the "animist belt."

The Archbishop did not advocate blind progressiveness. However, some of his remarks sound strange coming from a man who would later be scornfully called "the fundamentalist." He wrote:

> On the one hand, one must avoid narrowness of mind, an outdated and fossilized traditionalism that closes its eyes to the materialism and atheism running amok among the young: it locks itself away in its church, content with the presence of a few good parishioners and children. On the other hand, one must avoid a spirit of novelty *qui sapit haeresim* (which smacks of heresy), the heresy of activism that neglects prayer, preaching, the parish Mass on Sunday, or religious instruction. (NM 53)

Thus, while respecting the guidance of canon law concerning the ministry, "the Church increases the range of means she uses to bring home the message of the Gospel through the initiatives of priests and bishops inspired by enlightened zeal" (NM 54). In these conditions, Archbishop Lefebvre concluded, the spirit of our Lord and the spirit of the Church will inspire the missionary's initiatives, and give him "the ingenuity that comes from true zeal" (NM 52).

"He Was in Charge without Seeming to Be So"

Like many superiors, by 1957 Archbishop Lefebvre was confronted with the effects of the general crisis of authority in the Church. He responded by writing two circular letters, one on authority (1957), and one on the priestly spirit (1958). He wrote: "We lack the spirit of faith in obedience" (ES 100). However, the Archbishop insisted little on obedience as such. Rather, he preferred to ask the superiors to make a good use of their authority, and thus to avoid the problems that lead to a lack of obedience.

He denounced the weakness of certain local superiors who "give up their authority, and put themselves on the same level as their curates." Some situations had arisen where superiors "realize that they can no longer ask a measure of discipline from their collaborators" (ES 100). He explained that the superior holds authority "with a properly divine character" (AU 92). It is, therefore, truly humble of him to respect his own authority, and to exercise "the mandate which has been given him not for himself but for the common good." A good superior knows how to trust his subordinates and how to delegate, but he maintains control and demands to be in constant touch with his collaborators (AU 92-93). A good priest is a good leader who "ruleth well his own house" (I Tim. 3:4).

The Archbishop knew that the word "authority," from the Latin "auctoritas," comes from the verb "augere," "to increase." Therefore, the good leader does not put down his subordinates, but helps them to develop. This is what the Archbishop did with respect to his African priests. He looked after them, providing for them in the ways we have described, and wishing to see them rise through the ranks of the hierarchy. In 1960, he spoke of "the need to give our Senegalese confreres the responsibilities that correspond to their abilities." He added: "They must show that they are truly priests, true shepherds of souls, 'non implicate saecularibus negotiis' (II Tim. 2:4). They must be perfectly submissive to the guidance of their bishop by properly managing their apostolate and taking care of the goods of the Church that have been confided to them" (LC 70, 1).

The Archbishop found it painful to be obliged to change priests' appointments. He would make these changes "for the good of the apostolate and for the personal good of the individual," but as he admitted: "I suffer a lot knowing that I must hurt one or other among you" (LC 70, 1). Experience had taught him that a leader must take pains to make obedience easier by exercising authority humanely. One day, he came to the cathedral presbytery as he often did to take a quinquiliba (little drink) with the priests. At the end he took a priest aside and said:

"Fr. Carron, I must have a word with you." When they were alone, he said: "So, I am most worried…"

Straightaway, the priest said, "Monseigneur, I know what you're going to say."

He understood and let the embarrassed bishop explain the problem. At the end, Archbishop Lefebvre was greatly relieved to hear him say: "Monseigneur, you are the boss: tell me what to do and I will obey!"

The supernatural spirit of this priest impressed the Archbishop and changed the hasty judgment that he had formed about him.[95]

The remarks of Fr. Bussard, the Vicar General from 1959 to 1962, confirm the Archbishop's smooth style of leadership, and his ability to bring about ever so gently what he alone had thought through and decided upon: "He had a special gift for exercising authority with kindness. He didn't look like he was in charge, but he was well and truly in charge....He was not a heavy-handed or authoritarian bishop. No, he was a bishop full of authority."[96]

This type of fatherly or even brotherly authority was "much appreciated" by the missionaries. We could say he knew how to keep the machine running smoothly, thanks to his spirit of consultation and co-operation, and the great freedom he gave his priests. "He wanted his parish priests to be parish priests one hundred percent." In this he followed the advice of the Venerable Father Libermann: "Don't impede the development of a confrere's zeal nor stop him acting in a matter for which he is responsible."[97]

Besides, his subordinates knew that whatever happened, Archbishop Lefebvre would back them with his own authority. This was the case for Fr. Bourdelet after a sermon he preached in the cathedral on the feast of Christ the King. He was summoned by the Archbishop who said to him with a smile: "Father, I have to remonstrate with you...Well, I got a phone call from the Governor General about your sermon. You said that all those in authority receive their power ultimately from Christ the King, even if they believe neither in God nor the devil and reject totally the supernatural domain. And this, you said, is because everything has been created by Him, even if we obstinately reject it." The Archbishop went on to explain that the High Commissioner[98] had not been very pleased. When he was finished, he added: "Excellent! There we are, I have remonstrated with you as I was obliged to... Now, Fr. Jules, what about a whisky?"[99]

That was not all. The following Sunday, Archbishop Lefebvre himself stood in the pulpit and drove the message home, "All authority comes from God"!

---

[95] Fr. Louis Carron, ms. I, 58, 62; cf. Bussard, ms. I, 11, 28-31; Gravrand, ms. II, 69, 50.

[96] Bussard, ms. I, 11, 21-34.

[97] Notes and documents on Venerable Libermann, XIII, 335; cf. *Mémoire Spiritaine*, no. 2 (1995): 138.

[98] Bernard Cornut-Gentille, High Commissioner of French West Africa (1951-1956), Minister for France Overseas (1958-59), a high-ranking Freemason.

[99] Fr. Jules Bourdelet, ms. II, 56-57; 64, 31-33.

VIII. A LIVING PARADOX

PIETY AND LITURGY

In the pulpit Archbishop Lefebvre was not an orator. When preaching, he set out to explain one or two points of doctrine, and did so with the sort of admirable assurance and precision that he also liked to see in his priests. There were few who had his ability to analyze a theological question and make it understandable for the faithful.[100]

His vicar general considered him to be "very pious and profoundly religious," and the rector of his seminary saw in him "an example of that profound interior life of union with God which is the source of spiritual fruitfulness." On Sundays when he was in Dakar, he attended Mass in the various parishes and would be given a seat and a prie-dieu in the sanctuary. There he would appear "completely absorbed in his prayers."[101]

Each year he endeavored to lead the national pilgrimage or the military pilgrimage to Notre Dame of Popenguine. According to the wishes of Pius XII he made 1949 a Marian Year. In 1950 for the Holy Year, he organized the French-speaking African pilgrimage to Rome, and was one of the bishops who took part in the proclamation of the dogma of the Assumption of Our Lady. From the holy Virgin who was venerated at Popenguine and in his beloved oasis at Sébikotane, he hoped for the grace of conversion for the unbelievers, to which end he was constantly working.

During ceremonies, he pontificated with a simple dignity that edified and pleased the Africans. He wanted "ceremonies to be well done, even in the bush," "with dignity, grandeur, and respect for the sanctuary and the liturgical objects."[102] While he demanded that the priests wear the cassock during the celebration of Mass, he understood the difficulty of celebrating Mass while dying of thirst in the torrid heat, and he granted them permission to drink the ablutions of the chalice, even if they had to celebrate a second Mass. In his own case, however, he was very strict, and when he performed pontifical ceremonies at the cathedral, he still wore the tunics beneath the chasuble as the rubrics prescribed.[103]

PRINCIPLES AND GOODNESS

According to Fr. Bussard, Archbishop Lefebvre's private life was as orderly as his conduct at the altar. "He was a man with total self-control. I admired this marvelous way of being 'ascetic' without showing it." During

---

[100] *Ibid.,* 54, 36-40; 57, 38-42; 65, 47-53.
[101] *Fideliter*, no. 59: 102; Fr. Bussard, ms. I, 18, 46-54; Gérard Dubois-Burthe, Interview, July 1998, 3.
[102] Circular Letter 14: 4; 18: 9; (April 17, 1960): 6.
[103] Bussard, ms. I, 18-19.

meals, "he was charming company and appreciated the food." When he received some good cigars from his brother-in-law in Colombia, he offered them around after the meal and even smoked himself...

"That man was a paradox. He was so gentle and so kind...for example with respect to two or three priests he ought to have sent home to France, he ended up taking one back. I used to say to myself: 'You know, he is harder on rubrics than on people.'"

The Archbishop was very understanding with Fr. Berhaut, the distinguished botanist and zoologist, who used to send his snakes to the Institut Pasteur. He gave him a free hand to pursue his research.[104]

At the bishop's residence, as at the diocesan offices, he was always willing to see people, even those without an appointment: "When his secretary showed you into his office, he would get up and come towards you, smiling, hands outstretched, as if your arrival was the highlight of his week, as if you were doing him a great honor by coming to see him." After 1959, at the bishop's residence, he often opened the door himself.[105] When he went out, he liked to drive himself in his big American car which was sturdy and suited a man with the role of Apostolic Delegate. He didn't drive slowly, but smoothly without stalling, just like he guided his priests.[106]

However, there were different sides to his character. The man who smiled calmly, was infinitely kind, and who had a great respect for other people, their choices and initiatives, was also the man whose manner and tone would change completely showing him to be inflexible when principles were called into question,[107] and who acted with uncompromising firmness when the flock in his care was threatened. Thus, he imposed a local interdict—privation of the sacraments—on the Christians in Fadiout who had got themselves into debt with Muslim merchants: these latter would claim this or that boy as a slave in part payment and the slaves would soon become Muslim. Moreover, the Christians acquired all sorts of talismans from the marabouts. The punishment imposed by the bishop did more good than a long sermon on the subject. The peril was averted, and the marabouts had to leave the island.[108]

"When principles were called into question..." This was the case not only in the apostolate, but also in the social domain where we will now study Archbishop Lefebvre's activities.

---

[104] *Ibid.*, 12-13; 19, 17-24, 27-28; 20, 1-6.
[105] René Duverger, memoires, 3; Bussard, ms. I, 9-10; 19, 45-46.
[106] *Ibid.*, 10, 42-45; Fr. Christian Winckler, ms. I, 67, 28-48.
[107] Fr. Louis Carron, ms. I, 57, 41-46.
[108] Marziac, *Mgr. Lefebvre, soleil levant*, 118.

IX. CATHOLIC ACTION AND SOCIAL PROJECTS

THE "PROJECTS CENTER"

From his arrival, Archbishop Lefebvre was faced with the problems of an urban proletariat as we have already seen, and with the issue of the unions–permitted in Africa by the French law of August 7, 1944—some of which were inspired by Marxism. Archbishop Lefebvre decided to develop, co-ordinate, and organize initiatives for Catholic Action and social projects. He quickly worked out who was the best man for the job, and took Fr. Georges Courrier from his post as professor at the major seminary and appointed him director of the vicariate's projects in June 1948.

In two meetings (with Africans, then Europeans) on July 11, 1949, in the projects room that he had had built over the new print shop, Archbishop Lefebvre gave his orders:[109] "Be Catholic everywhere you go, persevere: study the nature of politics, Marxism, and secularism. The young men should meet together, and the young women too, to talk about marriage; young families should get together to talk about the Catholic family. You young women, only be members of sound union organizations."

This appeal was answered. Family Catholic Action was founded by the Africans. ACI (Independent Catholic Action) was created by the Europeans. In July 1951, Senegalese Social Action met in Dakar at the project center. Then Fr. Courrier was promoted director-general of Catholic Social Action for French West Africa, while Fr. Louis Carron became diocesan director. Fr. Carron was trained in the techniques of Catholic Worker Action and helped develop the Young Catholic Workers (JOC). The Legion of Mary, Senegal Catholic Aid, and an association of Catholic doctors, nurses, and midwives were also founded.

In his circulars, Archbishop Lefebvre asked his priests to be "innovative" with such projects (LC 18, 2-3), and called upon Catholic militants not to shun rural unions, co-operatives, council meetings, or the meetings of elders (LC 38). In 1951, despite his mistrust of the unions' inclination for protest, he asked the faithful to support the CFTC (LC 18, 21), and in 1957 he asked them again to support its latest incarnation, the African Workers' Confederation of Believers(ACTC), since he considered that its actions were inspired by Catholic social doctrine.

Faced with rivalry between projects and the tendency among the lay people to want to operate independently of the clergy, the Archbishop appointed Fr. Thiandoum as project director in 1956. He knew that being an African, Fr. Thiandoum was indifferent to the "anti-white" racism which had come from France (LC 53 [1956], 16-17). Fr. Thiandoum was

---

[109] Biarnès, *Les Français en Afrique*, 323; Marziac, *op. cit.*, p. 110-111; *Horizons Africains*, June 1948; Jul. 1949; Delcourt, *Histoire religieuse du Sénégal*, 93-94.

helped by a specialist, Fr. Chartier from the Lyons-based *Chronique Sociale*. With the help of Ernest Milcent, they launched an economic and social review called *Afrique Documents*, and opened a "People's University" where teachers and politicians, such as the future minister Daniel Cabou, came to teach political economy and "social doctrine."

Elsewhere, the Brottier Cultural Center organized a cycle of lectures, and in 1954 it became a platform on which important figures in Dakar could speak openly. Fr. Courrier opened "social offices" throughout French West Africa and gathered together "social teams." He was also helped by Ernest Milcent, and together they increased the numbers of lectures on doctrine and social action.

The Dominicans arrived in Dakar in 1955 and established their priory opposite the university on the road to Ouakam. The Archbishop entrusted them with the chaplaincy of the university, the JEC,[110] and the JOC, and gave them responsibility for Catholic radio broadcasts and relations with Islam. On December 19, 1957, they opened their cultural center, which had a lecture hall with four hundred seats where Fr. Louis-Joseph Lebret, O.P., gave the first conference on "The Conditions and Demands of a New Civilization," a civilization "inspired by Christianity," said the speaker…but which should renounce forever the desire to "restore all things in Christ" (Eph. 1:10).

To meet growing demand and in view of the JEC International Congress to be held in Dakar in 1958, the Project Center moved to Rue Sandiniéry in a converted building with the five-hundred-seat Daniel Brottier Lecture Hall. Sociologists such as Fr. Lebret and Joseph Folliet, and eminent lecturers such as President Senghor and Maître Abdoulaye Wade, spoke in this auditorium. At the end of 1958, Canon Robert Prélot became director of social action in Dakar. Later in 1959,[111] he became federal director for Western Africa, replacing Fr. Courrier.

A liberal, naturalistic, and quasi-socialist tendency began to appear in these activities, and the Archbishop, who was behind the growth of social initiatives in the diocese, seemed not to have control of the situation. In 1958, Family Catholic Action, which Archbishop Lefebvre was attached to, was ruined by Canon Prélot and his campaign for "A United Home for the Development of the Spouses" that made a mockery of the Catholic doctrine concerning the hierarchy of the two ends of marriage, as reiterated by Pius XII.[112]

The Apostolic Delegate reacted. With the backing of the other archbishops, he decided to reduce the "West Africa Project Center" to a simple

---

[110] A sister group to the JOC but for students.

[111] *Horizons Africains*, May 1958; Delcourt, *Histoire religieuse du Sénégal*, 96-99.

[112] *Horizons Africains*, Spring, 1959; *Enseignements pontificaux*, Marriage, appendix; Marziac, *Des évêques français contre Mgr. Lefebvre*, 139.

"Catholic Project Center" to provide help for national charities. Thus, the local hierarchy's authority would be more respected.[113] When Cardinal Tardini questioned the Archbishop in 1960 in view of the coming Council, he admitted to having been outmanoeuvred by "priests' committees" involved in Catholic social action: "The bishops no longer rule in their own dioceses. A bishop ends up merely ratifying what happens under his nose. His orders are not followed because of orders given out by the leaders of Catholic Action organizations."[114]

However, the same year on September 29, the Archbishop told his priests that he intended to retain control over "the progress of Catholic social action."[115] But would he really be able to make himself understood, or impose anti-liberal policies on the ideologues who had the wind in their sails? Let us look at some of the clashes that occurred.

ARCHBISHOP LEFEBVRE CLOSES DOWN THE JOC

Archbishop Lefebvre had been unhappy with the JOC from the beginning. This movement had existed in Senegal before he arrived and its founder, Canon Cardijn, who was supported unreservedly by Rome, had been to visit the JOC centers in Dakar and Thiès in October 1948.[116] In 1951 Canon Noddings sent JOC activists from Lille to Dakar to establish an African headquarters. One of them, Etienne Delattre, marched on May Day with the unions, and was reproached by Archbishop Lefebvre. However, the blacks were angered by this and told the Archbishop that they needed neither Delattre nor him: "We're big enough to make our own decisions."[117]

The bishop felt increasingly suspicious of the JOC and criticized a number of faults in their set up: firstly, its methods were consciously non-doctrinal and its activities were consequently ill-informed.[118] Ever since his days at Santa Chiara, Marcel Lefebvre knew that "action must be preceded by studying doctrine, and by learning the clear and precise principles that should guide it."[119] The bishop also criticized the JOC's motto "See, Judge, Act," preferring the traditional motto of the Association of French Catholic Youth (ACJF) approved by Saint Pius X: "Prayer, Study, Ac-

---

[113] Meeting of the Archbishops of West Africa, Dakar, April 1959. Archives of the Pontifical Missionary Works (Paris), 742-59-6 (Circular no. 2 from Canon Prélot).

[114] Reply to Cardinal Tardini, Dakar, Feb. 26, 1960.

[115] Circular Letter 70 (1960): 3.

[116] Letter of Pius XII to J. Cardijn, March 21, 1949; *General Bulletin* 621-622, 535.

[117] Catholic University of Lille, *Mémoires de Science Religieuse* 54, no. 3 (1997), Memoirs of Etienne Delattre, formerly a CGT representative and member of JOC at the same time, 85-87.

[118] Cf. JOC Manual (1930), 73-77; Fievez and Meert, *Cardijn*, 37, 127.

[119] Conference of Fr. Lebrun at Académie de Saint-Thomas, *Échos*, 119: 183.

tion."[120] Secondly, the JOC opted for "class-based pastoral care" and thus destroyed the unity of the parish community "which brought together rich and poor around the altar." They developed a parallel apostolate, following another agenda.[121] The bishop also criticized its systematic support for workers' demands,[122] a practice that, intentionally or unintentionally, contributed to the class warfare fomented by Communists themselves, albeit with other goals in mind. This created an atmosphere of criticism and discord that was contrary to charity.[123] Finally and most importantly, Archbishop Lefebvre intuitively perceived that their ambivalent apostolate was based essentially on purely human resources—social studies, workers demands—and suffered from a naturalism that lacked faith in supernatural means.

Archbishop Lefebvre encouraged Catholic Family Action and the Legion of Mary, neither of which sought primarily the suppression of social injustice. His family background and sense of hierarchy led him to think that social reform ought to be achieved by Catholic social action led by business leaders. Independent Catholic Action could have played this role. The fact remains that during the Mass on May Day to which the unions had been invited, Archbishop Lefebvre did not hesitate to "criticize workers' demands." According to Fr. Carron, "it took us months to 'restore the confidence' of the activists."[124]

In French-speaking Africa, Archbishop Lefebvre's opposition to the JOC became well-known. He used his position as Apostolic Delegate to limit Canon Noddings's[125] activities, and thus upset Bishop Bonneau, whose diocese of Douala, twinned as it was with Lille, was the JOC's stronghold. In Douala from September 12-17, 1956, the first pan-African meeting of the movement took place in the presence of Canon Cardijn.[126]

In Senegal the "inaugural National Congress" of the JOC took place around 1957. It voted on motions couched in violent language concerning the country's independence.[127] That was the straw that broke the camel's back. The Archbishop decided that the JOC had to be radically reformed.

---

[120] Archbishop Lefebvre, conference to students in Paris, May 2, 1965; Lefebvre, *Retreats preached at Econe*, Oct. 8, 1982, 6 P.M.; Lefebvre, *Spiritual Conferences at Econe*, 107 A, Feb. 28, 1984; St. Pius X, Allocution on Sept. 25, 1904, replying to an address given by Jean Lerolle, president of ACJF; (Bonne Presse) I, 228-230; (Éd. Courrier de Rome) I, 206-208; Bishop Antonio de Castro Mayer, *Catéchisme des vérités opportunes*, *Verbe* supplement, no. 25 (1953): 19.

[121] *Horizons Africains*, July 1949, 17; spiritual conference in Fribourg, Nov. 19, 1969.

[122] Fr. Louis Carron, ms. I, 58, 1-6.

[123] Archbishop Lefebvre, *Reply to Cardinal Tardini*, Feb. 26, 1960.

[124] Fr. Louis Carron, ms. I, 58, 29-35.

[125] *Mémoires de Science Religieuse* 54: 78-79.

[126] Fr. Joseph Bouchaud, *Mgr. Pierre Bonneau, évêque de Douala* (Yaoundé: Éd. de l'Effort Camerounais, 1959), 35-45.

This was obviously impossible, and in practice the movement was suppressed in the archdiocese.[128]

CLASHES WITH THE DOMINICANS

It is not clear whether the Dominicans had already taken charge of the JOC at that moment in time. However, it is interesting to go over the circumstances of their coming to Dakar and the events that brought them into conflict with the Archbishop, who incidentally had not asked them to come to the diocese.

Impressed with the missionary preaching of Fr. Petit–whom we shall talk about later–Fr. Maurice Corvez, superior of the Dominicans in the Province of Lyons, wrote to Archbishop Lefebvre on May 8, 1954, mooting the possibility of a foundation in Dakar and French West Africa. The Archbishop replied favorably, and in June 1954 Fr. Marie-Bernard Nielly came to make initial preparations for the foundation at Dakar. The priory was finally established on June 2, 1955, with the arrival of three other priests: Vincent Cosmao (who became chaplain of the JEC and the university), Jean-Bernard Rouxel (chaplain of the JOC but recalled to France in February 1956), and Martin Balzeau (who succeeded Fr. Rouxel as chaplain of the JOC). In March 1956 came Fr. Jean-Pierre Lintanf, who was responsible for Catholic radio broadcasting. In 1957 came Fr. Victor Martin, who belonged to the group Economics and Humanism[129] which began studying religious sociology with the financial backing of the Sacred Congregation for the Propagation of the Faith. Finally Fr. Luc Moreau arrived in 1958 and was made responsible for relations with Islam.

Soon, the founder of Economics and Humanism, Fr. Lebret, O.P., who was in Africa at the invitation of Léopold Senghor, brought his quasi-socialist ideas to Dakar. On the grounds that private property was supposedly not suitable for Africa and that collective property was "a norm required by man's progress,"[130] he wanted, in the words of Archbishop Lefebvre, "to set up kolkhozes and kibbutzim in Africa."[131] Lebret had some influence with Mamadou Dia, the president of the Senegalese State Council, and in 1960 he made a proposal to reorganize the administration of Senegal and implement a four-year development plan to be overseen by a team from Economics and Humanism.

---

[127] In September 1957, the JOC International Council met in Rome to vote on motions for the following: an end to all testing of atomic bombs, an end to all discrimination based on race, color, and religion, and mutual respect and trust to bring about world peace, etc. *Documentation Catholique* 1261 (Sept. 29, 1957), 1270-1271.

[128] Fr. Louis Carron, ms. II, 30-31; Circular Letter 57 (1957): 8.

[129] See Chapter VII, "The Battle of Mortain."

[130] Fr. Vincent Cosmao, O.P., *Développement et foi* (Cerf, 1972), 88, 115.

[131] *Fideliter*, no. 59: 25; Marcel Lefebvre, *Retreats preached at Ecône*, Sept. 19, 1979.

Elsewhere, the Islamic-Christian dialogue initiated by Fr. Moreau quickly seemed to the Archbishop to be favoring Islam more than anything else. The sympathy shown by Moreau when speaking of Islam only encouraged young Catholic women who wished to marry Muslims. Therefore, Archbishop Lefebvre complained to the Father Provincial about Frs. Lebret, Cosmao, and Moreau, and asked for the recall of Moreau to France. However, the priests in Dakar had no intention of listening to the Archbishop's orders. In a letter to the Father Provincial, Cosmao, the new superior in Dakar, declared that giving in to pressure from Archbishop Lefebvre[132] would constitute an admission of weakness by the Dominican Order, and would harm the Church's interests in West Africa.[133] With the support of Bishop Maury,[134] the new Apostolic Delegate, the Father Provincial refused to recall Fr. Moreau,[135] although he was now required to submit his pastoral projects for the approval of the Ordinary.[136]

Failing to secure the recall of this priest, Archbishop Lefebvre considered himself obliged to ask Fr. Michael Browne, Master General of the Order and a future cardinal, simply to close down the Dominican priory in Dakar. He replied that even if it were possible to secure the reappointment of one priest or another, it was impossible without the *placet* of Rome, under the terms of Canon 498, to close a religious house for which the local bishop had given his approval. Archbishop Lefebvre would not or could not have recourse to Rome, and the revolutionary activities continued.

In 1968, after the Dominicans had supported the student uprising, President Senghor asked the Nuncio to remove them. Archbishop Thiandoum, the new archbishop, was unhappy with this request and proposed a more amicable solution: the Dominicans ceased to serve the university chaplaincy, but their church was made into a parish. In 1977 the prior, Fr. Vincent Cosmao, gave perhaps a most beautiful testimony to Archbishop Lefebvre's doctrinal consistency, admitting at the same time to his own progressiveness:

> Until that moment, the Church made kings and thereby consecrated the social order. When that social order no longer corresponded to the relations between the social groups, it was necessary to deconsecrate society and thereby remove the Church from her position....Vatican II is the outcome of the Church's growing realization of this fact....It is the

---

[132] Letter of Archbishop Lefebvre, March 11, 1961, after Fr. Nielly, whom he liked, was recalled to France. Dominican Archives in Dakar.

[133] Letter of March 12, 1961.

[134] Letter of March 23, 1961.

[135] Letter of Sept. 28, 1961.

[136] Letter of Fr. Nicolas Gobert, socius of the Provincial, to Fr. Moreau, Oct. 3, 1961. Most of these details and their references are taken from *Mémoire dominicaine*, special edition IV, *Histoire des dominicains en Afrique* (Paris: Cerf), chap. 7.

Church which has changed, not Archbishop Lefebvre. He really is the witness of that Church which was certain of her truth, rights, and power, and which considered herself alone capable of saying how best to organize society.[137]

THE CITÉ CATHOLIQUE IN DAKAR

The Cité Catholique promoted the proper organization of society according to the constant doctrine of the Church. Towards the end of 1948, Gérard Dubois-Burthe, a young official from INSEE (the French Institute of Statistics and Economics) in Dakar came to see Archbishop Lefebvre to discuss establishing the Cité Catholique in Senegal.[138] But what was this organization about?

On August 15, 1939, two young laymen, Jean Ousset and Jean Masson, had solemnly promised in the presence of Fr. Jean Choulot, parish priest of Montalzat-en-Quercy, to work for the social reign of Christ. Their ideas took shape after the war in the summer of 1946 thanks to the help they found in the Spiritual Exercises of St. Ignatius as preached by Fr. François de Paule Vallet's Parish Co-operators of Christ the King. Working in study circles with a maximum of ten people, the Cité Catholique soon spread. Its review, *Verbe*, and its annual conferences examined all the social questions and sought to combat liberalism and socialism in the same spirit as Cardinal Pie and in the light of the teachings of the magisterium.[139]

Archbishop Lefebvre received his young visitor warmly and listened favorably to his proposals. In the Cité Catholique, the bishop saw an excellent doctrinal support for the Catholic social action initiatives that he wished to develop. In Solesmes around 1951, he met the prior, Dom Georges Frénaud, who was a former fellow student from Santa Chiara. The monk asked him to support the movement since it had recently been attacked as "Right-wing and monarchist" in an article written by Fr. Marie-Joseph Nicolas, O.P., and published in *La Vie Spirituelle*.[140] Certain priests of Catholic Action were behind this assault which made the French episcopate suspicious about the work of Cité Catholique and the "Priests of Chabeuil." Archbishop Lefebvre promised his help, met Jean Ousset, and visited the headquarters in Paris. He also showed more interest in the Dakar study circle which met each week at the home of Louis Galéa who ran "Française des pétroles."[141]

---

[137] Interview on Télévision Romande (Switzerland) Sept. 8, 1977, in *Le Courrier de Rome*, no. 175: 12.

[138] G. Dubois-Burthe, Interview with Michel de Penfentenyo, July 1998, 3.

[139] Jean Ousset, *Pour qu'Il règne* (La Cité Catholique, 1959), 723-725; Marziac, *Des évêques français contre Mgr. Lefebvre*, 133-136; Savioz, *Essai historique*, I, 18-19.

[140] Dec. 1951, no. 368; Marziac, *Des évêques français contre Mgr. Lefebvre*, 143.

[141] Lefebvre, *Spiritual Conferences at Ecône* 26 B, Feb. 10, 1976; F. Lagneau, Letter, June 5, 1997.

This first Senegalese "cell" was soon replicated in many places and at all levels, to such an extent that Louis Galéa was able to invite Jean Ousset and Jean Masson to oversee the first general meeting of the Cité Catholique on March 17, 1957. Despite growing opposition from some quarters, Archbishop Lefebvre accepted an invitation to chair the meeting in the Catholic projects center. Later, an African delegation which was mostly Senegalese attended the movement's Eighth Congress in Poitiers in June 1957. A Senegalese delegate, Louis Sané, delivered a speech on "The Church and the African Civilizations" in which he expounded with expertise the antidote to the ideologies imported from Europe.[142] The delegation returned to Senegal much encouraged.

While these "cells" of the Cité Catholique remained a "white concern," the central project office ignored them. However, when they gained some influence among the blacks, Catholic Family Action saw them as "a competitor harmful to the general good of Catholic Action." Archbishop Lefebvre manoeuvred skilfully: apparently giving in to the critics by requiring the "cells" to obtain permission from their parish priests to meet and to submit their program of studies to the project office, he "permitted the groups associated with *Verbe*" and warmly recommended them as "a school for the leaders of Catholic Action, inspired by the pure spirit of the Church." The following year when Fr. Louis Carron, parish priest of Rufisque, complained about a "cell" operating in his parish without his permission, and which was attended, *horresco referens*, by the bishop's own secretary Fr. Perraud, Archbishop Lefebvre answered him with a broad, disarming smile.[143]

Cité Catholique's ability to organize and purify Catholic Action in Africa was becoming clear. Using this organization to combat revolutionary activities in the Church and civil society, Archbishop Lefebvre invited Michel de Penfentenyo, the Secretary General of Cité Catholique, to give a presentation to the missionaries and lay people in Senegal, Ivory Coast (where there were already several "cells"), Dahomey, and Cameroon in spring 1959. This voyage was followed by another the following year, and everywhere the Africans were anxious to learn about the authentic Christian social order.[144]

The visits of the Cité Catholique delegates was opposed by Fr. Courrier who, having been informed by Michel de Penfentenyo of Archbishop Lefebvre's invitation, dared to write a circular to all the bishops and Cath-

---

[142] *Horizons Africains*, April 1957; *Verbe*, no. 84 (June 1957): 81 and supplement, no. 11 (Aug.-Sept. 1957); Ousset, *Pour qu'Il règne*, 728.

[143] Circular Letter 57 (Aug. 25, 1957): 4; Fr. Carron, ms. II, 31, 65-72.

[144] *Verbe*, no. 103: 51-54; no. 112: 53-56; Ousset, *Pour qu'Il règne*, 730; Marziac, *Des évêques français contre Mgr. Lefebvre*, 148.

olic project leaders in French West Africa and Togo in which he stated (our summary):

> Supporting this movement is especially inadvisable because of its French patriotism. It smacks of Action Française and has influenced some of the leaders of the 13 May Movement. It is the spiritual cousin of Chabeuil, *La Pensée Catholique, Défense du Foyer, Itinéraires, etc.*, and is dangerous because it confuses the building of a "temporal civilization" with the establishment of the kingdom of God. It makes ill-considered use of quotations from encyclicals, the majority of the French bishops hold it in some suspicion, and it is unable to adapt itself to the problems and mindset of Africa.[145]

This pathetic diatribe—the servile echo of the omnipresent instructions from the anonymous offices of an abstract "episcopate"—proved to the Archbishop that the rot had set in. So, very calmly, he called Fr. Courrier and without dramatizing the situation, simply and kindly took him to task:

"Tut tut tut...your circular letter was too strong. You're going to change it."

"But, *Monseigneur*, I cannot. It has already been sent!"

"Yes, but you're going to write another one saying that you've made a mistake and that the delegates of the Cité Catholique ought to be welcomed."

"But, *Monseigneur*, I cannot do any such thing because I am opposed to it..."

The Archbishop said to himself, "I will not change his ideas; let's not insist, and try to maintain good relations."

A circular was indeed sent out, but it was signed "Lefebvre." Fr. Courrier was replaced by Fr. Prélot as projects director in French West Africa, and he came back to Dakar to take charge of social action. Since the Archbishop had a lot of respect for Fr. Courrier, he appointed him the following year as a curate at the cathedral with "responsibility for relations with the trade unionists."[146]

Nonetheless, the Cité Catholique did find other protectors among the hierarchy. In 1957 Bishop Vion, bishop of Poitiers, "noted that high up in the Church in Rome they were following with interest the efforts of the Cité Catholique." Every year Cardinal Ottaviani wrote a letter of congratulations to whichever bishop hosted the annual congress in his diocese. In France, Cardinal Grente and Bishops Pic (Valence), Lallier (Marseilles), Chappoulie (Angers), Rupp, Morilleau (La Rochelle), and Ménard (Ro-

---

[145] Circular Letter of Feb. 29, 1959 (Paris: Archives of the Pontifical Missionary Works), 742-59-1. The circular referred to two articles of Fr. Le Blond in *Études* (Nov. 1958 and Feb. 1959).

[146] Ms. III, 12, 35-70; Circular Letter, April 1960 and no. 70 (Sept. 29, 1960).

dez) were all in favor of the movement. Archbishop Marmottin, the Archbishop of Reims, was known as its "chief champion."[147]

Archbishop Lefebvre's association with the movement did not stop there. On August 23, 1956, he wrote a first letter of encouragement to the committee on the tenth anniversary of its foundation. Taking account of the growing opposition that the movement met even in his own jurisdiction, he wrote a magnificent foreword on March 24, 1959, for Jean Ousset's *Pour qu'Il règne*, published that year: "Our Lord will reign in civil society when a few thousand disciples…believe in the truth that is given to them, and are convinced that this truth is a force capable of transforming everything."

Convinced of the strength in the principles of Christian order, an entire French and African elite began to occupy positions of responsibility across society in the name of Christ. Captain Gérard de Cathelineau, who died in Kabylia in 1957, observed in his "Notes on the role of an operational unit's leader": "Creating a 'cell' in the army…is to work for the nation."[148]

The activists' convictions and resolutions were strengthened by the Spiritual Exercises of St. Ignatius through which they meditated on life's goal and contemplated the love of Christ. Following the comments of various popes, Archbishop Lefebvre saw in these exercises "an irresistible spur and reliable guide for souls who would change their lives and reach the peaks of spiritual perfection."[149] He invited the Parish Co-operators of Christ the King to Dakar. Thus during the rainy seasons of 1960 and 1961, Frs. Augustin Rivière and Noël Barbara came to preach two series of retreats to numerous groups of retreatants, both priests and lay people.[150]

Thanks to the exercises and to the Cité Catholique, a new and healthy form of Catholic Action was born within the diocese. Its agenda and leaders were sound, and they accepted the guidance and direction of non-liberal prelates. This was a Catholic Action which escaped the ruts of social studies and worker demands, and as St. Pius X had requested, its goal was "to combat anti-Christian civilization by all just and legal means,…and to give back to Jesus Christ His place in families, schools, and in society."[151]

---

[147] Ousset, *Pour qu'Il règne*, 727, 780-787; Marziac, *Des évêques français contre Mgr. Lefebvre*, 142.

[148] *Le Monde*, July 9, 1958, under the pen name of Henri Fesquet.

[149] Pius XI, encyclical *Mens Nostra*, Dec. 20, 1929.

[150] *Marchons*, Nov-Dec. 1960; Nov.-Dec. 1961.

[151] St. Pius X, encyclical *Il Fermo Proposito*, June 11, 1905.

X. The Fortunes and Misfortunes of the Catholic Press

Afrique Nouvelle

Among the many projects in Dakar, the Catholic press was a fairly new initiative when Archbishop Lefebvre arrived in 1947. Two newspapers had just in fact been launched at the same time: *Afrique Nouvelle* and *Horizons Africains*. *Horizons Africains* was founded by Fr. Biard, the parish priest of the cathedral, and at first it was meant to bring together all the Catholics in French West Africa. When he arrived in the diocese, Archbishop Lefebvre gave the paper much encouragement while realigning its sights on the more realistic objective of being a Catholic monthly for Senegal. It brought together news items concerning the Church at home and abroad, with brief feature articles keeping the readers "in communion with the bishop and the Pope."[152] While the paper did sometimes not appear, it owed its survival and its progress (its distribution was 2,400 in 1956, and 7,000 in 1961) to the determination of the Archbishop whose views could be read in the leader articles.[153]

The new print shop established in 1949 was still expanding when the Little Sisters of St. Paul—also present in Cameroon from 1949—took charge. On state-of-the-art machines, they printed numerous periodicals for Catholic Action and the Catholic social projects in French West Africa, from *Jeunesse d'Afrique* (JEC in Dakar), and *Savoir et Agir* published by the Daniel-Brottier Cultural Center, to *Equipe Ouvrière d'Afrique* (JOC activist).[154] In 1957 they began printing the weekly *Afrique Nouvelle*.

Afrique Nouvelle is a story in itself. The creation of an inter-regional periodical had been discussed as early as November 1945 by the West African bishops gathered together at Koumi near Bobo Dioulasso. Their meeting was chaired by Bishop Thévenoud, the Vicar Apostolic of Ouagadougou in Upper Volta. They sought to define a common line of action with respect to the Dakar government, and the bishops divided the work between the various congregations, confiding education to the Lyons African Missions (Father Bertho came to live in Dakar), Catholic Action to the Holy Ghost Fathers, and the press to the White Fathers. This was why Fr. Patenot, a White Father, came to Dakar and founded *Afrique Nouvelle*.

Intended for French West Africa, French Equatorial Africa, and Cameroon as well, the paper first appeared on June 15, 1947, in Dakar. It aimed to make the voice of the Church heard and give Catholics a platform from which to speak. The political parties—among which was the Communist-aligned RDA—and the Protestants had their own plat-

---

[152] Koren, *Les Spiritains*, 507; *Horizons Africains*, April 1948, 1-2; Circular Letter 14: 4.
[153] Circular Letter 53 (1956): 17-18.
[154] *General Bulletin* 661; 685, 117; Delcourt, *Histoire religieuse du Sénégal*, 97-98.

forms.[155] Archbishop Lefebvre encouraged the paper for a long time and made it recommended reading in his diocese. It printed his pastoral letter on "Secularism, the Forerunner of Communism" in its entirety on February 11, 1953. Women and the family were well defended in its columns. Catholic education was championed too, although when the paper affirmed the importance of "truly nondenominational" schools (July 5, 1952), its liberal tendencies started to become apparent.

The first serious clash came in 1951 when High Commissioner Béchard filed a lawsuit against *Afrique Nouvelle*. Some members of Parliament sent a petition in favor of the paper to President Vincent Auriol. The symbolic condemnation of the paper with a suspended fine of fifty francs assured its popularity and brought about a crisis in the government in Paris. The resignation of the Minister for France Overseas, François Mitterand, was discussed, and an inquiry blamed the High Commissioner, whose salary was subsequently reduced.[156]

The rumpus caused by the paper which from a Catholic perspective was quite unnecessary annoyed the vicar apostolic and persuaded him to shelve a request for funds addressed to the Association for the Propagation of the Faith which the French West African bishops' commission had voted for in January 1952. Instead, the vicar delegate obtained a grant for his own central project office. The White Fathers were consequently furious, and complained to Rome in 1953. Meanwhile on August 15, 1952, Fr. Paternot had handed on the reins to one of his assistants, Fr. Robert Rummelhardt, another strong personality. The new editor did not improve relations, and having made some insolent remarks about the bishop in his newspaper, he was punished with an ecclesiastical censure…This caused another hue and cry among the White Fathers, who again appealed to Rome at the end of 1954.[157]

His replacement, Fr. Joseph-Roger de Benoist, supported decolonization. On March 15, 1955, he wrote: "The attitudes of certain churchmen amount to racial segregation and colonialism…the relations between European and African priests are not always the friendliest." On March 5, 1957, Fr. de Benoist, who had been present for the ceremonies marking Ghana's independence, wrote: "I saw N'Krumah cry as they proclaimed independence."

---

[155] Msgr. André Dupont, Letter of Aug. 1, 1996; Annie Lenoble-Bart, *Afrique Nouvelle, un hebdomadaire catholique dans l'histoire, 1947-1987* (Toulouse: Éd. de la Maison des sciences de l'homme d'Aquitaine, 1996); Guy Pannier, *L'Église de Pointe-Noire* (Paris: Karthala, 1999), 56.

[156] *Afrique Nouvelle*, Feb. 10 and Apr. 14, 1951; Lenoble-Bart, *op. cit.*, 57-58.

[157] *Afrique Nouvelle* Aug. 9 and 16, 1952; Lenoble-Bart, *op. cit.*, p. 21; Msgr. Dupont, Letter of Aug. 1, 1996; Letter of Fr. Bertho to Msgr. Bertin, Archives of the Pontifical Missionary Works, Paris, 742-54-7.

The Archbishop was increasingly unhappy, his warnings went unheeded, and the paper was suspended on more than one occasion. On October 1, 1959, the management was put in the hands of laypeople, and Ernest Milcent took charge, assisted by Fr. Michel Chartier. In Yaoundé, Bishop Graffin had the same difficulties with *L'Effort Camerounais* which, although it was printed in Yaoundé, owed its existence and inspiration to Bishop Bonneau, bishop of Douala. The paper was suspended, and the Apostolic Delegate—Archbishop Lefebvre—had the editor admonished: "I have good reason to call to Fr. Fertin's attention the fact that his paper is known throughout Cameroon as the paper of the Catholic Mission, whatever he does.…He must not be on the lookout for every injustice to turn it into a polemical article." In the end Bishop Graffin acted to prevent the expulsion of Fr. Fertin (who was in fact finally expelled in February 1962), and withdrew from circulation the edition of January 21, 1957, concerning Pierre Messmer's "repression" of the UPC insurgents.[158]

These two episcopal censures angered the courageous albeit liberal bishop of Douala. Shortly before his death he refused a visit from Archbishop Lefebvre, who was in the diocese: "He has made me suffer too much," he said. He also rejected the proposal of a visit from Bishop Graffin, saying: "It's useless for him to come and see me."[159] But what is more tragic than a lack of principle?

XI. SOCIAL DOCTRINE

The writings of the Archbishop of Dakar[160] are a handbook of the natural and supernatural principles relating to the social order but adapted brilliantly to the needs of Africa. Whether in his pastoral letters or his circulars to missionaries, whether they concern "the condemnation of Communism" (1950), "social and economic problems" (1951), "social and political evolution" (1955), or "the duty to avoid ambiguity" (1961), Archbishop Lefebvre "wrote everything himself, varying neither in essence, tone, nor style,"[161] and his faithfulness to the Magisterium of the Church and the reigning Pope was always manifest.

The social order willed by God is nothing other than the social reign of our Lord Jesus Christ (AI 10, 12, 13; P33; ESP 65). The real possibility of man fulfilling his purpose on earth to "know, love, and serve God" (68), in which lies the dignity of the human person (68-69)[162] in possession of certain fundamental rights (68-69), is dependent in fact upon the estab-

---

[158] Criaud, *La geste des spiritains*, 225; *General Bulletin*, 702: 69-70; Pierre Messmer, *Après tant de batailles* (Albin Michel, 1992), 226.

[159] Bouchaud, *Mgr. Pierre Bonneau*, 52; Criaud, *loc. cit.*

[160] References are to the *Lettres pastorales et écrits*, published in 1989.

[161] Testimony of Fr. Perraud, *Fideliter*, no. 59: 20.

lishment of the reign of our Lord. This reign also ensures true family life, excludes polygamy and the slavery of women (71, 78-79, 84), values women's dignity (80-84), respects work, validates parents' concerns for their children's future, honors prudent thriftiness (PES 31) and attachment to the land (80), teaches the notion of private property (30) as willed by God (79) and the need for suitable living conditions (30, 32). Professional organizations are established to oppose economic liberalism and the "money men" (EPS 74). In co-operatives, rural unions (NM 57-58), and local politics, "exemplary Christians" (58) should seek to rise to those positions that the administration prefers to see in the hands of polygamist chiefs and Muslims (58).

Despite the well-known weaknesses of the Africans (29-30, 58), the people possess a "down-to-earth wisdom" (84), and their customs uphold "certain essential values such as a sense of hospitality, the sacred character of authority, the spirit of mutual help, faithfulness, respect for motherhood, and in certain tribes a sense of modesty"(78). The missionary role of the Church is to "deliver these people from a type of civilization that is sanctioned by a false religion and oppresses human dignity."[163] It does this by calling them "to act under the guidance of the Christian religion and rise to a superior model of humanity and culture" (78) which assimilates their native values. The nuts and bolts of this new civilization are not within the province of the priest who, being aware of the interdependence of religion and society, will be responsible, nevertheless, for certain temporal affairs such as education, the training of an elite, and the organization of rural life.[164]

The European administration has worked towards this transformation by ensuring the freedom of movement and work, public safety, and education (81-82), but unfortunately "it has not believed in its own civilization" because it has not been willing to "recognize the reasons for its superiority, which consists entirely in its Christian principles" (82). On the contrary it has brought with it the European evils of socialism and secularism.

Infected with this socialism, the new local assemblies are tempted "to fulfil the role of private associations and families because they consider these insufficient" (PES 27, January 25, 1951). On the other, hand individuals and private organizations tend to "expect everything from the public services that are seen as the voters' heaven-sent safety net" (27). Far from wishing to encourage this mentality, the government must "help and encourage private initiative and not try to take its place" (28, 31). One

---

[162] For Archbishop Lefebvre, these rights as expounded by Pius XII were purely conditional in view of man's need to fulfil his duty (68-69).

[163] Archbishop Lefebvre, critical commentary on the scenario of the film *Le missionnaire*.

[164] *Ibid.* There is an allusion here to certain remarks of Pius XII.

cannot solve the problems of the urban proletariat by direct government funding (48), nor by conceding to union demands "that come from a continual spirit of conflict" (57), but rather by encouraging private organizations to promote justice and social charity (48-49). By secularism they remove from the hearts of African children "the most beautiful treasure and the best investment in the world: a fear of God and respect for His law" (30). "In spite of the incessant exhortations of the Vicar of Christ, they codify, legislate, and draw up national or international constitutions taking no account of the teachings of Him who said: 'Without me, you can do nothing' (Jn. 15:5)" (34).

However, secularism is "the forerunner of Communism" (CA 48). In 1949 the Holy Office established the punishment of excommunication for Communist propagandists and exclusion from the sacraments for their collaborators. From this time on, numerous prominent Africans such as Houphouët-Boigny in Ivory Coast affiliated their newly founded political parties, the RDA for example, to the French Communist party (although Senghor joined up more tamely with the Socialist party, SFIO). Therefore, the errors, the illusions, and traps of Communism (45) had to be denounced, and the practice of Leninist dialectics at work in Africa "taking advantage of everything that could divide men and provoke hatred and conflict" (44) had to be revealed. The orders given by certain African politicians to "destroy the monstrous lie of religion" called for counter-orders that indirectly target the great leaders: "A Catholic cannot follow such men" (CC 25).

Archbishop Lefebvre gave this latter order in 1950. Eleven years later he would take the risk of denouncing the persistent ambiguity in the "African socialism" of Senghor, the Head of State.

CHAPTER 9

APOSTOLIC DELEGATE

I. THE WILL OF THE POPE

On October 1, 1948, Archbishop Lefebvre visited the motherhouse of his congregation where he had gone in search of more funds and more personnel. He had only just arrived when Archbishop Le Hunsec saw him, came down, and straightaway said to him, "Come on, *Monseigneur*, come on. I've got something to tell you."

"What's up?" wondered Archbishop Lefebvre, "What's the matter?"

"Come into the parlor…you're not going to say no! The Pope has appointed you Apostolic Delegate."[1]

The "Apostolic Delegation of Africa," which was established in 1930 at Mombasa in Kenya, had been rechristened "Apostolic Delegation of British East and West Africa"[2] on January 2, 1947. Ever since, it had been expected that a similar delegation would be established for French-speaking, or rather French Black Africa.[3] However, what no-one yet knew was that Pius XII had not only chosen Dakar as the delegation headquarters,[4] he had also chosen the Vicar Apostolic to be the Apostolic Delegate. Even before naming him Vicar Apostolic, Pius XII already had his eye on Marcel Lefebvre. He simply waited a year in order to see him in action.

The letter, signed by Montini, which the Pope wrote to his "venerable brother" Marcel Lefebvre left no doubt on the subject, nor on the esteem or affection that the Pope had for the young bishop: "You have governed the Apostolic Vicariate of Dakar so prudently, wisely, and actively, and you are driven by such zeal for the reign of Christ…that We judge it right to choose you for this Delegation, being convinced that your gifts—principally your tried and tested ministry and the personal qualities that make you perfect for this post—will be immensely useful in this Delegation."[5]

Moreover, since the Apostolic Delegate ought to have the rank of Archbishop, on the same day Bishop Lefebvre received a letter appointing him titular Archbishop of Arcadiopolis *in Europa*.[6] However, that was

---

[1] Lefebvre, *Petite histoire,* 64; *General Bulletin,* 619-620: 487; *C.S.Sp. French Bulletin,* 41: 5.

[2] *A.A.S.* 39 (1947): 96; *General Bulletin,* 602-603: 171.

[3] There were already three in the Belgian Congo.

[4] Apostolic Letter Sep. 22, 1948, *A.A.S.* 42 (1959): 429; *Horizons Africains,* Jan. 1949.

[5] Brief of Sept. 22, 1948, *General Bulletin,* 630: 318-319.

nothing in comparison with his totally new situation. The bishop had two posts that were incompatible. On the one hand, he had pastoral responsibility for a particular flock; and on the other, he was juridically responsible for forty-four ecclesiastical territories and for diplomatic relations with the French government and its High Commissioners.

This is what Pius XII explained to him in October, and at the beginning of December the Sacred Congregation for the Propagation of the Faith and the Secretariat of State filled in the details. In his own words, he was "terrified" by the size of his task. He was the Pope's representative in one diocese, twenty-six vicariates, and seventeen apostolic prefectures, from Morocco and the Sahara to Madagascar and La Réunion, by way of French West Africa, French Cameroon, French Equatorial Africa and Somalia. These territories, whose Catholic population stood at more than 2,100,000, were in the care of twelve missionary institutes. Therefore, he had to manage Holy Ghost bishops (13), White Fathers (10), African Missionaries of Lyons (6), Jesuits (3), Capuchins (3), Fathers of La Salette (2), etc. "I, a poor Holy Ghost Father, going to preach to Jesuits!" he exclaimed.[7] However, his simplicity forestalled the possibility of his wounding the pride of members of other congregations.

When he returned to Dakar on December 12, the Archbishop was received at the government headquarters. Then, early in 1949, the Minister for France Overseas, Paul Coste-Floret, came to Dakar in person, and in a ceremony that took place in the square before the cathedral he decorated the Delegate with the cross of a *chevalier de la Légion d'honneur*.[8]

For the post of Delegation Secretary, Archbishop Lefebvre immediately asked for Fr. Emile Doutremépuich, a former fellow student from the French Seminary (1922-26). At first he had been a student mentor at Santa Chiara and a youthful but dependable assistant to Fr. Le Floch. Later he was rector at Chevilly and at the seminary in Carabane, Casamance. He was a hard-working man with a lively intelligence. He was also a man of principle who did not mince his words. "Fr. Doutre" became the most attentive, meticulous, and loyal secretary to Archbishop Lefebvre until, burnt out by overwork and terminally ill, he took early retirement on July 1, 1957.[9] His successor, who was just as hard-working and capable, was Fr. Isidore Perraud.

---

[6]   Nowadays Lüleburgaz, near Istanbul.

[7]   *Horizons Africains*, Dec. 1948, 12; *C.S.Sp. French Bulletin*, 41: 5; *General Bulletin*, 621-622: 512; *Fideliter*, no. 59: 17.

[8]   *Horizons Africains*, Jan. 1949, 8-10; C.S.Sp. *General Bulletin*, 623: 11-12; Marziac, *Des évêques français contre Mgr. Lefebvre*, 105-106.

[9]   *C.S.Sp. French Bulletin*, 128: 348-351.

THE INSTRUCTIONS OF PIUS XII

The Pope's instructions to his Delegate stemmed from a panoramic view that took in two principal concerns: on the one hand, the Church should no longer be a foreign institution in Africa, whence the urgent need to train a hierarchy of native bishops, and whence also the order to safeguard African customs in so far as they were reconcilable with God's law. On the other hand, Catholic works should be developed: the number of laypeople actively collaborating in the apostolate of the clergy should be considerably increased; others should work to reform social and political institutions according to the Gospel to counter Communist propaganda; and education must show the beauty of the Catholic religion to the non-Christians who will be tomorrow's elite.[10]

Archbishop Lefebvre accepted the instructions dutifully. The last of them, which was a little delicate, corresponded to the situation in Senegal. He also wished to use Catholic Action to implant Christianity anew in the real life of the natives. Finally, training a native clergy was indeed his goal. Nevertheless it seemed to him that the true objective of schools was to form a Catholic elite. Indigenization in all its forms—whilst an attractive theory that paid Africa a compliment—could not replace evangelization.

Pius XII did not conceal from his Delegate the fear that gripped him. Like Pius XI, his predecessor, he was concerned that in the wake of revolutions the Church in countries that were new to Christianity would be ruined by not having "a network of indigenous priests"[11] and bishops. The Communist threat in the Far East showed how right the Pope was in this respect.

For the Vicar of Christ, Marcel Lefebvre was both a docile instrument and a down-to-earth adviser. At the Secretariat of State, the Apostolic Delegate had his role explained to him. It was a limited, diplomatic function that, without making him an Apostolic nuncio, was designed to give a voice to the Church and to facilitate relations with the Minister for France Overseas.[12] At the Sacred Congregation for the Propagation of the Faith, Cardinal Fumasoni Biondi and Bishop Celso Costantini, the Secretary of the Congregation, explained to him in detail his missionary objectives of which we will now give a brief overview.

---

[10] Cf. Pius XII, encyclical *Summi Pontificatus*, Oct. 20, 1939; allocution, June 24, 1944; encyclical *Evangelii Præcones*, June 2, 1951.

[11] Pius XI, encyclical *Rerum Ecclesiæ*, quoted in Pius XII, enc. Cited above.

[12] Code of Canon Law, can. 267, §2; Joseph Greco, S.J., *Vingt ans de pastorale missionnaire* (Issy: St. Paul, 1958), 13-14.

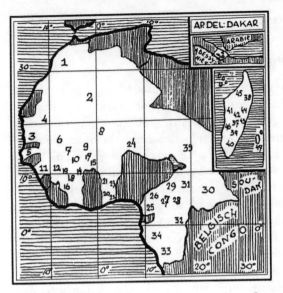

THE APOSTO[
DELEGATION
DAKAR IN 19

CONGREGATION INDEX

I.C. = indigenous clergy
C.M. = Lazarists
C.S.Sp. = Holy Ghost Fathers
C.SS.R. = Redemptorists
A.M.L. = African Missionaries of Lyons
M.S. – Missionaries of La Salette
O.F.M. = Franciscans
O.F.M. Cap. = Capuchins
W.F. = White Fathers
Q.P.S.H. = St. Quentin Priests of the Sa[
S.J. = Jesuits
S.M.M. – Monfortians

OTHER ABBREVIATIONS

Vic Ap = Apostolic Vicariate
Pr Ap = Apostolic Prefecture

I. MOROCO

1. Vic. Ap. Rabat .... O.F.M.

II. SAHARA

2. Vic. Ap. Ghardaia.. W.F.

III. FRENCH WEST AFRICA (A.O.E)

Senegal

3. Vic. Ap. Dakar.. C.S.Sp.
4. Pr. Ap. St. Louis.................................... C.S.Sp.
5. Pr. Ap. Ziguinchor................................. C.S.Sp.
6. Pr. Ap. Kayes .... W.F.

Sudan

7. Vic. Ap. Bamako .... W.F.
8. Pr. Ap. Gao .... W.F.
9. Pr. Ap. Nouna .... W.F.
10. Pr. Ap. Sikasso .... W.F.

French Guinea

11. Vic. Ap. Conakry .... C.S.Sp.
12. Pr. Ap. Kankan .... C.S.Sp.

Ivory Coast

13. Vic. Ap. Abidjan .... A.M.L.
14. Vic. Ap. Bobo-Dioulasso .... W.F.
15. Vic. Ap. Ouagadougou .... W.F.
16. Vic. Ap. Sassandra .... W.F.
17. Pr. Ap. Ouahigouya .... W.F.
18. Pr. Ap. Korhogo .... A.M.L.
19. Pr. Ap. Nzérékoré .... W.F.

Togo

20. Vic. Ap. Lomé .... A.M.L.
21. Pr. Ap. Sokodé .... A.M.L.

Dahomey

22. Vic. Ap. Ouidah .... A.M.L.
23. Pr. Ap. Parakou .... A.M.L.

Niger

24. Vic. Ap. Niger .... C.SS.R.

Cameroon

25. Vic. Ap. Douala .... C.[
26. Vic. Ap. Foumban .... Q.P[
27. Vic. Ap. Yaoundé .... C.[
28. Vic. Ap. Doumé .... C.[
29. Vie. Ap. Garoua .... C.[

IV FRENCH EQUITORIAL AFRICA (A.E.F)

Oubangui-Chari

30. Vic. Ap. Bangui .... C.[
31. Pr. Ap. Berbérati .........................O.F.M. [

Mid-Congo

32. Vic. Ap. Brazzaville .... C.[
33. Vic. Ap. Loango .... C.[

Gabon

34. Vic. Ap. Libreville.............................. C.[

Chad

35. Pr. Ap. Fort-Lamy ....

V. SOMALIAN FRENCH COAST

36. Pr. Ap. Djibouti .........................O.F.M.

VI. MADAGASCAR AND LA RÉUNION

Madagascar

37. Vic. Ap. Antsirabé ....
38. Vic. Ap. Diégo-Suarez .... C[
39. Vic. Ap. Fiaranantsoa ....
40. Vic. Ap. Fort-Dauphin ....
41. Vic. Ap. Majunga .... C[
42. Vic. Ap. Miarinarivo ....
43. Vic. Ap. Tamatave .... S.[
44. Vic. Ap. Tananarive ....
45. Pr. Ap. Ambanja .........................O.F.M.
46. Pr. Ap. Morondava ....

Island of la Réunion

47. Diocese de la Réunion ....C[

II. NEW TERRITORIES AND NEW BISHOPS

The Delegate was responsible for identifying where new ecclesiastical territories should be established and for proposing candidates for the new episcopal sees. Secondly, he was to prepare the ground for the setting up of a hierarchy of Ordinaries and for establishing episcopal assemblies. There then remained the third objective: the creation of an indigenous hierarchy. Besides these specific tasks, the Delegate had to ensure that the local churches were in good order, report to the Holy See (Canon 267), and oversee the equitable distribution of grants provided by the Pontifical Missionary Works.

THE CREATION OF NEW ECCLESIASTICAL TERRITORIES[13]

As the local churches grew, it was the Delegate's responsibility to subdivide the territories by creating new vicariates and new apostolic prefectures. In Senegal Archbishop Lefebvre divided his diocese of Dakar to such an extent that its area was reduced from 163,000 square km. to 15,000 square km. In 1953-54, Pierre Messmer, the governor of Mauritania, had suggested to the Vicar Apostolic of Dakar that he re-establish the Apostolic Prefecture of Saint Louis and include Mauritania within its boundaries. Archbishop Lefebvre agreed and added also the northern third of Senegal. Thus, the Prefecture of Saint Louis that had been suspended since 1899 was re-established on January 28, 1955, and given into the care of Monsignor Joseph Landreau, C.S.Sp. Two years later the whole east of the country became the Prefecture of Kaolack under Monsignor Théophile Cadoux, an Issoudun Father.

In Ivory Coast the Vicariate of Abidjan, which had been divided in 1911 and 1940, was divided again in 1951 at the request of the Delegate, and entrusted to Monsignor André Duirat. Later in 1956 Archbishop Lefebvre divided the territory of Daloa, which had itself become a diocese, in order to create the diocese of Gagnoa. Bishop Etrillard, who was bishop of Daloa, was offered the choice of succeeding to the new diocese and thus became its bishop. The Apostolic Delegate's latitude in this matter was meant to soften the blow of such territorial dissection.

Sometimes, the separations were painful since the "new-born" territory might be richer or, on the contrary, poorer in numbers and in resources than its severed "mother." This could cause dissent, and after having heard, although not necessarily accepted, Archbishop Lefebvre's opinion, Rome would come to its own decision. Archbishop Lefebvre also wisely

---

[13] *Annuaire des Missions Catholiques d'Afrique*, Apostolic Delegation of Dakar, 1959; Marziac, *Mgr. Lefebvre, soleil levant*, 123-24; P. Messmer, letter, March 10, 1999; Diary of the Carmel in Sébikotane, Feb. 8, 1952.

THE DIOCESE OF MADAGASCAR (1956)

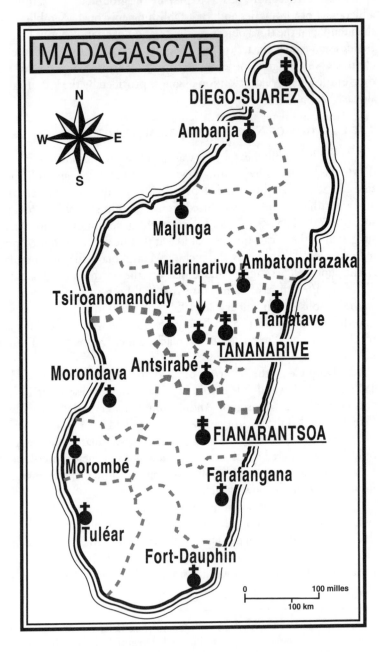

decided on the division of southern Madagascar, where the diocese of Fort-Dauphin gave birth to Farafangana and Tuléar.

APPOINTING BISHOPS

As well as establishing twenty-one new territories, the Apostolic Delegate was also responsible for appointing bishops, vicars apostolic, and apostolic prefects to those territories and elsewhere. Thus, according to Archbishop Lefebvre, he had "to draw up thirty-seven *ternae.*" After possibly consulting with the priests in the area, and hearing the suggestions of local bishops and the opinion of the motherhouse[14] of the congregation to which the candidates belonged, the Delegate would send a list of three names with his own report on them to the Sacred Congregation for the Propagation of the Faith. According to Pierre Messmer, who was several times Governor and then High Commissioner, "Archbishop Lefebvre's criteria were doctrinal rigor and solid virtue."[15]

The Delegate was also careful to see that these standards were observed in choosing seminary professors, determining seminary curricula, and establishing the rules of discipline for the seminarians. How many times had considerations that were inimical to the sanctity of the Church's mission come into play: political intrigues, nepotism, and promotions inspired by the saying *promoveatur ut amoveatur* (promote him to get him out of the way, or boot him upstairs)![16]

Although it was rare, the appointees would sometimes reject their promotion, as happened at Oubangui-Chari in Berbérati. This apostolic prefecture had been vacant since 1951, and Archbishop Lefebvre had it raised to the status of vicariate on March 13, 1952.[17] After making his visit to the new vicariate, the Apostolic Delegate proposed the appointment of Fr. Gabriel Tissot as the new vicar apostolic. This priest was a Capuchin of the Savoy Province that was responsible for Berbérati, and had been in the region since 1947. The selection was approved by the Pope and announced in a letter of April 3, 1952. However, Father Gabriel uttered a *"gran rifiuto"*: he simply refused the appointment. The Apostolic Delegate was obliged to visit the Capuchin monasteries in Savoy looking for new candidates where he was accompanied by Fr. Basil Baud, Father Provincial since 1948.

In the end the Delegate said to himself: "This Father Provincial is not so bad, he could do the job!" The information about him was positive: "a former student of the Catholic University of Lyons, he has remained or-

---

14 Gérard Vieira, *Sous le signe du laïcat, l'Eglise catholique de Guinée, 1925-1958*, II, 477.
15 Marziac, *Mgr. Lefebvre, soleil levant*, 122; Messmer, Letter, March 10, 1999.
16 Archbishop Lefebvre, Letter to Cardinal Tardini, Feb. 25, 1960.
17 *A.A.S.* 43 (1951): 656; 44 (1952): 705.

thodox." His circular letters to fellow priests spoke of "Mary, model of the interior life and of the apostolate, community life, prayer, penance, and charity." On his return to Paris, Archbishop Lefebvre invited the Father Provincial to Rue Lhomond. The Archbishop came to the point forcefully: "Your priest Fr. Gabriel even refuses the post of mission administrator. This is a serious matter before the Church! I only see one solution."

Fr. Basil was all ears.

"The solution is that you, most Reverend Father, accept the post of administrator instead!"

The priest did not even try to point out that he had never been to a mission country...

"I expect a favorable answer straightaway," the Archbishop insisted.

"Oh! *Monseigneur*, you've well and truly tricked me," was the monk's reply.[18] Under Rome's orders, he was sent to Berbérati on January 9, 1953.[19]

However, the Delegate still had one "trick" left to play, and on May 20, 1954, Fr. Basil was appointed Vicar Apostolic of Berbérati. He was consecrated bishop at Annecy on June 24, 1954. He was a good pastor and initiated much building in the diocese. He was also dedicated to his seminary and to his catechists' training school.

The Delegate also had to deal with some sensitive issues. For example, Monsignor Maurice Le Mailloux, the zealous Apostolic Prefect of Kankan in Guinea, was unfortunately a poor administrator, and the Delegate was ordered by the Sacred Congregation to ask him for his resignation. Happily, the Prefect consented with "splendid, supernatural self-denial."[20]

Another difficult case was that of Bishop Graffin, the Vicar Apostolic in Yaoundé, who was subject to hostility from the indigenous clergy or at least from some black priests. However, behind them were the whites— among whom was a Freemasonic administrator—stirring up racism against "white colonialists." While visiting Mvolyé at Pentecost 1949, Archbishop Lefebvre met with the priests. "A deluge of infamous calumnies," noted Bishop Graffin. However, the Delegate did not know what to think, and suggested to Bishop Graffin that he resign. The bishop would have done this willingly, had his colleagues in Cameroon not advised him to stay on. The Delegate reported the matter to Rome, and wrote to the bishop advising him to resign in a year's time but Bishop Graffin did nothing. Finally, a solution was found in March 1955. The bishops of Cameroon who had met at Nkongsamba "decided with the Delegate" that Bishop Graffin and Bishop Bonneau would each ask for an auxiliary.

---

[18] *Alpes-Afrique*, no. 325 (April 1982); Marziac, *Mgr. Lefebvre, soleil levant*, 131.

[19] Through a misunderstanding Pius XII appointed Fr. Gabriel as the first Vicar Apostolic of Berbérati on Jan. 12, 1953. *A.A.S.* 45 (1953): 80.

[20] Vieira, *Sous le signe du laïcat*, 406-408.

Upon his return to Yaoundé, Bishop Graffin sent the *terna* to Archbishop Lefebvre. Thus, Fr. Paul Etoga, an indigenous priest, was consecrated as auxiliary bishop of Yaoundé on November 30, 1955, by Bishop Graffin.[21]

III. SETTING UP THE HIERACHY (1955-1956)

Meanwhile, Pope Pius XII had taken the major decision to establish a hierarchy right across black Africa. This was first implemented in English-speaking Africa[22] where the presence of a Protestant "hierarchy" made it all the more urgent. Then on September 14, 1955, the hierarchy was established in French-speaking Africa and made dependent on the Apostolic Delegation of Dakar. Hitherto the Ordinaries had been attached to the Sacred Congregation for the Propagation of the Faith. Thirty dioceses and eleven archdioceses were established, the latter becoming capitals of ecclesiastical provinces. All the vicars apostolic became residential bishops or archbishops of their former vicariates. The archbishops were attached to Dakar, Bamako, Ougadougou, Conakry, Abidjan, Lomé, Cotonou (formerly the vicariate of Ouidah), Yaoundé, Brazzaville, Bangui, and Tananarive.

The Apostolic Delegate had helped to bring about this decision, and supported Pius XII's plans. In his bull *Dum tantis Ecclesiae*,[23] Pius XII stated that the Delegate's "prayers were answered" according to "his request...for the establishment of a regular hierarchy of local Churches and bishops." Archbishop Lefebvre's own actions had made this decision necessary, since by inviting so many different congregations to work in Dakar and elsewhere, he had rendered the vicariate system obsolete. He was able to explain to the Pope the advantages of setting up a hierarchy: the establishment of an ordinary hierarchy in Africa would mean that the Church was no longer a foreign institution, the native priests could take a proper pride in this work and be more inclined to take their responsibilities seriously, and vocations would hopefully increase. Moreover, it would ease the relations of the Church with the civil authorities since whereas before there was one civil governor but five or six directors of missions having no sole representative, from now on one of them could fill this role: the local archbishop.

The decision of the Holy Father was followed by the consecration of Bishop de Milleville as Archbishop of Conakry, and the consecration of Monsignor Etoga as auxiliary in Yaoundé. Archbishop Lefebvre was present at both ceremonies,[24] the second of which was commonly recognized

[21] Criaud, *La geste des spiritains*, 231-234; *L'Effort Camerounais*, no. 10 (Dec. 1955).
[22] Bull of Apr. 18, 1950, *A.A.S.* 42 (1950): 615.
[23] *General Bulletin*, 664: 242-244; *A.A.S.* 48 (1956): 113-118.

as a step towards implementing Pius XII's plans for the Africanization of the hierarchy.

To speed up this process of indigenization, the Pope ordered the search for native candidates for consecration to be intensified. In order to train such candidates, he founded St. Peter's College in Rome in 1946. Cardinal Eugene Tisserant, the secretary of the Sacred Congregation for the Eastern Church and a member of the Sacred Congregation for the Propagation of the Faith, had dozens of officials studying the dossiers of African and Asian candidates for the episcopacy.[25] The Cardinal begged Pius XII's permission to be allowed to perform the solemn ceremony of Archbishop Lefebvre's enthronement as Archbishop of Dakar on February 19, 1956. After Bishop Guibert had read the papal bull in French, His Eminence rose from the throne and installed Archbishop Lefebvre in his place. The new archbishop then received the obedience of each of his priests, and in his address he explained that the happiness caused by the establishment of the archbishopric of Dakar was the result of the spirit of faith and the devoted work of all the missionaries who had preceded them. The Cardinal, who was president of the Sacred Congregation for Ceremonies, had an imperious and demanding nature that made him the terror of masters of ceremonies. But in the midst of the general confusion in the sanctuary, Archbishop Lefebvre remained calm, smiling gently as was his wont.[26] However, he would later say of the Cardinal: "He gave us a hard time!"

As the one responsible for carrying out the orders of papal bulls, Archbishop Lefebvre could have kept for himself the honor of enthroning archbishops or could even have delegated it. However, the Cardinal was keen to do the majority of the enthronements himself. Nonetheless, the Apostolic Delegate was able to enthrone Bishop Victor Sartre, S.J., at Tananarive and three other bishops on the Grande Ile. He also enthroned his suffragan bishop, Prosper Dodds, C.S.Sp., at Ziguinchor on May 27, after having enthroned his friends Bishop Bonneau at Douala on April 2 and Bishop Fauret at Pointe-Noire on April 6. However, the Cardinal consecrated Bishop Thomas Mongo, auxiliary of Bishop Bonneau.[27] All things considered, the Cardinal said he was "amazed" by what he had seen the Archbishop do in Dakar.[28]

Archbishop Lefebvre had a diocesan-style setup in his archdiocese. He established an episcopal curia run by Father Neilly, O.P., of whom he thought highly. The existing districts became deaneries. Finally the Arch-

[24] Échos, Jan. 1956, 41-41; General Bulletin, 664: 255-256.
[25] Jean Chelini, L'Église sous Pie XII, II, 131.
[26] Horizons Africains, Feb. 1956; Fr. Bussard, Interview in Vevey, Aug. 21, 1997.
[27] Pannier, L'Eglise de Pointe-Noire, 100-101; General Bulletin, 666: 324-325.
[28] Ms. II, 68, 35-36.

Countries of French-Speaking Africa in the Apostolic Delegation of Dakar in 1959

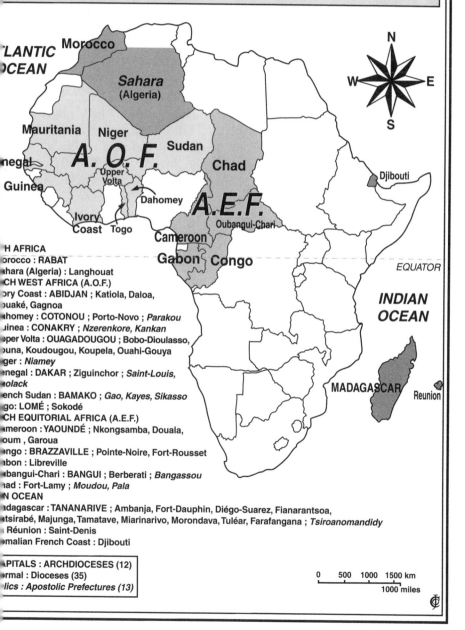

LANTIC OCEAN

Morocco

Sahara (Algeria)

Mauritania   Niger   Sudan

A. O. F.   Chad   Djibouti

negal   Upper Volta

Guinea

Dahomey   A.E.F.

Ivory Coast   Togo   Oubangui-Chari

Cameroon

Gabon   Congo   EQUATOR

INDIAN OCEAN

MADAGASCAR   Reunion

H AFRICA
rocco : RABAT
hara (Algeria) : Langhouat
CH WEST AFRICA (A.O.F.)
ry Coast : ABIDJAN ; Katiola, Daloa,
uaké, Gagnoa
homey : COTONOU ; Porto-Novo ; *Parakou*
inea : CONAKRY ; *Nzerenkore, Kankan*
per Volta : OUAGADOUGOU ; Bobo-Dioulasso,
una, Koudougou, Koupela, Ouahi-Gouya
ger : *Niamey*
negal : DAKAR ; Ziguinchor ; *Saint-Louis,*
olack
ench Sudan : BAMAKO ; *Gao, Kayes, Sikasso*
go: LOMÉ ; Sokodé
CH EQUITORIAL AFRICA (A.E.F.)
meroon : YAOUNDÉ ; Nkongsamba, Douala,
um , Garoua
ngo : BRAZZAVILLE ; Pointe-Noire, Fort-Rousset
bon : Libreville
bangui-Chari : BANGUI ; Berberati ; *Bangassou*
ad : Fort-Lamy ; *Moudou, Pala*
N OCEAN
adagascar : TANANARIVE ; Ambanja, Fort-Dauphin, Diégo-Suarez, Fianarantsoa,
tsirabé, Majunga, Tamatave, Miarinarivo, Morondava, Tuléar, Farafangana ; *Tsiroanomandidy*
Réunion : Saint-Denis
malian French Coast : Djibouti

PITALS : ARCHDIOCESES (12)
rmal : Dioceses (35)
lics : Apostolic Prefectures (13)

0   500   1000   1500 km
1000 miles

bishop again promulgated the "instructions and faculties" granted to his priests according to the Sacred Congregation's ten-year priestly faculties system. This diocesan set-up overlapped the organization of the religious orders, and each male congregation had its own "principal superior" who was responsible for the common and religious life of his congregation in that district.

The establishment of Dakar's archdiocese was made at the same time as the establishment of the ecclesiastical province of Dakar. On it depended the new bishopric of Ziguinchor, the Apostolic Prefecture of Saint-Louis, and from January 21, 1957, the Apostolic Prefecture of Kaolack.

IV. FOUNDER OF BISHOPS' ASSEMBLIES

There was already an embryonic bishops' assembly in Madagascar. Under orders from Pius XII, Archbishop Lefebvre granted it statutes, and created three others—the Bishops' Assembly of French West Africa, the Bishops' Assembly of Cameroon, and the Bishops' Assembly of French Equatorial Africa—on the same model. He would himself chair their meetings biannually.[29] Each assembly had to create a permanent commission of six elected bishops whose president would choose a permanent council staffed by the federal directors of Church projects, although the president would remain responsible for decision-making.[30]

COMMON PROJECTS—DIFFERENCES—UNITY

Common pastoral standards were discussed in the light of Fr. Joseph Greco's 1958 study *Twenty-five years of Pastoral Work in the Missions*[31] commissioned by the Apostolic Delegate. All the bishops were warned against the danger of interreligious initiatives, such as the taking up the defense of "non-denominational education" instead of fighting for Catholic education.[32] In these assemblies they discussed common projects: intervicariate or even regional seminaries, Catholic education, Catholic Action, and the press.

Sometimes Catholic Action was a special bone of contention between the bishops according to their traditional or liberal mentality. In these clashes Archbishop Lefebvre could clearly see a battle between two attitudes of mind. Those with strong personalities tended to have more influence in the discussions and usually "directed manoeuvres."[33] Fortunately,

---

[29] *Fideliter*, no. 48: 28-29; no. 59: 23; *General Bulletin*, 679: 373-374.

[30] Archives, Pontifical Missionary Works, Paris, 742-54-1.

[31] This concerned Madagascar but applied equally to Africa: Lefebvre, *Spiritual Conferences at Ecône*, 65 B, June 9, 1979.

[32] *Ibid.*, 26 B, Feb. 10, 1976.

[33] Archbishop Lefebvre, Interview with Ralph Wiltgen, in Wiltgen, *The Rhine Flows into the Tiber*, 89.

some non-liberal bishops such as Bishop Strebler of Lomé,[34] and even more so Bishop Graffin,[35] expressed the same reservations as the Apostolic Delegate about certain types of apostolate. For example, while Bishop Bonneau eagerly welcomed the Little Sisters of Jesus (founded by Fr. Voillaume), Bishop Graffin did not understand their form of religious life, and found Sister Magdeleine "very neurotic."[36] That was in 1951. This did not stop Archbishop Lefebvre welcoming the help of these sisters in a poor quarter of Dakar in 1958, even though he considered it imprudent for them to live at close quarters with the population.

The Archbishop of Tananarive, Monsignor Sartre, gave a good description of the Delegate's attitude in the course of discussions: "Despite the differences in our ways of looking at 'social issues,' we could exchange views without conflict or hostility." Besides, "Archbishop Lefebvre did not impose his own opinions on the bishops of Madagascar" because the Delegate "respected the opinions of other people" and did not go beyond the limits of his powers. However, he knew how to "underpin his instructions by relying on the authority of the Holy See."[37] In other words, without hiding his own views, he attempted to advance the thinking of the Holy See and put it into practice.

EARLY DANGERS OF COLLEGIALITY

In the instructions given for the foundation of these bishops' assemblies, Archbishop Lefebvre made it clear that they were not meant to have more authority than the bishops since that would have undermined the bishops and hampered their freedom in their own dioceses. On the contrary, they were meant to foster mutual help between bishops in establishing interdiocesan foundations, or co-ordinating Catholic Action. There was no question of establishing those "permanent secretariats" which would later come to have authority over the bishops. In Madagascar (where the bishops already met quite often), Archbishop Lefebvre said that he encountered some difficulties: "The Jesuits who were organizing things had already created various commissions for the press, schools, Catholic Action, *etc.* I reminded them that these should be consultative rather than decision-making commissions. The bishop was to remain master in his own diocese, and was free to accept or reject their suggestions."[38]

Ten years later on February 26, 1960, when replying to Cardinal Tardini's questionnaire in preparation for the coming Council, Archbishop

[34] *Terre d'Afrique Messager,* Nov.-Dec. 1984, 66; Marziac, *Mgr. Lefebvre, soleil levant,* 131.
[35] Antoine Grach, C.S.Sp., "René Graffin missionnaire au Cameroun," in *Revue d'Allex,* no. 791: 18.
[36] Criaud, *La geste des spiritains,* 221, 236.
[37] Bishop Victor Sartre, Letter, Aug. 7, 1997.
[38] *Fideliter,* no. 48: 29; no. 59: 23.

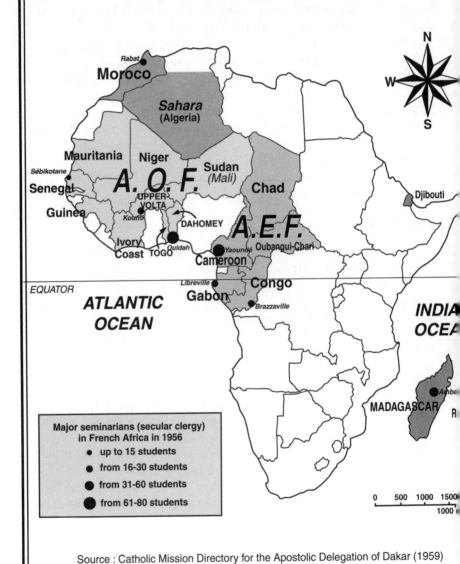

Major Seminaries in the Apostolic Delegation of Dakar in 1956

N
W
S

Rabat

Moroco

Sahara
(Algeria)

Mauritania   **Niger**

Sébikotane

Senegal   *A.O.F.*   **Sudan**
(Mali)

Chad

Djibouti

Guinea   UPPER-
VOLTA

Koumi

DAHOMEY   *A.E.F.*

Ivory   *Ouidah*   Oubangui-Chari
Coast   TOGO

Yaoundé
Cameroon

Libreville   **Congo**

EQUATOR

**ATLANTIC
OCEAN**   **Gabon**

Brazzaville

INDIA
OCEA

Amba

MADAGASCAR   R

**Major seminarians (secular clergy)
in French Africa in 1956**

- up to 15 students
- from 16-30 students
- from 31-60 students
- from 61-80 students

0   500   1000   1500
1000

Source : Catholic Mission Directory for the Apostolic Delegation of Dakar (1959)

Lefebvre made known his rather off-putting experiences with these bishops' assemblies, and asked for an "exact definition of their nature" and a "limitation on their powers and the number of times they should meet"; "the bishops," he said, "become paralyzed by these assemblies." On the other hand, the Archbishop of Dakar wished to encourage "more frequent gatherings of the provincial bishops' assemblies with their archbishop," as frequently happened to the benefit of the ecclesiastical province of Dakar.

Other useful meetings were organized by the Apostolic Delegate: meetings of the bishops from the Holy Ghost Congregation, meetings of archbishops, etc.[39] As one bishop from Ivory Coast remarked, in all these circumstances Archbishop Lefebvre "impressed me with his calm, his serenity, his smile, his patience when listening, and his questions that were always relevant and appropriate. He had a profound sense of the Church and the papacy."[40]

V. THE NEW FACE OF AFRICA

THE PRESTIGE OF THE CHURCH

Archbishop Lefebvre commented on how his mission served the honor of the Church: "When I went for the first time to Madagascar,[41] there was a crowd of 100,000 Malagasies, and the High Commissioner was present with the government and the army. They honored me as the representative of the Holy See. There was a reception at the High Commissioner's.…It was the first time that an envoy of the Pope had stood on Malagasy soil, and the type of welcome I was given served the purposes of the Catholic Church well. In the face of all that, the Protestants were rather over-shadowed."

Once, Archbishop Lefebvre traveled from Dakar to Gao on board the same plane as François Mitterand, Minister for France Overseas. Secular protocol meant that on landing the government minister would disembark before the Pope's Delegate. However, during the flight, the radio announced the downfall of the French government! The Delegate disembarked first and passed through the cordon of honor that now greeted him instead of the humiliated ex-minister. As the Archbishop recognized: "The Church acquired considerable prestige from such things. I was received several times by President René Coty at the Elysée Palace, and twice by General de Gaulle. All that helped with the carrying out of my mission."[42]

---

[39] *General Bulletin*, 679: 383.
[40] Marziac, *Mgr. Lefebvre, soleil levant*, 123.
[41] In Sept. 1949, C.S.Sp. *General Bulletin*, 627: 172-173.
[42] *Fideliter*, no. 59: 24; Conferences to the leaders of the MJCF, Dec. 23, 1984, 23.

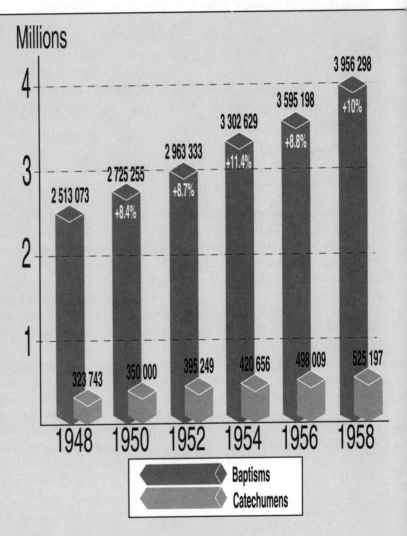

Statistics for Apostolic Delegation of Dakar: Numbers of Faithful (1948-1958)

Millions

| | 2 513 073 | 2 725 255 +8.4% | 2 963 333 +8.7% | 3 302 629 +11.4% | 3 595 198 +8.8% | 3 956 298 +10% |

| 1948 | 1950 | 1952 | 1954 | 1956 | 1958 |

323 743 · 350 000 · 395 249 · 420 656 · 498 009 · 525 197

◆ Baptisms
◆ Catechumens

Source : Catholic Mission Directory for the Apostolic Delegation of Dakar (1959)

ENCOURAGING AND ADVISING

The Apostolic Delegate set out to advise, encourage, and promote the foundation of this or that project, and put to good use the extensive, personal knowledge that he had acquired of each region, race, and custom.[43] Thus in Guinea, he recommended the foundation of student halls of residence at Conakry, and the revival of the congregation of indigenous sisters at Kankan.[44]

Letters of thanks came thick and fast from bishops and project directors: "I'm extremely grateful for your understanding and most discreet help and 'monitoring,'" wrote Bishop Fauret in 1959. Bishop Etrillard thanked him for his "constant support" in the matter of the minor seminary.

Fr. L. Danel, the federal director of Catholic education in Madagascar, wrote to him: "I do not think that the [interdiocesan] center would have been possible had you not helped get the idea off the ground, given encouragement and help, and insisted on its having proper statutes....You have done so much for education throughout all the dioceses, encouraging them to make the effort needed to build schools, and securing considerable help from the religious congregations."

Fr. Ravitariva from the mission of Fihaonana in the diocese of Miarinarivo stated: "We'll never forget all you have done for us: material help, moral support, the smooth running of the diocese, all of which we owe to your care...securing the services of the sisters [and] building the presbytery and the school."

The charitable Delegate not only knew how to encourage and advise the bishops—"Like a father you have guided me in my new responsibilities," wrote Monsignor Alphonse Chantoux, the Apostolic Prefect of Upper Volta—he also knew how to help them with appropriate financial aid.

THE UNWEARYING SEARCH FOR FUNDS

Monsignor Robert Chopard-Lallier, Apostolic Prefect of Pakarou in Dahomey (Benin) wrote to him saying: "To obtain manna from heaven, one has to be a Delegate to whom people listen." The Apostolic Delegate obtained this manna firstly from several organizations such as FIDES (Investment Funds for Social and Economic Development), which became FAC in 1959, but he secured most of it from the PMW, attached to the Sacred Congregation for the Propagation of the Faith. For the major and minor seminaries, he requested money from the St. Peter Apostle Funds; for the catechumens and schools he went to the Society of the Holy Child-

---

43 Canon A. Carette, member of the Lille-Cameroon twinning committee, Letter Aug. 29, 1959.
44 Vieira, *Sous le signe du laïcat*, 383, 384, 490.

hood, which was run by his great friend, Msgr. Adrien Bressolles, aided by Monsignor Richard Ackerman in the United States. For other projects he applied to the Association for the Propagation of the Faith (Rome, Paris, and Lyons). The general board of the PMW was not always very understanding. "When money was involved, people's conduct was not always edifying," said the Archbishop. One had to know how to insist and how to beg.[45] One day, tired out by the difficult negotiations, a clerk in the Vatican finance department threw a bundle of dollars in front of him on the table! The Apostolic Delegate calmly gathered them together, saying, "I'll manage on my own!"

On the other hand, the Paris headquarters of the PMW on Rue Monsieur run by Monsignor Henri Chappoulie, and later by Monsignor René Bertin, greatly supported the Archbishop's work. The same went for the Swiss Missionary Council, thanks to the Archbishop's friendship with Dr. Edgar Schorer from Fribourg, "God's millionaire hobo." The doctor supported many applications but only after medically examining the missionary who was seeking funding![46]

The funds and the additional grants that the Delegate secured for the various vicariate and intervicariate projects in his delegation amounted to a considerable sum.[47] He distributed this money himself according to the finance plan submitted to the PMW. Rather than using the diocesan twinning system—"Lille-Cameroon," "Lyons-Koupéla," "Cologne-Japon"—that tended to reduce the funding from the PMW, Archbishop Lefebvre preferred to contact this parish or that diocese in Europe through the PMW network with a specific African or Malagasy project in mind.[48] This often induced the people to be remarkably generous.

He often reminded the bishops and the project directors of their debt of gratitude. "Don't forget to give your benefactors or the PMW a report on how you have spent their money," he wrote, and he did not hesitate to visit major benefactors in order to thank them.[49] When he traveled to Europe or Canada, the Delegate would also give lectures and go in search of more funds.

---

[45] *Fideliter*, no. 59: 18; Interview with Fr. Edward Black, May 3, 1998; Interview with Fr. Du Chalard, June 28, 1998.

[46] Emile Marmy, *Millionnaire et clochard de Dieu, le Dr. Edgar Schorer* (Fribourg: Éd. S. Canisius, 1989), 34, 83, 86; Fr. Gravrand, ms. II, 79.

[47] For 1958, he asked the Pontifical Missionary Works for 234 million francs in normal funding and 119 million francs of extra funding (in total, $15 million by 2003 standards). This does not include the extra funding secured by the Ordinaries without going through the Delegation.

[48] Archbishop Lefebvre, Letter of March 6, 1958, to the PMW (Paris: Arch. PMW), 742-58-1. The building of the church at Fatick was made possible by the generosity of Catholics from the Fribourg diocese.

[49] He went to Ibach near Schwyz especially to thank Mrs. Elsener, manager of Victorinox (Swiss Army Knife manufacturer).

Statistics for Apostolic Delegation of Dakar: Number of Missionaries (1948-1958)

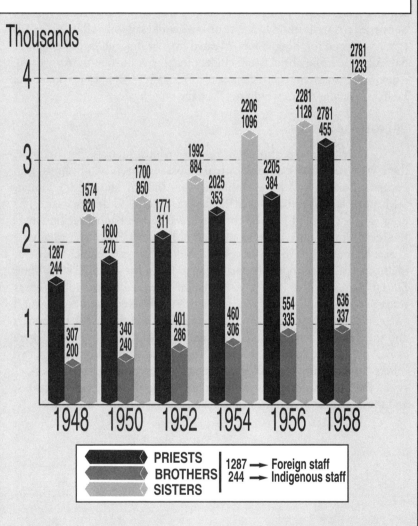

Thousands

	PRIESTS	1287 → Foreign staff
	BROTHERS	244 → Indigenous staff
	SISTERS	

Source : Catholic Mission Directory for the Apostolic Delegation of Dakar (1959)

It cannot be emphasized enough that Catholic French-speaking Africa owed its considerable development in the 1950's to the tenacity, tactical genius, and ceaseless, wide-ranging work of the Apostolic Delegate. All the witnesses agree with this, and were they to be silent the very stones would cry out! Wherever one goes, foundation stones, commemorative plaques, visitors' books, and archives commemorate the hundreds of churches, schools, health clinics, and project centers that were consecrated, blessed, or opened by Archbishop Lefebvre or—we could say—that Pius XII's Delegate canvassed for, begged for, "sweated for," or dragged into the light of day. All these stones, bricks, and cinder blocks gave birth to so many living stones, *i.e.,* so many Christian souls. Yes, after Archbishop Lefebvre, French-speaking Africa would never be the same again.

BRINGER OF PEACE

The Delegate was also able to settle various quarrels. For example, there was "endless discussion" in Ivory Coast between two bishops–Jean Baptiste Boivin, S.M.A., Archbishop of Abidjan, and André Duirat, S.M.A., Bishop of Bouaké–over the best place to build the seminary. The political class favored Bouaké because it was in the Baoulé region where President Houphouët came from. Archbishop Lefebvre came to advise. "Let it be in Anyama in the diocese of Abidjan," he said, emphasizing Abidjan's position as an intellectual center. Later he would say: "Bishop Duirat blamed me for it." However, the matter was settled, and peace was restored.[50] In Madagascar there was a dispute between two bishops and two congregations. The parties to the squabble were the La Salette Fathers and the Lazarists who occupied adjacent territories. Archbishop Lefebvre came[51] and decided to use a third congregation as a buffer between the two others.[52] In Guinea, the Delegate oversaw an exchange of territories between the Apostolic Prefecture of Kankan run by the Holy Ghost Fathers, and the Apostolic Prefecture of Nzerekoré served by the White Fathers.[53]

---

[50] Fr. Marziac, ms. II, 67, 7-15.
[51] In August 1951.
[52] The Parisian Assumptionists of Providence, in Tuléar in 1953; diocese established in 1957 by dividing the diocese of Fort-Dauphin. Cf. Marziac, *Mgr. Lefebvre, soleil levant*, 126-127.
[53] Vieira, *Sous le signe du laïcat*, 355-356; boundaries were changed: July 19, 1951.

VI. New Workers for the Harvest

Increasing the Number of Battalions

What the Archbishop did for Dakar, he also did for numerous territories in his delegation. He brought new congregations into the missionary fields: "In that sense, I was an innovator," he said.[54] This caused a few difficulties with the superior generals of the clerical congregations already there. The White Fathers refused the help of any other male congregation in their territories. The problem was such that Rome had to come to a decision and settled for restricting the interpretation of the "commission" given to priestly societies in mission countries. However, this was an easy decision since Rome was already planning for indigenous bishops[55] to take over these territories in the near future. Following the example of Dakar, many bishops understood the need to open up their dioceses to other male and female apostolic "battalions."

The Apostolic Delegate said:

I was very fortunate to enjoy the exceptional collaboration of Fr. Petit.[56] He was talented and confident. He was an accomplished missionary and excellent speaker. His superiors gave him permission to travel to Europe and Canada. He visited congregations, and was able to convince them to send priests, brothers, or nuns to Africa, Madagascar, and even to La Réunion. His argumentation was simple: if you have missions, you will have vocations. In this way he attracted almost seventy congregations to Africa. He would come to see me regularly and we would draw up a plan: we need sisters here, priests there, teachers for such a diocese, etc. Then he went off on the campaign trail. Certain congregations owe their survival only to their decision to go to mission countries.[57]

The Archbishop also benefited from the indispensable help of Fr. Joseph Bouchaud, C.S.Sp., "the Apostolic Delegation of Dakar's representative in France," who carried out several "delicate missions" for him.[58] However, the Delegate had no qualms about becoming a "priest prospector" himself. At the wheel of his Citroën with the licence plate "CD," he drove throughout Europe. In May and June 1955, he traveled across French-speaking Canada where he visited not only St. Alexander College and the houses of the Holy Ghost Fathers, but also three dioceses, three seminaries, two other colleges, and sixty-two male and female religious

---

[54] Interview with André Cagnon, 1987, 42.
[55] Second interview with Fr. Marziac, 3; Marziac, *Des évêques français*, 68-69.
[56] Fr. Henri Petit, whom Fr. Criaud called "a charismatic man"; he had his "office for religious congregations" in Paris at 94 rue Saint-Roch (*Annuaire des Missions Cath.* [Apostolic Delegation of Dakar, 1959], 13; Criaud, *La geste des spiritains*, 243); Vieira, *Sous le signe du laïcat*, 383.
[57] *Fideliter*, no. 59: 25.
[58] Fr. Joseph Bouchaud, Letter of Aug. 25, 1959.

houses at the astonishing rate of between two and six per day. He persuaded some of them to come to Africa, and convinced others to expand their existing African foundations. The Christian Brothers of Montreal went to Togo and Dahomey, the Brothers of the Sacred Heart from Granby went to Ivory Coast, the Servants of the Holy Heart of Mary from Quebec went to Nkongsamba in Cameroon, and the Sisters of Our Lady of Perpetual Succour from St. Damien de Bellechasse went to Niamey, *etc.* On May 24, while visiting the Trinitarian Fathers in Montreal,[59] he questioned his audience of priests, brothers, seminarians, and school students: "An immense harvest—forty million human beings—is waiting for the divine message. Will enough workers be found to labor in this part of the Lord's vineyard in order to convert all the people? We need many, and we need them now."

The Delegate stopped for a moment and looked at his audience. Everyone looked questioningly at the speaker. The Archbishop said: "This is the reason of my trip to French-speaking Canada: to seek your help in the immense work of evangelization in French Black Africa."

At the end of his conference the Archbishop went to speak to the members of the audience, and asked the school students who had listened to him attentively what they dreamed of doing in the future.[60]

As he visited and revisited all these congregations on both sides of the Atlantic, the Delegate showed tenacity and patience, and followed the motto "Never get worked up, and always try a second time."[61] An anecdote is told of his visit to the major seminary in Madagascar which was under the direction of the Jesuits of Ambanidia. He arrived a little late and after supper students came to chat with the Apostolic Delegate, who enjoyed chatting with them. At that moment, the rector arrived: "*Monseigneur*, it's the grand silence now so…I'm sorry because I know you are leaving early tomorrow." "Oh! No matter, I understand completely," smiled the Delegate. He left with the same smile, and three days later he came back, and this time without warning, at 9 A.M.: "Ah! I think that now I will be able to see your seminarians and professors, and we will have time to speak before the grand silence."[62]

That same year, 1955, the Archbishop created a Directory for the Apostolic Delegation of Dakar. It was published every two years and provided statistics and precise descriptions of the staff and the various projects in each mission. It was a testimony to the considerable development of the missions brought about by the Apostolic Delegate's work. The bishops and

---

[59] Who had already been in Madagascar since 1953.
[60] *Trinitas*, Review of the T.O. and the Archconfraternity of the Most Blessed Trinity in Canada, May-July 1955; *Communicantes*, SSPX review in Canada, no. 62 (Jul. 1997): 48-49.
[61] Savioz, *Essai historique*, III, annexe 3. 4.
[62] Ms. I, 66-67.

those responsible for missionary projects remembered him as the "courageous and smiling Archbishop Lefebvre who worked indefatigably"[63] and recalled his "kindly interest" in them.[64] Archbishop Louis Parisot was the most frank when he paid his "most sincere tribute to the virtues" the Delegate showed in carrying out his responsibilities: he had "honesty, perseverance, and a charming, uncomplicated goodness" and his mission was marked by many "apostolic initiatives."[65]

MONASTIC FOUNDATIONS

One of the Delegate's initiatives would be launched in response to the directive that Pius XII gave him during an audience in April 1950. The Pope said: "We insist that the wish of our venerable predecessor, Pius XI, be fulfilled: let the monastic life take root in the mission countries, and firstly in Africa. Very few Apostolic Vicariates acted on the encyclical *Rerum Ecclesiae*." When he returned to Dakar, the Archbishop wrote a circular letter to the vicars apostolic in his delegation to tell them of the Pope's desire. Then, in July he went to Notre Dame of Aiguebelle to persuade the Father Abbot, Dom Eugène Court, to make a visit to Africa in view of establishing a foundation. The monk arrived in Dakar on January 7, 1951, and the following day visited the oasis of Sébikotane.

Archbishop Lefebvre said: "There is ample space given the nine hundred hectares of land. Carmelites from Angers will move here this year, and a site has already been set aside for my major seminary. However, a monastery could easily be built two or three kilometers on."

"Yes," said the Abbot, "but...we can't spend such a large sum just to acquire the property."

"Oh!" replied the Archbishop, "that's a minor detail."

Finally, the Trappists opened a monastery further to the south in Cameroon where the Delegate considered that "a monastic presence would be more fruitful." At the regional conference for vicars apostolic in mid-February 1954, Archbishop Lefebvre proposed the foundation of a monastery without a parish that would be purely contemplative.[66] The Benedictines of Solesmes would later found their abbey of Keur Moussa at Sébikotane.

---

[63] Raymond de La Moureyre, C.S.Sp., Bishop of Mouila, Gabon, Letter of Sept. 5, 1959.
[64] Bernardin Gantin, Bishop of Cotonou, Letter of Aug. 24, 1959.
[65] Louis Parisot, Archbishop of Cotonou, Ouidah, Letter of Aug. 31, 1959.
[66] Fr. Charbel Gravrand, *Fils de saint Bernard en Afrique* (Beauchesne, 1999), 20-21, 37, 63-64, 79.

VII. AN INDIGENOUS HIERARCHY

One day in 1953, Archbishop Lefebvre came to visit Fr. Bourdelet in Thiès: "Fr. Jules, pack your bags—I want you to go to Rome to further your studies by doing a doctorate in theology and Canon Law." The priest packed his bags. It did not take long. The Archbishop returned just as the man was finally ready: "There's been a change of plan! I have just received orders from Rome that preferably I must send African priests."[67] Thus, St. Peter's College took in two new potential bishops as guests: François-Xavier Dione and Hyacinthe Thiandoum.

Since the beginning of his pontificate, Pius XII had wished for the establishment of an indigenous hierarchy for two reasons in particular found in his writings and allocutions. Firstly, the coming independence of former colonies—and the current Communist threats against missionaries in China[68]—made it essential to have indigenous bishops without whom the local Churches risked finding themselves in serious difficulties. Secondly, the catholicity of the Church and its "unity and supranationality" among the various races and cultures logically demanded an indigenous hierarchy.

Archbishop Lefebvre understood these reasons. Nevertheless, he had been unhappy with a remark that Bishop Costantini had let slip in his presence: "You're wrong if you think that the European bishops are really going to convert Africa. You need African bishops to do that."[69] Such scorn for the work of missionary bishops seemed to him incredible in the Secretary of the Sacred Congregation for the Propagation of the Faith.

The Archbishop feared that Roman idealism made Africa's future uncertain. Would the young African Catholic Church have enough maturity to govern herself? The Delegate had to work to ensure that the Church in Africa grew up much faster. The first African bishop in modern times, Bishop Otunga, auxiliary of Kisumu in Kenya, had been consecrated in Rome on October 29, 1939. The very first Malagasy bishop, Ignazio Ramanosandratana, had been consecrated in the same year for the new vicariate of Miarinarivo. After the war, Archbishop Lefebvre played an essential albeit variable role–as we shall see–in choosing several African bishops. He was "a pioneer"[70] when in 1955 he proposed Fr. Paul Etoga as auxiliary of Yaoundé and Fr. Thomas Mongo as auxiliary of Douala. Later, there was Dieudonné Youkbaré, first bishop of Koupéla in Upper Volta who was consecrated by Cardinal Gerlier in 1956, and then—and he was not the

---

67 Fr. Jules Bourdelet, ms. II, 58, 45-58.
68 The hierarchy was established in China on April 11, 1946, barely three years before Mao Tse-t'ung proclaimed the People's Republic. It had been established in Japan in 1940.
69 Lefebvre, *Petite histoire*, 77-78. This must have been around 1951 or 1952.
70 According to a Jesuit based in Madagascar. Marziac, *Mgr. Lefebvre, soleil levant*, 127.

last—Bernadin Gantin, auxiliary bishop of Cotonou, who was consecrated by Cardinal Tisserant in Rome on February 3, 1957.[71]

However, Archbishop Lefebvre admitted to "intervening from time to time for prudential reasons."[72] Thus, when Bishop Bonneau died, and the priests in Douala suggested that Bishop Mongo, his auxiliary, succeed him, the Delegate passed on this request to Rome but told the priests that he did not agree with them (not that he was opposed to the appointment of an African, but because he thought that a good auxiliary does not necessarily make a good leader). When, in spite of the Delegate's opposition, news of Bishop Mongo's appointment came from Rome, the auxiliary initially refused the post and looked "very unhappy,"[73] although he accepted three weeks later. However, the Delegate's concerns were fortunately eased by the new bishop's wise management and his firm resistance to the secularism of the young Cameroonian government.[74]

VIII. THE APOSTOLIC DELEGATE IN ROME

At least once a year, the Apostolic Delegate saw Pope Pius XII to give him a report and to get fresh orders. Archbishop Lefebvre said: "There was a certain empathy that brought us together. The Pope was always very friendly with me and provided a lot of support and encouragement. He was a true father, very good, very simple, and at the same time very dignified and very noble. He was a man that commanded respect in those who had dealings with him."[75]

FIDEI DONUM

Archbishop Lefebvre answered the questions of Pius XII—who was meticulous and precise in everything—concerning the growth of the faithful, the subdivision of territories, Catholic Action, and the prospects of indigenization. With the use of figures and examples, the Archbishop delicately explained to the Pope the reality of the missions in Africa and Madagascar. The establishment of the hierarchy and the consecration of the first indigenous bishops did not mean that missionary activity was over. The local clergy was growing bit by bit, but could not yet replace the missionaries who were needed more and more. During these meetings with his Delegate, Pius XII listened, absorbed the amazing figures of charitable donations to missions, and admired the growth in the number of religious

---

[71] Chelini, L'église sous Pie XII, II, 130-131.
[72] Fideliter, no. 59: 22.
[73] Note of Fr. J.-B. Coudray, Criaud, La geste des spiritains, 228-229.
[74] Bishop Mongo's letter "Principles for the Country" was very successful: General Bulletin, 688; cf. also General Bulletin 689: 264, on the resignation of Bishop Mongo from the constitutional consultative committee.
[75] Fideliter, no. 59: 18.

foundations in the delegation of Dakar. Between 1955 and 1958, the number of male congregations rose from thirty-two to thirty-nine, and the number of female congregations rose from eighty-two to one hundred thirty.

One can say that it was thanks to the initiatives and suggestions of his Delegate that Pope Pius XII wrote the encyclical *Fidei Donum*.[76] Certain paragraphs in this document directly express the concerns that Archbishop Lefebvre had mentioned to the Sovereign Pontiff:[77] the lack of priests and resources to convert the eighty-five million African animists and protect them against "workers other than those of our Lord," the call to bishops to support recruitment for missionary congregations and to fund missions, the need to "found schools and spread Christian education at all levels" and to create "organizations for social action to help the Christian elite serve civil society," and finally the fear that "the African peoples who, through short-sighted nationalism, have just been deprived of the influence of Europe, and might be led unwittingly into disorder and slavery."[78]

What does not seem to come from the thinking of Archbishop Lefebvre is a principle invoked by Pius XII which "makes each bishop, insofar as he is by divine institution a legitimate successor of the Apostles, jointly responsible for the apostolic mission of the Church." On the other hand, what was less foreign to the Archbishop's thinking was the idea of "making diocesan priests [from developed countries] available to African bishops" for special apostolates or schools "for a limited period." Nonetheless, a definitive commitment to missionary work was for Archbishop Lefebvre a traditionally recognized requirement.[79] Besides, some of the visiting missionaries imbued with fashionable European theories gave the Archbishop considerable trouble.[80]

Archbishop Lefebvre was criticized for bringing to Africa so many congregations who were new to the missions. However, he said, "Pius XII supported me." The influence of the Delegate on the Pope proves to have been considerable, as much in giving the Pope a realistic view of the difficulties of converting Africa, as in making him recognize the continuing, central importance of the missions. The best proof of this beneficial influence and of the Sovereign Pontiff's gratitude is the remark that Pius XII made to Monsignor Veuillot, an attaché of the Secretariat of State and the

---

[76] Encyclical of April 21, 1957, *A.A.S.* 49 (1957): 226-248; *Documentation Catholique*, 1251: 581-593.

[77] Marziac, *Mgr. Lefebvre, soleil levant*, 128; *Fideliter*, no. 59: 11.

[78] Cf. Pius XII had already remarked on this in his 1955 Christmas message.

[79] Cf. Archbishop Lefebvre, *Projet de restauration de l'œuvre du P. Claude Poullart des Places*, Jan. 26, 1968. Speaking of the "desire of a number of secular priests to dedicate themselves to the missions," the Archbishop said this "desire was already partly fulfilled following the encyclical *Fidei Donum*."

[80] Fr. Bussard, ms. II, 35-38.

Pope's "scribe" while writing *Fidei Donum*. "Archbishop Lefebvre is certainly the most efficient and the most qualified of the Apostolic Delegates."[81] This was why the Roman pontiff kept him on as Apostolic Delegate beyond the end of his statutory six year mandate.

KNOWLEDGE OF THE ROMAN CURIA

The Delegate also had to give a report to the Roman dicasteries, and firstly to the Sacred Congregation for the Propagation of the Faith. He rarely saw the Cardinal Prefect, but he regularly met with the secretary, Archbishop Pietro Sigismondi, who was unfortunately overworked and hardly had time to talk with delegates. Why did he not secure the services of under-secretaries to meet with the seminarians and nuns who occupied much of his time? Then the delegates could have been received methodically and at greater length when some question needed to be studied. The most urgent matters were not really looked at properly, and it was those that were important to Archbishop Lefebvre: major seminaries, universities, and organizations for training elites. Moreover, the finance secretary categorically refused to hear talk of such precise projects, and thus Africa wanted for a Catholic, intellectual elite that was truly educated and firm in its convictions.[82] This incompetence annoyed the Delegate because of what was at stake. Sometimes he deplored the snail's pace of Roman bureaucracy and longed to get things done more quickly.[83]

At the Secretariat of State where he went in his diplomatic capacity, Archbishop Lefebvre got to know the two substitutes and noticed a contrast between them. In Domenico Tardini, he saw a man of faith, for whom the service of our Lord was the most important thing. Tardini was firm, and was not afraid to fight for or state the truth. On the other hand, in Gianbattista Montini he perceived a man who was slippery and vague, and who was also afraid of conflict and difficulties. Certainly, Montini received the Delegate politely, but he showed no liking for his ideas. Once, Montini spoke to him about "Réarmement Moral," an organization founded by the Freemasons whose center in Vevey, Switzerland, welcomed African visitors in an atmosphere of universal brotherhood. The Africans said: "It's marvelous! At Caux all religions get on, while in Africa the missionaries are always warning about Protestants, atheists, and Islam."

"We can't let such ideas spread without doing something," Archbishop Lefebvre suggested.

---

[81] Savioz, *Essai historique*, I, 17; III, annexe 3.4; Fr. Henri-Louis Valentin, O.S.B., ms. III, 44.

[82] Archbishop Lefebvre, reply to Cardinal Tardini, Feb. 26, 1960.

[83] Marziac, *Mgr. Lefebvre, soleil levant*, 127; Letter from Dakar, Aug. 27, 1957; Arch. PMW, Paris, 8240-57-7.

"Oh no!" Archbishop Montini replied, "We cannot always be making condemnation after condemnation after condemnation! The Church will look like a wicked step-mother."[84]

Fortunately, other prelates in the Curia were completely devoted to the reign of Jesus Christ. Cardinal Ottaviani, Secretary of the Holy Office, was dedicated to the Church. Ildebrando Antoniutti, Apostolic Nuncio in Canada and Spain (later a Cardinal), and many others "were deeply humble men primarily concerned with the honor of the Church and the defense of our Lord's rights. That's what they lived for."[85]

IX. LEAVING THE DELEGATION

The Apostolic Delegate of Dakar also worked in that same spirit. Without being a career man, and without looking for it, he had become "one of the most important figures in the Church."[86] In Africa "he dutifully carried out his responsibilities by obedience, keeping his own thoughts to himself and representing publicly only the thinking of the Holy See."[87]

Gérard Dubois-Burthe recalled that Archbishop Lefebvre had "a level of intelligence way above most clergy." He was a "keen observer of the political scene." The bishop was well acquainted with the counter-revolutionary political thought then being explored by Léon de Poncins, Jacques Ploncard d'Assac, and Jean Madiran whose review *Itinéraires* he regularly read in Dakar. In spite of being a Freemason, Bernard Cornut-Gentille, Governor General of French West Africa, recognized the Archbishop's qualities: "Archbishop Lefebvre is the most intelligent man I have met in Africa. Moreover, when he comes to see me, I'm careful about what I say to him, and I listen very closely to what he wants to tell me."[88]

Had Pius XII reigned longer, such a man would have been made a cardinal. However, appointing cardinals was a "cross" for Pius XII who with his sensitive and impressionable nature always feared allowing himself to be influenced. Thus, in a twenty year reign, he only held two consistories for the creation of cardinals, and the last of those was in 1953.[89] However, in summer 1956, *La Voix du Nord* announced that "Archbishop Lefebvre, Archbishop of Dakar, could be appointed cardinal at the next

---

[84] Lefebvre, *Spiritual Conferences at Ecône*, 33 B, Aug. 20, 1976 ; 55 B, Jan. 17, 1978 ; 97 A, Jan. 11, 1983; *Fideliter*, no. 59: 18 ; Marziac, *Des évêques français contre Mgr. Lefebvre*, 98. The "Réarmement Moral" would be finally denounced by Rome.

[85] Lefebvre, *Spiritual Conferences at Ecône*, 55 B; *General Bulletin*, 710: 548-550: said in praise of Cardinal Valerio Valeri.

[86] Fr. Vincent Cosmao, O.P., *Courrier de Rome*, no. 175: 12.

[87] Fr. Jean Watine, S.J., Letter of May 21, 1998.

[88] G. Dubois-Burthe, interview with M. de Penfentenyo, July 1998.

[89] Cardinal Tardini, conference given on October 20, 1959, *Documentation Catholique*, 1328 (1960): 625-628; German version: *Pius XII als Oberhirte, Priester und Mensch* (Freiburg: Herder, 1961), 63, 146; Chelini, *L'église sous Pie XII*, II, 38-41; 519-523.

consistory." This rumor had been created...by the Archbishop's aunt, Marguerite Lemaire-Lefebvre, who wanted him to be named cardinal at any price, and who approached Rome concerning the matter. She could not have done more to torpedo his chances![90] Indeed, the matter was never raised at all, and Pius XII died on October 9, 1958, without having been able to boost a dying Sacred College with a few faithful servants of Christ the King.

Besides, prior to this, Archbishop Lefebvre "had felt a growing opposition to the principles he defended," even in Rome. He was not one of the cardinals created by John XXIII at his first consistory on December 15, 1958. When he was still Apostolic Nuncio in Paris, Angelo Roncalli often invited the Apostolic Delegate to lunch, and on more than one occasion he told the Archbishop he did not believe diocesan bishops should also be Apostolic Delegates with diplomatic responsibilities. Moreover, he once reproached him for having praised Fr. Le Floch during a speech after his consecration. It was doubtless Cardinal Liénart who had told him about the Archbishop's remarks. "Certainly" said Archbishop Lefebvre, "Pope John XXIII had much less esteem for me than Pope Pius XII."[91]

Knowing the new Pope's mind, the Delegate thought it right after the conclave to inform the Roman Curia of his desire to resign from one of his two posts. John XXIII sought to learn which of the two he preferred.[92] The Archbishop answered that since he had not appointed himself, it was not his place to choose: the decision was Rome's. A letter containing the decision arrived on July 22, 1959, signed by Cardinal Agagianian, Prefect of the Sacred Congregation for the Propagation of the Faith. "In view of the preference expressed by Your Excellency" to remain Archbishop of Dakar....The gentle, diplomatic sleight of hand could not hide the truth: they no longer wanted him to be Apostolic Delegate. In letters he wrote to his brother Joseph and Fr. Bussard after receiving this news, he could not hide his feelings about the decision, but calmly concluded: "Good, now I am bishop of Dakar. That's the end of it."

Bishop Jean-Baptiste Maury, who was appointed Archbishop Lefebvre's successor as Apostolic Delegate of Dakar, was at that moment coadjutor of Bishop Théas in Lourdes and was handling the crisis caused by the financial difficulties of the Marian sanctuary. His new appointment in Africa came as a relief. Like his predecessor, he was not a career diplomat, but he had chaired the French board of the PMW at Lyons. Therefore, Archbishop Lefebvre knew him, and warmly welcomed him to Dakar on October 15, 1959, when he also presided at the new delegate's inauguration

---

[90] Joseph Lefebvre, ms. I, 43,8-21.

[91] *Fideliter*, no. 59: 20, 21.

[92] Testimony of Jean Letourneur, C.S.Sp., passed on by Monsignor Bressolles, Letter to Archbishop Lefebvre, summer 1959.

ceremony. Bishop Maury arrived at a difficult time, and tried in vain to prevent Sekou Touré nationalizing Guinea's Catholic schools.

Later, the Delegation became "the Apostolic Delegation of West Africa" and included Gambia, Sierra Leone, and Ghana. In 1961 it became an inter-nunciature, and in 1966 it became a nunciature under the direction of Monsignor Giovanni Benelli, pro-nuncio of Dakar, who was also Apostolic Delegate for West Africa. In recognition of Archbishop Lefebvre's "effective ministry" as Apostolic Delegate of Dakar, John XXIII made him an Assistant to the Pontifical Throne. The Archbishop of Dakar also remained president of the Assembly of West African Archbishops. Their first meeting was chaired by Bishop Maury and established six permanent episcopal commissions. Archbishop Lefebvre became president of the commission dealing with the press, radio, and cinema.

CHAPTER 10

AFRICAN SKIRMISHES

From that moment on, Archbishop Lefebvre gave all his time to the diocese of Dakar, and started by "getting reacquainted with people and even with things."[1] He no longer needed an auxiliary bishop, but he retained the services of Bishop Guibert until November 7, 1960, when the Holy See appointed him as bishop of Saint-Denis in La Réunion.[2] During his final two years as Archbishop of Dakar (from the end of 1959 to the beginning of 1962), debate concerning Senegal's independence was widespread.

I. INCULTURATION AND ECUMENISM

LITURGY AND INCULTURATION

In his 1956 foreword to the collectively written *Des prêtres noirs s'interrogent*,[3] Archbishop Lefebvre appeared in favor of some Africanization of the liturgy. He admitted that there was "no obligation to stick strictly to melodies from Europe" and that there was "work to be done with all languages and indigenous melodies."[4] He recognized the practice of "religious dance" during open-air celebrations and processions, although not in the liturgical processions. He suggested that indigenous artists should be commissioned to make paintings and sculptures for churches. He called for an "investigation" into more or less fetishist or superstitious ceremonies attached to the African lifestyle, stating that "there is no law against studying the possibility of adopting ceremonial customs that could be Christianized, especially for funerals and weddings. The ritual could be expanded to include blessings, especially for African traditions and customs."

This wish for limited liturgical inculturation, dictated by and subject to the authority of the Church, corresponded to Pius XII's own desires.[5] Soon it would be overtaken by more radical demands such as those ex-

---

[1] Circular letter "On the Apostolate," 1960, *Lettres pastorales et écrits*, 129.
[2] To replace Msgr. François Cléret de Langavant, *General Bulletin* 694: 431.
[3] Paris: Éd. du Cerf, 1956.
[4] To those seminarians who were attracted to "creativity," he said: "Well, give me some suggestions!" However, they could make no suggestions as regards new chants.
[5] Allocution to the Assisi Congress, Sept. 22, 1956, quoted by Archbishop Lefebvre, Circular Letter 53 (1956), 9. Pius XII spoke of the "liturgy of the present looking to the past to create something new." *Les enseignements pontificaux: La Liturgie*, ed. Monks of Solesmes (Desclée), 807, 817, 822.

pressed by the Third International Congress of the Pontifical Institute for Sacred Music held in Rome in July 1957. The Congress wanted to "promote indigenous liturgical music"[6] and thus opened the doors of the churches to tom-toms and balafons. The Benedictines of Keur Moussa made use of these instruments instead of preserving Gregorian chant.[7] But even when instruments are not used, one must ensure that the rhythms of the music do not induce people to clap their hands and bob their heads,[8] since this is not fitting in church. Archbishop Lefebvre rightly asked that the "Negro spiritual" style be avoided.

Moreover, even though he was opposed to any unconventional conduct during the rites,[9] he was always open to some liturgical innovation, provided that it was approved by higher authorities. In 1957, he promoted lay "liturgy teams" in order to "bring more to life the participation of the faithful in the Holy Sacrifice," and also permitted evening Masses.[10] In 1960 he adopted the *Directoire pour la pastorale de la messe à l'usage des dioceses de France* (Pastoral Guide to the Mass for the Dioceses of France) which promoted "active community participation by the faithful," the slogan for liturgical reform being prepared by the CNPL in Paris and Annibale Bugnini in Rome. Without as yet appreciating the ambiguity of this principle, the Archbishop was conscious of some of the conclusions that could be drawn from it, and he asked that "care be taken to ensure certain periods of silence during the Mass."[11]

What is admirable here is the Archbishop's prudence which, albeit principled, was not blighted by prejudice. His pastoral sense was inventive, but he was careful to remain subject to higher authorities.

AN INTERRELIGIOUS CEREMONY IN DAKAR

One day the Archbishop had a disagreement with his vicar general. It was after Independence, and while the Archbishop was away in Nouakchott an airplane attempting to land at Yoff airport overturned and ended up in the water. There were 160 victims of various religions, but their bodies were in such a state that Catholics could not be distinguished from Muslims. Air France's chief executive was a practicing Catholic and came to see Fr. Bussard. The vicar general gave the following account of their conversation and its consequences:

---

6   *General Bulletin*, 675: 198 (agency *Fides*, July 20, 1957).
7   *Fideliter*, no. 59: 25.
8   Like the hymn to the Virgin Mary, in the musical style of the Pahouins of Southern Cameroon, intoned on Aug. 8, 1954, in Yaoundé's stadium. Criaud, *La geste des spiritains*, 237-238.
9   Ms. I, 19, 52-53.
10   Circular Letter 57 (1957), 4.
11   Circular Letter, May 20, 1960, 13.

"Couldn't you do a joint ceremony?" said the Chief Executive. "Not all the religions at the same time," I replied. "I do see one solution. The ceremony could take place in the courtyard of the bishop's residence, the three religions could do their ceremonies one after the other, and I'll ask the Apostolic Nuncio to come and give the absolution."

Bishop Maury consented on the condition that he be the first to conduct the ceremony, and that he not assist at the ceremonies of the other religions. The whole government was there, and when the Nuncio intoned the *Libera me* all the Catholics joined in singing heartily. Then the Protestant pastor gave a dull address. As for the marabout, he did not want to appear. I had to ask Mamadou Dia to make him come, "otherwise," I said, "people will believe that we didn't want him to take part, while the opposite is true." The marabout came in the end and read from the Koran, and that was the end of the ceremony.

The Catholics said, "Wow! We were really able to show the others what it's all about! They were pitiful!"

The following day Archbishop Lefebvre returned, and I went to fetch him from the airport.

"I heard on the radio," said the Archbishop, "that there was a ceremony in the cathedral grounds. Did you give your permission for that?"

"Yes."

"But it's *communicatio in sacris!*"

"No, *Monseigneur.* The expression is exact but does not apply to the ceremony. The Catholic part was separate. And, well, the Apostolic Nuncio..."

"Oh, yes!" he replied, "that's nothing to go by!" He was kind with everybody but sometimes he could be a little sharp like that.

"*Monseigneur*, there was no *communicatio in sacris.* It was a triumph for the Catholics; you can ask anybody."

Then Archbishop Lefebvre spoke to his secretary who was there and who was very strict on such matters, "What do you think, Fr. Duguy?"

"No, *Monseigneur*, Fr. Bussard did the right thing."

"Not you as well!" replied the Archbishop.

That was the end of it, and the matter was never raised again. I said to him, "*Monseigneur*, if you think I did the wrong thing, you know, I'll resign straightaway."

He said nothing more. However, I think he didn't approve.[12]

Certainly Archbishop Lefebvre did not approve and could not approve: the juxtaposition of these three religious rites, even one after the other, smacked of relativism and indifferentism. One could not compromise principles by allowing an ambiguous fraternization that amounted to casting doubt on the only true religion. On this matter, Archbishop Lefebvre would never budge an inch: he said "no" to Assisi in 1986, as he did to Yoff in 1960. However, he was not about to begin discussing the application of this principle: it was so clear him, and he was disconcerted at

---

12 Fr. Bussard, ms. I, 12-13.

seeing his most reliable collaborators waver. The expression *"communicatio in sacris"* had sprung to mind because in his indignation his intuitive faith could find no stronger terms to denounce such a debasement of Christ and His Church.

II. ISLAM

THE CROSS AND THE CRESCENT

Ever since becoming Archbishop in Dakar, Archbishop Lefebvre had been careful not to offend the Muslims, and he frequently met the leading marabouts to whom he showed a friendly politeness. During his address in the cathedral when he was made Apostolic Delegate, he said in the presence of the Muslim guests that there was "a fundamental link that brought Christians and Muslims together: belief in God."[13] In 1953 he was happy to see "the increasing number of contacts between Christians and young Muslims" made possible through the cultural centers. "It is to be hoped that a more direct apostolate can be relaunched among the Muslim youth who hardly practice their religion and surely wonder about the Faith."[14] Besides, he said, "secularization has had catastrophic effects in Africa: delinquent children, theft, *etc.*"[15] The youths, who were more or less freed from Islamic law and also ignorant of Christ's law, were certainly involved in all kinds of corruption. In 1956 it seemed to the Archbishop that "the blows that are shaking Islam—we shall come to them—are bringing down the social barriers that imprison the masses and stop them from turning to the Catholic Church." "Already" he added, "many Muslims come to the study circles to find out about the teachings of the Church and the Popes. The elite are turning their eyes towards the Church."[16]

The Archbishop's hopes were accompanied by a realistic evaluation of Islam's influence on morality and the Catholic Faith in Black Africa: "Let us reread the letter in which St. Pius V, the conqueror of Lepanto, asks Philip II, King of Spain, to act decisively against Islam in an effort to stop the corruption and immorality that it spreads in Catholic areas."[17] The Archbishop also spoke of "the frightening immorality" in Senegal. He condemned the "constant divorces, the traffic in women, and open prostitution, which are essentially the work of the Muslims."[18] In a letter to the

---

[13] *Horizons Africains*, Jan. 1949, 11. Archbishop Lefebvre does not say "faith in God."
[14] Conference of Archbishop Lefebvre at Santa Chiara, Nov. 20, 1953. *Échos*, Jan. 1954, 24.
[15] Conference of Msgr. Lefebvre. at Santa Chiara, *Échos*, July 1955, 31.
[16] Conference at Santa Chiara, Nov. 19, 1956, *Échos*, Jan. 1957, 33-34.
[17] Cf. Msgr. Bressolles, "L'Islam et l'Afrique noire," *Revue des Travaux de l'Académie des Sciences Morale et Politique*, 110th Year, 4th Series, 1957, 1st trimester, lib. Siren.
[18] *Fideliter*, no. 59: 29-30.

faithful in 1954 Archbishop Lefebvre denounced the continuing use of slavery: "People who think Africa has been liberated know nothing about it. Every missionary who has crossed the Sahara or traveled in the desert regions has quickly seen the slaves and masters in the nomadic tribes who wander about these vast lands. Sometimes one can tell from something in their face, or else in the jobs that only slaves do."[19]

As for the conversion of the Muslims, Archbishop Lefebvre knew from experience that it was unlikely among the young since they were so dependent on their families: "If they are unfortunate enough to convert, they risk ill-treatment or even imprisonment."[20] The social pressure of Islam was like a vice that kept souls in error.[21] In 1900, Monsignor Roy wrote: "It is only some Europeans that are under the illusion that Islam can be a first step for pagans on the road to Christianity. Islam is not a stepping stone to stand on, it is a wall that stands in one's way."[22]

However, according to the Archbishop of Dakar, conversion is possible in some intellectual circles that are freed from the domination of socio-religious customs: "Some Senegalese, some politicians or high-ranking officials, have thus converted." On the other hand, the tribal chiefs who are "staunch polygamists rarely convert to Catholicism, for they would have to abandon their wives. They find it difficult to renounce this presumptuous prerogative which is a kind of totalitarianism[23] practiced even by minor village leaders." In 1965, some harkis[24] who had taken refuge in France and no longer found themselves under the domination of their milieu, wanted to convert. Archbishop Lefebvre wrote to Fr. Maurice Avril: "I pray with all my heart for the success of your apostolate so you might prove that the Muslims are also called to partake of the Body and Blood of our Lord."[25]

In 1987 he wrote: "If the Western nations who were responsible for educating the people of Africa had not betrayed their mission,[26] and if the Church had not gone back on everything she stood for, today instead of seeing the worrying progression of Islam, most of Africa would today be Catholic."[27]

---

[19] Letter quoted in *Trinitas*, May-July 1954; *Communicantes*, Review of the SSPX in Canada, no. 62 (July 1997): 50. Cf. *Vigilance Soudan*, no. 67 (May 1998): 4, denouncing "more than a thousand children kept in slavery by the Mujahedeen militia."

[20] *Fideliter*, no. 59:29-30.

[21] Cf. Lefebvre, *Retreats preached at Écône*, Apr. 3, 1977.

[22] *Dictionnaire de théologie catholique*, I, col. 535 (s.v. *Afrique*).

[23] *Fideliter*, no. 59, 29-30.

[24] [The *harkis* were Algerian nationals who fought on the side of the French during the Algerian war for independence (1954-1962). Trans.]

[25] Letter of July 7, 1965, in Fr. Maurice Avril, *La XII⁰ croisade* (Salérans, 1990), 84.

[26] Liberal and Freemasonic governments forbade the missionaries to convert Muslims. In the Church, Massignon was opposed to their conversion.

ISLAM UNDER THE INFLUENCE OF COMMUNISM

Speaking at the French Seminary in Rome in 1956, Archbishop Lefebvre revealed the antagonism in African Islam between the traditionalists and reformers, purists and Pan-Arabs, as fomented by Cairo. When they went home, the black students of El-Azhar University were "preaching in the mosques about waging war on the Westerners and the missionaries." The Archbishop explained that this Pan-Arabism favored Communism: "The Addis-Ababa Congress, held in a city that the Marxists are leading into anarchy, came to the conclusion that 'One must "Islamicize" to "communize."'" As Cardinal Tisserant said: 'Those who think Islam is a rampart against Communism are totally mistaken.'"[28] Did not the Senegalese Muslim Mamadou Dia, the future head of government, declare in 1957 that Senghor's dream of a federation of French-speaking African countries would "only be worthwhile" "if it brought together the teachings of Marx and Lenin"?[29]

At the request of a writer from the Canadian daily *Le Devoir*, Archbishop Lefebvre wrote an article on November 2, 1959, entitled "Will the Christian states surrender Black Africa to the Communist star?" In the piece he stated: "The countries in which there is a Muslim majority are separating themselves as quickly as possible from the West, and using Communist methods…fanaticism, collectivism, slavery of families": these countries were especially open to Islamic customs. Thus, said the Archbishop, Guinea and Sudan (later Mali) were already internally organized "according to methods inspired by an essentially Marxist mentality." He raised this specter: "Senegalese wisdom will perhaps carry the day. Otherwise, in a short while Communism will rule from Dakar to Gao." In other words, would the Catholic Senghor be able to stand up to the Marxist Modibo Keita? For since January, the two independent countries of Senegal and Sudan had been joined together in "The Mali Federation," and while the Sudanese Modibo Keita was the head of the government, Senghor was only president of the federal assembly.

The article, which was reprinted on the December 18, 1959, by *La France catholique*, reached Senegal. The head of the government, Mamadou Dia, who had just had an audience with John XXIII, was overcome by "an unbelievable rage."[30] Modibo Keita wrote a virulent article to denounce the "anti-Islamic" attitude of the Archbishop. Archbishop Lefeb-

[27] *Fideliter*, no. 59: 31.
[28] *Échos*, Jan. 1957 (conference given on Nov. 19, 1956).
[29] International Congress of African Political Parties, Dakar, Jan. 11-13, 1957. Paul Auphan, *Histoire de la décolonisation* (Paris: France-Empire, 1975), 160.
[30] Fr. Louis Carron, ms. I, 61, 6-14; Archbishop Lefebvre had been happy about the prime minister's audience with the Pope: *Horizons Africains* no. 114 (Nov. 1959). Fr. Gravrand, ms. III, 10, 48-65.

vre was immediately taken to task on the radio by the Minister for Information, Lamine Diakhaté: "We did not know that Archbishop Lefebvre harbored such ideas about Islam."

The Archbishop was very embarrassed. Obviously, his remarks on Islam were not meant for a Senegalese audience, and he had not foreseen that his article would be distributed in Senegal just one week after a visit from General de Gaulle, who in principle had agreed to the independence of the "Mali Federation." Through his auxiliary, Archbishop Lefebvre arranged a secret midnight meeting with the great marabout Seydou Nourou Tall to assure him that he had not meant to attack Senegalese Islam.[31] The French ambassador, Boislambert, asked the Archbishop to come and see him "to explain these objectionable assertions that are at the very least risky and inappropriate."[32] Having first resolved to keep his silence on the subject, Archbishop Lefebvre attempted to explain himself in *Horizons Africains* in March 1960.

The split between Senegal and Mali on August 28, 1968, came as a relief to the Archbishop of Dakar. Senegal would become neither an Islamic republic nor a popular democracy.

III. INDEPENDENCE

DECOLONIZATION

In September 1949 representatives from many missionary congregations working in Africa gathered together in Paris at a meeting chaired by the Apostolic Delegate, Archbishop Lefebvre, and by Monsignor Chappoulie, bishop of Angers and president of the PMW. The decision was taken to establish a chaplaincy for the Catholic students from Overseas France who were studying in France. At Archbishop Lefebvre's request, this work was entrusted to the young Fr. Joseph Michel, C.S.Sp., who distinguished himself in Congo-Loango by his courage in trying to "stem the flow of socialist propaganda among the Catholics."[33] Fr. Michel was the chaplain from 1950 to 1958. In his bimonthly newsletter *Tam-Tam*, the priest became a bold advocate of independence in order to get black students interested. He gave a lecture on February 23, 1954, at a *Pax Christi* meeting in Paris in which he spoke of the "duty of decolonization." The very aim of colonization was decolonization, he said. The idea was bold but correct. Archbishop Lefebvre approved[34] and maintained his support for the chaplaincy and the chaplain.

---

[31] Ms. I, 24, 33-42.
[32] Claude Hettier de Boislambert, *Les Fers de l'espoir* (Plon, 1978), 540-541.
[33] Cf. Guy Pannier, *L'Eglise de Pointe-Noire*, 65-66, 69.
[34] "Joseph Michel and the Duty to Decolonize," *Mémoire Spiritaine*, no. 4: 132-133; Fr. Dominique Desobry, O.P., Letter to Archbishop Lefebvre, Sept. 6, 1959.

Nonetheless, it must be said that the lecture made too much of an abstraction from the reality of Africa, especially concerning the conversion of the people to Christ. The speaker said nothing about the predictably damaging effects of decolonization when it chose to ignore such circumstances. Moreover, in the middle of the lecture Monsignor Bressolles, president of the Society of the Holy Childhood, conspicuously left the room. François Charles-Roux, former French ambassador to the Vatican, tried afterwards to refute Fr. Michel, but the debate was already based on a false premise, and could only go from bad to worse.

Archbishop Lefebvre was not opposed to possible decolonization. The real question for him was how it would come about. What form would these future nascent states assume, since in spite of their Catholic faith there were many ethnic divisions? Would it not be condemning them to chaos to implement the European democratic principles of secularism and egalitarianism in their countries?

TOWARDS INDEPENDENCE

The conference in Brazzaville that met from January 30 to February 8, 1944, under General de Gaulle was officially opposed to any idea of independence, although it had recognized that in future the French African colonies would "move step by step towards...having a separate political identity." The loss of Indochina (1954), the rebellions in Algeria (starting on November 1, 1954) and Cameroon (from May 1955), and the independence granted to Morocco and Tunisia (March 2 and 20, 1956) persuaded the French government to establish internal autonomy for its territories in Black Africa. The "framework law"[35] proposed by Gaston Deferre and voted for on June 23, 1956, ruled that the governor in each territory should share his powers with a government council whose members were to be elected from a territorial assembly formed by popular suffrage.[36]

In Senegal, Senghor was elected president of this council while the vice president, the Muslim Mamadou Dia, effectively became the head of government.[37] In May 1957 the decree implementing the "framework law" established a quasi-legislative assembly in Senegal as elsewhere.

The military strike on May 13, 1958, in Algiers in support of French Algeria worried the political classes of Black Africa. Was this not a return

---

[35] [A "*loi cadre*" is a general act of legislation outlining the general principles of some reform. Trans.]

[36] Biarnès, *Les Français en Afrique Noire*, 286, 339-341; Delcourt, *Histoire religieuse du Sénégal*, 101. Consultation was carried out through motions submitted to all the members of a "collège unique" *i.e.,* one which made no distinctions regarding its members' origins, race, or religion. This was egalitarianism crushing natural hierarchies and minorities.

[37] Sorel, *Léopold Sédar Senghor*, 125.

to "armed colonialism"? Archbishop Lefebvre told the seminarians at Santa Chiara[38] that the Africans found General de Gaulle reassuring, but de Gaulle, who was carried to power by the enemies of independence, was now determined to rid France of "the expense of her colonies." Using the notion of "*communauté*" (community), he was determined to define the internal autonomy of African countries and their external union to France in the terms of the Constitution of the Fifth Republic. Consequently, he came to Africa and used his prestige to ask the people to vote "Yes" in the coming referendum.

However, at Conakry on August 25, the Guinean leader Sekou Touré delivered an aggressive speech demanding immediate independence. It signaled a breakdown in relations. De Gaulle, who felt threatened, left the following day saying, "Farewell, Guinea!" News of the clash in Conakry spread like wildfire, and on August 26 in the Place Protêt in Dakar, a few protesters paid by French Communists yelled slogans and brandished placards that read "Independence Now." Looking at the placard carriers, de Gaulle himself yelled, "If they want independence, they can vote for it on September 28..." The people of Dakar were surprised. Immediate independence was not what they wanted. If this promise quietened the protesters, it was a cause of concern to the Minister for France Overseas and to the Archbishop, who perceived in the General's hasty remark an ill thought out concession to artificial, popular pressure. While Senghor was conspicuous by his absence, the Minister for France Overseas, Cornut-Gentille, saved the situation. He met the marabouts and persuaded them to maintain their position in favor of union with France. The "Yes" of the marabouts in the referendum on September 28 led to a landslide majority in favor of the idea of the "*communauté*." On November 25, 1958, under the presidency of Senghor, Senegal became a Republic within the "*communauté*."[39]

ARCHBISHOP LEFEBVRE AND INDEPENDENCE

The Archbishop of Dakar had not yet expressed his views on independence publicly and openly. His position as a delegate of the Holy See and his chairmanship of various bishops' assemblies had forced him when addressing his episcopal colleagues to adopt the role of optimistic leader. The "Joint Declaration of the Bishops of French West Africa and Togo"[40] of April 24, 1955, bearing the Archbishop's signature, is no indication of his own thinking. Nonetheless, in 1957 he persuaded Pius XII to give a warn-

---

[38] Conference at Santa Chiara, 1958, *Échos*, Jan. 1959, 43-44.
[39] De Gaulle, *Mémoires d'espoir*, I, 60-62; Sorel, *Léopold Sédar Senghor*, 135-139.
[40] *Documentation Catholique*, 1200 (1955): 670; 1259 (1957): 1130.

ing to the people of Africa in *Fidei Donum* concerning "a short-sighted nationalism which might lead them unwittingly to disorder and slavery."

Fully aware of the circumstances and fearing the realization of Pius's fears, he met with General de Gaulle on August 26,1958, at the general's request. The Archbishop told the general of his concerns, and de Gaulle related to him the incident in Conakry:

"I could do nothing else," said the general, "but I think that we can come to an arrangement with Sekou Touré."

"But he is obviously a Communist," replied the Archbishop.

"No, no, no! He isn't a Communist; we will be able to come to an agreement."[41]

Obviously no agreement could be made, and at Santa Chiara on November 14, Archbishop Lefebvre explained why: already Sekou Touré was threatening Catholic schools, establishing people's courts, and forbidding Catholic organizations. "Guinea is no longer that far from China," the Archbishop observed. Soon in fact, Monsignor de Milleville was expelled from Guinea for having protested against the regime,[42] and later all the missionaries were thrown out. Nevertheless, the Archbishop had high hopes for Senegal: "The Muslim politicians in power are far from rejecting the Church. The head of the government, the Muslim Mamadou Dia, asked Fr. Lebret to chair the commission for economic affairs that is working on the forthcoming Constitution."[43]

However, when Senghor gave up his dream of bringing together the former countries of French West Africa under his own aegis, he secured the union of Senegal and Sudan on January 17, 1959, in the "Mali Federation." The Archbishop of Dakar was very concerned that the Sudanese president Modibo Keita was a Marxist and a Muslim, even if the Federation's State Prosecutor Isaac Forster, who was a staunch Catholic, declared as he took office: "I pray to God to come to my aid and preserve me from perjury and malfeasance."[44] However, the Bamako extremists demanded total independence. Senghor caved in and came to Paris on September 28 to petition the President. De Gaulle accepted the request in principle, and on December 12, 1959, he addressed the Heads of State during a meeting of the Community's Executive Council in Saint-Louis, accepting that the

---

[41] Fr. Marziac, first interview with Archbishop Lefebvre, 18.

[42] *General Bulletin*, 693: 418; the archbishop was expelled on Aug. 26, 1961 (*ibid.*, 699: 655-656) and Archbishop Lefebvre welcomed him in Dakar that same evening. Still shaken, Msgr. de Milleville barely replied to his host's questions. It was only after a few days that he said to the Archbishop: "You know, it's unheard of. They watch you so much down there that you end up not daring to say anything" (*C'est moi l'accusé*, 335-336).

[43] Conference of Archbishop Lefebvre at Santa Chiara, Nov. 14, 1958.

[44] Delcourt, *Histoire religieuse du Sénégal*, 101. Cf. Archbishop Lefebvre, sermon, Sept. 23, 1979.

"*Communauté*" would become an "Association." The next day at the Federal Assembly in Dakar, he ratified the existence of the "Mali Federation," stating that Mali would attain "internationally recognized sovereignty" with "the support, help, and agreement of France."[45]

On this occasion he sought Archbishop Lefebvre's views once again: "This independence," he asked, "will the Europeans be opposed to it?"

"No, I don't think so; they won't do anything."

De Gaulle got the answer he wanted to his first question but not to his second: "I think," he said, "that the union of Sudan and Senegal is a very good initiative. Wouldn't you agree, *Monseigneur*?"

"General, if you want my opinion, I don't think it will last long. The mentalities in Sudan and Senegal are very different."

"Oh, no, no, no! I think it's a very good thing. Just wait and see."[46]

A week later, there was general uproar in Dakar against the Archbishop who, as we have seen, had dared to write: "Senegalese wisdom perhaps will carry the day. Otherwise in a short while Communism will rule from Dakar to Gao." However, de Gaulle would make the same observation in his memoirs: "The attempt [to form the Mali Federation] would fail because the liberal, democratic leaders in Senegal feared being overwhelmed by the Marxists in Bamako."[47]

On June 28, 1960, Senghor proclaimed the independence of "Mali," and exactly two months later on August 28,[48] he had Mobido Keita arrested. On Senegal's Independence Day, June 3, 1961, Archbishop Lefebvre led a thanksgiving ceremony in the cathedral attended by Senghor, four other heads of state, and André Malraux. The joint letter of the Senegal bishops that he signed on this occasion seems rather bland: "Let us learn how to rise above differences of race, language, or religion. Let us close our eyes to the things that divide us, and be united with one heart as we pursue the same ideal: the greatness of our country. Let us be ready to sacrifice all forms of selfishness and let go of our own personal ideas."

We will not find the personal thinking of the Archbishop in this collegial text. In reality, for him "the great benefit" of independence would only be achieved if it were done "with dignity and order" and not "with hatred and violence."[49] What good is independence if it leads to chaos and totalitarianism? "Wisdom" or the Christian social order "must prevail." Thirty years later he would define this order as "a hierarchy of well-organized inequalities" and express the wish that African heads of state might under-

---

[45] De Gaulle, *Mémoires d'espoir*, 71; Sorel, *Léopold Sédar Senghor*, 143 ; Messmer, *Après tant de batailles*, 246.

[46] Gravrand, ms. III; Marziac, interview, I, 19.

[47] De Gaulle, *Mémoires d'espoir*, 70.

[48] Sorel, *Léopold Sédar Senghor*, 147-148.

[49] *Horizons Africains*, no. 128 (April 1961): 2.

stand how to bring about peace with justice, *i.e.*, the *Pax Christiana*, the peace of Christ the King of nations, and not create a peace with injustice, like the *Pax Sovietica* or the *Pax Islamica*.[50]

THE AMBIGUITY OF "AFRICAN SOCIALISM"

Around 1950, the Apostolic Delegate wished the bishops to condemn Houphouët-Boigny's pro-Communist RDA movement. Bishop Parisot of Dahomey objected that the RDA had not attacked the Church, and Archbishop Lefebvre gave in. Bishop Dupont of Bobo Dioulassou was personally able to indicate the bishops' disapproval to the Ivory Coast leader, who soon steered the RDA away from Communism.[51] In 1959 and 1960, Léopold Senghor, president of the Mali Assembly, expounded to the PFA his theory of "the path of African socialism" while warning against the dangers of a European socialism that was not adapted to Africa's problems.[52] The Archbishop was indignant at the ambiguity of this position, especially since Senghor was hardly opposing the collectivist and dictatorial socialism promoted by the head of government, Mamadou Dia.

A year later, Archbishop Lefebvre made up his mind to denounce this ambiguity in a pastoral letter "On the duty of living according to truth and avoiding ambiguity." He asked his vicar general to check the text:

"*Monseigneur*, get rid of this part here. You are talking about French style socialism, but here we have Senegalese socialism, Senghor's socialism, and he is a practicing Catholic."

"Do you reckon so? I'll think about it."

The text came back a few hours later, and when Fr. Bussard had read it he said: "But *Monseigneur*, you haven't made any changes!"

"Well, no! One has got to tell the truth."[53]

Written on March 26, 1961, the letter told a few home truths to the supporters of Senghor's "socialism for believers" (our summary):

> It is claimed that these ideas are inspired by socialism but reject atheism, hoping thereby to be more compatible with the doctrine of the Church. However, by accepting its vocabulary, one ends up approving its ideas. It is not enough to believe in God; one must recognize that God and not the State is the foundation of law. The socialist State "suppresses private initiative" and requires "monstrous bureaucracy." It monopolizes all the resources of intelligence, creativity, innovation, charity, and the spirit of enterprise, bringing them under its control and blocking them off.[54]

---

[50] Archbishop Lefebvre's Foreword and Afterword to Fr. Marziac's *Précis de la doctrine sociale de l'Eglise à l'usage des chefs d'Etats* (Caussade, 1991). Cf. *Fideliter*, no. 59: 22-23.

[51] Msgr. André Dupont, Letter to J.-M. L., Aug. 1, 1996.

[52] Sorel, *Léopold Sédar Senghor*, 141, 144.

[53] Fr. Bussard, ms. I, 11-12.

[54] *Lettres pastorales et écrits*, 146-148.

In other words, the African socialism of the believer Senghor was a contradiction in terms. As Pius XI wrote in *Quadragesimo Anno*,[55] "religious socialism and Christian socialism are contradictions: nobody can be at one and the same time a good Catholic and true socialist." As Fr. Garrigou-Lagrange had said, "it is as perilous to play with the principle of contradiction as it is to play with fire or with a tiger. Whoever denies such a principle will be hoist with his own petard."[56]

However, Archbishop Lefebvre hardly needed to add such a colorful quotation to his letter to enrage Senghor. The Head of State summoned the Archbishop: "*Monseigneur*, let me say how amazed I was by your letter..."

"Listen, Mr. President, I am only repeating what the Popes have said about socialism."[57]

The Archbishop would not concede any ground, and when the rumor spread that he had withdrawn his letter, he refuted it.[58] He would not retract any of his "timely truths"[59] concerning socialism since he always believed that "the most pressing duty of the shepherd...is to diagnose the soul's illnesses."[60] Sometime later, and doubtless on Senghor's advice,[61] the Apostolic Delegate Archbishop Maury agreed with Ambassador Boislambert that "while the ambassador could do with visiting Paris, the Delegate could do with visiting Rome."[62]

RESIGNATION

Archbishop Lefebvre suspected that Dakar would be in contact with the Holy See. Would this be enough to decide his future? In any case, the appointment of indigenous candidates to archiepiscopal sees was well underway ever since John XXIII had accepted the resignations of Bishop Boivin (1959), Bishop Sartre, and Bishop Socquet (1960) and consecrated three indigenous priests in Rome on May 8, 1960, appointing them to the

---

[55] Pius XI, *Quadragesimo Anno*, May 15, 1931 (Bonne Presse), 7, 156.

[56] *De virtutibus theologicis* (Turin: Berruti, 1948), 151.

[57] Marziac, interview, I, 1. In *Mater et Magistra* on May 15, John XXIII would follow Pius XI in saying that "Catholics can in no way approve the principles of socialism." *A.A.S.* 53 (1961), 408.

[58] Meeting of Superiors, April 18, 1961; Circular Letter 71, 7.

[59] Cf. Bishop de Castro Mayer, "Catéchisme des Vérités Opportunes" (political, economic, and social questions). Supplement to *Verbe*, 1953.

[60] Lefebvre, *Lettres pastorales*, 142.

[61] Senghor's role in the affair was confirmed by Fr. Philippe Béguerie who later met Bishop Benelli, former Delegation secretary during Archbishop Maury's tenure and his immediate successor: ms. I, 72, 48-49; 74, 11-20; Fr. Bussard conjectured that "Senghor perhaps overdid it when getting rid of Archbishop Lefebvre" (Savioz, *Essai historique*, I, 22), but he also said: "I know that a complaint was made to Rome" (ms. I, 12, 22-23).

[62] Boislambert, *Les Fers de l'espoir*, 540-541.

sees of Abidjan, Tananarive, and Ougadougou. Archbishop Lefebvre's pro-posal of a white candidate for Abidjan in 1959 was rejected unanimously by the other bishops: "Only a genuine black African should be promot-ed."[63]

It was thought that in view of independence, African archbishops were henceforth required as a parallel to the indigenous heads of state. Archbishop Lefebvre did not at all reject this principle, but he thought it was applied hastily just as he had found the granting of independence to be premature. Later he said that he had "sometimes intervened for the sake of prudence"; this was how he described his attitude to the hastiness fash-ionable at the time: "Wherever there were two African priests, one had to become bishop....All the same they might have checked whether he had the qualities required! Before they made them archbishops they could have chosen them as auxiliaries at first, as was done elsewhere."[64]

However, the "winds of change" were blowing as strongly in Rome as in Paris, and from time to time either Rome or Dakar made him or others like him feel that it was time to think about moving on.[65] Thus, he decided to make his own preparations, regardless of when it should happen, by naming Fr. Hyacinthe Thiandoum as second vicar general on May 7, 1961.[66] His two friends Archbishop Joseph Strebler in Lomé and Arch-bishop René Graffin in Yaoundé resigned on June 16 and September 6, 1961, respectively,[67] and the search began to find successors for them among the indigenous clergy. Rome seemed to wish for a similar process in Dakar. Besides, Archbishop Lefebvre's resignation would enable Rome to appoint African prelates in all four archiepiscopal sees of ex-French West Africa without seeming to concede ground to Sekou Touré in Conakry.[68]

The Archbishop said: "I was not going to impose myself and stay there, seemingly refusing to go."[69] On September 18, at the evening Mass for the fourteenth anniversary of his consecration, he said in his sermon that he "longed with his whole soul for the day when a Senegalese priest would receive the fullness of the priesthood and become his collaborator or even replace him." He then took the initiative, and wrote to Rome ask-ing for an African coadjutor.

---

[63] Bishop Pierre Rouanet, Letter to Fr. J.-M. L., Dec. 5, 1996.

[64] *Fideliter*, no. 59, 22.

[65] Fr. Marziac, Interview with Archbishop Lefebvre, 16 ; A. Cagnon, *id.* (1987), 8; Lefebvre, *Petite histoire,* 77.

[66] Archbishop Lefebvre expected to be often absent in Rome at the meeting of the Central Preparatory Commission, and Fr. Bussard was often traveling around the diocese. *Horizons Africains,* June 1961.

[67] Ant. Grach, *René Graffin, missionnaire au Cameroun,* end.

[68] Archbishop Strebler, Letter to Archbishop Lefebvre, Jan. 30, 1961; ms. I, 44, 31-38.

[69] Fr. Marziac, Interview, 16.

One has to believe that the Holy See was embarrassed by this request because the Archbishop received no reply. It became clear that they simply wanted him to resign. In his Christmas message he mentioned the obedience of bishops to the Pope and the example "of Him who made Himself obedient even to the death of the cross."[70] At the beginning of January, a little while before leaving to attend a session of the Central Preparatory Commission for the Council to be held from January 15 to 23, 1962, he made up his mind to write to the Sacred Congregation for the Propagation of the Faith: "If the Holy Father wishes me to withdraw, I am at his disposal."

He had barely arrived in Rome when he was received by Cardinal Agagianian, Prefect of the Sacred Congregation, who took him by the hand and thanked him effusively. Archbishop Lefebvre gave an account of the incident to his dear Carmelites:

"You should have seen it, the Cardinal's joy! You should have seen it!"

A few days later while visiting Cardinal Cicognani, the Secretary of State, the Archbishop told him of his wish for a six-month breathing period before the receiving any new appointment, "This summer we have our General Chapter Meeting and it may be that the Fathers…" He was thinking that six months would be enough to improve his English in order to be useful to the congregation. However, the Cardinal interrupted him: "No, the Holy Father does not wish to leave you without work. When a Delegate or a Nuncio leaves his post and returns to his country, we give him a diocese. The Holy Father is going to give you the diocese of Tulle."

The Archbishop was surprised and tried again: "Still, some rest would be useful…could I not explain my thinking to the Holy Father?"

"No, no, I'm responsible for this matter."

"But, I can see the Holy Father!"

"Only to thank him. That's what he wishes you to do."

The Archbishop said to the Carmelites: "A wish of the Pope is an order. I ask for obedience, and I have to practice it…but thanking the Pope, I admit, I did not feel up to it."[71]

On January 23, 1962, the Pope signed the decree of the Sacred Congregation of the Consistory and the two apostolic letters transferring Archbishop Marcel Lefebvre from the archiepiscopal see of Dakar to the episcopal see of Tulle with the personal title of archbishop. Henceforth, the Archbishop's days in Dakar were numbered. He did not waste time, but redoubled his efforts.[72] On January 25, he wrote a pastoral letter from Rome concerning the necessity of prayer. On February 2, he announced to

---

[70] *Horizons Africains*, Sept. and Dec. 1961.

[71] *General Bulletin*, 701: 9; 702: 65; diary of the Carmel at Sébikotane, Feb. 2, 1962; Interview with Fr. Marziac, 16; *Petite histoire*, 78-79; Fr. Gravrand, ms. III, 15, 3-25.

[72] *Horizons Africains*, no. 137 (March 1962); Delcourt, *Histoire religieuse du Sénégal*, 103.

Dakar that he was leaving and bid farewell to the seminary at Sébikotane. A few days later he did the same at Fadiout, Thiès, and Mont-Roland. On February 2, he broadcast a radio message to the Senegalese. On the 10th he blessed the foundation stone of the chapel at the college in Hann, and on the 11th he blessed the church of Our Lady of the Angels in Oukram. Also on February 10 and 11, he presided at the ACJF Congress. Finally on February 12, the Archbishop celebrated a farewell Mass in the cathedral in the presence of Monsignor Joseph Landreau and Bishop Prosper Dodds.

Monsignor Landreau recalled the saying of a Senegalese minister: "To be Senegalese, one does not have to be born in the country. It is enough to love the country and work for it." He concluded: "Your Grace, you have been a great Senegalese."

Controlling his emotion, Archbishop Lefebvre spoke "the language of faith." By appointing "a child from among the Senegalese families" as Senegal's chief shepherd, the Holy Father was showing his confidence in "Senegalese Christianity, which was truly alive and solid in its faith." This had been the mission of a line of bishops who for 150 years had worked with their collaborators to achieve this goal.

His final words revealed the deepest feelings of a shepherd who leaves his flock on orders from above: firstly, they had always to "remain faithful to the path that the good God has shown [them]" and secondly, in order to do that, they had to "be attached to our Lord throughout [their] lives"[73] by "being in a state of habitual prayer."[74] The following day he advised Fr. Bussard to do "everything possible" to ensure the appointment of Fr. Thiandoum,[75] and then he left Senegal for Rome.

---

[73] *Horizons Africains*, no. 137, 3-4.
[74] "The Necessity of Prayer," *Lettres pastorales et écrits*, 158.
[75] Fr. Bussard, ms. I, 13, 17-21. Fr. Bussard had nothing to do; the appointment was a foregone conclusion; ms. I, 13, 50-52.

PART III

THE COMBATANT

CHAPTER 11

THE TULLE INTERLUDE

I. A VERY NICE, SMALL DIOCESE

AN ARCHBISHOP FOR A SMALL DIOCESE[1]

When the French cardinals and archbishops heard in late summer 1961 about the possibility of the Archbishop of Dakar being appointed to France, they were concerned. What? Archbishop Lefebvre! A religious: that is out of the ordinary. And what is more, his "fundamentalist tendencies and brazen patronage of *Verbe*"[2] are well-known! Worse still, Bishop Maury had suggested to Rome that Archbishop Lefebvre be appointed in the archiepiscopal see of Albi which had been vacant since the death of Bishop Jean Emmanuel Marquès on August 2. That was quite beyond the pale!

Soon at the request of the cardinals and archbishops, Cardinal Richaud, Archbishop of Bordeaux, made a special trip to Rome. The Secretariat of State accepted their objections, and on December 4, 1961,[3] Bishop Claude Dupuy was promoted to the post of Archbishop of Albi in record time. Moreover, it was made clear that Archbishop Lefebvre could only be given a small diocese such as Tulle, which had been vacant since October 18.

When the Nuncio Bishop Bertoli learned of the Archbishop's resignation from Dakar, he informed the cardinals and archbishops who in turn approached the French government: "Archbishop Lefebvre can have a small diocese, but he must not be a member of the Assembly of Cardinals and Archbishops." The government's representative, Jean-Marie Soutou, passed their demands on to the Nuncio who was urgently requested to come to the Interior Ministry on January 17. Professor Gabriel Le Bras, who was then a chargé d'affaires at the Ministry, came later to see Archbishop Lefebvre and told him what had been said.[4] The Nuncio had given

---

[1] Fr. Marziac, first interview with Archbishop Lefebvre, 7, 16; Lefebvre, *Petite histoire*, 81-82; Jean Vinatier, *Histoire religieuse du Bas-Limousin et du diocèse de Tulle* (Éd. Lucien Souny, 1991).

[2] An account of the audience of January 17, 1962.

[3] *Informations Catholiques Internationales*, Year 1976; A.A.S. 53 (1961), 528; 54 (1962), 106.

[4] Account, supra; *Fideliter*, no. 59: 47.

in, and even promised that "Archbishop Lefebvre's case would not set a precedent."

In Rome a few well-intentioned bishops said to Archbishop Lefebvre: "Tulle! You should have complained!" The Archbishop thought to himself: "People see nothing but the career ladder: promotion after promotion. Those things are just human considerations. We are not worthy to have responsibility for a single soul. As St. Francis de Sales says, one soul alone is a whole diocese. I will have 220,000 souls and that's a big diocese"!

However, it was a diocese that was hardly known in Rome, where one of the cardinals said to him: "So you are going to Toul?"

"No, Tulle."

"Toulon?"

"No, Tulle!"

"But there's no such place!"

"Look in the Pontifical Directory: there, Tulle!"

"Oh yes! Tulle."[5]

TULLE'S CATHOLIC HISTORY

Pope John XXII created the diocese of Tulle in 1317 when he separated the whole of Bas-Limousin from the diocese of Limoges. Since 1823 this area has corresponded to the Department of Corrèze. The area is studded with hills marked by craggy outcrops and verdant summits, and a thousand silvery streams run into a network of deep tributaries. The region's water flows finally into the Rivers Vezère, Corrèze—tributary of the Vezère—and the Dordogne. Ussel and Bort-les-Orgues stand to the East, and Brive and Argentat lie to the West. In the twelfth century, the region developed under the influence of the Benedictines who built abbeys at Vigeois, Beaulieu, Tulle, Aubazaine, Meymac, and Bonnaigue. In the 14th century, Bas-Limousin had an exceptional influence given that three popes emerged from two of its parishes, and the diocese of Tulle subsequently gave the Church an impressive number of bishops and cardinals.[6] The Protestant Reformation did deep and lasting damage to the people of the region, and its effects were so much the worse for remaining largely beneath the surface. The seventeenth century Counter-Reformation saw the foundation of the seminary in Tulle where the Sulpicians trained priests who were both knowledgeable and effective. In the eighteenth century, the Freemasons—descendants of the first Reformers in disguise—under-

---

[5]   Diary of Sébikotane; Lefebvre, *Petite histoire*, 82; Lefebvre, *Spiritual Conferences at Ecône*, May 24, 1984.

[6]   One hundred and seven bishops and thirty cardinals. Canon A. Leyrich, Letter to Archbishop Lefebvre, Feb. 5, 1962.

mined Christian society. There were liberal bishops, abandoned chapels, and deserted monasteries.

During the Revolution, the majority of the clergy refused to take the oath to the Republic (247 non-jurors as opposed to 195 who took the oath[7]), especially those who lived in the countryside around Tulle and Brive. Ussel and Uzerche were more "enlightened." The cathedral was profaned by the enthronement of the "Goddess Reason" and ransacked on November 27, 1793. Its majestic dome collapsed, ruining the apse. The priests went underground and their ministry became clandestine. Some emigrated (eighty) and unfortunately some married (forty-five)! Other priests were deported and died in captivity.

The nineteenth century saw the rapid spread of female congregations. The Sisters of Nevers did marvelous work in the hospitals. A Carmel was founded at Tulle in 1836. However, as early as 1830, the bishop noted: "The faith is getting weak, and impiety is gaining ground everywhere." Bishop Berteaud, a friend of Louis Veuillot and a strong, pro-papal voice, was Tulle's greatest bishop (1842-1878). During his reign, he saw two junior seminaries founded at Brive and Servière, a Catholic school at Ussel, and a major seminary. In 1878, the diocese had 458 priests and eleven ordinations.

Despite the plundering of Church property in 1906, the seminaries made progress. Under the Roman Bishop Nègre (1908-1913), a two thousand strong legion of female catechists taught the love of Jesus in the Blessed Sacrament. Unfortunately, the falling birth rates, migration to the cities, secular schools, and Masonic propaganda ravaged the faith. The number of vocations declined inexorably, and the number of priests fell from 375 in 1918 to 300 in 1940.

Bishop Jean Castle (1918-1939) organized Catholic Action zealously but was weak when it came to the principles of sound doctrine and supernatural means. Edmond Michelet got involved with the "Social Teams" of Robert Garric, and the speakers at his "Circle Duguet" included the Christian Democrat inheritors of Sillonist ideas such as Georges Bidault, Georges Hourdin, and Fathers Maydieu, Ducattillon, and Montcheuil. Following the influence, both good and bad, of the Resistance in Corrèze, Bishop Amabile Chassaigne (1940-1962) asked the priests of the Mission of France to be responsible for the mostly dechristianized areas of Lapleau, Bugeat, and Treignac. He also gave a second wind to specific Catholic Action projects. He ordained 87 priests and presided at the funerals of 155 others. In 1961 he was seriously injured in a car accident and resigned on October 18.

---

[7] [The juring clergy were those members of the clergy who during the French Revolution agreed to swear an oath accepting the Civil Constitution for the Clergy as dictated by the revolutionary government. Trans.]

II. THE CITÉ CATHOLIQUE AND THE BISHOPS

GIVING SUPPORT AGAIN TO THE CITÉ CATHOLIQUE

Even before the "bishop elect" had contacted anyone in Tulle, his attention was drawn to recent attacks made against his friends in the Cité Catholique. In Dakar he heard that the French bishops—or rather the group that directed it, the Assembly of Cardinals and Bishops (ACA)—had in March, 1960, produced a critical study of the movement. Some extracts were passed on to Jean Ousset in which he was criticized for acting without the permission of diocesan bishops, and also for promoting the "Counter-Revolution." Ousset accepted the criticism in the second instance and avoided using such vocabulary in future.

However, in November 1961, other extracts of this "Memorandum reserved to the bishops" began doing the rounds in the press.[8] They referred to far more serious faults: in the Cité Catholique "the systemization of certain ways of thinking leads to the death of true thought," and, "the thinking expressed in *Verbe* permeates everything, and prevents Catholic Action from being fruitful." Soon a pamphlet[9] by Fr. Soras, S.J., backed by Fr. Villain, S.J., in *La Croix* in March 1962, raised some questions about this "Memo": "It is a warning against the Cité Catholique," stated *La Croix*. On the other hand, an Algerian daily claimed: "It expresses approval." Léon-Étienne Duval, Archbishop of Algiers, replied: "No, it really is a warning." Therefore, the ACA was required to issue its own interpretation; a duly solemn warning was inevitable.

To prevent this, Archbishop Lefebvre intervened straightaway. "I would be failing in my duty to the truth," he wrote to Jean Ousset and his collaborators on March 4, "if I kept silent." His letter was published in part in *Le Monde* on March 15,[10] and then published in full in *L'Homme Nouveau* on March 18. This letter totally contradicted the Jesuit:

> Are you criticized for not having the bishops' permission? Such permission is not needed for any activity which is not properly speaking Catholic Action. All that is needed is for an activity to be fully in accord with the spirit of the Church and her discipline, and every bishop can judge that for himself in his own diocese.
> Are you criticized for the way in which you interpret papal documents? Would to God that all Catholics had such a fine command of these documents! In any case, be sure not to interpret them according to the

---

[8]   *France Observateur*, Nov. 9; *La Croix*, Nov. 10. Cf. the article of the very liberal Canon G. Bavaud in *La Liberté* of Fribourg, March 7, 1961. *Verbe*, no. 122.

[9]   A. de Soras, *Documents d'Église et options politiques* (Éd. du Centurion), questioning Archbishop Lefebvre's role as the "protector of the Cité Catholique."

[10] Then in *Itinéraires*, no. 62 (Apr. 1962): 225-228; *Nouvelles de Chrétienté*, etc.

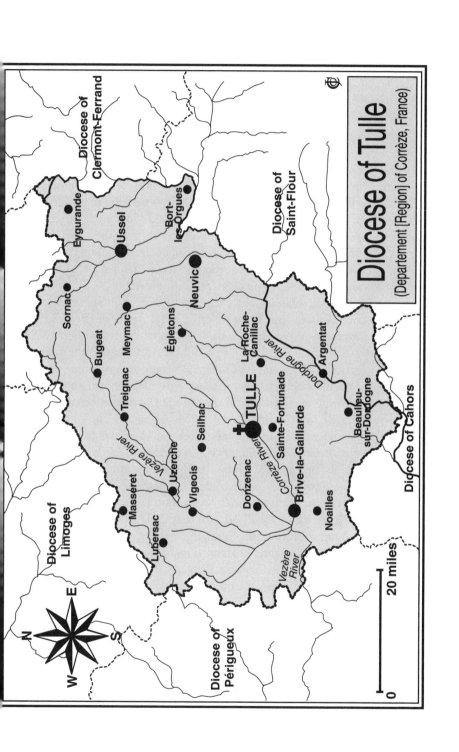

Diocese of Tulle
(Departement [Region] of Corrèze, France)

Diocese of Clermont-Ferrand

Diocese of Saint-Flour

Diocese of Cahors

Diocese of Périgueux

Diocese of Limoges

Eygurande

Sornac

Bugeat

Treignac

Masséret

Lubersac

Uzerche

Vigeois

Seilhac

Ussel

Meymac

Bort-les-Orgues

Neuvic

Égletons

La-Roche-Canillac

Argentat

TULLE

Sainte-Fortunade

Donzenac

Brive-la-Gaillarde

Noailles

Beaulieu-sur-Dordogne

Dordogne River

Corrèze River

Vézère River

Vézère River

20 miles

0

N E S W

rules laid down by our Jesuit friend. One could not do a better job of removing all moral authority from papal documents!

Are you criticized for your thinking on the temporal power of the Church and her authority over society? The direct and indirect power as explained in your pamphlets is exactly what is taught in the Roman universities and in the documents that come from the Holy See.

Nothing is missing from this lucid and hard-hitting defense. One or two well-aimed arrows were meant for *La Croix*, the "newspaper rightly or wrongly considered as the voice of the Church in France" that used its columns "in this odious campaign." As a parting shot the Archbishop added that the Cité Catholique was criticized for not wanting to put up with "the sight of your children growing up in a climate of materialism, secularism, and atheism.... While this atmosphere is ruining the supernatural spirit, *i.e.,* the spirit of prayer and self-denial, and consequently the birth of priestly vocations, they want to stop you rechristianizing society. Your initiatives are crucial and only strengthen Catholic Action."

On reading these timely but uncomfortable truths, the French bishops were seized with horror. What we can call the "Lefebvre effect" stirred some deep feelings. Although three bishops supported Archbishop Lefebvre, others such as Cardinal Liénart,[11] Bishop Ancel, and Bishop Brault reacted negatively. The members of the ACA could not hide their embarrassment at Archbishop Lefebvre's challenge: they felt he had beaten them to it by publishing his views first in the press. They contented themselves with publishing extracts from the 1960 "Memorandum" in *La Croix* on March 16, a move that brought more well-aimed arrows from another quarter in the form of Jean Madiran's commentaries in *Itinéraires* (nos. 61, 62, 64, and 67). The Pope had to come to the rescue, and on May 10,[12] his Secretary of State assured Fr. Wenger, chief editor of *La Croix*, of the Pope's "fatherly confidence." This was after Archbishop Lefebvre had been given an hour's audience with John XXIII[13] on May 7. The Pope gave the Archbishop a kind but firm word of warning:[14] "You see, when I was professor of Holy Scripture at Bergame, I defended the theories of Fr. Lagrange and I was labeled a 'modernist.' That has dogged me throughout my life. I've seen my files: they read "modernist tendencies." I'm not a modernist. That is why I was never given an appointment in Rome. I was always kept at a distance from the Roman Curia because I was—so it was said—a modern-

---

[11]   President of the ACA. His letter of March 22 told Archbishop Lefebvre of the "surprise" and "pain" of the ACA members and that they wished him to show "a more prudent and brotherly attitude."

[12]   *Documentation Catholique*, 1377 (June 3, 1962): 716.

[13]   From 1 P.M. to 2 P.M. *Sem. Rel. de Tulle*, no. 12 (June 1, 1962).

[14]   Monsignor Joseph Cucherousset, Letter to Archbishop Lefebvre, July 1, 1962.

ist. So, you be careful not to declare yourself such an out and out conservative."

What the Pope was implying was that such a course was necessary if Archbishop Lefebvre wanted to make a career for himself.[15] Archbishop Lefebvre cared little about making a career for himself. However, seeing "good Pope John" trustingly and naively relating the setbacks of his own life gave him an insight into this easy-going Pontiff's liberal personality. "You be careful," John had warned him, but Marcel would take no notice since he was quite resolved to state the undiminished truth at all times.

EPISCOPAL COLLEGIALITY IN THE DOCK

Archbishop Lefebvre's contribution to this debate drew a number of spectators to openly express their own views. Many priests rallied to his support, seeing the former Archbishop of Dakar as a sign of hope. Fr. Bénéfice[16] wrote to him: "At last, the voice of a bishop who sounds like a bishop!" Fr. Lacheteau[17] stated: "Your voice, which is unique among the French bishops, is so full of courage that the sons of the Church are beginning to hope again." Fr. Collin[18] wrote to express his "thanks to the brave bishop who, while all others were silent, has had the courage to take up the defense of excellent Catholics who have been unjustly discredited."

Encouraged by these responses to his actions—and following a suggestion of Cardinal Ottaviani—the Archbishop wrote to Cardinal Liénart asking to be invited to the meetings of the Cardinals and the Archbishops,[19] where he would have the chance to explain his actions. During a meeting of the Central Preparatory Commission in Rome towards the end of March or the beginning of April, Liénart spoke to the Archbishop and gave him his reply in person:

"Your Grace, I'm sorry to have to tell you, but you know, we took a decision and you will not be able to, *etc.*"

"Oh!" replied Archbishop Lefebvre, "it's not important, you know."

Just then Cardinal Cerejeira, Patriarch of Lisbon, suddenly appeared and taking the Archbishop by the hand congratulated him in a loud voice: "Well done for your letter to Jean Ousset. It was a good thing for you to stand up for them."

Liénart slipped away quickly.[20]

On May 17, the new bishop went to meet General de Gaulle, who was visiting Tulle. The President was obviously aware of Archbishop Lefebvre's

---

[15] Archbishop Lefebvre, Interview with A. Cagnon; interview, Fr. Marziac, I, 5.
[16] Parish Priest of Malaucène, Vaucluse; March 16, 1962.
[17] Priest at St. Léger-de-Montbrillais, Vienne, March 17.
[18] Parish Priest of Saint-Cloud, March 23.
[19] I.C.I., 1976; ms. III, 11, 52-62.
[20] Archbishop Lefebvre, first interview with Fr. Marziac, 7.

support for those the press labeled as "Right-wing Catholics" who were carrying out "a politico-religious blockade in the name of doctrine";[21] such language could have implied that they had contacts with the OAS.[22] Charles himself might well have had a few reasons to talk about the OAS, and Marcel might have had his own reasons to talk about the French army officers imprisoned at Tulle. Whatever happened during the meeting, the press had already stated on May 10: "Regardless of his standing, the Elysée Palace will not countenance Archbishop Lefebvre's (Archbishop-Bishop of Tulle) taking part in the meetings of the Cardinals and Archbishops of France."[23] In reality the government and the bishops had been hand in glove with each other since January.

In haste the ACA which met in March had Archbishop Guerry[24] write a memorandum on its own powers and competence. In the universal Church, jurisdiction belongs not only to the Pope, but "collegially to the episcopal corps participating in the supreme jurisdiction of the Pope as head of the Church." Certainly the ACA had no such jurisdiction, but it had "moral authority." Archbishop Lefebvre replied in two letters to Archbishop Guerry stating that collegiality was only exercised "exceptionally in the case of a council." He said that if the ACA went beyond its remit, "it risks either muzzling the bishops or being contradicted by them." The Archbishop criticized the ACA for promoting a kind of Catholic Action "that has not kept the supernatural character that ought to belong to all apostolic action." He denounced the "iron-fisted methods" of Catholic Action at the national level, and the pastoral centers that excluded the Legion of Mary and the five-day retreats. With these things in mind he recalled a very valuable truth: "The whole history of the Church shows that the Holy Ghost uses people more than organizations....The bishops have spoken freely, and the Spirit of Truth is better manifested precisely through that freedom. [This Spirit] is moreover approved by the successor of Peter."

Here the Archbishop was warming up for the Council, where he would wage war on collegiality with the same apostolic freedom. However, this healthy freedom met the ACA's distinct disapproval. They made it known that "only those cardinals and bishops exercising archiepiscopal responsibilities were invited to the ACA meetings." This obviously excluded Archbishop Lefebvre, who was only Archbishop by personal title.[25] None-

---

[21] La Croix, March 16, 1962 ; I.C.I., Apr. 1, 1962.

[22] The Communist weekly Le Travailleur de la Corrèze saw Archbishop Lefebvre as the "official protector of those who inspired the OAS" and as a support for "those who confuse the Bible with Mein Kampf" (start of April 1962).

[23] Robert Havard de La Montagne in Aspects de la France, May 10, 1962.

[24] Archbishop Lefebvre, Letters to Monsignor Guerry, Apr. 20 and June 10, 1962.

[25] Semaine Religieuse de Cambrai, end of May; Le Monde, June 3-4, 1962.

theless, the ACA's declaration was a flagrant lie. Archbishop Rémond of Nice and Archbishop Girbeau of Nîmes, both Archbishop-Bishops, were definitely invited to the ACA meetings. It mattered little to the Bishop of Tulle who had enough to be going on with in his own diocese.

III. BUILDING UP CONFIDENCE AGAIN

A DIOCESE IN DECLINE

Around March 10, 1962, Archbishop Lefebvre paid a short visit to Tulle. He traveled from Paris with Monsignor Layotte, his Vicar Capitular, and when he got off the train at Uzerche he was met by Bishop Chassaigne. They took the road from Uzerche that winds down the valley, passing through hamlets and chestnut groves. During this quiet springtime visit to his diocese, he learnt and memorized many details of the history and life in Corrèze. On the day of his enthronement, the regional prefect was "knocked out" by his accurate knowledge of the area.

Soon they came to Tulle. It was grey, quiet, and seemed crammed into the valley with its arms factories, the rococo prefecture, and the longer grey seminary buildings that were unfortunately empty! At last they could see the bishop's residence and the spire of the cathedral which rose into the sky. The former was brand-new and functional but it seemed poor and sat uncomfortably between the hillside and the noisy road. The faces around him were pleasant, even though some had been warned about "the bishop who talks politics"—a fabrication that was quickly dispeled by his actions.[26] The following day, he said Mass at the Carmel where he asked for prayers. He spoke about the state of the diocese with his predecessor,[27] and left the following day to return to Paris.

On March 16, Bishop Chassaigne retired to Thiers where he died on April 6. The previous day, Archbishop Lefebvre had written his first message to the diocese to be read out at Mass on April 8. He said that he would encourage "all initiatives, everything that could really contribute to the salvation of souls." He denounced "everything that could separate souls from God, from our Lord, from His holy Mother, and everything that comes from the father of lies."[28]

On April 10 and 11, he took part in a meeting of bishops at Bordeaux for the new "Apostolic Region of the South-West." It was chaired by Cardinal Richaud, and he met once again some fellow students from Rome:

---

[26] Archbishop Lefebvre, Letter to his former diocese of Dakar, March 1962; Monsignor Monéger, Interview with Fr. Marziac, ms., 2.

[27] This unusual visit, which was not dictated by protocol, was much appreciated since it indicated a desire to have continuity, as his official arrival barely one month after Monsignor Chassaigne's departure would show.

[28] *Sem. Rel. de Tulle*, March 30, 1962, 83-84.

Roger Johan (bishop of Agen), Robert Bézac (auxiliary bishop of Dax), and his friend Xavier Morilleau (bishop of La Rochelle). On the 12th, he went back to his diocese via the Bordeaux road.

On April 15, he went to Tulle for the Blessing of Palms, and then on to the Carmel to celebrate Mass.[29] Later in the presence of Jean Montalat, deputy mayor of Tulle, he placed a wreath of carnations on the war memorial and another at the memorial for the Martyrs of the Resistance (he was, of course, the son of a Resistance fighter who had died after being deported). In the afternoon after the ceremony of enthronement in the cathedral attended by the civil authorities, he held a reception for the clergy and town's leaders. This gesture, which was unusual in France, impressed the prefect, whom the bishop had visited the evening before. Afterwards Archbishop Lefebvre said: "I could go and see him without any problem, and when we met in the street we would shake hands."[30]

Coming from Dakar, where African Christianity was expanding rapidly, Archbishop Lefebvre keenly felt how different things were in the diocese of Tulle, which had undergone a sharp decline since the war. The number of clergy had fallen from 300 in 1940 to 240 in 1962 (of whom sixteen were religious). Although the seminary had twenty-one seminarians in 1958, it had closed and its students were sent[31] to Clermont-Ferrand with other seminarians from Saint-Flour and Limoges. While there had been six ordinations in 1961, there would only be two in 1962, one of which was the ordination of Fr. Yves Puyjalon, performed by Archbishop Lefebvre on July 15, in the abbatial church of Beaulieu-sur-Dordogne. What had become of Xaintrie to the south that was formerly a breeding ground for vocations? And what of Treignac to the north that had been called "the holy town on the Mountain"? Of the twenty-one congregations present at the end of the nineteenth century, there remained only the Little Brothers of Mary at Lacabane, the Sisters of Providence at Portieux (working in the parishes), the Sisters of Mercy at Beaulieu (care of the sick and parish work), the teaching Sisters of Charity from Nevers (in Brive), and the diocesan congregation of the Sisters of the Holy Heart of Mary.[32] However, one after the other these orders were closing their houses and their schools. Archbishop Lefebvre stated: "One had this feeling of a kind of inevitability for which there was no answer. It was crushing."[33]

---

[29] Which had thirteen choir nuns, four postulants, and three sisters on reception.

[30] *Fideliter*, no. 59: 50; the mayor made the town's function room available for the reception, *Sem. Rel. de Tulle*, Apr. 20, 1962, 130-131.

[31] There were five at Clermont, one in Rome, one in Paris, one in Lyons, and seven doing National Service.

[32] Vinatier, *Histoire religieuse du Bas-Limousin*, 214, 216; *Sem. Rel. de Tulle, passim*.

[33] *Fideliter*, no. 59: 47-48.

Moreover, Catholic Action had policies and chaplains imposed from the national level. It was committed to projects with a purely social scope that were lacking a supernatural basis. The pastoral team sessions organized by Fr. Fernaud Boulard[34] followed the same paths. In fact, just as the new bishop arrived, this priest had organized an interparish mission to be preached by Redemptorists, Jesuits, and Dominicans—about twenty in all—who caused trouble in the factories, set the workers against the management, and insulted the factory owners.[35] The latter complained and Archbishop Lefebvre was obliged to put a stop to this mission. As for the priest teams from the Mission of France, they understood the need for priests to lead the common life but they were too taken up with social concerns and were leading what remained of the faithful into a secular way of thinking. In their newsletter *Monédières*, they even had the temerity to claim that a region full of marvelous little Romanesque churches "had never been evangelized."

At Écône, Archbishop Lefebvre remarked: "I can still see the Dean, appointed by the Mission of France, who came to see me before I left and wept in my office. 'I did not enter the Mission of France to end up in an atmosphere like this. I can no longer live with my colleagues! I don't want to stay.' He felt that his colleagues were no longer priests or no longer acted like priests."[36]

From his arrival in the diocese, Archbishop Lefebvre was aware of the threat being posed by this secularizing spirit in the priesthood. He spoke out against it but with great tact. In the address he gave during his enthronement in the cathedral, considered by some to be "as simple as a country priest's sermon," he spoke directly to his priests: "Let Christ shine through you, so that the faithful feel closer to heaven when they are with you, so they feel closer to God and further away from the things of the earth, and so you can really lead them to our Lord and to heaven!"[37]

Some found this overly transparent language to be full of "blunders, inaccuracies, and generalities."[38] He drove the message home in his "bishop's letter" of June: "Primacy of the supernatural! In Catholic Action, let us

---

34 Pierrard, *Les Diocèses de Cambrai et de Lille*, 319. The priest who was resident at the presbytery of St. Sulpice in Paris was at that time in Peru.
35 Archbishop Lefebvre, *Retreats preached at Ecône*, Sept. 18, 1979. It was a "general mission" of the "Home Missionary Pastoral Center." Bishop Jean Gay, a former student at Santa Chiara and bishop of Basse-Terre, wrote Archbishop Lefebvre on June 8, 1962, to tell him of the difficulties he had had during a diocesan mission preached in Guadeloupe: "If I had to do it again, I would certainly not call upon the HMPC. Many of those missionaries seem to belong to a demolition company!"
36 Archbishop Lefebvre, Interview with A. Cagnon, 1987; Lefebvre, *Retreats preached at Ecône*, Sept. 19, 1988.
37 *Sem. Rel. de Tulle*, Apr. 20, 1962, 127.
38 Monsignor F. Monéger, Interview with Fr. Marziac, ms., 2.

always join our activities to prayer and union with our Lord: otherwise, they will no longer be Catholic."

The Archbishop also recommended the five-day Ignatian retreats. In July he invited the faithful to come to the aid of Algerian refugees, and expressed the wish "that these events should remind us that our understanding of the notions of justice, law, charity, and respect for the human person—all of which belong to the natural law—has been transformed through the grace of our Lord Jesus Christ. Let us always recall this principle: 'The less we are Christian, the less we are human.' Consequently, our first duty in restoring human relations between men is to work for the reign of our Lord with all our strength."[39]

COMFORTING AND ENCOURAGING HIS PRIESTS

Archbishop Lefebvre was not just all talk. Shortly after his enthronement, he called a meeting of all the senior parish priests to whom he put the following question: "Would it be a good thing for the bishop to visit the priests in their presbyteries in order to cheer them up and encourage them?"

One of the deans, Fr. Chèze, who was parish priest of La Roche-Canillac and who easily spoke his mind, replied: "You ask us that, but you will be like the others. We will never see you!"

"Father," replied the bishop, "do you have a diary so we can settle on a date for my visit?"

"I must have a scrap of paper here somewhere…" came the reply.

The Archbishop then took out his diary, and a date was decided upon. Later that week, he went to La Roche-Canillac where he stayed for two days with the parish priest and visited his five parishes.[40]

Archbishop Lefebvre said: "Coming to Tulle with my missionary experience, I brought a glimmer of hope. People started to take heart again, even the priests. They felt that I had not despaired, and that to me the situation did not appear to be irreversible."[41]

In fact, the bishop was able to make three similar visits to other parish priests. He would inform them of his visit at the last moment, arrive alone behind the wheel of his own car, have supper just with the parish priest, spend the night at the presbytery, celebrate Mass the following morning, meet a few zealous laypeople, and visit the churches attached to the parish.

The Archbishop recounted his experiences: "I saw priests living in truly stark poverty. We were much less poor in the Holy Ghost Fathers, even

[39] *Sem. Rel. de Tulle*, June 1, 1962, 172; July 13, 1962, 208-209.
[40] Monsignor Marcel Meyssignac, Interview with Fr. Fabrice Delestre, April 8, 1997; Lefebvre, *Retreats preached at Ecône*, 8 B, June 1979.
[41] *Fideliter*, no. 59: 49.

as missionaries in Africa, than some priests in France who lived in poverty."

This poverty in a spiritual desert led some priests to be discouraged.
The Archbishop recalled: "I can still see this young priest, ordained two or
three years before, who wept in my office. 'But *Monseigneur,* what use am
I? Why did I become a priest? You have given me three or four parishes,
but there's not that much to do. There are two or three old people at Mass
on Sunday and seven or eight children at catechism who I know will never
set foot in church after their communion and confirmation. I am lonely. I
have to go to the cafe to eat. I cannot carry on like this.'"[42]

The Archbishop inquired firstly about the material conditions in
which the poor priest lived: "So, you have to pay off the car that the diocese gave you? So, you keep warm with a gas stove?" Then moving on to
more spiritual matters, the Archbishop consoled and comforted the man:
"Prepare well for daily Mass. Do this carefully. When a priest has celebrated his Mass, he has accomplished the most important part of his priestly
ministry....Have faith in the graces which come from your Holy Mass,
even if only two or three people attend."[43] Humility was also necessary: "It
is our Lord Jesus Christ who acts. We are but poor instruments. If you tell
yourself that, it will stop you becoming discouraged with an unsuccessful
apostolate."[44]

Such private meetings with their bishop provided "enormous support" for the priests. They felt that the Archbishop was confident and not
desperate. Rather, he was "convinced that they could turn the situation
around because there was still priestly holiness—holy priests and holy religious."[45]

RECOVERY WAS POSSIBLE

All was not lost. It was only a matter of turning again to the traditional, tried and tested means. Firstly, the priests would be reorganized into
deaneries.[46] The bishop proposed this at the Deans' meeting. It was the
idea for the future priories of the Society of St. Pius X in embryonic form.

It was necessary to provide support for the diocesan congregation of
the Sisters of the Holy Heart of Mary. They ran health clinics, small primary schools, and the orphanage at Treignac, and they visited the sick and

---

[42] Lefebvre, *Retreats preached at Ecône,* 2 B, Sept. 21, 1979; *ibid.,* 1 B, Sept. 8, 1981;
      Lefebvre, *Spiritual Conferences at Ecône,* 140 A-B, Feb. 9, 1991.
[43] Msgr. Lefebvre, sermon at La Cascade de Bord, June 21, 1962, *Sem Rel. de Tulle,* 1962,
      199; spiritual conference at Fribourg, Oct. 15, 1969; Lefebvre, *Spiritual Conferences at
      Ecône,* Dec. 1, 1971.
[44] Spiritual Conference at Fribourg, Jan. 21, 1971.
[45] Lefebvre, *Retreats preached at Ecône,* 1 B, Sept. 8, 1981.
[46] *Sem. Rel. de Tulle,* no. 13 (June 7, 1962): 187-188.

provided material back-up for the priests in the parishes. They gave great service and were loved by the people. As the Archbishop said to his priests: "We have to send them vocations, and seek to pick out good young women."

They would open new Catholic primary schools, drawing pupils from several villages, and organize transport to collect all the children. The parents were in favor. The young priests in the diocese could be brought together and would find in this apostolate a worthy objective for their zeal. They would maintain the junior seminary at Ussel with its 110 pupils because the lower classes were very promising.[47] However, the Archbishop wanted to found an additional junior seminary in some large unused buildings to the south of Brive. He said he would reopen "a seminary to train priests to be zealous and sound in doctrine: Saint-Antoine de Brive seems like a good place to me."[48]

Moreover, to enable Catholic families to withdraw their adolescent children from the public schools where they were "like poor orphans,"[49] Archbishop Lefebvre envisaged opening a new Catholic secondary school for boys in Tulle, with the help of a few priests from the Vendée whom Bishop Antoine Cazaux, bishop of Luçon,[50] promised to send.

There was a lot of criticism concerning the "teaching priests" from the west of France, but it was mistaken criticism according to the Archbishop: "With such schools one can begin evangelizing from the bottom up. Catholic schools are a great means of evangelization as long as they are truly Catholic. Such schools are willed by God to inculcate children with religion.[51]…The future of the Church and her mission lies in teaching, especially in those schools run by priests or religious who preach by word and by example. The future of seminaries, religious vocations, and Catholic homes lies with Catholic schools."[52]

Wishing to develop these schools in Tulle as he had done in Dakar resulted from the sound realism of the Archbishop, a man of practical experience.

---

[47] M. Marcel Mangematin, P.S.S., superior of the major seminary, Letter to Archbishop Lefebvre, Jan. 26; Bishop Chassaigne, Letter Jan. 29, 1962.

[48] Vinatier, *Histoire religieuse du Bas-Limousin*, 259.

[49] This remark of the Archbishop did not please the lay people working in the public high school chaplaincies.

[50] Lefebvre, *Spiritual Conferences at Ecône*, 140 A and B, Feb. 9, 1991. There were two junior high schools at Brive: the Bossuet School and St. Antoine's, formerly a "minor seminary for the missions."

[51] Spiritual Conference at Fribourg, Nov. 25, 1969.

[52] Note for André Cagnon, June 11, 1987.

IV. AN EXTRAORDINARY PRESENCE

AN EXCELLENT "HANDS-ON" BISHOP

Let us look at some examples of the "very good relations" that Archbishop Lefebvre had with his priests.[53] Two people had died in questionable circumstances, and the parish priest of Brive telephoned the bishop's residence. The bishop came on the line straightaway: "You are there, have a look, judge for yourself and make a decision. Whatever you decide, I will back you up."

The priest later said: "I really appreciated his reply. It was realistic, and just what a priest has the right to expect from his bishop."

On July 7, Archbishop Lefebvre decided he would go himself to see the apostolate at Brive. He arrived in the evening at the appointed hour.

"*Monseigneur*," said the parish priest, "excuse me. I have a meeting to organize hospitality and some temporary accommodation for refugees from Algeria. Two thousand of them arrive every day in Brive!"

"Go ahead! But would it be useful if I came to this meeting? That would give me some ideas for when I organize the same thing in Tulle."

"I didn't dare ask you..."

The bishop was very attentive, and during the meeting he tactfully passed some unassuming but realistic comments on the matters for discussion.

At that time fifteen generals and high-ranking officers who were responsible for the putsch on April 22, 1961, in Algiers, were incarcerated in Tulle prison. Archbishop Lefebvre decided to visit them personally, and made a request to the Ministries of Justice and the Interior. Unfortunately, authorization only arrived after he had left the diocese... This was a diplomatic way of handling the situation: in reality the government rejected any mention of the imprisoned officers meeting an archbishop who asked to see them. Archbishop Lefebvre would later write: "I would have been happy to meet them, but three ministers refused me permission to go and visit these heroes whose prison I could see from the bishop's residence."[54]

His successor, Bishop Donze, was able to meet the officers. The visit went badly since the new bishop barely said a word. However, later on Marcel Lefebvre was able to do at least something for the prisoners. The chaplain of the hospital and prison in Tulle was Fr. R. Lory, an eccentric priest who was a conscientious objector and did not look favorably upon

---

[53] Msgr. Marcel Meyssignac, former arch-priest of Brive, Interview with Fr. Fabrice Delestre, April 8, 1997.

[54] Note to André Figueras on March 15, 1984. In his fictionalized account of the OAS, *Les funérailles de l'honneur* (published by author, 1984), André Figueras imagines what the meeting of the Archbishop and the officers would have been like (137-139).

the army. Thus, the putsch officers, whose numbers had risen to seventeen since the arrival of Generals Salan and Jouhaud on December 7, 1962, were deprived of real spiritual support. Raoul Salan was "converted" in the Santé prison by the Ignatian exercises preached by the Jesuit Fr. Joseph Vernet.[55] He wrote to a Jesuit friend[56] who passed his letter to Archbishop Lefebvre. The Archbishop persuaded Bishop Donze to appoint Fr. Meyssignac as the new chaplain, and he ministered to them devotedly for the rest of their stay in prison.

As parish priest, Fr. Meyssignac was responsible for building a new church (the Sacred Heart) in the northwest quarter of Brive (Les Rosiers). However, he was in some difficulty. None of the four architects in the town were capable of designing such a construction. Archbishop Lefebvre came to see the site chosen for the building, and in fifteen minutes he had gone through all the reasons for building the church on this site. He then advised the priest to contact the architect of Colmar, Joseph Muller, who had designed thirty-five churches in Africa free of charge. The Sacred Heart was completed and consecrated in 1965.

In spite of his dislike for official Catholic Action, Archbishop Lefebvre was persuaded by Canon Paul Gouygou, his Chancellor, to change his plans so that he might chair the diocesan meeting for the ACGH (Men's Catholic Action) on June 24, 1962, in Ussel. Naturally, during the meeting he set forth the plan of "piety, study, action," recommending prayer, the study of the Popes' encyclicals, and action that was above all supernatural. Monsignor Meyssignac would later say: "Of the eight bishops I have known in Tulle, he was the one who was most like what a real bishop should be. In the field he was 'incredible.' He was only bishop of Tulle for six months and all in all he only spent thirty-one days in the diocese. He was an excellent, 'hands-on' bishop with an extraordinary presence—I don't know what he did to be so present!—and as a bishop he was very close to his priests. I say that because it's true, even if not everyone likes to hear it."

FAREWELL TO TULLE

In July 1962 the General Chapter of the Holy Ghost Fathers took place. On July 26, as was expected, they chose Archbishop Lefebvre as the new Superior General. From May 14 to June 7, the bishop had done a round of confirmations in his diocese and conferred the sacrament of Christian combat on more than two thousand children and teenagers. Soon after the Chapter, he returned to Corrèze on August 14, and bid fare-

---

[55] Cf. Edmond Jouhaud, *O mon pays perdu* (Fayard, 1969), 495, 513; Hélie de Saint-Marc, *Mémoires: Les champs de braises* (Perrin, 1995).

[56] Fr. Robert-Marie Louisgrand. Archives, Fr. Marziac.

well to Lacabane on the 15th and to Beaulieu on the 16th. He took his leave of the Prefect and the Mayor of Tulle on the 17th and held a gathering for the cathedral chapter and parish priests. He finally left the diocese for Paris on August 18.

However, faithful to his word, he welcomed pilgrims from Corrèze to the Eternal City of Rome where they had come for the sixth centenary of the death of the Corrézian Pope Innocent VI. He arranged an audience with John XXIII for them on August 29 at Castel Gandolfo. At the end of the audience, the Archbishop, together with Monsignor Monéger, the pilgrimage leader, came up to the Pope:

"Most Holy Father, you appointed me at Tulle, and I really thought I would spend the rest of my days there. Now, you have confirmed my election as the Superior General of the Holy Ghost Fathers."

"Such were the wishes of your confreres," replied John XXIII, "and one must respect them."[57]

Monsignor Monéger's testimony will help us conclude this chapter. When the pilgrims were leaving from Roma Ostiense, Archbishop Lefebvre came to say goodbye. As they were getting on the train, a woman who must have bought too many souvenirs struggled past the bishop with her case. The Archbishop took hold of the bag, asked for the number of her carriage, and accompanied her to her seat in a gesture of tactful and benevolent charity.

---

[57] Monsignor F. Monéger, Interview with Fr. Fabrice Delestre, April 8, 1962.

CHAPTER 12

IN THE TURMOIL
OF THE COUNCIL

I. MEMBER OF THE CENTRAL PREPARATORY COMMISSION

"THROUGH AN INSPIRATION OF THE MOST HIGH..."

"What would your Very Reverend Eminences think about my convening an ecumenical council to continue the Vatican Council interrupted in 1870?" This was the question Pius XI put to a secret consistory on May 23, 1923. The cardinals were almost unanimously opposed to the idea. The advantages that a council might bring could be obtained, they said, without a council and would be outweighed by the disadvantages it would surely entail. When it came to Cardinal Billot's turn, he got to his feet: "One cannot shut one's eyes to the profound differences among the bishops....They could give rise to discussions that would go on indefinitely." "Should we not fear seeing the council 'manipulated' by the worst enemies of the Church, the modernists, who are already making preparations—as certain signs indicate—to take advantage of the Church's 'Estates General'[1] in order to provoke a revolution, a new 1789?" He concluded: "Let us fear seeing the infiltration of propaganda and discussion; they are practices that belong more to democratic custom than to the traditions of the Church."[2]

Thirty-six years later on January 25, 1959, Pope John XXIII spoke[3] to the cardinals gathered at the monastery of St. Paul Outside the Walls and announced his "humble resolution" to convoke an ecumenical council.[4] His idea of the council was irenic. "[It will be] an admirable spectacle of the cohesion, unity, and concord of the holy Church of God....In itself, it will be an invitation to our separated brethren...to come back to the uni-

---

1   [The Estates General was a French pre-Revolutionary assembly composed of representatives of the clergy, nobility, and commoners. It was convoked by the king at times of national crisis, and its last meeting was one of the preludes to the outbreak of the Revolution of 1789. Trans.]
2   Giovanni Caprile, S.J., *Il concilio Vaticano II* (Rome: Civiltà Cattolica, 1968), V, 681-701, cited by Raymond Dulac, *La collégialité épiscopale au deuxième concile du Vatican* (Paris: Cèdre, 1979), 9-10.
3   *A..A.S.* 51 (1959): 68; *La Documentation Catholique*, 1300: 387-388.

versal flock that Christ freely entrusted to the guidance and care of St. Peter."[5]

However, the announcement on January 25, 1959, had caused deep unease, notably among the Pope's curia,[6] with the exception of Cardinal Ottaviani. Archbishop Lefebvre would later judge the stubborn optimism of Pope John severely: "He wanted to ignore the fact that his predecessor Pius XII, who also wished to call a council, had had the wisdom to give up the idea because of the enormous risk that it posed to the Church. John XXIII literally clung to his opinion. He decided not to listen to any of those who tried to dissuade him. Lots of people advised him against calling a council. They pointed out to him the pressure that the media would exert. 'No,' he retorted, 'that's not important.'"[7]

Even before John's election as Sovereign Pontiff, those who knew his mind did not doubt his intention to "solemnly bless ecumenism."[8] Early on, this former diplomat who later on was Apostolic Delegate in Bulgaria (1925-1934) stated his opposition to the missionary activities of the Eastern Catholics (Uniates), preferring an apostolate aimed at "the union of Churches so that all together they could form the true and unique Church of our Lord Jesus Christ."[9]

CARDINAL TARDINI'S SURVEY

Naturally, Archbishop Lefebvre was still not aware of what was going on behind the scenes prior to this already virtually booby-trapped Council. He received Cardinal Tardini's letter of June 18, 1959, asking the bishops of the world for suggestions about the topics that the Council ought to discuss. On May 17, John XXIII had announced[10] the setting up of a Preparatory Commission chaired by Domenico Tardini, the Secretary of

---

[4]   In February 1948, Pius XII returned to Pius XI's idea. Cardinals Ruffini and Ottaviani saw in it a good opportunity to condemn the errors of the "new theology." However, the sixty-five bishops who were consulted suggested all sorts of new and puzzling topics. Pius XII finally grew weary of the business and decided that a council was not necessary. Thus, he himself defined the Assumption of our Lady in 1950 and condemned contemporary errors the same year in his encyclical letter *Humani Generis*.

[5]   Speech for the Fédération des Universités Catholiques, April 1, 1959, *Documentation Catholique*, 1302: 515.

[6]   Giuseppe Alberigo, *Jean XXIII devant l'histoire* (Seuil, 1989), 204, nn.17, 18.

[7]   Cagnon, *Les Relations de Rome avec Ecône*, 5; cf. *Fideliter*, no. 59: 41.

[8]   According to the prediction of Roncalli's old friend Dom Lambert Beauduin, O.S.B., cf. Louis Bouyer, *Dom Lambert Beauduin, un homme d'Eglise* (Casterman, 1964), 180-181.

[9]   Letter of July 27, 1926, to C. Morcefki, a young Orthodox Catholic who wanted to study at the Catholic seminary and whom Roncalli had turned away. Alberigo, *Jean XXIII devant l'histoire*, 19.

[10] Sermon for the Vespers of Pentecost, *A.A.S.* 51 (1959): 420; *Documentation Catholique*, 1306: 770, 782.

State, and composed of ten members among whom were the very Reverend Fr. Arcadio Larraona (a Claretian), Archbishops Pietro Palazzini and Dino Staffa, and Fr. Paul Philippe. Some of the bishops' replies deserve to be better known. Bishop Carli, bishop of a tiny Italian diocese, who was very keen to address the inconveniences of such a small jurisdictional territory, had at the same time some doctrinal concerns and wanted to see the Council condemn "materialist evolutionism" and "moral relativism." He was also concerned about the plotting of international Judaism. His concerns were shared and exceeded by the worries of a Brazilian bishop, Antonio de Castro Mayer, who asked for the Council "to denounce the existence of a conspiracy against the City of God," and considered that "priestly training ought firstly to form priests ready for combat against the anti-Christian conspiracy." His compatriot Geraldo de Proença Sigaud was no less perceptive or belligerent, denouncing "the implacable enemy of the Church and Catholic society...the Revolution." He called for "counter-revolutionary combat," especially against Communism.[11]

The Archbishop of Dakar, who, as we shall see, would soon form a holy alliance with these bishops, differed from them by his essentially pastoral concerns. In his reply to Cardinal Tardini,[12] he recommended accelerating the annulment process, simplifying the rules for Church benefices, extending the power to hear confessions, and granting wider permission for the celebration of evening Masses. He envisaged the more general use of the black clerical suit and Roman collar with a little cross on the lapel, and advocated an increase in the number of bishops so that no diocese would have more than 200,000 faithful. He also suggested adapting the ceremonies of baptism for the catechumenate, and strongly criticized the failures of the Sacred Congregation for the Propagation of the Faith while proposing a program of radical reform.[13]

Such suggestions correspond well to the bold pastoral innovations, practical sense, and essentially apostolic vigilance that we have already noted in the Archbishop of Dakar. He was open to modernity insofar as it involved a better adaptation of means and structures to achieve missionary objectives.

The proper management of dioceses was one of his particular concerns. He also wished to preserve the free exercise of the bishops' authority that was being threatened by the highly invasive episcopal assemblies and by the influence of Catholic Action guided by extra-diocesan directives. He asked moreover for clarification on the lay apostolate.

---

[11] *Acta et documenta de concilio Vat. II apparando*, series I (antepræparatoria), vol. II; hereafter *A. Doc.*

[12] From Dakar, Feb. 26, 1960.

[13] Cf. *Fideliter*, no. 140 (March-April 2001): 20.

However, he also expressed his concerns about sound doctrine and suggested remedies to the doctrinal deviations that were spreading in the seminaries. He recommended especially that teaching should follow the *Summa* of St. Thomas and that a summary of the social doctrine of the Church be created as a teaching aid. He focused on two particular points of doctrine: the dogma that "outside the Church there is no salvation" required clarification in the light of "serious errors[14] that ruin the missionary sense of the Church." It also seemed "desirable to define or at least affirm" the Marian doctrine "that the Most Blessed Virgin Mary, Mother of God, is the Mediatrix of all Graces."[15] This truth would only confirm the spiritual motherhood of the Virgin Mary.

Archbishop Lefebvre's suggestions and those of the three other bishops we have quoted contrast sharply with the "average" suggestions made by the bishops of the world,[16] who rarely called for any doctrinal clarifications.

THE TROJAN HORSE IN THE CITY OF GOD

On June 5, John XXIII appointed Archbishop Lefebvre (then Archbishop of Dakar) and Bernard Yago, Archbishop of Abidjan, to represent French-speaking West Africa on the Central Preparatory Commission for the Council. The 120 members were responsible for examining the schemas that had been written by the ten preparatory commissions working from the suggestions made by the world's bishops. Up until June 1962, the Archbishop—who became bishop of Tulle in the meantime—took part in all the sessions of the Central Commission that were sometimes chaired by the Pope. He was able to observe the care that went into preparations for the Council, and also the terrible battles of influence between the two camps that had been created by Pope John himself. On one side were the "Romans" with the Theological Commission of Cardinal Ottaviani, Pro-Secretary of the Holy Office; on the other were the Liberals and their "Trojan horse," the Secretariat for the Promotion of Christian Unity, that was chaired by Cardinal Agustin Bea with the help of the young Dutch prelate Jan Willebrands.[17]

---

[14] Cf. R. P. Retif, "La doctrine missionnaire des pères de l'Eglise" (The Missionary Doctrine of the Fathers of the Church), in *Missions Catholiques,* no. 77 (Jan.-March 1960): 38.

[15] Bishop de Castro Mayer made the same request.

[16] Simoulin, "Les *vota* des évêques," in *Église et contre-Eglise au concile Vatican II* (Éd. Courrier de Rome, 1996), 89.

[17] Secretary for the Catholic Conference for Ecumenism founded in 1952 in Fribourg, Switzerland (and chaired by the local bishop, François Charrière), as an official link with the Ecumenical Council of Churches. Cf. Harold E. Frey, in Rouse and Neill, *A History of the Ecumenical Movement,* WCC, 4th ed. (London: SPCK, 1993), 320.

The First Skirmishes

Like all Council Fathers, Archbishop Lefebvre received a list of the experts appointed by the Pope to the various preparatory commissions;[18] he read it attentively. When it came for his turn to speak during the first session of the Central Commission on June 15, 1961, he did not hesitate in denouncing—all alone—the contradictions between what had been said and what was being done.

As for the standards required of the Council's theologians and canonists, it is clear, as the advisers have explicitly stated,[19] that firstly they must have the sense of the Church, and adhere with all their heart in word and deed to the doctrine of the Sovereign Pontiffs found in all their documents.

This principle needs restating all the more since we were, in my humble opinion, very surprised to read on the list of the preparatory commissions the names of certain theologians whose theology does not meet the standards demanded by the advisers.[20]

Three of the consultants at least had in fact fallen under censure or sanction from higher authority.[21]

"At the time," said Archbishop Lefebvre, "Cardinal Ottaviani did not pick up on my remarks, but after the meeting during coffee, he took me by the arm and said, 'I know! What can be done? The Holy Father wants it like that. He wants experts with a reputation!'"[22]

Archbishop Lefebvre later commented on this decision of Pope John: "He tended towards laxity. Maybe his head was quite traditional, but certainly not his heart. Under the guise of holding very broad opinions, he had fallen into the clutches of a liberal spirit. And when [later on] he discussed the difficulties of the Council, he told those he spoke with that he was certain 'everything will work out,' and that 'everyone will agree.' He didn't want to accept the idea that someone could have bad intentions, or that one had to be wary....In the same way he insisted on choosing experts condemned by the Holy Office, in spite of the upset caused by such a decision."[23]

From November 1961, the Central Commission began to examine and discuss the schemas prepared by the commissions. In general the

---

[18] A list of the "consulters," appointed in June 1960. *Documentation Catholique*, 1346: 267ff. A complementary list in *Documentation Catholique*, 1367: 67ff.

[19] In particular Wynen, a judge at the Rota [One of three tribunals established by Pius X in 1908 to deal with contentious cases. Trans.], and Vaccari.

[20] *A. Doc.*, series II (præparatoria), vol. II, pars I, 316.

[21] Yves Congar, O.P., Henri de Lubac, and Karl Rahner, S.J.

[22] *Spiritual Conferences at Ecône*, Dec. 11, 1972, Sept. 20, 1973; *Fideliter*, no. 59: 39; interview with Fr. Marziac, 5-6.

[23] *Fideliter*, no. 59: 41.

Archbishop gave them his *placet*, his "yes" vote. As he later said: "Through the preparatory commissions the Council was preparing to proclaim the truths opposed to these [modern] errors in order to drive them from the midst of the Church for as long as possible....It readied itself to be a light in today's world, which it would have been had it used the pre-conciliar texts in which were found a solemn profession of sound doctrine concerning modern problems."[24]

Archbishop Lefebvre considered that the Church could not keep the deposit of the Faith without fighting error. So, on January 20, 1962, when Cardinal Ottaviani had finished presenting his schema "Keeping purely the deposit of the Faith," the Archbishop declared: "The Council must talk about modern errors—how can we defend the Faith if we have no principles?"[25] On January 23, he suggested that the Council should formulate two types of documents: in addition to the proposed schemata which would be coupled with "canons" rejecting modern errors "precisely and almost scientifically," the Council could "more positively" elaborate a short text containing a synthesis of the entire Christian plan of Redemption "from which it would be clearly apparent that no salvation is possible outside of Jesus our Savior and His mystical body which is the Church[26]...following the idea of numerous members of the Commission."[27]

Already the insidious criticisms of the liberal Fathers worried Archbishop Lefebvre. On January 20, Cardinal Alfrink criticized one of Ottaviani's schemas for being "bound to one school of philosophy." Cardinal Bea attacked the document's "scholastic language." Foreseeing that during this second preparatory session, the liberals were attempting to get rid of all the schemas that were not to their liking, the Archbishop made the bold and original suggestion noted above. The liberals were no fools, and understood that in Marcel Lefebvre they would have an adversary who was determined to throw a wrench in the works. Cardinal Ottaviani approved of and praised Archbishop Lefebvre's idea, as did numerous Fathers. Unfortunately, they took it no further.

In meeting after meeting the same thing happened. After each schema had been presented by the president of the commission that wrote it, discussion was opened and was usually led by the cardinals. On the one side were Liénart, Frings, Alfrink, Döpfner, König, and Léger and on the other Ruffini, Siri, Larraona, and Browne: six cardinals against four. Archbishop

---

24 Msgr. Lefebvre, *J'accuse le concile* (Martigny: Éd. Saint-Gabriel, 1976), 108-109. [English version: *I Accuse the Council* (Angelus Press, 1982).]

25 Manuscript record of voting. [Including members' remarks. Trans.]

26 Like the Council of Trent which, in addition to its declarations and canons, produced "that admirable synthesis of the Catholic Faith in her catechism" (*ibid*).

27 *A. Doc.*, II, II, II, 417-418.

Lefebvre explained: "It was clear to all the members who were present that there was a division inside the Church. It did not come about by chance and neither was it superficial. It was a deep division, and deeper still between the cardinals than between the archbishops or bishops." In time Marcel Lefebvre's interventions in these meetings became more numerous. Either he prepared them while reading the schemas which he received several weeks in advance, or he would jot them down during the meetings while listening to the liberal Fathers. With gravity and with a supernatural spirit, the Archbishop rose and made his pertinent remarks, giving voice to the *sensus Ecclesiae*. Thus, on January 17, 1962, when Cardinal Aloisi Masella's schema on the Sacrament of Orders proposed the idea of married deacons, Archbishop Lefebvre protested: "In our missionary regions, it seems to me that this new practice would be interpreted as a step on the road towards married priests, *quod non placet*. Moreover, it certainly risks reducing the number of vocations to the priesthood....On the other hand, I quite like the new idea of a permanent diaconate."

DEFENDER OF GREGORY AND ROME'S TRADITIONAL LATIN MASS

During the meeting in March-April 1962, the subject of the liturgy was addressed. Unwillingly, Cardinal Larraona presented the schema of Fr. Bugnini signed by his predecessor, the late Cardinal Gaetano Cicognani.[28] It was a detailed plan for a systematic reform (*instauratio*) of the entire liturgy along the lines of the innovative principles already used by Frs. Antonelli and Bugnini in the reform of the Holy Week Liturgy. It overturned the 1960 reform of the Code of Rubrics "under the prevailing pressure of the new mood of innovation."[29]

While the liberal Fathers tried to outdo each other in praise of the schema "that must be counted as one of the most remarkable schemas that has yet been proposed to our Central Commission," as Döpfner said, Ottaviani denounced its "spirit that opens wide the door to excessive innovation, or at least gives in to an urge for novelty." Archbishop Lefebvre himself denounced "the definition of the liturgy [which] seems incomplete because the sacramental and sanctifying aspects are given more emphasis, and the aspect of prayer is not emphasized enough. Now, the fundamental aspect of the liturgy is the worship given to God, an act of *religion*."

He was opposed to the increase in the number of readings at Mass and widening the use of the vernacular ("What will remain of those most beau-

---

[28] Who died on February 5. On February 1, he eventually signed the schema for the liturgical commission, something he had long refused to do....His successor, Larraona, was most unhappy to have to ratify Bugnini's schema.

[29] Bugnini, *La Riforma liturgica*, 26.

tiful Gregorian melodies?"), and he attacked those that had come up with the initiative and the idea of a sudden, artificial reform:

> Certainly, it is stated that only the hierarchy can change something in the liturgy...but...we know by experience that it is not the bishops who are asking for changes, but certain priests in the liturgical pastoral commissions who have nothing else to do but change something in the liturgy!...
> We must not forget that we have to "hold on to the traditions." These changes must only be allowed with great prudence. What is Tradition if not the work of the Church throughout time? And generally this work is born of the efforts of numerous generations.[30]

The Archbishop's insights are admirable. The reform proposed was anti-liturgical because it suppressed what was essential—the divine cult—and also because it scorned the work of Tradition. On March 27, Fr. Bugnini attended the meeting at which the unfortunate Cardinal Larraona[31] explained to the Fathers the plan for the reform of the Ordinary of the Mass. While Lercaro, Döpfner, *et al.* went into raptures of approval, the "Roman" cardinals went on the offensive. Godfrey dissected the text, refuted a few of its sophisms, and rejected one after the other the suggested modifications and suppressions. Ottaviani hurled a thundering *non placet*: "There is such an accumulation of changes that it seems to be a revolutionary reform which will stun the Catholic people." Browne restated the principle that "the sanctification of man...is brought about at Mass by the very act of oblation and sacrifice, the supreme act of the virtue of religion. The innovators[32] have forgotten this truth, and emphasized instead the hearing of God's word and the celebration of the Last Supper."

As for Fr. Paul Philippe, he explained that in the light of the doctrine proposed by Pius XII, concelebration blurs the unique, hierarchical role of the priest who at Mass is assimilated to Christ the Priest. It diminishes the principal effect of propitiation and impetration for the living and the dead because this effect "is not the same in one concelebrated Mass as in many Masses celebrated by several priests."

When it came to his time to vote, Archbishop Lefebvre firstly said: "*Placet juxta modum*:[33] according to the observations of their Eminences Cardinals Godfrey, Ottaviani, Browne, and Fr. Philippe."[34] It was a "yes" to a reform of the Mass of the Catechumens, but "no" to a revolution. The commission for reform will have to work under the Pope's authority but

[30] *A. Doc.*, II, III, 71, 76, 98-99.
[31] On Larraona's resistance, see Bugnini, *La Riforma liturgica*, 41.
[32] He was speaking about Protestants but also indirectly criticized the liturgical commission and especially Professor Josef Jungmann, spokesman for the subcommission for the reform of the Mass.
[33] "Yes on condition such and such a *modus* [change in the text] is added."
[34] *A. Doc.*, II, III, 121, 125, 126, 128, 142.

"once the changes are made, things should be left for a while because continual change lessens esteem for the dignity and value of the Church's liturgical rites as much among priests as among the faithful."

On March 30, 1962, he opposed the innovations to the liturgy for mission countries as found in the schema of Cardinal Agagianian. He said that they destroyed the unity of the rite and the liturgical language which "for our faithful in the mission regions is a very strong argument in favor of the Faith, especially given the diversity of Protestant rites that reflect their divisions." He illustrated this truth with two facts:

> When the Sacred Congregation for the Propagation of the Faith gave us permission to translate the chants for High Mass into the vernacular: *Kyrie, Gloria, Credo, etc.*, all the priests and especially the indigenous priests dismissed the translation as useless, because they and their faithful knew all of the chants perfectly, and understood that the Latin language is a sign of the unity of the Faith.
>
> For the Dakar Pan-African Congress, the presidents of the civil governments—Senghor from Senegal, Tsirana from Madagascar, Maga from Dahomey, and Yaméogo from Upper Volta—came to the cathedral for High Mass and sang loudly together all the Latin chants, including the *Graduale*. After Mass they told us expressly how happy this unanimity made them.
>
> For all the Catholics present, what a great example of unity and brotherhood in prayer and worship!
>
> If then we accept the principle that the bishops' conferences can act and legislate in liturgical matters and sacramental rites, even with the consent of the Holy See, there will be a return to national liturgies and rites. All the efforts of the last two centuries in favor of liturgical unity will have been in vain. Art and Gregorian music will fall into ruin....We run the risk of creating anarchy.[35]

THE LAY APOSTOLATE AND CHRIST THE KING

At the seventh and last preparatory meeting, the Archbishop acted decisively in support of the reign of Christ the King even over temporal affairs. On June 18, he spoke about the lay apostolate and asked for a reaffirmation of its dependence on the priestly apostolate. Following Pius X,[36] he distinguished two ways in which this dependence operates: the first regards the lay apostolate in the broadest sense— "the sanctification of professions and civil society"—in which the laypeople are "subject to the bishops' *vigilance*"; the second is through an apostolate in the strict sense in which laypeople "unquestionably depend *directly* and *immediately* on the

---

[35] *Ibid.*, II, III, 384-385.
[36] St. Pius X, enc. *Il Fermo Proposito,* June 11, 1905; *Les Enseignements pontificaux, Le laïcat,* nn. 364-365.

authority of the bishops and the priests appointed by them, since they then collaborate in the very mission entrusted by Christ to the bishops."[37]

Having made this enlightening distinction, Archbishop Lefebvre added that nevertheless, one cannot separate the temporal and the spiritual domains; on the one hand the temporal is in fact subject to the supernatural order, and on the other the clergy cannot be excluded from the care and possession of temporal things. Lastly he denounced the false principle that states "Let us restore the natural order so that it might become supernatural," since this idea was "disastrous for the true apostolate." He said: "Christ our Lord never taught us such a principle since He was Himself the restoration of order in the natural and supernatural domains. His grace both heals us and raises us up."

POPE JOHN'S DOUBLE DEALING

John XXIII then brought to this initial battle a second Trojan horse through the agenda of Léon-Joseph Suenens, Archbishop of Malines. The Pope had just appointed him to the Central Preparatory Commission and he would soon make him a cardinal. From March 1962, Suenens complained to John XXIII about the "excessive" number of schemas—no less than seventy. John XXIII, who had provided no guidelines for the preparatory work[38] and who did not want to face Ottaviani, secretly gave Suenens the job of clearing the way ahead. The Suenens plan consisted of taking all the preparatory schemas and reworking them to fit one of two categories: what the Church had to say to her children, *ad intra*, and what the Church had to say to the world, *ad extra*. The second category was obviously a revolutionary innovation.

The plan was ready by the end of April and the Pope liked it. In mid-May he ordered it to be sent to a few influential cardinals whom he wanted to win over to the idea: Cardinals Döpfner, Montini, Siri, Liénart, and Lercaro.[39] Did this not begin the process that led to the eventual ditching of the preparatory schemas? Thus, John destroyed with one hand what he was building with the other. He allowed the Preparatory Commission to continue with its work while at the same time planning for others to destroy it.

According to the Bishop of Tulle, John thought that the Holy Ghost would take care of everything. He gave his diocese an account of his meeting with the Pope on June 7, 1962,[40] during which they had discussed the

---

[37] Voting, 18 June 1962, *A. Doc.*, II, IV, 558-559.
[38] Cf. talk of Cardinal Bea, Sept. 1962, Etienne Fouilloux, *Vatican II commence* (Catholic University of Louvain, 1993), 72, n. 56; Lovey in *Eglise et contre-Eglise*, 141.
[39] Alberigo, *Jean XXIII devant l'histoire*, 191; Fouilloux, *Vatican II commence*, 149; Lovey in *Eglise et contre-Eglise*, 138.
[40] Not mentioning that John had reproached him. Cf. Chapter 11 on "Tulle."

work of the Central Commission: "The Holy Father follows the work with great interest and an impressive spirit of Faith. He bases all his hopes on the Holy Ghost and not on human calculations."[41] That was not all. The Secretariat for the Promotion of Christian Unity had not remained idle.[42] It had its experts in the ten sub-commissions make suggestions or draft schemas on subjects that were also being tackled by other commissions. However, it dealt with these matters from an ecumenical point of view. It also prepared three special schemas on ecumenism, religious liberty,[43] and the question of the Jews. The Secretariat sent the projects on its first three topics to Ottaviani's Theological Commission, which took as little notice of them as possible. Cardinal Bea also asked if the Secretariat could form a joint commission with the Theological Commission (as he had done with other preparatory commissions). Ottaviani refused.[44] To avoid these deep divides without solving them himself, John XXIII decided on February 1, 1962, that the last two schemas of the Secretariat, one of which was on religious liberty, would be directly sent to the Central Preparatory Commission without going via other commissions.

A Dramatic Showdown

On June 19, the penultimate day of the final meeting, two rival schemas were to be discussed by the Central Commission. The first, Chapter IX of the schema "On the Church" prepared by the Theological Commission and worked on personally by Cardinal Ottaviani, concerned "Relations between Church and State and religious tolerance." There were nine pages of text and fourteen pages of endnotes with numerous quotations from the papal teachings of Pius XI and Pius XII. The second, written by Cardinal Bea's Secretariat for Christian Unity,[45] was entitled "On Religious Liberty." There were fifteen pages of text and five pages of notes but no references to the Magisterium of the Church.

---

[41] *Semaine Religieuse de Tulle*, June 1, 1962, p. 1.

[42] Stjepan Schmidt, *Augustin Bea, der Kardinal der Einheit* (Graz: Styria, 1989), 431, 441-444, 467ff.

[43] This theme soon appeared on the Secretariat's agenda, but Schmidt does not mention it. Fr. P. Jérôme Hamer, O.P., recounts how they drew up the first version of the schema, the "Fribourg Document," on November 27, 1960, at the bishop's residence in Fribourg: that day the sub-commission consisted of Bishops François Charrière and Emile De Smedt, Canon Bavaud, and Fr. P. Hamer. Cf. *Vatican II, La liberté religieuse*, Unam Sanctam (Cerf, 1967), 53-57.

[44] Cf. Dr. Werner Becker, "Das Dekret über den Ökumenismus," in *LThK*, vol. 13, pp. 12-13.

[45] And more specifically by the sub-commission chaired by Bishop Charrière of Fribourg and attended by Bishop Emile De Smedt, Bishop of Bruges; the Belgian Jérôme Hamer, O.P.; the Canadian A. Baum, A.A.; and the American Weigel, S.J.

When he received these two texts in advance, Archbishop Lefebvre said to himself: "The first is Catholic Tradition, but the second? What on earth is that? They want to introduce Liberalism, the French Revolution, and the Declaration of the Rights of Man into the Church! This cannot be! We'll soon see what happens at the meeting."[46]

And plenty happened. Cardinal Ottaviani began presenting his schema and openly attacked the other schema: "In expounding the doctrine of the relations between the Catholic State and other religions, it seems to me we must recognize that the Holy Synod (Council) must follow the undisputed doctrine that belongs to the Church and not some doctrine that pleases non-Catholics or gives in to their demands. This is why I think we must eliminate from our discussion the constitution proposed by the Secretariat for Christian Unity insofar as it smacks greatly of the influence of non-Catholics."

Having given a few examples to illustrate this influence, he presented his schema whose central concern was the protection of the Catholic Faith and the safeguard of the temporal common good based on the unanimity of citizens in the true religion. He then made a distinction between the very different situations in which people live: entirely Catholic nations, nations with religious diversity, and non-Catholic States. In the first case the principles would be implemented in full; there would be the union of Church and State with civil recognition and protection for the true religion and, if need be, some tolerance of false religions. In the second case the Church would enjoy the same rights accorded by the State to all religions that do not contravene natural law. In the third case the Church would ask for mere freedom of action.

When it came to his turn, Cardinal Bea rose and presented his concept of religious liberty which applied in all cases and for every man, even those "who erred as regards the Faith." Until this moment the Church had only supported the rights of her own children. Would she now claim those rights for members of all religions? That was the case, as Bea soon explained, and he underlined the ecumenical significance of the topic: "Today this is a question of interest for non-Catholics who repeatedly criticize the Church for being intolerant when she is in the majority and for demanding religious liberty when she is in the minority. This objection totally undermines all the efforts made to lead non-Catholics to the Church. When the Secretariat wrote this schema in accordance with its responsibilities, it bore in mind these circumstances and asked itself what the duty of the Church was as regards religious liberty, and how that liberty ought to be exercised."

---

[46] Talk in Sierre, Switzerland, Nov. 27, 1988.

How right Ottaviani was! This schema had indeed been written to satisfy the demands of non-Catholics. Now, they wanted to make these demands into Catholic doctrine. How could Ottaviani co-operate in such a venture? Besides, by reading the schema he could see that it had a completely subjective philosophy and was opposed to the realism of sound Thomist philosophy.

The schema said that sincere men want to do God's will, and since they perceive God's will through their conscience, they have "the right to follow their consciences in religious matters." Moreover, human nature demands that man express his conscience exteriorly and collectively. Therefore, men have the right not to be hindered in practicing their religion, alone or in a group, except where that opposes the clear rights of a third of society or of society as a whole. Finally, this religious liberty "must be inscribed in strong laws, and expressed by the civil equality of religions." Thus, in the name of liberty of conscience expressed in all its crudity, the notion of the Catholic State was to be done away with.

To justify his assertions that ran counter to former universal Catholic practice—and which still applied in several countries—Cardinal Bea did not hesitate to claim that "in present-day conditions, no nation can be said to be properly speaking 'Catholic'…and that none could be considered alone or separate from the others," a claim that implied a common international rule of religious liberty.[47] Besides, as he added, "the State as such perceives neither the existence nor the power of the supernatural order."[48] Finally, the reigning pontiff wanted "an *aggiornamento*," or "[he wanted people] to adapt to conditions of life today, and not to re-establish what had been possible or even necessary in other sociological structures."[49] Bea concluded: "Our two documents…do not agree on the fundamental is-

---

[47] Pius XII (allocution *Ci Riesce*, Dec. 6, 1953) had recognized for the sake of peace the legitimacy of a regime of religious tolerance in a community of states whose peoples differed in religious allegiance. However, the civil right thus granted to members of false religions would only depend on the needs of the common good and not on a natural right of conscience. Cf. Davies, *The Second Vatican Council and Religious Liberty*, appendix VI. On the contrary, Cardinal Bea was promoting a natural right to religious liberty.

[48] Since 1951, the American Jesuit John C. Murray had argued, in *The American Ecclesiastical Review* (May 1951, 327-352), that the distinction between the true religion and those that are false could not enter into the constitutional sphere. He had been fought in the pages of the same journal by Fr. Joseph C. Fenton (*AER*, June 1951, 451ff.) and in Rome by Cardinal Ottaviani himself (allocution at the Lateran Atheneum, March 3, 1953, in Ottaviani, *L'Eglise et la Cité* [Imp. Polygl. Vat., 1963], 276).

[49] *A. Doc.*, II, IV, 689. The regime of a Catholic State, taught by Pope Leo XIII, that officially recognizes the Catholic Church as such was not a doctrine, according to Fr. Murray and Jacques Maritain, but only a practice that was linked to a former sociological context.

sues presented in Nos. 3 and 8. It is up to this distinguished gathering to pass judgment."

Irritated by the historical relativism that his opponent applied to the public law of the Church, a subject he had taught for twenty years, Cardinal Ottaviani thought it right to reply by strongly underlining his opposition: "The commission of the Secretariat for Christian Unity ought to have submitted its schema (which concerns doctrine and not just sociology, because this 'sociology' is founded on doctrine) to the Doctrinal Commission for us to see whether it accorded with the thinking of the Doctrinal Commission. Now we see that there are certain matters on which we do not agree, and those matters are doctrinal!"[50]

Thus as Archbishop Lefebvre remarked, "they were there like that, both stood up. The rest of us were seated, looking at the two cardinals confronting one another, two eminent cardinals who were in conflict over such a fundamental thesis of theology."[51] The cardinals that spoke afterwards came down on one side or the other. Frings considered that "the Church no longer needs the secular arm to protect the Catholic Faith against the spread of religious errors." He added that "the State cannot prevent the spread of another religion if the temporal common good is not at stake." Léger, inspired by Fr. Murray, believed he was giving a learned explanation when he said that "only people can profess a religion and not the State. The State is a function....The State is not competent to decide which is the true religion." On the other hand, the realist Ottaviani predicted that "religious liberty would enable the Protestants to conquer Latin America." Ruffini declared that, "Liberty in itself is for truth and for virtue, not for error or for vice. In practice, tolerance is necessary from the point of view of charity." "As regards the State,…and what his Eminence Cardinal Bea has claimed—that the State as such cannot and must not know or recognize the [true] religion—I'd consider that to be completely false." Larraona considered that it was "naïve" to think one can attract non-Catholics by recognizing that they have the same freedom as we do. Finally, Browne said: "It seems to me childish to suppose that the doctrine expounded by Leo XIII in his encyclical *Immortale Dei* is a contingent doctrine."

Cardinal Ruffini asked "that the question be resolved by referring it to our Holy Father the Pope." Nonetheless, they proceeded to the vote when Archbishop Lefebvre was able to give his own opinion:

---

[50] *Ibid.*, 691.
[51] Cagnon. The best observers have underlined the seriousness of this face to face confrontation which fills fifty-four folio pages in the *Acta*: firstly the cardinals' long explanations of their positions and then the votes of all the members. Cf. Schmidt, *Augustin Bea, der Kardinal der Einheit*, 469.

On Religious Liberty: *non placet* ...since it is based on false principles solemnly condemned by the sovereign pontiffs, for example Pius IX,[52] who calls this error "delirium" (Denzinger 1690). *On the Church*: *placet.* However, the exposition of the fundamental principles could be done with more reference to Christ the King as in the encyclical *Quas Primas.*....Our Council could have as its aim to preach Christ to all men, and to state that it belongs to the Catholic Church alone to be the true preacher of Christ who is the salvation and life of individuals, families, professional associations, and of other civil bodies.

The schema on religious liberty does not preach Christ and therefore seems false. The Theological Commission's schema expounds the authentic doctrine but does so like a thesis; it does not sufficiently show the aim of this doctrine which is nothing other than the reign of Christ....From the point of view of Christ as source of salvation and life, all the fundamental truths could be expounded as they say "pastorally," and in this way the errors of secularism, naturalism, and materialism, *etc.* would be excluded.[53]

This intervention which was original by its supernatural perspective, and which brought the debate back to its fundamental principle, could only have struck a note in the minds of the Fathers of the Central Preparatory Commission. A man filled with the spirit of wisdom had stood up and proclaimed not the Rights of Man but the Rights of Christ the King. The voting continued. The Latino Fathers—Italians, Hispanics, and Latin-Americans—were in favor of the Ottaviani schema whereas the American, English, German, Dutch, and French Fathers supported Bea's project. The numbers were evenly divided.[54]

Therefore, on the eve of the Council, as Archbishop Lefebvre explained, "the Church was divided on a fundamental subject: the social reign of our Lord Jesus Christ. Ought our Lord to reign over nations? Cardinal Ottaviani said 'Yes!' The other said, 'No'! So I said to myself: 'If this is how it has started, what will the Council be like?'"[55]

He made known his concerns to his diocese in Corrèze on July 13, 1962: "Let us have no illusions. The powers of darkness will use every means to thwart the Council or to direct it in such a way as to ruin the Church." The bishop advised his people: "Like the Apostles before Pentecost, let us hide our souls away in piety, adoration, humility, recollection, and prayer."[56]

---

[52] Encyclical *Quanta Cura*, Dec. 8, 1864.
[53] *A. Doc.*, II, IV, 740-741.
[54] When one thinks about the novelty of the Secretariat's thesis and even about the novelty of this Secretariat in itself, such a result was already a victory. Cf. Schmidt, *Augustin Bea, der Kardinal der Einheit*, 469.
[55] Talk in Sierre, Switzerland, Nov. 27, 1988.
[56] *Semaine Religieuse de Tulle*, 208.

Besides, as the Archbishop thought, there were plenty of reasons to hope. He would later say that the preparation for the Council "was very serious and completely in accord with Tradition," enabling the Church to "proclaim the truth in the face of modern errors in order to drive them out from the midst of the Church for as long as possible." He thought the Council could be "a light in today's world."[57]

II. THE REVOLUTION BEGINS

JOHN XXIII REVEALS HIS HAND

The Central Preparatory Commission's work ended on June 20. The sub-commissions altered their schemas. Some were dropped, others were sent to the Commission for Reform of the Code of Canon Law. Yet more were condensed to such a degree that their number was reduced from seventy-three to twenty.[58] Seven of them were sent to the future Council Fathers in July 1962.

On the morning of October 11, 1962, the rain that had drenched Rome for the previous two days stopped. The clouds parted to reveal a bright sun. In rows of six, the 2,400 Council Fathers—the bishops in cope and mitre—ascended the steps of St. Peter's Basilica, crossed the vestibule, and passed through the main door. Then they were shown to their places on the right and left in galleries constructed on either side of the nave. Archbishop Lefebvre's place was numbered D 1090. It was a temporary seat that was uncomfortable since it was too narrow and had little legroom. Like the other Fathers he was given a small, white, plastic document holder and he put it on the armrest-*cum*-writing desk attached to his chair. Looking inside the document holder he found texts of the Council prayers, a calendar for October, a pamphlet with instructions for how to vote, *etc.*

The Pope made his entry, knelt at the small altar in the nave before the cardinals, and intoned the *Veni Creator Spiritus.* Yes, "Come Holy Ghost, fill the hearts of Thy faithful....O Guide our minds with Thy blest light....Far from us drive the deadly foe." The Archbishop, who had been Superior General of the Holy Ghost Fathers since July 28, fervently invoked the divine patron of his order. Certainly, the two sides that had faced each other during the preparatory meetings were readying themselves for new battles, but Archbishop Lefebvre thought that the help of the Holy Ghost and the Pope's chairing the Council as successor of Peter—head of the Church by divine right—would guarantee the triumph

---

[57] Lefebvre, *J'accuse le concile*, 108-109.
[58] Ralph Wiltgen, S.V.D., *The Rhine Flows into the Tiber* (Augustine Publishing Co., 1978), 22.

of the Spirit of Truth in "a Church still entirely obedient to the wind and fire of Pentecost."[59] He shared this confidence with the members of his congregation in a letter that was, if the truth be told, quite standard for such an occasion.

This confidence was immediately knocked by John XXIII as he delivered his opening address inspired by Cardinal Montini.[60] All his predecessors from the last 150 years up to Pope Pius XII had unanimously denounced a "terrible and deep-rooted malady which, developing every day and eating into its inmost being, is dragging it to destruction. You understand, Venerable Brethren, what this disease is—apostasy from God."[61] However, Pope John contradicted them, showing a curious optimism: "We believe we ought to disassociate ourselves entirely from those prophets of doom[62] who are constantly predicting the worst, as if the end of the world were near....According to them, contemporary society would lead to nothing but ruin and calamity; compared to past centuries, our own age show nothing but deterioration."

John suggested a new method for the Council: "This sure and unchangeable doctrine, [Christian doctrine] must be studied and expounded according to methods demanded by modern-day thought. The deposit of faith is one thing, but the way it is presented is something quite different. In our teachings, we must have recourse to a style of presentation that is especially pastoral."

The keyword had been spoken: "pastoral." In the past, they had been pastoral by warning the flock about "the ravenous wolves"—as Ottaviani thought they still should—and the errors that were infiltrating the seminaries and the Catholic universities. However, John cared little about such things: "Today the Spouse of Christ prefers to have recourse to the medicine of mercy, rather than brandishing the arms of severity. She considers that rather than condemning, she better responds to the needs of our age[63] by emphasizing the wealth of her doctrine." However, as Archbishop Lefebvre asked himself, how was the Church going to present the truth "effectively" without condemning error? Was the idea of an "especially pastoral Council" a cover-up for surrendering in the combat for the Faith?

---

59   "Letter of His Grace Archbishop Lefebvre, Superior General, to all the members of the Congregation on the occasion of the Second Vatican Council," *General Bulletin*, 222ff.

60   Cf. J. Madiran, in *Itinéraires*, no. 285: 158.

61   St. Pius X, Encyclical *E Supremi Apostolatus*, Oct. 4, 1903, §3 (Bonne Presse) I, 33; *Courrier de Rome*, I, 34-35 [English version: Angelus Press, 1998.]

62   John XXIII read the third part of the secret of Fatima and considered that it did not concern his age...

63   This was the leitmotiv of the petition recently sent to the Pope by Cardinal Léger, and also signed by Cardinals Frings, Alfrink, Suenens, Döpfner, König, and Liénart. G. Routhier, "Le Cardinal Léger et la préparation de Vatican II," in *Revue d'Histoire de l'Église de France*, no. 205 (1994): 301. Lefebvre, *Lettre ouverte aux cath. perplexes*, 136.

FIRST LIBERAL VICTORIES

Archbishop Lefebvre often spoke about the victories of the liberal wing who from the outset began shaping the way the Council would develop. The Council was "controlled by the forces of modernization. We felt it, we sensed it, and when I say 'we' I mean the majority of Council Fathers at that time; we had the impression that something unusual was happening."[64] The first thing was the rejection of the list of Fathers drawn from the preparatory commissions and proposed by Archbishop Felici as the ones best suited for election to the conciliar commissions. Together with the German bishops, Cardinal Frings, Archbishop of Cologne, decided to push for the acceptance of another list that would be made up of liberal bishops. Cardinal Liénart was to lead the attack.[65]

At the entrance to the Basilica, he received from Cardinal Lefebvre a Latin text written by Archbishop Garrone, Archbishop of Toulouse. He stood up at the table of the Council Presidency where he had been sitting, and after Cardinal Tisserant had refused him permission to speak merely to keep up appearances, he read his speech "in a shaky voice" referring to "the liberty of the Fathers." He was applauded, and Frings himself spoke in turn. The applause was twice as loud, and the meeting was brought to a close.[66]

Hastily the bishops' conferences from the banks of the Rhine—Germany, Austria, France, the Low Countries, Belgium, and Switzerland—together with some African bishops, drew up a common list to which were added the names of a few liberal Fathers from other countries. When Cardinal Siri complained about this monopoly, Frings replied: "If you do not accept the Italians we propose, none of your Italians will be elected."[67] Thus on October 16, "the European alliance" won 49% of the seats. As Wiltgen commented: "The Rhine had begun to flow into the Tiber."

The liberal Fathers' second victory was to have the discussion of the first four doctrinal schemas put off indefinitely. This followed on the Dutch initiative to distribute Fr. Schillebeeckx's commentary of these documents as soon as the Council Fathers arrived in Rome. John XXIII accepted the request of Cardinals Frings, Liénart, and Alfrink, and on Octo-

---

[64] *Ibid.*

[65] Cardinal Tisserant, speaking to Jean Guitton of the Académie Française, mentioned "the meeting we all had before the Council opened [with five other cardinals], when we decided to hold up the first session by rejecting the tyrannical rules laid down by John XXIII"; cf. Jean Guitton, *Paul VI secret*, 123, quoted in Romano Amerio, *Iota Unum* (NEL, 1987), 80.

[66] *A. Syn.*, I, I, 207-208; *Spiritual Conferences at Ecône*, Dec. 11, 1972; Wiltgen, *The Rhine Flows into the Tiber*, 17; Claude Beaufort, Cardinal Liénart's memories in *Pèlerin Magazine*, Nov. 22, 1985.

[67] *Spiritual Conferences at Ecône*, Dec. 11, 1972.

ber 16, it was announced that the first schema for discussion would be the constitution on the liturgy.

This second liberal victory was fully secured when the first doctrinal schema "On the Sources of Revelation" finally came up for discussion on November 24. The liberal group mobilized itself: its aim was to deny divine Tradition's independence from Sacred Scripture in order to establish the primacy of the Bible for ecumenical ends. The arguments raged back and forth between thirty "Romans" and forty liberals who spoke one after the other during five general meetings.

The Council Presidency decided to ask the Fathers to vote on whether discussion of this schema should be suspended. Sixty-two percent were in favor of the motion but the two-thirds majority necessary was not reached. Nevertheless, John XXIII gave in to entreaties from Cardinals Bea and Léger and, notwithstanding the rule that he himself had made, decided to have the schema revised along "pastoral and ecumenical lines."[68] This decision sounded the death knell for the three other dogmatic schemas.

Archbishop Lefebvre would later say that after the death of John XXIII on June 3, 1963, and the election of Paul VI on June 21, the two early liberal *coups* were crowned by yet another when the new Pope changed the role of the Council Presidency—whose members grew from ten to twelve cardinals—so it was only responsible for procedural matters. He gave power to four Cardinal moderators: Döpfner, Suenens, Lercaro, and Agagianian "to direct the Council's activities and establish the order of discussion." The first three were liberal and the last was deemed to be the most acceptable of the Curia cardinals.[69] Thus, Paul VI ensured a liberal hegemony over the Council.

III. THE *COETUS INTERNATIONALIS PATRUM*

HUMBLE BEGINNINGS

The *Coetus Internationalis Patrum* was founded to provide an effective opposition to the liberal domination of the Council. Early in the first session of October 1962, Archbishop Lefebvre met Bishop Antonio de Castro Mayer, bishop of Campos in Brazil and the author of *Pastoral Letter on the Problems of the Modern Apostolate* (1953) which had been published in *Verbe*. The Brazilian introduced the Archbishop to his colleague and compatriot Bishop Geraldo De Proença Sigaud, who was bishop of Jacarèzinho and would soon be archbishop of Diamantina. From the beginning Sigaud was determined to organize the scattered forces that would be able to provide some opposition to the progressive "majority" at the Council.

---

[68] Wiltgen, *The Rhine Flows into the Tiber*, 46-51; *Le Sel de la Terre*, no. 34: 231.
[69] Wiltgen, *op. cit.*, 81-82. Paul VI announced this reorganization on Sept. 13.

In 1934, Canon de Castro Mayer and Fr. Sigaud, both professors at the major seminary in São Paolo, began contributing to the newspaper *O Legionario*, the official mouthpiece of the Marian Congregation of Saint Cecilia edited by Plinio Corrêa de Oliveira. When they supported a book written[70] by Plinio to combat leftist and progressive infiltrations into Brazilian Catholic Action, the canon and the priest were both sanctioned (respectively in February 1945 and March 1946).[71] This did not prevent the Nuncio Aloisi Masella from secretly intervening on behalf of the two courageous men. Pius XII appointed Fr. Sigaud bishop of Jacarèzinho (1947) and Canon de Castro Mayer was named auxiliary bishop of Campos (1948).

In Campos in 1951, Bishop de Castro Mayer founded the monthly *Catolicismo* in which his writings would be published, and he entrusted the paper to a group led by Professor Plinio in São Paolo. From 1951 to 1967, the *Catolicismo* youth groups grew more numerous in Brazil, and in 1960 they gave birth to the Brazilian Society for the Defence of Tradition, Family, and Property under Plinio's direction. With the impetus of the professor and the two bishops, the *Catolicismo* groups (and from 1963 the TFP groups) were successful in opposing Communist attempts at "agrarian reform"[72] during the "Goulart era." They created an ideological and spiritual climate that brought about the fall of the crypto-Communist president João Goulart. Archbishop Lefebvre himself later said: "We must recognise that the TFP saved Brazil from Communism."

Meanwhile in 1962, a *Catolicismo* group established an office in Rome in order to follow the unfolding of the Council on the spot.[73] Consequently, Archbishop Lefebvre accepted the suggestion of the two Brazilian prelates to form a *piccolo comitato* or "study group" to oppose liberal ideas in the Council in keeping with Cardinal Ruffini's thinking. They met on Corso d'Italia at the Holy Ghost Fathers' headquarters, and during the first session on the Council in Rome they organized lectures and discussions expressly for the Council Fathers.

---

[70] Canon de Castro Mayer, who was Vicar General, had given the Archbishop's *imprimatur*; the Nuncio, the future Cardinal Aloisi Masella, had written the book's foreword.

[71] The Vicar General, Canon de Castro Mayer, was removed and made the curate bursar of a country parish but also given a teaching post at the Pontifical Catholic University of São Paolo; Fr. Sigaud was sent to Spain.

[72] Supported by the Archbishop, Dom Helder Cámara, secretary of the Brazilian Bishops' Conference. Professor Plinio's book, *Reforma agraria, cuestión de conciencia*, to which the two future bishops had contributed, was criticized by Gustavo Corção, who was suspicious of Plinio's personality.

[73] Cf. *TFP, Medio Siglo de epopeya anticommunista* (Madrid: Covadonga-TFP, 1983); David Allen White, *The Mouth of the Lion* (Kansas City: Angelus Press, 1993), 83.

It is was not until April 18, 1963, that Bishop Sigaud wrote to Archbishop Lefebvre and suggested setting up the study group for the next session. On May 4, Archbishop Lefebvre agreed to this as yet modest project with prudent reserve. He secured the involvement of the Fathers from the Abbey of Solesmes, and the help of a private theologian (as the rules of the Council allowed), who was none other than Fr. Victor Alain Berto (1900-1968), another Santa Chiara student who had been ahead of the Archbishop in seminary. On October 2 or 3, 1963, at the beginning of the Council's second session, a general gathering was called at the Divine Word Society of which Bishop Sigaud was a member—they later met at the headquarters of the Congregation of the Holy Savior—and fifteen Council Fathers met with Bishop Sigaud (secretary), Archbishop Lefebvre (chairman) and Dom Jean Prou, Abbot of Solesmes. The group as yet had no name. A small committee was formed consisting of Archbishop Lefebvre, Bishop Sigaud, Fr. Berto, and Dom Frénaud, the Prior of Solesmes and private theologian to Dom Prou.

On October 8, a group of twenty gathered to hear a lecture by Cardinal Ruffini. On the following day during the forty-fourth general assembly of the Council, Bishop Sigaud spoke in the *aula* and attacked the chapter on collegiality in the new schema on the Church (Nos. 12, 13, and 16) because it taught a "new doctrine." When he returned to his place, he received a note from Bishop Luigi Carli congratulating him. Afterwards Bishop Sigaud introduced Bishop Carli to Archbishop Lefebvre. Luigi Carli was one of the theologians of the Italian Bishops' Conference. He was unanimously recognized as the best theologian at the Council, and was equally the most feared. He was invited to the meeting of the Fathers on October 15, and agreed to join them, although he maintained his independence to make interventions himself, notably against Cardinal Bea's project exonerating the Jews from responsibility for the death of Christ.

Archbishop Lefebvre later explained: "The soul of the *Coetus* was Bishop de Proença Sigaud as secretary. I myself, as a former Apostolic Delegate and Superior General of a congregation, was the 'public face' in the role of chairman. Bishop de Castro Mayer was vice-chairman and 'the thinker,' while Bishop Carli was 'the pen,' with his talents, his lively mind, and his Italian know-how."[74]

We must underline the strong commitment of the Abbey of Solesmes which hosted three *Coetus* study sessions. From January 11 to 14, 1964, with the help of Dom Paul Nau, Dom Frénaud, and Msgr. Lusseau, a biblical scholar and Dean of the theology faculty at Angers, Dom Prou, Archbishop Lefebvre, and Bishop Sigaud prepared a *compendium* of ecclesiology,[75] Mariology, and material on ecumenism and religious liberty, the

---

[74] Cf. *Fideliter*, no. 59: 43-44.

latter understood as "freedom to profess the true religion." It was a veritable summary of the thinking of the *Coetus*, and it was sent to many Fathers. The second meeting took place at Solesmes in July 1964 before the *Coetus* unveiled itself officially. Solesmes also hosted the last meeting from July 15 to 21, 1965, attended by Archbishop Lefebvre, Bishops Sigaud and Morilleau, Dom Prou, and Dom Meugniot, who was then theologian for the Abbey of Solesmes. At this time, they planned their strategy for the Council's fourth session.

HIGH-PLACED PATRONAGE, LOOSE STRUCTURE, MEAGER FUNDS

Towards the end of the second session on December 6, 1963, Archbishop Lefebvre had an audience with Pope Paul VI. To his great satisfaction, the Holy Father explained to him his thoughts regarding the suggestion of some Fathers to group together the various interventions into collective propositions, or even *systematic exposés* of the thinking of those known as the "minority." Paul VI alluded to this idea in his address at the closing of the second session. With this unlooked for support from the highest authority, Archbishop Lefebvre had no more doubts and after the meeting at Solesmes he notified Archbishop Pericle Felici on February 8, 1964, of his intention to organize the traditionally minded Fathers into one group.[76]

A first letter dated August 5, 1964, signed by Bishops Sigaud and de Castro Mayer and Archbishop Lefebvre, to which were added the signatures of Bishops Caban, Silva, Lacchio, and Cordeiro, stated that a number of Fathers attached to the tradition of the Church had formed a group. The letter justified this move by the recent additions made to the Council rules allowing Fathers who wanted to make the same arguments to band together so that one of them could speak for all, provided that there were at least seventy of them.

The birth of this group was announced at the beginning of the third session of the Council in a document dated October 2, 1964, and distributed to the Council Fathers. It was signed by Bishop Sigaud and announced the formation of the group under the highly placed patronage of Cardinals Santos (Manila),[77] Siri (Genoa), Ruffini (Palermo), Browne (Curia), and Larraona (Curia). Santos proved to be ineffective, while Larraona, whose name disappeared from the definitive document on October 6, was the closest and the most effective of all the cardinals in his support

[75] *A. Syn.*, III, I, 621-628. Text signed by Archbishops Marie and Lefebvre, Bishops Sigaud and Grimault, and Dom Prou, sent to the Council Secretariat.

[76] Archbishop Lefebvre, Letter to Archbishop Felici, Feb. 8, 1964.

[77] Who on September 29 finally gave in to Bishop Sigaud's request for him to be the group's spokesman in the Sacred College. *Fideliter*, no. 59: 45.

of the *Coetus*'s actions. The other cardinals supported the group but remained on the margins, considering that the Roman purple prevented them being more deeply involved. It was only in November 1964 that the group chose its definitive name of *Coetus Internationalis Patrum*—the International Group of Fathers. Thus, the creation of this association of Fathers came late in the day compared with the progressive groups that had been in operation since the first session. At last, the simple children of light reacted to the feverish plotting of the innovators.

Potential supporters of the *Coetus* were invited to meetings at the Augustinian headquarters to hear a series of lectures. On October 13, Cardinal Ruffini spoke about Schema XIII, and on October 27, Fr. Ermenegildo Lio, O.F.M.[78] spoke about marriage. Bishop Franic gave a talk on "Communism and the Church." On November 3 and 10, Bishop Carraro gave a lecture on the institution of the priesthood, *etc.* Only Cardinal Ruffini touched on a theme that would be considered in detail by the Council. These meetings succeeded little by little in spreading the spirit of the *Coetus*, but did not aim at organizing any concerted action, which remained the province of the group's inner core. This was made up of the three founders and Bishop Carli, and to these were added Archbishop Cabana, archbishop of Sherbrooke in Canada, and Bishop Morilleau, bishop of La Rochelle. This committee led a body of 250 bishops who appear on the mailing list that was drawn up, added to, and changed throughout the Council.[79]

The *Coetus* was nebulous, a network with vague limits, which allowed it to refute all accusations of being a secret organization within the Council. No formal membership was required of any Father. Personal contacts played a great role. The most notable of these were Bishop Carli's circle of Italian friends, the links between former students from Santa Chiara (three bishops and a French Father Abbot in addition to Archbishop Lefebvre), friendships created through the journals *Verbe* and *La Pensée Catholique*, and the Portuguese-speaking friends of Bishop Sigaud. Through Bishop Carli, the *Coetus* had contacts with the Lateran University where two professors, Msgr. Piolanti and Msgr. Lattanzi, joined in the fight. Through Cardinal Siri, they had contacts with the Council's Co-ordinating Commission, and Cardinal Ruffini was their permanent contact on the Council's Presidency.

The *Coetus*'s financial means were extremely meager in comparison with the European alliance that had many resources it could call upon,

---

[78] He was the author of the pre-conciliar schema *De Castitate* (On chastity) that was dropped.

[79] No complete list ever seems to have existed. There are only a few partial lists, which together with the list of the bishops in favor of the future review *Fortes in Fide*, allow us to compile a reliable albeit incomplete one.

especially the all-powerful IDOC, which towards the end of the third session admitted having distributed more than four million leaflets. Archbishop Lefebvre said: "On our side, the conservative bishops, we had certainly tried to counterbalance this influence, thanks to Cardinal Larraona, who placed his secretariat at our disposal. We had typewriters and copiers and a few people, three or four."[80]

In November 1963, the Archbishop had already acquired a duplicator, but the *Coetus* also got hold of an offset printing machine. Cardinal Larraona in effect "lent" them his two Claretian secretaries, Don Jesús Torres Llorente and Don Ruiz. The machines would print the *Coetus* texts, and then early in the morning the young Brazilians and Frenchmen from *Catolicismo* went throughout Rome in Archbishop Lefebvre's Peugeot 403 to distribute advice to the Fathers on the *Coetus* list about how to vote. Moreover, ever since the first session, Fr. Ralph Wiltgen, S.V.D., had willingly given over the pages of his news agency, the Divine Word News Service, to interviews with Bishop de Castro Mayer, Archbishop Lefebvre,[81] and subsequently other members of the *Coetus*, thus giving greater publicity to the Roman positions.

AN EFFECTIVE, DIVERSE CAMPAIGN

The Tuesday evening lectures organized in 1963 and 1964, the texts of which were published, only prepared the way for the *Coetus*'s real strategies and campaigns. According to a letter sent to Cardinal Siri on October 30, 1963, the tactic first envisaged by Bishop Sigaud would be to give a role to the Cardinal Chairmen of the episcopal conferences. They would be asked to meet once a week to assemble advice and guidance for voting on the schemas which would then be passed on to the bishops. The majority had successfully set up such "inter-conference" contacts in 1962. However, Bishop Sigaud quickly understood that trying to do the same in favor of the minority would be quite hopeless.

Thus, the strategy that was finally adopted was to "federate the Romans," as Fr. Berto said,[82] at least to prevent there being moral unanimity for the schemas that were supported by the majority. The priest thought it was realistic to expect to be able to win over a quarter of the Fathers to the Roman theses, but this goal was only twice achieved: in February 1964 with the petition[83] for the consecration of the world to the Immaculate Heart of Mary (510 signatures) and in 1965 with the petition asking for

---

[80] Marcel Lefebvre, *They Have Uncrowned Him* (Kansas City: Angelus Press, 1988), 166.
[81] Wiltgen, *The Rhine Flows into the Tiber*, 39-40, 88-90.
[82] Secretary of the *Cœtus* during the third session.
[83] Organized by a group of Brazilian and Portuguese Fathers supported by the Fathers of the *Cœtus*. Bishop Sigaud gave it to Paul VI on Feb. 3, 1964.

the condemnation of Communism (454 signatures). On another occasion in December 1964 the *Coetus* distributed six hundred tracts with suggested amendments and managed to obtain 574 votes *placet juxta modum*.

The *Coetus*'s "style" was characterized by great attention to the juridical aspect of questions under discussion and to the correct procedural unfolding of the Council. This is why it frequently had recourse to the Council's rules and launched impeccable, procedural manoeuvres with the intention of blocking or slowing down the progress of the innovators. However, the *Coetus*'s essential work lay in producing an "almost uninterrupted flow" of circulars, commentaries on schemas, suggested amendments—*modi*—as clear as possible, and their explanations—*ratio modi*—with the object of correcting, replacing, or clarifying ambiguous terms, phrases, paragraphs, and intentional omissions from schemas being considered by the Fathers.[84] The *Coetus* would then encourage them to vote *placet juxta modum*.

Moreover, the members of the *Coetus*'s inner core would often speak publicly in the *aula* to restate principles of sound philosophy, truths of revealed doctrine, or the common teaching of theologians. Archbishop Lefebvre especially excelled in recalling the teachings of recent popes. He himself gave testimony to the effectiveness and limitations of the *Coetus*'s activities:

> ...We were able all the same to limit the damage, to change these inexact or tendentious assertions, to add that sentence to rectify a tendentious proposition or an ambiguous expression.
>
> But I have to admit that we did not succeed in purifying the Council of the liberal and modernist spirit that impregnated most of the schemas. Their drafters indeed were precisely the experts and Fathers tainted with this spirit. Now, what can you do when a document is in all its parts drawn up with a false meaning? It is practically impossible to expurgate it of that meaning. It would have to be completely recomposed in order to be given a Catholic spirit.
>
> What we were able to do was, by the *modi* that we introduced, to have interpolated clauses added to the schemas; and this is quite obvious: it suffices to compare the first schema on religious liberty with the fifth—for this document was five times rejected and five times brought back for discussion—in order to see that we succeeded just the same in reducing the subjectivism that tainted the first drafts. Likewise for *Gaudium et Spes*, the paragraphs can easily be seen which were added at our request and which are there, I would say, like pieces brought back onto an old coat. It does not stick well together. The logic of the early drafting is no longer there. The additions made to lessen or to counterbalance the liberal assertions remain there like foreign bodies.[85]

---

[84] Luc Perrin, "Le *Coetus internationalis Patrum* et la minorité à Vatican II," in *Catholica*, s.v. "Histoire religieuse contemporaine," *passim*; Berto, *Notre-Dame de Joie*, 42, 290-291.

We will not give here a complete history of all the fights in which the *Coetus* was involved, but only those in which Archbishop Lefebvre took part. We must also recognize that the Fathers of the *Coetus* spoke in the *aula* in a personal capacity, and even when they were speaking for the *Coetus*, they kept to their own style and expounded their own opinions. Archbishop Lefebvre had attended a talk given to the French Fathers by Fr. Congar, and was shocked by the cavalier manner in which the theologian handed out various jobs: "Bishop X, you will speak on this topic. You, Bishop Y, you will contribute to the debate on this question. Don't worry, we will prepare the text, and you will only have to read it." The *Coetus*'s spokesmen never became the message boys of their theologians. Fr. Berto spoke about the nature and extent of his work for Archbishop Lefebvre:

> I had the honor, a very great and unmerited honor—and I say this before God—to be his theologian. The secrecy to which I am sworn covers the work I did under him, but I am betraying no secret in saying that the Archbishop is far superior as a theologian to me—and would to God that all the Fathers had his knowledge of theology. His theological *habitus* is perfectly sure and acute, and his very great devotion to the Holy See adds to it the connaturality which enables the Archbishop, even before the discursive *habitus* comes into play, to discern intuitively what is and what is not compatible with the sovereign prerogatives of the Rock of the Church. He in no way resembles the Fathers who, as one of them had the effrontery to boast publicly,[86] took from the hands of an "expert" in the very car that was taking them to Saint Peter's, the "ready-baked" text of their intervention in the Council hall. Not once have I submitted to him a memorandum, a note, a draft document, without his having reviewed, revised, re-thought, and sometimes reworked it from beginning to end. I have not "collaborated" with him; if such a word existed, I would say I have truly "sub-laborated" with him, in accordance with my capacity as private theologian and in accordance with his honor and dignity as one of the Fathers of an ecumenical Council, Judge and Doctor of the Faith with the Roman Pontiff.[87]

Archbishop Lefebvre would never accept being a bit-part player or a "name" to push ideas that he had not personally considered and reconsidered.

Through his activities as a member of the *Coetus* he took part in three battles: the fight against collegiality, the request for the condemnation of Communism, and the bitter struggle against religious liberty. This did not prevent him also battling for the honor of the Most Blessed Virgin and for the integrity of Christian marriage.

---

[85] *Spiritual Conferences at Ecône*, 63 B, Dec. 14, 1978; Lefebvre, *They Have Uncrowned Him*, 167-168; Lovey, in *Eglise et contre-Eglise*, 41-42.

[86] Archbishop Maziers, Archbishop of Bordeaux. Cf. Cagnon, *Les Relations de Rome avec Ecône*, 74.

[87] Letter to the Mother Superior of a religious house, Lefebvre, *J'accuse*, 5-6.

THE FIGHT AGAINST COLLEGIALITY

In the minds of numerous conciliar Fathers, the object of the Second Vatican Council was to be a counterbalance to the teachings of the First Vatican Council. Vatican I had expounded the doctrine of the Pope's primacy. In their view, Vatican II ought to declare the right of the bishops to rule the Church with him. The new schema for the constitution of the Church that replaced the abandoned preparatory schema had been passionately debated during the second session in 1963. Three rival theses clashed: the extreme liberal thesis said that the bishops formed a college of which the Pope was merely the head and which the Pope would consult before taking any decisions. The moderate liberal thesis—Paul VI's—claimed that the bishops formed a college under the Pope who was their leader by divine right. Independently of the college, the Pope retained his personal powers as defined by Vatican I. Consequently, supreme power over the Church was exercised by two authorities: the Sovereign Pontiff on one hand, and the episcopal college "with and under its leader" on the other.

Faced with this mitigated liberal thesis, the *Coetus* objected that by divine right the bishops could logically demand (when they wanted or even regularly) that the Pope exercise this supreme power which supposedly belonged to them by virtue of the divine constitution of the Church. The supreme power of the Pope was thus in danger of being reduced accordingly. The *Coetus* held to the thesis of Roman theology expounded by Fr. Berto[88] in his draft schema and supported by Archbishop Lefebvre. Referring to all tradition and history, it demonstrated that the Pope was the only leader of the universal Church by divine right, and that in him alone resided the plenitude of supreme power. As for the episcopal corps, it did not constitute by divine right a college in the juridical sense of being the subject of common action. It only acted collegially in the exceptional circumstances of an ecumenical council, and had no authority over the universal Church except that granted it by the Pope, as and when he wished and when delegating part of his own supreme authority.

Given these objections, a new draft text was prepared, and since Paul VI was not satisfied with it, the draft had to be revised and corrected. He finally approved it on July 3, 1964, as the basis for discussion in the third session. It proposed the moderate liberal thesis of the Church in a permanent state of Council by divine right.

The *Coetus* was determined to defend the primacy of the Pope, even against the Pope, and to defeat the so-called divine right of collegiality. In Solesmes on July 15, 1964, Archbishop Lefebvre, Bishop Morilleau, and

---

[88] Berto, *Pour la sainte Église romaine*, 236-265 (texts from 1964); *Itinéraires*, no. 115 (July-Aug. 1967) and no. 132 (April 1969); supplement: *L'abbé Berto*, 119.

Dom Prou drew up a petition or *postulatum* to Paul VI that was signed by at least thirteen Fathers. It asked the Pope to proclaim the Most Blessed Virgin Mary as "Mother of the Church" and to banish from the discussions of the third session all schemas that were contrary to traditional doctrine. Peter, they said, was head of the Apostolic College because he was the Vicar of Christ: he was not Vicar of Christ because he was head of the Apostolic College, as was now being insinuated.

Not content merely with trying to block the schema approved by Paul VI, Archbishop Lefebvre and his friends met at Solesmes to broaden their field of fire in a letter to the Pope that denounced the decisions and ambiguities hidden in certain schemas. It was signed by several conciliar Fathers. Curiously, their concerns were similar to Fr. Schillebeeckx's. Although he was an extreme liberal, he had been scandalized during the second session when he heard experts admitting to him that the schema on the Church presented the moderate liberal thesis in a deliberately ambiguous fashion.[89] The expert said to him: "We are using diplomatic language, but after the Council we will draw all the implicit conclusions out of the text." Fr. Schillebeeckx had the decency to "find this tactic dishonest."[90]

Archbishop Lefebvre considered that by such subliminal messages carrying resurgent errors, the Council was discrediting and lowering itself. If Paul VI did not take action, it was going to infect the Church. He wrote to the Pope: "Already the studies made by some of the Council's 'experts'...reach conclusions which we were always taught to consider as imprudent and dangerous, if not fundamentally false. Certain schemas...are thus exploited...in such terms and in such a sense that if they do not always contradict, they are at least formally opposed as much to the teaching of the ordinary Magisterium as to the pronouncements of the extraordinary Magisterium, made by the Church during the past century."[91] This letter, which is crucial for the honor of the Council and for the judgment that we should pass on it, went unanswered.

THE *"NOTA EXPLICATIVA PRAEVIA"*

At the opening of the third session on September 15, 1964, Archbishop Staffa asked to speak on behalf of seventy Fathers. His request was denied. The *Coetus* resigned itself to suggesting some amendments in the chapter concerning collegiality in the schema *On the Church*. From September 21 to 29, the text was put to the vote paragraph by paragraph. The

---

[89] "Are we speaking of two inadequately distinct subjects in which resides supreme power or simply of a unique subject that is still collegial? Our text (schema) provides us with no answer to this question." Yves Congar, unpublished study, July 11, 1963, cf. Dulac, in *La Pensée Catholique*, no. 87, app. I.

[90] Art. in *De Bazuin*, Jan. 23, 1965; Wiltgen, *The Rhine Flows into the Tiber*, 238.

[91] Letter on ambiguities, in Lefebvre, *J'accuse*, 54.

results included 572 *placet juxta modum* or a "yes" on condition that certain amendments were made. The theological commission began to examine the *modi*. However, before this work was completed, the *Coetus* learnt that its *modi* had been left out while other less important ones had been accepted.

Archbishop Staffa could not accept this, and wrote to Paul VI denouncing the procedural misdeeds that aimed at silencing Roman theology in favor of an "extreme form" of the collegial thesis.[92] The letter was sent to twelve of the most committed *Coetus* Fathers, and Archbishop Lefebvre asked each one to obtain the signatures of twelve other Council Fathers. This initiative, known as "Operation Staffa," succeeded since Paul VI passed this letter to the theological commission ordering an inquiry into the violation of procedural rules.

Meanwhile, on the eve of the opening of the third session, Cardinal Larraona managed to persuade thirty-five cardinals and five Superior Generals—Archbishop Lefebvre among them—to send to Paul VI a "private memorandum," dated October 18, expressing their "apprehension" concerning the novelty of the doctrine sponsored by the Pope: "The schema changes the face of the Church: from being monarchical, the Church becomes episcopalian[93] and collegial according to divine right and by virtue of episcopal consecration; the [papal] primacy is separated from or emptied of its meaning,…serving only to maintain a united and undivided hierarchy….The hierarchy of jurisdiction insofar as it is distinct from the hierarchy of orders,…is shaken and destroyed." The signatories denounced the "pressure groups, bold experts, and the influence of the press which make calm discussion difficult and hinder or shackle true freedom." They asked for the Council to have a period of reflection and "time to consider the new doctrine at length."

Paul VI felt himself personally under attack, and replied to Cardinal Larraona in a handwritten letter full of sarcastic remarks, asking him to "think deeply about the harmful consequences that could come from this attitude (if it were divested of true and solid justifications) so contrary to the majority of the bishops and so prejudicial to the success of the Council."[94] Paul VI decided not to see the dangers in the schema's ambiguity until a liberal Father made the mistake of putting an extreme interpretation in writing, claiming that the text would be thus understood after the Council. Seeing himself tricked and deceived the Pope collapsed in tears. Then he asked Cardinal Ottaviani to rework the wording of some of the

---

[92] Wiltgen, *The Rhine Flows into the Tiber*, 228.
[93] [In the sense of its hierarchy being based on the authority of the episcopal corps, the bishops. Trans.]
[94] Cf. Lefebvre, *J'accuse*, 70.

text and had a "preliminary explanatory note" drawn up indicating how the text should be interpreted.

The *Nota explicativa praevia* was presented to the Fathers on November 14, 1964, and was bitterly criticized by the liberal Fathers. Among the announcements he made on November 16, the first day of the week that the liberals would call "Black Week," Archbishop Pericle Felici, Secretary General of the Council, said that the doctrine in the schema concerning collegiality was to be interpreted "according to the meaning and tenor of the said *Nota*" in an attempt to put an end to the discussions.

The *Coetus*'s actions had saved the primacy of the Roman Pontiff from mortal danger. The note established the interpretation of the conciliar text—that contained the moderate liberal thesis—in a restricted sense that Archbishop Lefebvre could accept. It became an integral part of the constitution *Lumen Gentium*, while showing at the same time the intrinsic weakness of a text which without it would be ambiguous.

THE REQUEST FOR THE CONDEMNATION OF COMMUNISM

We now come to one of the *Coetus*'s greatest initiatives, and one that earned the greatest sympathy and the most support. Already on December 3, 1963, on the eve of the closing of the second session, Archbishop de Proença Sigaud brought a petition to Cardinal Cicognani with the signatures of 213 Fathers from forty-six countries, asking that a special schema be prepared in which "Catholic social doctrine would be clearly expounded and the errors of Marxism, socialism, and Communism refuted." This request echoed the anti-Communist battles of Bishops de Castro Mayer and Sigaud in Brazil, and reflected the constant concerns of Archbishop Lefebvre in Dakar and in Africa.

On February 3, 1964, Archbishop Sigaud personally gave Paul VI another petition signed by 510 prelates that begged the Holy Father to act together with the Council Fathers to consecrate Russia and the world to the Immaculate Heart of Mary according to the request made by our Lady to Sister Lucy, one of the seers of Fatima. Through this consecration, "Russia would be converted." The Pope let this request gather dust before finally rejecting it in January 1965.

On October 21, 1964, discussion focused on the part of the schema on the *Church in the World* —Schema XIII—which dealt with atheism. The word "communism" was still carefully avoided. In the face of this constant silence, the *Coetus* went into action on September 29, 1965, at the beginning of the fourth session. A letter asking the Council to examine Communism and condemn it was signed by twenty-five bishops and distributed. It was written by Bishop Carli and handed around by Archbishop Sigaud and Archbishop Lefebvre who, not wishing to appear too prominent, had not signed it. It stated that the Council's silence on

Communism would be a disavowal of the recent Popes. To the letter was joined a petition asking for the condemnation of Communism, on which there were already 332 signatures.[95] In the end the signatures totaled 454.[96] Archbishop Lefebvre submitted the petition and the 332 original signatures in person[97] at the Council Secretariat on November 9 when there was sufficient time for it to be considered. He was given a receipt acknowledging that the document had been received.

The result? On November 13 the new version of the schema made no reference to the wishes of the petition. Communism was still not named. Thus, Bishop Carli made a protest on the same day to the Council Presidency and lodged a complaint with the administrative tribunal. Moreover, he decided to make the request once more in the form of an amendment, and at the same time proposed a debate specifically on the topic. The *Coetus*'s helpers spent the evening of Saturday, November 13, and Sunday, November 14, chasing around Rome by car distributing the two documents to all the Fathers. Before November 16, another twenty-nine signatures were added, and on November 15, the vigorous protest of Archbishop Sigaud shook the Council. But it was all in vain.

Nevertheless, Cardinal Tisserant ordered an inquiry that revealed...that the petition had unfortunately been "lost" in a drawer. In fact Msgr. Achille Glorieux, secretary for the relevant commission, received the petition but had not passed it on to the commission. Archbishop Garrone apologized publicly for Msgr. Glorieux's "forgetfulness," but there was nothing that could be done. Time had been made for a paragraph on Communism to be added, but it had now passed. Besides, the condemnation of Communism would contrast too severely with the pastoral vision of Pope John, who had decided that the Council would condemn no errors. Moreover, in his encyclical *Pacem in Terris* on April 11, 1963, John XXIII put aside all criticism of Communism, even accepting that one can "recognize in it positive elements that are worthy of approval."[98]

This was to deny Pius XI's condemnation of Communism as "intrinsically perverse" and to allow Catholic co-operation with Communism. In a written intervention on September 9, 1965, Archbishop Lefebvre denounced this denial: "Page 18, §19 [of Schema XIII]: Communism is discussed merely from the point of view of atheism, without any explicit

---

[95] Bishop René Graffin had collected these signatures. Archbishop. Lefebvre. E 01, 16 B, A 712.

[96] Among whom were 104 Italians and 30 Chinese Fathers (expelled from the country). Twenty-six African and 23 Latin American countries were represented. All in all 86 different countries.

[97] Accompanied by Bishop Sigaud. Cf. Marcel Lefebvre, *C'est moi l'accusé qui devrais vous juger* (Fideliter, 1994), 340. [English version published under the title *Against the Heresies* (Kansas City: Angelus Press, 1997).]

[98] No. 157 (159) of the encyclical, *A.A.S.* 55 (1963): 300.

mention of Communism itself. From this text, it can be deduced that Communism is condemned solely on account of its atheism; this is clearly contrary to the doctrine constantly taught by the Church. It is thus better to have a text, it would seem, which either does not mention Communism at all, or which speaks of it, on the contrary, excplicitly, to show its intrinsic evil."[99]

Paul VI, who chaired this debate but was also the heir of John XXIII, kept his silence concerning the word "communism." He was content merely to make mention on December 2 of the "former condemnations of atheism," thus falsifying Pius XI's doctrine which condemned Communism for being a system and method that organized perverse social action (a technique for enslaving the masses and for the practice of dialectics, as Jean Madiran said) and not only for its atheism.[100] The reference in a footnote to Pius XI's encyclical *Divini Redemptoris* enables the reader to observe this betrayal.

Archbishop Garrone's excuses and quibbles could neither satisfy the *Coetus* nor quench its zeal. Thus, in a last-ditch effort, on December 3, 1965, they distributed to eight hundred Fathers whose names were on their files a final letter containing five reasons why the sections on Communism, the ends of marriage, and the topic "War and Peace" in schema XIII, were not as yet satisfactory.

THE ENDS OF MARRIAGE

Archbishop Lefebvre was the prime mover behind the great initiative against Communism. He played the same role defending Christian marriage and the traditional doctrine that places procreation over human love as the primary end of marriage.[101] He had already denounced during the Council the reversal of the two ends of marriage sought by the Liberals:

> The chapter on marriage, page 47, line 16 ff., presents conjugal love as the primary element of marriage from which comes the second element, procreation. Throughout the chapter, conjugal love and marriage are identified, as on page 49, lines 24 and 25....This is also contrary to the traditional doctrine of the Church, and if it were approved it would lead to the most serious consequences. One could say in fact, "No conjugal love, therefore no marriage!" Yet how many marriages there are without conjugal love! They are nevertheless true marriages.[102]

---

[99] Lefebvre, *J'accuse*, 89-90.

[100] Jean Madiran, *La vieillesse du monde, essai sur le communisme* (DMM, 1975), especially 107-110.

[101] Cf. Leo XIII, encyclical *Arcanum*, Feb. 10, 1880, *Enseignements pontificaux de Solesmes, Le mariage*, n. 147; Code of Canon Law (1917), can. 1013, §1; Pius XI, encyclical *Casti Connubii*, Dec. 31, 1930, Denzinger, 2227-2231; *Enseignements pontificaux de Solesmes, Le mariage*, n. 274; judgment of the Rota, Jan. 22, 1944; *A.A.S.* 36 (1944): 179-200; *Enseignements pontificaux de Solesmes, Le mariage*, appendix, n. 11.

The stakes were high. Accepting the new doctrine meant also promoting the limiting of births and contraception, or even excusing abortion. In any case it surely meant destroying the Christian family. The Archbishop remembered the feelings that had been stirred the previous year on October 29, 1964. Cardinal Suenens directed an attack against procreation, and Ottaviani protested magnificently, giving the example of the poor family with twelve children from which he had come. Then Cardinal Browne had shouted: "*Cauti ergo esse debemus!* Let us be on our guard when exaggerated claims are made for the rights of conjugal love!"[103]

A year later on November 25, 1965, Paul VI intervened, imposing four amendments on this topic in Schema XIII,[104] one of which was on contraception. However, he did not re-establish the order of the two ends. Therefore, Archbishop Lefebvre made a last attempt to have it changed but without success.[105] The final text gave official approval to the reversal of the ends of marriage,[106] just as it refused to condemn Communism explicitly. The promulgation of the pastoral constitution "On the Church in the Modern World," *Gaudium et Spes*—Joy and Hope—was, as Cardinal Ruffini wrote, more like a "*Giorni di dolore.*"[107]

THE ROME-MOSCOW AGREEMENT

Moscow feared nothing as much as an Ecumenical Council's solemnly renewing Pius XI's condemnation of Communism. To prevent this happening, the Kremlin offered a deal to the Vatican: for ecumenism, you want observers from the Moscow patriarchate to come to the Council? They are not very keen. However, we will help them to decide as long as Rome gives the patriarchate a special invitation and the Council does not mention Communism.

Such was the tenor of the agreement made in Paris in August 1962 between Metropolitan Nikodim and Archbishop Jan Willebrands, and confirmed at Metz by Nikodim and Cardinal Tisserant, who spoke Russian. *France Nouvelle*, the centrally-published weekly of the French Communist Party,[108] gave a report on the agreement, then *Le Lorrain* of Febru-

---

[102] Written intervention on schema XIII, Sept. 9, 1965. Cf. also the intervention of Bishop Carlo Maccari, submitted on October 1, 1965, also signed by several members of the *Cœtus*, including Archbishop Lefebvre. A. Syn., IV, III, 209 ff.

[103] A. Syn., III, IV, 57, 85 and 87; Wiltgen, *The Rhine Flows into the Tiber*, 269.

[104] *Ibid.*, 270; Lefebvre *Un évêque parle*, 155; Peter Hebblethwaite, *Paul VI: The First Modern Pope* (New York: Paulist Press, 1993), 367. (Page refs. are to Spanish version.)

[105] At the vote on Chapter I of Schema XIII on December 2, only 131 Fathers had rejected the part on atheism, and 155 rejected the chapter concerning marriage and the family. During the vote for the entire document on Dec. 7, 1965, the *non placet*s were reduced to 75.

[106] *Gaudium et Spes*, no. 48, §1.

[107] [Day of sorrow. Trans.]

ary 9 and *La Croix* of February 15 gave details of the meetings. In fact, Archbishop Willebrands had been able to visit Moscow from September 27 to October 2, 1962, taking with him the invitation and assuring the patriarchate that the Council "would not embark on anti-Communist polemics."[109]

Thus, two Russian Orthodox observers arrived in Rome on October 11 for the opening of the Second Vatican Council, and on orders from above, "each time one of the bishops wanted to address the question of Communism, Cardinal [Tisserant] from the table of the Council Presidency intervened and recalled the Pope's order concerning silence on this topic."[110]

"The Council that had taken it upon itself to discern the 'signs of the times' was condemned by Moscow to silence on this most obvious and monstrous sign of the times!"[111]

FOR THE HONOR OF THE MOST BLESSED VIRGIN MARY

At the outset, the schema on the Blessed Virgin was an independent text and amongst other titles gave Mary the name of Mediatrix of all Graces. During a meeting of the Preparatory Commission, Cardinal Liénart had protested against this title, but nevertheless it was kept. In the period between the sessions in 1963, the theologian Karl Rahner thought that this text "would do incalculable harm from an ecumenical point of view"; his opinion was shared by his colleagues Grillemier, Semmelroth, and Ratzinger. As soon as the second session was opened, it was proposed that the schema on Mary be reduced to a simple chapter in the schema on the Church. References were made to "an excess of Marian piety." Thus, on October 27, Bishop Grotti, a Servite and one of the original members of the *Coetus,* had a refutation of these arguments handed out: "Does ecumenism consist in professing or hiding the truth?" He developed an argument we saw Archbishop Lefebvre use in Dakar, stating: "Hiding the truth hurts us because we look like hypocrites. It also harms those who are separated from us because it makes them look weak and liable to be offended by the truth." Unfortunately, the vote on October 29, 1963—1,114 for

---

[108] January 16-22, 1963, p.15.

[109] Ulisse Floridi, *Moscou et le Vatican* (Éd. France-Empire, 1979), 146-147, quoting R. B. Kaiser, *Pope, Council and World*; cf. Jean Madiran, in *Itinéraires*, no. 70 (Feb. 1963): 177-178; 72 (April 1963): 43; 84 (June 1964): 39-40; 280 (Feb. 1984): 1-11; 285 (July.-Aug 1984): 151ff., quoting a letter of Bishop Georges Roche, a longtime collaborator of Cardinal Tisserant.

[110] Letter already cited of Bishop Roche to J. Madiran, May 14, 1984.

[111] Lefebvre, *They Have Uncrowned Him*, 215; cf. Madiran, *op. cit.*, 158-159; *Spiritual Conferences at Ecône*, 102 B, Oct. 28, 1983, "the three betrayals."

and 1,097 against—gave victory, albeit a slim one, to the sensitive souls and ecumenists.

During the summer of 1964, the *Coetus* asked Paul VI in a petition for Mary to be proclaimed "Mother of the Church…because in her maternal charity, she wants all that her Son wants for His Mystical Body which is the Church, thus begetting the Church from the beginning to the end, and also because by that same charity the Blessed Virgin Mary truly intercedes without ceasing for the universal Church and for each member of the faithful, and even for the men that God wants to save." Not only was this beautiful theology scorned, but to the indignation of the *Coetus*, the text proposed at the third session had suppressed the title of "Mother of the Church," in spite of the wish Paul VI had expressed at the end of the previous session. Thus, Bishop Castán Lacoma, a member of the *Coetus*, demanded on behalf of eighty Fathers its reintroduction.

In spite of these protests, neither the Theological Commission nor the voting re-established this title. On the last day of the session, November 21, 1964, Paul VI had to go above all their heads and announce *motu proprio* that the Blessed Virgin Mary would be invoked under the title of "*Mater Ecclesiae.*" Applauding with the majority of Fathers this triumph of one of our Lady's privileges, the *Coetus* also saw it as the Pope's reaffirming his primacy independently of the Council.

TRADITION AND SACRED SCRIPTURE

Another arena in which the *Coetus* fought was the schema on Divine Revelation, which replaced the preparatory text on "The Sources of Revelation." A mitigated form of Protestant error was re-emerging at the Council in the tendency to reduce divine oral Tradition to nothing more than an interpretation of Sacred Scripture and also dependent on it.

This was why, in spring 1964, Archbishop Lefebvre and his friends La Chanonie, Grimault, Morilleau, and Prou made a written proposal with an amendment stating that "Tradition was broader than Scripture."[112] This was so that the Council would not seem to exclude, as they said, "the possibility of finding in Tradition truths that are not contained explicitly in Scripture."

This amendment was rejected. Curiously, the fight led by the *Coetus* was limited to defending Scriptural inerrancy (absence of error) and did not include the immutability of divine Tradition. Tradition "progresses in the Church" as *Dei Verbum* would say. The post-conciliar error of "living" and evolving Tradition would be supported by this notion. However, the Fathers of the *Coetus* did question the Secretariat about the authority of the text which was going to be voted on. On November 15, Archbishop

---

[112] *A. Syn.*, III, III, 889 s.

Felici mentioned the note issued by the Theological Commission on March 3, 1964. Only those things would be defined that were explicitly defined. For the rest, the authority of the text depended on its genre. This clarification is essential: since it defined nothing as such, the Council would not be infallible of itself.

However, the *Coetus* Fathers were above all preoccupied by their fight against religious liberty.

RELIGIOUS LIBERTY

The initial clash between Cardinals Ottaviani and Bea during the final preparatory meeting echoed unendingly throughout the Council. No text was subject to as many revisions as the schema on religious liberty under strong pressure from the *Coetus,* which threw its best resources into this battle. During the first session, the Ottaviani schema on relations between Church and State was discarded like the others by the manoeuvres of the "European alliance." At the second session in 1963, only the Bea schema survived, reworked and transformed into Chapter V of the schema on ecumenism. It was presented by Bishop De Smedt, bishop of Bruges, but met considerable opposition, and it was not put to the vote in order that its content could, so it was said, have time to grow in the Fathers' minds...although rapid growth is not at all the same as the spontaneous heritage of a long tradition.

In the third session, the text had become an independent "declaration" that incorporated 380 amendments submitted between sessions in 1963 and 1964. The debate on the question was brief. From September 23 to 25, 1964, supporters of the two theses clashed on the Council floor, and Cardinals Browne, Ruffini, Quiroga y Palacios (Saint James of Compostella), and Bueno y Monreal (Seville) jousted with the advocates of liberalism, Cardinals Ritter (Saint Louis, Missouri), Cushing (Boston), Meyer (Chicago), Silva Henriquez (Santiago in Chile), and König (Vienna).

Fr. Fernandez, Master General of the Dominicans, maintained that the text should be entirely revised since it was sullied with naturalism. Msgr. Carlo Colombo, Dean of theology faculty of the major seminary in Milan and personal theologian to Paul VI, asked that the schema should be better founded on Catholic doctrine. The Secretariat for Christian Unity undertook to redraft the text once more. This work was underway when on Friday, October 9, Cardinal Bea received two letters from Archbishop Felici, one of which requested "on higher authority" that the declaration on religious liberty be submitted to a radical revision for which a mixed commission would be responsible. It would be formed from members of the Secretariat and the Theological Commission, and the Pope had already designated four of its members: Msgr. Carlo Colombo, Fr. Fernandez, Cardinal Browne, and Archbishop Marcel Lefebvre.

The very mention of the last name spread panic in Rome. Ten cardinals, one of whom was Augustin Bea, gathered on October 10 in the apartment of Cardinal Frings—refuge of sinners—and wrote a letter to the Holy Father expressing their "pain," their "great worry," and "deepest concern" at seeing the Declaration "put into the hands of a mixed commission to which four members have already been appointed, three of whom seem opposed to the Council's orientation in this matter." After this denunciation made in the name of an all-powerful "orientation," they came to their threats. The signatories said it would be "a violation of the rules of the Council" and "would badly affect universal public opinion." To be sure of excluding the formidable archbishop from the Holy Ghost Fathers, the only one of the four not to be a member of any conciliar commission, the cardinals considered that if His Holiness were to keep this mixed commission, it "ought to be formed from the conciliar commissions." The good apostles charitably referred Paul VI to Article 58, Paragraph 2 of the rules of the Council.[113]

When Archbishop Lefebvre was asked about the subject, he replied with a calm smile that he "knew nothing about it." Paul VI gave in, and the mixed commission that finally sat on October 27 did not count Archbishop Lefebvre among its members. He would later say: "I was the only one eliminated. My interventions on this topic during the Council and my membership in the *Coetus* frightened them."[114]

During the one and only meeting of the commission, the declaration was approved and sent to the Theological Commission to be examined and given the *nihil obstat*, which it just scraped on November 9. The new draft (*textus emendatus*) was given to the Fathers on Tuesday, November 17, for a vote on Thursday, November 19. The *Coetus* then acted, and the liberal wing would speak of its "Black Week." The *Coetus* pointed out that the amended text was not a simple revision of the previous schema (*textus prior*) but a new text which was twice as long and in which the issues and arguments were new. It spoke of the dignity of the human person and his rights; conscience's need to express itself; the need of religion to be exercised in external, public acts; the need for an unhindered search for the truth through dialogue; and, finally, the competence of the State which was limited to the temporal order.

Thus, on November 18, the *Coetus* submitted to the Council Presidency a petition based on Article 30, §2 of the Council's rules and on the impossibility of properly examining the text in such little time. They asked

---

[113] Antoine Wenger, *Vatican II, chronique de la troisième session* (Paris: Centurion Press, n.d.), 137; Wiltgen, *The Rhine Flows into the Tiber*, 166. Cardinal Bea did not sign the letter as had done seventeen other cardinals: Frings, Döpfner, König, Ritter, Meyer, Alfrink, Leger, J. Lefebvre, Silva, then Liénart, Suenens, Lercaro, *etc.*
[114] Lefebvre, *J'accuse*, 48.

for the vote to be deferred. The chairman, Cardinal Tisserant, agreed that Archbishop Felici should put this request to the Council and that there should be a preliminary vote on the matter. Afraid that this vote might prejudice their stalling tactics, Bishop Carli, one of the signatories of the *Coetus's* letter, had recourse to Cardinal Roberti, chairman of the administrative tribunal of the Council. This appeal was successful and obtained the Pope's approval.[115] On November 19, Cardinal Tisserant had to announce "that we will not proceed to a vote during the present session."

The liberal wing of the Council was absolutely furious. As Wiltgen states: "Never were so many harsh and angry words heard in the *aula* as in that moment of panic." The *Coetus* had jammed up the progressives' machinery. On December 18, 1964, they sent to the Fathers on their mailing list fifteen pages of amendments for the schema on religious liberty. On December 30, Archbishop Lefebvre, who was in Mauritius, sent to the Council Secretariat seven pages of observations on the schema.[116] Then in June 1965, the *Coetus* again sent twenty-four pages of new amendments to be added to the fourth version of the schema (*textus reemendatus*). They criticized this version for abstracting from the distinction between the notions of true and false in laying out the juridical criteria for determining true religious liberty. They also found fault with the fact that it emphasized the need for public order in limiting the exercise of any religion, rather than basing its arguments on the common good.[117]

BOLD REQUEST, THREAT OF SUPPRESSION, PERSEVERANCE[118]

In July, the important meeting already mentioned took place at Solesmes. On this occasion Archbishop Lefebvre and Bishops Sigaud and Carli sent a letter dated July 25 to the Holy Father asking that the views of the minority and the majority on the great debates of the Council be presented by one or two speakers from each side one after the other. In this way all the Fathers would have a synthesis of the theses being presented. An answer came dated August 11 from Cardinal Cicognani, Secretary of State, and addressed to Bishop Carli. It rejected the request out of hand, and criticized the Fathers of the *Coetus* for their name and for forming a group that was likely to divide the assembly of bishops.

Worried, Bishop Carli wrote about the matter to Archbishop Lefebvre on August 17, and on August 20, the Archbishop forwarded the letter to Archbishop Sigaud, remarking, "It seems that the Holy Father or the Car-

---

[115] René Laurentin, *L'enjeu du concile, bilan de la 3ᵉ session* (Paris: Seuil, 1965), 275-276.
[116] Cf. Lefebvre, *J'accuse*, 41-49.
[117] The Common Good includes respect for natural moral law and, in Catholic countries, protection for the true religion.
[118] Wiltgen, *The Rhine Flows into the Tiber*, 244 ff.

dinal Secretary of State have been alarmed by our name, which suggests a powerfully organized association capable of causing divisions....We can quite easily get rid of the title, and personally I would not be opposed. In any case, it won't change the reality." That meant: let us carry on!

Thus, on September 18, 1965, the third day of the debate on religious liberty during the fourth session of the Council, the *Coetus*, acting in the name of one hundred Fathers and under the rules of the Council, submitted to the Cardinal moderators a petition asking permission to read a paper that would present its perspective on this doctrine "in a complete and systematic manner." The request was rejected, and on September 21 the Council Fathers voted 1,997 for and 224—the hardcore of the *Coetus*—against the schema *textus recognitus* as the basis for the definitive declaration.

The *Coetus* wondered whether the Council would give up discussing principles and radically reform the text to begin again on a sound foundation. Would it be necessary, as had often proved to be the case, to focus on changing little details[119] in an attempt to prevent the worst? The *Coetus* did not resign itself to this strategy, but decided to mobilize all its forces for the crucial battle over principles. Already the fifth version that was discussed and put to the vote on October 26 and 27, 1965, had had to be changed to take into account the hundreds of *modi* of the Fathers. However, the sixth draft that came from this revision (*textus denuo recognitus*), which was presented on November 17 by Bishop De Smedt, was not acceptable to the *Coetus*. On November 18, the *Coetus* sent a final text to eight hundred Fathers with two dense pages analyzing the fundamental logic of the Secretariat's thesis and refuting its principal claims. Its conclusion: "We are compelled to say *non placet*."

Despite the improvements made to No. 1 concerning "the traditional Catholic doctrine of the moral duty of men and societies towards the true religion and the unique Church of Christ," this principle was not satisfactorily applied in the rest of the text, while the Secretariat's fundamental thesis was stubbornly maintained. The *Coetus*'s arguments can be summarized as follows:

The "right to freedom from constraint in religious matters" that the document tries to attribute to the "person" (no. 1) and to "religious groups" (no. 4) is, according to the schema itself, entirely based on man's right to *act* in a religious manner in his "search for the truth" (no. 2), a right based on "the social nature of man" which "requires that he express the interior acts of religion exteriorly, and which demands that in religious matters he have contact with others who *profess his religion*[120] in a communal form" (no. 3). The *Coetus* said that the problem here was that neither

---

[119] Cf. *Spiritual Conferences at Ecône*, Dec. 15, 1972.

reason, Sacred Scripture, nor the Magisterium accepts that the religious right can be legitimately expressed, claimed, or exercised as a natural right when it concerns religious error or false worship.

Pius XII had again recently taught that "what is not in accord with truth and the moral law has objectively no right to exist, to be promoted, or to be practiced,"[121] and that no human authority can give a positive mandate or positive permission to teach or to do things contrary to religious truth."[122] This same Pope taught that, consequently, the natural right to freedom from constraint in the profession or practice of religion only applies concretely to the true religion. Thus, he said, man has "the right to be free to venerate *the true God*,"[123] and "is wholly free to practice *true divine worship*."[124] Archbishop Lefebvre summed up the question in a pithy expression which horrified the liberals: "Only truth has rights, error has none."

The *Coetus* text added two corollaries to this basic truth. Firstly, religious error, or rather its exterior manifestations, could be tolerated, as Pius XII said, "for higher or greater interests" [the common good],…in certain circumstances."[125] This tolerance would be guaranteed by conceding a civil right to a degree of freedom from interference. Secondly, the rights of religious truth meant, as Pius XII again taught, that "the Church…in principle considers collaboration [with the State] as normal, and holds as an ideal the unity of the people in the true religion, and unanimity in practice between that religion and State."[126] Thus, two claims of the schema collapsed: the right to religious liberty in all circumstances which was not merely civil but also natural, and the general neutrality of the State which would only recognize a given religion "in particular circumstances."

What a shame that this final text of the *Coetus* could not be presented and expounded upon in the *aula*! In any case, the vote on November 19 on the sixth text saw the number of *non placet*s rise higher than ever: 249 against 1,954 *placet*s. Bishop di Meglio, a specialist in international law, had his own commentary handed out on December 3: "For a notable number of Council Fathers the teaching and practical applications of the schema are not acceptable in conscience. In fact, the fundamental principle of the schema has remained unchanged despite the amendments that

---

[120] Thus, the negative right to freedom from constraint in one's religion is founded on the affirmative right to profess one's religion. Whatever one says, one could not escape from this logic the conclusion that the *Cœtus* strongly underlined.

[121] Pius XII, allocution to Italian lawyers *Ci Riesce*, Dec. 6, 1953, *Documents*, 614.

[122] *Ibid.*, 616, *PIN* 3038.

[123] Allocution to the Congress of Business Administration, August 5, 1950, *PIN* 1119.

[124] Allocution to the Christian Democrat Youth of West Berlin, March 28, 1957, *PIN* 1252.

[125] *Ci Riesce*, *PIN* 3041.

[126] Allocution at the Tenth International Congress of Historical Studies, Sept. 7, 1955.

have been introduced: that is, the right of error....Since the declaration on religious freedom has no dogmatic value, the negative votes of the Council Fathers will constitute a factor of great importance for the future studies of the declaration itself, and particularly for the interpretation to be placed upon it."[127]

The 249 *non placet*s prevented there being moral unanimity in favor of religious liberty. Paul VI made it known that he supported the text and wished for such unanimity. Some Hispanic bishops who up to that point had voted *non placet* then said: "How can we not now vote *placet*? Besides, Article 1 mentions that the traditional doctrine on the duties of the State towards the Church is safe." Archbishop Lefebvre complained about this attitude, "Yes, Paul VI had this little sentence added [on November 17], but it has no effect on the text, which states the opposite. It's too easy to approve error with the help of a little sentence like that." Unfortunately, the Archbishop's voice was not heard, and on December 7, in a public session attended by the Pope, the final vote showed that the *Coetus*'s numbers had fallen to seventy *non placet*s, one of which was Archbishop Lefebvre's.

PROMULGATION OF RELIGIOUS LIBERTY[128]

That day, each Council Father had signed his attendance slip as usual. Then, the Holy Father made his solemn entry. Next, the Secretary General read the four texts that the Fathers would vote on. The final vote on religious liberty was followed by three other final votes concerning the decree on the missionary activity of the Church (*Ad Gentes*), the priesthood in the Church's mission (*Presbyterorum Ordinis*), and the pastoral constitution on the Church in the modern world (*Gaudium et Spes*). This last document was opposed by seventy-five votes, Archbishop Lefebvre's among them.[129]

For each conciliar document, the Fathers filled out and signed an individual voting slip using a special magnetic pencil that could be read by machine. The voting was secret and was required to be done in person. Even if a Council Father was representing an absent Father, he could not vote for him. This was required by Canon Law, as Archbishop Felici reminded them, although a Father's representative could sign an act once it was promulgated.[130]

At the end of Mass, Archbishop Pericle Felici came to the Pope and announced the results of the four votes. The Pope then approved the four

---

[127] Wiltgen, *The Rhine Flows into the Tiber*, 251.

[128] Cf. *Sedes Sapientiæ*, review of the Society of St. Thomas Aquinas, no. 31: 41-44; no. 35: 32-45.

[129] According to the records conserved in the Council archives, Archbishop Lefebvre would claim to have voted *non placet* on the subject of religious liberty and the Church in the modern world.

[130] Code of Canon Law (1917), can. 224, §2; A. Syn., III, VIII, 184.

documents and promulgated them orally to the sound of a loud applause. Then, four large sheets were passed around the Fathers, each one bearing the titles of the four promulgated documents. The Fathers were asked to sign their names with the word "Ego" preceding their Christian name. The word meaning "I" was added to signify the union of each Father in the act of promulgation by the Pope, head of the Conciliar College. A Father's representative could show the Father's approval by writing: "*Ego procurator...*—I, procurator of..." Thus, on one of these large sheets,[131] the following signatures appear in the same hand: "Ego + Marcellus Lefebvre arch. Tit. Synnada in Phrygie," "Ego procurator pro Epis. Augustinus Grimault, epis. tit." And on another: "Ego Antonius de Castro Mayer, ep. Camposinus, Brasilia."

What these indisputable facts show is that, having voted against religious liberty to the bitter end, Archbishop Lefebvre, like Bishop de Castro Mayer, finally signed the promulgation of the declaration *Dignitatis Humanae*. What could seem like a volte-face should not be surprising in the least. Once a schema was promulgated by the Pope, it was no longer a schema but changed in nature to become an act of the Magisterium. Archbishop Lefebvre himself underlined the weight of papal approval in his talk on September 15, 1976, when he admitted having signed lots of Council texts "under moral pressure from the Holy Father," because, as he said, "I cannot separate myself from the Holy Father: if the Holy Father signs, morally I am obliged to sign."[132] According to Wiltgen:

> Basically, this was the attitude of all Council Fathers...; each was convinced that his own position on a given topic was the correct one....But these men, trained in Church law, also realized that both sides could not be right. And ultimately they went along with the majority view, when this finally became clear and was promulgated by the Pope as the common doctrine taught by the Second Vatican Council.[133]

There was neither dishonor nor inconsistency in this submission. After all, the clauses included in *Dignitatis Humanae* on "the true religion" or on the "just limits" of religious liberty made it just about possible to interpret the eleven lines that strictly speaking were the declaration (no. 2) in a Catholic manner, even if that was not the obvious meaning of the text, as the rest of the document makes clear. In any case, Archbishop Marcel Lefebvre's and Bishop Antonio de Castro Mayer's support was officially registered in the Council's *Acta*.[134]

If later Archbishop Lefebvre stated several times that he did not put his signature on the declaration of religious liberty—as with *Gaudium et*

---

[131] Kept in the Council archives and summarized in *A. Syn.*, IV, VII, 804-859.
[132] *Itinéraires*, special edition, April 1977, pp. 224, 231.
[133] Wiltgen, *The Rhine Flows into the Tiber*, 252.
[134] *A. Syn.*, IV, VII, 809, 10th line and 823, 8th line.

Spes—it was a claim in line with his opposition before and after the promulgation, and the result of an error or a memory slip.[135] He seems to have confused his final votes against *Gaudium et Spes* and *Dignitatis Humanae* with refusing to sign. Such a mix-up appears from the denials that the Archbishop made in 1976 and 1990.[136] This would seem to imply that while on the one hand he gave his final *placet* to all the conciliar schemas except two, he did not think of the signatures as a promulgation of the Council documents with the Pope, even though he signed them all (as appears in the *Acta Synodalia*).

Putting that to one side, if we compare the number of voters on religious liberty (2,386) and the number of Fathers present who signed the promulgation, we find that at least twenty-two Fathers who voted for or against did not sign the documents. Archbishop Lefebvre was not one of them. Nonetheless, if certain facts prove to have escaped us, or if another interpretation is found to be more plausible, we would be quite open to accepting it. In our opinion, the Archbishop's signing *Dignitatis Humanae* takes nothing away from the value of his fight against religious liberty.

It now remains for us to study more closely his participation in this fight against religious liberty and against two other major themes of the Council: collegiality, of which we have spoken, and ecumenism.

---

[135] Ms. II, 32, 33-34.
[136] *Le Chardonnet*, no. 57 (June 1990); no. 59 (Sept. 1990); no. 61 (Dec. 1990); *Tradi Presse*, no. 8 (June 15, 1990); *Fideliter*, no. 79 (Jan.-Feb. 1991): 7.

CHAPTER 13

HERALD OF CHRIST THE KING

I. ARCHBISHOP LEFEBVRE'S INTERVENTIONS AT THE COUNCIL

"IT WAS MY DUTY TO SPEAK"

"I certainly made more interventions than other bishops, but I considered that it was my duty to speak."[1] By these words, Archbishop Lefebvre explained the state of mind that led him to intervene publicly at the Council. Already on October 20, 1962, barely ten days after the opening ceremony, he immediately reacted to the "Message to All Men" proposed for the Fathers' approval:

> We were given a quarter of an hour to familiarize ourselves with this. Those of us who wished to introduce any modifications had to inform the Secretariat of the Council by telephone, draft our intervention and present ourselves at the microphone when called by the Secretariat. It was abundantly clear to me that this message was inspired by a concept of religion wholly orientated towards man and, in man, towards temporal advantages in particular, in the search for a theme to unite all men, atheists and religious men—a theme of necessity utopian and liberal in spirit.[2]

Holding to his resolution to intervene when necessary, Archbishop Lefebvre asked to speak and came to the microphone to criticize the very content of the message: "It [the message] considers primarily human and temporal benefits and does not pay sufficient attention to the spiritual and eternal values; it concentrates on the welfare of our earthly city and takes too little account of the heavenly city towards which we are journeying and for which we are upon this earth."[3] Archbishop Lefebvre later commented on his attack on the spirit of the Pope's words: "I was clashing with those who had written it, and after the meeting His Eminence Cardinal Lefebvre spoke to me bitterly. He had overseen the writing of the message that was no doubt done by French experts like Fr. Congar."

---

[1] In Marziac, *Monseigneur Lefebvre, soleil levant*, 12.
[2] Lefebvre, *J'accuse le concile*, 14.
[3] *Ibid.*, 16.

This first skirmish only helped the Archbishop to sharpen his sights. This was even more the case on October 30: when Cardinal Ottaviani, the guardian of the faith, went over the time limit in his address to the *aula*, Cardinal Alfrink, who was chairing the session, ordered his colleague's microphone to be switched off. Humiliated, the old warrior had to sit down again to applause from his adversaries.[4] Scandalized by this incident, Archbishop Lefebvre was more than ever resolved to speak. He explained why in detail in 1987:

> I did not seek to be different…far from it. I think it was the training I received in the French Seminary in Rome which led me to react along the lines of certain principles, the principles the Popes expound in all their encyclicals. I acted in that spirit, the spirit that builds Catholic societies so that our Lord Jesus Christ might reign.
>
> When the Council came, it became almost necessary to stop thinking about the Social Reign of our Lord so that all religions could be free to express themselves in a liberal and ecumenical spirit. Obviously, I could accept nothing of the sort!
>
> What surprises me is that out of all those who were with me at the Seminary and who also become bishops, many accepted it all: Bishop Ancel, Archbishop Garrone, Bishop Lebrun, Bishop Michon, and I don't know who else…they were all keen, some of them more than I, on the thought of taking part in the Pope's battles or in the fight for the Church. They had given brilliant lectures at the Seminary which had remained legendary. But having been appointed as bishops in France, they had been recycled. They had sold out totally to liberalism and to the liberal theses. It is pitiful. It is one of the saddest things of my life.[5]

"I HAVE NOT CONCEALED THY TRUTH FROM A GREAT COUNCIL" (PSALM 39)

However, some bishops from the Holy Ghost Fathers who were full of human respect said that they were embarrassed by the public interventions of their Superior General in the *aula*. "They had a meeting. They criticized me because I was out of step with the French bishops."[6] The Archbishop did not care. Besides, some Holy Ghost Fathers supported him, and simple missionaries wrote to him to express their admiration for the fighting spirit of a "lone knight." One of these did not mince his words:

> Those who admire you just to be diplomatic and your ideological opponents who fear you[7] will continue their work. You can tell them all that at least one Holy Ghost Father is proud of your attitude, because you have had the courage to express your ideas before the entire Church for its

---

4   Wiltgen, *The Rhine Flows into the Tiber*, 28.
5   Cagnon, 1987, 3, 18-19.
6   Cagnon, *Les Relations de Rome avec Ecône*, 11.
7   Within the Holy Ghost Fathers.

greater good (even at the price of your reputation), thus showing that liberty is not an empty word among the brothers of Christ.[8]

The prospect was not at all inviting of having to mount resistance against the mood that was increasingly becoming the predominant spirit of the Council. Despite being anti-liberals, some bishops did not have the psychological strength to get involved in the fight. Such was the case of Bishop Nestor Adam, bishop of Sion in Valais. Archbishop Lefebvre said,

> He was completely opposed to what happened at Vatican II. We were quite close at the time and he told me of his concerns, saying: "I'm no longer going to come to the Council. I do not want to come back to such a gathering where they are establishing principles that will demolish the Church." He saw things very clearly. I said to him: "But, Your Excellency, that is not the thing to do. If you are against it, you must stay and fight with us, so that we can resist this invasion, this tidal wave which is engulfing the Church." "Oh, no," he said, "it is too strong for me." He did not return to the Council for a whole year.[9]

MAKING CLEAR THE GOALS OF THE COUNCIL

Archbishop Lefebvre wrote[10] that the ambiguities of the Council were apparent from the first meetings. Why were they gathered together? Pope John XXIII had clearly spoken of how he wanted to guide the Council towards a pastoral *exposé* of doctrine (address of October 11). But the ambiguity remained, and one can see through the interventions and discussions the difficulty they had in knowing what the Council intended. It was said: "The Council is not dogmatic; we do not want to define new dogmas but to expound the truth pastorally." Liberals and progressives love living in a climate of ambiguity. On the pretext of not defining anything, would they also give up clearly expounding sound doctrine? "Whence my proposition of November 27, which I had already submitted to the Central Preparatory Commission and which was approved by the majority of its 120 members. At the Council the proposition was backed by a few people including Cardinal Ruffini and Archbishop Roy.[11] It would provide an opportunity to establish exactly what the 'pastoral' character of the Council was."

The Archbishop came to the microphone: "How can we define our doctrine so as to leave no place for today's errors, and how in the same text can we make truth accessible to people who are unfamiliar with theology?"

---

[8]   Letter from M'bour, Senegal, Nov. 23, 1965.
[9]   *Spiritual Conferences at Ecône*, 125 A, June 9, 1988, transcription, 206.
[10] Lefebvre, *J'accuse le concile*, 17.
[11] Archbishop of Quebec, who chose Charles De Koninck († 15 Feb. 1965) as his private theologian at the Council. De Koninck was a lay professor in the theology faculty at the University of Laval.

All the innovators pricked up their ears. What would Lefebvre propose to resolve the ambiguity of the word "pastoral" which worked in their favor?

> Each commission could produce two documents: a more dogmatic document to be used by theologians, and a pastoral document to be used by other people whether Catholic, non-Catholic, or unbelievers.[12]

The Archbishop explained the advantages of his solution. However, they no longer wanted to listen to him. What? Two documents! That would be twice as much work. Anyway, there was no question of using scholastic language. Of course, Archbishop Lefebvre refuted these two objections with scrupulous precision: the work would, on the contrary, be simplified, and everyone would draw maximum benefit from the Council. But the liberals and the neo-modernists were quite resolved to keep the cloak of ambiguity. "The idea of clearly stating the goals of the Council irritated them immensely. Therefore, my proposition was rejected."

AN ELOQUENT SYNOPSIS

To get a better grasp of the Archbishop's work in the Council, a synoptic table will speak louder than words.

I[ST] SESSION - AUTUMN 1962[13]

R — Message to All Men	Oct. 20, 1962	Naturalism; purely human ideas (p. 16) (I, I, 240)
S — The Liturgy	Oct. 29, 1962	Against the hegemony of the C.P.L. (I, I, 633)
R — Goals of the Council	Dec. 1, 1962	With the pastoral *exposé*, there must be a precise doctrinal text (18-21) (I, IV, 144 s.)

---

12 Cf. also *General Bulletin*, 708 (March-April 1963): 434.
13 Explanation of letters: R = read in the *aula*; S = submitted to the Secretariat; M = mailed. The numbers are for the pages referred to in *J'accuse le concile*; the Roman numerals are for the *Acta Synodalia*.

IIND SESSION - AUTUMN 1963

R — Collegiality	Oct. 11, 1963	The two dangers of collegiality (25-27) (II, II, 471 ff.)
R — Collegiality	Nov. 8, 1963	Against juridical collegiality (30-31) (II, IV, 643 ff.)
S — Ecumenism and Religious Liberty	November 1963	"The Holy Ghost does not decline to make use of..." (33-34) (II, V, 797 ff.)
S — Religious Liberty	Nov. 26, 1963	False dignity of the person (39-41) (III, II, 832 ff.)

IIIRD SESSION - AUTUMN 1964

R — Religious Liberty	Sept. 24, 1964	False definition of liberty as immunity (74-76) (III, II, 490 ff.)
S — The Church in the World (observations)	Oct. 23, 1964	The Church has an answer to all problems; do not disdain the teachings of Pius XII (83-85) (III, V, 477 ff.)
S — Missionary Activity	Start of Nov. 1964	It is Peter who sends; personal authority of the bishops (77-82) (III, VI, 561 ff.)

INTERSESSION 1964-65

M — Religious Liberty (observations)	Dec. 30, 1964	False notions of conscience and liberty; role of authority; common good and truth (41-48) (IV, I, 792 ff.)

IVTH SESSION - AUTUMN 1965

S — The Church in the World	Sept. 9, 1965	"New doctrine" (88-93) (IV, II, 781 ff.)
R — Religious Liberty	Sept. 20, 1965	Philosophers of 18th Century and Freemasons; divine law (95-98) (IV, I, 409 ff.)
R — Missionary Activity	Oct. 2, 1965	Naturalism and latitudinarianism (99-104) (IV, IV, 551 ff.)

METHOD OF ARGUMENTATION

This synoptic table shows the major themes and the arguments of the Archbishop's interventions in the Council. Some of these texts were read in the *aula*, others were handed to the Secretariat since they could not be read, and others were merely sent. The advantage of interventions that were read was that they could have an effect on all the Fathers. Those that were sent to the Secretariat were only made known to the commissions that were responsible for amendments.

The Archbishop's early interventions are couched in gentle language and are usually preceded by a long *captatio benevolentiae* (see interventions of December 1, 1962, on the goals of the Council). Already, however, on October 29, Archbishop Lefebvre's intervention on the liturgy attacks the power of the Pastoral Center for Liturgy over the diocesan bishops. During the second session (Autumn 1963), the language very quickly becomes lively and incisive. On November 6, 1963, the Fathers heard the Archbishop speak on collegiality, saying: "Now, this is grotesque and without the slightest foundation." Speaking on religious liberty in October 1964, he said: "The declaration against constraint in No. 28 is ambiguous, and in certain respects, false." The final sentence of his intervention concerning the *Church in the Modern World* that he submitted on September 9, 1965, to the Secretariat reads thus: "This pastoral Constitution is not pastoral, nor does it emanate from the Catholic Church."

His serious and solemn warnings to the Fathers are numerous. Concerning collegiality, he declared: "[I]t would then be logically necessary to assert, as one of the Fathers has almost declared: The Roman Church has erred in not knowing the fundamental principle of her divine Constitution" (November 6, 1963). In October 1964, he spoke on religious liberty: "Should this statement in its present terms come to be solemnly accepted, the veneration that the Catholic Church has always enjoyed among all men and all nations, because of her love of truth, unfailing to the point of martyrdom, will suffer grave harm, and that to the misfortune of a multitude of souls whom Catholic truth will no longer attract."[14]

Sometimes the Archbishop even questioned his listeners or readers. Thus on December 30, 1964, he spoke from the very depths of his heart when he wrote these moving words concerning the practical indifferentism of religious liberty: "What good are these sacrifices? What good is priestly celibacy or the virginity of religious? What good is the blood of the missionaries if it is not for the truth? Because Christ is the truth, because the Church of Christ is the truth!"

The supple, natural style of his line of argument revealing the spontaneity of its composition was always united to arguments from reason,

---

[14] Lefebvre, *J'accuse le concile*, 76.

proofs drawn from Sacred Scripture and the authority of the Sovereign Pontiffs. Thus, on November 26, 1963, the Archbishop took apart piece by piece the notion of religious liberty based on a "poorly defined human dignity": "From what, in fact, does the person derive his dignity? He draws his dignity from his perfection. Now the perfection of the human person consists in the knowledge of the Truth and the acquisition of the Good. This is the beginning of eternal life and eternal life is 'that they may know Thee, the only true God and Jesus Christ Whom Thou hast sent' (Jn. 17:3). Consequently, so long as he clings to error, the human person falls short of his dignity." The scriptural proof is repeated and expanded: "The dignity of the human person does not consist in liberty set apart from truth. In fact, liberty is good and true to the extent to which it is ruled by truth. 'The truth shall set you free,' said Our Lord (Jn. 8:32). The truth shall give you liberty."

This line of argument abundantly shows *a priori* and *a posteriori* that the destruction of the dignity of the person comes from the impact of error on morals:

> The dignity of the person also comes from the integrity of his will when it is ordained to the true Good. Now error gives birth to sin. "The serpent deceived me" (Gen. 3:13) said Eve, who was the first sinner. No truth can be clearer than this to all mankind. It is sufficient to reflect upon the consequences of this error on the sanctity of marriage, a sanctity of the greatest interest for the human race. This error in religion has gradually led to polygamy, divorce, birth control, that is to say, to the downfall of human dignity, above all in women.

While here he used such a lively and concrete example to defend a principle that was all too often denied by the liberals, his proofs were also based on the Magisterium of the Church. Since error, especially religious error, destroys the dignity of the human person, there is no place for giving it free rein: "In truth, it is opportune to recall the words of Pius IX, in his Encyclical *Quanta Cura*: 'And also, contrary to the teaching of Sacred Scripture, of the Church, and of the most holy Fathers, they do not hesitate to assert that "the best condition of society is the one in which there is no acknowledgment by the government of the duty of restraining, by established penalties, offenders of the Catholic religion, except insofar as the public peace demands' (Denzinger 1689)."

Then comes the inevitable conclusion: "To conclude, the chapter on 'religious liberty'[15] should be drawn up anew, in accordance with the principle which conforms to Catholic doctrine: 'For the very dignity of the human person, error must be repressed to prevent it from spreading, unless greater evil can be foreseen from its repression than from its tolera-

---

[15] Then merely Chapter V of the schema on Ecumenism.

tion.' I have spoken."[16] The tightly marshalled reasoning of this doctor of the faith is far from the theorizing of an "armchair intellectual."[17] It is dominated by the sense of sin and the concerns of a pastor of souls.

THE DOUBLE ERROR OF COLLEGIALITY

The first topic that the Archbishop spoke about in the *aula* was the supposedly collegial nature of the episcopacy as stated in the new schema on the Church (Chapter 2, §§ 16 and 17). In two spoken interventions in October and November 1963, Archbishop Lefebvre put on trial not the intentions but the tendencies[18] of the schema. Without analyzing the text of the schema as Bishop Carli would do, he perceived its harmful tendencies and dangerous applications. In October, he said: "This text claims that members of the college of bishops have a right of government either with the Sovereign Pontiff over the universal Church, or with the other bishops[19] over the various dioceses."

Thus the Pope should share his universal authority with a permanent college, and the bishops should share their power as pastors of a particular flock with the national bishops' assemblies.

Moreover, the Archbishop repeated his denunciation of this position in an interview with Fr. Wiltgen's Divine Word News Service on October 15: "[It is] a new kind of collectivism invading the Church....individual bishops would be so restricted in the government of their dioceses as to lose their initiative."[20] His experience as Apostolic Delegate and his more recent clashes with the French Assembly of Cardinals and Archbishops had made him aware of the danger that powerful bishops' conferences could pose to the pastoral responsibility of individual bishops. On November 6, 1963, the Archbishop deployed with subtle irony the arguments of history against the principle of juridical collegiality: "If, by some miracle, this principle should be discovered in this Council, and solidly affirmed, it would then be logically necessary to assert, as one of the Fathers has almost declared: 'The Roman Church has erred in not knowing the fundamental principle of her divine Constitution.'"[21]

Finally, on October 2, 1965, during the debate concerning the missionary activities of the Church, he noted that when in *Fidei Donum* Pius XII talked about the common responsibility of the bishops as regards the

---

16 ["I have spoken" was the standard phrase used to indicate the end of the intervention. Trans.]

17 Note for August 1963, Archbishop Lefebvre. Interview 01, 16 A, 008, B 5.

18 Cf. Berto, *Pour la sainte Eglise romaine*, 252.

19 Nevertheless, the schema gives the assurance that the "solicitude" of each member of the [bishops'] college for the Universal Church "is not an act of jurisdiction" (§17).

20 Wiltgen, *The Rhine Flows into the Tiber*, 89-90.

21 Lefebvre, *J'accuse le concile*, 31.

Church's universal missionary concerns, it was only in the sense of a moral solicitude by virtue of charity and not as demanded by justice: "...according to the law, bishops belong to their diocese, to their own particular flock; then, out of charity, they owe their solicitude to every human soul."[22]

These timely clarifications confirm the well-founded nature of the Preliminary Explanatory Note that Paul VI had added to the Constitution on the Church.

IS THE CHURCH OF CHRIST NO LONGER THE CATHOLIC CHURCH?

One crucial debate addressed by the Council centered on the definition or the very identity of the Catholic Church. The schema on the Church sent to the Fathers in 1963 replaced the text of the Preparatory Commission that was shelved during the first session in November 1962. It still claimed that the unique Church referred to in all the creeds as "one, holy, Catholic, and Apostolic" "is the Catholic Church constituted and ordained as a society in this world." However, in July 1964 the text sent to the Fathers provoked a wave of reaction. The Church of Christ, it said, "subsists in the Catholic Church." The "*est*" of identity had been replaced by a "*subsistit.*" Thus, the Church of Christ was simply *present* in the Catholic Church, or *constant* in, or *fully constituted* in the Catholic Church. This substitution of words had been suggested by the Protestant Pastor Schmidt[23] to Cardinal Frings's theologian, Fr. Ratzinger. The Doctrinal Commission explained: "*Subsistit* is used instead of *est* so that the expression corresponds better with the recognition of elements of the Church found elsewhere."[24]

At the opening of the third session, Bishop Carli's reaction was the most hard-hitting: "The words *subsistit in* are not acceptable, for one could believe that the Church of Christ and the Catholic Church are two distinct things, the first being present in the second as in a subject. With greater accuracy let us simply say '*est*' because that is what the sources say."[25] By "sources" he meant the recent texts of the Magisterium to which the text referred without remaining faithful to them. These included Pius XII's encyclical *Mystici Corporis,* which well and truly identified the Church of Christ with the Catholic Church (§13), and the encyclical *Humani Generis.*

By moving away from this traditional teaching, the Council was turning the Church into a nebulous form without precise shape, made up of a

---

22 *Ibid.*, 100.
23 Letter of Pastor Wilhelm Schmidt to Fr. Matthias Gaudron, Aug 3, 2000.
24 In cap. I, *A. Syn.*, III, I, 440.
25 *A. Syn.*, III, I, 653.

dense core, the Catholic Church, around which "ecclesiastical realities: true local Churches and diverse ecclesiastical communities" gravitate in concentric circles. These churches do not have a singular subsistence like the Catholic Church but rather (illogically) an ecclesial existence.[26]

The Archbishop opposed this error during the debate on ecumenism in November 1963. The schema dared to affirm that, "These separated Churches and communities are not totally deprived of meaning in the mystery of salvation; the spirit of Christ does not refuse to use them as means of salvation."[27] The refutation of this claim was made in a few enlightening lines submitted to the Council Secretariat: "A community, insofar as it is a separated community, cannot enjoy the assistance of the Holy Ghost. He can only act directly upon souls or use such means as, of themselves, bear no sign of separation."[28]

FALSE ECUMENISM

In the same intervention, Archbishop Lefebvre said that by looking for or giving value to the "sanctifying elements" that our separated brethren might have retained, one supported them in their errors. Thus, by saying "the separated brethren are disciples of Christ, regenerated by baptism" we deceive them because often their baptism "is invalid by defect of form, or matter, or of intention,"[29] and it generally bears no fruit because in those that have reached the age of reason, the absence of divine Catholic Faith is an obstacle, an *obex*, to grace. We also deceive the Orthodox by "false ecumenism" by which "the Primacy is injured and emptied of its content," and this leads people "to believe and state that the Bishop of Rome is no more than a *primus inter pares*, a first among equals." They regard the Primacy "almost uniquely for maintaining a united and undivided hierarchy," *i.e.*, as a simple "link of exterior unity."[30]

---

[26] Cf. Card. J. Ratzinger, talk on Feb. 27, 2000; *L'Osservatore Romano*, March 4, 2000, 7-8.

[27] Schema *Decreti de Œcumenismo*, 1963, p. 8, n. 2; cf. Conciliar decree *Unitatis Redintegratio*, §3.

[28] Lefebvre, *J'accuse le concile*, 34.

[29] *Ibid.*, 103. Archbishop Lefebvre would always emphasize the fact that the *error* of a sacred minister concerning the effects of a sacrament can influence his *intention*, either by leading him to make an act of will positively against the effect of the sacrament, or by determining the will precisely and resolutely to desire something quite other than that effect. This had not been clarified by the declarations of the Holy See; cf. Denzinger-Schönmetzer, *Enchiridion Symbolorum* (Herder, 1965), 3101-3102 (hereafter, DS); Archbishop Lefebvre was concerned about it.

[30] *Ibid.*, 60, 62: passages taken from the Private Memorandum of Cardinal Larraona, also signed by Archbishop Lefebvre.

Archbishop Lefebvre said that if "these truths are diminished"[31] by dint of the Council's "half affirming an essential truth in order to encourage unity" (namely the primacy of the Sovereign Pontiff), it would confirm the separated Eastern Churches in their false concept of unity according to which they do not "fully accept the consequences of primacy."[32]

We can see to what degree John Paul II later followed these diminished truths of the Second Vatican Council when he asked in his encyclical *Ut Unum Sint* "that an acceptable [to the Orthodox] way of exercising the primacy be sought."

THE CHURCH, SACRAMENT OF THE UNITY OF THE WORLD

On September 9, 1965, the Archbishop's intervention—not read publicly—contained not only numerous criticisms of the infamous Schema XIII (the future *Gaudium et Spes*), but also two attacks directed against the new ecclesiology: "Page 28, lines 22 and 23: The Church is defined thus: 'The Church is, as it were, the sacrament of intimate union with God and of the unity of the whole human race.'[33] This conception requires explanation: the unity of the Church is not the unity of human race." With his customary intuition, the Archbishop perceived the underlying spirit in this ambiguous concept, as in many other concepts contained in the schema. "Innumerable propositions contain ambiguities because in reality the doctrine of those who drafted them is not traditional Catholic doctrine, but a new doctrine, made up of a mixture of Nominalism, Modernism, Liberalism, and Teilhardism."[34] Among many other ambiguous sentences, the Archbishop singled out this one that was derived from the thinking of Teilhard de Chardin and Karl Rahner:[35] "By His Incarnation, God the Father's Word assumed all of man's nature, body and soul ('This is true, certainly,' said Archbishop Lefebvre). Thereby, he *sanctified* (Archbishop Lefebvre's emphasis) all nature created by God, matter included, so that in its own way every creature calls to its Redeemer" (p. 39, lines 19-22).[36]

The Council would correct this assertion by suppressing the ambiguity as regards all nature, but it would maintain the ambiguity regarding man: "By his Incarnation, the Son of God has united himself in some way

---

[31] *Ibid.*, 33.

[32] Memo of Cardinal Larraona, *ibid.*, 63.

[33] This idea that already appears as an axiom in *Lumen Gentium* (no. 1) was taken up again in schema XIII and used in *Gaudium et Spes*, no. 42, §3. It comes from Dutch-speaking theologians: P. Smulders, B. Willems, E. Schillebeeckx, J. Witte, as well as K. Rahner.

[34] Lefebvre, *J'accuse le concile*, 91-92.

[35] Cf. Karl Rahner, *XXᵉ siècle, siècle de grâce?* Selected lectures (Mame, 1962), 63, 84, 85.

[36] Cf. The commentary of Fr. Chenu in *Un théologien en liberté: Jacques Duquesne interroge le P. Chenu* (Centurion, 1975), 186.

to every man."[37] In this can be seen the leitmotiv of Pope John Paul's theology of Universal Redemption, which omits redemption from sin, the necessity of baptism, and the need to belong to the Church for salvation.

Archbishop Lefebvre criticized Schema XIII (pp. 6-10) for "always remaining silent about original sin and its consequences," for "speaking of the vocation of the human person (p. 13 ff.) without speaking of baptism and of justification by supernatural grace," and for defining the Church not as a perfect society necessary for salvation but as "the evangelical leaven of the whole mass of humanity."[38] He concluded his intervention, which, unfortunately, he was not able to read in the *aula*, with this extraordinary outburst:

> This pastoral Constitution...does not feed Christian men with the Apostolic truth of the Gospels and, moreover, the Church has never spoken in this manner. We cannot listen to this voice, because it is not the voice of the Bride of Christ....The voice of Christ, our Shepherd, we know. This voice we do not know. The clothing is that of the sheep. The voice is not the voice of the shepherd, but perhaps that of the wolf. I have spoken.[39]

RELIGIOUS LIBERTY: A FALSE DEFINITION

The battle against religious liberty was where Archbishop Lefebvre excelled as the "spirited, shrewd defender of Catholic truth"—*veritatis catolicae defensor acerimus*, as one cardinal called him. Although he often supported the remarks of his friends, Cardinals Ruffini, Bacci,[40] and Browne, the Archbishop nevertheless put forward his own thinking—which was the most traditional. Holding to the doctrine passed on by Leo XIII in *Immortale Dei*,[41] he taught:

> At the risk of destroying all authority, human liberty cannot be defined as freedom from any constraint. Constraints can be physical or moral. Moral constraint in the religious domain is extremely useful and is found throughout Sacred Scripture. "The Fear of God is the beginning of wisdom" (Ps. 110:10). Authority is there to help men do good and avoid evil. It is meant to help men use their freedom well. (42 and 75)

Thus, the "new basis" in the search for truth that the authors of the schema thought they had found amounted to mirrors and smokescreens: "This paragraph clearly shows the unreality of such a declaration. The search for truth, for men living on this earth, consists above all in obeying and submitting their intelligence to whatever authority may be concerned:

---

[37] *Gaudium et Spes*, no. 22 §2.
[38] Schema of May 28, 1965, p. 40, l. 13; cf. *Gaudium et Spes*, no. 40, §2.
[39] Lefebvre, *J'accuse le concile*, 93.
[40] *Op. cit.*, 33.
[41] *PIN* 149.

be it familial, religious, or even civil authority. How many men can reach the truth without the help of authority?" (43 and 75).

As for this "new basis": "this statement is based on a certain relativism....It considers individual and changing situations of our own times and seeks new guiding lines for our activity, after the manner of those who consider one particular case alone as, for instance, the United States. But such circumstances can, and in fact, do change" (76).

This pointed remark was aimed at the thesis of Fr. John C. Murray, who wanted to base the religious ideal of the State on the American model of religious pluralism and general mutual tolerance. It showed the fragility of a theory based on the sand of changing circumstances, and also threw into relief the strength of the traditional doctrine based on the rock of the rights of truth: "As this declaration is not based on the rights of truth, which alone can supply a solution that is true and unshakable in every event, we inevitably find ourselves confronted by the gravest difficulties" (76).

In other words, religious liberty is not a doctrine but sheer opportunism.

RELIGIOUS LIBERTY: HYPOCRISY

Bishop De Smedt was the great defender of this opportunism in the *aula* and acted as a reporter for the commission. Following Fr. Murray's idea, he held that civil authority is not competent to judge the truth or falsehood of a religion.[42] The schema is less explicit (Chapter 2, no. 4), but assumes this principle which Cardinal Ruffini, it may be remembered, had declared "completely false." Archbishop Lefebvre emphasized the fact that denying the State this competence "explicitly contradicts Catholic doctrine," especially as expounded by Leo XIII in *Immortale Dei* (44):[43] "Those who drafted this statement are clearly in error in refusing to allow to the Christian heads of state a sense of the truth. Experience proves the utter falsity of such an opinion: in some way or other everyone perceives the truth, those who contradict and persecute true believers, as well as unbelievers who respect the truth and those who believe in it" (76).

---

[42] *Relatio de Reemendatione Schematis Emendati,* May 28, 1965, pp. 48-49, *A. Syn.*, IV, I, 191.

[43] "The heads of state must hold as holy the name of God and count among their principal duties that of promoting religion, protecting it by their benevolence, and shielding it with the authority of laws....Civil society must...make the holy and inviolable observance of religion respected" (*PIN,* 131). As for knowing which is the true religion, it is not difficult, even for non-Catholics, because "one can recognize it without difficulty at least in Catholic countries from the signs of truth whose striking character she bears. This religion must be preserved and protected by the heads of state" (Leo XIII, Enc. *Libertas,* June 2, 1888).

In the light of this paradox which was very much in the style of the venerable Fr. Voegtli, State secularism—be it clerical like Bishop De Smedt's or anti-clerical like the Freemasons'—appeared in its true light: hypocrisy.

RELIGIOUS LIBERTY: VICTORY FOR THE FREEMASONS

Archbishop Lefebvre held that historically religious liberty was not found in Sacred Scripture—as Father Congar would later admit:[44] "Holy Scripture can only prove the obligation of submitting to God, to Christ and to the Church, not only one's conscience but one's whole....Nowhere and to no one does Holy Scripture make scandal permissible, even in the case of a conscience that is erroneous through no fault of its own" (46). On the contrary, the origin of religious liberty is to be found "outside the Church. Clearly it made its appearance among the self-styled philosophers of the [seventeenth and] eighteenth centuries: Hobbes, Locke, Rousseau, Voltaire." In the middle of the nineteenth century, "with Lamennais, the Liberal Catholics attempted to reconcile this conception with Church doctrine: they were condemned by Pius IX. This conception, which in his Encyclical *Immortale Dei*, Leo XIII calls 'a new law,' was solemnly condemned by that Pontiff as contrary to sound philosophy and against Holy Scripture and Tradition" (96).

Finally, the Archbishop denounced the disreputable dens where religious liberty was originally concocted:[45]

> This very year [1965], Yves Marsaudon, the Freemason, has published the book *L'oecumenisme vu par un franc-maçon de tradition* (Ecumenism as Seen by a Traditional Freemason). In it the author expresses the hope of Freemasons that our Council will solemnly proclaim religious liberty....What more information do we need? (96)

[Marsaudon] writes that, "Christians should, nevertheless, not forget that every path leads to God (in my Father's house there are many mansions) and be faithful to the courageous idea of liberty of thought that—one can speak truly here of a revolution that has come from our Masonic lodges—has magnificently spread its wings over the dome of Saint Peter's."[46]

---

[44] Eric Vatré, *La droite du Père, enquête sur la tradition catholique aujourd'hui* (Éd. de la Maisnie, 1994), 118.

[45] Cf. Schmidt, *Augustin Bea, cardinale dell'ecumenismo e del dialogo* (Milan: Éd. San Paolo, 1996), 139-141, recounting the important meeting in New York on April 1, 1963, of the American Council for Democracy under God, chaired by Bea. The meeting's theme: "Liberty and civil unity under God."

[46] (Paris: Éd. Vitiano), 121; quoted by *Permanences*, no. 21 (July 1965): 87.

THE RIGHT TO CAUSE SCANDAL AND ITS CONSEQUENCES

The Archbishop often said, "Religious liberty is the right to cause scandal" since it gives civil rights to the spread of religious error and its moral consequences. Among these consequences, the Archbishop pointed out the following:

- Immorality: "The liberty of all religious communities in human society, mentioned in No. 29, cannot be laid down, without at the same time granting moral liberty to these communities: morals and religion are very closely linked, for instance, polygamy and the religion of Islam" (75).
- The death of Catholic States: "A civil society endowed with Catholic legislation shall no longer exist" (47).
- "Doctrinal relativism and practical indifferentism" (47).
- "The disappearance in the Church of the missionary spirit for the conversion of souls" (47).

On the contrary, all these grievous problems would disappear if instead the Council proclaimed that "the Church of Christ [the Catholic Church] alone possesses the fulness and perfection of divine law, natural and supernatural, as she alone has received the mission to teach this law and the means to observe it; it is in her that Jesus Christ, Who is our law, is found in reality and truth. Consequently, she alone, always and everywhere, possesses a true right to religious liberty" (97).

II. BETWEEN ANGUISH AND HOPE

Although he was so involved in the battle for the faith in the conciliar *aula*, the Archbishop often liked to withdraw from the action and commit his personal thoughts to writing, either in sympathetic journals or even in the *General Bulletin* for the Holy Ghost Fathers. These writings reveal his thoughts on the work of the Council, and his feelings which moved between anguish and hope. Archbishop Lefebvre was not a two-dimensional figure. Although he saw the negative, he tried also to find the positive.

LOOKING FOR A FRUITFUL MIDDLE WAY

Following the second session which had seen the promulgation of the Constitution on the Liturgy, he gave an overview of the situation "as directed by the successor of Peter" in the review *Itinéraires*.[47] He approved of the conduct of Paul VI and blamed those who took it upon themselves to "anticipate arbitrarily how the Constitution should be implemented." However, the Archbishop considered that "what is worse than liturgical

---

[47] *Itinéraires* no. 81 (March 1964): 28-41; Lefebvre, *Un évêque parle*, 28-41.

improvisation by priests is the practice and example of public disobedience."

In the Holy Ghost Fathers' *General Bulletin*,[48] he explained to the congregation that the envisaged reform seemed to preserve the essentials. *Sacrosanctum Concilium* did not suppress Latin or Gregorian chant. Consequently—and this was his basic attitude—they must trust Rome and strictly obey its orders, thus guaranteeing a sensible implementation of the reformed norms. That said, the Archbishop did not disguise the weaknesses of the conciliar constitution and the dangerous spirit behind it: "Would it not be a dishonor to the liturgy to consider it merely as a tool of the apostolate and no longer to consider it as the public worship and praise of God?" That would induce "low regard for the liturgy" and "lessen the spirit of faith and religion among the faithful."

In June 1965, he tried to find "a productive middle way" for the reforms that were taking place, and asked himself: will that line be found? He recognized a very clear distinction between the first part of the Mass or "the Mass of the Catechumens" and the properly sacrificial part which began at the Offertory: "The first part of the Mass which was designed to instruct the faithful…needed to attain its objectives more clearly. So, let the priest be near the faithful, communicate with them, pray and sing with them, stand at the lectern, say the Collect in their language and also the readings of the Epistle and the Gospel."[49] Archbishop Lefebvre wanted the second part of the Mass to be said at the altar. He also wanted it said in Latin in a low voice.

The prelate's broad views on the first part of the Mass are interesting. He considered that the readings and the sermon were indispensable in preparing the faithful for the sacrifice. Naturally, the Offertory and the Canon remained the impregnable bastion of that sacrifice.

"I ADMIT I WAS TOO OPTIMISTIC"

Archbishop Lefebvre passed severe, lucid judgment on the spirit behind some of the conciliar schemas: "[they have] a spirit of rupture and suicide," as he said in 1964. "[There exists] a spirit of non-Catholic or rationalist ecumenism that has become a battering ram for unknown hands to attempt to pervert doctrine."[50] Some "of the Council Fathers' very legitimate wishes" were "as if unbeknown to them" used "by a group of Fathers and *periti*" to secure approval for theses "that the majority of

---

48 *General Bulletin*, 708 (March-April 1963): 416-437: Letter on some aspects of the first session of the Second Vatican Council.

49 *Itinéraires*, no. 95 (Jul.-Aug 1965): 78-79; Lefebvre, *Un évêque parle*, 58.

50 Article of Oct. 11, 1964, published on June 1, 1970, in *Critica Cattolica*, no. 6, Rome. Lefebvre, *Un évêque parle*, 110ff.; Lefebvre, *Lettres pastorales*, 189ff.

Fathers had never thought about." The Archbishop as yet refrained from accusing the Council itself. He attacked instead the perverse spirit that lived parasitically on the Council and was turning it away from its true objectives.

In 1965 before the fourth session, he also denounced "the magisterium of the modern world: public opinion" which poisoned the Fathers and influenced the debates. How many interventions had been made or were justified "by the fear of not conforming to this new magisterium"! However, the Archbishop remained optimistic:

> There is another magisterium here other than the Magisterium of the Church. This claim is corroborated by the Popes' addresses at the close of sessions and their interventions. But the Church in the person of Peter's successor has not yet substituted the traditional Magisterium with this new one and neither has the Church in Rome....The majority of the Cardinals and especially the cardinals of the Curia, and therefore of the Church in Rome, do not look to the new magisterium. Neither collegiality nor the ill-conceived religious liberty, both of which are contrary to the doctrine the Church, will succeed.[51]

Only later when he reread what he had written during the Council did the Archbishop say: "I admit that the optimism I showed regarding the Council and the Pope was ill-founded."[52]

PASTORAL CHARITY AND PRIESTLY HOLINESS

The end of the Council and the promulgation of the conciliar decrees that (in spite of the efforts of the *Coetus* and Archbishop Lefebvre) were influenced by the same spirit as the schemas, left the Archbishop momentarily silent. After four years of fighting, it was necessary to step back and take account of what had happened.

The one conciliar document that the Archbishop had any regard for was the decree on the ministry and life of priests, *Presbyterorum Ordinis*. He shared his very positive thoughts[53] on the document with the Holy Ghost Fathers. Those things that would eventually be the Archbishop's prime concerns were already becoming clear: to protect the priesthood against any deviation and refocus it on what was its essence and sanctity. In this respect he did not fail to note that the document moved the emphasis away from the priest's role of offering sacrifice and on to his role as preacher.[54] He corrected this idea: "This ministry is not an end in itself, it is a

---

[51] *Itinéraires*, no. 95: 68-77; Lefebvre, *Un évêque parle*, 46-56.
[52] Letter to André Cagnon, Jan. 6, 1988.
[53] "The Priest of Our Lord Jesus Christ in the Conciliar Decree *Presbyterorum Ordinis*," Thought for the Month, March, May and Sept. 1966, in *General Bulletin*, 726, 727, 729; *Lettres pastorales*, 239-252.
[54] Cf. *Spiritual Conferences at Ecône*, 6 A, 1974.

preparation, it leads to another ministry which is more essential and which is the particular goal of the priesthood."

However, the Superior General picked out the better part of the Council text. First was the definition of the priest: "...priests, by the anointing of the Holy Spirit, are marked with a special character and are so configured to Christ the Priest that they can act in the person of Christ the Head" (§2). [55] Then, concerning the very goal of the priest's functions: "Through the ministry of priests, the spiritual sacrifice of the faithful is made perfect in union with the sacrifice of Christ, the sole Mediator. Through the hands of priests and in the name of the whole Church, the Lord's sacrifice is offered in the Eucharist in an unbloody and sacramental manner....The ministry of priests is directed toward this work and is perfected in it" (§2). Finally, with respect to uniting the interior life with the apostolate, something that many priests found difficult to do: "Thus...they will find in the very exercise of pastoral love the bond of priestly perfection which will unify their lives and activities. This pastoral love flows mainly from the Eucharistic Sacrifice, which is therefore the center and root of the whole priestly life. The priestly soul strives thereby to apply to itself the action which takes place on the altar of sacrifice" (§14).

A NEW DOGMA: THE DIGNITY OF THE HUMAN PERSON

Even if, like his fellow bishops, the Archbishop simply praised the document concerning the priesthood, he was far more critical and realistic in an article—already quoted—dated October 11, 1964, and written during the third session. Its deliberately provocative title was: "To Remain a Good Catholic, Should One Become a Protestant?" On Bishop Morilleau's insistence, however, he did not publish the piece, which finally appeared only in 1970. It identifies the damage to the "truth of the Church" that would be caused by collegiality, ecumenism, and religious liberty: "The truth of the Church obviously has consequences that trouble the Protestants and unfortunately a number of Catholics imbued with liberalism. Henceforth, the dogma that will replace the truth of the Church is the dignity of the human person and the superior good of liberty."[56]

By the "truth of the Church," Archbishop Lefebvre firstly understood the Church as "the one true religion established by God which cannot without great injustice be put on the same footing as other religions."[57] He

---

[55] "Christ the Head" sounds strange if we are speaking of "the Eucharistic sacrifice in which priests fulfil their principal function" (§13, c). The accent on the spiritual sacrifice of the faithful in the action of the priest is also strange.
[56] *Lettres pastorales*, 193-195.
[57] Leo XIII, enc. *Humanum Genus*, Apr. 20, 1884 (Bonne Presse), I, 254.

also meant the unique ark of eternal salvation, the Mistress of Truth who "enjoys total certitude beyond all heterodox systems and possesses the absolute and unchangeable truth."[58]

The Council replaces this truth of the Church with the "truth of the person,"[59] *i.e.,* his transcendental dignity regardless of the choices he makes, his liberty however he uses it, his independence untrammeled by interference from any authority, his very search for truth without a magisterium, and the primacy of his conscience over every human law.[60]

The Archbishop notes that "to define liberty as the absence of constraint is to destroy all authority established by God," the authority of the Magisterium of the Church, and also the authority of parents in families, and especially in Christian families. "The doubts concerning the legitimacy of authority and the demands of obedience caused by giving greater importance to human dignity, autonomy of conscience, and liberty, are shaking every society beginning with the Church, religious orders, dioceses, civil societies, and families."[61]

Similarly, "the truth of the Church is the reason for Catholic schools. With this new dogma they imply it would be better to merge" with secular schools. The new dogma kills zeal for vocations and vocations themselves. "The truth of the Church is the very reason for her zeal in evangelizing and proselytizing. Consequently, it is the ultimate reason for the vocations of missionaries, whether priests and religious." Finally, the truth of the Church is a source of zeal for lay Catholics "to work to establish or to re-establish the Catholic State." According to the new dogma, they should favor pluralism and "they would have a duty to maintain the religious indifferentism of the State." Now subordinate to the dignity of the person, the Church should give up being the truth. She would only bear her own truth, and be one truth amongst many.

Behind the new dogma can be discerned the primacy of man over God and the dethronement of Christ. The Church should submit her truth, her institutions, her worship, and, finally, her priesthood to this new dogma.[62] What gave Archbishop Lefebvre the greatest pain was his increasing awareness of the complicity of Popes John XXIII and Paul VI in the proclamation of the new dogma. In spite of their personal interventions that were sometimes heartening and encouraging, they almost always supported the plotting of the liberals and modernists by "muzzling the Cu-

---

[58] Msgr. Sarto, future St. Pius X, in Pierre Fernessole, *Pie X, essai historique* (Lethielleux, 1952), I, 54.

[59] John Paul II, encyclical *Veritatis Splendor,* August 6, 1993.

[60] Such is the tendency if not the letter of the following texts of the Council: *Gaudium et Spes* 4,4; 9,1; 11,2; 12,1; 16; 17; 22,1; 25,1; 26,2-3; 29,2; 41,2; *Dignitatis Humanae,* 1, a, c; 2, a, b, c; 3b, d; 6a ; 9.

[61] Letter to Cardinal Ottaviani, Dec. 20, 1966, *Fideliter,* no. 98: 57.

[62] Fr. Paul Aulagnier, *La Tradition sans peur* (Paris : Éd. Servir, 2000), 114.

ria," that "most noble part of the Church of Rome, Mistress of Truth." Very often in the name of conciliar unanimity, they silenced "those who wanted to express their disagreement or simply warn"[63] about the new dogma and its implementation.

THE GREATEST TRAGEDY THAT THE CHURCH HAS EVER SUFFERED

Barely nine months after the closing of the ecumenical Council, Pope Paul VI thought it necessary to alert the bishops and ask them to report on "the growing abuses in the interpretation of the Council's doctrine," the "wild and bold opinions," and "the errors" touching upon "dogma itself and the foundations of the faith."[64] How had the Church reached this point so quickly?

The French bishops tried to minimize the danger: "There are always tendencies, currents, uneasiness, wavering, or leftist tendencies" (Archbishop Veuillot spoke of "blunders"[65]). On the other hand, Archbishop Lefebvre, Superior General of the Holy Ghost Fathers,[66] revealed a most serious crisis in the "extremely confused ideas" and also "the break-up of Church institutions: religious orders, seminaries, and Catholic schools."

The Archbishop set out to identify the cause of the crisis. Little by little he came to place the blame on the Council itself: "Through the preparatory commissions, the Council readied itself to proclaim the truth in the face of these errors....It was horrible to see all this preparation rejected, to be followed by the most serious tragedy that the Church has ever suffered. We have witnessed the *marriage of the Church with liberal ideas.*"

This expression of Archbishop Lefebvre, which was crucial to his thinking, contained a secret intuition concerning the objectives of the Council: by bringing about a "new synthesis"—the "marriage of the Church with liberal ideas"—the liberals aimed to overcome past and recent opposition between Catholicism on the one hand, and Protestantism, the Rights of Man, and modernism on the other.

Was it the Council itself, the spirit of the Council, or a spirit foreign to the Council which was to blame for this tragedy? At first the Archbishop was inclined to denounce a spirit foreign to the Council: "The Council allowed those who believe in the errors and tendencies condemned by the Popes[67] to believe legitimately that their doctrines were henceforth ap-

---

[63] *Fideliter*, no. 59: 34; *Lettres pastorales*, 191-192.

[64] Letter of Cardinal Ottaviani, pro-prefect of the SCDF, to the chairmen of all the world's episcopal conferences, July 24, 1966. *A.A.S.* 63 (1966): 659; *Doumentation Catholique*, 1481: 1843ff.

[65] Summary of the reply of the French bishops by Fr. Dulac, *Le Courrier de Rome*, Feb. 20, 1967, original: *Documentation Catholique*, 1488: 327ff.

[66] Reply to Cardinal Ottaviani, Rome, Dec. 20, 1966; *Fideliter*, no. 98: 55ff.

[67] Pius IX, *Syllabus*; St. Pius X, *Lamentabili*; Pius XII, *Humani Generis, etc.*

proved of." However, if they believed this "legitimately," then the very spirit of the Council if not the letter of the Council was to blame: "*One can and one must unfortunately state that generally speaking, when the Council made an innovation, it struck at the certainty of the truths taught by the authentic Magisterium of the Church and which rank definitively among the treasures of Tradition.*"[68]

The Council, therefore, was not only a sounding board for the new heretics who were present at the Council or on the fringes; by its innovations it also struck at Catholic truth. Listing the consequences of this process, which he predicted in 1964, the Archbishop said he was "driven by the facts" to conclude: "In an inconceivable fashion, the Council promoted the spreading of liberal errors. The Faith, morality, and ecclesiastical discipline are shaken to their foundations as all the Popes have predicted. The destruction of the Church is advancing rapidly."

However, because he was a pastor as much as a theologian, Archbishop Lefebvre did not hesitate to indicate to the Cardinal a course of remedies for the Holy Father's consideration: Suppress those spreading error and reduce them to silence; urge the bishops to reform their seminaries and to restore St. Thomas to the curricula; encourage the Superior Generals to maintain all the principles of Christian asceticism, and especially obedience, in the novitiates and communities; encourage the development of Catholic schools.

These things were exactly what he had tried to do in his own congregation ever since his election as Superior General.

---

[68] Underlined in the text.

CHAPTER 14

SUPERIOR GENERAL

THE LAST ATTEMPTED RESCUE

I. A HARD FOUGHT ELECTION

FACING PROBLEMS

To give a continuous overview of Archbishop Lefebvre's contribution to the Council, we have considered his role as a Council Father up to 1966. We must now go back over his election as Superior General of the Holy Ghost Fathers and consider his work in that capacity.

The name of Archbishop Lefebvre had already been mooted during the General Chapter of 1950. He came second in the first round of elections for the delegates from the province of France,[1] and in the second round he was elected to the chapter as the third delegate for the fourth mission group.[2] During the chapter "his election as Superior General would surely have happened if the members of the chapter had not been warned not to vote for a man who was at that time fulfilling the sensitive role of Apostolic Delegate."[3] Thus, when Fr. Francis Griffin, Superior General from 1950 to 1962, made it known that he would not stand for re-election, many Holy Ghost Fathers backed Archbishop Lefebvre for the post. He was close to his missionaries and was "hospitality itself,"[4] unlike Fr. Griffin who, once he was elected Superior General, no longer willingly met missionaries who were passing through Rue Lhomond. "You're on holiday? Good. Get back to your mission and your work quickly! I've got my own work to do."[5]

Choosing the former Apostolic Delegate would do honor to the congregation, and his perfect knowledge of the Roman Curia would help settle matters in high places. Archbishop Lefebvre was aware of all this, and many colleagues said to him: "Next time, it's your turn!"[6] Nonetheless, the

---

[1] With 380 votes, behind Fr. Côme Jaffré elected as delegate with 521 votes in the first round; *French Bulletin*, 45.
[2] *General Bulletin*, 632.
[3] *Clartés*, diocesan bulletin in Guadeloupe, May 18, 1963.
[4] Fr. Bussard, ms. I, 17, 6.
[5] *Ibid.*, ms. I, 16-17.
[6] Lefebvre, first interview with Fr. Marziac.

opinions of the Archbishop's colleagues differed, depending on where they came from. On one hand, the Irish admired Archbishop Lefebvre as a great missionary bishop and emulator of Bishop Shanahan. He had been to Dublin to the Fathers' Congress,[7] and on that occasion visited the scholasticate at Kimmage and the college at Blackrock. On the other hand, the Germans had been impressed by the Delegate's practicality. When he arrived at Knechtsteden to pay them a visit, he got out of the car, opened the hood, and immediately began fiddling with the engine to fix some problem. As the admiring Fathers and students might have said: "Well, he is not afraid of getting his hands dirty. Here's the man we need!"[8] As for the Portuguese, they knew and respected him as a man of sound doctrine who came to preach a retreat to the seventy-three fathers of the province in Carcavelos in 1959.[9]

Among the French, whose province was the biggest in the congregation, many admired and even loved the Archbishop. By voting for him, they were determined to make up for the affront to the congregation caused by the Archbishop's removal from Dakar—not transferred but "Tulle-ferred," as they said.[10] However, for an active minority, Archbishop Lefebvre's thinking and his contribution to the African mission said a lot about his fundamental attitudes. Every month[11] a group of forty missionaries from various countries met together and worked at redefining the relations that ought—so they said—to exist between the young African churches and the religious congregations and churches in Europe. With this in mind one of them was given the job of studying the thinking of the Archbishop of Dakar. Thus, Fr. Philippe Béguerie, Professor at the Chevilly Theology scholasticate and Director of Studies for the French province, wrote a study of the Archbishop's writings and distributed it among the missionaries who came to France on holiday or for retreats. This "exegetical" study concluded that "the best description" for the Archbishop was to be found in Dostoïevski's *The Legend of the Grand Inquisitor*: "The most dangerous thing for man is freedom. Freedom is only given to the race of those who command, and not to the race of those who obey."[12] Therefore, so it was said, the Archbishop wanted to keep his subordinates in blind obedience and prevent the African churches from obtaining their majority. This woeful analysis of Pius XII's former Delegate was echoed elsewhere. Fr. Courrier in Dakar distributed a tract that spoke out against the Archbishop's election,[13] and on the eve of the general chapter, Fr. Jo-

---

7   June 1961. *General Bulletin*, 698: 606-607.
8   Fr. Philippe Béguerie, Interview in *Golias*, no. 27-28 (1991): 21-22.
9   From September 16 to 23. *General Bulletin* 687: 204.
10 Béguerie, article quoted, 21.
11 Inspired by several bishops including Bishop Cucherousset. Ms. I, 75, 36.
12 Ms. I, 76-77; 80, 41-57; II, 3, 8-54.

seph Michel gave a small dossier on Archbishop Lefebvre[14] to Fr. Jean Le Gall, chapter delegate for the Congo.

On the other side an opposing group of French Fathers led by Fr. Jean Letourneur—Procurer General of the motherhouse since 1942, a former student from Santa Chiara, a true religious, and a man of quality with a gift for organization[15]—saw in Marcel Lefebvre the man sent by Providence who would save the congregation from indiscipline, and also from the doctrinal deviations that were spreading through the French province. These were especially noticeable at Chevilly, despite the warnings from Rome to those training clerics and religious.

A letter from the Sacred Congregation for Seminaries and Universities spoke out against tendencies in the younger clergy towards a slackening in the prayer life and neglect of custody of the heart. These led to activism: "Very quickly, one becomes exhausted by fruitless efforts, and one ends up being lukewarm and discouraged." Love of the Church is lost in disobedience: "In ecclesiastical training institutions, it is not rare—and this Sacred Congregation had sometimes had to intervene—to witness experiments that give too much unbridled freedom to students… [and to] independent learning."[16]

Similarly, in a letter on the training of the clergy, the Sacred Congregation for Religious spoke out against "a lack of humility, an attitude of mind that is quick to criticize the acts of superiors, a wholly inaccurate concept of obedience, a real distaste for sacrifice, and an often inexact appreciation of certain doctrinal problems." It saw the root of these attitudes in the "often worldly and secular milieus" from which these vocations came. It asked "that the training of religious be intensified to enable them to face the perversions of the modern world without giving up. This involves learning solid doctrine and acquiring the necessary virtues, especially humility, obedience, and the spirit of sacrifice. Young candidates for the priesthood should most especially be trained in the *sound social doctrine of the Church*."[17]

As in other scholasticates or seminaries directed by the Holy Ghost Fathers, some of these deviations were developing at Chevilly. Too much emphasis was put on students' personal research, and there was a general craze for acquiring expertise in Scriptural Studies or Patristics, without

---

[13] Ms. I, 63, 8-11.

[14] *Mémoire Spiritaine*, 4 (1996): 87—the Béguerie dossier?

[15] *General Bulletin* 743: 438; *Bulletin for the Former Students of the French Seminary in Rome.*

[16] Letter signed by Pizzardo (prefect), Staffa (secretary), *Documentation Catholique*, Aug. 16, 1959; *General Bulletin* 687: 196.

[17] Underlined in the text. Letter of Oct. 6, 1961, signed by Valerio Valeri (prefect). *General Bulletin*, 700: 677-678. Archbishop Lefebvre seems to have inspired more than one of these lines; he held Cardinal Valeri in high esteem.

making this learning subject to the system of the Angelic Doctor. Warnings given about authors in Pius XII's encyclical *Humani Generis* and about those recently censured by the Holy Office were not properly heeded. In liturgy, the vernacular compositions of Fr. Lucien Deiss, Professor at Chevilly until 1957, were gradually taking the place of Gregorian chant. Moreover, since 1958 the already ordained seminarians in Fifth Year spent their six months of apostolate experience at the Dominican Pastoral Center on Rue Glacière in Paris (Fr. Jean Le Gall had been appointed Director of Apostolate Experience at Chevilly and later at Brazzaville). In addition, since 1953 the refresher courses for missionaries had been organized at the Missionary Catholic Action Center in Lille—previously they had taken place in the congregation's house at Ruitz—which was already affiliated to Workers' Catholic Action (ACO).[18]

Although they were aware of these harmful tendencies, Fr. Griffin and the general council felt powerless to stop them. The Superior General no longer even wanted to go to Chevilly where the staff openly criticized the motherhouse before the students. The situation seemed "incurable"[19] without taking radical steps which they much preferred leaving to their successors. So, people looked to the Archbishop of Dakar whose resignation was foreseen. He would be the key man who would, if necessary, generously undertake the thankless task of reform. To whomever would listen, the Archbishop said quite openly: "If I'm elected as Superior General, I will clean out Chevilly,"[20] and before his election he even said at Chevilly that he would "tidy it up."

AN EVENTFUL ELECTION

Since he was not a religious superior, the Archbishop of Dakar had no strict right to be a member of the general chapter. In order to take part, he therefore had to be elected as a delegate either for the second constituency of Senegal and Guinea or for the sixth constituency of France and Rome.[21] Brought together by this common danger, the French progressive lobby spread its stories about the Archbishop, and at the first round of elections for French delegates it was moderately successful. However, the motherhouse was scandalized by this group's disgraceful attempts to exert pressure, and with the backing of some highly placed figures in Rome declared the vote null and void. Another letter from Rome, probably from the Sacred Congregation for Religious or the Apostolic Signatura, seems to have

18 *French Bulletin* 92, 97, and 104; *General Bulletin* 723: 200ff.; ms. I, 71, 36-38.
19 Lefebvre, Letter to Msgr. Paul Philippe, Dec. 28, 1965.
20 Béguerie, article quoted, 22; Fr. Michel Legrain, C.S.Sp., Letter to J.-M. L., Nov. 30, 1998.
21 Convocation to the general chapter, May 28, 1961, *General Bulletin*, 697.

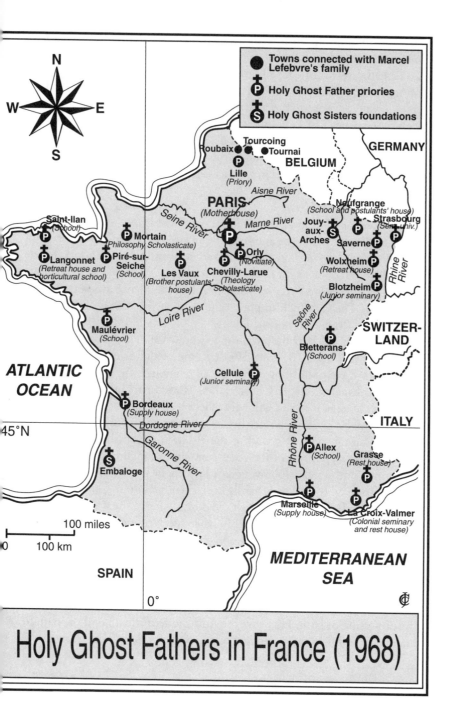

Holy Ghost Fathers in France (1968)

declared that the election's results were to be respected.[22] However, a "second first round" in September 1961 resulted in the election of Fathers Louis Ledit (rector of Chevilly), Jacques Lacroix, Joseph Hirtz (opponent of Archbishop Lefebvre), and Henri Barré. In Africa the first round (whose results were uncontested) was won by Archbishop Lefebvre with thirty-eight votes, ahead of Fr. Courrier with nine votes. In the second round, Archbishop Lefebvre was elected as delegate for Senegal and Guinea with 59 votes out of 103, while in France the same four priests who had won the first round also won the second. At least two of them were enemies of the Archbishop.[23]

On the eve of the chapter, Fr. Joseph Michel advised an English delegate: "Vote for whomever you like, but not Archbishop Lefebvre."

The Englishman was amazed. "But Cardinal Feltin, Archbishop of Paris, made it known that the Holy Father wanted Archbishop Lefebvre elected!"

Fr. Michel rushed over to the Archbishop's residence and was told the real story: "The Cardinal simply meant to relate the wishes of the French Seminary in Rome and not the Pope's."[24]

The truth was that the Archbishop's presence in Tulle was a thorn in the side of the French bishops. While Rome was in principle opposed to the appointment of bishops at the head of religious congregations, it made it known that if the Holy Ghost Fathers elected Archbishop Lefebvre as Superior General, it would willingly relieve him of his post in Tulle.[25]

Finally the general chapter began at Chevilly on July 20, 1962. On July 25, during the first round of the election, Archbishop Lefebvre received nearly two-thirds of the votes cast, almost obtaining enough to be voted in at one go. The following day, July 26, he got up to speak: "Leave me as Bishop of Tulle. I have hardly been there six months, and I have just got to know the priests and to visit the diocese. Leave me where I am."

He should not have bothered! He then received more than two-thirds of the votes. However, since he was in charge of a diocese, he could not be relieved of his pastoral charge by anyone else but the Pope. The chapter could, therefore, only "propose" him as Superior General. This was done and John XXIII accepted the proposal. In the evening of July 28,[26] Archbishop Lefebvre was solemnly enthroned in the chapel after having made the profession of faith. He swore the Anti-modernist oath and the oath to maintain the spirit and objectives of the congregation.[27] He received the

22   Lefebvre, Letter quoted; Béguerie, article quoted; ms. I, 72, 11-12; 77, 28-39.
23   *General Bulletin* 699: 630ff.; 701: 3-4.
24   *Mémoire Spiritaine*, no. 4, page quoted.
25   Koren, *Les Spiritains*, 546.
26   *Petite histoire*, 86; *Fideliter,* no. 59: 49; *General Bulletin* 704 (July-Aug 1962): 170.
27   *General Bulletin* 432, 735: prescriptions of the constitutions.

mandate to be Superior General for twelve years. On August 7, the Pope made the Archbishop-Bishop of Tulle titular Archbishop of Synnada in Phrygia.[28]

The elections continued, and on August 1, the members of the new general council were elected. The two assistants were Heinrich Hack from Germany and Joseph Hirtz from Alsace; Hirzt was elected in opposition to Archbishop Lefebvre. The four general advisers were Lambertus Vogel (Low Countries), William Higgins, Charles Connors, and Avelino Costa, and none of them was involved in the plot against the Archbishop. All four men were able, and the Superior General said he enjoyed "working with them in a positive atmosphere."[29] But this was only at the price of a constant effort, not at friendliness, which Archbishop Lefebvre never lacked, but at seeing eye to eye with Fr. Hirzt. He could make no important decisions concerning the congregation without the agreement of both of his assistants.

The work of the general chapter continued until October 13. The Archbishop strictly implemented the chapter's resolutions, but gave them, as we shall see, his own personal mark.

II. CLEANING AND REFORMING

"I WILL CLEAN OUT CHEVILLY!"

The first task that the new Superior General undertook was to clean out, as he had promised, the major scholasticate at Chevilly. The rules of the congregation[30] gave the Superior General the prime duty of watching over sound doctrine in the spirit of the congregation's founder, Poullart des Places. Rome encouraged this by a second letter from the Sacred Congregation for Seminaries signed by Pizzardo and Staffa.[31] It denounced those priestly training institutions where the rule was scorned and in which a "wind of naturalism" was blowing, "often with the complicity of those who dismiss out of hand the practices of the past which they consider insufficient to form a new generation of priests, and who take considerable trouble in ceaselessly seeking up-to-date 'methods'....Prayer, intimate union with God, the spirit of mortification, humility, obedience, the hidden life, and separation from the world are with increasing frequency played down in the name of a form of activism which dresses itself up as charity."

---

[28] *L'Osservatore Romano*, Aug. 10, 1962; *General Bulletin* 705: 251.
[29] Cf. *Petite histoire*, 88.
[30] Rules of the Seminary of the Holy Ghost, p. 2, no. 2; First Holy Ghost Father Rule, 1734, no. 78; Libermann's Rules, p. 5, nn. 154, 162, 146.
[31] Letter of Sept. 20, 1960, to the bishops. *General Bulletin*, 694: 438-455.

At the beginning of the Council, the Superior General jotted down his deepest worries in his personal notebook:[32]

> We, the Superior Generals, hear about so many novelties and see the "new theology" invading the minds of some of our professors and theology students. We are astounded and we wonder how to eradicate and stop so many errors.... When a *monitum* comes from the Holy Office, the last line in the defense of the Faith, one week later the troublemakers are already contradicting it....What must we think about the claims of the authors of this new theology as regards Revelation, miracles, the origin of man and of the world,[33] original sin, personal sin, the pains of hell and purgatory, the presence of our Lord in the Eucharist, chastity in marriage, priestly chastity, and the Blessed Virgin Mary? All these things are put in doubt.

Archbishop Lefebvre visited the province of Portugal[34] from August 31 to September 10 and again admired the discipline and doctrinal purity preserved in the scholasticate at Carcavelos. Soon, he devised a plan which he shared with the other members of the council: "Let's transfer the theology students from Chevilly to Portugal!" Unfortunately, this bold solution, which would have brought about the radical reform he desired, was not welcomed by everyone on the general council. He would have to be content with half measures. "Well," he decided, "no matter. Let's do it now."

Marcel Lefebvre methodically went about the "clean-out" of Chevilly following the directives of St. Pius X in *Sacrorum Antistitum*. In the first year, his practical wisdom told him to make no sweeping changes, but he demanded that the books of Congar, Chenu, and others be removed from the scholasticate's library,[35] and that imprudent initiatives and the disrespectful attitudes to the motherhouse be suppressed. However, when he learnt about the proposals of theology professor Fr. Fourmand to change the face of the theology curriculum (getting rid of apologetics and the treatise on the Virgin Mary, revising the treatise on the Church), he sent him

---

[32] Archives of Archbishop Lefebvre at Ecône. Dossier on collegiality first session: draft of spoken intervention, text in Latin.

[33] This was in 1962 when "Teilhard de Chardin was the most widely read author in both the lodges and the seminaries" (Yves Marsaudon, *L'œcuménisme vu par un franc-maçon de tradition*, 25).

[34] *General Bulletin*, 705: 248-249.

[35] But could he also have banned the book of the Holy Ghost Father Joseph Lécuyer, *Le sacerdoce dans le mystère du Christ* (Cerf, 1957) in which among other errors the author claims that "the principal act [of sacrifice and the priesthood of Christ] only takes place in the heavenly sanctuary"(p. 22)? Published in a series of CPL books, this work, which moved the emphasis from the Passion of Christ to His Resurrection and Ascension, falsified Redemption, the priesthood, and the Mass all in one go.

to Martinique.[36] During 1963 when Fr. Béguerie, another professor, asked to leave the congregation, he was moved away from Chevilly.

In April 1963, the Superior General called a meeting of the rectors of the major scholasticates, and in May did the same with the provincial superiors. The practical directives that he gave to them were also contained in two letters. He requested the Father Provincials "to remove from teaching posts those who are more or less imbued with modernist ideas, according to the prescriptions of the Church"[37]:

> Watch over the Faith in all communities, advising superiors to choose wisely when seeking retreat masters, lecturers, or journals.[38] We must avoid everything that is likely to undermine respect for the Church and the Pope, and everything that minimizes the historical truth of the Scriptures, the value of Tradition, the fundamental notions of morality and sin, and personal responsibility. We must prevent the invasion of the spirit of the world in religious communities.

He recommended the rectors of the major scholasticates to exercise, not abdicate, their authority. His letter is very revealing about the situation before the Church's own revolution: "This authority will doubtless be fatherly, but the rector must guide and direct the students and not let himself be controlled by an active minority.…You must absolutely avoid asking the students for comments on how the scholasticate is run, discussing essential points of discipline and studies, and considering them as having some right to exercise authority and organize the scholasticate.…You must avoid all collective demands.…A familiar manner of speaking between students is regrettable.[39] That must never be the case when the rector addresses the students, and especially not when the students address the rector."

The Superior General appointed new "Deans of Studies" over whom he placed Fr. Gerald Fitzgerald[40] (who would be Archbishop Lefebvre's confessor for several years). In philosophy, Archbishop Lefebvre denounced "those great evils of our time, idealism and subjectivism. Thomistic philosophy alone gives us knowledge of the real." In theology he recommended the treatise on the justification of the impious (i.e., the conversion of sinners or unbelievers): "[This treatise is] very important in deciding what conduct one should adopt towards pagans and towards the faithful as they grow in 'justification' (sanctification). The students will

---

[36] *General Bulletin*, 705 (Council meeting of 21 Aug 1962).
[37] Sentence suppressed in the published text in *General Bulletin*, 710: 556.
[38] Fr. Lombardi, founder of "Pour un Monde Nouveau" [For a New World] who at first gained Pius XII's trust and then wreaked havoc in Italy. He had been to Chevilly to give a talk in December 1958. *General Bulletin*, 683: 19.
[39] [The students were addressing each other using *tu* (the familiar or affectionate form of *you*) instead of *vous* (the formal or hierarchically nuanced form of *you*). Trans.]
[40] *General Bulletin*, 710: 564.

learn in this treatise how grace and freedom work together." Does not all priestly pastoral work stand in need of this treatise on grace? Without it, the apostolate would be sheer naturalism or, what amounts to the same thing, sheer Protestantism.

Finally, he wrote that "one must insist on the importance of the Magisterium, and on Tradition and its relations with the ministry of sacraments and sacrifice." To this end he prescribed refectory readings of "the main encyclicals and papal documents from Pius IX to the present," especially the acts of St. Pius X, and made a precise list of those that were to be read.[41]

The Superior General also laid down two pithy liturgical norms: "Follow the prescriptions of Rome" and "Avoid everything that comes from the personal initiatives of so-called liturgists."[42] As for the number of practical rules that had been laid down, they suggest the growth of rubric "experimentation."[43] Yet is there anything surprising about this? Faced with the growing number of "experiments" in concelebration and Masses facing the people, Pius XII said nothing concerning the roots of the problem.[44]

Archbishop Lefebvre himself prescribed the following:

- "True piety will be maintained and developed by the true liturgy and not in disobedience to the decisions of the Church.
- The liturgical language must be the one chosen by the Church.
- The para-liturgy must never be more important than the liturgy and must never be fused with it.
- Explanations during services must be subject to the liturgy and not the liturgy to the explanations (other than with a brief pause).
- Communion must not be received when the communicant is standing.
- Mass must not be celebrated facing the people in the chapels of our scholasticates, other than exceptionally and after necessary permission has been obtained."[45]

Even here, certain decisions were only half measures or else left the door ajar...the door that Rome was leaving wide open. At least once Archbishop Lefebvre himself concelebrated facing the people on December 26, 1966, in the novitiate at Baarle-Naussau in the Low Countries.[46]

---

[41] Publicly reading papal documents was called for around 1950 in the major Irish scholasticate in Kimmage and supported by Fr. Denis Fahey. Unfortunately, it never happened. Archbishop Lefebvre's decision was mostly ignored and even criticized.

[42] Letter to the Father Provincials, May 1963.

[43] Cf. Reply of the Sacred Congregation of Rites to questions posed by the professors of the Seminary of the Holy Ghost (Croix-Valmer) on July 24, 1961, concerning seven innovations in Solemn High Masses. *General Bulletin*, 698: 626-627.

[44] Cf. Pius XII, discourse to the World Congress of Pastoral Liturgy in Assisi, Sep. 22, 1956. *Enseignements pontificaux de Solesmes, The Liturgy*, nos. 807, 808, 817.

[45] Letter to the rectors of the major scholasticates, April 1963.

RESULTS OF THE "CLEAN OUT"

At the beginning of the school year in 1963 Archbishop Lefebvre visited the major scholasticate in Gemert (Low Countries), and gave Chevilly a second "going over" by accepting the resignation of the rector, Fr. Louis Ledit, and replacing three professors all at once. "A real purge," as Fr. Thibault remarked.[47] At the end of the same year, inspired by the "concerns expressed by our Holy Father Pope Paul VI in his apostolic letter *Summi Dei Verbum*,"[48] the Archbishop wrote another letter to the provincials and rectors of the major scholasticates and novitiates,[49] reminding them of his "grave responsibility as Superior General" and his "present concerns caused by the numbers leaving the scholasticates,[50] the lack of esteem for the religious life, and the false ideas or total lack of understanding concerning the priesthood."

The picture he draws of the situation that prevailed in certain Holy Ghost Fathers houses is amazing:

> Ruin of authority, unbridled freedom, the right to judge and criticize everything, the absence of humility. The loss of respect for colleagues, authority, and for themselves. The loss of modesty in dress, in looks, in reading and television.... From these things come the lack of the spirit of piety that is both personal and deep, and a collective piety that is superficial. [This leads to] scorn for traditions, giving up Latin and Gregorian chant, and abandoning scholastic philosophy and theology.

Thus, the Superior General planned to take certain practical measures "in order to bring about a true conversion and reform," notably sending "visitors responsible for assisting superiors."

Was this "assistance" effectively planned and implemented? When at the opening of the school year in 1964 Archbishop Lefebvre appointed Fr. Georges-Henri Thibault as rector of Chevilly, he said to himself: "He is young, intelligent, and little by little will get rid of those who have a bad influence."[51] When questioned on this matter, Fr. Thibault answered our questions very frankly.

"Did Archbishop Lefebvre give you orders?"

"No! He trusted me. I greatly disappointed him, I suspect."

"Did he give orders to the professors?"

---

[46] Photo archives, Gemert, Low Countries, ms. II, 39, 55-59.
[47] Ms. II, 45, 34.
[48] Apostolic Letter of Nov. 4, 1963, *A.A.S.* 55 (1963): 979ff.
[49] Draft of letter.
[50] Seventy-six gave up in 1964, the same number in 1965, out of 850 students in the major scholasticates. This is equal to more than half over six years, the minimum period of studies.
[51] Lefebvre, reply to Msgr. Philippe quoted.

"I don't remember. He trusted people. I pulled the wool over his eyes and used methods that were not to his liking. The students were my brothers, not my inferiors!"[52]

This open confession shows what caused the failure of Archbishop Lefebvre's attempted reform. Sometimes he appointed men who did not meet his expectations.[53] This was the case for G.-H. Thibault at Chevilly, whom he had known and liked as a professor at Sébikotane, and Roland Barq, formerly a model seminarian at Mortain who was appointed rector at the French Seminary after Fr. Henri Barré resigned.[54] He overestimated their ability to exercise a truly fatherly authority that was both strong, capable of training priests, and able to withstand the craze for the new theology and for revolutionary teaching methods. These men failed him.

A DIFFERENT LEADERSHIP STYLE

Fr. Koren described Archbishop Lefebvre in the following way: "He was imposing, had a confident manner, and his face shone with interest and goodness. He was a model leader who was loving and beloved."[55] Fr. Michael O'Carroll knew a "wonderful man, with self-control, courteous, suaveness itself, and amazingly open in his conversations, saying what he thought, describing his stances that were so subtle and so certain...and in contrast, he had a very gentle voice."[56]

A young priest whom he ordained remarked that "beneath his affable and very courteous exterior, he was inflexible in his ideas."[57] This did not impress some young colleagues and students who were warned about him, but when they saw him he was "so suave, kind, and spoke so gently" that they felt a "seductive strength" that needed to be resisted.[58] Many witnesses comment on Archbishop Lefebvre's obstinacy in his ideas in spite of the opposition he met, which made little impression on him. According to Koren, he was defined as "a gentle, pig-headed man." Some people denounced the roots of the Archbishop's "stubbornness" as an attachment to personal and outdated views: "It is because of his training under Father Le

---

52 Interview in Chevilly, Nov. 9, 1997, ms. I, 46, 36-45; *General Bulletin*, 723: 196.
53 Cf. P. Muller, bursar at Rue Lhomond, Interview with Fr. J.-Y. Cottard, ms. II, 20, 39.
54 *General Bulletin*, 710 (July-Aug. 1963): 562-563. Fr. Barcq was not appointed by Archbishop Lefebvre but proposed by the French bishops to the Holy See. On the other hand, Archbishop Lefebvre appointed Fr. François Morvan as rector at Mortain: *General Bulletin*, 704 (July-Aug 1962): 172.
55 Koren, *Les Spiritains*, 545.
56 Fr. Michael O'Carroll, C.S.Sp., *A Priest in Changing Times* (Dublin: Columba Press, 1998), 95; Interview with Fr. L.-P. Dubrœucq, 1997.
57 Fr. Bernard Boulanger, C.S.Sp., Letter to J.-M. L., March 21, 1999.
58 Fr. Michel Legrain, former professor at Chevilly, kept in this post by Msgr. Lefebvre, Letter to J.-M. L., Nov. 30, 1998; cf. Fr. O'Carroll, Interview May 9, 1998.

Floch," said some, while according to others, "it was because of his Maurrassian[59] education." While recognizing the Archbishop's "tremendous courage" in maintaining his doctrine against all comers, Michael O'Carroll thought he could explain all: "He was so convinced [of his own views] that he found it hard to see other people's point of view. It was not his fault, he was made like that. He was convinced that he was right, and he had great confidence in himself," to such an extent that "when discussing with Archbishop Lefebvre, you would sometimes find you had a psychological hurdle to negotiate."[60]

Marcel Lefebvre's tenacity was well founded. In reality his views seemed so clear-cut and original because they were rooted in the most authentic traditions. His personal ideas overturned a prevailing sloppiness only by the innovative daring that came from his expansionist zeal.[61] Many a thoroughly upright and unprejudiced individual recognized Archbishop Lefebvre as the very contrary of a narrow-minded person. He was open, realistic, and attentive to people. One colleague who worked with him in the bursar's office at Paris said: "What a superior he was! Goodness, hospitality, uprightness, a good listener. It was a pleasure to work with him. In his hands everything had a simple solution. He never got lost in the details, and he never failed to encourage us."[62]

Another Holy Ghost Father said perceptively: "He knew how to express his thinking clearly and gave the impression of understanding practical things as much as keeping things in order in his mind. These considerations were the basis of various projects that were sometimes apparently contradictory, but they were ready to be done as his sense of events dictated. He had the ability to evaluate a sudden opportunity."[63]

Another colleague from the bursar's office in Switzerland noticed especially the Archbishop's determination to carry out his resolutions: "They called him the 'iron fist in the velvet glove.' He never gave in. Once he had decided, he followed whatever line he had adopted, and then he started organizing things."[64]

His stubbornness in getting things done both puzzled and bothered his subordinates. It silenced the armchair experts and went against the hard-baked liberals, convincing the more intelligent among them that they had to be dishonest in their conduct. The unfortunate priests who

---

[59] [Referring to his training in systematic thinking, or to the early influences of Action Française noted in Chapter 3. Charles Maurras was famous for his classical, systematic thought. Trans.]
[60] Fr. Michael O'Carroll, Interview, Nov. 27, 1997.
[61] Cf. Chapter 8, "Archbishop of Dakar: Inventive and Ingenious Zeal."
[62] Fr. Bernard Aguillon, C.S.Sp., speaking with Fr. Lacheteau, ms. II, 68, 14-15, 32-33.
[63] Fr. Antoine Nibel, C.S.Sp., Letter to J.-M. L., Dec. 21, 1998.
[64] Fr. Christian Winckler, C.S.Sp., Interview, 1997, ms. I, 66, 28-31.

were hampered by these vices of the mind often felt that Marcel Lefebvre had what they took for a psychological block. In fact, it was only the spontaneous reaction of a healthy mind faced with the impenitent enemies of principles. How in fact can one discuss with anyone who denies the absolute value or practical effectiveness of principles?[65] In these cases, the Archbishop's quick intuition was reluctant to argue over truths that were only too obvious.

Moreover, his great respect for neighbor made him avoid any new, painful breaches that would hurt others and destroy the cordial relations that existed.[66] If he gave the impression of avoiding dialogue or if he seemed to be stubborn in a personal opinion, his interlocutor only needed to question his own conduct or blame his own intellectual confusion. The Archbishop was silent when he saw intellectual insincerity, but if the person was too impertinent, the Archbishop could become indignant and in a moment of exasperation[67] blurt out some hard home truths. Sometimes he would cut the conversation short by saying "Let's talk about something else."[68] Otherwise, he simply called for obedience without discussion by saying: "You're not asked to think, but to obey!"[69]

On other occasions, Archbishop Lefebvre's deep sensitivity and his care for subordinates led him to use great tact when persuading a colleague to accept a difficult reappointment. In the middle of the school year, he said to Fr. Joseph Michel who was in the middle of writing a biography of Fr. Laval: "You would really help me if you agreed to go to the seminary college in Martinique to take over as superior."[70]

Occasionally the embarrassment he felt in telling a priest about a new appointment led to misunderstandings. One priest was approached by a colleague who said: "Congratulations on your new appointment!" Unfortunately, the priest had not yet been informed of his new post overseas. On another occasion in 1966, the Archbishop was passing through Mortain, and at the end of the meal gave a short address to the community. He ended by saying: "Since I am here, I have some news to give you. I am going to introduce you to your new superior." The professors on the high table were stunned, for nobody—not even the current superior, Fr. François Morvan—had been notified of the change.[71]

In these matters, one must bear in mind that Marcel Lefebvre had not spent six or seven years in one of the congregation's scholasticates. Thus he

---

[65] "One can no longer discuss with people for whom there is no fixed truth": Interview with Fr. Marziac, *Monseigneur Lefebvre, soleil levant*, 8.
[66] Fr. E. du Chalard, Interview June 28, 1998, 2.
[67] Ms. I, 57, 41-46; II, 4, 12-17.
[68] Ms. I, 74, 45-48.
[69] Béguerie, article quoted.
[70] *Mémoire Spiritaine*, no. 4: 79.
[71] Ms. I, 34, 24-27; Fr. du Chalard, Interview 1-2; *General Bulletin* 725: 18.

did not know his colleagues well enough to smooth troubled waters or know whom he could count on.[72]

His important decisions were only the more remarkable. This was the case when he decided to move the motherhouse from Paris to Rome in the light of his predecessor's wishes and the resolution[73] of the 1962 general chapter. Some French colleagues bore him a grudge for doing this. However, on the one hand, he felt more at ease in Rome—since he was Roman in heart and soul—than in the Paris of the Catholic Institute, Saint Sulpice, etc., that was dominated by the progressives. One the other hand, he wanted the motherhouse to be in the capital of Christianity, near the Pope and the Roman congregations.[74] To do this, he needed special permission from General de Gaulle.[75] In spite of the move, the Holy Ghost Fathers were able to retain their civil status through keeping an office in Paris. They thus continued to benefit from their continued recognition under French law.

The house in Rome was situated on the slopes of Monte Mario, a quiet, ideal location near the Vatican. It was surrounded by attractive grounds and could accommodate thirty people. It had housed a school run by the Sisters of the Society of Mary the Helper, a congregation founded in Paris in 1854 by Marie-Therese Soubiran (1834-1889). The Archbishop took charge of the conversion of this property into the motherhouse[76] to ensure that it would be wholly functional. The conversion was completed on September 14, 1966, the very day on which the staff moved in. However, in his impatient zeal, the Superior General had already moved in on July 15. The bursar's office on the Corso d'Italia remained separate, but Archbishop Lefebvre appointed as priest in charge Fr. Matthew Farrelly, whom he trusted completely,[77] in place of Fr. Lécuyer with whom he did not get on.[78]

MALIGNED AND CALUMNIATED MANAGEMENT

However, opposition to Archbishop Lefebvre among a group of French priests only continued to grow. Some of them even left the congregation rather than remain under the authority of a superior whose stances they did not accept.[79] The Archbishop did everything to stop these eight

---

[72] Petite histoire, 88.
[73] Chapter Statutes, 22.
[74] General Bulletin 730: 234 (Monthly Message, 7 Nov. 1966).
[75] Michael O'Carroll, C.S.Sp., A Priest in Changing Times, 96-97; General Bulletin, 708: 438.
[76] Interview with A. Cagnon, 65; General Bulletin, 729: 158.
[77] On June 29, 1966, General Bulletin, 728: 132.
[78] Lécuyer, appointed as an expert at the Council by John XXIII (General Bulletin, 705: 230). Paul VI admired him as a theologian.

priests leaving, since their conduct was a bad example. During the first session of the Council, a group of ten bishops from his congregation came to speak to him at Santa Marta. Bishop Jean Gay had been nominated to open the discussion: "Your Excellency, it troubles us that you speak publicly in the Council as Superior General of the congregation."

The Archbishop listened and let them speak. They expected a discussion or an argument, but nothing of the sort happened. When they had finished, the Archbishop simply said: "I'm going to tell you something. I don't force any of you to vote this way or that way or to think this or that. You have your consciences, follow them. I have mine."[80]

It was quite obvious but Archbishop Lefebvre refused all dialogue. But the gap between them was too wide, and a discussion would only have poisoned relations without gaining anything. In this respect, the Archbishop recounted a revealing incident: "The French Seminary where many French bishops were staying belonged to the congregation. When I went there, I presided at meal times as Superior General. Then one fine day, I was reseated at another table, a small table with the bishops. And yet I was under my own roof! So I never went back."[81]

In December 1963 at the end of the second session at the Council, the same missionary bishops, with the signed approval of Archbishop Hascher,[82] repeated the grievances of the same group of priests, attacking Archbishop Lefebvre on four counts: for his support for *Verbe*; for choosing Father Berto, who was not a Holy Ghost Father, as his theologian at the Council; for his circular letter on wearing the cassock; and for his isolation from the "French bishops."

In April 1964, Fr. Hirtz wrote him expressing his "anxieties and worries," and in May 1964 the provincial superiors and other leading members of the congregation who were attending a meeting at the motherhouse asked him not to impose on the congregation his "own personal ideas"; this was especially because they ran counter to the majority of Council Fathers, although the superiors recognized that he was perfectly within his rights to put them forth at the Council. In August 1964, ten priests on retreat at Chevilly wrote to the Archbishop expressing the same wishes, although they were opposed by the twenty other priests on retreat.

[79] Ms. I, 34, 31-36; 80, 1-5. Especially regarding public interventions made by Archbishop Lefebvre at the Council.

[80] Bishop de Milleville, interview at Chevilly, Feb. 1, 1997, ms. I, 40, 48-55.

[81] Interview with Cagnon, *Les Relations de Rome avec Ecône*, 72; *Fideliter*, no. 59: 52; *General Bulletin*, 709: 540-544.

[82] Who then admitted to Archbishop Lefebvre that he had been "pushed into doing it by others even though he was perfectly in agreement with [the Archbishop's] way of thinking and doing things." (Reply of Archbishop Lefebvre to Bishop Paul Philippe, Dec. 28, 1965).

Fr. Joseph Lécuyer amassed these complaints and others: authoritarianism, failing to undertake a consultation process before making decisions as was required by the congregation statutes, management based on personal opinions, imposing personal ideas on liturgical language and collegiality, stances contrary to the "decisions of the French bishops" which threatened to undermine confidence in the French Seminary. Finally, there was the fear that Archbishop Lefebvre would not implement the decisions of the Council.[83] The "Lefebvre file" was submitted to Paul VI and examined by the Sacred Congregation for Religious, who subsequently asked the Superior General for an explanation of these issues.

Archbishop Lefebvre had no difficulty in refuting the web of inept accusations that were at times malevolent and calumniating. His defense, sent in writing to Msgr. Paul Philippe on December 28, 1965, highlighted his keen desire to hear the views of his colleagues by his having called an increased number of meetings with various superiors. It also underlined his desire to implement not personal ideas but "the fundamental principles of religious and priestly training." Finally, the Archbishop pointed out that the complaints came from a small group of priests who had been opposed to the orientation of the congregation under his predecessor. They were, he said, taking advantage of the Council to push their already hackneyed ideas.

The incident seemed to be a repeat of the manoeuvre that led to the ousting of Fr. Le Floch from the French Seminary: the same liberal and modernising spirit, the same malicious plotting, and the same recourse to the Holy See. However, Msgr. Philippe was wholly satisfied by the defense provided by Archbishop Lefebvre in his letter of December 28. In addition the Archbishop justified his actions at the Council: was it wrong to fight a schema? No. "It seems to me that improving a text is a positive contribution" and "I do not see why one would oblige all the bishops to conform to the thinking of a few bishops, even the most influential. That would be incredibly tyrannical." He stated: "The majority of bishops and priests [of his congregation] entirely approve of the way I am running things and of the thinking which guides my actions. They know full well that my submission to Rome is complete and unconditional, and that I'm ready to follow the directives to be issued after the Council. I have proved this ever since the beginning of the Council."

Pope Paul VI said that he was satisfied with the Archbishop's answers, and when he received him in audience he made the following proposal: "Do you want me to write a letter to all the members of your congregation to ask them to be subject to you?"

---

[83] Letter of the Sacred Congregation for Religious (Bishop Paul Philippe, Secretary) to Archbishop Lefebvre, Dec. 9, 1965.

"No," replied the Archbishop, "Holy Father, as long as you give no credence to these accusations, that is all I ask. If my colleagues think that I have asked you to help me prop up my authority, I won't last."[84]

III. BETTER ORGANIZATION

Archbishop Lefebvre would "last," and where he was most successful was in reorganizing the congregation according to the decisions of the 1962 general chapter in the light of the new circumstances in which the Holy Ghost Fathers were operating: five thousand professed members[85] meant their numbers were steady, but there was a decline in vocations. It was, therefore, necessary to decentralize authority by making the provincials responsible for appointments, and also by regrouping the priests working in missionary areas, and by initiating recruitment drives in the older provinces. Being faithful to the objectives of the congregation, the Superior General was able to propose and implement his personal views that were nevertheless traditional.

ORGANIZATION AND RECRUITMENT IN THE PROVINCES[86]

The provincials were given permanent assistants to enable them to be free to travel about their provinces. Distinct and effective departments were created in each province (in France, Ireland, Portugal, Germany, the United States, the Low Countries, Belgium, Canada, Poland and the vice-province of Switzerland): education (training for teachers in schools and minor scholasticates), information and recruitment, finance ("It is better to rely on the regular help of benefactors than on farming or industrial profits"), archives, journals (several times revamped or merged with those of other congregations, a process that indicated some problems), provincial visitors responsible for information in the districts under each province.

Moreover, following the wishes of previous general chapters, the headquarters of the French province were separated from those of the motherhouse, whose standing was accordingly increased. The French province headquarters and the motherhouse to-ed and fro-ed between Rue Lhomond and Rue des Pyrénées[87] until the motherhouse moved to Rome in 1966.

---

[84] Lefebvre, Interview with André Cagnon for *Fideliter*, no. 59.
[85] 5,100 members (priests, brothers, and students) in Dec. 1963. *General Bulletin*, 715: 933. There would be 5,075 in Dec. 1965: the decline was already becoming apparent, *General Bulletin*, 727: 122.
[86] Letter to Father Provincials, Oct. 28, 1962; *General Bulletin*, 708: 456.
[87] *General Bulletin*, 708: 454.

It was necessary to close some minor scholasticates that only had a few students. Nevertheless, Archbishop Lefebvre wished to preserve these types of institutions[88] since the majority of novices still came through them: all vocations in Portugal and Switzerland and two-thirds in France. "Going against the opinion that considered such solutions outdated" on the grounds that vocations were no longer as evident at a young age, Archbishop Lefebvre considered that "suppressing the minor scholasticate at the present would represent suicide for the congregation."[89]

The role of recruitment directors was vital for the future of the congregation. The Superior General detailed their duties: "Firstly they will use supernatural means: prayer, sacrifice, putting up with difficulties....Vocations—true vocations—must be won by sacrifice and prayer." Next they should use "the best natural means: the press, radio, films, missionary exhibitions, but especially preaching, talks, keeping in contact with bishops, parish priests, chaplains of schools, and families. This requires a lot of organization from true apostles living in community."[90]

APPROPRIATE REORGANIZATION OF MISSIONARY DISTRICTS

The missionary districts also found themselves in a new situation that—as we have seen—the former Apostolic Delegate had helped to create through his avant-garde initiatives that quickly rendered obsolete the system of Prefectures and Apostolic Vicariates under the care of one missionary congregation. In their place were founded genuine dioceses in which many different religious institutes and a growing number of indigenous clergy operated.

The "group of forty" of whom we have spoken were wrong to think that by dreaming up theories and projects they could do the impossible. Archbishop Lefebvre was one step ahead of them and knew that even without their help he could implement his views that were both realistic and based fundamentally on doctrine.[91] In the Holy Ghost Fathers' "missionary districts," the increase in the number of congregations meant that diocesan headquarters could no longer serve as focal points for the congregation. The Superior General asked the bishops to permit the establishment of "Holy Ghost Houses" where Holy Ghost Fathers could meet from time to time. The bishops would sign *contracts* with the congregation—an idea devised by Archbishop Lefebvre and backed by Fr. Lambertus Vogel—

---

[88] Although most of the students might not have had real missionary ambitions. Cf. report on the Belgian minor scholasticate of Gentinnes.

[89] *Réflexions sur les petits scolasticats*, 1966.

[90] Project for reorganizing recruitment in the French Province, March 8, 1963; *Letter to Father Provincials*, May 1963.

[91] Draft agreement with African Ordinaries, Sept. 20, 1962; Letters to ordinaries and district superiors, Aug. 19, 1965; *General Bulletin*, 714: 835.

which specified the nature, location, duration, and financing of the Holy Ghost Fathers' activities and recognized the religious authority of the "principal superiors" over their subjects. He begged the Ordinaries[92] to give the congregation at least one parish in a town in addition to the bush missions that, according to the congregation's objectives, were located in the most difficult areas, allowances being made, nevertheless, for the missionaries as they got older.

However, the declining numbers of staff compared with the growing Catholic population[93] forced the priests to amalgamate their priories to continue community life (an aspect of the rule on which Archbishop Lefebvre put great emphasis). Some mission stations, therefore, became the responsibility of indigenous clergy. Similarly, the Holy Ghost Brothers would form effective and mobile teams.

Finally, since the congregation could not find enough missionaries in its provinces, the African bishops would have to allow the Holy Ghost Fathers to recruit religious missionaries in Africa itself. Already in Nigeria, a Holy Ghost Father novitiate and scholasticate was in full operation, and some vocations it produced[94] were sent as missionaries even to countries other than their own. Archbishop Lefebvre considered it wrong to think of such indigenous recruitment as creating competition with indigenous seminaries. "It is rather," he said, "a mark of living and generous Christian communities."

"Let's be realists," he concluded. "Faced with the present difficulties, let us call on the 'Spirit of wisdom and charity' and on 'the spirit of the Church.'"

The Archbishop asked Fr. Vogel to remind the congregation of the solid doctrinal basis (defined by Vatican I as a matter of divine faith) for the presence of missionary congregations in the dioceses of missionary countries. Such a presence did not represent an "intrusion by foreigners"[95] because "the religious or other priests sent by the Pope to a diocese (or supported by his orders) have every right to be in the diocese since it is firstly the diocese of the Pope before being the diocese of the bishop."[96] It was a powerful and timely truth!

ENCOURAGING PERSECUTED MISSIONARIES

Archbishop Lefebvre's time as Superior General coincided with new persecutions directed against the Church in many countries where the

---

[92] *I.e.,* the bishops or the Apostolic Prefects and Vicars Apostolic.
[93] Fifty thousand new Catholics annually just in Owerri and Onitsha, in Nigeria.
[94] Four new priests ordained by Archbishop Lefebvre at Pentecost 1965.
[95] Even when an Apostolic Vicariate (of the Pope) becomes a diocese and its bishop is no longer merely a vicar of the Pope.
[96] *General Bulletin,* 714 (March-April 1964): 834.

Holy Ghost Fathers were working. In his "Monthly Message" in September 1964 he spoke of the situation that he had foreseen before independence was granted to the young African republics that would fall through Communist plotting. He wrote:

Dear Colleagues,

At this time our Belgian colleagues are suffering persecution in the regions occupied by Mulelistes, a situation which brings to mind the painful memory of our colleagues massacred in Kongolo.[97] Meanwhile our colleagues in Poland are suffering an incessant persecution that one could say is scientifically organized. [When one sees] missionaries in numerous countries suffering humiliations and being threatened with expulsion, it is good for us to renew our faith in our vocation.[98]

The Holy Ghost Fathers had their schools in Congo-Brazzaville confiscated (August 1965), and they were also expelled from Haiti[99] and Guinea. On this last occasion in May 1967, Archbishop Lefebvre came especially from Rome to Paris to greet the expelled missionaries as they disembarked from the plane. Shortly after, the congregation also suffered because of the war in Biafra (1967-1970).[100] The Superior General wrote again in 1964: "It is obvious to the eyes of faith that the sufferings of our colleagues past and present logically make them conform to and resemble our Lord." He did not shy away from drawing the conclusion that missionaries who were persecuted "if only because they are from another country are entitled to be called martyrs" since "the only reason for their being there is their faith in our Lord and in his Church."

This message was welcomed by the Holy Ghost Fathers suffering in these upheavals. Thus, Fr. Brumbeck, religious superior at Pointe-Noire (Congo Brazzaville) wrote on January 8, 1965, to his subordinates who were still reeling from the shock of sweeping nationalization:

Faced with these events, many of you have understood the right attitude to adopt. Our duty is to remain, to work calmly, and to keep up our morale. Thus, one of you wrote me: "We continue our wholly spiritual, disembodied[101] ministry. By the example of our life and by practising prayer and recollection, we take on the role of witnesses. That also is an apostolate; at least they cannot attack that one."

As to your practical conduct, I refer you to the article "Stratégie missionnaire" [Missionary Strategy] in the Cor Unum[102] of October 1964.

---

[97] During the war in Katanga (Belgian Congo), twenty Holy Ghost Fathers were massacred by government troops on Jan. 1, 1962. General Bulletin, 701; Koren, Les Spiritains, 478-481.

[98] General Bulletin, 717: 1050-1054.

[99] Under the dictatorship of François Duvalier, "Papa Doc," where persecution began in 1961. Koren, Les Spiritains, 485.

[100] Cf. Koren, Les Spiritains, 565-575.

[101] I.e., deprived of the educational work essential to the mission.

For those who stand in need of a little extra encouragement, let me straightaway recommend meditating on the last "Monthly Message" of our Most Reverend Father [the Archbishop]: cf. *Bull. Gen.* n. 717. Each paragraph is relevant to our current situation.[103]

THE SUPERIOR GENERAL'S TRAVELS

In addition to writing such "messages," the Superior General sent his provincials to visit provinces and districts and also visited them himself, while continuing nevertheless to govern the congregation and prepare for the various sessions of the Council. His unceasing and diverse work is astounding and obliged him to manage his time and the work of his collaborators perfectly. A brief list of these visits will give us an idea of what he accomplished.

- September 1962. Portugal.
- January-March 1963. France: scholasticate and novitiates; in Tulle for the consecration of his successor, Bishop Henri Donze.
- April. Spain (re-establishing a scholasticate).
- May-June. United States: Duquesne University in Pittsburgh, visit to Archbishop John Wright; novitiate in Richfield, scholasticate in Ferndale, Cornwell's High School. There are eighty Holy Ghost priories, fifty-two of which serve parishes for blacks. Hence the decision taken on January 1, 1964, to divide the districts in two. Then, Trinidad: centenary of high school; Guyana, West Indies, and England.
- July 1963. Kenya: centenary of Holy Ghost missions in East Africa.
- February-March 1964. Nigeria. Later, Ireland: centenary of Rockwell School where Archbishop Lefebvre celebrates Pontifical High Mass at the faldstool in the presence of Cardinal Browne. He meets Archbishop McQuaid, Fr. Griffin, and President Eamon de Valera (who serves Mass for him on one occasion). Scotland: Motherwell scholasticate.
- December. Bethlehem (South Africa), where he notes: "The Fathers are happy and work well. However a spirit of novelty is appearing among certain Jesuits." Mauritius: centenary of Fr. Laval, and La Réunion.
- January-February 1965. Angola, where he notes: "The blacks cannot have their children baptized in the city parishes intended for Europeans…this seems truly intolerable." Cabinda. Sierra Leone: centenary; established a Holy Ghost house and parish, and obtained

---

[102] Internal newsletter of the Holy Ghost Fathers.
[103] Pannier, *L'Eglise de Pointe-Noire,* 175-176.

the bishop's permission to open a minor scholasticate. Cape Verde Islands.

- June 1965. Nigeria: priestly ordination for students trained in the country.
- June 1966. Cameroon.
- June-August 1967. Trinidad: new scholasticate; Brazil, especially the Amazon and the South:[104] Manáus (parish), Belem (bursar's office), Téfé (prelature under Dutch Holy Ghost Fathers) whose main superior lived at Manáus and neglected Téfé. Bishop Joaquim De Lange is wrongly criticized by some visiting Dutch as "not modern." Carauary; Itamarity; Cruzeior do Sul (six missions manned by German Holy Ghost Fathers—Archbishop Hascher had just passed the diocese (the prefecture of Juruá) on to Archbishop Rüth. Archbishop Lefebvre notes: "We could have a lot of vocations if the superior thought about opening a minor scholasticate."
- Then the southwest of the country: districts of Florida Paulista (Irish Fathers who run the seminary at Emilianopolis, which is unfortunately too isolated); São Paulo and Santa Catarina (German priests run the parish at Blumenau and the seminary and Brothers' novitiate in Salete, brand-new but too remote); discusses the new division of the territories that would be more equal and more useful to the missionaries. From there, visit to Belo Horizonte, Itauna, and Divinopolis, where Archbishop Lefebvre is shocked by the relaxed dress of the students under the Dutch Fathers. He asks for this to be corrected and meets with a refusal.[105]
- The voyage includes a short visit to Colombia and visits to Paraguay (village of Lima where he stays three days and is impressed by the good management of the mission, Arequipa, Asunción, and Concepción).
- In each place he gives the Holy Ghost Fathers a spiritual talk and news about the congregation. He briefly surveys the work and proposes certain measures; he emphasizes at the same time the primacy of supernatural means, preparing souls well to receive the sacraments, maintaining the hours of personal and community prayer, and the wearing of religious clothing. Unfortunately, two missionaries are already asking for laicization!
- December 1967. Portugal.
- March 1968. Trinidad.

---

[104] *General Bulletin*, 736: 438ff.; 737: 42ff.
[105] Handwritten notes on his trip; Joseph Lefebvre, ms. I, 45, 49-56.

IV. RELIGIOUS LIFE AND APOSTOLATE

WEARING THE CASSOCK

The Superior General's first stance concerning the religious life focused very practically on the wearing of religious and priestly clothing. Archbishop Lefebvre—who was not "two-dimensional" but often full of contrasts[106]—had written to Cardinal Tardini and said to Fr. Bussard[107] that he would be happy either with the cassock or with the clerical suit and Roman collar, as long as a simple cross were worn conspicuously on the lapel and recognized universally as the sign of a Catholic priest.[108]

However, in 1962 while he was Bishop of Tulle, he attended a meeting of the bishops of Southwest France and was scandalized, like many of his colleagues, at the suggestion from Paris read out by Cardinal Richaud: they should "do away with the cassock" since it was considered "a hindrance," and they should gradually bring priests around to this point of view.[109] As Superior General of an international congregation, he was happy with the use of the clerical suit for traveling and in Anglo-Saxon countries, where the cassock was not worn publicly. In 1962, the French bishops decided to give general permission for the wearing of the clerical suit. Archbishop Lefebvre noticed that in the space of a few months, priests were going "far beyond" the terms of that permission. He saw that it led "in many dioceses to abandoning any distinctive sign of belonging to the clergy" and to the wearing of lay clothes. Therefore, he decided to write a circular letter to the congregation "On Wearing the Cassock,"[110] knowing full well that some Holy Ghost Fathers would take no notice.

This letter is remarkable for its profoundly spiritual line of reasoning. "Until the present day clerical dress seemed designed to distinguish a person consecrated to God, but with the least outward sign...." But can the least outward sign be enough for religious, of whom Christ has said "You are not of the world" (Jn. 15:19), or for priests "*ex hominibus assumpti*, chosen from among men" (Heb. 5:1), or for apostles sent into the world by the Lord's word: "You shall be witnesses unto me" (Acts 1:8)! "The priest's cassock achieves both these ends clearly and unequivocally," marking his separation from the world and his witness to our Lord.

Then the Superior General became incisive and spoke with all his episcopal power: "This disappearance of any outward witness by means of

---

[106] Michel Lefebvre, Interview April 28, 1997, ms II, 11.

[107] Letter to Cardinal Tardini, Feb. 26, 1960; *Relations between Rome and Ecône*, 49; *Fideliter*, no. 140: 20; ms. I, 14, 30-40.

[108] To distinguish Catholic priests from Protestant pastors.

[109] *Retreats at Ecône*, 57 A, Feb. 1, 1983; *Spiritual Conferences at Ecône*, 140 A and B, Feb. 9, 1991.

[110] Letter of Feb. 11, 1963, *General Bulletin*, 707: 328ff.; *Fideliter*, no. 59: 93-94.

dress clearly indicates a lack of faith in the priesthood, a failure in respect for the religious attitude of one's neighbor, besides cowardice and a lack of courage in one's convictions." Exploring these three problems, he denounced the "desire to fit in with a secularized and dechristianized world," and he showed that "they know nothing of the human soul who believe it to be indifferent to spiritual things and to the desire for heavenly things." He stated that "the cassock makes the priest a living sermon": "the [apparent] absence of any priests in a large city" is "a step backwards in preaching the Gospel."

Long passages from the text were published by *Le Monde* on April 19 and by *Rivarol* on May 9, *etc*. The letter became public and Archbishop Lefebvre had it printed and sent to numerous priests, laymen, and publications who asked for it. On May 9, Cardinal Ottaviani sent a letter congratulating him on his stance. It is superfluous to add that this position won Archbishop Lefebvre many friends but also many enemies. For him, the important thing was to combat evil, and to say what was true in season and out of season, as St. Paul exhorts us (2 Tim. 4:1-2).

Defending the Religious Life of His Missionaries

Whether in his letters to the members of the congregation or in his "Monthly Message" in the *Bulletin Général* (which he made bilingual, publishing it in English and French—an initiative appreciated by the English speakers), Archbishop Lefebvre took it upon himself to defend the religious life of his missionaries, drawing, as he stated, on the Tradition of the Church. In his first letter to members of the congregation, he spoke about "belonging to the Church" and said he desired "there to be no place for our own ideas, but that all our ideas might be those of the Church and the Pope."[111] He said that like his predecessors, he was anxious "to draw from the true sources of piety, from faith in the Holy Sacrifice of the Mass."[112] He asked the rectors of the major scholasticates to "make their young Levites into truly priestly souls" who seek to "resemble the Priest *par excellence* in His obedience, His union with the heavenly Father, His humility, His simplicity, and His deep and merciful charity."[113]

From the beginning, he attacked the scornful attitude that was corroding the value of the religious life. On the grounds that the Venerable Libermann wanted his congregation to be an institute for missionary priests and not primarily for religious (although all its members, whether priests or brothers, would take the three vows of religion), some tried to argue: "We are firstly missionaries," while others reacted and said: "No!

---

[111] Letter to members, Oct. 11, 1962, *Lettres pastorales*, 169.
[112] *General Bulletin*, 711 (Sep-Oct. 1963): 604.
[113] Letters to rectors of major scholasticates, 1963.

We are firstly religious." Archbishop Lefebvre denounced "this vain argument that shows a lack of understanding of both the religious life and the apostolic life." He explained: "A soul perfectly formed by the gift of piety which is given abundantly in the priesthood and in the religious life will thirst for religion and the religious life—in other words, adoration, devotion, and prayer."

The goal of the apostolate is nothing other than "reviving in men's souls the virtue of religion under the influence of the virtues of Faith, Hope, and Charity." Consequently, there is no opposition or separation between the religious life and the apostolic life. "The contemplative's life is essentially active," said the Archbishop in a striking summary, meaning that the contemplative, religious life, which by extension becomes active and apostolic, "is nourished by the same sources, and has the same goal."[114]

Archbishop Lefebvre had lived this union of priestly and religious life for many years. It was a topic he returned to in 1964 desiring to inculcate the congregation with this idea. He quoted Paul VI who had said: "Be deeply convinced of the pre-eminence of the interior life over the active life. You are called to conquer the world spiritually... without becoming part of the world. St. Bernard of Clairvaux reminds the apostle: 'If you are wise, be a reservoir and not a canal,' because a canal simply lets water run through it without retaining any, while a reservoir begins by filling up before letting itself overflow." The Pope concluded: "By remaining faithful to your meditation, you will nourish this interior life and preserve it from being harmed by your activities."[115]

At the end of that year, the Superior General emphasized the point, quoting again from Paul VI: "Do not carry the religious life as a burden or treat it as an obstacle to the apostolic life!"[116] Keeping to religious poverty, he firmly dismissed the idea of allowing the priests of the congregation a "certain gratuity": "No," he said, "although the priests are able to keep money they inherit, they cannot without special permission use as they wish the revenues generated by it."[117]

Some priests misunderstood the Council decree on the renewal of the religious life and wanted to make themselves popular by putting the brothers on the same footing as the priests. The Archbishop answered: "No, the brothers are equal to the priests as regards the general goal of the congregation, which is the glory of God and the sanctification of its members. However, as for the specific goal of "evangelizing black unbelievers," the

[114] Letters to members, Lettres pastorales, 173.
[115] General Bulletin, 715 (May-June 1964): 900-904; Paul VI, allocution to the Brazilian College, April 28, 1964.
[116] General Bulletin, 718 (Nov.-Dec. 1964); Paul VI, allocution to Superior Generals.
[117] Letter to Father Provincials, May 1963, General Bulletin, 710: 558.

brothers only help the priests. In fact, they are attached to their status as brothers and do not wish to become clergy. They see their specific goal as helping the priests by their trade or their know-how."[118]

This did not stop the Archbishop thinking that it would be desirable to give minor orders to the brothers. But his reasons were quite different: he wanted to give the brothers the graces corresponding to the offices of acolyte and catechist so they could fulfill such roles on the missions.

V. Towards a True *Aggiornamento*

"I Gave a Cry of Alarm"

In 1965 while the Council was promoting the modernization or *aggiornamento* of religious congregations by its decree *Perfectae Caritatis*, Archbishop Lefebvre wrote a letter[119] on the topic to the members of his congregation. Dated January 6, 1966, it asked local superiors to have the conciliar texts studied and to gather together members' suggestions concerning the Holy Ghost Fathers' constitutions. This was in preparation for the administrative general chapter which would take place at Rome. The Archbishop asked that these suggestions be made "in a state of simplicity, objectivity, realism, and peace."

He announced that he was setting up four modernizing commissions: one for the rule of the congregation, one for training, one for religious discipline, and one for their apostolate. Beforehand, however, in a letter to provincials and rectors of novitiates and scholasticates,[120] he gave, as he would later say, a "cry of alarm"[121] asking for a "true *aggiornamento* of the congregation regarding the religious virtues and the formation of minds and wills. If two years hence, there is not a clear recovery,…we will be leading the congregation towards extinction."

He reminded superiors of scholasticates of their duty to be vigilant over doctrine "and over the errors of evolutionism, materialism, the confusion between the natural and supernatural, and the error that minimizes personal responsibility and exaggerates humanity." The remedy was "philosophy according to Thomistic principles," especially in "political, social, and family ethics" and "not only positive[122] but speculative theology in or-

---

[118] *Note* of Jan. 15, 1967: Brothers in the Congregation of the Holy Ghost. The Sacred Congregation of Religious were consulted on this subject by Archbishop Lefebvre on February 16, but answered evasively. *General Bulletin*, 733: 332-335.
[119] *General Bulletin*, 725 (Jan.-Feb. 1966): 6-8.
[120] In 1965; *Lettres pastorales*, 217ff.
[121] Interview with André Cagnon, 1987, 11.
[122] Positive theology: the study purely of the sources of revelation—Sacred Scripture, the Fathers of the Church, Councils, *etc.*

der to show through the thought of St. Thomas the compatibility of reason and faith."

In the liturgical domain, Archbishop Lefebvre implemented a decision of the general chapter proposing *ad libitum* a revision of community prayer. The "Holy Ghost Fathers' prayers" were replaced by Lauds in the morning and Vespers or Compline in the evening. The priests were very satisfied with this change involving a custom which was encouraged by the Church in her canon law.

However, as the itch for liturgical experimentation spread in the congregation's provinces of France and the Low Countries, the Superior General reminded them of the principles which would enable it to "give liturgical adaptations their rightful place [and make them] at the proper time."[123] It must of course be admitted that these principles have little to do with the conciliar constitution on the liturgy. This was why a growing murmur of criticism was soon heard against the Archbishop for not being faithful to the Council. Since, moreover, the malcontents were promoting innovations in the name of the Council, Archbishop Lefebvre was quick to intervene and correct new deviations: "We will continue to give the Blessed Sacrament the place of honor it deserves in the middle of the main altar" and "we will avoid discrediting private low Masses by wrongfully increasing the number of concelebrations." He gave permission for "only two Masses a week in the vernacular."

The doors that Rome had opened willy nilly could hardly be closed by the authority of the Superior General, who was caught between the experiments of his subordinates and the cowardly decisions or the indecisive cowardice of his superiors. While others talked openly about "independent learning" and "independent training," the Superior General spoke up forcefully against this "abdication of authority in what is its essential role," and against "the lack of realism which ends up causing chaos and indiscipline, represents a bonus to those who are daring and strong-headed, and leads to good, humble, and submissive religious being scorned."

Three years later when he met with the malcontents, he added: "Those in authority serve, therefore,...": those in authority serve, but they serve the common good and not the agenda of one or other individual. This is why authority "must crack down on scandals (public faults against religious discipline, bad examples that can spread) that do serious harm to the *common good*." He repeated what he had said in Dakar concerning authority: that in order for it to be exercised and respected, authority must firstly respect itself. He asked them to avoid the double pitfall of "those who believe they must apologize for their position" by being on too famil-

---

[123] *General Bulletin*, 798 (March-April 1963): 424.

iar terms with their subordinates, and "those who cannot find the right balance that true simplicity and dignity would bring."[124]

In this same letter of 1965 from which we have quoted extensively, he deplored the damage caused by the spinelessness of authorities who go back on what they should stand for. The sloppy exercise of authority leads to casual dress among priests and seminarians. Ceasing to imitate Jesus Christ leads to "a lack of modesty, a lack of self-respect and respect for one's neighbor. Such tendencies oppose self-possession and the order willed by God, and lead to licentiousness and lust."

"Let us have our *aggiornamento* not in the spirit of a destructive neo-Protestantism that ruins the sources of sanctity" but "driven by the holy desires that have inspired all saints who were involved in reform. They were reformers because they loved our Lord on the Cross, and practiced obedience, poverty, and chastity. There, they acquired the spirit of sacrifice, oblation, and prayer which made them into apostles."

THE APOSTOLIC RELIGIOUS LIFE

It can well be said that ease does not engender fervor. Around 1967 following the Council the rule of the Holy Ghost Fathers tended to lose its austerity. Now and then instead of getting up at 4:50 A.M., they got up about 6 A.M. Private morning Masses where the missionary priests could communicate intimately with Christ sometimes gave way to concelebrations. The time for community prayer was no longer fixed.

Bishop Coudray (recently expelled from Guinea), the visitor sent by Archbishop Lefebvre to the district of Pointe-Noire from February 20 to April 9, 1968, noted: "One cannot say that the prayer life has been abandoned, but there is some slackness. The priests are first to recognize it and want to do something about it. Thus, in many parishes, they recite the office with the sisters. They know that the sisters are more regular than themselves, which is a good incentive. Besides, it is a good example for the Christian community."[125]

Certainly, common recitation of certain hours of the Divine Office with nuns is a good thing, but the visitor already speaks of translating the office into the vernacular to sing the psalms using indigenous melodies. Above all, he does not foresee a return to the customs that were being abandoned, which are, nevertheless, the great traditional means of union with God.

Also in 1967, increasing unsteadiness and immaturity among candidates to the religious life was apparent in the numbers of those who were giving up during their training. This convinced the Union of Superior

---

[124] "De l'autorité," Monthly Message, *General Bulletin*, 738 (March-April 1968).
[125] Quoted by Pannier, *L'Eglise de Pointe-Noire*, 231.

Generals to write to the Sovereign Pontiff[126] asking him to permit "periods of apostolic experience during the novitiate, a lengthening of temporary probation, and the taking of temporary promises other than vows" (nn. 5, 6, 7, 23-25, 34-37).

Archbishop Lefebvre also noted that in his congregation "certain initiatives for 'updating' the novitiates were being taken very far."[127] He was opposed to the underlying spirit according to which "the present style of novitiate differs so much from the life for which it prepares [the novices] that they are not able to see whether this life suits them or not."[128] Archbishop Lefebvre reacted by highlighting the central place of the religious life and novitiate with respect to the apostolic life of priests: "It is said that the religious life is only a means for the apostolic life," and therefore not indispensable. The Superior General considered this rather short-sighted:

> Our novitiate and religious life are special means of union with God and of knowing our Lord Jesus Christ through experience [of contemplation], things that are eminently apostolic because they bring about love for neighbor. Blessed, blessed is he who during his novitiate has grown close to Christ Jesus in mind, heart, and soul! He will have increased tenfold if not a hundredfold his apostolic potential.[129]

This simple but splendid doctrine reflects the experiences of the novice Marcel Lefebvre at Orly. It also echoes the teachings of St. Thomas Aquinas as expounded at this time by his friend Msgr. Paul Philippe, Secretary for the Sacred Congregation of Religious, in a work entitled *The Goals of the Religious Life According to Saint Thomas Aquinas*. The Angelic Doctor clearly explains: "With many who are taken up with their work, it is not divine charity which moves them, but rather dislike of contemplation."[130] The author concludes: "Those who speak against contemplation show thereby that they have no charity or very little. Perfect charity, according to St. Thomas, exists when one's preaching flows from the depths of contemplation."

Msgr. Philippe thus shows how mistaken are those who want "to change the religious rules with the sole intention of effectiveness in the outside world." The "true *aggiornamento*" that Archbishop Lefebvre called upon his colleagues to make was not, as Fr. Koren wrote, "a nostalgic plea in favor of the past," nor an "About-face!"[131] but a return to the authentic

---

[126] Written on Dec. 8, 1967; *Documentation Catholique*, 1534: 168ff.

[127] From the beginning of the school year in 1963, Archbishop Lefebvre agreed to delay the novitiate by one year, *i.e.*, after the first year of philosophy. Ms. II, 17, 16.

[128] *Ibid.*

[129] *General Bulletin*, 733 (May-June 1967): 348ff.

[130] *De perfectione vitæ spiritualis*, ch. 23; Bishop Paul Philippe, *The Goals of Religious Life* (Athens, 1962), 70.

[131] Cf. *Fideliter*, no. 59: 55; Koren, *Les Spiritains*, 545, 549.

sources of the priestly and religious life. Far from dreaming nostalgically of the past in an effort to cope with the new conditions of Africa and the conciliar crisis, Archbishop Lefebvre was able to draw from the sources of the Church's Tradition the courage to make the necessary changes to missionary activities, and the strength to defend the ways of the Holy Ghost Fathers against the deadly infection of neo-modernism.

BRINGING BACK THE "GENTLEMEN OF THE HOLY GHOST"

Although he was thoroughly opposed to a reform that would destroy the Holy Ghost Fathers' approach to the novitiate, he was however thoroughly open to overhauling the training and putting the novitiate after priestly ordination. Here we see the breadth of the Archbishop who, far from being two-dimensional, was open to extensive reforms as long as they were in line with the thinking of the founders of the congregation. In light of the fact that "many young religious have their vows dissolved" while "many professed priests seem little attached to their religious life," and "the number of requests for dispensation from vows is increasing steadily,"[132] it was apparent that many were entering the religious life "out of necessity and not out of conviction, and only to belong to a society that sends its members to the missions, or through feeling an attraction for the spirit of the congregation."

On January 25, 1967, he opened his mind to the members of the congregation by publishing his "Proposal for Restoring the Work of Father Claude Poullart des Places"[133] alongside a proposed reform for admitting prospective members. The minor scholasticates would be maintained to direct students towards the missionary ideal without forcing them into a vocation pursued from an early age. The major scholasticates would begin with "a preparatory year of ecclesiastical studies for the priestly life and the life of a professed missionary" during which students would study Latin and Apologetics and be introduced to Sacred Scripture, patrology, and theology. Curiously, a course on spiritual doctrine is totally absent from the first year curriculum.

Then, the Superior General proposed, there would be five years of ecclesiastical studies according to the *Summa* of St. Thomas with brief courses on Scripture, patrology, the Magisterium, and Canon Law. This would provide a unique route by which "the student would discover and marvel at the greatness and the depths of the knowledge of God, Jesus Christ, the soul, and its path towards God. He will be fascinated by his discoveries and his soul will be filled with zeal, piety, faith, and a great desire to make his

---

[132] Handwritten notes on minor scholasticates and the re-establishment of the "Gentlemen of the Holy Ghost," 1967.
[133] Cf. *Fideliter*, no. 59: 87.

true and deep knowledge of God known to others." Sound philosophy would find a place in this synthesis as well as the "true principles of social and political studies."[134]

Finally, only after ordination performed "*ad titulum servitii Ecclesiae*"[135] would the young priest be able to choose to enter the congregation with a year's novitiate, followed by taking perpetual vows or being incardinated either in a missionary diocese or one that lacked priests. In the latter case, these priests would be, according to Archbishop Lefebvre, "the renewal or rebirth of the Gentlemen of the Holy Ghost established by Claude Poullart des Places, our first founder." This institute would take nothing away from the status of professed Holy Ghost Fathers with whom they would have "spiritual ties."[136]

The Archbishop underlined the advantages of such a move. Attempts at recruitment in dioceses would be better received, the secular and religious clergy would be brought together, and there would be a better distribution of priests between rich and poor dioceses. He added that "the Gentlemen of the Holy Ghost could form an association, a *fraternity* [society] that would be organized and supported by the congregation." The common seminary shared by the Gentlemen and Fathers of the Holy Ghost would be an "*international seminary* in the way it distributed its priests."[137]

We have emphasized two keywords that opened up completely new possibilities and went beyond a mere return to the original model. Unfortunately, the plan of Archbishop Lefebvre that was so traditional and so innovative was unable to attract the interest of either the most traditional or the most progressive members of the congregation. However, outside the congregation it would receive an unexpected echo.

VI. EXTRAORDINARY CHAPTER MEETING—RESIGNATION

REVOLUTION OF THE COUNCIL IN MINIATURE[138]

By 1967, Archbishop Lefebvre could see that "it was impossible to continue running a congregation that no longer either listened to me or wanted me." He told his friend Archbishop Sigaud that he intended to resign as Superior General.[139] However, preparation for the extraordinary

---

[134] *Notes* quoted.
[135] "For the service of the Church," a new canonical status for being ordained priest.
[136] *Notes* quoted.
[137] Thus would be realized "certain objectives of the Council" as Archbishop Lefebvre wrote. See: *Presbyterorum Ordinis*, 8, 3; 10, 1 and 2, and motu proprio *Ecclesiæ Sanctæ* of Aug. 6, 1966, I, 3, §§ 1, 2; *Documentation Catholique* 1477, 1444.
[138] *General Bulletin*, 742: 241ff.; O'Carroll, *A Priest in Changing Times*, 98-100; *Fideliter*, no. 59.
[139] Interview, Cagnon, *Relations between Rome and Ecône*, 1987, 11; Archbishop Sigaud, Letter to Archbishop Lefebvre, Feb. 2, 1967, Archives of *Fortes in Fide*.

general chapter for reform undertaken by the chapter's preparatory commissions continued, according to the permission granted by the Sacred Congregation for Religious[140] and the norms[141] issued by Paul VI on August 6, 1966, implementing the conciliar decree *Perfectae Caritatis.*

The Superior General allowed the commissions to be free in bringing together the various motions from the provinces. Similarly the central preparatory commission was unhindered in its work of making an overall synthesis of the propositions. The results of this work were inspected by an independent expert, who praised them: "This chapter is better prepared than any other I have studied."[142] As to the basis of the reforms Archbishop Lefebvre would say: "I prepared an exhaustive reform of our congregation certainly taking into account its evolution but also restating decisively the essential principles of our religious life."

Before the chapter in May 1968, Archbishop Lefebvre and his general council, whose mandate was due to last until 1974, decided to offer their resignation on the first day with "the desire to stop personal issues emerging in the course of this chapter and becoming more important than a sound and genuine reform."[143] However, it was understood that their common resignation would only become effective when the chapter had elected another general council. Until then the present Superior General was to chair the chapter according to the constitutions.

One Easter Monday 1967 (March 27), the Archbishop went to visit Padre Pio at San Giovanni Rotondo to ask him to pray for the general chapter. He arrived at the wrong time because the Superior General of the Capuchins had come with the same request for the Capuchin general chapter. "Pray for our Capuchin general chapter which will be held to draw up new constitutions."

At these words, Padre Pio angrily reacted, exclaiming: "It's all idle chatter and destruction!"[144]

Seventeen weeks later when Paul VI was due to give an audience to the Capuchin chapter, Padre Pio wrote to the Pope on September 12, 1968: "I pray to our Lord that it [the Capuchin order] continue its traditions of serious religious austerity, evangelical poverty, and observance of the rule and constitutions, while renewing its vitality and interior spirit according to the directives of the Second Vatican Council."[145]

---

[140] Letter of Cardinal Antoniutti, Prefect, May 5, 1966, *General Bulletin*, 727.

[141] Motu proprio *Ecclesiæ Sanctæ, General Bulletin*, 729: 162-174.

[142] O'Carroll, *A Priest in Changing Times*, 98.

[143] Report of Archbishop Lefebvre to general chapter; *L'Osservatore Romano*, no. 41, Oct. 11, 1968.

[144] Reaction reported by Fr. Jean, Capuchin at Morgon in the "Letter to Friends of St. Francis," no. 17, Feb. 2, 1999; *Fideliter*, no.129: 52.

[145] Cf. *Roma Flix*, monthly newsletter of the SSPX in Italy, vol. 1, no. 5 (March, 1999): 4-5.

When the new constitutions were announced, Padre Pio reacted in a similarly sharp manner: "What are you doing in Rome? What are you planning? You even want to change the rule of Saint Francis!"

However, the conversation between the Archbishop, who was accompanied by Fr. Barbara and another priest, and Padre Pio flanked by two Capuchins, was simple, brief, and to the point. The priest with the stigmata promised to pray for the Holy Ghost chapter. The Archbishop was moved to veneration and asked him for his blessing. Padre Pio replied: "No, Your Grace, it is your place to bless me!"

Thus, Archbishop Lefebvre implored heaven's blessing on Padre Pio.[146]

The general chapter opened in Rome at the *Domus Mariae* on September 8, 1968. In his general report, the Superior General mentioned the completion of new projects and some difficulties that had arisen, and then proposed several reforms: giving assistants and general council members a new role and considerably more responsibility; reorganizing the large provinces; delaying religious profession; and accepting young aspiring missionaries who did not want to take the three religious vows, in keeping with the spirit of the work established by Poullart des Places, *etc.* Finally, he submitted the general council's resignation that had already been announced.

He let the chapter members decide whether they would elect the new general council at the end of the chapter (as had been the case in 1962), from the beginning (as had been done previously), or following "a third solution suggested by some of you" to name one of several moderators so that the meetings might be "led by members other than the Superior General, who would nevertheless continue to chair the sessions."

Archbishop Lefebvre attempted to dismiss this third solution by adding that in this case the posts of Superior General, assistants, and general council members would be vacant and the Congregation would be left without a head.[147] He knew very well that the progressive wing among the chapter members feared most of all his keeping control of the direction of the general chapter and preventing them from bringing about their reforms. As a shrewd leader, the Archbishop put forth their proposition but took pains to show its great disadvantage: the sidelining of the Superior General in the congregation's most important gathering. This would be a repeat at chapter level of the Council coup that led to elected moderators replacing the Council chairman appointed by the Pope.

---

[146] About 1976, a totally different version of their meeting began to do the rounds. Padre Pio supposedly prophesied: "You will disobey…you will divide the Church." Needless to say, this so-called "prophecy" of the Capuchin was sheer invention. The Archbishop denied it categorically.

[147] *Report* quoted.

In accordance with the plan of the progressive priests, the chapter put off the election of a new general council but voted immediately to suspend constitution 91 concerning the powers of the Superior General to chair the meetings and to choose the members of commissions for the chapter. One question remained to be answered: would the Superior General, who was entitled to chair the chapter, also chair the central commission according to the rules laid down by the general council?

Soon the Archbishop's enemies made their case: "The chapter, which is a legislative power, cannot be placed under the authority of the executive power as represented by the Superior General. The members of the central commission would have to be elected without exception." Answering this specious argument, Fr. Michael O'Carroll asked: "What will the members in the provinces and missions think about us if the first thing we do is to sideline our Superior General?"

Archbishop Lefebvre was against electing the members of the central commission and concluded: "Every one of us is free to express his opinion and vote according to his conscience; as for me, I will abide by the results of the vote."

Had the vote taken place straightaway, it would perhaps have gone in the Archbishop's favor. However, for some unknown reason that was no doubt providential, he delayed the voting until the following day, leaving the reformers a night to hold secret meetings and exert pressure on the chapter. The Archbishop lost the vote on September 11, sixty-three votes against forty, and saw himself reduced to the unacceptable role of "theoretical and honorary chairman." Remaining calm, he merely remarked: "The situation in which the Superior General has been put is certainly contrary to the spirit of the Church and to the spirit of Canon Law, and is in contradiction with our traditions and constitutions."

He continued to chair the morning session, but at midday he was faithful to his promise and left the chapter. He asked Fr. Hack, the first assistant, to stand in for him at the meetings; returning to the motherhouse he confined himself to "settling current business." The chapter was momentarily stunned, but then elected three moderators, and continued on its way, getting bogged down in unreasonable motions and endless paperwork. It lasted for four months, two in Rome in 1968 and two in Chevilly in 1969.

RESIGNATION

The following day, September 12, Archbishop Lefebvre wrote to Cardinal Antoniutti, Prefect of the Sacred Congregation for Religious, and made him aware of what had happened and of his decision. Then on September 16, he put to the congregation his doubts concerning the validity of the vote taken by the chapter since it was contrary to the constitutions.

Although in *Ecclesiae Sanctae* Paul VI gave authority to chapters involved in reform to modify *ad experimentum* (experimentally) certain constitutional rules, he did not allow them to "alter the very nature of a religious society or its fundamental structures."[148] The Archbishop said that such was the case by removing the Superior General's powers over the chapter.

The Archbishop "turned several projects over in his mind" which he shared with his closest associates. One of them was to hold a chapter in Assisi—the peaceful city of St. Francis—with the chapter members who had been in favor of him during the vote: they would undertake a reform of the Holy Ghost Fathers in the spirit of its founders. Before the chapter, the possibility of a split had occurred to him. On August 15 he wrote: "Already the certainly painful but necessary purification of the Church and its religious societies is taking shape. Some are divided, and others will become divided. Some who remain true to the teachings of the Church and her holy traditions will have vocations. The others will break up and disappear."[149]

According to Fr. Michael O'Carroll,[150] it seemed to the Archbishop on second thoughts that "it was not possible. He thought it would be a sign of division in the congregation. Besides, how many would follow him?" Finally, he went to spend a few days in peace in Assisi where he wrote a text that he came to read during his brief appearance at the chapter on September 28. It was a solemn admonition to remain faithful to the spirit of the Venerable Libermann, who clearly saw that the apostolate amongst abandoned souls "would always consist in spreading and giving an example of our Lord's holiness present in the souls of missionaries." He said that the Venerable Liberman "could not conceive of an apostolate, and especially not of the apostolate he proposed to his sons, as distinct from holiness....For him, holiness was essentially apostolic."

He set out to give the means of holiness to his sons. "These means are: the religious life and community life which bring about the life of self-denial, the life of prayer, and the life of fraternal charity (all of which are needed for holiness to develop) and apostolic zeal or real union with our Lord by which holiness is spread." However, Archbishop Lefebvre noted:

> Many of you no longer want these things. What is the use in hiding it from us?...Their [*sic*] individualism, their selfishness, and their thirst for freedom and independence have prevailed against the religious life, community life, the life of obedience, and prudence with respect to the world,

---

[148] Motu proprio, Aug. 6, 1966 - II, 6, *Documentation Catholique* 1477: 1459; *General Bulletin*, 729: 164.

[149] "Nos raisons d'être optimiste" (Reasons for being optimistic), article publication details unknown, *Lettres pastorales*, 325.

[150] Interview with Fr. Michael O'Carroll, May 9, 1998, 3; O'Carroll, *A Priest in Changing Times*, 100.

the life of real detachment from the goods and comforts of this world. They have prevailed against the realities of life in community which is our mortification and compels us to practice charity and live the life of prayer....[However], their individualism can only live parasitically.

Calling upon the chapter members to seek inspiration for their decisions in the writings of the Venerable Libermann, he quoted an admirable extract from the writings of the founder precisely on the statutes of the Holy Ghost Fathers:

> The unfortunates who left their country to be missionaries always held to this idea: I am above all a missionary! Consequently and without realizing it, they did not give any importance to the religious life and became, I believe, too involved in their activities....In truth, the mission is the objective, but the religious life is the means *sine qua non* [indispensable]....If they are holy religious, they will save souls. If they are not, they will do nothing because God's blessing is attached to their holiness.[151]

Only on October 4[152] was the Archbishop received by the new secretary[153] of the Sacred Congregation for Religious, Msgr. Antonio Mauro. Cardinal Antoniutti was absent on a visit to South America. "If I had dealt with the Cardinal," Archbishop Lefebvre would say, "things might have turned out differently. But (Providence was there) I had to speak to the secretary who was dismissed three months later because he was ignorant and not up to the job."[154]

Archbishop Lefebvre said to him: "There is a revolution in the chapter. I have been sidelined. I am not even a member of any of the commissions, as are the other chapter members. I'm just a spectator, I, the Superior General!"

"You understand," replied Msgr. Mauro, "after the Council, you have to understand...I am going to give you some advice that I have just given to another Superior General who came to see me about the same thing. 'Go on,' I said to him, 'take a little trip to the United States. It will do you good.' As for the chapter and even for the congregation's present business, leave it to your assistants!"

However, his assistants insisted that Archbishop Lefebvre continue to deal with the congregation's affairs. He did this, thinking: "The chapter

---

[151] Ven. Francis Libermann, *Directoire spirituel*, 2nd ed. (Paris, n.d.), 189; *General Bulletin*, 741: 172-180.

[152] Cf. Letter of Fr. Paul Dentin to Archbishop Lefebvre, Oct. 4, 1968.

[153] Cf. *A.A.S.* 59 (1967): 650, appointed on Jan. 29, 1967; his predecessor, Bishop Paul Philippe, was the same day appointed as Secretary to the Sacred Congregation for the Doctrine of the Faith. On Jan. 8, 1968, Cardinal Franjo Seper was appointed as Prefect to the CDF, replacing Cardinal Ottaviani, the Pro-prefect.

[154] *Fideliter*, no. 59. Bishop Mauro was appointed vice chairman of the Secretariat for Non-Believers on April 12, 1969. *A.A.S.* 61 (1969): 292.

members can come and speak to me and good relations will be maintained, even though the situation is totally abnormal."[155]

On October 13, he wrote to the chapter offering fourteen pages of suggestions regarding the objectives and nature of the congregation, religious and common life, apostolic zeal, and allowing brothers to have certain posts on the general council. Among the suggestions were two "quite new" projects regarding a new role for the assistants and the restoration of the work of Claude Poullart, while faithfully maintaining the religious congregation founded by the Venerable Libermann." None or almost none of his suggestions were followed.

On October 28, Fr. Joseph Lécuyer was elected as Superior General. Archbishop Lefebvre, now relieved of his responsibilities, returned the same day to present the chapter to Cardinal Agagianian. To a close associate, the Archbishop said of his successor: "He's the best of a bad lot."[156] On November 11, he attended the audience that the Pope gave to the chapter.

Apart from these sporadic occasions, the Archbishop let the chapter get on with its work "in complete freedom." The "directives and decisions"[157] published in 1970 show the destructive revolution brought about by the chapter.

- Authority: concern for the common good is replaced by respect for personalities and individual freedoms.
- Obedience: becomes co-responsibility, dialogue, the common search for God's will, taking part in decisions, working as a team, and group dynamics.
- Religious training: provided by several stages of spiritual formation that replace the novitiate. "Retraining" courses, and "revising the evangelical life."
- Mission: revised and corrected ecumenically as a "dialogue for salvation" between the minister of Christ and those who belong to religions that "the Catholic Church respects" in accordance with the Council.

A HOMELESS BISHOP

The Archbishop left the motherhouse, one simple bag in hand. A French seminarian saw him and asked: "Where are you going like that, Excellency?"

""I don't know…"

"Can I be of assistance?"

---

[155] Lefebvre, reply to Fr. Paul Dentin, Oct. 9, 1968; talk at La Villa Aurore, May 2, 1976, *Courrier des A.F.B.*, no. 34: 16; O'Carroll, *A Priest in Changing Times*, 100.

[156] Fr. Bussard, ms. I, 15, 46-48.

[157] Rome, motherhouse, *General Bulletin*, supplement to no. 784.

"Thank you, that's all right."

He found refuge firstly on November 1 at the Institute of the Holy Ghost on Via Machiavelli. A little later, he found a small room at the Villa Lituania on Via Casalmonferrato. It was maintained by the sisters who were attached to the Lithuanian seminary. He bought himself a desk, a wardrobe, and some shelving,[158] and he had just enough to pay his rent with the ninety thousand lira he received monthly from the Sacred Congregation for the Propagation of the Faith for his work as a consulter and as president of the commission responsible for catechisms in Africa. It was a role he kept until 1972.

Although the establishment of the Secretariat for Non-Christians virtually ruined the *Propaganda Fide*, he was happy to make his knowledge of Africa available to the Sacred Congregation.[159] He could have traveled to Africa to visit the training centers for catechists to which he attached such great importance. But this possibility did not attract him. At sixty-three, and in fact at "the end of his career," he felt dissatisfied with such meager responsibilities. He felt himself pushed from within, urgently compelled to do other work.

On one hand, as he had told Archbishop Sigaud, he wanted to "dedicate [himself] entirely to the fight against the progressives"[160] through the press, as he had been doing since 1966. On the other hand, he still had the idea of an international seminary that he shared with his friend Bishop Morilleau[161] and his confidant, Fr. Michael O'Carroll.

"Father O'Carroll," he said to him one day, "if ever I have to leave the congregation, I will found a traditional seminary and in three years I will have 150 seminarians."[162]

[158] He moved his furniture to Albano in 1973.
[159] *Fideliter*, no. 59: 58-59.
[160] Archbishop de Proença Sigaud, Letter to Archbishop Lefebvre, Feb. 2, 1967.
[161] Cf. Letter of Bishop Morilleau to Archbishop Lefebvre, Jan. 11, 1967.
[162] O'Carroll, *A Priest in Changing Times*,100.

CHAPTER 15

CHARTER OF RESISTANCE (1965-69)

I. FIGHTING IDEOLOGICAL OPPRESSION

For Marcel Lefebvre the end of the Council did not mean an end to the hostilities of the four previous years, any more than the engrossing albeit painful reform of his congregation absorbed all of his zeal. Reflecting on the Council and on the crisis that was beginning to grip the Church, he tried to organize resistance among some of the remaining orthodox priests.

POST-CONCILIAR CRISIS, CRISIS OF AUTHORITY

Although the Archbishop still refused to question the authority of the Council, he was beginning to wonder about it: "The Council's texts, especially *Gaudium et Spes* and that on Religious Freedom, have been signed by the Pope and bishops, so we cannot doubt their content....Yet, how are we to interpret, for example, the document on Religious Freedom which carries within itself a certain intrinsic contradiction? It begins by stating that it nothing of tradition is altered, whereas, in fact, nothing in the text squares with tradition!"[1]

In those Council documents that glorify the individual and his private conscience, the Archbishop could already see the cause of the general crisis in authority that was rapidly spreading after the Council:

> To exalt the personality and the personal conscience of the child to the detriment of family authority is to store up unhappiness for the children and drive them to rebellion and scorn for their parents....A child is born so weak, so imperfect, one might almost say incomplete, that we can infer from it the absolute necessity for permanence in the home and the indissolubility of the family....We are straying from the way laid down by God when we claim that truth alone, by its own power and light, should point men to the true religion whereas, in reality, God's plan was for the transmission of religion by parents and witnesses worthy of the trust of their hearers.

---

[1] "Après le concile, l'Eglise devant la crise morale contemporaine" (After the Council: The Church and the moral crisis of today), talk given at the quarterly dinner of the Union of Independent Intellectuals, Paris, end of 1968, *A Bishop Speaks*, 65-72.

The role of civil authority that some wanted to secularize through religious liberty is also providentially appointed in the religious education of nations:

> ...It is undeniable that in fact the test of the history of Catholic nations, the history of the Church, the history of conversion to the Catholic Church, shows the providential part played by the State, so much so that it may fairly be said that its share in humanity's attainment of eternal salvation is of capital, if not preponderating, importance. Man is weak, the Christian wavering. If the whole machinery and social conditioning of the State are secular, atheistic, areligious and, still worse, if it persecutes the Church, who will venture to say that it will be easy for non-Catholics to be converted and for Catholics to remain faithful?...It would be criminal to encourage Catholic States to secularise themselves, lose all interest in their religion, see with indifference error and immorality spread and, under the false pretext of human dignity, introduce into society with an exaggerated religious liberty, a ferment for its dissolution, elevating the individual conscience at the expense of the common weal.[2]

Archbishop Lefebvre had a wise perspective that had many real applications. He concluded that authority is ultimately a participation in the Divine Love that wishes to spread itself and to draw men towards Divine Goodness while punishing those who reject it. It follows that when civil authority refuses to legislate or punish in religious matters, it is denying God an occasion to spread His love.

A NATURALIST GNOSIS

However, the crisis in authority was only a sign of the crisis in the Faith itself, and the Archbishop analyzed it in the pages of a review published by his friend Fr. Luc J. Lefèvre.[3] He denounced "man's constant tendency to rebel against God's authority," and showed how in the writings of the neo-Modernists, "reason is opposed to the authority of God who reveals the road to salvation along which it has pleased the Eternal Wisdom to make us journey." He quoted St. Pius X's condemnation of the heresiarchs who began by distorting the fundamental postulates, *i.e.*, the realities that lie at the very origins of Redemption: "Original sin, the fall of man....The whole structure of the Faith is ruined from top to bottom."[4]

---

2   "L'autorité dans la famille et dans la société civile au service de notre salut" (Authority in the Family and in Secular Society as an aid to our Salvation), Feb. 22, 1967, in *La Pensée Catholique*, no. 107: 19-27; article republished on Nov. 23, 1967 and Feb. 5, 1968, by *Rivarol*, Jan. 1968, and *Les Ecrits de Paris*, April 1968; *A Bishop Speaks*, 55-64; *Lettres pastorales*, 309-320.

3   "L'hérésie contemporaine" (The contemporary heresy), Feb. 21, 1968, in *La Pensée Catholique*, no. 113; *Lettres pastorlaes*, 229ff.

4   Encyclical *Ad Diem Illum*, Feb. 2, 1904 (Bonne Presse), I, 85-87.

Did not the rationalist postulate of the continuous progress necessary to humanity lead the Council to say in *Gaudium et Spes* that "the human race has passed from a rather static concept of reality to a more dynamic, evolutionary one. In consequence, there has arisen a new series of problems, a series as important as can be, calling for new efforts of analysis and synthesis."[5] When at the beginning of the century this thesis was applied to religion by the heirs of Lessing, Herder, and Hegel, it led to a "liberal, modernist Christology" that was expertly criticized at the time by Fr. Léonce de Grandmaison.[6]

However, in 1967 it was now the heirs of Teilhard de Chardin and Rahner who corrupted the penny catechism with their evolutionist and rationalist gnosis, publishing the Dutch Catechism (issued in French without *imprimatur*) and the "basic fundamentals" of the French catechism. The latter was approved by a plenary gathering of the French bishops in 1966, although it said nothing about original or venial sin, the title of the Immaculate Conception, the devil, angels, and hell. Moreover, the declaration of the Bishop of Metz at Saint Avold[7] outraged readers of *Itinéraires*[8] who had learned of it through Jean Madiran. The bishop had dared to say: "The changes in our civilization that we see around us bring transformations not only in our conduct but also in the ways we think about Creation and the salvation wrought by Jesus Christ. This far reaching re-evaluation requires not only new pastoral approaches but more importantly a more evangelical understanding—at once more personal and more communal—of God's plans for the world."[9]

How right the Archbishop was to denounce the reinterpretation of the basics of the Faith with its high-minded assumptions concerning collective salvation and the evolution of humanity!

To counter this heresy of the twentieth century, Pope Paul VI called for a "Year of Faith" in 1967 that was aimed more specifically against a "post-conciliar mentality" which he accused of "spreading the vain wish to give the Christian religion a new interpretation."[10] When, on June 29, 1968, the Sovereign Pontiff proclaimed his *Profession of Peter's Faith* to

---

[5] *Gaudium et Spes*, §5, quoted by Lefebvre, "L'Eglise accomplira-t-elle à temps sa véritable rénovation?" Aug. 30, 1968, *Lettres pastorales*, 331.

[6] Quoted by Lefebvre, "L'hérésie contemporaine" (The contemporary heresy), 304.

[7] Official Bulletin of the Diocese of Metz, Oct. 1, 1967.

[8] *Itinéraires*, nos. 118 and 119: "La religion de Saint-Avold ou l'hérésie du XXᵉ siècle" (The religion of St. Avold or the heresy of the twentieth century). Jean Madiran republished the Catechism of St. Pius X in *Itinéraires* no. 116 (Sept.-Oct. 1967), rightly stating that today laymen must "stand in" and give the Catholic catechism to the faithful who can no longer find it. (*Itinéraires*, no. 121: 71).

[9] *Itinéraires*, no. 118: 12.

[10] Apostolic Exhortation *Petrum et Paulum*, Feb. 22, 1967, *Documentation Catholique*, 64, 486.

close the Year of Faith, Archbishop Lefebvre was full of hope: "There are real grounds for optimism," he said.[11]

People everywhere were looking to the Pope for support. Unfortunately, his actions often contradicted his words: Rome did not censure the new catechism (it was even given some encouragement), and the Roman Curia was subverted by a reform that confirmed the dominance of politics (Secretariat of State) over the Faith (the Sacred Congregation for the Doctrine of the Faith [CDF]), reducing the former Holy Office to a mere office for "promoting doctrine." Cardinal Seper, prefect for the CDF, explained: "Although the motu proprio *Integrae Servandae* speaks of condemning errors contrary to the doctrine of the Faith, it highlights the fact that the Congregation's main task will involve promoting theological research. Therefore, there is a change of emphasis that favors the more positive and dynamic aspect."[12]

Archbishop Lefebvre had asked Cardinal Browne, formerly of the Holy Office: "This change of name and role, is it a superficial or an essential change?"

"Oh," replied the Cardinal, "essential. It is obvious!"

"Yes," the Archbishop would conclude, "it is no longer a courtroom for the Faith but a theological research office with a commission of theologians from all over the world who are forever 'seeking the truth.' The situation is very serious."[13]

SMASHING THE INTELLECTUAL DICTATORSHIP

Even before the Council finished, the neo-Modernist clique had its hands on the levers of power in the Church's courts, administration, and media. By May 1965 they had already promised that there would be "a schism by the end of the year," brought about by "a movement of independent groups reacting against the Council's decisions" and whose "unease would increase" after the promulgation of religious liberty and Schema XIII.[14]

Writing in *Itinéraires*, Fr. Calmel denounced the dominant progressive forces' use of "sociological relegation"[15] that was becoming extreme and insidious: in order to exclude people utterly, they spoke of schism. However, none of the "leading lights" of the Catholic resistance in France (or elsewhere)—neither Archbishop Lefebvre in his commentaries, nor eminent

---

[11] "Nos raisons d'être optimiste," Rome, Aug. 15, 1968, *Lettres pastorales*, 321ff.; "Lueurs d'espérance" (Glimmers of Hope), Rome, Aug. 15, 1968, in *Itinéraires*, no. 127: 226ff.

[12] *ICI*, no. 316 (July 15, 1968): 27; motu proprio of Dec. 7, 1965, *A.A.S.* 57, 953.

[13] *Spiritual Conference at Ecône*, 45 A, Oct. 10, 1977; 55B, Jan. 17, 1978.

[14] Declaration of Bishop Pailler, coadjutor of Rouen, at the congress of ACI in Amiens, May 12, 1965; *AFP* 178 B 100; *La Croix*, May 8-9; *Le Figaro*, May 13.

[15] *Itinéraires*, no. 206: 5-6.

laymen such as Jean Madiran in his review *Itinéraires*, and still less Jean Ousset in *Verbe* or Marcel Clément in *L'Homme Nouveau*—showed the least sign of questioning the decisions of the Council. Jean Madiran would explain his position in July 1965.[16]

In the same edition of *Itinéraires*, Archbishop Lefebvre denounced in his usual, frank manner "a new magisterium: public opinion." In the conclusion to the article he claimed for each bishop freedom from the episcopal administrative departments which were tending to "take control." He said: "It is inconceivable that a majority impose upon a minority just by voting. That would be the end of episcopal authority....The bishop in his diocese must remain entirely free at the risk of being no more than a civil servant, or even, let it be said, a minor."[17]

We must conclude that the leading core of the French bishops felt attacked because they sent Cardinal Lefebvre to admonish his rather rebellious cousin: "After your attacks on the French bishops in your article on June 6 and in a conference given to the Benedictines of Ozon on Easter Tuesday, the bishops wanted to have recourse to the Holy See. However, having regard to the position of Your Excellency, I have been asked to make known to you the bishops' sorrow and condemnation."[18]

The Archbishop replied sharply:

> The pretension of certain influential members of the episcopacy to impose their way of thinking on all the bishops is inadmissible, and contrary to the very nature of the episcopacy and to the most basic, legitimate freedom of thought. This desire to monopolize minds is becoming all the more obvious in the memos from the episcopal secretariat, in the press officially supported by the bishops' offices, in particular *La Croix*, and by the episcopal secretariat's choice of theologians. Blackballing is being used against those who are out of step with this general tendency.
>
> Now, the ideas that these influential members of the episcopacy want to impose are clearly liberal, and generally speaking run counter to traditional Roman theology....In private, many bishops do not want to conform, but dare not act in public for fear of being reprimanded and criticized by the press. This intellectual dictatorship over the bishops is unbearable.[19]

To break this ideological stranglehold and repel the invasion of error, Archbishop Lefebvre had the idea of establishing links between the bishops who had been members of the *Coetus*, as we will see.

As an epilogue, let us add that three years later when the first new catechisms based on the "basic fundamentals" appeared, Archbishop Lefe-

---

[16] *Ibid.*, no. 95, editorial entitled "A Schism for December."
[17] *Perspectives Conciliaires*, June 6, 1965, 82.
[18] Text reconstructed from Archbishop Lefebvre's reply.
[19] Letter of Sept. 1965 to Cardinal Lefebvre, Archives of Archbishop Lefebvre at Ecône.

bvre personally got involved in the fight.[20] In the pamphlet "What Should We Think of the New Catechism?" published by Pierre Lemaire, director of *Défense du Foyer* (Family Defense) and received by the French bishops on the eve of their meeting in Lourdes in November 1968, the Archbishop wrote: "The Church of France is bringing God's curse upon itself. The children have asked for bread and they have been given scorpions."

The Archbishop of Bourges (Cardinal Lefebvre) was angry,[21] and wrote Archbishop Lefebvre for the umpteenth time saying that "all the bishops" on whom Archbishop Lefebvre cast "suspicion and discredit"[22] were "sad and astonished." However, the Cardinal, who had authored a catechism suspect of heresy,[23] richly deserved the title of "goose-stepping oppressor" given him by Fr. Berto.

II. ORGANIZING RESISTANCE AND RECONSTRUCTION

BRINGING TOGETHER THE BISHOPS WHO WERE READY TO REBUILD

Archbishop Lefebvre recalled: "At the end of the Council, we held a modest get-together for the most active, devoted, and solid members of the *Coetus*—there were about thirty—before going our separate ways. We had our picture taken and promised we would produce a bulletin to help us keep up our fight for Tradition."[24] This was Archbishop Lefebvre's own idea: for the bishops who shared his Roman spirit he wanted to do what his friend Professor Francesco Leoni was doing with his review *Relazioni*, in bringing a traditional Catholic spirit to the study of politics and economics.[25]

Faithful to his promise, the Archbishop informed his colleagues on February 20, 1966, of his proposal to publish a combative, multilingual interepiscopal bulletin of information and analysis which would help the bishops "to take practical measures against progressivism and in favor of a sound interpretation of the Council." This would also enable them "at the right time to take action together on a worldwide scale," or at least "to help Rome with its task of defending and promoting the truth." Writing to Archbishop Sigaud, the Archbishop added: "When the Holy Father realiz-

---

[20] Like Pierre Lemaire, Jean Madiran, and Louis Salleron; cf. *Itinéraires* and *Documents-Paternité* of March 1968.

[21] He had already got "annoyed" with Messers Madiran and Salleron. Fr. Berto, his former fellow student at Santa Chiara, wrote an "Open Letter to His Excellency the Archbishop of Bourges" in September 1968, published in *Itinéraires*, no. 127 in November 1968.

[22] Letter of Nov. 14, 1968.

[23] "It is heretical," Fr. Coache said of the new catechism in *Le Combat de la Foi* in October 1968.

[24] Interview with André Cagnon for *Fideliter*, no. 59: 64.

[25] Letter of F. Leoni to Archbishop Lefebvre, Nov. 5, 1965.

es that those whom he trusted are leading the Church to her ruin, he will find himself a group of bishops in the world who are ready to rebuild. Unfortunately, the time has not yet come, because the Holy Father himself must change what he is doing, and that conversion will be painful."[26]

The review which originally was to be called *Notitiae Postconciliares* was never published under that name. In fact it took time to find good regional contributors, and it was only in July 1966 that Providence gave the Archbishop a sign to undertake the work.

Visiting Rue Lhomond, the Archbishop was getting ready to fly to Rome when the telephone rang. Short of time, the Superior General agreed to a meeting at Orly Airport. Hearing his name called over the loud-speaker, he came to the desk and met Lady Claude Kinnoull, a close friend of Léon de Poncins. She was a Scottish countess educated in France but now living in California. "This is a donation for your work," she said, "I'll willingly give more."[27] This is in fact what she did through her right-hand man, the English lawyer Vernor Miles.

With this unexpected gift and the encouragement of Cardinals Ottaviani and Siri,[28] Archbishop Lefebvre bought an IBM word processor, an offset press, and a photocopier in order to ensure a "careful and clear presentation."[29] *Relazioni* offered him office space for the review which finally appeared in August 1967 under the more combative title of *Fortes in Fide*, *i.e.*, "Strong in the Faith." Bishop Castán Lacoma allowed one of his priests, Fr. Luis Viejo Montolío, a student in Rome, to man the review's office, where he worked with the Carmelite friar Fr. Philippe de la Trinité.

The first editions of *Fortes in Fide* published a pastoral letter of Bishop Carli, a lecture of Archbishop Graber, and a review of Pierre Virion's book *Avant le gouvernement mondial, une super contre-Eglise?* However, the involvement of even the best bishops proved to be sensitive. Bishop de Castro Mayer, whom Archbishop Lefebvre planned to visit in Campos, wrote to him: "It will be better for us—you, Archbishop Sigaud, and me—to meet in another, larger town where we can be anonymous....It would be better still if we could meet at a farm...in São Paulo State, two hours from the city by car." Besides, according to Bishop de Castro Mayer, Archbishop Sigaud's clergy in Diamantina were "with few exceptions in favor of innovation, and unfortunately Archbishop Sigaud, especially after his last illness, no longer has the courage needed to face such a situation."[30] As for the over-prudent Nestor Adam, bishop of Sion, who had "warmly greeted

[26] Letter of Jan. 28, 1967.
[27] Interview with Joseph Lefebvre, ms. I, 46, 18-28.
[28] Letter of Ottaviani of July 27, 1966, cf. L. de Miles, Oct. 15, 1966; Letter of Siri of Aug. 30, 1966. Siri supported the Italian theological review *Renovatio*.
[29] Letter to V. Miles, March 3, 1967.
[30] Letter from Campos, May 21, 1967.

the setting up" of the bulletin the year before, he asked if they did not mind his judging it inopportune to subscribe or to allow his pastoral letters to appear in its pages.[31]

Thanks to benefactors the review struggled along with a few hundred subscribers, but this idea of interepiscopal links proved not to be viable. Meanwhile, the Archbishop rented a property in Rome and opened an international bookshop to sell good books. It was in operation between 1968 and 1969.

BRINGING TOGETHER THE TRADITIONAL PRESS

Archbishop Lefebvre's links with the directors of the main traditionalist reviews across the world gave him the idea of changing *Fortes in Fide* into an international information service for the traditionalist press. On the one hand, only thirty bishops maintained an interest in *Fortes in Fide*, and on the other, since the Archbishop had ceased to be Superior General, he no longer had the support of those Holy Ghost Fathers who had translated articles for him. After moving to a new apartment on Via Casalmonferrato, Archbishop Lefebvre visited various places in Europe because, as he said: "More than ever, I want to work to maintain the Faith."[32]

There were already some excellent journals. In France there was Canon P. Doazan's *Nouvelles de Chrétienté*, principally written by Dom Edouard Guillou, and André Lucq's[33] *Revue de la Presse Internationale*, published in Giles de Coüessin's CICES bulletin. Thus, Archbishop Lefebvre kept the same title for his review *Fortes in Fide*, but from March 1969 it became a weekly compendium of documents sent to forty different journals across the world. This made him freer to distribute polemical documents such as the invitation given by Fr. Louis Coache to his Corpus Christi celebration on June 16, 1968. The director of the newly founded *Combat de la Foi* wrote: "I invite priests and faithful…to come in large numbers to this corner of Vexin to proclaim their love for God, and their fidelity to the Faith of all time against modern heresy." He also published Fr. Coache's tract "Let Us Purify Our Churches!" which called on the faithful to remove from the piety stalls of their local churches all "so-called Catholic reviews that are in fact anti-Catholic." As the priest explained: "Besides, they are free, and it would be a wrong to leave a donation for them. So, Catholics, act in conscience!"

Moreover, from 1964, the Archbishop, who was at that time Superior General, took steps against "so-called Catholic journals that are 'filthy and immoral'" which were filtering into the minor scholasticates and apostolic

---

[31] Letter from Sion, Feb. 28, 1968, signed by Camille Grand.
[32] Letter to André Lucq, Jan. 19, 1969.
[33] Archbishop of region of Savoy, Chambéry, dos. 120 F, I, 5-6.

schools (St. Ilan, for example). To the mother of a family who was alarmed, he wrote: "Unfortunately, it is possible that they might be brought in without permission. They are in fact in all parishes and schools. It is insane! I can assure you that I am doing all I can to support the campaign against these reviews. I am outraged at the thought that these reviews are approved by the bishops. I am sorry that I am no longer a bishop in France for I would certainly have publicly protested. That is more difficult for me since I have no jurisdiction here."[34] On the other hand, in 1968 the Archbishop was free once more to support publicly the fight against the so-called Catholic press that was in fact corrupt.

The publications working together through *Fortes in Fide* needed to have more discussion in an effort to focus the war effort. This was why Archbishop Lefebvre called a meeting in Rome on March 8, 1969, for the directors of the newspapers and journals concerned. This small traditionalist press congress was a success: for example, Dr. Inge Köck from Ratisbonne, who translated for *Fortes in Fide*, refereed *Itinéraires,* and co-founded *Nunc et Semper,* wrote the Archbishop to express her gratitude for the "memorable few days in Rome that were terribly useful and encouraging."

The Archbishop helped co-ordinate the efforts of thirty-seven journals in fourteen countries. His moral authority was strengthened and he raised the courage of that section of the press that had been put out in the cold because of warnings from the bishops.[35]

ENCOURAGING PRIESTLY ASSOCIATIONS

It would be inaccurate to speak of March 8, 1969, as the date of the founding of the "traditionalist movement": it was nothing of the sort. However, Archbishop Lefebvre, whose inventive mind was full of ideas, had for a time thought about "setting up in Rome an international secretariat for the various traditionalist lay movements."[36] Dr. de Saventhem made the Archbishop think about another possibility for *Fortes in Fide*: "Provide the spiritual and administrative framework for an international secretariat" to help those priestly associations that are being founded here and there to bring together priests in the fight for the Faith and clerical discipline."

The Archbishop had already given his support to Fr. Coache and to the priests who put their name to the *Vade Mecum of the Catholic Layman.* He encouraged them "in the battle they are waging to preserve Catholic

[34] Letter to Mrs. Antier, Feb. 10, 1964.
[35] Cf. Warnings of the French episcopate in 1962 against *Verbe*; June 27, 1966, against *Défense du Foyer, Itinéraires, Le Monde et la Vie* (André Giovanni), *etc.*; warning of the Brazilian episcopate against *Catolicismo.*
[36] Project presented to Eric de Saventhem. Cf. Letter of Eric de Saventhem, Aug. 9, 1968.

Faith and Catholic morality which lead to, and are expressed by, Catholic worship. May God bless their efforts!"[37]

Archbishop Lefebvre also made contact with the *Asociación de sacerdotes y religiosos de San Antonio Claret* in Barcelona.[38] He drew up a list of seven such associations among which were the *Cephas* of Fr. J. W. Flanagan in Polegate, England, established to "prevent the spread of false doctrine by emphasizing pontifical teachings," and *Opus Sacerdotale* founded by Canon Etienne Catta in France. Hundreds of priests gathered at the congress in Segovia in 1969, and on November 11, a group from Barcelona sent Fr. Bugnini and Paul VI a petition signed by its six thousand priest members refusing "responsibility" for "casting good people into heresy"[39] through the New Mass. However, of the six thousand priests very few remained faithful to this resolution. Moreover, when the international congress of priestly associations met in Madrid in February 1970 to consider the proposal of an international federation,[40] it could not come to an agreement due to lack of unanimity and perseverance in rejecting the liturgical reforms.

After painfully racking their consciences, many priests who adopted the reformed Mass felt it was death to their souls. A parish priest from the archdiocese of Florence wrote in June 1969 to Bishop Celada: "I am living in a state of soul that I cannot describe. I am suffering, and sometimes I weep bitter tears. As the day gets nearer, I think about it in terror and I shudder. I would like to write, or go [*sic*] and throw myself at the feet of Paul VI to beg him to dispense me from offering this 'mass.'"[41] Archbishop Lefebvre would say: "I know priests who have died from the sorrow of having to say this New Mass," not to mention those who remained faithful to the Mass of all time, who were persecuted by their bishop, driven out of their parishes, demoted by their superiors, and only overcame these trials by a rare strength of character or heroic virtue.

SUPPORTING LAY MOVEMENTS

Unable to create a secretariat for lay movements, Archbishop Lefebvre maintained his support for the existing groups, and especially for Cité Catholique, which had become the *Office international des oeuvres de formation civique et d'action doctrinale selon le droit naturel et Chrétien* (International Office for Civil Training and Doctrinal Activities according to Natural and Christian Law). The Archbishop was often present at the an-

---

[37] Ferrey Printers, 4th Quarter, 1968.
[38] Letter of Frs. José Bachs and José Mariné, Sept. 22 and 29, 1969.
[39] Text in *Itinéraires*, no. 140 (Feb. 1970): 32.
[40] Letter of Fr. Dulac to General Lecomte, Nov. 16, 1969, and Feb. 21, 1970.
[41] Celada, "La mini-messa contro il dogma," in *Lo Specchio*, June 29, 1969.

nual[42] congress of the Lausanne office. In 1965 Roger Lovey, a lawyer from Valais (Switzerland), spoke on the topic "Church, State, and Information."

In 1966 Archbishop Lefebvre was given an audience by Paul VI and he asked the Pope for his blessing on the congress whose theme would be the role of lay people in civil society. The Archbishop said to Pope Paul VI: "These are people who are working for the Reign of our Lord Jesus Christ. This is the list of speakers."

"Ah," said Paul VI, "I don't know that one; I don't know that one. Oh! Michel de Saint Pierre....But Michel de Saint Pierre is not a Gaullist!"[43]

Taken aback, the Archbishop looked at the Holy Father. What did he mean? It was the only remark he passed. Finally he concluded: "Well, that's very good. I'm happy to be kept abreast of things. Can I keep the paper?"

Vatican radio broadcast its wishes for the success of the congress, but there was no papal blessing from Paul VI.[44]

The following year, the Archbishop turned to Cardinal Ruffini since the Congress was about the theme "Politics and Natural Law." The Cardinal sent his blessing, and spoke very highly of Archbishop Lefebvre: "I am sure that under the guidance of Your Grace, whose wisdom and total fidelity to the Magisterium of the Roman Church I have always admired, it [the Congress] will bring forth all the fruits that are hoped for."[45]

Through the International Office, Archbishop Lefebvre got to know the Knights of Our Lady. The *Militia Sanctae Mariae* was founded in 1945 by the future monk of St. Wandrille Dom Gérard Lafond. It was made an order of knights by the bishop of Chartres, Bishop Roger Michon, who was a former fellow student of Marcel Lefebvre at Santa Chiara (1922-28). Its members "by virtue of being dubbed Knights direct their efforts to bringing about a Christianity that will maintain the reign of Christ on earth which is as it were the apparel of His Mystical Body."[46] The Order was soon established in Valais and also in German-speaking Switzerland, where its name was *Marienritter vom Kostbaren Blute*.

---

[42] The Tenth Congress of the Cité Catholique had been held in 1960 at Issy-les-Moulineaux. The following congresses were held in Switzerland, at first at Sion, Valais.

[43] [Gaullists were the supporters of General de Gaulle, whose politics were situated on the French Republican Right. Pope Paul's assimilation of de Gaulle's politics with the agenda of the Cité Catholique is astounding; even if the Gaullists held to a conservative nationalist line that he might have supposed the Cité Catholique preferred, they nevertheless accepted the regime of the Republic with all its liberal and Freemasonic sympathies. Confusing this with the social reign of Christ the King is sloppy, to say the least, for a former diplomat. Trans.]

[44] *Spiritual Conferences at Ecône*, 26 B, Feb. 10, 1976.

[45] Letter from Palermo, March 13, 1967.

[46] Rule of the Knights of Our Lady, 1958, *imprimatur* 1965.

Through the Knights of Our Lady, the Order of Rouve, founded in 1960 by students at the University of Louvain, also rediscovered the chivalric traditions. Its first knights were dubbed in Riaumont by Bishop Rupp in 1967. Archbishop Lefebvre dubbed others at Serville at the home of the Count de Ribaucourt on May 25, 1969. One of them, a Belgian lawyer called Gerald Walliez, had already been present in Rome at the gathering of the traditionalist press. The Archbishop wrote a "Knight's Spiritual Guide" for the Knights of Rouve based on the theological and cardinal virtues; in it the knight is described as "a true companion-in-arms of our Lord, of her who is as strong as an army in battle array, and of the leader of the heavenly armies, the Archangel Saint Michael."[47]

Archbishop Lefebvre also gave much encouragement to the various movements of young Catholics springing up everywhere as if "by spontaneous generation." He admired their enthusiasm, writing in 1968: "We see the rise of a new generation,...young people thrilled by their discovery....They see that their minds' and hearts' desire has been hidden from them, and it is that treasure that has *transformed the world*. They have discovered...the true history of Christian civilization, and henceforth it becomes their life, their interior life, their life in society, and their ideal. They will never again abandon it."[48]

These words foreshadow the future work of Archbishop Lefebvre in the service of the Catholic priesthood and more precisely in priestly training. However, even from the beginning this work would be providentially hurled into an heroic battle for the Catholic Mass.

III. FACING THE REFORM OF THE MASS

ACTIVELY PARTICIPATING AND UNDERSTANDING WITH EASE[49]

On the grounds of providing for the faithful's "full, conscious, and active participation" as demanded by the conciliar constitution on the liturgy (promulgated on December 4, 1963), the theories of the innovators eventually came to corrupt the liturgy and the jewel in its crown, the Holy Sacrifice of the Mass. Since March 1963, Archbishop Lefebvre had fought against this ambiguous principle: "The ultimate end of prayer does not lie in understanding the texts, but in union with God. Sometimes focusing on the texts can be an obstacle to prayer. The soul finds union with God more in religious chant, the piety of the liturgy, recollection, the beauty of

---

[47] La Croix-Valmer, Jan. 6, 1970.
[48] "Lueurs d'espérance" (Glimmers of Hope), Rome, Aug. 15, 1968, in *Itinéraires*, no. 127: 227-228; cf. also *"Pour une vraie rénovation de l'Eglise"* (For a true renovation of the Church), in *A Bishop Speaks*, 54-55.
[49] Lefebvre, talk in Montréal, 1982, *Fideliter*, no. 85.

the architecture, the nobility and piety of the priest, symbolic decoration, the odor of incense, *etc.*"[50] The *Consilium for Liturgical Reform* instituted on February 26, 1964, was chaired by Cardinal Lercaro and run by Fr. Bugnini. It soon began not the "revision" asked for by the Council (*Sacrosanctum Concilium*, §5) but a radical and systematic overhaul of the liturgy and of the Mass in particular—a "genuine creation," as Bugnini would say. In doing this he applied the guiding principle of *Sacrosanctum Concilium* already put forth before the Council by Fr. Ferdinando Antonelli:[51] "Everything is directed to one end: to do whatever is necessary for the faithful (1) easily to understand the rites and (2) to become again what they must be: not only spectators but active participants in the liturgy."[52] According to Antonelli and Bugnini, these two things had been lost for centuries.

When he found this assertion later in Bugnini's *La Riforma liturgica*,[53] Archbishop Lefebvre was outraged: "It is false! The real teaching of history proves the very contrary. Imagine saying that all the faithful who were there for centuries—long before Bugnini existed—took part silently in Mass as spectators and strangers! Nothing could be further from the truth. Is the active participation of the faithful not their spiritual participation, which is far more important than exterior participation?"[54]

As he read *La Riforma*, Archbishop Lefebvre could discern in these false principles a doctrinal error and an underlying heresy: "Beneath it all—beneath, not formally—there is a heresy: it holds that the priesthood of the faithful and the priesthood of priests is the same; that everyone is a priest and that the People of God must offer the Holy Sacrifice of the Mass." Antonelli himself blamed Bugnini for "having involved in the work [of the *Consilium*] some individuals who were capable but who were also theologically progressive. He did so without resisting their thinking because [he said] certain tendencies could not be foiled." He recognized that "the current theories amongst forward thinking theologians concern the sacramental forms and the rites."[55]

---

[50] *General Bulletin*, 708 (March-April 1963): 428 and 430, our summary.

[51] With Fr. Bugnini a member of the commission set up by Pius XII (1948-1960), the Preparatory Commission for the Council (1960-62) and the *Consilium* (1964-1969).

[52] Nicola Giampietro, O.F.M. Cap., *Il card. Ferdinando Antonelli e gli sviluppi della riforma liturgica del 1948 al 1970* (Rome: Studia Anselmiana, 1998), 60, 64, 73, 79, 89, 101, 200, 203-204.

[53] Annibale Bugnini, *La riforma liturgica* (Rome: Centro Liturgico Vincenziano—Ed. Liturgiche, 1983), 1st ed., 50; 2nd ed., 55.

[54] *Spiritual Conferences at Ecône*, 111 A, June 12, 1982. Was the most traditional and effective exterior participation not the Gregorian chant popularized by Solesmes, in conformity with the wishes of St. Pius X? Cf. St. Pius X, *Motu proprio* on the restoration of sacred music and the reintroduction of Gregorian chant for the people, Nov. 22, 1903.

[55] Antonelli, *Diario*, April 1969, in N. Giampietro, *Il card. Ferd. Antonelli*, 264, 257.

These were the theories of the "new theology." Subtly changing the emphasis, this new theology highlighted the common priesthood of the baptized and no longer saw in the priest the individual who properly speaking carried out the functions of the priesthood;[56] the priest was now the one who "brings together the votive offerings of the faithful in the sacrifice of their Head" rather than the one who himself offers the sacrifice as the Minister of Christ the Priest.[57] The "Paschal mystery" celebrated in the Mass was more the triumphant Christ in His Resurrection than the Christ who expiates by His Passion;[58] sin was no longer considered as an injustice towards God and His rights, but only as something that harmed man and human solidarity; the Redemption brought about by Christ's offering of satisfaction and by the Father's propitiation was thus emptied of its substance: the cross of Christ was made void. A symbolic, sacramental theology made the Mass into a "memorial" of Christ's work of salvation, a memorial that re-presented, i.e., made that work present in the "living moment" of the community's liturgical action; in this sense the Mass was only a sacrifice because it was a "memorial."[59] The substantial presence of Christ in the species was buried in the memorial. The transubstantiation of bread and wine became superfluous: a transsignification sufficed.[60]

The harmful influence of this multiform albeit coherent and omnipresent gnosis escaped the notice of the uninitiated; Archbishop Lefebvre picked up on certain signs that were present in the logic of the successive, liturgical upheavals cleverly achieved step by step: turning the altar around, moving the tabernacle aside, suppression of the "individual prayers" of the priest (prayers at the foot of the altar), signs of the cross, etc., the Canon recited in a loud voice, and finally the invasive use of the vernacular to the point of its totally supplanting Latin—reforms all approved by Paul VI between 1964 to 1967.[61]

---

[56] Yves Congar, *Jalons pour une théologie du laïcat* (Cerf, 1953), 155, 178, 199-200, 243-244; criticized by Fr. Berto, *La Pensée Catholique*, no. 11 (1949): 31-46.

[57] *Lumen Gentium*, no. 28.

[58] J. Lecuyer, *Le sacerdoce dans le mystère du Christ* (Cerf, 1957).

[59] Cf. Odo Casel, *Faites ceci en mémoire de moi*, Lex Orandi, vol. 34 (1962), 165; *Le mystère du culte*, Lex Orandi, vol. 38 (1964), 26, 300. Benedictine monk of the German abbey of Maria Laach, Dom Casel put about his "mysteries" theory of the liturgy. Cf. *Jahrbuch für Liturgiewissenschaft*, from 1921.

[60] Y. de Montcheuil, *La présence réelle*, photocopy distributed by hand, analyzed by Garrigou-Lagrange (1946) and Piolanti (1951); Ed. Schillebeeckx, "Une question de théol. eucharistique: transsubstantiation, transfinalisation, transsignification," in *Revista di pastorale liturgica*, no. 16 (1966): 228-248, Queriniana, Brescia, analyzed by Msgr. Ugo Emilio Lattanzi: *Il misterium fidei nella teologia nuova e nella rivelazione*, March 23, 1967, photocopied for Archbishop Lefebvre.

[61] Instruction *Inter Œcumenici*, Sept. 26, 1964; *Tres Abhinc Annos*, May 4, 1967; *Eucharisticum Mysterium*, May 25, 1967.

On May 25, 1967, the association *Una Voce*, founded to preserve liturgical Latin and Gregorian chant, made a protest to Paul VI about the spread of the vernacular that was contrary to *Sacrosanctum Concilium* (no. 36, §1). Bishop Romoli, bishop of Pescia, wrote about the matter on August 17 to the Italian bishops' conference. Archbishop Lefebvre published this letter in *Fortes in Fide*.

However, up to this moment the reforms had only been provisional "alterations." For Bugnini and the *Consilium*, "it was a matter of giving new structures to entire rites ... and in certain respects creating something new." While the bishops waited for this reform, they had to "take initiatives, suggest adaptations and experiments, *etc.*" or else risk through their "opposition to change" being overrun by arbitrary[62] and individual experiments about which Paul VI was bitterly unhappy.[63] Against this permanent revolution in the liturgy encouraged "by the upper echelons" and incited "from below," Fr. Dulac spoke out in *Courrier de Rome*.

THE NORMATIVE MASS

On October 21, 1967, a synod of bishops was opened. They were told that Fr. Bugnini, secretary for the *Consilium*, would come to present his "normative Mass," the draft of the new Mass. In its inexorable logic it would apply the principles of *Sacrosanctum Concilium* which foresaw "rites of remarkable brevity"[64] (no. 34), "more ample reading from Sacred Scripture" (no. 35), the supposed logical restoration of the *Ordo Missae*, the suppression of "parts which with the passage of time came to be duplicated" (no. 50). The sacrificial Offertory was one of them: according to Fr. Bugnini did it not illogically anticipate what was said at the consecration? "Other parts which suffered loss through accidents of history are to be restored" (no. 50), *etc.* In addition, this normative Mass, so named because it was to become the norm for celebrating the reformed Mass, was deliberately conceived of as a "celebration with the people," thus diminishing the essential value of the Mass which is independent of the prayers of the faithful, as the Council of Trent recalled (DS 1747, 1758).

Archbishop Lefebvre soon saw the danger. Using an article of his collaborator Fr. Gerald Fitzgerald, C.S.Sp., to which he made some alterations, the Archbishop had the text "Regarding the New Mass" quickly photocopied. Before the meeting on October 24, it was secretly distributed to the bishops at the synod between the covers of *Fortes in Fide*.[65] The

---

[62] A. Bugnini, press conference, Jan. 4, 1967.

[63] Allocution to the *Consilium*, April 19, 1967, *Documentation Catholique*, 1493: 769.

[64] [This is translated as "noble simplicity" in the English version published in *Vatican II: The Conciliar and Post-conciliar Documents*, ed. Austin Flannery, O.P. (Northport, NY: Costello, 1975). Trans.]

Archbishop concluded: "The normative Mass or what is used as the basis for the liturgical reform cannot be a Mass requiring the participation of the faithful since this participation is accidental and not essential to the Mass."

The "Lefebvre effect" was considerable. The majority of Fathers, as Bugnini recognized, went to the Sistine Chapel on October 24 "on their guard and ill-disposed" to attend a "normative Mass" celebrated in Italian by the liturgist himself: welcoming rights, brief ceremony of penance all together, *Gloria*, three readings, *Credo*, bidding prayers, three short prayers for the "presentation of the gifts," an entirely new Canon, modified words of consecration, fewer signs of the cross or genuflections, *etc.*[66] Soon, several bishops, Archbishop Slipyj among them, left the Chapel in protest.[67]

On October 26, the Synod Fathers answered the question "Does the structure of the new Mass in general have your approval?" Out of 180 votes, 71 voted yes, 43 voted no, and 62 *juxta modum*. Paul VI asked the *Consilium* to get to work again and draw up a Mass apparently less revolutionary but which nevertheless would have, as Bugnini wished, "a completely different appearance from what it had before."[68]

In December 1967, during the gathering of the World Union of Superior Generals attended by Archbishop Lefebvre, Fr. Annibale Bugnini was invited to present his normative Mass. He did so very calmly: he said that to help the faithful to participate, (Rome) would change everything in the first half of Mass, suppress the Offertory, which only said what the Canon said, get rid of the prayers of the priest before communion, change and produce new Eucharistic prayers, *etc.* The Archbishop remarked:

> While listening to this conference, which lasted one hour, I said to myself: "How on earth can this man be trusted by the Holy Father? How can he have been the one chosen to reform the liturgy?" We had before us a man who was trampling on the ancient liturgy off-handedly and with unimaginable scorn. I was shattered, and even though I find it easy to speak in such gatherings, as I had done at the Council, I did not feel up to speaking. The words just stuck in my throat.
>
> However, two Superior Generals stood up to speak. The first said: "Father, if I understand rightly, now you've suppressed the *Confiteor* and the Offertory, shortened the Canon, *etc.* A private Mass is going to last ten or twelve minutes!" Fr. Bugnini replied, "We can always add something!" One could see what little importance he attached to the Mass and the way in which it was said.

65 A. Bugnini, *La riforma liturgica* (2nd ed., 1997), 347, and note 14; Archives of Archbishop Lefebvre at Ecône. Archbishop Lefebvre's name did not appear.
66 *Documentation Catholique*, 1506: 2077.
67 *Spiritual Conferences at Ecône*, 86 A, June 24, 1981.
68 A. Bugnini, press conference, Jan. 4, 1967, already quoted.

The second, a Benedictine abbot, spoke: "This active participation: is it a corporal participation or a spiritual participation?"—it was the right question—"The normative Mass is meant to be attended by the faithful, but we Benedictines say Mass without the faithful being there. What are we going to do now?" This was Bugnini's reply: "To be honest, we haven't thought about that!" That tells you a lot about this reform.[69]

BUT WHO IS THIS BUGNINI?[70]

Fr. Annibale Bugnini, C.M., who directed the *Ephemerides Liturgicae,* had been a member of the *commissio piana* (1948-1960), then secretary of the pre-conciliar commission (1960-62). However, in 1962 on the insistence of Cardinal Larraona, president of the conciliar commission for the liturgy, John XXIII had removed Bugnini from his chair for liturgy at the Lateran University. "I was accused of being an iconoclast," Bugnini admitted. The same "good Pope John" had not confirmed Bugnini's appointment as secretary to the conciliar commission and appointed instead Fr. Ferdinando Antonelli. Paul VI had wanted to "undo the injustice"[71] by appointing Bugnini as secretary of the *Consilium* in 1964. It is known that Annibale had asked for six Protestant ministers to be admitted as observers during the plenary meetings of the *Consilium*. In 1965 did not Bugnini alter the solemn prayers of Good Friday, removing, as he said, "anything that could constitute even the shadow of a stumbling block or cause displeasure" to the separated brethren?[72]

Besides, Archbishop Lefebvre had heard Archbishop Cesario D'Amato, abbot of St. Paul Outside-the-Walls,[73] say: "Excellency, don't talk to me about Fr. Bugnini. I know too much about him. Don't ask me what he is!" When the Archbishop insisted, the Abbot replied: "I can't talk to you about Bugnini."

Ferdinando Antonelli wrote similarly:[74] "I could say a lot about that man. I must add that he has always been supported by Paul VI. His most notable failing is his lack of training and theological sense."

In February 1969, the Archbishop visited Cardinal Amleto Cicognani, who was still Secretary of State, to tell him how sad he was about the

[69] *Spiritual Conferences at Ecône,* 30 B, March 26, 1976; 85 B, June 23, 1981; *Fideliter,* no. 85: 13.
[70] Lefebvre to A. Cagnon, *Relations between Rome and Ecône,* 17-24.
[71] Bugnini, *La Riforma* (2nd ed.), 44 and n. 5.
[72] *L'Osservatore Romano,* March 19, 1965; *Documentation Catholique,* 1445: 604.
[73] He was appointed in 1960 to the preparatory commission for liturgical reform to which Antonelli and Bugnini belonged (Giampietro, *Il card. Ferd. Antonelli,* 46-47).
[74] When Bugnini was appointed to the secretariat for the Congregation for Divine Worship that brought together the Sacred Congregation for Rites and the *Consilium* on May 8, 1969; Giampietro, *Il card. Ferd. Antonelli,* 264.

new Canons. Archbishop Lefebvre asked him: "Your Eminence, you cannot let this go! It's a revolution in the liturgy, in the Church."

The Cardinal put his head in his hands saying: "Oh, Your Excellency, I agree with you. But what do you want me to do? Fr. Bugnini can go to the Holy Father's office and get whatever he wants signed!"

The Archbishop added: "I am not the only one who heard it. He was speaking to me, but other people in the Secretary of State's office heard it too."[75]

Next he went to the Sacred Congregation for Worship with Fr. Coache. There he spoke to Cardinal Gut about Communion in the hand (for which the decree permitting the practice was being prepared in the *Consilium*). In the presence of Msgr. Antonelli, secretary of the congregation, the cardinal admitted to him: "I am Secretary for the Sacred Congregation for Worship, but I'm not in charge; you can easily guess who is." Turning to Antonelli, he continued: "If I'm asked, I'll kneel in front of the Holy Father and beg him not to allow such a thing, but only if I'm asked!"[76]

Bugnini's influence on Paul VI and the "dictatorial" manner of his decisions that went above the heads of the Prefects for the Congregation for Worship, was an enigma to Archbishop Lefebvre. In 1974, the Archbishop said: "It is certain that some unacceptable things went on between the Holy Father and the organizations controlled by Archbishop Bugnini. All of that will be come out later."[77] The Archbishop believed he had confirmation when at the merger of the Sacred Congregations for Divine Worship and the Sacraments on July 11, 1975, Paul VI relieved Bugnini of his duties and six months later appointed him pro-nuncio in Teheran. The rumor spread that Bugnini had lost compromising documents that revealed he was a Freemason. However, he said to Paul VI that he knew nothing about Freemasonry, or "what it is, what they do, or what its goals are."[78] In 1976, a series of apocryphal letters between Bugnini and a so-called grandmaster went the rounds, along with a list of many Curia prelates and others who had belonged to a secret society in Rome between 1963 to 1971. Bugnini, "Buan" to the other members, supposedly became a member on April 23, 1963.

---

[75] *Spiritual Conferences at Ecône*, 30 B, March 26, 1976, *Retreats Given at Ecône*, 2 A, Sept. 20, 1979.

[76] *Spiritual Conferences at Ecône*, 86 A, June 24, 1981. The cardinal was greatly pained to sign the instruction permitting Communion in the hand and did it only to obey the will of the Pope (instruction of May 29, 1969): *La Riforma*, 101.

[77] *Spiritual Conferences at Ecône*, March 12, 1974.

[78] Letter to Paul VI, Oct. 22, 1975, *La Riforma*, 104 (1st ed., 101). It was saying too much and too little at the same time...

Archbishop Lefebvre put faith in the rumor and the suspect documents. He wrote: "In Rome it has been discovered that he who was the soul of the liturgical reform is a Freemason."[79]
The mystery or the mystification remains.

THE *NOVUS ORDO MISSAE*—FIRST REACTIONS

Annibale Bugnini tried again and again six times, besieging Paul VI for ten months, to secure permission for three new Canons in the Mass with new words of consecration and the words "*Mysterium fidei*" removed: in fact they were to become an invitation to the faithful to acclaim the Paschal and eschatological mystery. The Holy Office under Ottaviani had no major objections.[80] Paul VI agreed, and it was to obey the Pope that on May 23, 1968, Cardinal Gut, Prefect of the Sacred Congregation for Rites, reluctantly signed the decree allowing the use of the three Canons from August 15.

When Archbishop Lefebvre said to him that in France Canon II, the shortest, was the one most commonly used, the cardinal was shattered: "I said it would be like that!"[81] Nevertheless, the letter of the *Consilium*, dated June 2, 1968, signed by Gut the president and Bugnini the secretary, was sent to the bishops' conferences with the texts of three "anaphores." An accompanying commentary praised their "linear construction and clear form," saying nothing about the role of the priest or the word *consecration*, and expressing pleasure at the "faithful's enthusiasm now that they are lively participants and no longer silent spectators in the sacred actions."[82]

Una Voce reacted on August 14 with a communiqué denouncing "a clear change of emphasis" that was also underlined by Dom Edouard Guillou in *Nouvelles de Chrétienté* in October 1968: transubstantiation was obscured in the "memorial" by removing the words "*Mysterium fidei*" from the consecration and making them into an acclamation of the faithful. However, the *Consilium* was coming to the final, heavy pruning in its changes to the Ordinary of the Mass: it suppressed the sacrificial Offertory "to remove the ambiguity of the 'little Canon,'" and modified the Roman Canon (words of consecration) in harmony with the new Canons.[83] At the

[79] Letter to Friends and Benefactors, no. 10, March 27, 1976; *Itinéraires*, no. 204.
[80] Bugnini, *La Riforma* (2nd ed.), 182 and note 66; 456 and note 10.
[81] On Feb. 13, 1969; *Spiritual Conferences at Ecône*, 86 A; *Nouvelles de Chrétienté*, no. 536.
[82] *Notitiæ*, no. 40 (May-June 1968): 147; *Documentation Catholique* 1520: 1171ff.
[83] *La Riforma* (2nd ed.), 375-380. On June 2, 1968, Paul VI had asked the prefects of the Curia's dicasteries their opinions on the latest reforms. Cardinal Seper, Ottaviani's successor, was thus consulted but seems not to have thought it useful to have a meeting of his congregation (the CDF). *Ibid.*, 369, 372; *Fideliter*, no. 85: 15.

consistory on April 28, 1969, Paul VI announced the new *Ordo Missae*. On May 2, in the press conference room, the Apostolic Constitution *Missale Romanum* (dated April 3), and the texts of the new *Ordo Missae* (NOM) (introduced by a long *Institutio Generalis*), were made public. Some Protestants very quickly declared themselves in favor of the NOM. Brother Max Thurian from the ecumenical community of Taizé stated in *La Croix* on May 30: "Perhaps one of the fruits will be that non-Catholic communities will be able to celebrate the Holy Supper with the same prayers as the Catholic Church. Theologically it is possible."

Fr. Dulac reacted on June 25 in *Courrier de Rome*: We refuse to give any support whatsoever to an ambiguity....We refuse to follow the new *Ordo Missae*." On July 10, he made clear the meaning of this refusal by organizing a petition to be sent to Paul VI, asking him "to revise radically" the NOM: "While we await an answer to our petition, we will openly, modestly, and with peace of soul continue to use the freedom protected by St. Pius V's[84] Constitution and by a four-centuries-old universal custom."

THE SHORT CRITICAL STUDY OF THE NOM

With the idea of presenting a petition to Pope Paul so that he might delay the introduction of the *Novus Ordo Missae* (planned for the end of November 1969) and see to its revision, Vittoria Guerrini (who inspired *Una Voce*) met with Archbishop Lefebvre to whom she was well known. Her *nom de plume* was Cristina Campo,[85] and together with her friend Emilia Pediconi, another lady of Roman society, she came to find the Archbishop. Since they could call whenever they wanted upon Cardinal Ottaviani, they were able to act as go-betweens. It was decided that a document would be written to be passed on to the cardinal who agreed in advance to revise it and submit it to the Pope.[86]

Vittoria Guerrini managed to assemble five or six churchmen including Msgr. Renato Pozzi, former Council expert and member of the Sacred Congregation for Studies, Msgr. Guerrino Milani from the same Congregation, and notably Msgr. Domenico Celada, who had a reputation as a liturgist and had written some hard-hitting articles.[87] Archbishop Lefebvre

---

[84] Granting to every priest in perpetuity power to offer freely the Mass he was codifying.

[85] Cf. Christina de Stephano, *Belinda e il mostro, vita segreta di Christina Campo* (Milan: Ed. Adelphi, 2002), 127-139.

[86] *Spiritual Conferences at Ecône*, 69 A, Feb. 8, 1979; *Fideliter*, no. 85, p. 14, P. Guérard des Lauriers, *Introduction to the BCS*, published by St. Jeanne d'Arc Publishers, minimizes Archbishop Lefebvre's role.

[87] Cf. *Sodalitium*, French ed. no. 49: 74 and article of Msgr. Celada, "La mini-messa contro il dogma," in *Lo Specchio*, June 29, 1969; *Contre Réforme Catholique*, no. 23, Aug. 1969.

also asked Fr. M.-L. Guérard de Lauriers, O.P., who contributed to *La Pensée Catholique*, to take part.

As a bishop, Archbishop Lefebvre chaired the first meeting and some of the night-time gatherings which took place "at a punishing rhythm" on the premises of *Una Voce* in Rome between May and June 1969. Fr. Guérard de Lauriers wrote the text which was discussed in the meetings, dictated by him as they went along, and immediately translated into Italian by V. Guerrini. She herself clarified and completed the document, notably as regards the liturgy. Without having studied theology, these Roman ladies "had it in their blood."

The Italian text was sent to Cardinals Ottaviani and Bacci. Archbishop Lefebvre begged other friends amongst the cardinals to help, but although they read it they were afraid to sign it. The Archbishop also hoped to secure the signatures of numerous bishops among whom were sixty Italians. In the meanwhile, he had the text translated into French (Fr. Guérard), German (Elizabeth Gerstner), Spanish (Don Luigi Severini), and English (Professor Anderson). He also arranged to have it published by various reviews and organizations friendly to *Fortes in Fide* after it had been sent to the Pope.

However, time was passing. The cardinal had kept the document "on the back burner" for several months. Doubtless he thought he had to study it in-depth before submitting it to the Holy Father. Besides, he was without doubt embarrassed by the fact that two years earlier he had given his *nihil obstat* to the three new anaphora. Pen and paper in hand, Msgr. Pozzi came to speak to the cardinal, who was blind. Ottaviani passed remarks on numerous points and said in particular: "It's radical to claim that the new Mass is contrary to Trent, but as uncomfortable as it may seem, it's true."

Finally on September 13 after much insistence, Cardinal Ottaviani's approbation for the *Short Critical Study* was secured and he signed a letter addressed to Paul VI. Cardinal Bacci signed it in turn on September 28. Other signatures were sought in vain: there were none, not even Bishop Carli's. Meanwhile, on October 15, Fr. De Nantes prematurely published the letter of the cardinals—with only Ottaviani's signature—in his *Catholic Counter-Reformation* newsletter. There could henceforth be no delay and the petition dated September 3, the feast of St. Pius X, was submitted to Paul VI with the *Short Critical Study* on October 21.[88]

---

[88] Michael Davies, *Pope Paul's New Mass, The Liturgical Revolution*, vol. III, (Kansas City: Angelus Press, 3rd ed., 1992), 493-494. We have corrected some errors in dates and facts. Antonio Bacci, a fine Latinist and active propagandist for liturgical Latin, had written a preface to Tito Casini's book *La tunique déchirée*, a work that provoked Paul VI's anger.

A "STRIKING DEPARTURE" FROM THE DOCTRINE OF THE MASS

The *Short Critical Study* firstly analyzes the *Institutio Generalis*, and picks out from Article 7 this wholly new description of the Mass: "In the Mass or Lord's Supper, the People of God are called together into one place where the priest presides over them and acts in the person of Christ. They assemble to celebrate the memorial of the Lord, which is the sacrifice of the Eucharist. Hence the promise of Christ: 'Wherever two or three are gathered in my name, there am I in the midst of them' (Mt. 18:20)." According to the *Short Critical Study*, this quasi-definition does not present the Mass as a sacrifice but rather as a meal.[89] It obliterates the intrinsic value of the Mass by making it depend upon the gathering of the people. It reduces the minister of Christ the Priest to a simple president of the assembly, and the substantial presence of Christ to a mere spiritual presence. Finally, according to other passages from the *Institutio Generalis*, the "memorial of the Lord" is the memorial of Christ's Resurrection as well as His Passion.

Going next onto a rigorously organized analysis of the *Ordo Missae* itself, the *Short Critical Study* notes that: (1) By suppressing the prayers of the Offertory and the prayers to the Holy Trinity, the propitiatory end of the Mass is passed over in silence. (2) The subtle changes to the words of consecration suggest a simple narration of what Jesus did at the Last Supper and not the actual change of the bread and wine into the body and blood[90] of Christ by the action of the priest. They remove the emphasis on the actions of the priest to highlight the idea of commemoration in which the "priesthood of the people" comes into play.[91] (3) The suppression of numerous signs of the cross, bows, genuflections, the purifications and care taken with regard to particles of the host, *etc.* suggest that the presence of Christ in the Eucharist is only real when it is received (in Communion) or that it is only spiritual. (4) Finally, the suppression of the "personal" prayers of the priest along with the other changes dilutes the hierarchical priesthood and the ministry of the priest, who no longer appears to be alone capable of consecrating and offering the body and blood of the Redeemer "in the person of Christ the Priest."

This was why the letter of the two cardinals came to the following judgments: "...the *Novus Ordo Missae*...represents, both as a whole and in

---

[89] Cf. also nn. 8, 48, 55 d, 56 and the expressions "Lord's Supper or Mass," "*Convivium paschale*," "participating together at the Lord's table," in spite of no. 259: "At the altar, the sacrifice of the Cross is made present under sacramental signs," which says both too much and too little since it omits transubstantiation.

[90] The *Short Critical Study* does not comment on the introduction of "take and eat," "take and drink" in the words of consecration, but focuses on the question of punctuation that Archbishop Lefebvre considered secondary.

[91] Here we see the major themes of the new theology of the sacraments.

its details, a striking departure from the Catholic theology of the Mass as it was formulated in Session 22 of the Council of Trent. The 'canons' of the rite definitively fixed at that time erected an insurmountable barrier against any heresy which might attack the integrity of the Mystery."

THE "LEFEBVRE EFFECT" AGAIN

In conclusion, the cardinals believed that "the subjects for whose benefit a law is made have always had the right, nay the duty, to ask the legislator to abrogate the law, should it prove to be harmful," and they begged Paul VI not to "deprive us of the possibility of continuing to have recourse to the integral and fruitful Missal of St. Pius V, so highly praised" by His Holiness.

Paul VI received the petition on October 21, 1969. Moved by the authority of the two signatories, he sent the documents the following day to Cardinal Seper, asking the CDF to carry out a "rigorous examination of the criticisms made." Franjo Seper was concerned and spoke to Cardinal Gut. Both of them were deeply shocked and spoke to Fr. Bugnini.[92] Seper asked Bugnini to suspend the definitive publication of the *Ordo Missae*[93] and have the *Short Critical Study* examined by three theologians of the CDF.

The cardinals' intervention—the new "Lefebvre effect"—was succeeding. Already, Ottaviani's name, the objective of the petition, and the nature of the documents that accompanied it were made public in the press without the Cardinal making a retraction.[94] Bishop de Castro Mayer received the *Short Critical Study* in September and made a résumé of the document for his priests. He also sent a copy to Paul VI, accompanied by a letter dated September 12, asking the Pope's permission to continue to make use of the *Ordo Missae* of St. Pius V. Elsewhere, from October 10 to 15, *Una Voce Romana* brought together seventy noteworthy laymen and priests,[95] among whom was Archbishop Lefebvre.[96] In a final press com-

---

[92] Antonelli's diary, Oct. 31, 1969, in *30-Tage*, no. 11 (1998) and *Dokumentation zum Zeitgeschehen*, no. 6 (Jaidhof, 1998), following Giampietro, *Il card. Ferd. Antonelli*, 259.

[93] Letter of the CDF, Oct. 25, 1969; Bugnini, *La Riforma* (2nd ed.), 287-288.

[94] However, he wrote Dom Lafond on February 17, 1970, congratulating him on the "doctrinal note"—we will return to this—but regretting that his letter to Paul VI had been published without his personal permission, which was false since Fr. Dulac had received his permission, and he said he was "extremely happy" with the doctrinal clarifications given by Paul VI in his addresses of November 19 and 26.... Jean Madiran rightly accused the blind cardinal's secretary of dishonesty for having had the cardinal sign this most unlikely letter. Cf. Dom Lafond, *Note doctrinale sur le N.O.M.* (Doctrinal Note on the NOM), supplement of *Défense du Foyer*, Feb. 1970; commentary of Jean Madiran, *Itinéraires*, April supplement, 1970; Davies, *Pope Paul's New Mass*, 495.

muniqué, they asked for the abrogation or, at the least, the reform of the *NOM*.

Archbishop Lefebvre had already asked his canonist friend Fr. Dulac to prepare a case "showing that numerous reasons allow and encourage the keeping of at least the Offertory and Roman Canon."[97] Fr. Dulac produced his arguments on December 24: on the one hand, Paul VI had surreptitiously added a sentence of twenty-two words to the first edition of the Apostolic Constitution fixing the implementation of the *NOM* for November 30; on the other hand the desire expressed at the end of the constitution "that these laws and prescriptions be firm and effective now and in the future," only concerned the new formulae of the consecration introduced for "pastoral reasons" and "convenience"—motives which were, said Dulac, "so doubtful in themselves that their doubtfulness redounds on the prescription, if indeed it is a prescription."

Lastly, the final clause was neither precise enough in its content nor firm enough in its resolve to abrogate or obrogate[98] St. Pius V's constitution *Quo Primum*. Therefore one could apply Canon 23: *In dubio revocatio legis praeexsistentis non praesumitur, sed leges posteriores ad priores trahendae sunt et his, quantum fieri possit, conciliandae.* (In doubt, the revocation of a previous law is not presumed; rather, later laws are to be related to earlier ones and, as far as possible, harmonised with them.) The conclusion followed that Paul VI had certainly "not wanted to make his missal obligatory, in a truly juridical sense."[99]

Fr. Dulac had already raised two other arguments in *Courrier de Rome* on July 10: The perpetual indult given to every priest by St. Pius V to use the missal he promulgated did not seem to be revoked by Paul VI's constitution; and it could be asked whether the custom of a millennium that the Pope had only codified could ever be abrogated. In fact, as early as 1967, Raymond Dulac had stated a very radical juridical principle: "Every law is ordained to the common good; insofar as it falls short in that respect, it has no binding force."

---

[95] Among whom were Louis Salleron and Frs. Coache, Dulac, Lefèvre, Guérard, and Michel André, C.S.Sp.; the last of these had been expelled as a missionary from Guinea and was parish priest of Monte Coman in Argentina. Invited to the meeting by Archbishop Lefebvre, he became a "missionary" for fidelity to the traditional Mass in South America before returning to Angers in France in April 1971.
[96] Archbishop Lefebvre left Rome on October 11 for Fribourg.
[97] Letter to Bishop de Castro Mayer, Fribourg, Oct. 16, 1969.
[98] Abrogation or *express revocation* comes from a formal stipulation [that a law no longer applies. Trans.]. Obrogation or implicit *revocation* comes, for example, from the publication of a new law whose details contradict the existing law, or which completely reorganizes the matter as it is dealt with by the law (Can. 22).
[99] *Itinéraires*, no. 140 (Feb. 1970): 39-40.

All that was very well and good, but it was Jean Madiran who raised the most fundamental objection to Paul VI's reform: "To reject systematically the rites *handed down*, to replace them by rights *which have not been handed down* is to ruin entirely the traditional character of the liturgy."[100]

PAUL VI SACRIFICES THE MASS

To nip in the bud the campaign that was developing and the resistance being organized against the NOM, Paul VI acted swiftly. On October 30, Msgr. Bugnini was ordered by Archbishop Benelli from the Secretariat of State to publish the instruction straightaway—it had already been sent to the bishops' conferences on October 20—announcing a gradual introduction of the New Mass[101] and allowing use of the old *Ordo Missae* until November 28, 1971.

On receiving the instruction, the Italian bishops' conference decided to wait until 1971. Around November 3, in *L'Osservatore Romano*, an anonymous note appeared claiming that the Italian bishops were implementing the NOM from November 30, 1969. When Cardinal Poma, president of the Italian bishops' conference, was questioned, he was not aware of the matter. Outraged, Bishop Carli wanted to open canonical proceedings against the newspaper, suspecting that the *Consilium* were really behind this attempt to apply pressure.

On November 12, through the Secretariat of State, Cardinal Seper sent the Pope the results of his theologians' analysis of the *Short Critical Study*: "The work *Short Critical etc.* contains lots of superficial, exaggerated, inaccurate, intemperate, and false statements."[102] In the end, Paul VI asked the *Consilium* to correct Article 7 of the *Institutio Generalis* (which nonetheless remained ambiguous), but he did not correct the *Novus Ordo Missae* that went with it. He thought it necessary to give two addresses justifying his reform in the name of "obedience to the express will of the recent Council." In the first, on November 19, he claimed that the new Mass was orthodox, and confirmed that it would be "obligatory" in Italy ten days later. In the second, on November 26, he justified "a change that affects a venerable tradition of many centuries, and thus the inheritance of our religious patrimony that it had seemed one ought not to touch." Paul VI said it was "a very great sacrifice" but "understanding the prayers is more important than the worn-out silk vestments with which it [the old liturgy] was bedecked; what is also more important is that people nowadays take part: they want to be spoken to clearly and in a way that is under-

---

[100] *Ibid.*, no. 137 (Nov. 1969): 298.
[101] By giving the episcopal conferences the power to decide (when the vernacular translations were approved) when the NOM could be *allowed*.
[102] Bugnini, *La Riforma* (2nd ed.), 288.

standable and can be translated into their everyday language." The Pope concluded: "If the noble Latin language cut us off from children, young people, and the world of work and business, and if it was a dark screen instead of being as clear as crystal, would we who fish for souls be calculating wisely by keeping it as the exclusive language of prayer and religion?"[103]

Archbishop Lefebvre had refuted these specious arguments as long ago as 1963 and was scandalized by the idea invoked by Paul VI of obeying the Council, and even more by the unusual praise the Pope heaped on the Roman Mass, "the inviolable, traditional expression of our religious worship and of the authenticity of our Faith," just prior to sacrificing it to modernity. The internal contradiction and tyrannical weakness of a profoundly liberal man seemed to him glaringly obvious. The Archbishop would eventually come to oppose this Pope: Archbishop Lefebvre was resolved to keep the authentic Catholic priesthood for the Church, and could not imagine doing so without the Catholic Mass.

---

[103] *Documentation Catholique*, 1552 (Dec. 7, 1969); the *Contre Réforme Catholique*, Jan. 1970.

PART IV

THE RESTORER

CHAPTER 16

FOR THE CATHOLIC PRIESTHOOD

I. SEMINARIANS IN DISTRESS

In Libreville, Mortain, and Dakar, Archbishop Lefebvre had ended up training future priests without having ever intended getting involved in such work. He would now be led by "providential circumstances," as he said, to do what he did not intend. As Superior of the Holy Ghost Fathers he attempted to reform the scholasticates, and from 1962 onwards priests, families, and candidates for the priesthood who were looking for solid training came to seek his help at Rue Lhomond. "Hoping to revive the solid traditions of the French Seminary manned by the congregation, I directed these vocations to Rome. There were around twenty of these young seminarians. Unfortunately, I soon had to recognize that, with one or two exceptions,[1] those running the seminary were leading it towards its ruin, just like the seminaries in France, despite all my efforts to avert such a thing."[2]

ATTEMPTED REFORM AT SANTA CHIARA

Fr. Barq, who was rector of the seminary from 1963 onwards, had seemed to Archbishop Lefebvre the right man for a difficult job: there were thirty-nine French bishops staying at Santa Chiara for the Council. However, this priest, who owed his appointment to a proposal of the French bishops, felt quite independent of his Superior.

"He [the Archbishop] took me to task for having told the bishops who were staying at the Seminary that I was determined to train students to work for them in their dioceses, according to their directives and in the spirit of the Second Vatican Council. He reminded me that the Holy Ghost Fathers and not the French bishops had founded, and were responsible for, the French Seminary."[3]

The Superior General's observation was not received favorably according to Fr. Paul Aulagnier, a seminarian at the time:

---

[1]   Fr. Aulagnier singles out Fr. Simon and Frs. Larnicol and Rozo.
[2]   Diary of Fribourg, 1969-1970, 1.

Not one day went by without some speaker, bishop, or theologian telling us in the corridors or in a spiritual talk about how the Conciliar debates were progressing. I was once in a corridor when Fr. Congar, who was staying at the seminary, emerged from the elevator: Old Barq bowed deeply to him...he was the master. The Council dominated the seminary and everything was called into question. The liturgy underwent official innovations: the altar was turned round, there was concelebration, the office was said in French, and "liturgical teams" dreamed up improvisations. As for the cassock, there were only three of us wearing it by 1968.

Archbishop Lefebvre, who was the canonical superior, sometimes came to the seminary. The first of his talks that I attended really struck me: he was the only bishop who spoke to us about the priesthood or about our vocation, making merely a simple allusion to the Council. His talk was about the ideal of the priesthood, and from that moment I was impressed by this bishop's wisdom, his calm, and his peace, this blend of simplicity and stature.

From then on with one of two other seminarians, we would use all kinds of ruses to go and ask his advice on the spiritual life as inconspicuously as possible. "Be edifying," he said, "be diligent in your morning prayer, maintain a positive attitude, work, don't let yourselves be dragged down."

With this hardcore, we hoped, like Archbishop Lefebvre, to be able to have a positive influence on the way the seminary was going. For example, I managed to have Dom Guillou's *Nouvelles de Chrétienté*, *Permanences*, *La Pensée Catholique*, and *Itinéraires* ordered for the reading room.[4]

At first Fr. Barq was not hostile to the seminarians for whom Fr. Aulagnier was the spokesman and initiator, if not the leader. However, the rector had his own perspective on the matter: "Archbishop Lefebvre had been an influence on some of the followers of Canon Berto, Fr. de Nantes,[5] Fr. Coache and Salleron,[6] in line with the thinking of *La Pensée Catholique*. They told him about my decisions, talks, and sermons. But I must say that they did not manage to change the general direction the seminary was going in, nor create open opposition or trouble. I always welcomed them kindly and listened as best I could."[7]

---

[3] Fr. Roland Barq, a former pupil of Fr. Lefebvre in Mortain, sent by him to Rome to study theology; he was a missionary in Madagascar from 1951 onwards. As Apostolic Delegate, Archbishop Lefebvre appointed him Vicar General to Bishop David in Majunga. As Superior General, he appointed him as rector of the French Seminary with the agreement of the French bishops. R. Barq, Letter from Mahajanga to Fr. J.-M. L., July 21, 1998.

[4] Fr. Paul Aulagnier, *La Tradition sans peur* (Paris: Ed. Servir, 2000), ch. 3; *Fideliter*, no. 59: 109-113; Interview with Bishop Tissier de Mallerais, 1996 and 1997.

[5] Doubtless this is inaccurate.

[6] Louis Salleron, the father of Fr. Bruno Salleron who was then a student at Santa Chiara, Fr. Georges Salleron, and Fr. Joseph de Sainte-Marie, O.C.D.

[7] Letter from Mahajanga to Fr. J.-M. L., July 21, 1998.

On the defensive, the rector could only see the least important aspect of what was a healthy reaction against the innovations that he authorized. At the Gregorian, Fr. Dhanis showed the same weaknesses: one day during class, he suggested that teaching no longer be conducted in Latin. Fr. Aulagnier was the only one to challenge him, explaining his position in Latin to the priest: "If the courses are no longer taught in Latin, the seminarians will not be able to understand their breviaries or the Fathers. They will no longer read the commentators of St. Thomas, and the liturgy would not be able to remain in Latin. It would be a terrible impoverishment for the priests, who would be cut off definitively from the Church's inheritance." The priest agreed: "You are right." Latin still disappeared. Later, when a professor of Patristics was openly scornful of scholasticism and Thomistic teaching, Paul Aulagnier conspicuously left the *aula* and later returned to explain the reason for his reaction to the teacher.

FR. THEODOSIUS'S SOCIETY

According to Archbishop Lefebvre "the persecution against good, sound seminarians" soon began. The review *Nouvelles de Chrétienté* was banned for "openly criticizing the Conciliar constitution on the liturgy." Other similar journals suffered the same fate. Then, said Paul Aulagnier: "Several of us asked to receive the tonsure and the minor orders but were refused. As for me, I understood that it was useless asking. We turned more and more towards Archbishop Lefebvre." In anguish, the seminarians became more insistent: "Your Grace, if you do not intervene, the priesthood will be closed off to us."

The Archbishop would later say: "I could not have imagined where that cry of distress would lead. With great sorrow we had to give in and look for other places, other universities. Two were still sound in what they taught: the Lateran and Fribourg. So, we had to look for somewhere near these places for our good seminaries to be trained properly for the priesthood. Faced with the difficulty of entering the Lateran seminary, we had to look at a Society then being sponsored by the wonderful Cardinal Siri, Archbishop of Genoa."

The Society of the Most Blessed Virgin Mary[8] was founded in Athens by Fr. Theodosius Sgourdelis,[9] a Greek diplomat and ship-owner who converted from Greek Orthodoxy and was ordained by Cardinal Siri. His Society was established in Genoa, and consisted of a community of sisters and an embryonic male community. Thanks to the generosity of the Countess de Kinnoul, this society was able to move to Rome, and at the

---

[8] Archbishop Lefebvre had heard talk of *Renovatio* from Dec. 1966, cf. Letter of Dr. Giovanni Baget Bozzo, Nov. 30, 1966.

[9] Theodosius-Mary of the Cross, his name in religion, † May 19, 1989.

beginning of the school year in 1967, it welcomed a group of eight students from Santa Chiara, led by seminarian Christian Charlot. These young men followed courses at the Lateran University; Archbishop Lefebvre watched over them attentively, and the generosity of his benefactors enabled them to rent a larger house which the Archbishop blessed on August 15, 1968. Nevertheless, Paul Aulagnier was not attracted by the atmosphere of a community that he found too cloistered; he remained at Santa Chiara. Later, Archbishop Lefebvre was sorry to lose five or six solid students to Fr. Theodosius; had they stayed, the Archbishop would have had enough students to make his Fribourg foundation viable.

"It was wise not to ignore the advantages of Fribourg.[10] That is why I took advantage of our residence[11] on Rue du Botzet and sent some seminarians to Fribourg University, all the while regretting that these young candidates for the priesthood would not find the desired training at the priory. There, at least, they were in peace, far from the bullying of rotten seminarians. That was the situation until 1968 when I resigned as Superior General."

AT THE CROSSROADS—THE DREAM OF DAKAR

Archbishop Lefebvre found himself at a crossroads. Retired at sixty-three, he could have contented himself with his salaried post as consulter for the Sacred Congregation for the Propagation of the Faith. He could have led the quiet life that Paul VI referred to in 1972 as his "calm retirement."[12] However, the growing disintegration of the institution of the priesthood led him to form a plan to transmit the precious inheritance he had received at Rome from the hands of Fathers Le Floch, Voegtli, Frey, and Le Rohellec. When still an archbishop in Africa, he had a premonition of this work, but did not know when it was to be carried out. Only late in his long life, in his *Spiritual Journey* (December 8, 1989), did he reveal to his sons the vision of the future that had inspired his actions:

> ...The dream was to transmit, before the progressive degradation of the priestly ideal, in all of its doctrinal purity and in all of its missionary charity, the Catholic Priesthood of Our Lord Jesus Christ, just as He conferred it on His Apostles, just as the Roman Church always transmitted it until the middle of the twentieth century.

---

[10] University of Fribourg, founded in 1889 by Georges Python as a sign of Swiss Catholicism's freedom and the Thomist revival promoted by Leo XIII. The theology and philosophy faculties were entrusted to the Dominicans. Prestigious figures such as Pierre Mandonnet or Santiago Ramirez had taught St. Thomas there. It still had an illustrious faculty including the great Dominicans Ceslas Spicq, Thomas Mehrle, Jean Henri Nicolas, Louis-Bertrand Geiger, Arthur F. Utz, and M.-Dominique Philippe.

[11] [*I.e.,* The priory of the Holy Ghost Fathers. Trans.]

[12] Letter to Archbishop Lefebvre for his 25th episcopal jubilee.

How should I carry out that which appeared then to me as the sole solution to revive the Church and Christianity? It was still a dream, but there appeared to me already the need, not only to confer the authentic priesthood, to teach not only the *sana doctrina* approved by the Church, but also to transmit the profound and unchanging spirit of the Catholic priesthood and of the Christian spirit essentially bound to the great prayer of Our Lord which His Sacrifice on the Cross expresses eternally.

The priestly truth is totally dependent upon this prayer; that is why I have always been haunted by the desire to show the means for true priestly sanctification according to the fundamental principles of Catholic doctrine concerning Christian and priestly sanctification.[13]

Ever since his return to Europe, one desire had gripped him more and more: to found an international seminary according to these principles. During Easter week 1964, with two cousins from Châteauneuf-de-Galaure, he met Marthe Robin[14] and told her of his preoccupation. Marthe said without hesitation: "Your Grace, you must found this seminary!"

The Archbishop objected: "My responsibilities as Superior of the Holy Ghost Fathers prevent me from doing so."

Marthe repeated: "You must found this seminary and God will bless you."[15]

The idea of this international seminary started to take shape two years later: Archbishop Lefebvre was offered a property in the diocese of Aire and Dax. He entered into negotiations with the bishop, Robert Bézac, who had been his friend at Santa Chiara. While visiting Maylis Abbey in the diocese on July 31, 1966, he told the Father Prior, Dom Fulgence-Marie Lagrâce,[16] about his project (which would come to nothing). Six months later, his friend Bishop Morilleau brought him back to the subject: "Then, there is your great 'international seminary'! That really would be the mother of all projects! Is your 'Maylis idea' providential perhaps?"[17]

If asked, Fr. Berto said he would be ready to take part in such a project and leave his work at Pontcalec[18] at a moment's notice. However, God called him home on December 17, 1968.

While the benefactors of the Archbishop were supporting the seminarians studying in Rome whom we have mentioned (as well as several others), eight or ten candidates who had never been seminarians were sent to him between 1967 and 1968 by his former fellow students: Luc Lefèvre, V.-A. Berto, and Bernard Le Roux, and also by Canon Poncelet. Moreover,

---

[13] Marcel Lefebvre, *Spiritual Journey* (Angelus Press, 1991), iii.
[14] A privileged soul, bedridden by her pains. Her spiritual director was Fr. Finet, a former fellow student of the Archbishop at Santa Chiara.
[15] Lefebvre, Letter to Mrs. Peyret, of St-Etienne, Jan. 9, 1983.
[16] Letter of Dom Augustin-Marie Joly, abbot emeritus of Flavigny, March 11, 2001.
[17] Bishop Morilleau, Letter from Malaga, Jan. 10-11, 1967, Archives of *Fortes in Fide*.
[18] Cf. Berto, *Notre Dame de Joie*, 23.

by the end of 1968, Fr. Theodosius said he did not want to take more than ten seminarians, whom he meant to train as religious. In addition, during a brief visit to Fribourg at the end of March 1969, Archbishop Lefebvre heard from Fr. Bussard that they no longer wanted to house his seminarians at Botzet. He said: "I had this conviction which nothing could shake, that to save and continue the Church, one had to train priests: holy priests and true priests."[19]

Haunted by this overwhelming thought, he looked for houses in Fribourg whose university was certainly attractive and where the seminarians could really get good training. The Ordinary, Bishop Charrière, was consulted and gave his approval to the plan and even pointed the Archbishop in the direction of the interdiocesan seminary, the *Salesianum*. Charrière was, however, pessimistic about the future of priestly training.[20] Archbishop Lefebvre went to the *Salesianum* but remarked: "Here again, everything was wanting, and the rector of the *Salesianum* openly admitted it. The Marianist prior was equally frank: 'Here we no longer have a rule.'"

The Archbishop then went to Valais where he saw a property with possibilities, and wrote a letter about it to his friend Bishop Adam, the bishop of the diocese. Adam wisely—or prudently—advised him: "Setting up a seminary such as the one you envisage would certainly be easier at Fribourg. Being near a university where St. Thomas is still honored would make things a lot easier."[21] Such was also the opinion of his friend and confidant Dom Jean Roy, Abbot of Fontgombault, who wrote to him on May 5, 1969. He had just visited Fribourg where he met Fr. Marie-Dominique Philippe:[22] "The international seminary must be opened in the town next October."

However, Archbishop Lefebvre would not yet admit he was convinced: "I was searching in France in despair. The Brothers of St. Vincent de Paul[23] at Erigné took in two seminarians. But that was not the solution. The only thing for me to do was to make a foundation myself at Fribourg."

II. THE FOUNDATION AT FRIBOURG

THE DECISION

Fr. Aulagnier witnessed the decisive scene:

---

[19] *Retreats at Ecône*, 83 A, Holy Week 1988.
[20] Lefebvre, *Petite histoire*, 57-58.
[21] Bishop Nestor Adam, Letter of April 13, 1969.
[22] Professor of Greek philosophy and especially of Aristotle at the University of Fribourg.
[23] Who remained faithful to the spirit of their founder Jean-Léon Le Prévost.
Archbishop Lefebvre knew Fr. Paysant, superior of their "Seminary for Workers' Missions" at Murs-Erigné.

I was doing my national service. I came to Fribourg on leave to visit my fellow student from Rome, Pierre Piqué, whom Archbishop Lefebvre had sent to Rue du Botzet. I arrived and found the Archbishop himself who invited me with my friend to a meeting. There we were on Grand'rue in the library of our host, Professor Bernard Faÿ,[24] an upstairs room in a grand house overlooking the Sarine. There were Fr. Marie-Dominique, O.P., Dom Bernard Kaul, Fr. d'Hauterive, and Jean-François Braillard, who was the father of a young family and headed the Fribourg state education department. We were amazed to see these individuals exchanging reflections on the decline of the priesthood.

Archbishop Lefebvre recalled:

They literally took me by the scruff of the neck and said: "Something must be done for these seminarians!" It was useless my saying that I was sixty-five and retired, or that it was foolish to begin something that I could not continue if I should die within the next few years... They wouldn't have it.

They said: "Get it going. You will have more students!" "We can find you some," added Fr. Philippe, "I know a few. We have to have good elements straightaway at the university to support the teachers who are still holding on."

"Okay," I said to them, "I'll go and see Bishop Charrière. If he says yes, that will be a sign of Providence."[25]

Fr. Aulagnier reminisced: "I can still see Fr. M.-D. Philippe fervently kissing Archbishop Lefebvre's ring at the end of the interview. His effusion and intensity were extraordinary."

Two days later, the Archbishop had a meeting at the bishop's residence. Their friendship forged in Senegal in 1952 was strengthened when Bishop Charrière was cordially invited to bless the Church at Fatick in 1959: now it counted for everything. Archbishop Lefebvre explained to his friend that some bishops especially from South America would send their candidates to the seminary.[26] In fact, he had an Argentinean sent by Fr. André and who would enter in October. The Archbishop said: "His Excellency Bishop Charrière received me warmly and was enthusiastic about my projects. He willingly gave me permission to open this 'orphan-

---

[24] French historian (1893 † 1978), professor at the Collège de France, specialist in 18th Century history, the United States and Freemasonry. Administrator of the National Library (1940-1944), he also directed the Secret Society Department for Marshal Pétain's regime and went through the archives of the Grand Orient of France, *etc.* Condemned to perpetual forced labor in 1946, incarcerated at the penal colony of St-Martin-de-Ré and later at the prison of Fontevrault, he escaped during a stay in hospital at Angers on September 30, 1951, and fled to Switzerland where he was helped by his writer friend Gonzague de Reynold. Savioz, *Essai historique sur la fondation de la Fraternité Saint-Pie X*, 35-37.

[25] *Spiritual Conferences at Ecône*, 1 A, May 30, 1971.

[26] Lefebvre, Letter to Cl. de Kinnoul, June 17, 1969.

age' for seminarians from all countries, especially South America. This happened on June 6, 1969, at 3 P.M. in the bishop's residence at Fribourg. The seminary was born! Now we had to think about getting down to business."[27]

PREPARATIONS

The "Saint Pius X Association for Priestly Training" was formed on July 2 at the home of J.-F. Braillard. All five of its committee members hailed from Fribourg; their chairman was Mr. Braillard and their vice-chairman Msgr. John Rast. This kindly prelate would sometimes invite the seminarians to services at his Church of Notre-Dame, and acted as their confessor for the first year. Archbishop Lefebvre related: "On July 16 after a long search,[28] I secured twelve rooms in the Foyer Don Bosco at 106, Route de Marly for the school year 1969-70. Providentially, benefactors who were visibly guided by their guardian angels brought the necessary financial support since many seminarians could not pay for their lodgings. The only thing missing was someone to work with me, which I considered indispensable."

Archbishop Lefebvre thought about asking Fr. George Delbos,[29] but Fr. Henri C. agreed to work with him. In the end, however, he was very hesitant and the Archbishop said: "I asked him not to come to Fribourg because I am keen for the foundation to be run by someone with solid convictions and not vacillating ones!"[30]

Thus, Providence decided that he, Archbishop Lefebvre, and no other, would be the rector of the seminary he was founding. He would be completely involved in the work.[31]

COMMON LIFE AND PRIESTLY TRAINING

On October 13, 1969, the "new boys" arrived at 106, Route de Marly, most of them in lay clothes. Apart from Pierre Piqué and Paul Aulagnier—both from Santa Chiara—there was the Swiss M. Doyon, the Argentinean E. Eraso, and J. Antier, R. Fillion, G. Monti, B. Pellaboeuf, and B. Tissier de Mallerais, all of whom were French. Archbishop Lefebvre himself welcomed them. Paul Aulagnier was already there, keeping his thoughts to himself: "I felt disappointed and worried. The nine students assembled for

---

[27] Diary of Fribourg, 1969-70, 3; Letter to Miles, June 17, 1969; Letter to Friends and Benefactors, no. 29.

[28] For a little while Archbishop Lefebvre planned to buy a house from the Fathers of the Holy Family in Fribourg; Letter to Miles, June 7, 1969; Letter to Cl. Kinnoul, June 26, 1969.

[29] Missionary of the Sacred Heart of Issoudun. Other priests were also asked.

[30] Letter to Fr. Paul Aulagnier, Sept. 19, 1969.

[31] Diary, introduction dated Nov. 17, 1969.

this first academic year did not seem reliable to me. It was far from the ideal that I had dreamed of: a breeding ground for young, traditional Catholic Levites, spiritually pumped up and having no qualms."[32] The weakness of the troops was soon apparent as regards their clothing. No sooner had they been invested with the holy livery of Christ after a simple blessing of cassocks on October 17 than some of them showed embarrassment at having to wear them in the university's corridors and *aula*. Nevertheless, the Archbishop put all his energy into sharing with this fragile and disparate group of men the deepest convictions of the Faith of a priest and missionary. On the third day, he wrote to Bishop de Castro Mayer: "I would like to rebuild the true priesthood with true priests. It will be a consolation to me in the mad age in which we live."[33]

From October 16 to 20, Fr. Theodosius came to preach a retreat which aimed at purifying the priestly candidates from the spirit of the world. Soon, in the community's humble meeting room, the Archbishop began to explain to seminarians the "directory," the heart of the seminary rule, that he had written in the previous weeks. It was inspired by canon law, a passage from the conciliar decree on Priestly training,[34] and to a small degree the rule of the French Seminary in Rome. This latter text was marked by the spirit of Fr. Le Floch, although, it must be said, it cannot hold a candle to Marcel Lefebvre's Directory.

Discipline is hardly spoken of, and the duties of this or that function even less. Not one line defines the role of the rector, or the prefects of discipline or studies. It was perfectly puzzling. Only the spirit, the virtues, and the priestly life in which the students were being initiated, were described. In fourteen concise articles, every word of which is thick with meaning, the founder sums up "the spirit in which the Church means to form her priests…[it is] the spirit of our Lord Himself, handed down through the ages…." With its unique view of the priesthood that is also pure Thomism, the Directory is based on "faith and knowledge of Our Lord Jesus Christ," "of His mystery" and of "His Redemptive work," a faith which they will increase "by studying and meditating upon the natural and supernatural realities taught them in Philosophy, Theology, Sacred Scripture, Church History, and Canon Law, always striving to bring everything back to Our Lord Jesus Christ, 'recapitulare omnia in Christo' under the guidance of St. Thomas Aquinas. They will acquire a perfect knowl-

[32] Aulagnier, *La Tradition sans peur*, 65.

[33] Letter of Oct. 16, 1969, Archives of Archbishop Lefebvre in Ecône.

[34] *Optatam Totius*, no. 16: "…theology should be taught in such a way that students will accurately draw Catholic doctrine from divine revelation, understand that doctrine profoundly, nourish their own spiritual lives with it, and be able to proclaim it…in their priestly ministry…students should learn to penetrate [the mystery of Christ and the mysteries of salvation] more deeply with the help of speculative reason exercised under the tutelage of St. Thomas."

edge of the writings of the Angelic Doctor and notably of the *Summa Theologica*, in which they will find the surest nourishment of an enlightened faith, of a profound piety, and of effective and ardent preaching" (no. 5).

Then comes charity, firstly towards God: "Their love of God should blossom forth to be manifested and nourished in their piety or in their exercise of the virtue of religion," the essential virtue of the priest, who is "the religious of God because he is the one chosen by God for the principal act of the virtue of religion: offering sacrifice" (no. 7). These lines sum up the tradition described by St. Paul to the Hebrews, St. Thomas, and Jean-Jacques Olier. From this comes "their desire to offer themselves to God with Jesus in the Blessed Sacrament, to take part in His expiatory sufferings, to join in His praise and thanksgiving," as does their "life of prayer" that will be "the soul of their apostolate" (no. 8).

Charity is also exercised in the common life, "which is none other than a form of family life, showing on all occasions an affectionate respect for the one who partakes in the authority of Our Lord and for those who work with him in the exercise of this fatherhood" (no. 9). From this should come joyful and faithful obedience, mutual affection between seminarians devoid of over-familiarity, and full of concern for the common good (no. 10). All this is based on the idea that a proper attitude among subordinates depends on the proper exercise of authority.

Through "the consequences of the priesthood, which will make them like Jesus Christ, a priest for eternity," through their priestly character, the future priests must be "separated in heart from the world" and thus "detached from the goods of this world and…far removed from the concupiscence of the flesh"; they must acquire the virtue of temperance and its subordinate virtues: chastity, poverty, self-denial, modesty (wearing the cassock to show "their faith and membership of the clergy"), mortification, and "generous acceptance of suffering in union with Our Lord Jesus Christ" (nos. 11-13).[35]

The last article (no. 14) refers to the seminarians' being introduced to the pastoral ministry during their holidays "in rectories or priories in contact with fervent and zealous priests."[36]

In five pages that are astoundingly simple, this gem of priestly spirituality combines the Church's theological sense, the supernatural breath of infused wisdom and knowledge, and experience of the humblest virtues flowing from faith and charity, the chief perfections.

---

[35] Archbishop Lefebvre would always have great respect for the sick; he recommended the intentions of his Apostolic Delegation to the prayers of "The Mission for the Sick of Our Lady of Bourguillon" on Aug. 7, 1952. See Appendix I.

[36] The example he had seen at the community at St-Léger-de-Montbrillais had struck him.

In the daily spiritual conferences,[37] the Archbishop passed on this doctrine with great simplicity! The writer—who witnessed and took part in the early work of Archbishop Lefebvre—must confess that although he rubbed shoulders with him daily in chapel, in the refectory, during recreation, or while doing the dishes, he struggled to perceive beneath the Archbishop's constant modesty the riches and depth of his soul.

LITURGICAL LIFE

Coming and going from the university, the community at the Foyer Don Bosco could not lead a very intense liturgical life. The community prayers in the morning and evening were taken from the prayer book of the Salesian students. Only during the second year were they replaced fortuitously with the hours of Prime and Compline. Why be deprived of the magnificent liturgical prayers of the divine office? Archbishop Lefebvre chose Prime rather than Lauds: "The prayer of Prime is the simplest and the best preparation for all human work. How many now say it? The Martyrology offers us the marvelous example of martyrs and saints."[38]

Of course, to these prayers were added silent morning meditation in community, community rosary in the evening—with its contemplation of Mary and prayers for the benefactors—and occasionally Benediction: "Prayer gives the priest stability and courage."[39]

The community Mass in the morning was the center and source of the seminarians' daily activities. The missal of St. Pius V was said in Latin with the psalm *Judica me* and the Last Gospel omitted according to the reforms of 1965. Moreover, up to the *Credo*, the priest stood at the sedilla and not at the altar. "That is the 'Mass of the Catechumens,' but afterwards the Mass is truly the concern of the priest" (October 29, 1969). The two readings were given from lecterns on the Epistle and Gospel side. The reading aloud of Holy Scripture while the priest faced the congregation "was meant to increase our faith." "He that believeth in the Son hath life everlasting (Jn. 3:36); but he that believeth not the Son shall not see life" (November 21, 1969).

On the other hand, the Offertory and the Canon were said by the priest alone in a quiet voice so that the faithful could not hear him. Otherwise, "in the long run, the faithful could lose their grasp on the significance of the priestly character, and even the meaning of the prayers" (November 26, 1969).

---

[37] ["Une conférence" is not strictly the equivalent of the English "conference." However, in the idiolect of the international Society which is dominated by such "Frenchisms," it has come to mean the same as "lecture" or "short talk." It is used here and throughout the rest of the book in that sense. Trans.]

[38] *Spiritual Conferences at Ecône*, Nov. 5, 1973.

[39] *Ibid.*

However, Archbishop Lefebvre realized that he was out of step with all the other priests saying the old Mass, and in 1974 he gave up the clear separation between the "Mass of the Catechumens" and the "Mass of the Faithful." Henceforth, in the main chapel at Ecône—which for a while was only a low barn with some furnishings—the entirety of the Mass took place at the altar. The magnificent ceremonies and Gregorian chant would grace numerous solemn pontifical Masses of ordination, sung Masses and Vespers of every sort, months dedicated to the Rosary and to our Lady, *etc.* Ecône would live the rhythm of the liturgy, forming its students in liturgical piety.

A PROBLEM: ASSISTING AT THE NEW MASS

Since Archbishop Lefebvre was opposed to the New Mass, he would not have it in the seminary. On the eve of the first Sunday of Advent 1969 when the *Novus Ordo Missae* came into force in the diocese of Fribourg, the Archbishop simply said: "We'll keep the old Mass, eh?" Everyone agreed. Nonetheless, Dom Lafond's acceptance of the New Mass would soon divide the Order of the Knights of Our Lady and trouble Pierre Piqué and Bernard Pellabeuf. The Archbishop deplored the monk's bias in favor of hastily obeying the edict: according to Rome, the New Mass would only be obligatory at the end of 1971. Until then at least, the old Mass could be maintained.

It is true that prudence might suggest to this or that priest "not to refuse the new *Ordo* for fear of scandalizing the faithful" by their witnessing his apparent disobedience to the bishop.[40] Such a priest should, however, "keep the Roman Canon which is still permitted, and say the words of consecration in a low voice according to the old form, which is still allowed."[41] When Archbishop Lefebvre was absent on a Sunday, the seminarians would go and assist at Mass together at the Bernadine convent of La Maigrauge where an old monk celebrated the New Mass in Latin. The Archbishop was not a man to rush souls. He allowed himself time to see the fruits more clearly in order to pass better judgment on the tree. He also wanted to hear the opinions of his colleagues in the episcopate, and find a consensus among his friends.

His friend Bishop de Castro Mayer found himself with a very painful problem of conscience with respect to his priests: "Can we, the bishops, be silent? Can we, pastors of souls, follow a *via media*, saying nothing and leaving each priest to follow his conscience as he wishes at such risk to so many souls? And if we say openly what we think, what will be the conse-

---

40 Spiritual Conference, Fribourg, Nov. 9, 1969.
41 Letter to a young priest, Sierre, Feb. 16, 1970.

quences? We will be removed…leaving many of the faithful in confusion and scandalizing the weakest souls."[42]

In January 1978 the Bishop of Campos had already solved his doubts. He translated the *Short Critical Study* and distributed it among his priests. "It seems to me preferable that scandal be given rather than a situation be maintained in which one slides into heresy. After considerable thought on the matter, I am convinced that one cannot take part in the New Mass, and even just to be present one must have a serious reason. We cannot collaborate in spreading a rite which, even if it is not heretical, leads to heresy. This is the rule I am giving my friends."[43]

At the time, Archbishop Lefebvre's position was not quite as categorical. He considered that the New Mass was not heretical, but as Cardinal Ottaviani had said, it represents serious dangers; thus in the course of time, "Protestant ideas concerning the Supper would be unconsciously accepted by the Catholics." This was why children had to be taught the fundamental notions about the Mass. However, "it is an exaggeration to say that most of these Masses are invalid." One should not hesitate to go a little further to have Mass according to the Roman *Ordo*; but "if one does not have the choice and if the priest celebrating Mass according to the *Novus Ordo* is faithful and worthy, one should not abstain from going to Mass."[44]

A TRIED AND TRIMMED FOUNDATION

Archbishop Lefebvre's wait-and-see attitude based on practical and doctrinal resistance was not accepted by all the seminarians. Outside influences were pushing some of them to reject out-right the *Novus Ordo Missae* and persuading others to accept it. All this would not have mattered if the Archbishop had not been absent so often and for so long. Fortunately, at those times two exemplary religious came to stand in for him, providing Holy Mass and spiritual conferences. They were Fr. Auguste Rivière, C.P.C.R., who lived at Grolley with the Fathers of Chabeuil, and Fr. Guérard des Lauriers.

Then, however, having been absent for the whole of December, the founder fell ill at Dijon at the end of the year. A period of rest at the house of the Holy Ghost Fathers in La Croix-Valmer was insufficient. He was hospitalized in Fribourg, felt very ill, and unbeknownst to the community, he asked Fr. Bussard for extreme unction. The priest reassured him: "Now is not your time, Your Grace!"

---

[42] Bishop de Castro Mayer, Letter to Archbishop Lefebvre, Oct. 5, 1969.
[43] Letter of Jan. 29, 1970, to Archbishop Lefebvre. Unfortunately, Bishop de Castro Mayer states that Archbishop Sigaud "has drawn up a decree for the implementation of the New Mass in his diocese."
[44] Letter of Feb. 17, 1970, to Gérald Wailliez.

At last on January 30, test results reassured the patient and his spiritual sons: he was suffering from strongyles contracted in Africa and lodged in his liver. For the rest of his life he would suffer from sudden coughing fits. He underwent prompt and extensive treatment in Sierre which succeeded in putting him more or less back on his feet. He remained tired and on February 17, 1970, he wrote to Maître Walliez: "Providence has put me to the test with this illness for the last two and a half months. Doubtless it is because suffering is essential to the works of God."

Meanwhile, and until June, the community was governed by Fr. Cler, a former chaplain at the school for children of Armed Forces personnel in La Flèche. He was very good on spiritual matters but could be influenced by opinion: in his view the seminarians should not "present themselves as being necessarily the ones who are right and pure." They could leave their cassocks in the wardrobe when they went to the university "so that others might not once again say: 'Saint Pius X, they're a sect'!"

Not all the seminarians were quite so sensitive, and some of them did not like "the new gems that can be found in the innovations in the liturgy"[45] such as the new system of readings at Mass. Fortunately, Archbishop Lefebvre's return put everything back in order. He simply recommended to his disciples to "keep a balance between charity and stating the truth."[46] However, not everyone was good at keeping balance. While on one side there were extremists, on the other there were those who had little stomach for the fight. By April 15, only five of the original nine seminarians remained.

Returning from Fribourg on April 30, Archbishop Lefebvre noted this decline in numbers. Having been recently tried by illness, he was now beset by doubts: what was the use of carrying on with troops so weak and without a reliable collaborator? However, thanks to the Cité Catholique and the Knights of Our Lady, seven solid recruits were acquired. With his customary simplicity, he stated his worries to the five remaining students:[47] "That would make twelve. It's not many, and I am a little afraid. Let me have in writing your suggestions for the future. I won't conceal from you the anxiety that I feel at the thought of taking the decision to accept new seminarians with all the risks that could pose to their future. Will they be accepted in dioceses? Should we form a priestly society? I am putting my whole confidence in the holy providence of God."

The Archbishop was encouraged at this time by Fr. Jean-Yves Cottard who was living at the French Seminary in Rome but who wanted to come to Fribourg. The Archbishop replied: "No, wait: things are not doing very well. We do not know where we are going. Stay there as long as you can."[48]

---

45   Spiritual Conference of Fr. Cler, Feb. 17, 1970.
46   Archbishop Lefebvre, Spiritual Conference, May 9, 1970.
47   By May 13, only four remained.

Sometime after his return to Fribourg, on May 19, 1970,[49] Archbishop Lefebvre made a quiet visit to Bishop Adam in Sion. He had heard that his friend had made up his mind to transfer his seminary from Sion to Fribourg.[50] Why not ask Nestor to look after them? But Nestor Adam turned down the request out of prudence. Then, the Archbishop put a second request to him: he could give the Archbishop permission to use a house in Valais that some laypeople had put at his disposition; he intended to use it to house young men who would do a year's study there before going on to university in Fribourg. Bishop Adam did not dare refuse his enterprising friend's second request, and gave his *placet*.[51] As long as it was just the first year, that was acceptable; he could not see a full seminary being founded in Valais where there was not only the diocesan seminary but also seminaries for the Canons of St. Bernard and the Capuchins. Archbishop Lefebvre could sense the Bishop of Sion's reticence, and on the way home he was again beset with doubts.

He had left Fribourg very early in the morning without having said his Mass and returned in the early evening. Paul Aulagnier prepared the Archbishop's vestments for him and asked about the success of his trip and the possibilities it might represent the future of the little group. He later said: "Just then I saw him weep from discouragement. While I knew how serious the situation was, my morale was high, doubtless by the grace of God. I respectfully shared my optimism with Archbishop Lefebvre: 'Your Grace, we're not going to stop now; we have to continue!' He looked doubtful, but I think in the end he was deeply touched."[52]

For a while the Archbishop spoke of sending his Fribourg seminarians to the *Salesianum* where, under the guidance of Fr. Philippe, a group of theology students were leading a common life and readying themselves to form the future congregation of the Brothers of St. John. This time, it was Bernard Tissier de Mallerais who said that such an initiative was impossible: "I confess," he said, "I never doubted that the Archbishop would continue."

---

[48] *Fideliter*, no. 59: 121. On May 26, 1970, from the balcony of the French Seminary hung a red banner that read: "Vota comunista !" Cf. *Il Borghese*, June 14, 1970, p. 407.
[49] Archbishop Lefebvre's diary, 1970, Archives of Archbishop Lefebvre at Ecône.
[50] The decision to move had been taken in 1967, but was not realized until the new school year in 1970 when a Jesuit property was rented. Cf. Paul Martone, *Geschichte des Priesterseminars des Bistums Sittens (1545-1988)* (Buch und Offsetdruck Simplon, 1990), 72-75. Two thirds of the seminarians consulted said they were in favor of the move in order to "open up to the world" and to get "better training," two arguments that Archbishop Lefebvre would refute when he did exactly the opposite in 1971.
[51] Archbishop Lefebvre always stated that he received the *placet*, and Bishop Adam never contested this.
[52] Aulagnier, *La Tradition sans peur*, 68; *Fideliter*, no. 59: 112.

Archbishop Lefebvre simply said: "For me, the reactions of the seminarians manifested the designs of Providence."

The loyal support of the Fribourg committee certainly helped the Archbishop to persevere. Professor Faÿ came to give talks about Freemasonry to the seminarians. District Judge Albert Volanthen also supported the work; in spite of everything Fr. Philippe remained friendly and encouraged the Archbishop; he came to the Foyer to give spiritual conferences, and the seminarians took part several times in mini-retreats that he preached at Hautrive. Other clergy visited the seminary: Fr. Edmond Wéry from Brussels, Bishop Morilleau himself, who once directed the schola at short notice, Fr. Pierre Caillon, and Fr. Noël Barbara. Laymen also came to the Foyer: Gérard Mercier from *Vers Demain,* Jean Ousset and Michel de Penfentenyo, Dr. Schorer, Dr. Eric de Saventhem and his wife, *etc.*

Thus, the Archbishop set out once again to find an independent property for the four remaining Fribourg seminarians for the start of the school year in 1970. A suitable house on Route de la Vignettaz soon went up for auction, and on June 26 while the Archbishop prayed in the cathedral, the architect Antognini won the bidding for him.[53] However, the Archbishop had found another house for the new students who would arrive that year: Ecône!

III. ECÔNE

A MAGNIFICENT ACT OF FAITH

Archbishop Lefebvre was going to launch a project that was dear to his heart: a year of spiritual formation before beginning studies for the priesthood. Well before Fribourg in fact, Providence and our Lady were preparing Ecône for him on this blessed plot of land in a corner of Valais. There between the two most anti-clerical villages in the area, Saxon and Riddes, would take root the work willed by God for the restoration of the Catholic priesthood.

In the autumn of 1967, Fr. Pierre Epiney[54] had just accepted from his bishop the post of Riddes parish priest that had been refused by four other priests. He began by visiting his parish. He rang the doorbell at Ecône, but there was no answer. He went into the deserted courtyard: on the left was the barn and on the right the kennels. In a flash, he saw in his mind's eye the courtyard of a large seminary full of seminarians. Very quickly he

---

[53] A gift from Bishop Bressolles made this purchase possible. Cf. Bishop Bressolles, Letter of June 27, 1970.

[54] While still a curate at Savièse, he had been to Rome for some reason and had met Archbishop Lefebvre who was still Superior General of the Holy Ghost Fathers. The Archbishop invited him to dinner and gave him lodgings at the French Seminary.

chased away the meaningless image and found himself again in the deserted courtyard. Canon Roserens who still maintained the property came down to greet him: "Here, it's all over, there's nothing left to do." Was that certain? In Valais many men had been "reinvigorated" by the Spiritual Exercises of St. Ignatius thanks to Fr. Barrielle and his colleagues in the CP-CR: among these was Roger Lovey,[55] a lawyer, and like his friends Gratien Rausis[56] and Alphonse Pedroni,[57] a member of the Knights of Our Lady. Everything began on Holy Thursday, 1968. Alphonse Pedroni, a young man from Valais who assisted at daily Mass, heard during a conversation in a cafe that the house and grounds of Ecône were to be sold by the Great St. Bernard Canons. He opened his heart to Gratien Rausis, who came to see him that day over a business matter: "It breaks your heart to see another religious place disappearing. There are several buyers who have lots of money and one of them is a Communist group who want to blow up the chapel!"

"Alphonse," Gratien replied, "if it's only a question of money, we have to do something."

They knew Ecône well. The Canons of St. Bernard bought the lands of Econnaz from Pierre de la Tour, Lord of Châtillon, in 1302, and six centuries later in 1892 they opened an agricultural school. In 1895 they built a chapel dedicated to Our Lady of the Fields and in 1922 the agricultural school moved to Châteauneuf near Sion. The congregation continued to use Ecône to produce fruit and vegetables, and it housed kennels for St. Bernard dogs. For a decade from the end of the 1940's, the house, a solid nineteenth-century building with schist floors and tuff walls, provided accommodation for the younger theology students of the congregation under the guidance of Canon René Berthod. Even in the middle of winter, they used the attic space as sleeping accommodation. Afterwards the theology students moved to Martigny, leaving Ecône to be looked after by one old Canon and just a few brothers. The roof had just been redone but there was not enough money to pay for the repair: hence, the house was put up for sale.

---

[55] Parishioner at Fully (1929-1988), notary and lawyer practicing in Sion, future public prosecutor for Lower Valais (1977-1988). Originally from Châtelard, he was the son of Jules Lovey (1903-1978) and Marie Tornay (1905-1996), and the eldest of five children. He himself had seven. He was also the secretary of the Valais Democratic Party and the Valaisan French-speaking president of *Una Voce Helvetica*.

[56] From the village of Reppaz, in the district of Orsières, the fourth of a Catholic family of fourteen children. His father Henri Rausis was leader of Orsières Council for twenty years, a Valais councilman for sixteen years, and finally became the leader of the Valais State Council in 1961.

[57] From a Saxon family; 1921-1978. His quarry later provided stone for the church at Ecône that was built twenty years after he died.

Gratien Rausis telephoned the very same day. The Canons replied: "Make an offer." Alphonse Pedroni thought: "We cannot do that alone." He suggested that his brother Marcel[58] join them, while Rausis put forward the names of Roger Lovey and Guy Genoud.[59] On April 18, Roger Lovey wrote to the Provost: "Because of Ecône's past, it means a lot to us. We could say that it has a religious vocation which we refuse to see abandoned without greater scrutiny."[60]

On May 31, 1968, the feast of the Queenship of Mary, contracts were exchanged by the five friends and Canon Bernard Rausis. The Provost of St. Bernard, Msgr. Angelin Lovey, had said: "We will do you no favors." How were they to pay? They would borrow from the bank. The manager sought information: "But have you assets?"

"No," replied Pedroni, "we don't have any. You only need give us the loan: it's for a religious work. You only have to lend us everything!"

Amazed, the bank manager gave them a loan for the entire sum.[61]

But how would they repay the loan? They would have to develop the farming land around the house. Therefore, these gentlemen became farmers. They began by raising cattle although the beasts were not strong and caught cold easily. Thanks to a sick cow, Lovey one day got his trousers covered in dung just one hour before going into court. Then they built a large hen-house and at one point had the best yield in French-speaking Switzerland. Their selfless enthusiasm and faith was allied with great realism. Finally they planted vines, and farm worker Claude Telani, whose zeal became legendary among generations of seminarians, took charge of Ecône Farm with its grape and apricot harvests.

There remained the religious house comprising the St. Bernard wing and the chapel of Our Lady of the Fields. The latter had been empty ever since the last Canon left, but on their first day, the men and Fr. Epiney sang there a *Salve Regina* that was full of faith. The chapel was but waiting for the return of the perpetual sacrifice: it called out to priests and—who knows!—even to future priests.

ARCHBISHOP LEFEBVRE IN ECÔNE

Nine months passed from May 1968 to February 1969. Then Divine Providence led Archbishop Lefebvre to Ecône:

---

[58] A builder in Saxon; in 1966 he had taken part in the First CPCR Congress in Argentina.

[59] Future Valais state representative; then a State councilor, *i.e.*, a representative in the federal parliament at Berne.

[60] L.-M. Jugie, *Ecône, le séminaire de l'espoir* (Orme Rond, 1986), 39.

[61] M. Pedroni, May 17, 2001, ms. III, 27.

The possibilities of something in Rome were dwindling....I had the idea of asking the Order of the Knights of Our Lady about a project of priest-knights who would depend on his Excellency Bishop Michon, protector of the order. I made known this suggestion to Colonel Jehan de Penfentenyo, Grand Master of the Order. The reply was slow in coming, but after Dom Lafond[62] had discussed and thought upon the question, it proved to be practically impossible. However, the Grand Master very kindly suggested that I contact the Knights in Valais who had a building that could be used as a seminary. I decided to go to Valais to get more information.[63]

Through his friend and former fellow seminarian Henri Bonvin, who was parish priest at Fully in Valais, the Archbishop got himself invited at the end of March 1969 to preach a Lenten retreat at Monthey and a First Communion retreat at Fully. While there,[64] he explained his seminary project to Fr. Bonvin; he had not yet decided to begin things in Fribourg and had heard talk of a house in Valais. Henri Bonvin guessed straightaway that he meant Ecône. At the end of Mass the following day while giving out Holy Communion, he whispered as he passed his parishioner Roger Lovey: "Come and see me at the presbytery after Mass!"

At the presbytery, he said to Lovey: "I've got Archbishop Lefebvre here and he is looking for a property to house his seminarians. Might Ecône be suitable?"

Had Roger Lovey already been informed by the Grand Master about the Archbishop's search? The fact remains that the designs of Providence became clear to him. God was pleased with the magnificent act of faith that the five friends had made. He had guided their initiative, and now they would become the instrument of a work which would exceed their wildest dreams and reward their unconquerable hope. The Archbishop and the Sedunois lawyer soon met, and Archbishop Lefebvre made his first visit to Ecône one day during Holy Week 1969. There he found an oasis of apricot trees in blossom bordering the rocky slopes of an arid vineyard and protected from the nearby torrent by a strong earthen dyke. During summer its banks were lined with anthyllis, rosebay willowherb, and coquesigrue.

Ecône was being readied to welcome a chapter of the Knights of Our Lady (after their Lausanne Congress) which Bishop Adam of Sion would

---

[62] *Note* of Dom Lafond of March 25, 1969, sent to Archbishop Lefebvre by Colonel de Penfentenyo on May 15.

[63] Diary of Ecône, 1970-71, introduction.

[64] The presbytery at Fully provided much hospitality. On July 4, 1961, it had welcomed a reunion of former Santa Chiara students from Burgundy, Franche-Comté, and Switzerland including Monsignor Joseph Bayard, rector of the major seminary at Sion, Canon Clément Schnyder, dean of the chapter, Fathers Léonce Rey, and de Grimentz, Archbishop Marcel Lefebvre, Canon Liger-Bélair, *etc.*, and Fr. Larnicol. (*Échos de Santa Chiara*, July 1962, 7).

honor with his presence. The house was in fact the seat of the Sion Precep-torat[65] and the "Preceptor" François Lagneau addressed these words to the gathering: "Let's have no more triumphalism! I confide this house to the protection of Fr. Berto; may he do his best for us from heaven! Here, yes, here, we are in a land of saints!"[66]

Roger Lovey invited his knight friend Gratien Rausis to Ecône. He also asked Marcel Pedroni, a practical man who could get things done. They showed Archbishop Lefebvre around Ecône, and he was soon en-chanted by the lonely tranquillity of the setting and the religious austerity of the house. The Archbishop later said: "I didn't really think it was a good spot for a seminary since it was so far away from any major town, but it was very suitable for a novitiate. Besides, His Excellency Bishop Adam[67] did not want a seminary to be founded there[68] and wished the house to be outside his jurisdiction. I asked these gentlemen to give me some time to think and, if possible, to give me first refusal for one year. They willingly accepted to do this until October 1970."

However, the "dream," as the Archbishop called it, "of giving the be-ginners a year of spirituality" began to take shape during summer 1969; he wrote about the matter to Vernor Miles on September 3: "Concerning the property in Valais, I intend to make it into a house for the first year of spiritual and liturgical formation; it will be a kind of broad novitiate with-out the name or the legal status. It will also provide a year of transition between secular and ecclesiastical studies. I'm counting on a little group of very good priests who have five parishes in the region of Vienne."[69]

The Archbishop continued: "During the first trimester of the 1970-71 school year, this wish seemed to me to be an absolute necessity. I decid-ed to look for priests who would help me. Faced with the difficulty of find-ing any, I met Dom Roy, abbot of Our Lady of Fontgombault, and dis-cussed the possibility of the seminarians' spending a year in the abbey. Dom Roy kindly accepted the suggestion in principle, although he raised some objections that might come from the diocesan authorities."

Just then, the Archbishop received an offer from two young priests who wished to help him out. Fr. Maurice Gottlieb, a former student at Santa Chiara, was a friend of the St. Léger priests and curate at La Châtre

---

65   [A chapter of the Knights of Our Lady. Trans.]
66   François Lagneau, Letters of June 5, 1997, and Aug. 22, 1998.
67   "I visited the building," wrote Archbishop Lefebvre to Miles on April 9, 1969, "and I have written to Bishop Adam." Maître Lovey soon went to see Bishop Adam to tell him about their discussion.
68   Cf. Bishop Adam, Letter of April 13, 1969, cited above.
69   Including Fr. Mulot, parish priest of St-Léger-de-Montbrillais, and his colleagues Jacques de Fommervault, a retreat master, and Fr. Albert Hus, a Montfortian Father. They only left the St-Léger area in 1972, moving to Loublande, near the community of Claire Ferchaud, where the chaplain, Fr. Lacheteau, was already residing.

(and was at that time visiting Fribourg), and Fr. Jacques Masson was a teacher at the minor seminary of Meaux who came to see the Archbishop at Rue Lhomond and declared his enthusiasm. Nonetheless, their definitive offers[70] were not made until the end of May 1970 when the Archbishop also secured the collaboration of Fr. Claude Michel during a visit to Rome.

Without waiting for the outcome of the negotiations with Fontgombault, Archbishop Lefebvre met Maître Lovey during the Lausanne Congress at Easter 1970 and discussed with him his dream of a year of spirituality; on May 24 with Paul Aulagnier he returned to Ecône for another visit and was welcomed with open arms by Maître Lovey, Marcel Pedroni, etc.

"*Monseigneur,*" said Lovey, "will you allow us to invite the parish priest from Riddes?"

"Oh! What kind of man is he? Will he not try to put a spanner in the works?

"No, there is no danger of that. He is not like other parish priests."[71]

In a nearby restaurant the two visitors, Fr. Pierre Epiney, and the five friends sat down to eat. At the end of the meal, Alphonse Pedroni, who until then had remained mysteriously silent, opened his mouth to speak these words which proved to be prophetic:

"Well, *Monseigneur,* I tell you: they'll talk about this seminary of Ecône throughout the world."

The final decision to begin the renovations needed before the house could lodge seminarians was taken on June 24 when the Archbishop's proposal of going to Fontgombault was finally rejected.[72] The Archbishop promised to pay them a substantial sum (from his benefactors) by way of rent. However, the final material problem remained to be solved: finding nuns to staff the kitchen and laundry. Where would they find them in such an isolated region? After an unsuccessful visit to the Sisters of Chabeuil, Archbishop Lefebvre, who was increasingly worried by the matter, thought "about good old Fr. Berto and his nuns," the Dominicans of the Holy Ghost. Before leaving for Rome he sent them an SOS.

"Then," he said, "on September 3 I received a positive response by telephone in Rome. It was the feast of St. Pius X. Such thoughtfulness on

---

[70] Fr. Gottlieb was allowed a secondment of two years by his bishop and Fr. Masson a secondment of three years by his (cf. Letter of the two priests to Archbishop Lefebvre, May 21 and May 26, 1970).

[71] Archbishop Lefebvre immediately recognized Fr. Epiney, whom he had already met in Rome.

[72] Lefebvre, Letter to Maître Lovey, June 24, 1970. In September Fr. Bernard Lecareux established an embryonic priestly fraternity in the presbytery at Mérigny near Fontgombault.

the part of Providence, the holy Pope, and the Reverend Mother de Pont-calec![73]

IV. THE YEAR OF SPIRITUALITY

Archbishop Lefebvre still had to obtain the *placet* of the bishops concerned. To undertake this work of the Church, he could do nothing without first presenting his proposals to the Ordinaries to secure their permission. In April 1969 the Archbishop had written to the Bishop of Sion proposing the foundation of either a first year or even a full seminary[74] at Ecône. We have already mentioned that Nestor Adam[75] was not really in favor of this latter proposal, and suggested the Archbishop try at Fribourg. On June 30, 1969, the Archbishop met the Bishop of Sion[76] to present his plans for Fribourg in detail and his idea for Ecône. Again, as we have already mentioned, he secured on May 19, 1970, the Bishop of Sion's approval for a preparatory year at Ecône.

As for the Bishop of Fribourg, the Archbishop wrote him a *memorandum* on June 29, 1970. He had explained to the bishop his proposal that the students complete a preparatory year before beginning university studies. He had also described his plans for a priestly society—to which we shall return. Bringing these two ideas together, he said: "If the foundation is approved, the preparatory year or year of spirituality required before making an engagement in the Society will take place at Our Lady of the Fields at Ecône in the diocese of Sion. Bishop Adam has already given us his agreement."[77]

On July 1, 1970, Archbishop Lefebvre had a meeting with Bishop Charrière and his auxiliary, Bishop Pierre Mamie, at the bishop's residence in Fribourg. He gave Bishop Charrière a draft of the Society's statutes and obtained his permission to continue with the work in Fribourg. They met again on August 18 and Bishop Charrière confirmed orally to the Archbishop and in writing the same day his "authorization...given to His Grace Archbishop Marcel Lefebvre in the meeting of June 6, 1969: to make an international foundation at Fribourg for priestly candidates who will follow courses at the University."[78]

---

[73] Diary of Ecône, 1970-71, 2-4.
[74] Cf. Lefebvre, Letter to Roger Lovey, April 2, 1969.
[75] Adam, Letter of April 13, 1969, quoted above.
[76] Lefebvre, Letter to Roger Lovey, June 25, 1969.
[77] *Memorandum* of June 29, 1970, Diocesan Archives of Lausanne, Geneva, and Fribourg VIII, R, I, 42; Savioz, *Essai historique sur la foundation de la Fraternité de Saint-Pie X*, annex 1. 23.
[78] Archives of the FSSPX, Menzingen; Diocesan Archives of Lausanne, Geneva, and Fribourg , classer I, doc. 4.

Thus, after Fr. Rivière had preached a retreat in Ecône to the two communities from October 8 to 13, the second year at Fribourg and the first year in Valais would begin in tandem with complete legal regularity. The Archbishop shared his time as equitably as possible between his two groups of sons.

PROGRAM OF THE YEAR OF SPIRITUALITY

On August 25, 1970, Archbishop Lefebvre and Frs. Gottlieb, Masson, and Michel met at Fontgombault to beat out the details of the year of spirituality with the help of Fr. Dominique Marc, the abbey's Master of Novices. It was a matter of repairing a weakness in ordinary priestly training, a weakness that the young Marcel Lefebvre had felt in Rome. In contrast, he remembered the benefits he had gained from his novitiate at Orly. He wished his seminarians to benefit similarly from learning about and practicing the interior life which would be the soul of their priestly existence and "help them to make their theology understood by the faithful who also aspire to the interior life."[79]

Without this spiritual training, as Archbishop Lefebvre explained, "we would risk making the seminary a place for purely intellectual studies. We would train heads but not always hearts…hearts which are made to grow in sanctity and to live an interior life of intense union with our Lord." Thus he concluded, "I think that this innovation is certainly very important."[80] At the Council's Central Preparatory Commission, the Archbishop had already made the suggestion: "Studying and being initiated into the spiritual life for a year seem to be of the utmost importance. This year of spiritual life is more necessary than studying Pastoral Theology."[81] Vatican II, in its decree on the training of priests, *Optatam Totius*, asked the bishops "to establish an appropriate period of time for more intense spiritual apprenticeship, so that spiritual training can rest upon a firmer basis and students can embrace their vocation with a decision maturely weighed" (no. 12). The Archbishop was consulted by the Sacred Congregation for the Propagation of the Faith concerning priestly training in Nigeria. Given his recent experiment in Ecône, he was able to recommend six months or a whole year for this "period of spirituality."[82]

This was the substance of the meeting at Fontgombault. For practical and pedagogical purposes, the course in spiritual doctrine would explore the practice of mental prayer, spiritual direction, confession, *etc.* The first year seminarians would study the catechism and the theology of the Coun-

---

[79] *Spiritual Conferences at Ecône*, 59 A, May 16, 1978.
[80] *Ibid.*, 80 A, Nov. 3, 1980.
[81] Manuscript of oral intervention, Jan. 17, 1962; *A. Doc.*, II, II, 17, 167.
[82] Opinion given on Feb. 6, 1972, in answer to inquiry of Oct. 12, 1971, prot. 4899/71.

cil of Trent concerning the Holy Sacrifice of the Mass, and subsequently a theological critique of the New Mass. Then, the writings of the Angelic Doctor would be used to initiate the seminarians in the theology of the Trinity, grace, sin, penance, the discernment of spirits, and, finally, the Christian virtues and gifts of the Holy Ghost.

The first seminarians remember how happy they were to enter this garden of graces, virtues, and gifts under the Thomistic iron rule of Maurice Gottlieb. What solid theological spirituality! What an invitation to explore St. Thomas, just like their founder!

A SPECIAL COURSE: THE "ACTS OF THE MAGISTERIUM"

Alongside the course in spirituality would go a Latin class and an introduction to Sacred Scripture focusing especially on Jesus' life according to the Gospel and referring to the solid but accessible Thomistic commentary of Dom Paul Delatte. There would be an introduction to Gregorian chant and a Liturgy course given by Fr. Claude Michel following Dom Guéranger's *Institutions liturgiques*.

The Valaisan Canon René Berthod would also give a hand teaching the course "on modern errors" known usually as the "Acts of the Magisterium Class." This course was devised in the spirit of Fr. Le Floch's talks on the papal condemnations of Freemasonry, liberalism, and modernism. Later, from 1979-1982, Archbishop Lefebvre himself taught this subject. As he explained:

> The aim of this course is not so much to make a logical study of such errors, but rather to go over the encyclicals themselves and especially those in which the Popes have given an in-depth study of the truths opposed to these errors, or a detailed analysis of the errors themselves. One can only admire the zeal and faith of these watchful guardians of the deposit of the Faith, and it is all the more stupefying to note that this relentless fight was suddenly abandoned through a false ecumenism amounting to a betrayal of the truth, in favor of making pacts with the authors of these errors and the inheritors of their ideas.[83]

The course is introduced through St. Pius X's papal agenda: "To restore all things in Christ" (*E Supremi Apostolatus*, 1903). In this encyclical, the Pope prophesies the coming of "the religion of man who makes himself God"—which was blessed by Paul VI, the apostle of the "Rights of Man." This was a new religion that Pius X said was the religion of the Antichrist "in which man substitutes himself for God."[84] According to Archbishop Lefebvre, this demand for man's independence from Jesus Christ and from

---

[83] Marcel Lefebvre, plan for the course of Acts of the Magisterium, in *C'est moi l'accusé*, xvi.

[84] Encyclical *E Supremi Apostolatus*, Oct. 4, 1903 (Bonne Presse), I, 35-39; *C'est moi l'accusé*, 5-10.

God is the quintessence of liberalism, which itself is "one of the causes of the Church's present crisis, and consequently one of the reasons for the birth of this seminary; in the course of history, the good Lord gives us remedies to the evils as we fight and combat them."[85]

V. THE PRIESTLY SOCIETY OF SAINT PIUS X

THE ORIGINAL IDEA

How could priests who were trained to fight for Christ the King, according to the sublime ideal of the priesthood, subsequently maintain the doctrinal purity and missionary charity of their calling if not by some rule of life? And after they had returned to their dioceses as priests, how could they be protected against the growing liberal corruption of the clergy? It was logical but also in keeping with the grandest traditions of the Church that the idea of an international seminary and a year of spirituality should lead to the founding of a priestly society of common life. Implicitly, if not explicitly, the "dream of Dakar" was in fact a plan for that society.

In early times St. Augustine, Bishop of Hippo (396-430 A.D.) led a common life with his clergy. Later, numerous reformers of the clergy sent by God imposed this common life on their disciples. This was certainly not the life of religious who take the vow of poverty; rather it consists of living under the same roof and eating at the same table. This same rule of common life was adopted by Jean-Jacques Olier's priests of St. Sulpice, St. Jean Eudes's Congregation of Jesus and Mary, the Paris Society for Foreign Missions, and obviously the Holy Ghost Fathers founded by Claude Poullart des Places. The 1917 Code of Canon Law (Can. 174) stated that "the observance of the common life among the clergy must be praised and recommended."

From 1966 to 1967, Archbishop Lefebvre, as we have said, was thinking about re-establishing Poullart des Places's "Gentlemen of the Holy Ghost" alongside the Holy Ghost Fathers. Did the "dream of Dakar" have a part in this plan? In our opinion, yes. However, by throwing the Archbishop "out on the street," Providence would ensure, unbeknown to the Archbishop, that his plans would be brought to even greater fruition.

Claire Ferchaud[86] heard about his idea for a seminary and wrote to him on May 8, 1969: "Your Grace, would you not consider coming yourself to pitch camp on the chosen hillside and inaugurate a Mass of expiation and redemption? So many priests would follow you!" The Archbishop replied on May 13 saying that he wished he could "come to the help" of the proposed perpetual Mass at Loublande. He added:

---

[85] *Spiritual Conferences at Ecône*, 6 A, Jan. 1974, 7th conference on liberalism.

However, like you, I wish to follow the signs of Providence....I believe that at this moment in time, my most urgent duty is to train priests. This is my constant concern and it fills all my time. Perhaps by this means your own projects will be brought to fruition....I am also convinced that it is the holiness of the priesthood that will save us. This is why I'm devoting all my energy and prayers to that end.

The constitution of a society in the same mold as the "Foreign Missions" could easily include a more contemplative branch devoted primarily to this perpetual Mass.

I will ask the Holy Ghost to show me His ways so that all present opposition might disappear. Already very clear signs are showing me that the good Lord wills this new foundation for training priests.[87]

He wrote in the autumn to his friend Vernor Miles and told him about the house at Ecône that he had visited in the spring. The Archbishop explained not only his idea of a "novitiate broadly speaking," as we have seen, but also his proposal of a new Society: "This house will probably become the headquarters of an international Society of secular priests: a pious union that would come to the help of priests in their ministry and encourage them to keep the true traditions. In the course of this year we will organize this project, so that next year we will be able to welcome the first group of young men."[88]

However, before the arrival of this "first group" in 1970 which would in fact be the second, the Archbishop shared his grand idea with the group of nine who came in October 1969. In his spiritual conference on November 12, barely a month after their arrival, the founder spoke to the students not only of "a preparatory year of study of the vocation which could take place in Martigny," but most importantly of a Society:

Let me offer you some considerations for the future: [we could] form a society, not of religious like Fr. Theodosius, but a society of seculars. It

---

[86] Claire Ferchaud (1896-1972) was a French girl who, during World War I, received messages from the Sacred Heart. One of these messages was to ask the French government to place an emblem of the Sacred Heart of Jesus on the national flag borne by the armed forces. She had an interview with the President of the Republic, Raymond Poincaré, to ask him to comply; he did not. Later, she received heavenly revelations asking her to found a work of perpetual Masses: priests would relay each other at the altar at Loublande (in Poitou), celebrating Mass unceasingly. The Church has made no pronouncement on these revelations. Cf. Claude Mouton, *Au plus fort de la tourmente...*, *Claire Ferchaud* (Montsurs: Éd. Résiac, 1978).

[87] Letter sent from La Croix-Valmer, *Lecture et Tradition*, no. 179: 25-27. Claire Ferchaud's included the request that the priests come to Rinfillières at Loublande and ascend one after the other to the altar to offer Mass. With this in mind, Fr. Georges Roche founded his "Cenacle," but did not include this objective in the statutes. This is why his plans came to nothing. In the 1960's, a group of priests who were keen on Loublande were living in the presbytery at Saint-Léger-de-Montbrillais and Fr.Gottlieb went there often. Archbishop Lefebvre visited them in 1969 (cf. ms. II, 68).

[88] Letter to Miles, Sept. 3, 1969.

would be a society of priests without vows, apostles focused on the priesthood, even for non-priest members. The fundamental cause of the crisis is the weakening of the priesthood. Now, the priesthood is centered on the Holy Sacrifice of the Mass. The possible aims of this society could include seminaries and the priestly apostolate, excluding everything which does not specifically belong to priests. It would be possible to leave this society after a three-year trial period. I ask you to think about it and to pray. Should we be scattered throughout dioceses or existing congregations? Or should we remain together, at least living in small groups?

THE APPROVAL OF THE CHURCH

The seminarians were quite embarrassed by this proposal. Those who had been sent by their bishops or even already incardinated in their home dioceses considered that they were destined for those dioceses. The new students had no clear ideas on a topic that went beyond their present concern of becoming good priests. Archbishop Lefebvre did not push the matter. However, on February 21, 1970, did he not have a few good reasons to persevere with his project? With some difficulty, he obtained from the bishops of Clermont-Ferrand and Dax dimissorial letters authorizing him to tonsure Paul Aulagnier and ordain Pierre Piqué to the subdiaconate in the charming pilgrim chapel of Our Lady of Bourguillon[89] on the outskirts of Fribourg. This first ordination ceremony in the history of the Seminary of Saint Pius X encouraged Archbishop Lefebvre greatly; but did God will the foundation of this priestly Society he was planning for? With no visible indications of Providence, the problem remained unsolved.

The Archbishop put this question to several people[90] in Rome in March 1970. His friends Cardinal Ildebrando Antoniutti, prefect of the Sacred Congregation for Religious and Secular Institutes, and Archbishop Pietro Palazzini, secretary of the Sacred Congregation for the Clergy, encouraged him. However, in April the Bishop of Dax asked the seminarian Pierre Piqué to leave Archbishop Lefebvre's seminary.[91] The Archbishop was only half-surprised by this first act of aggression against his foundation from a member of the French episcopate; it was a sign of Providence. He considered that, henceforth, a priestly society could offer some protection against this type of opposition which would most likely recur.

This was why he raised the matter again with the seminarians during his talk on April 30. He asked them to tell him what they thought about the idea of a "priestly Society": should it be founded as distinct from the seminary? Bernard Tissier de Mallerais replied: "It's a possibility to be con-

---

[89] On October 20, the seminary went on pilgrimage to Bourguillon to consecrate themselves to "Our Lady, Guardian of the Faith," who is honored there under this title.

[90] Cf. spiritual conference, Fribourg, April 30, 1970.

[91] Diary of Fribourg, April 15, 1970.

sidered...if it becomes difficult or even impossible to be incardinated directly into dioceses." Paul Aulagnier thought that the Society[92] "would one day become inevitable. Events and Providence will show it the path to follow....We should still make a distinction between the seminary and the Society."[93]

The Archbishop expected more of a response, if not more enthusiasm. After a few days of doubt—as we have related—he took heart again. He went to Rome on May 25, and in his "hermitage" on the Via Casalmonferrato, he wrote the "Draft Statutes of the Society of the Apostles of Jesus and Mary," dated June 17, 1970. On June 29, Archbishop Lefebvre sent Bishop Charrière a *memorandum*[94] concerning his idea for a priestly society. On July 1, he went to the Bishop's residence in Fribourg and gave the Bishop his draft of the statutes: "I have been asked by some young priests and seminarians to found a society for secular priests. I have written these draft statutes in accordance with Canon Law."

"I see nothing to object to in such a useful and timely initiative," replied François Charrière.

"If you agree to the foundation, the year of spirituality will take place in Ecône; Bishop Adam has already given his permission. During this year, candidates can prepare to join the Society—it is a novitiate by another name—although the seminarians will not be obliged to join. The Society will have its headquarters at Fribourg on Rue de la Vignettaz."

"Very well, I'll consider your statutes at leisure."

On August 18, the Archbishop again met the Bishop to talk about the proposed society; unfortunately Bishop Charrière had not had time to study the statutes. The Archbishop wrote to him after their meeting: "I hope that during October I will be able to speak to you again on this topic which is, in my opinion, of great importance for the good of the priesthood which today is under such attack. I have but one desire and the statutes give expression to it: to train good and holy priests filled with zeal for their own sanctification and the salvation of souls."[95]

Trying again—as only he knew how—Marcel Lefebvre wrote François Charrière on October 13, 1970, reminding him of their meetings and the statutes under consideration. Since time was growing short (was there not talk of the coming resignation of the Bishop of Fribourg?), he hurried his friend a little: "Respectfully, I am submitting for your consideration a draft

[92] [Used hereafter as a proper noun and abbreviation for the Society of Saint Pius X. Trans.]

[93] Archives of the foundation at Fribourg, motherhouse, written replies of the seminarians.

[94] Manuscript, Diocesan Archives of Lausanne, Geneva, and Fribourg, VIII. R.I. 42.

[95] Letter of August 18, Diocesan Archives of Lausanne, Geneva, and Fribourg, classer I, doc. 3.

decree of erection authorizing the foundation of the Society. On this day, October 13, I confide this intention to our Lady of Fatima."[96]

Finally, on November 7, still awaiting a reply, Archbishop Lefebvre telephoned the bishop's residence; he was worried since he knew that the auxiliary bishop, Pierre Mamie, was opposed to the foundation. Nevertheless, Bishop Charrière said eagerly: "Yes, Your Grace, come over straightaway." After a brief conversation at the bishop's residence, he said: "There's no point in waiting any longer." He had Archbishop Lefebvre's draft in his hands: "You can leave with this straightaway. I'll give the decree to my secretary to type up." There was just time to go and say a prayer in the chapel while the document was being prepared. Then Bishop Charrière signed it. He was at the end of his episcopal career. Three months later he resigned.[97]

Archbishop Lefebvre had certainly put a little pressure on the Bishop. However, he declared: "I'm absolutely delighted to see my wish so quickly fulfilled!"

The document ruled that:

> The International Priestly Society of St. Pius X is erected in our diocese as a "Pia Unio" (pious union)….We approve and confirm the Statutes, here joined, of the Society for a period of six years *ad experimentum,* which will be able to be renewed for a similar period by tacit approval; after which, the Society can be erected definitely in our diocese by the competent Roman Congregation….Done at Fribourg, in our palace, November 1, 1970, on the Feast of All Saints, François Charrière.

The decree was deliberately predated by six days. Returning to Rue de la Vignettaz, Archbishop Lefebvre, who was obviously delighted, showed the letter to the seminarians, who passed it from one to another: they could not resist re-reading it, looking at the signature and checking the seal. Everything was in order. The Archbishop later said: "Was it not providential? That date of November 1, 1970, is to my mind an event of great importance in our history: it was the day that saw the official birth of the Society. It was the Church which brought it into the world that day. The Society is a work of the Church. For me, I would have been horrified at the thought of founding anything without the bishop's approval. It had to be of the Church."[98]

AN APPROPRIATE BUT PROVISIONAL CANONICAL STATUTE

This same spirit of the Church is expressed in the thirteen pages[99] of the Society's statutes which bring together, in the same brief and concise

---

[96] Diocesan Archives of Lausanne, Geneva, and Fribourg, classer I, doc. 5.
[97] *Fideliter,* no. 59: 65-66.
[98] *Ibid.,* 66.

style and following the same rigorous Thomistic plan as the seminary directory, its identity, patrons, aims, activities, structure, and the virtues and means of sanctification to be practiced by the members of the Society. Firstly, its identity: "The Society is a priestly Society of common life without vows, after the pattern of the Societies of Foreign Missions. However, it is founded in a spirit of profound Faith and perfect obedience, in the steps of the Divine Master" (I, 1).

Therefore, the Society is clearly placed in the category of societies of common life without vows, according to Canon 673 of the Code of Canon Law. It is similar to religious congregations except for the vows, which are replaced by simple promises. "You are not religious," explained the founder to his sons, "but you must have a religious spirit."[100]

This Society of common life would, however, have the provisional statute of a simple pious union: "In its beginnings, the Society shall be subject to the local Ordinary who erected it as a "Pious Union" and approved its statutes, in conformity with the prescriptions of Canon Law" (IV, 1). This was clarified by the decree of erection signed by Bishop Charrière. A *pia unio* is an association of the faithful with some pious or charitable objective, as for example a confraternity; however a *pia unio* might very well be formed by the clergy and is usually the first obligatory stage for a future clerical society. After, with the diocesan bishop's permission and the Holy See's *nihil obstat*, the *pia unio* can become a society of diocesan right properly speaking when it reaches fifty members.[101] The acquisition of pontifical right through a "decree of eulogy" comes much later on. Such was the process described to Archbishop Lefebvre in December 1970 by his friends Cardinal Agagianian,[102] prefect for the Sacred Congregation of the Propagation of the Faith; Cardinal Antoniutti; and Msgr. Paul Philippe, a member and former secretary of Cardinal Antoniutti's congregation.[103]

To establish the most solid base possible for the Society, the decree of erection referred to the conciliar document *Presbyterorum Ordinis*[104] which, aiming at a better distribution of the clergy, encourages in para-

---

[99] Having had to suffer the length of the Holy Ghost Father rule (four hundred articles in 1957), Archbishop Lefebvre confined himself to forty-six articles for the Society, leaving all the details to a future spiritual and pastoral "directory."

[100] *Spiritual Conferences at Ecône*, 35 A-2, Nov. 29, 1976.

[101] *Memorandum* of Archbishop Lefebvre to Bishop Charrière, June 29, 1970. Diocesan Archives of Lausanne, Geneva and Fribourg, VIII, R.I. 42; Letter of Archbishop Lefebvre to Cardinal Antoniutti, Nov. 6, 1972.

[102] Report of Archbishop Lefebvre to Bishop Mamie, Jan. 18, 1971. Diocesan Archives of Lausanne, Geneva, and Fribourg, Class. I, dos. 5.

[103] Archbishop Lefebvre, Letter to Bishop Charrière, Dec. 19, 1970. Diocesan Archives of Lausanne, Geneva, and Fribourg, Class. I, dos. 8.

[104] And not the decree *Optatam Totius* as the decree of erection mistakenly says, even though the Archbishop had prepared both documents.

graph 10 the founding of international seminaries, "personal prelatures, and other institutions to which priests can be transferred or incardinated for the common good of the whole Church." Cardinal Antoniutti had no objections to making the Society a "secular institute" like the priests of the Prado of Lyons, France. This was a new and very flexible model[105] established by Pius XII in his constitution *Provida Mater*, issued on February 2, 1947. Nevertheless, according to Church law, it was the diocesan bishop's responsibility to watch over the life, recruitment, and apostolic usefulness of the pious unions he instituted. He was also responsible for incardinating its members.

As for the seminary whose legal existence was suggested by the statutes, in light of its preparatory year in Valais, its house in Fribourg, and the studies at the University, it could be considered as an appropriate training center needed by the institute even at its embryonic stage of clerical pious union.

THE HEART OF THE SOCIETY: THE MASS

The goal of the Society as fixed by its statutes was "the priesthood." This vast agenda was clarified by a particular spirit:

> The Society is placed specially under the patronage of the priesthood of Jesus. For Our Lord's whole existence was and remains priestly, and the Sacrifice of the Cross was the reason for His incarnation. Thus will the Society's members, for whom "*Mihi vivere Christus est*" (Phil. 1:21) is a reality, live in a way entirely directed towards the Sacrifice of the Mass and our Lord's sacred Passion. (I, 3)

> It is also under the aegis of Mary, Mother of the Priest *par excellence*, and through Him Mother of all priests, in whom she forms her son. She reveals to them the profound motives for their virginity, a condition for the flowering of their Priesthood. (I, 4)

From these things follows an ardent devotion that the members will have towards the Blessed Virgin "in her Compassion for Jesus, Priest and Victim, for the redemption of our sins" and "ever present at His Offering" (I, 3).

The entire life of the priests—their studies, piety, and works—is centered on the Mass: "A profound theological knowledge of the Sacrifice of the Mass will convince them ever more firmly that in this sublime event is realized all of Revelation, the Mystery of Faith, the completion of the Mysteries of the Incarnation and Redemption, the whole effectiveness of the apostolate" (II, 3). "Nothing, therefore, shall be neglected to the end that piety be directed towards, and flow from, the Liturgy of the Holy Mass, which is the heart of theology, of pastoral activity, and of the Church's life"

---

[105] Cf. J. Beyer, S.J., *Les instituts séculiers* (DDB, 1954), 208-213.

(III, 1). "The Society is essentially apostolic, because such is the Sacrifice of the Mass" (I, 2).

Therefore, the Mass is the priest's source of sanctity, the source of his union with Christ, the victim of the cross, and of his zeal to pour out the Precious Blood on souls. Archbishop Lefebvre left the development of this doctrine to a future "spiritual and pastoral directory," but he often explained to his priests why he did not feel the need to make them religious: like St. Jean Eudes, he was convinced that priests can find in their dignity alone—a dignity which puts them above religious—the inspiration and means to raise themselves to a greater perfection. He considered that a high ideal of the priesthood and of the sanctity that it demands was the most effective means of training seminarians.[106]

In fact, such is the foremost of the Society's activities: "...all the works necessary for the formation of priests and whatever pertains thereto." Thus, seminaries, whether they are those of the Society or not, must take care that the training "attain its chief goal: the priest's holiness, together with sufficient knowledge" (III, 1). This is why the Society was placed under the patronage of St. Pius X. The primordial concern of this holy Pope was the integrity of the priesthood and the sanctity that flows from it.[107] "In accord with the wishes and prescriptions so often renewed by Popes and Councils, the *Summa Theologica* of St. Thomas Aquinas and his philosophical principles shall be the chief subject of study in the Seminary. The seminarians shall thus carefully avoid modern errors, particularly liberalism and all the ideas it engenders" (III, 1).

In addition to this work of training seminarians, the Society was founded to sanctify priests by preaching retreats, looking after old priests, and even helping fallen priests[108] to reform. True Catholic schools would be encouraged and founded by the members of the Society, but at the beginning it was not foreseen that the Society would actually run them (subsequent events made this an eventuality). From these schools "will come vocations and Christian homes." Finally, the priests of the Society would be devoted to the parish ministry and to preaching parish missions (III, 4-5).

Taking the idea of Loublande and expanding it, the statutes also foresaw "a community of somewhat contemplative character devoted to the celebration of the Holy Sacrifice of the Mass, adoration of the Blessed Sacrament, and preaching retreats in-house" (VII).

---

[106] *Dictionnaire de théologie catholique*, V, 1473, 2° (s.v. Eudes, Bienheureux Jean). Another of the Archbishop's reasons for this: the modern apostolate constantly exposes active religious to transgress their vow of poverty.

[107] St. Pius X, encyclical *E Supremi Apostolatus*, Oct. 4, 1903 (Bonne Presse), I, 39-41.

[108] Like the Missionaries of Nazareth founded for this end by Fr. Boissard in Lendreville, France.

Along with the priests and future priests, the Society would include "members who are not priests" as well as affiliated nuns "when God raises them up" (II, 4). It shall seek to "inculcate a sense of the greatness and nobility of the vocation of helpers in the service of the Altar and all that is related to it" (III, 3).

The virtues recommended to the members of the Society include firstly "a great love of God," a charity such "as to naturally engender virginity and poverty" as well as "the gift of self through faith and by a ready, generous, and loving obedience" (VI, 1); also[109] "a great simplicity and frankness, through constant evenness of temper and contagious joy" (VI, 5). The virtue of poverty will break the enslavement caused by tobacco and television: "Our true television is the Tabernacle" (VI, 7).

This same charity should excite a hunger and thirst for the virtue of justice towards God, *i.e.,* the exercise of the virtue of religion above all in the Holy Sacrifice of the Mass, "the act of the most sublime Christian prayer." The virtue of religion would also be expressed by wearing the cassock. The cassock is "a witness, a sermon. It repels wicked spirits and those subject to them; it attracts upright and religious souls. It greatly facilitates the apostolate" (VI, 6).

This same charity which surrounds and thus guides the whole life of the Society's members should be apostolic, "avidly desirous of saving souls" at the cost of humiliations and trials like our Lord Jesus Christ, winning souls by "humility, gentleness, discretion, and magnanimity" (VI, 4). The community life including four times of prayer in common is the rule both for aspiring members and full members of the Society; it is "a chance to exercise fraternal charity."

It must be admitted that a reading of the statutes indicates no particular spirituality with Archbishop Lefebvre. We cannot speak of a "personal idea" on the part of the founder; the tradition is common among the clergy of leading an existence centered on the altar as the source of apostolic charity and in the context of the common life. He would later say: "If there is one thing I have always sought, it is not to have personal ideas. We have the ideas of the Church!...As I have already told you, I do not want to impose any special spirituality unless it be the spirituality of the Church..., *i.e.,* spirituality as St. Thomas conceives of it in his *Summa Theologica*: a spirituality based on the exercise of virtues, the truths of faith, the supernatural virtues, and the beatitudes. This is how our spiritual life normally works."[110]

Archbishop Lefebvre later reminded his sons of how the Society came to be founded. He emphasized certain things very strongly: "It was not

---

[109] Two Holy Ghost Father virtues that the Archbishop liked very much.
[110] *Spiritual Conferences at Ecône,* 36 A, Nov. 30, 1976.

born in the spirit of dissent and opposition, far from it. It was born as the works of the Church are sometimes born, *i.e.*, from a necessity which arose to ensure that there was proper priestly training....I looked for a solution. Providence allowed the creation of this seminary at Fribourg...and afterwards, to protect the priesthood, this little group became the Society...and later still the seminary moved from Fribourg to Ecône."[111]

VI. THE SEMINARY OF SAINT PIUS X IN ECÔNE

NEW DECISION—BISHOP ADAM'S AGREEMENT

Archbishop Lefebvre commented:

From November 1970 I had to think about the new school year in October 1971 and work out where we would lodge those who had finished the year of spirituality. In principle, it was to be at Fribourg[112] in an existing building that was rented or bought, or otherwise in a new building! So, we set about house hunting, visiting buildings and looking at properties.

Meanwhile, the university courses were no longer satisfactory; the students were becoming agitated, and Fr. Philippe looked like he would soon be proved right: for he had said to me since the beginning: "One day soon you will have to give the courses yourself."

Now, when I went to Ecône, it was good to see how the young men benefited from a true and simple curriculum and from being in an atmosphere of peace rather than dissent. They were also out in the Valais countryside where the people were still deeply religious. So, I thought to myself: why not put the seminary here?

Then I consulted with His Eminence Cardinal Journet, His Excellency Bishop Mamie, and my colleagues. The Cardinal was categorical: "The university does not suit the majority of seminarians and does not encourage seminary discipline; if you have the choice, you must not hesitate. Send only a few students to the university to get degrees."[113] Bishop Mamie understood what good could come from an independent seminary but thought that it would be difficult to set up....Lastly, my colleagues were unanimous: if it was going to provide training that was sound and solid in all respects, the seminary should be in Ecône.[114]

[111] *Ibid.*, 47 A and B, Oct. 10 and 11, 1977.

[112] Nevertheless, in summer 1970 Archbishop Lefebvre visited the château of the Duchess of Sabran in Anjou that was available for his use.

[113] Interview on Jan. 14, 1971 (according to Archbishop Lefebvre's diary). In his reply to the Archbishop, the cardinal was "careful not to say anything for or against his venture, not wishing to get mixed up in it." Journet, Letter to Bishop Mamie, Jan. 10, 1973, Diocesan Archives of Lausanne, Geneva, and Fribourg, classer I, doc. 22; Savioz, *Essai historique sur la foundation de la Fraternité de Saint-Pie X*, annex 1.78.

The Diary of Ecône notes on November 16 that at the end of a novena to St. Joseph, and "after a visit to the chapel," the Archbishop decided to build the seminary at Ecône. Bishop Adam's permission was still needed... On December 26, 1970, Maître Lovey drove the Archbishop and Fr. Gottlieb to the bishop's residence in Sion, and stayed in the car while they went in. "Getting permission was a little more difficult" than for the year of spirituality, said the Archbishop. At last, the Bishop of Sion gave in: "The last time, you asked me if you could use Ecône for your pre-seminary, I accepted; but when you asked permission for a seminary, I objected that we already had three in the diocese. Now, this year, my seminary is at Fribourg and the Capuchins have closed theirs. So, I no longer have any objection."[115]

In what form did Nestor Adam give his permission? We do not know. Archbishop Lefebvre stated that the authorization was "explicit": "Then, I asked him for written approval. But he smiled and said: 'You doubt the word of the Bishop?' So I had nothing in writing. I regretted it because a few years later, he dared to claim that he had not given permission for the seminary but only for the year of spirituality! Maître Lovey protested against Bishop Adam in turn because he well remembered how satisfied we were at getting Bishop Adam's agreement. Two of us could give witness."[116]

What was the reality? Later on, Bishop Henri Schwery, Nestor Adam's successor, heard his predecessor tell him more than once: "Archbishop Lefebvre tricked me!"—Bishop Schwery thought this concerned a "juridical" question. He was probably talking about this authorization that the Archbishop dragged out of him and that Bishop Adam conceded through gritted teeth. The former Vicar General of Sion, Msgr. Camille Grand, one day advised Bishop Schwery: "Be very careful! Bishop Adam was tricked a few times. Old man Lefebvre knows how to use things you say."[117]

We think the matter can be explained in the following manner. Nestor Adam was reticent about the proposal of his determined visitor, and began by raising certain objections: "Ecône? Is the spot well chosen? The St. Ber-

---

[114] Diary of Fribourg, "A look at the year 70-71 and what the future holds"; Notes of Archbishop Lefebvre to Cardinal Wright, Jan. 11, 1972, Sion Diocesan Archives 396.15; *Spiritual Conferences at Ecône*, Dec. 21, 1972; "Priests for Tomorrow," Paris, March 1973, in *A Bishop Speaks*, 143ff.

[115] Cf. Sermon for the Ordinations, Ecône, June 29, 1977.

[116] Roger Lovey, *Nouvelliste et FAV*, Jan. 16, 1975; Diary of Richenbach, Oct. 22, 1980; Msgr. Lefebvre, Letter to Bishop Tissier de Mallerais, May 5, 1990. Opposed to these: Adam, Letter to Hugo Maria Kellner, April 15, 1972; conversation with Nuncio, June 16, 1972; Letter to Cardinal Garrone, Feb. 21, 1973; instructions of April 23, 1974; instructions of Aug. 14, 1975, Sion Diocesan Archives 396, 91 (Savioz, *Essai historique sur la foundation de la Fraternité de Saint-Pie X*, ann. 1. 59; 1. 62; 1. 81; 1. 90; 1. 93).

[117] Cardinal Schwéry, Interview with Fr. J.-M. Savioz, in Savioz, *Essai historique sur la foundation de la Fraternité de Saint-Pie X*, ann. 2. 2, 2, 4.

nard Canons tried putting their own students there and gave up after a few years; besides, it might not be easy to find qualified teaching staff. Fribourg seems to me much better."[118]

The Archbishop had no trouble replying that he preferred the quiet of Ecône, which was much better for study than the noise of Fribourg. And he was trying hard to find professors who would agree to live at Ecône. Wearying of the struggle, the Bishop of Sion must have given in, but fudged the issue: "In that case, Your Grace, there is no objection." It is an "explicit" authorization without really being terribly explicit. The "Bishop's word" only stretched to this reticent and convenient ambiguity that nothing in writing would later clarify. And Bishop Adam could claim afterwards that he never really gave his permission (deliberate, positive, written, *etc.*).

For want of anything better, Archbishop Lefebvre considered himself nonetheless satisfied and got on with the work. Henceforth, things went very quickly. On February 3, the architect Ami Delaloye was commissioned. On February 15, 1971, he came to present his plans for the future St. Pius X wing, a first building providing accommodation, and his quotation: 1,500,000 Swiss francs. The Archbishop listened, saying nothing but thinking: "I need at least a third of that to begin without getting into debt; I don't have it, I can't go ahead."

Now, at that very moment, a telephone call from Fribourg informed him that a benefactor—Bishop Adrien Bressolles[119]—had just credited his account with a large amount of money. Providentially, it was just enough to get the project started![120] On April 28 at Mr. Delaloye's office, the timetable for the construction was drawn up. The Archbishop was helped by Fr. Charles Berclaz, C.S.Sp., who was a construction specialist. Fr. Berclaz remarked: "I really admired the spiritual atmosphere, the piety that he managed to bring to that construction site meeting. He began with a prayer; and quite a few of those people who were there gave their services for more or less nothing."[121]

It was true that some builder friends generously waived their fees and worked hard on the suppliers. The Archbishop, his brother Michel, and Marcel Pedroni went to order the carpets from "Tapis Sion" in the north of France. Marcel negotiated the price and the Archbishop later said he had "fought hard so that our new house might not be too comfortable." Ami

---

[118] Bishop Adam, *Notice sur le séminaire Saint-Pie X*, April 25, 1974, Diocesan Archives of Lausanne, Geneva, and Fribourg 396, 46; Savioz, *Essai historique sur la foundation de la Fraternité de Saint-Pie X*, ann. 1. 90.

[119] Bishop Bressolles, Letter to Archbishop Lefebvre, Jan. 29, 1971.

[120] Ms. I, 68, 29-34; notebooks and memoirs of Marcel Pedroni.

[121] Ms. I, 49, 40-47.

Delaloye often said: "But, Your Grace, your seminarians need this or that!" And the Archbishop would reply: "They also need renouncement."

The entry in the Diary of Ecône on April 29, 1971, notes that Bishop Adam made a visit; the bishop of the diocese was able to see the initial work on the foundations for the first building. On June 6, Archbishop Lefebvre blessed the foundation stone in the presence of the owners, Fr. Merhle (the prior of the Albertinum in Fribourg), the Fribourg committee, Canon de Soos from the Canons of St. Bernard, Mr. Jules Monet (leader of Riddes Council), and Fr. Epiney. At last on June 28, the vigil of the feast of Saints Peter and Paul, the Archbishop ordained the first priest, Fr. Peter Morgan, a member of the Society; he soon left to set up the Society in Great Britain.

As for Paul Aulagnier, he would be ordained by the Archbishop on October 17 at the end of the new school-year retreat preached in Grolley by Frs. Rivière and Barrielle; there were thirty-eight seminarians of whom five had come from Fribourg. A Pontifical Mass of Ordination took place in Riddes parish church where the parish priest decided that Tradition would henceforth reclaim its rightful place. The meal after the ceremony was held in the barn at Ecône, and Fr. Paul Aulagnier spoke a few words to the guests in the presence of Archbishop Lefebvre: "We will follow him everywhere!" The Archbishop corrected him: "We follow the Church! God forbid I should have ideas of my own!"

However, the accommodation at Ecône was not sufficient and some seminarians were put up temporarily in buildings kindly loaned by Mr. Guy Fellay, who was manager of Ecône's electricity plant.

ORGANIZING STUDIES—ST. THOMAS THE MASTER

On May 2, 1971, at Ecône, Archbishop Lefebvre with the help of the teachers who were present fixed the curriculum for philosophy and theology studies in view of the 1972 school year. Fr. François-Olivier Dubuis thought that the seminary studies should last seven years. Archbishop Lefebvre, who was more realistic and who was being asked by the faithful to supply priests, fixed the curriculum at five years: a year of spirituality, two years of systematic philosophy (Logic, Cosmology, Psychology, Metaphysics, Ethics) and two years of theology. It was short; it was also true that they would begin studying Sacred Scripture, the Treatise on the Church, and even moral theology at the same time as philosophy. However, a third year of theology would be added subsequently.

Besides the "specialist" subjects such as Sacred Scripture, Canon Law, History of the Church, and Liturgy, the former disciple of Fr. Le Rohellec wanted a unique philosophy-theology *cursus* in which the seminarians would study Aquinas's *Summa Theologica* question by question[122] from day one. He feared in fact that philosophy separated from theology would give a naturalistic understanding of reality:

> Does not the teaching of philosophy carry with it the disadvantage of focusing firstly on natural truths for two years...and only later on Revelation?
>
> For God has willed us to be raised to the supernatural state;...we cannot separate nature from grace now. No man has ever existed, nor now exists, in the state of pure nature; that does not exist! Adam and Eve were created in the state of grace and those who have not received grace are in want of it. They feel this lack of grace because their very nature is wounded and disordered because it is deprived of grace. No man can exist who does not either have or lack grace. Therefore, one cannot be indifferent to grace.[123]

A study of reality from a merely natural point of view carries with it the risk of seducing students with the pleasures of pure speculative thought or fascination with the logical and metaphysical subtleties which it gives rise to. For two long years, it deprives the seminarians of that wonderful synthesis of reason and faith contained in the *Summa Theologica*, which so accurately describes man's spiritual progress towards God. The seminary professors objected that philosophy and theology are two quite distinct disciplines because of their different "lights"—reason and faith—and that one must know philosophy before using it as the instrument and "servant" of theology. The Archbishop gave in and followed the opinion of his professors.

The first three teachers were quickly joined by priests of exceptional quality. Firstly there was Fr. François-Olivier Dubuis, a former married Protestant Pastor and a seminary professor at Sion and the scholasticate of the Grand St. Bernard Canons at Martigny: he taught patrology and history for three years. Archbishop Lefebvre knew that he celebrated the New Mass—not in Ecône—but he was broadminded enough to ask for his help after consulting Bishop Adam and Msgr. Lovey.

Then came Canon René Berthod,[124] a former pupil of Fr. Santiago Ramirez in moral theology at Fribourg University; like his teacher he had a great love for St. Thomas Aquinas. He taught theology to Grand St. Bernard students in Ecône and then became director of studies at Martigny. Later, he was a superb principal of Champittet School run by the Canons in Lausanne, and had just left his post as prior at Lens. With Msgr. Lovey's permission, he agreed to come and teach at Ecône: he gave courses in "Acts

---

[122] Lefebvre, Letter to Cardinal Ottaviani, Dakar, Feb. 26, 1960.

[123] *Spiritual Conferences at Ecône*, 9 A, Sep. 30, 1974.

[124] He came from Praz-de-Fort (1916-1996) and was the seventh child of Joseph Berthod (primary teacher and postal worker) and Hélène M. Thétaz (midwife). His great-grandfather Jean-Laurent Berthod was a cheese maker and had come from Courmayeur (Vald'Aoste) in 1843.

of the Magisterium," philosophy (from 1971-72 onwards), and moral theology (from 1972-73), commenting on the textbook written by Fr. Dominique-M. Prummer, O.P., which was faithful to St. Thomas and at the same time very practical. He was loved and respected by all the seminarians. And with his unequaled pastoral experience, his refined Valaisan humor, his endearing shyness and theological wisdom, he trained his students thoroughly in the great principles of moral theology.

At the beginning of the school year in 1972, Ecône also received the wholly unexpected support of Fr. Ceslas Spicq, O.P., a professor at Fribourg University, who came to give classes in New Testament exegesis. This learned expert and humble monk came each Wednesday for three years and commentated on the writings of St. Paul, St. Luke, and St. John. His interpretations were resolutely opposed to the slippery slope of "new symbolic exegesis." His perfect command of Greek philology meant he could easily expose the literal sense of a passage, without neglecting the commentaries of the Fathers or St. Thomas. He succeeded in giving the students a taste for Sacred Scripture, which is what Archbishop Lefebvre wanted most from this subject.

A year after Fr. Spicq, his colleague from Fribourg, Fr. Thomas Mehrle, began coming each Thursday to Ecône. His theology courses at Fribourg had been boycotted and he had lost his professorial chair. The dissenting students who were responsible accused him of judging everything from a Thomistic point of view: "Professor Mehrle is so hidebound by orthodoxy that he is totally unable to understand new trends of thought."[125]

"That's a good sign!" Archbishop Lefebvre thought to himself. This priest was encouraged to come to Ecône by Bishop Mamie and by the Master General of the Dominicans. He accepted Archbishop Lefebvre's invitation, and for two years he taught from the Angelic Doctor's *Summa*, as the Archbishop wanted, presenting the seminarians with the very marrow of St. Thomas's thought, adding—as Vatican II had reasonably asked theology teachers to do—a brief historical overview of each doctrinal question along with the relevant scriptural evidence and decisions of the Magisterium. Fr. Mehrle was a good teacher who was also very rigorous, and he did not hesitate occasionally to criticize Karl Rahner and the "New Theology"; his students were not quite so happy when he felt obliged to quote Vatican II to show that "there were some good things in the Council."

---

[125] *La Liberté*, Fribourg, Feb. 17, 1972; Savioz, *Essai historique sur la foundation de la Fraternité de Saint-Pie X*, annexe 2. 6.

A VARIED BUT UNITED TEACHING STAFF

The professors such as Canon Berthod who lived at Ecône were joined by Dom Edouard Guillou. He was a Benedictine from Notre-Dame de la Source in Paris and the liturgical editor of *Nouvelles de Chrétienté*. In light hearted, mocking tones, this liturgist monk invoked various grand axioms as he made fun of the deviations of the "new liturgy": "The liturgy," he said, "is not a lesson and is not meant for teaching." "Mass is not supposed to be all yack, yack, yack." But he warned the seminarians about going to the other extreme: "Legalism in the rubrics leaves you open to accepting any reform." Dom Guillou was a true son of Dom Guéranger, and reiterated his maxim: "Liturgy is Tradition in its most powerful and solemn expression."

Naturally, Dom Guillou used the principles of the "Liturgical Doctor's" fight for the Roman liturgy to expound a penetrating critique of Paul VI's reforms. Had not Prosper Guéranger already denounced "that blind and far too common hope of bringing back heretics by diminishing doctrine and Catholic practices"? Did he not condemn the New Mass in advance by identifying the characteristics of "anti-liturgical heresy"? He noted in particular "hatred for the traditional formulae of the divine cult" and the tendency to "replace ecclesiastical formulae with readings from Sacred Scripture" in order "to silence the voice of Tradition" by "cleverly selecting texts" and quoting "truncated passages" to propagate new dogmas. Thus, "the liturgy is a two-edged sword that in the hands of the Church saves souls and in heresy's hands mercilessly destroys them."[126]

Another particularly relevant subject was Apologetics. It was joined to the Treatise on the Church and was taught by a young discalced Carmelite, Fr. Dominique de La Presle. He meticulously went about training his students to argue scientifically. He unveiled the esoteric and satanic origins of ecumenism, foretold and planned by the great *illuminati*. History of the Church was taught by Fr. Christian Dumoulin from the major seminary at Bourges; he was a teacher noted for his logical rigor and his wonderfully entertaining acting abilities.

Social Ethics or politics in the broad sense, a controversial science if indeed it is a science, was taught with style by the enthusiastic Fr. Aulagnier, who faithfully followed Archbishop Lefebvre's directive:

> In politics we can have our personal convictions provided they are in accordance with the doctrine of the Church. But the seminary must not advocate any particular form of politics. We must stand above politics and look at things only from the principles of general politics as taught by ethics. Democracy remains dangerous because it wavers between anarchy and

---

[126] Dom Prosper Guéranger, *Les Institutions liturgiques*, I, 396-397 (ed. of 1878); II, 724 (ed. of 1861).

dictatorship. However, let us be wary! We must not be like the "pirate seminary" in Barcelona which split after a disagreement between Carlists and supporters of Juan-Carlos![127]

If, therefore, Fr. Aulagnier was happy to quote from the "natural politics" of Charles Maurras,[128] it was because Maurras's thought was in agreement with the Popes' condemnation of Jean-Jacques Rousseau's "Social Contract," the base of liberal democracy. However, the combative priest exhorted the seminarians to read preferably the Catholic, anti-liberal authors recommended by Archbishop Lefebvre such as Cardinal Pie, Louis Veuillot, Fr. Emmanuel Berbier and his *Histoire du catholicisme liberal*, Fr. Felix Sarda y Salavny's *Liberalism Is a Sin*, the works of Msgr. Henri Delassus, *etc*. "If you do not read," he told them clearly, "you will understand nothing about the crisis and you will give in!"

All these individuals, be they distinguished professors or humble beginners, and whether they resided in Ecône or not, ensured that the teaching staff was varied, occasionally very different, but always united on the essential mission of handing on Catholic doctrine. Archbishop Lefebvre made discreet and thoughtful use of the talents of each one; having expressed his wishes and intentions at the beginning of the year,[129] he took a back seat and trusted his men.

Other teachers came from time to time to make their own contributions: thus, Fr. Guérard des Lauriers came to give a class in Mariology for which he had scribbled his notes on the back of a subway ticket but which still went beyond the abilities of the average student to understand. Professor Faÿ's talks presented a grand historical overview of the successive epochs of the Counter-Church, from the cabal and esoteric sects up to Freemasonry with its present-day role, and touching upon humanism, the Protestant reformers, the Encyclopaedia,[130] and the French Revolution. The lively eloquence of this dignified invalid who walked with a limp went curiously well with the subtle metaphysical thinking of the "wizened, abstracted Dominican."

Such was Ecône in those intrepid early years. But Ecône would not have been Ecône if Providence not led Fr. Barrielle to its door!

---

[127] *Spiritual Conferences at Ecône*, Dec. 21, 1972.

[128] Ch. Maurras, *Mes idées politiques* (Fayard, 1937), preface.

[129] Fr. Thomas Mehrle, Interview with Fr. Savioz, Nov. 16, 1993, Savioz, *Essai historique sur la foundation de la Fraternité de Saint-Pie X*, ann. 2, 6.

[130] [This multi-volume reference work initially compiled by Diderot, and d'Alembert has as its philosophical undercurrent the ideas of the Enlightenment. It is a good summary of the prejudices of the eighteenth century "Philosophers" with their contempt for tradition, Catholic history and thought, and their belief in the absolute independence of reason. Trans.]

FR. BARRIELLE'S TREASURE: THE IGNATIAN EXERCISES

St. Thomas's solid spirituality based on the distinction of the soul's powers, the four wounds of original sin, the development of the theological and moral virtues and the gifts of the Holy Ghost, was soon to receive the support of an instrument that wedded the realism of sin and a sense of being in spiritual combat with the apostolic zeal that the Archbishop wanted to inculcate in his students. Archbishop Lefebvre was fortunate enough to find such a tool in the Spiritual Exercises of St. Ignatius of Loyola, as preached, explained and popularized at Ecône by Fr. Ludovic-Marie Barrielle.

He came from Château-Gombert near Marseilles. As a young man this enthusiastic Provençal had fought in the First World War. Later, he was parish priest at the Good Shepherd in Marseilles before becoming a Parish Co-operator of Christ the King (CPCR) at Chabeuil. He had been a close friend of the founder, Fr. Vallet, and was superior of the house at Chabeuil before distancing himself from the post-conciliar liberal tendencies. Thinking about refounding his order in the orbit of Tradition, he came to Ecône one day in October 1971...and stayed on. In the end he gave up on his idea, or rather achieved it in a better way as "spiritual director" of the seminary, passing on the torch of the exercises of St. Ignatius to the members of the Society of Saint Pius X.

In his "spiritual talk" in the evening, Fr. Barrielle dished out "milk for the novices." He excelled at giving the students a hunger for sanctity through meditation on the liturgy and the example of the lives of saints. He made them understand the irresistible logic of St. Ignatius's "Principle and Foundation" that has repercussions throughout the Ignatian vision.

Archbishop Lefebvre admired Ignatius's perfect Thomism. Man must always ask God for the grace that he wishes to obtain through meditation, be it the conquest of self, or knowing the love of our Lord, the ultimate goal and the greatest means of sanctification. "Accordingly as we love Him, our Lord enlightens the soul, and it instinctively feels within itself the obstacles to union with Him."[131] In fact, the founder was careful to repeat often: "I have no wish to impose a special spirituality unless it be the spirituality of the Church."[132] This was why he preferred the plan of St. Thomas's *Summa*. Nonetheless, the Archbishop recommended the "thirty days" that Fr. Barrielle preached every summer and which he once followed, stating later how profitable he had found them.

Fr. Barrielle knew very well that Ignatian meditation on the mysteries of Jesus Christ leads the soul to take the "high dive" into sanctity, the sec-

---

[131] *Retreats at Ecône*, 76, priestly retreat, Sept. 1986.
[132] *Spiritual Conferences at Ecône*, 36 A, Nov. 30, 1976.

ond conversion. He said: "I have sometimes seen retreatants being led along the very paths of mysticism after only an eight day retreat."[133] Without Fr. Barrielle, Ecône would not have been Ecône. One would not have had, as Bishop Morilleau remarked while visiting the seminary, the "impression of being in a novitiate."[134]

> [He was] a wonderful model of a priest, filled with an intense and continual desire for the salvation of souls. Haunted by the idea of eternal salvation, Fr. Barrielle lived by faith and was in touch with heavenly realities: the Blessed Trinity, the Sacred Heart, St. Joseph, the holy Angels. He lived on these devotions, taught them, and promoted them.[135]

He remained "on the go," preaching the exercises in the house at Montelenge, Piedmont, until he was totally exhausted. He gave up his valiant soul to God at Ecône on March 1, 1983, the first Friday of the month of St. Joseph in whom he had had unbounded confidence. It would have made the old soldier's joy complete to see his spiritual sons growing in number and preaching the Exercises, not only to lay people throughout the whole world, but also to priests as required by the statues of the Society. Thus, the Society fulfills "its true goal which is the sanctification of the priesthood" (Statutes, VIII, 3).

VII. THE SPREAD IN VOCATIONS

AMERICA COMES TO ECÔNE

Archbishop Lefebvre looked hopefully to the United States as a potential source of vocations. Faced with the devastation of modernism, this country could boast strong resistance from Catholic Tradition. There were organized movements such as the *Catholic Traditionalist Movement* of Fr. Gommar De Pauw, the Orthodox Roman Catholic Movement of Fr. Francis Fenton, Fr. Joseph Gedra's Committee for the Tridentine Latin Mass, *etc*. Numerous priests remained faithful to the Mass of all time, for example, Fr. Frederick Nelson at Powers Lake, North Dakota. Other Catholics belonged to the non-denominational, anti-Communist John Birch Society. The various tendencies of these diverse organizations would be reflected in Archbishop Lefebvre's first recruits.

In the United States, they quickly learned of the foundation of the Society of Saint Pius X's seminary in Switzerland. On December 29, 1970, a young Carmelite from California, Gregory Post, wrote to Archbishop Lefebvre. His application to the seminary was accepted, and he came to Rue de la Vignettaz in Fribourg in Autumn 1971. However, prior to this,

---

[133] *Ibid.*, March 13, 1972.
[134] *Ibid.*, 85 B, June 23, 1981.
[135] *Ibid.*, 99 A, March 8, 1983.

in March 1971 the Archbishop went "prospecting" in the United States; through Fr. Ramsay, a professor at the "St. Pius X Seminary" of his friend Bishop Ackerman in Covington, Kentucky, he met three seminarians from New York: Anthony Ward, Donald Sanborn, and Clarence Kelly.

On March 18, the Archbishop wrote from Covington to his friend and benefactor General Jean Lecomte: "I am in the United States; I want to avoid having to make American seminarians come to Switzerland. I hope to be able to have a house here to attract good vocations." For the time being this project was shelved and the three Americans entered the year of spirituality in Ecône on October 5 and 6, 1971.

For the European seminarians, the characters of their American colleagues proved to be something quite new: they were very relaxed during recreation or while doing the dishes, but amazingly rigid when it came to the liturgical rubrics. At first they not unreasonably deplored the omission of the psalm *Judica me* and the last Gospel from Mass at Ecône. The same was true for the readings of the Epistle and Gospel that were read from a lectern facing the people. In 1974, when the Archbishop returned to a strict observance of the 1960 rubrics, that was not enough to satisfy some of them who were determined that after they left seminary they would follow the pre-John XXIII prescriptions. The same students could not understand why Archbishop Lefebvre did not consider the New Mass to be invalid or the Apostolic See to be vacant.

Archbishop Lefebvre must have expected trouble from these young clerics who, quite simply, suffered from the classic American weakness coming from the contrast between a naturalistic daily life emphasizing material and technical means and an idealist and formalistic piety. The American seminary founded in Armada, Michigan, in 1974 and that moved to Ridgefield, Connecticut, and later on to Winona, Minnesota, would aim precisely at achieving a harmonious integration of truly "natural nature" with supernatural grace. However, neither Anthony Ward, who soon left the Society, nor Clarence Kelly, nor Donald Sanborn, who distanced themselves too much from Archbishop Lefebvre to be able to remain with him, would help achieve this ideal. It would take the methodical intelligence and the determined iron grip of a young Englishman.

IN THE ISLAND OF SAINTS

Opposition to the conciliar reforms had also been organized in Great Britain. Hamish Fraser of the review *Approaches* founded a lay movement, and Archbishop Lefebvre supported it from 1966 onwards. There was also the Latin Mass Society which was affiliated to *Una Voce*. Moreover, even before the implementation of the New Mass, some lay people began developing a network of Latin Masses that loyal priests offered either in churches or secretly in private houses, as in "penal days."

After 1969 when the Latin Mass Society undertook only to organize Traditional Masses with the permission of the bishops according to the indult secured by Cardinal Heenan—permission that was deliberately granted sparingly—some people turned to Archbishop Lefebvre. One of these was Miss Mary Nielsen, president of *Una Voce Scotland*, who met the Archbishop at the 1969 meeting in Rome. The Archbishop also visited the United Kingdom in 1971. During a trip to Edinburgh he met the young Edward Black who would become the second district superior of the Society in Great Britain.

Meanwhile, Fr. Peter Morgan, a sociable, jovial man who was extreme in his traditionalism, was ordained priest in Ecône on June 28, 1971. The Archbishop immediately sent him to England where he soon established a house of the Society in London within the diocese of Southwark. Archbishop Lefebvre wrote to Bishop Cyril Cowderoy of Southwark describing this foundation as a small pre-seminary; on May 1, 1971, Bishop Cowderoy answered stating that he would only give permission for "a house for prayer and study for the actual members" of the Society. The Archbishop accepted these terms on May 8. Little by little, Fr. Morgan was joined by several courageous priests. He organized a traveling apostolate that obviously was not backed by the various Ordinaries.

In autumn 1972 the earliest signs of revival in the Island of Saints were seen in Ecône: firstly the military and pragmatic Scotsman Edward Black, and two months later, a phlegmatic and impassioned Englishman devoted to Shakespeare and Beethoven, called Richard Williamson.

A FLOOD OF VOCATIONS

That year from 1972 to 1973, the Society's only apostolate was in Great Britain and California, unless we include the small chaplaincy served by Fr. Aulagnier at Mademoiselle Luce Quenette's girls' school in Malvières, France—a remote village that during winter the chaplain could sometimes only reach on skis.

However, vocations began flooding to Ecône. They were attracted by its growing reputation or sent by doctrinally solid priests who were faithful to the Mass of their ordination (of whom there were still hundreds in France). Twenty-seven new recruits entered in October 1971, most of whom were French: for example, Pierre-Armand d'Argenson, Didier Bonneterre, Louis-Paul Dubroeucq, and Maurice Monier. There was also a Swiss, Denis Roch, the son of a Protestant pastor from Geneva, and our three friends from New York.

Fearing that he would not have enough space in Ecône to accommodate the "litter" of 1972, Archbishop Lefebvre thought for a while about establishing the year of spirituality at Val d'Aoste; he even got permission from Bishop Ovidio Lari.[136] Nevertheless, the thirty-five new students who arrived in October 1972 began their introduction to the spiritual life in Ecône; they came from six European countries: the United Kingdom, Belgium, France (Denis Coiffet, Jean-Michel Faure, Philippe Le Pivain), Italy, Switzerland, and Germany.

In Germany, resistance to the revolution in the Church had begun at Munich University shortly before Christmas 1965 during one of Professor Reinhard Lauth's classes in transcendental philosophy. From then on, a growing group of students got together with the Professor to study the crisis in the Church and support the continuance of the Traditional Mass. Among them was a Swabian student of mathematics, Franz Schmidberger, and Klaus Wodsack, a philosophy student from Prussia.

In 1972 these two friends entered Ecône. Roger Bonvin, President of the Federal Council, had recently visited the seminary to see the new wing composed of communal rooms. A final accommodation wing was added in 1973. The new German speakers, including Josef Bisig from Zoug in Switzerland, opened up Germany and German-speaking Switzerland to the Archbishop, who was now traveling further and further afield.

THE ARCHBISHOP ON A SPEAKING TOUR

Far from restricting himself to the peaceful retirement that Paul VI ascribed him, the Archbishop was continually active. Answering the requests of eminent and committed laymen, he went on speaking tours throughout France and other European countries to draw attention to the Society and its three-fold combat: the true Mass, the veritable propitiatory sacrifice; the true priesthood through which is offered up the victim of Calvary; and the true Christian and religious life in which is made the offering of daily life in union with the cross of Christ: "There lies the whole mystery of the Church: Satan strikes at its heart by attacking the Holy Mass."[137]

In January 1973, the Archbishop traveled throughout France. At Fontgombault, he beseeched Dom Roy: "Keep the Mass: that's the aim we share. These last few weeks we have been increasingly under attack precisely because of the liturgy; there is no way we are giving up!" Unfortunately, Dom Roy gave up the following year.

In Rennes, Saint-Brieuc, Best, Vannes, Nantes, and La Roche-sur Yon, the faithful crammed by their hundreds into small halls that could not accommodate them all; in Montauban, the parish priest Jean Choulot had gathered together forty priests who almost all wore the cassock and who seemed to be in full agreement with the analysis and advice of the Arch-

---

[136] Notebooks of Marcel Pedroni, Jan. 3, 1972; Letter of Archbishop Lefebvre to Bishop Adam, Feb. 10, 1972.
[137] *Spiritual Conferences at Ecône*, Jan. 27, 1973.

bishop. The faithful expressed their worries, especially for their children. Everything—the new catechism, the New Mass, the decline in school discipline—was turning the youth away from Tradition and the Faith.

The Archbishop gave hope to priests and laymen alike by teaching them how to fight: he told the priests to gather together to examine how the New Mass "blurs and diminishes the expression of our faith in those realities that constitute the very essence of the sacrifice left to us by our Lord."[138] He was effectively calling on these priests to return to the Mass of their ordination. He also advised the faithful: "Learn how to do without television, support the loyal priests, organize catechism groups. I pray to God that you keep the Faith until your dying day, *so that the Church might continue.*"[139]

Everywhere, laymen began establishing "St. Pius V Associations," setting up temporary chapels in barns, garages, and public meeting halls. These were served by volunteer priests who followed the example of Catholic Vendée's recusant priests and their heroic deeds under the Reign of Terror, or else imitated the priests of Alexandria who resisted Arianism at the instigation of their indomitable, exiled bishop St. Athanasius.

Chauffeured by loyal and able drivers, Archbishop Lefebvre traveled throughout Europe; sometimes he would think of Ecône. In 1977, he said: "Throughout this tour, my thoughts have been turned to you, dear seminarians, because I cannot leave you. Seeing so many people before me, so many thousands, I said to myself: what work there is to do, what prospects for the apostolate!"[140]

IN THE ANTIPODES

If only there had been just Europe! The Archbishop crossed the oceans. On March 14, 1971, in Rougemont, Canada, he addressed the pilgrims of Saint Michel familiarly known as "the white berets," and spoke of the "moral martyrdom suffered by the priest" when the Mass—"everything that is most sacred, and for which he became a priest"[141]—is under attack. He warned his audience about the revolution in the Church. He could see how things had changed in the country since his visit of 1955: all the great values of Catholic Canada had been shattered by the "gentle revolution."

---

[138] "The Priest and the Holy Sacrifice of the Mass," Barcelona, March 8, 1971; "The Priest and the Present Crisis in the Church," Barcelona, April, 1972, in *A Bishop Speaks* (Edinburgh: Scottish Una Voce, n.d.), 85ff., 99ff.

[139] "That the Church May Endure," Rennes, Jan. 15, 1973, *A Bishop Speaks*, 117ff.; Brest, Jan. 17, 1973, in *DRM, Katholische Pilgerzeitung*, Apr. 7, 1975, 5-6.

[140] *Spiritual Conferences at Ecône*, 43 B, May 26, 1977.

[141] *Vers Demain*, Nov.-Dec. 1971.

In summer 1972 he went again to the New World; in August he was in the United States at Powers Lake with Fr. Nelson where he celebrated a Pontifical Mass for one thousand pilgrims at Our Lady of the Prairies.[142] There he ordained Fr. Post on August 28.

The southern hemisphere's summer of 1973 brought the Archbishop to Australia where he was invited by the Latin Mass Society to take part in the Eucharistic Congress in Melbourne. Credited with being the only French bishop present at the meeting, he was invited to take part in an ecumenical ceremony, but declined. He remained instead with Fr. James Opie at Armadale from where he went to visit three other bishops who also refused to take part in the ceremony (during which the Bible was carried in procession instead of the Blessed Sacrament). These bishops were Their Excellencies Bernard Stewart, bishop of Standhurst, William Brennan of Toowoomba, and F. X. Thomas of Geraldton. The Archbishop was able to offer three Pontifical Masses (one of which was held at the cathedral of Standhurst) assisted by Fr. Cummins, C.SS.R., or by Fr. Carl Pulvermacher, O.F.M. Cap., who would soon help the Society with its apostolate.

To the faithful he gave the following recommendations: "Keep the Faith without compromise. Read the catechisms of the Council of Trent and St. Pius X. And look for the Tridentine Mass or at least find a priest who says the consecration in the Latin; have confidence in God and don't be bitter. In my seminary in Switzerland, I am training priests who are loyal to the traditional Magisterium and liturgy. I also expect to found a congregation for nuns."[143] In fact, the Archbishop had just met the young Janine Ward, the first postulant of the Sisters' foundation. He had also met the first future Australian seminarian, Gerard Hogan (who brought the Society to Australia in 1982).

At Ecône in October 1973, he welcomed thirty-six new seminarians among whom were two French-speaking Canadians and ten English-speaking students (two Australians), who brought the seminary's population to ninety-five. In October 1974, the number of students stood at 104 without counting the small group who founded the seminary in the United States. The Archbishop said to himself: "The day the Society becomes international and crosses oceans, I will know that this work is really willed by God."

He could no longer have any doubts on the matter. Already, the annual priestly ordinations had brought the number of priest members to a dozen. And several Ordinaries were asking the Archbishop for priests: Bishop Viot Roberti was asking for some at his seminary in Caserta, Bishop Adolfo Tortolo in Argentina wanted priests for his seminary and for a

---

[142] *The Maryfaithful*, Sep.-Oct. 1972, 12-13.
[143] *World Trends*, April 1973; *Spiritual Conferences at Ecône*, March 10, 1973.

large parish; Archbishop Sigaud in Brazil had enough work for ten priests; Bishop Ndong in Gabon proposed the foundation of a minor seminary.[144] But none of this work could be undertaken.

FOR ROMANITY

On the other hand, the Society was able to establish itself in Rome. Already on July 12, 1972, Cardinal Ottaviani had met the Archbishop and encouraged him "to found a center for his apostolate at Rome itself."[145] But how could he find a house in Rome?

On May 3, 1973, the Archbishop went house hunting and was driven by his friend Rémy Borgeat. After crossing the Great St. Bernard Pass, the young Valaisan driver made the following bet: "Your Grace, you are worried, you've got to look for a house. I'm going to offer you a wager: let's go via San Damiano, since you don't believe in it. You are going to ask Our Lady of the Roses to find you something. If it works, it works; if it doesn't work, never mind, but if your prayers are heard, then..."

The following day, the telephone rang in the Archbishop's office at the Villa Lituania. Inexplicably, a wealthy benefactor asked for a meeting, and when he came he offered the Archbishop the money needed for the purchase. Thus, on the way home as they neared Piacenza, Archbishop Lefebvre said to the driver: "Leave the highway here. We are going to say thank you to Our Lady of the Roses."[146]

Soon, with Bishop Mamie's *nihil obstat*, the house at Albano (where the Archbishop meant to accommodate new priests for one or two "Roman years") was canonically erected by Bishop Raffaele Macario, the diocesan bishop, on February 22, 1974. It was of great satisfaction to Archbishop Lefebvre to be able to pass on to his sons his veneration for the successor of Peter, an attachment to the See of Peter, and everything that makes up "Romanity." The project was only launched two years after the clash with Paul VI. In the interim, Albano would be the novitiate for the Sisters of the Society.

VIII. THE SERVANTS OF THE PRIESTHOOD

THE SISTERS OF THE SOCIETY OF SAINT PIUS X

The simple faith and open countenance of the young Australian woman surprised the Archbishop. Janine Ward wished to enter a congregation that did not exist! "It existed in my head," the Archbishop said, and also on

---

[144] *Spiritual Conferences at Ecône,* Sep. 17, 1973.

[145] Emilio Cavaterra, *Il prefetto del Sant'Offizo: Le opere ed i giorni del cardinale Ottaviani* (Milan: Ed. Mursia, 1990), 136, quoting the diary of Ottaviani.

[146] Rémy Bourgeat, Interview, July 12, 2001, ms. III, 23-33.

MARCEL LEFEBVRE

paper: the statutes of the Priestly Society had foreseen "affiliated Sisters when God raised them up" (II, 4). The idea for the Sisters became gradually clear in the Archbishop's mind. In October 1972 he quietly announced "to friends and benefactors" his "hope of soon founding a Society novitiate for sisters who would serve the priests."[147]

But how would he go about this? Archbishop Lefebvre felt "unable" to found a society of sisters. Straightaway, he met his sister, Mother Marie-Gabriel, who was in the Holy Ghost Congregation and who nursed at the Stella Maris mission near Dakar. Providentially, she was on leave and resting in Montana, Switzerland. The sister had already visited Ecône in September 1971. Then, in summer 1972, Fr. Epiney, who was on a speaking tour[148] in Canada, Brazil, and Senegal, stopped at Dakar.

Sister Marie-Gabriel asked him: "What is going on? What is my brother doing? We hear talk about him!"

In 1973 the Archbishop asked her no more and no less than to free herself from her obligations in order to come and run the novitiate of the future Sisters of the Society! Her brother said: "I had to insist." And Mother Marie-Gabriel admitted: "It cost me a lot to take that step."

She gradually came to understand the importance of her brother's work, and felt more and more ill at ease in a congregation that was abandoning the habit and its traditional practices. However, although she was still attached to the congregation—she had been Assistant General from 1959 to 1965 before asking to be sent to Senegal as a simple sister—she felt herself free to go when, upon reading a letter from her superior, she understood that she would not be able to lead an authentic religious life when she returned to her community. She would be "exclaustrated" at first for six years and then definitively, though she never left her congregation nor stopped wearing her white missionary habit.[149]

In autumn 1973, she welcomed the first two postulants whom she took to Pontcalec where the Dominicans of the Holy Ghost had agreed to prepare them for entry to the novitiate. They remained there until Mother Marie-Gabriel was free and the house at Albano was ready to receive them in September 1974. Fr. Claude Michel was the superior, while Fr. L. Molin, and later Fr. Joseph Le Boulc'h, were chaplains.

The founder had already written draft statutes which he summed up thus:

> The Sisters will help the priests in all the work that the Priestly Society is asked to do. Just as the Mother of Jesus in her Compassion took part in

---

[147] Letter to Friends and Benefactors, no. 3, Nov. 1, 1972.
[148] He spoke about Ecône; his companion Albert Bochud spoke of the Blessed Virgin.
[149] Ms. II, 37. Nurse in the Antilles from 1940 to 1947, she was principal superior in Cameroon from 1947 to 1953 and then had the same responsibilities in Bangui from 1953 to 1959.

the priestly work of Jesus dying on the cross for the redemption of souls, so the Sisters of the Society of Saint Pius X will have a special devotion to the Sacrifice of the Mass and the Eucharistic Victim, and will unite themselves to the presence of Mary, the Coredemptrix. This is why in addition to the ordinary devotional exercises, they will usually spend an hour or two half-hours with Jesus in the Eucharist during the course of the day.[150]

The Archbishop's key idea came from bringing together the charisms of the Daughters of Charity and the Franciscan Missionaries of Mary whose work he had admired in Africa. The first of these orders is active: they are devoted to priests and work readily with laypeople. The second of these orders, which arose from a division of the Sisters of Our Lady of Reparation when they adapted their life to the missions in India, was distinguished for its devotion to priests and for a spiritual and supernatural solidity derived from a daily hour of prayer.[151] The Sisters of the Society, therefore, would bring together contemplation and action; "their interior life will make them practice both continual watchfulness and simplicity."[152]

Their first objective is spiritual: "To offer oneself with the divine Victim in imitation of Our Lady of Compassion."[153] Their second goal is apostolic and consists in "helping and contributing to the priestly apostolate": they help by performing "the most humble tasks" in the seminaries or priories: washing, cooking, cleaning, gardening; they contribute by undertaking work in primary school, clinics, or by visiting the poor (III, B). Catechism by correspondence would later fit perfectly with the apostolic vocation of the Sisters.

Canonically, the Sisters of the Society constitute a religious society in simple vows (poverty, chastity, and obedience—II, 7). They are independent of the Priestly Society since they have their own Superior General, local superiors, and houses. Nonetheless, the Sisters call upon the Priestly Society for the spiritual and doctrinal training of its members, and primarily help the Priestly Society in its ministry (II, 10).

Albano, where the first generations of Sisters learned to love the See of Peter, became in 1977 a base for priests during their Roman year, and later in 1978 the philosophy scholasticate. The novitiate moved to St. Michel-en-Brenne, and the Sisters later spread to the United States, Argentina, and Germany. The first clothing ceremony took place on September 22, 1974, in Ecône, and the first professions were made in Albano on September 29, 1976. After six months of postulancy, the candidates spent two years in the novitiate; Mother Marie-Gabriel considered that this was not

[150] Letter to Friends and Benefactors, no. 6, Feb. 27, 1974.
[151] *Spiritual Conferences at Ecône*, Sept. 19, 1973; Letter of March 6, 1980 to a sister.
[152] Letter of Aug. 21, 1985, to a sister.
[153] Spiritual Conference to Sisters, Nov. 20, 1974.

too long. The first foundation was established near the priory of St. Francis de Sales at Onex near Geneva in June 1977. Other communities were set up adjacent to retreat houses for the Spiritual Exercises (Le Pointet in 1979), seminaries (La Reja in Argentina), and retirement homes (Le Brémien). Often the Sisters took charge of priory schools.

Mother Marie-Gabriel was a model of regularity, prayer, generosity, and practical know-how; she lived by a spirit of faith. She retired as Superior General at seventy-seven when she felt herself slowing down, but she remained an example of joy and simplicity to her daughters until she died on January 26, 1987.

Living by the rules of their two founders, the Sisters of the Society of Saint Pius X are appreciated by the priests for their regularity and their effective but discrete support. Their prayers of adoration before the tabernacle are a hidden treasure. Archbishop Lefebvre wrote to them: "I am counting on your hour of adoration for the sanctification of the Society."[154]

THE BROTHERS OF THE SOCIETY

Brother François, the first brother, came from the Knights of Our Lady; for three years he was the conductor of the Gregorian schola at Ecône. Brother Gabriel, a spiritual son of Fr. Berto, arrived in 1972. He had been a postulant with the Holy Ghost Brothers and his training as a cook naturally made him useful in the seminary kitchens. The first five postulants entered in Autumn 1974. According to Archbishop Lefebvre, brothers' vocations "are rare in our age because they require a spirit of faith which is tending to disappear from a world wholly obsessed with human advancement."

The novices are trained in seminaries but sometimes there are separate novitiates. In any case, along with the common life, having a trade is an essential factor in their being naturally and supernaturally occupied in such a way as to foster stability and sanctity.

If the Brothers' general aims are the glory of God and their own sanctification, their specific role is to relieve the priests of the burden of material tasks: bookkeeping, filing and typing, cooking, cleaning, gardening, *etc.* Some brothers are sacristans, catechists, schola conductors, or school-teachers, performing many beautiful tasks that are spiritual or even apostolic. Some of them blossom into teaching brothers. On the missions, as the Archbishop foresaw, the Brothers can be builders or even run technical schools (Statutes, II, 6).

Their religious oblation is made "in a spirit of consecration to the priesthood of Our Lord, which is continued in His ministers and on the

---

[154] Letter from Rickenbach, Jan. 4, 1980.

altar. This is why they will have a deep desire to serve the priest respectfully and faithfully, considering in him the priestly character more than the person" (III, 9).

THE OBLATES OF THE SOCIETY

The Oblates were established at the same time as the Sisters of the Society. In autumn 1972, the three Dominican Sisters of the Holy Ghost who had worked in Ecône for two years returned to Pontcalec. This was because three other nuns, "affiliated to the Society," had come to the seminary.[155] During 1973 they became the Oblates of the Society of Saint Pius X. The first to make her engagement as an Oblate was Mathilde Pommeruel, the aunt of Pierre-Marie Laurençon, who was a seminarian and later a priest of the Society; she left her congregation and became an Oblate on May 17, 1974, at Suresnes, taking the name of Sister Marie Bernard.

The Archbishop wrote statutes for them which took account of the various backgrounds from which the Oblates came: in the beginning they were nuns "who were obliged in conscience to leave their religious congregations which had become unfaithful to their constitutions." The day one of the Oblates left her community, she heard her Superior say to her: "You are stopping this community from evolving according to the directives of the Council. Your behavior comes from an attitude of disobedience and your leaving is, therefore, a grace for this convent."[156]

Archbishop Lefebvre encouraged them, saying that their vows were still valid before God; nonetheless they still had to wear the Oblates' habit and make their engagement. However, others wanted to join the Oblates; they were mostly women who were living in the world but who wanted to leave secular life, and whose age or health prevented them joining the Society's Sisters. They too became Oblates and took the habit which was more or less the same as the Sisters' habit with a cross replacing the medal of Saint Pius X worn by the Sisters on their scapular.

The Oblates are not a congregation distinct from the Priestly Society; unlike the Sisters, they make no public vows; they pass quite quickly through their postulancy and novitiate before making their oblation. Their goal is to sanctify themselves through the Mass and by working with the Society. As their model, they take the Virgin Mary, Mother of the Eternal Priest. Like her, the Oblates offer their daily life for the redemption of souls, and they are content to take part in the sacrifice of our Lord, standing at the foot of the cross like Our Lady of Compassion (Statutes, II).

---

[155] Letter to Friends and Benefactors, no. 3.
[156] Sister Marguerite Le Boulc'h, notes, Dec. 4, 1996, 1.

They live in the priories of the Priestly Society in separate accommodation from the priests. If possible they are placed in small groups and thus exercise the precious virtues of the common life. They go about their work in a spirit of silence and prayer (Statutes, V).

Like his priests, Archbishop Lefebvre benefited from the invaluable work of the Oblates who took charge of his office and later staffed the office of the motherhouse. He greatly appreciated the discretion of his secretaries. On important occasions he was able to express his gratitude for the Oblates' effective but discreet and hidden work. Nevertheless, he was especially attached to the Sisters of the Society over whose training he particularly watched. During his confirmation tours in France, he often enjoyed spending a few days in the peace of St. Michel Abbey with his sister and his "daughters." He shared the confidences with them from which was drawn his autobiography, *The Little Story of My Long Life*. He was happy to preach the retreats in preparation for the religious professions on *Quasimodo* Sunday. "*Pax vobis*," the words of the resurrected Christ in the gospel of this Sunday became the title of the internal newsletter of the Society's Sisters: its readers—nuns, or biographers who also benefit from reading it—can find in its pages many details concerning life in the priories that one would look for in vain in newsletters written by the priests.

THE THIRD ORDER OF SAINT PIUS X

In Ecône, May 28, 1971, on the Vigil of Pentecost, some laymen came to Archbishop Lefebvre: "Your Grace," they said, "don't you have some sort of third order? Could not lay people attach themselves to your work?"

"It's true, the statutes say 'The Society also welcomes associates, whether priests or laymen, who wish to collaborate in working for the Society's purpose and to profit by its grace for their personal sanctification' (IV, 4)."

"Well, Your Grace, you must think of us as your first tertiaries."

"Well! Hang on. I've done nothing about this apart from alluding to the matter in the statutes. Let me have a breather to think it through!"[157]

The Archbishop would take a "breather" for ten years. However, in 1973, he had to think about sending back the devoted volunteers from the Holy Ghost Fathers who had been helping him manage the finances of the Society: Brother Christian Winckler in Fribourg and Fr. Marcel Muller in Paris were required by their superiors. It was then that he said, "a third order of lay people would be useful for work like this."[158] However, their spiritual aim remained of the utmost importance: they would live through "our spirituality based on the Holy Sacrifice of the Mass and on immola-

---

[157] *Spiritual Conferences at Ecône*, B, May 30, 1971.
[158] *Ibid.*, Jan. 10, 1973.

tion"; "being evermore filled with this great mystery of our faith, the treasure of the heart of Jesus, the source of all true and unalterable love."[159]

Nevertheless, the Third Order[160] was only established on January 29, 1981, when the General Council of the Society promulgated the rules written by the Archbishop at the end of 1980. The tertiaries must lead a Christian life of "sacrifice and coredemption" and be loyal to Tradition as expressed in the infallible Magisterium and the catechism of the Council of Trent, the Vulgate, the teachings of the Angelic Doctor, and the liturgy of all time.

Are the duties of the tertiaries demanding? Not really! They are well-balanced and within the limits of what one can expect from devout members of the faithful. There is nothing very difficult, and not even giving up television is that hard. But the rule that the tertiaries share conquers individualism, encourages imitation of the virtues, and above all emphasizes growth in charity and the offering of one's life to God. Thus the Third Order forms a lively, devoted spiritual elite who support the Society's priories.

---

[159] *Retreats at Ecône*, Sept. 19, 1973; Letter to Friends and Benefactors, no. 4, March 19, 1973.

[160] Canonically, the title "Third Order" is meant for members in the third rank of the great religious orders (Franciscans, Dominicans, *etc.*).

CHAPTER 17

"I ADHERE TO ETERNAL ROME"

I. FAITHFULNESS TO THE MASS OF ALL TIME

TWO MASSES—REJECTING THE *NOVUS ORDO*

Archbishop Lefebvre did not found his Society against the New Mass, but for the priesthood. However, the concerns of the priesthood now brought him to reject the new *Ordo Missae*. On June 9, 1971, the Archbishop returned from Paris where he had given a talk for his friends in the ROC (Union for the Christian West), an organization run by General Lecomte[1] and Admiral de Penfentenyo. At Ecône, he called together the teachers and seminarians and began by handing out a typed sheet (which he did only rarely) with a summary of his talk, written on November 25, 1970. Until then, he had kept to the "old Mass" because it was still permitted; now, however, he would reject the *Novus Ordo*.

"It was an historic moment of capital importance for the Church," said Fr. Aulagnier. "The Archbishop was making a choice and shared his conviction with us; it was the right choice and one that could not be changed. It was based on doctrine." It did not come from some personal preference but from the dogmas defined at the Council of Trent: "Three truths of defined Catholic faith—*fide divina catholica*, as he insisted—are essential to the reality of the sacrifice of the Mass: the priest, who by his sacerdotal character is distinct from the faithful and is alone capable of consecrating the Eucharist; the sacrificial nature of the Mass and its propitiatory role (communion only being a consequence of consuming the victim); and, finally, the real and substantial presence of the victim—the same victim as at Calvary—through transubstantiation."

Now, the liturgical reform "directly or indirectly undermines these three essential truths" and waters them down so that the Mass becomes a

---

[1] Former principal of two prestigious Parisian military academies (École de Guerre and the École d'État-Major), General Lecomte was one of the keenest minds in the French army. During the war in Algeria, his work in those posts "ensured that far more importance was given to solving daily problems of command through case by case studies of innovative methods." Cf. Hugues Kéraly, *Hervé de Blignières* (Paris: Albin Michel, 1990), 228.

community activity. The cross fades from the Mass, taking with it the spirit of sacrifice; vocations were drying up. The first solid, practical conclusion now had to be drawn: "If ever we accepted the *Novus Ordo Missae*, we would have no more vocations: the tree would wither just as if we had taken an axe to its roots."[2]

The Archbishop clearly based the doctrinal and pastoral rejection of the New Mass on Canon Law:

> The design of this reform, the way it was published with unjustified changes in successive editions, the way it was made obligatory—sometimes tyrannically, as was the case of Italy—the change of the definition of the Mass in Article 7 without any change to the rite itself:[3] all these things are unprecedented in the tradition of the Roman Church which always acts *cum consilio et sapientia*; they allow us to doubt the validity of this legislation, and thus to invoke Canon 23: "In doubt, the revocation of a law is not presumed. Rather, the later law must be related to the earlier law, and one must reconcile the two, as much as is possible."[4]

Archbishop Lefebvre was in contact with thinkers writing in the closely linked journals *Itinéraires* and *Courrier de Rome*, and he found some of their studies "amazing [and] convincing. They ought to be put in the hands of every bishop and priest."[5] He emphasized the differences between the work of Paul VI and St. Pius V, saying that they were diametrically opposed. The holy Pope maintained the Roman missal as codified by St. Gregory the Great, Pope from 590 to 604, who certainly did not create this Mass but must have received it from Tradition; so Pius V confirmed a tradition that was at least ten centuries old. On the contrary, Paul VI artificially created a new rite.[6]

Moreover, St. Pius V's act had the value of canonization: noting the rite's antiquity, its continual use, power, doctrinal soundness, holiness, and fruits, the holy Pope canonized it with the sort of declaration that is made concerning a person's heroic virtues. Therefore, his act was definitive and

---

[2]   *Fideliter*, no. 59: 118-119; Spiritual Conference, Fribourg, June 10, 1971.

[3]   According to Professor Emil Lengl, former consulter of the *Consilium*, the corrections made to the *Institutio Generalis*, "were brought in to satisfy the wishes of a few people but changed nothing essential to the first version." *Spiritual Conferences at Ecône*, 69 B, Feb. 15, 1979, 426.

[4]   Cf. Argument of Fr. Dulac, cited above. Four days later on June 14, 1971, a notice of the CDF decreed: "Starting from the day that the translations *must be* adopted for services in the vernacular, those who continue to use Latin must only use the renovated texts of the Mass and the Divine Office." *Documentation Catholique*, 1014: 732. Rome's arbitrary power was handed over to the arbitrary power of the episcopal conferences.

[5]   Letter to General Lecomte, Nov. 15, 1973, on the subject of the article "Les deux messes" (The two Masses) published in *Le Courrier de Rome*, no. 123.

[6]   Talk in Paris, May 26, 1971, schema in Letter to General Lecomte, May 19, 1971; *Spiritual Conferences at Ecône* 8 B, Jan. 19, 1982.

infallible. For all time, this Mass would edify the Church and serve her; nobody would be able to forbid it because forbidding and destroying what a pope has canonized is impossible: it cannot happen! A successor of St. Pius V might create a new rite and encourage it to be used, but he could never exclude the traditional rite.[7] In other words, the holy Pope's act was not a purely disciplinary measure to be always subject to change. It was by nature a doctrinal act which committed all his successors to upholding it.

THE ORTHODOXY AND VALIDITY OF THE NEW MASS

Archbishop Lefebvre did not hesitate to speak publicly on the question of the orthodoxy and validity of Paul VI's Mass. He considered that "one cannot say generally that the New Mass is invalid or heretical"; however, "it leads slowly to heresy." On this topic he said he did not share "the radical views of Frs. Guérard des Lauriers and Coache," but he admitted that "the number of invalid Masses is on the rise" because young priests trained to think of the Mass as a "memorial" have an intention that is more and more determined by this concept, which is completely different from what was defined at Trent. This is the case even without their being aware of the opposition because they are "under the influence of a relativistic and evolutionist conception" of dogma.[8]

In 1975, the Archbishop added that the New Mass "is ambivalent and ambiguous because one priest can say it with a totally Catholic faith in the sacrifice, etc., and another can say it with a different intention, *because the words he pronounces and the gestures he makes no longer contradict [other intentions]*."[9]

THE PROBLEM OF ASSISTING AT THE NEW MASS

Some priests were torn between the need to keep the Faith as expressed by the Traditional Mass and a desire to be obedient as they saw it. In the early days of the reforms, Archbishop Lefebvre advised them to keep at least the traditional Offertory and Canon and to say them in Latin. His advice to the seminarians as to the faithful was remarkably moderate in tone for one who was first to step up to the breach to repel the New Mass. He exhorted them: "Make every effort to have the Mass of St. Pius V, but if it is impossible to find one within forty kilometers and if there is a pious priest who says the New Mass in as traditional a way as possible, it is good for you to assist at it to fulfill your Sunday obligation."

---

[7]   Talk in Paris, 1971; *Spiritual Conferences at Ecône*, March 7, 1974.
[8]   Letter to Gérald Wailliez, Jan. 14, 1972; Letter to General Lecomte, May 21, 1971, 1st remark; Letter to Lecomte, May 8, 1974, note on the work of "Fidelis."
[9]   "La messe de Luther," Talk in Florence, Feb. 15, 1975. [In *A Bishop Speaks*, 192 ff.]

One can counter the dangers for the Faith through solid catechism: "Should all the world's churches be emptied? I do not feel brave enough to say such a thing. I don't want to encourage atheism."[10]

Thus, the Archbishop did not go as far as Frs. Coache and Barbara, who, during the "marches on Rome" which they organized[11] at Pentecost 1971 and 1973, made the pilgrims and children take "an oath of fidelity to the Mass of St. Pius V." Nevertheless, he added in 1973: "Obviously, our attitude will become more and more radical as time passes, and as invalidity spreads with heresy."[12] All the same, he took note of how the position of Fr. Thomas Calmel, O.P., changed. At first, like the Archbishop, he showed considerable pastoral prudence,[13] but later he became more categorical and eventually supported the seminary at Ecône where he preached the Easter retreat in 1974:

> "Don't drag St. Pius X along to the Masses of the new religion! Our position is only tenable if we have the souls of martyrs....It is no joke. God's love asks this of us: to give witness like this is hard and it wears you down with all the false problems of authority and obedience. It is love of God that made the martyrs, those who confessed the Faith. Our witness, our fight is to maintain the true rite. God does us a great honor in making us confessors of the Faith in our age. Whatever our feelings of being ostracized or abandoned, let us be true![14]

Little by little the Archbishop's position hardened: this Mass with its ecumenical rite was seriously ambiguous and harmful to the Catholic Faith. "This is why one cannot be made to assist at it to fulfil one's Sunday obligation."[15] In 1975 he still admitted that one could "assist occasionally" at the New Mass when one feared going without Communion for a long time. However in 1977, he was more or less absolute: "To avoid conforming to the evolution slowly taking place in the minds of priests, we must avoid —I could almost say completely—assisting at the New Mass."[16]

A POISONED LITURGY

Soon, Archbishop Lefebvre would no longer tolerate participation at Masses celebrated in the new rite except passively, for example at funerals. He did not say the New Mass was intrinsically bad in the sense in which one can say that something is intrinsically perverse; however he considered

---

[10] *Spiritual Conferences at Ecône,* Dec. 10, 1972.
[11] The first "march on Rome" had taken place in 1970. Cf. Fr. Louis Coache, *Les batailles du "Combat de la Foi"* (Chiré, 1993), 202.
[12] *Spiritual Conferences at Ecône,* June 26, 1973.
[13] "L'assistance à la messe," *Itinéraires,* no. 157 (Nov. 1971).
[14] Talk during retreat, Ecône, April 10, 1974.
[15] Letter to M. Lenoir, Nov. 23, 1975.
[16] *Spiritual Conferences at Ecône,* 42 B, March 21, 1977.

that it was bad in itself and not only because of the circumstances in which the rite was performed (*e.g.* a table instead of an altar or Communion in the hand).[17]

Yet how was it possible for a pope to have promulgated it? For in principle this Mass, which is apparently a universal law of the Church, is guaranteed to be free of all error or danger to the Faith because of the infallibility of the pope's magisterium, according to the common opinion of theologians. The Archbishop replied to this objection in 1981:

> Looking at the broader context (the circumstances of its institution) and at the Mass itself (the analysis of the rite) along with its fruits, it is manifest that, although it is not heretical, it leads to a loss of faith, and cannot be a true law. As Don Giuseppe Pace says: "It is blindingly obvious that the new legislation is not *ad bonum commune* as the law requires: it does not secure the common good."
>
> This Mass is not bad in a merely accidental or extrinsic way. There is something in it that is truly bad. It was based on a model of the Mass according to Cranmer[18] and Taizé (1959). As I said in Rome to those who interviewed me: "It is a poisoned Mass!"
>
> Who is responsible for this? Who decided to change our spirituality? They have poisoned our liturgy. Some say, "Yes, but it's a slow poison!" Yes, but a slow poison is still a poison all the same![19]

CRISIS OF THE CHURCH AND CRISIS OF THE PRIESTHOOD

Through talks which he gave everywhere, Archbishop Lefebvre made himself the herald of the combat for the Faith. At Tourcoing[20] in the presence of the Mayor he said: "If I agree to give talks, it is to defend, protect, and reawaken our faith at a time when it is attacked on all sides...indeed from within the Church." He quoted from publications issued by official and unofficial bodies attached to the French Episcopate. The catechism notes issued by the Jean-Bart Center put forth the traditional notion of salvation ("We lost grace but have been redeemed by Christ") alongside a new idea of "salvation-covenant": "The future of humanity is the Cove-

---

[17] Circumstances he considered decisive in 1974: *Spiritual Conferences at Ecône*, March 7, 1974, and April 1, 1974.

[18] Archbishop of Canterbury. He wrote the first edition of the *Book of Common Prayer* in 1548 that replaced the Catholic Mass. Cf. Michael Davies, *Cranmer's Godly Order* (Augustine Publishing Co., 1976).

[19] Archbishop Lefebvre quotes Fr. Joseph de Sainte-Marie, O.C.D., Professor in Rome: "Those who made this *Novus Ordo* built it on a theology that is flagrantly opposed to Catholic dogma" (Note to Archbishop Lefebvre around the time of the CDF questionnaire, 1979). Archbishop Lefebvre also referred to an unpublished study of Dom Guillou on the prayers of the new missal: no more enemies, no more spiritual combat! Cf. *Fideliter*, no. 86.

[20] "Crisis of the Church or Crisis of the Priesthood," Talk of Jan. 30, 1974, in Lefebvre, *A Bishop Speaks*, 163ff.

nant of God, sealed in Jesus on Easter Day."[21] In their notes on the liturgy, they explained the Mass in the following manner:

> "At the heart of the Mass, there is a narrative....The *memorial* is not the renewal of these events,...it means that we recognize God's action in the great events of the history of salvation."[22]

As for the Strasbourg Theology School, it rejected "a certain way of celebrating the Lord's *memorial* [which] was linked to a religious universe that is no longer ours, with a 'sacral' covering borrowed from Leviticus and based on the sacrificial cult of the religions at the time." In fact, "it is a symbolic action....It is not a question of a miraculous presence....One must begin with the glorious Christ and see in the Eucharistic presence a *special focus* of the *Paschal presence* of Jesus Christ. This presence ought to be called spiritual in the fullest sense of the word."[23]

Cardinal Seper, Prefect for the Congregation for the Doctrine of the Faith (CDF), was sent these edifying documents. His only answer was the following: "What you have sent me is frightening. What is left of Catholicism? I cannot understand why the Church authorities there do not react. Rome cannot intervene everywhere, and especially not quickly."[24]

It was an avowal of powerlessness and ignorance: Seper clearly was not aware that this aberration of a theory was the New Mass! Archbishop Lefebvre saw clearly how the two were linked. He said to his seminarians: "I can't see how one can have a seminary that uses the New Mass. I would not have the strength, even with all the good will in the world. The true Mass is the heart of a seminary, the priest, the Church, the Gospel, and of our Lord. St. Pius V saw it clearly: the Mass is also a rampart for the Faith against heresy."[25]

BOOBY-TRAPPED ORDINATIONS AND CONFIRMATIONS

On June 18, 1968, the ritual for priestly ordination was poisoned with the same venom. The prayer clarifying the form of the sacrament and recited as the ordinand touches the chalice no longer expresses "the power to offer sacrifice and celebrate Masses." It is replaced by the injunction: "Receive the oblation of the holy people to offer it to God." The intention of the minister—the bishop—can be perverted. The suppression of the rite for handing on the power to forgive sins (which repeats the words of our

---

[21] "La foi mot à mot," class notes, Jean-Bart National Teaching Center, Paris, edited by Jean Vernette, *Croissance de l'Eglise*, supplement 1972-73.
[22] Liturgical session, Paris region, Fr. Bernard Audras, March 17, 1973.
[23] Meeting of Feb. 2, 1972, Ch. Wackenheim.
[24] Letter of February 23, 1974.
[25] *Spiritual Conferences at Ecône*, Nov. 23, 1972.

Lord: "Receive the Holy Ghost: whose sins you forgive they are forgiven...") increases this doubt.

"Why have they suppressed these words? Doubtless the power is already given in the essential rite of the imposition of hands with the consecratory preface as defined by Pius XII.[26] But this Pope asked for nothing to be changed to the additional rites of ordination. The fact that they have suppressed the words of our Lord is enough to condemn this Conciliar Church."[27] Is not the meaning of the essential rite thereby corrupted "*ex adjunctis*"? Thus, Archbishop Lefebvre continued to use the pre-conciliar Pontifical to ordain priests and even to conditionally ordain some priests whose ordination in the new rite was doubtful.

Similarly, he continued to confer the clerical tonsure on seminarians, the four minor orders and the subdiaconate, in spite of their having been suppressed by Paul VI on August 15, 1972, and replaced by the two lay "ministries" of lector and acolyte. He based his action on the antiquity of these orders attested in 251 by Pope St. Cornelius and on the authority of the Council of Trent that defined in Session XXIII (Canon 2) the existence "beside the priesthood of other orders, major and minor, by which one tends by degrees towards the priesthood." He thought that this gradual progression gave the seminary an intense liturgical and hierarchical life that was destroyed by gloomy post-conciliar egalitarianism.

The Archbishop also believed that the validity of the sacrament of confirmation was affected by the new "form" of the sacrament published on August 15, 1971. It came from an Eastern confirmation rite and expressed less clearly the special character of confirmation, especially in the sometimes unreliable vernacular translations. When on November 30, 1972, Paul VI approved of the use of any vegetable oil and no longer only olive oil (contrary to a unanimous Catholic tradition) as the matter of the sacrament, the doubt became more serious. "The faithful have the right to receive the sacraments validly," said the Archbishop in 1975 to the cardinals who reproached him for confirming in dioceses without the permission of the bishops, and for even confirming conditionally. "I have a justified doubt," he said. Archbishop Ferrand, archbishop of Tours, his close friend from seminary, would not put up with this attitude: "How dare you doubt the validity of my confirmations!" And he broke with him. Archbishop Lefebvre said: "We live at a time in which natural and supernatural laws supersede positive, ecclesiastical laws when the latter oppose the former, instead of serving them."[28]

---

[26] Pius XII, apostolic constitution *Sacramentum Ordinis*, Nov. 30, 1947.
[27] Archbishop Lefebvre, ordination retreat 1989, 100, 3 A.
[28] *La messe de Luther*, Feb. 15, 1975, p. 11.

THE MASTERSTROKE OF SATAN[29]

Therefore, the Archbishop considered that he had to make a choice between true and false obedience: false obedience to an equivocal liturgy or an ambiguous catechism, promulgated through "a series of conflicting orders, circulars, constitutions, and orchestrated or manipulated pastoral letters." "From what authority do they come? From the Holy See? From the Council? From commissions? From episcopal conferences? We don't really know."

There was Rome and Rome: the "Rome that was eternal" in its Faith, doctrines, and concept of the sacrifice of the Mass, and there was the "Rome that was earthly" and influenced by the ideas of the modern world. Besides, the Pope managed to condemn in his addresses what he encouraged by his actions. "Eternal Rome condemns earthly Rome. We prefer to choose the eternal one." That is true obedience.

In fact "the masterstroke of Satan has been to trick the Church through obedience into disobeying her Tradition." The Church was going to destroy herself by obeying revolutionary principles brought inside the Church by the authorities of the Church. From 1968 onwards, did not Paul VI himself speak publicly of "the auto-demolition of the Church"? On June 29, 1972, he admitted: "Through some crack, the smoke of Satan has entered the temple of God....Satan...has come to spoil and wither the fruits of the Council." Paul did not want to see where that crack was. Marcel saw it and denounced it: it lay in the break with Tradition. Already, however, the Archbishop felt that his foresight would get him condemned: "Satan has played a masterstroke: those who keep the Faith are condemned by those who should defend and propagate it!"

II. THE OFFENSIVE AGAINST ECÔNE

PROBLEMATIC INCARDINATIONS[30]

"Bishop Mamie, Bishop Charrière's auxiliary, was opposed to our foundation," said Archbishop Lefebvre. Even before François Charrière's resignation, when the Archbishop asked the bishop of Fribourg to incardinate members of the Society in his diocese, the vicar-general, Msgr. Perroud, replied that although Bishop Charrière had been happy to establish the Society as a *pia unio* in his diocese, "he could not however undertake to incardinate its members."[31]

---

[29]   Oct. 13, 1974, published in 1977.
[30]   [Incardination is the technical term for the affiliation or permanent attachment of a cleric to a particular diocese or religious congregation capable of incardinating its members. Trans.]
[31]   Msgr. Téophile Perroud, Letter of Dec. 15, 1970, to Archbishop Lefebvre.

In fact, the refusal came from the auxiliary, Bishop Mamie. He later said: "At the time, it was I who made the decisions, and I was opposed to it."[32] Archbishop Lefebvre protested to Bishop Charrière: "His Excellency Bishop Philippe in Rome has confirmed for me the procedure that we have followed. The members 'are provisionally incardinated in the diocese that established the *pia unio*'"; to refuse us incardination "is to stop this association living and developing." Another solution would have been for the bishop of Fribourg to grant Archbishop Lefebvre the right to give his subordinates dimissorial letters according to an indult mentioned in Canon 964§4, from which the CPCR Fathers had benefited. Otherwise, the "*pia unio* would die almost as soon as it was born."[33]

This request went unanswered because Bishop Charrière was getting ready to leave his post. His successor, Bishop Mamie, received Archbishop Lefebvre on January 20, 1971, and told him that he refused to incardinate "those from outside the diocese"—a refusal that was canonically irregular and morally unjust. Bishop Adam, who was also asked, proved to be just as negative.[34]

Henceforth, Archbishop Lefebvre was reduced to finding sympathetic bishops outside Switzerland. He soon thought about his former auxiliary in Dakar, Bishop Guibert, who was now bishop of Saint-Denis in La Réunion; on January 21, the Archbishop wrote explaining Bishop Mamie's refusal and asking Guibert to incardinate in La Réunion those members of the Society who were ready for ordination. Visiting Rome at the beginning of February, he was assured that this procedure was quite correct. He wrote again to Bishop Guibert on February 14: "Archbishop Palazzini has encouraged me to find a bishop who would provisionally accept incardinations." On March 4, the Bishop of La Réunion wrote, saying that he agreed.

What a relief for Archbishop Lefebvre! However, he also asked other sympathetic bishop friends whom he met in March. Bishop Castán Lacoma, bishop of Sigüenza in Spain, readily agreed; on the contrary, Bishop Ackerman of Covington, United States, was evasive.[35] As for Bishop de la Chanonie at Clermont-Ferrand, at least he incardinated Fr. Aulagnier, who was a member of his diocese. In 1974 when Bishop Guibert was on the point of resigning, he returned the files of the individuals who were due to be incardinated in La Réunion. Archbishop Lefebvre looked to his friend from Campos, Bishop de Castro Mayer, as his last recourse.

---

[32] Bishop Mamie, interview, March 16, 1994. Savioz, annex. 2.7.
[33] Archbishop Lefebvre, Letter to Bishop Charrière, Dec. 19, 1970.
[34] Diary of Fribourg.
[35] Spiritual Conference, Fribourg, April 11, 1971.

Thus, as is proved by the dossier of dimissorial letters granted to Archbishop Lefebvre by diocesan bishops,[36] the Archbishop never conferred minor or major ordination without canonical provision before 1976.

AN ATTEMPT TO SECURE PONTIFICAL RIGHT

In order to solve the problem of incardinating the members of his Society, the founder soon approached the Roman dicasteries to obtain pontifical right which would allow him to incardinate clerics in the Society itself. He had conceived of the Society in such a way that it fell within the remit not only of the Sacred Congregation for Religious and Secular Institutes but also of the Sacred Congregation for the Propaganda (since its apostolate had no territorial limits)[37] and of the Sacred Congregation for the Clergy (as an association of priests established to help the priestly apostolate[38] and balance the distribution of the clergy). [39]

Recently, the Sacred Congregation for the Clergy had asked to supervise a few priestly Societies without vows, such as the Prado. Archbishop Lefebvre said: "The project is being studied, but the Sacred Congregation for Religious seems to be holding back."[40] In February 1971, he pleaded his cause with the Sacred Congregation for the Clergy, whose secretary, Archbishop Palazzini, was favorable towards him and gave him useful advice. Thus on February 11, Archbishop Lefebvre wrote from Rome to the Cardinal Prefect, John Wright, asking for a letter of encouragement as well as "the faculty to call candidates for ordination." The cardinal gave him the letter, probably written by Palazzini himself, but signed by Wright and Palazzini, and dated February 18; it praises the *sapientes normae*, "the wise rules that govern the Society" which, it was said, "can do much to help realize the plans of this dicastery for spreading the clergy throughout the world."

---

[36] Savioz, *La fondation de la Fraternité St Pie X*, 60. Only exception: priestly ordination of Fr. Sanborn on June 29, 1975. Later, Archbishop Rudolf Graber, of Ratisbonne, agreed to incardinate the Benedictines of Dom Augustin Joly ordained by Archbishop Lefebvre. Rudolf Graber, a former member of the *Cœtus*, would have liked to reform his seminary in a traditional manner; unable to do this, he founded a seminary parallel to his own diocesan institution but with the New Mass.

[37] Cf. mentions of the Society's role in foreign missions (statutes I, 1), the Sacred Congregation for the Propaganda (memo to Bishop Charrière, June 29, 1970), taking in seminarians from Latin America (meeting of June 6, 1969, with Bishop Charrière), putting priests at the disposition of the diocese of La Réunion (Letter to Bishop Guibert, Feb. 14, 1971).

[38] Cf. Statutes, I, 1; Letter to Cardinal Wright, May 13, 1971.

[39] Cf. Decree erection, Nov. 1, 1970; letter of Cardinal Wright, Feb. 18, 1971.

[40] *Spiritual Conferences at Ecône*, Nov. 29, 1971.

But the Cardinal granted nothing as regards incardination. Archbishop Lefebvre tried again: on May 11, he was received by Cardinal Wright and asked him (repeating his request two days later in writing) for "the privilege of incardinating in the Society."[41] "Carry on as you have done until now incardinating in some diocese," was the reply of the *porporato* on May 15. No matter! The Archbishop tried again in November 1971 when the Cardinal met with him and encouraged him: "Your Grace, the work you are doing is among the most important projects in the Church at the present time."[42] In a letter of February 11, 1972, the Archbishop insisted again, stating that things were developing quickly and that he had the support of the bishops of Sion and Aoste.[43]

None of these steps were by the book; according to canon law, Bishop Mamie, bishop of the diocese that had set up the *pia unio*, should have been responsible for doing this. Since Archbishop Palazzini knew that the Bishop of Fribourg was hostile, he wrote on March 10 to the Bishop of Sion, who had welcomed the establishment of the seminary, and asked him his opinion on granting pontifical right. Twice—on March 18 and again on April 15—Nestor Adam warmly supported Archbishop Lefebvre's request.

In fact, the Bishop of Sion would not have been unhappy to see the Society and its seminary directly attached to Rome. On the previous September 7, he had been irritated when eighteen priests and two brothers from a group responsible for the apostolate in French-speaking Switzerland had met in Montana, Valais, and written to Cardinal Garonne, Prefect of the Sacred Congregation for Seminaries and Universities, to complain about the seminary at Ecône: "[It was] spreading fundamentalism" in the neighboring parishes,[44] and "causing divisions among the clergy and unrest among the faithful."

During a meeting of a bishops' synod to which he belonged, Bishop Adam met the cardinal in Rome and courageously defended Archbishop Lefebvre against "these partisan attacks."[45] However, he asked Marcel Lefebvre straightaway to meet with Gabriel Garonne. On November 22, 1971,[46] the cardinal, who was "most kind," met with his former fellow student from Santa Chiara, but he merely asked about how Ecône was im-

---

[41] Letter of May 13, 1971, to Cardinal Wright.
[42] *Spiritual Conferences at Ecône*, Nov. 30, 1971. Cardinal Garrone also received Archbishop Lefebvre and said to him: "I'm glad that you have vocations."
[43] "The bishop of Aoste in Italy would willingly welcome us in his diocese." There was a plan to transfer the year of spirituality to Val d'Aoste; it failed because Bishop Ovidio Lari imposed unacceptable liturgical conditions.
[44] Frs. Gottlieb and Masson did some work for the parish at Saxon and Saillon and the parish priest of Riddes was happy to have support from Ecône.
[45] Expression used by Archbishop Lefebvre thanking Bishop Adam, Dec. 26, 1971.
[46] Diary of Ecône.

plementing the *Ratio fundamentalis* for priestly training issued by his dicastery. Archbishop Lefebvre was able to say: "Eminence, we are perhaps the only ones who are following your rule!"[47]

Following the interview, Garrone reminded Nestor Adam of his duty "to follow closely the life, progress, and pedagogical and doctrinal tendencies" at Ecône.[48] As things stood, one could say that in spite of Bishop Mamie's reticence and opposition from progressive Swiss clergy, Archbishop Lefebvre's approach to the Sacred Congregation for the Clergy was well on the way to succeeding in April 1972: the existence of his *pia unio*'s seminary was not a problem for Rome. Then, a troublemaker journalist, Hugo-Maria Kellner, who was living in the United States, "torpedoed the affair" by writing to Cardinal Wright: "Is it true that the Sacred Congregation for the Clergy supports Archbishop Lefebvre's seminary? But he does not respect canonical norms, and he has come to you because he does not like the way the other dicasteries are going!"[49] Wright was irritated and withheld his support.[50]

Without let up, Archbishop Lefebvre turned to the Sacred Congregation for the Propaganda where he was still a consulter. He made the case that the Society could exercise its apostolate "in those places where the priesthood is most in danger or else abandoned, as in Africa or South America."[51] The possibilities of an apostolate for the Society in those countries were very real, as we have seen. Nevertheless, the Cardinal Prefect, Angelo Rossi, said that his Congregation was not the one he should be dealing with.[52]

As Cardinal Rossi's evasive answer was late in coming, the Archbishop finally wrote on November 6 to Cardinal Antoniuttti at the Sacred Congregation for Religious and Secular Institutes—surely the right Congregation! Unfortunately, Ildebrando Antoniutti had still not replied to this final request when...he died in office on August 1, 1974.

So, the Society of Saint Pius X would not have pontifical right. Archbishop Lefebvre consoled himself. Was Bishop Mamie silent? Too bad! At least Bishop Adam visited the seminary at Ecône from time to time. He did not hide his admiration from Fr. Epiney, who brought him there twice: "Wow! It's fantastic, it's a great work; I am very pleased to see it."[53]

---

[47] Cf. *Rivarol*, April 5, 1973.
[48] Letter of the cardinal to Bishop Adam, Feb. 1 and March 3, 1972; Feb. 7, 1973.
[49] Letter to Cardinal Wright, April 1972; to Bishop Adam, April 4; reply of Bishop Adam, April 15.
[50] Personal letter, Archbishop Lefebvre, June 15, 1972.
[51] Letter of Archbishop Lefebvre to Cardinal Rossi, July 8, 1972.
[52] Reply of Cardinal Rossi, Nov. 11, 1972.
[53] Interview of Fr. Epiney with Fr. Savioz, Savioz, *La fondation de la Fraternité St Pie X*, 104.

Unfortunately, his positive attitude would soon crumble under pressure from Rome, egged on by the French bishops.

Ecône, a "Wildcat Seminary"?

The bishops in France could not but be worried by a seminary where "the Latin Mass" was still celebrated, the cassock worn, a strict rule followed, "pre-conciliar" training given, and where French priestly candidates were pouring in. During 1971, an inaccurate report from one of Archbishop Lefebvre's former Fribourg[54] collaborators came to the notice of the episcopate. They questioned Cardinal Garonne: What is this seminary where they accept defectors from other seminaries? Garrone soon spoke to Bishop Adam: "Is it true that Ecône accepts seminarians from diocesan seminaries? That would be against canon law."[55]

On February 10, 1972, Nestor Adam replied: out of forty-one seminarians, only three came from other seminaries and their cases were canonically regular with respect to their own dioceses. To the cardinal's other question concerning the impact of Ecône in Valais, the Bishop replied by sitting as usual on the fence: "The progressives are bitterly opposed, the 'fundamentalists' are for, and most people are indifferent. Personally, I think that for the sake of pluralism, they should have the right to exist."

Nestor was right: Ecône was becoming a sign of contradiction or a rallying point for all Switzerland. On March 18, seven hundred Catholics on pilgrimage at Fribourg[56] approved a resolution that was sent to the Swiss bishops, calling for "confirmation that the Roman Missal restored by St. Pius V is fully legal and also unreserved support from our bishops for the Priestly Society of Saint Pius X."[57]

One might as well aim high! However, let us add that Archbishop Lefebvre had nothing to do with this spontaneous action of the faithful. The French bishops shuddered, and Fr. Marcus, Rector of the Carmelite Seminary, took it upon himself during a meeting of priests from the Paris diocese to denounce "the pitfalls…of wildcat adventures in priestly training…and of an ultra-conservative seminary that accepts candidates who do not have the approval of their Bishop." "They claim to be giving the Church solid priests. But the Church will not be able to recognize them as her own." The barriers of exclusion came down sharp and swift. Surprisingly, however, this future bishop had again recently been in touch with

---

[54] According to information received by the Archbishop. Cf. His letter of Oct. 17, 1972, to Cardinal Marty.
[55] Letter of Feb. 1, 1972.
[56] Two hundred of them had spent the night in prayer in the basilica of Our Lady.
[57] Fribourg daily newspapers from March 19.

Archbishop Lefebvre concerning a Carmelite seminarian who wished to enter Fribourg.

To get information from the horse's mouth, the French bishops sent an official visitor, Bishop Jacques Delarue, bishop of Nanterre, to Sion and Ecône. On March 24, 1972, he was able to speak with some teachers and seminarians.[58] He was given a cautious welcome, but he said to Bishop Adam after his visit: "The atmosphere remained friendly....I told them that I had come neither to condemn nor to approve, but above all to get to know them."[59]

Archbishop Lefebvre was annoyed by the French bishops' interference in a project and seminary that had nothing to do with them and whose candidates wanted nothing from them (at least those who had come to Ecône to become members of the Society). However, he knew very well that the forty, and soon seventy, students who came mostly from France weighed heavily in the balance when set against the entries to French seminaries that had gone down to 237 in 1971. Bishop Ménager especially was unhappy at the loss of minor seminary students who went on to Ecône where they were attracted by their former spiritual director from Meaux, Fr. Masson. He shared his "thoughts" with Cardinal François Marty, archbishop of Paris.

Bishop François Fretellière, auxiliary bishop of Bordeaux, had to prepare a report on seminaries for the next plenary meeting of the French bishops; the cardinal asked him to question Archbishop Lefebvre about his seminary. The Archbishop replied with a frank offer: "As former Bishop of Tulle, I could come to the meeting at Lourdes to discuss things and put right any misinformation."[60]

Panic set in at Paris, and Cardinal Marty wrote to the Archbishop at Ecône: "Your coming to Lourdes seems to us neither appropriate nor feasible."[61]

The Archbishop telephoned him directly, and François Marty promised that there would be no discussion of Ecône in Lourdes.

The "resolutions" passed in Lourdes on October 30 show that they did discuss it. In fact it is stated: "Training for the priestly ministry comes under the responsibility of the bishops in a collegial context....This is why we undertake only to ordain [those candidates] who are preparing for the priesthood in seminaries chosen in agreement with us."[62] Cardinal Marty

---

[58] Archbishop Lefebvre was absent from Ecône on that day, the eve of diaconal ordinations that he would perform the following day.

[59] Letter of Bishop Adam, March 30, 1972.

[60] Cf. Letter of Archbishop Lefebvre dated Oct. 16 to all the bishops of France, and another dated Oct. 17 to Cardinal Marty; *Fideliter*, no. 59: 66.

[61] Letter of Sept. 21, 1972.

[62] *Documentation Catholique*, 1620 (Nov. 19, 1972): 1025.

remarked: "It is our duty to safeguard the priestly ministry as the Church wants it,…[and] the priesthood as the Council described it."[63] The avowal was clear: the Council had conceived of a new priesthood that was endangered by Ecône.

In the *Figaro* and the *Aurore* on December 11 and 13 respectively, Archbishop Lefebvre made his reply: the seminary had been founded "with the encouragement of Cardinal Journet[64] and the agreement of Bishop Adam." Moreover, Rome encouraged the Society. Finally, "the seminary does not depend on any episcopal conference in general and has no need of the French bishops' recognition in particular. It is the seminary of the Society of Saint Pius X, and, therefore, it is independent."

"I Am Asking to Perform the Experiment of Tradition"

At this stage of the debate, the Archbishop could fear that such agitation might have unfortunate consequences in Rome for his work. Nonetheless, since he was not a pessimist by nature, he remained confident: he only wanted to do the work of the Church, and it was for the Church to judge! On February 2, 1973, he was invited to Bouveret by the Holy Ghost Fathers, and in the animated conversation at table he went as far as to declare: "Some seminarians came to see me. Should I have abandoned them? My seminary is going against the tide, okay! If Rome intervenes, I'll throw in the towel. But training holy priests…we always need them. Several bishops have already placed their orders."[65]

Bishop Mamie took up the position of the French bishops[66] and declared: "One cannot prepare priests for the future by bringing back the methods of the past."

Speaking at the Mutualité Lecture Hall in Paris—"smiling sweetly but with characteristically steely resolve"—the Archbishop retorted that he taught his seminarians "to love their Mother the Church, that the sacrifice of the Mass is the center of priestly life, and that the catechism is the Deposit of Revelation passed on through Tradition."[67] As for the Mass of St Pius V, he said: "I follow the directives given for group Masses (laughter). I am asking to perform an experiment with Tradition (applause)."[68]

---

[63] *L'Aurore*, Oct. 30, 1972, 9a.

[64] The cardinal later denied having encouraged Archbishop Lefebvre. He wrote to Bishop Mamie on Jan. 10, 1973, saying he had carefully avoided saying anything that could be interpreted as encouragement. Savioz, *La fondation de la Fraternité St Pie X*, annexe 1, 78. See Chapter XVI, n. 6.

[65] Fr. Charles Rappo, C.S.Sp., personal diary, Feb. 2, 1973. Savioz, ann. 3. 1; ms. I, 29, 33-35.

[66] *Evangile et Mission*, Jan. 25, 1973; *La Suisse*, Jan. 26.

[67] Talk of March 29; cf. *L'Aurore*, March 30, 1973.

[68] *Rivarol*, April 5, 1973.

The newspaper articles and reports grew more numerous concerning "this prospering wildcat seminary." Fr. Coache, who had already bought the Maison Lacordaire in Flavigny in 1972, now acquired the minor seminary of the same small Burgundy village "to house his first minor seminarians there in 1974, remaining in touch with Ecône."[69]

But the growing unhappiness of the bishops of France, the increasing anxiety of Nestor Adam, the rather sympathetic press coverage, and the prudent silence of Rome only encouraged the lively and combative traditional initiatives that acted as healthy and legitimate forces within the Church.

NESTOR ADAM

Nestor Adam wanted to separate himself from Ecône. When speaking to Cardinal Garrone, he claimed that he had not approved the seminary but only the year of spirituality: "Without my permission, the pre-seminary became a seminary; I had to accept a *fait accompli.*"[70] He was playing with words: as shrewd as a fox, he was able to claim he had not given his permission since he had only given it verbally and not in writing. He reminded the cardinal that in Ecône "they keep to the missal of St. Pius V and claim that the Holy Father did not wish to abolish it." Therefore, he wished for a clarification from the Holy See.

On March 17, 1973 (having received clarification, we must believe), he wrote to Archbishop Lefebvre: "The Mass of Paul VI is obligatory....I cannot put up with the formation of a sect in the diocese....All the history of the Church teaches us that true reformers...do not withdraw themselves from obedience."

No, replied the Archbishop, Ecône is not a "center of revolt," and if we keep the old rite, it is "not at all in the spirit of revolt or disobedience, but with the desire to keep the Faith."[71]

The drama being played out here was at Sion and not Ecône. Marcel Lefebvre stated that the fight for the Faith was more fundamental than a poorly understood obedience; Nestor Adam was giving up the fight. He had chosen to believe blindly in the Council and resolved to obey, whatever it might cost his diocese. The progressive elements on his lay and priestly council paralyzed him. He drove the parish priest of Riddes out of his parish because he was "for St. Pius V"; but the valiant priest remained in the village in a sawmill converted into a chapel. One day the Bishop turned to him and said these lucid and terrible words: "The avalanche is

---

[69] *Le Monde,* Dec. 6, 1973. The enterprise failed and the building was sold back to the Benedictines of Dom Augustin Joly.

[70] Letter to Cardinal Garrone, Feb. 21, 1973; Bishop Adam's on Ecône, April 25, 1974.

[71] Letter of Archbishop Lefebvre, Rome, March 23, 1973.

coming down, let it come down! Why must you always put yourself in the way?"

Archbishop Lefebvre was surrounded by many young men whom he inspired with a love for principles, truth, and the Mass. He saw in the humanly unexpected growth of the movement a providential confirmation that "God wants this work for the good of the Church." He stuck to his guns in order "to give the Church true and holy priests," knowing perfectly well that he risked a confrontation with the "Council's destructive, reforming tendency."[72]

III. Suppression of the Society

Meetings in Rome and the Canonical Visit

A year would pass. The number of seminarians grew to ninety-five, throwing "more than one episcopate into a state of real alarm," as Cardinal Garonne wrote to Bishop Adam on March 9, 1974. One in every six or seven French seminarians went to Ecône!

Garrone was pressured into acting by the Secretary of State, Cardinal Jean Villot, who promised the French bishops that he would sort out the matter. The permanent secretary, Archbishop Etchegaray, gave an assurance that "in six months time, Ecône would be finished." The heads of the three congregations involved (Seminaries, Clergy, and Religious) met and decided on resolutions that received "the Holy Father's approval." Then on March 5, "in obedience to the directives received" (of Villot perhaps?), they organized a meeting with the two bishops concerned (Mamie and Adam). The meeting took place on April 26 at the headquarters of the Sacred Congregation for Seminaries. They examined the "resolutions" mentioned above and decided to ask Archbishop Lefebvre "to explain clearly and expressly how he was adhering to the conciliar directives" and to accept the norms governing "the opening of houses in other dioceses."[73]

On his return to Fribourg, Bishop Mamie summoned the Archbishop on April 30: "Where are you planning to open new houses?"

The Archbishop replied: "I am in fact going to Rome to see the secretary of the Sacred Congregation for Religious and I will tell him." On May 4, he had a meeting with Archbishop Augustin Mayer, who was intrigued by the foundation at Albano.[74] They also spoke of Suresnes (Paris) and Armada.

"Good," said the secretary, "but what about your liturgy?"

---

[72] "An anniversary," text of Archbishop Lefebvre, June 13, 1980.
[73] Letter of Cardinal Garrone, signed by Garrone, Wright, and Augustin Mayer, addressed to Bishops Mamie and Adam, March 9, 1974.
[74] Bishop Raffaele Macario had just given his *placet* on Feb. 22, 1974.

"I see no other option that would be useful to the Church," Archbishop Lefebvre explained. "It is a theological question. You recognize that there is a serious situation: there are causes and their remedies. Now, one cannot accept bits of this reform without accepting everything; but in that case the seminary would close in three weeks!"

"That's very serious," Augustin Mayer replied, both surprised and concerned.[75]

Things were not "very serious" in Ecône but they were in France. Recruitment was very poor in those seminaries where the liturgical reform and the corresponding concept of the priesthood were enforced: in October 1973, there were only 131 new seminarians![76]

In summer 1974, a holidaymaker passed by Ecône and asked to see Archbishop Lefebvre, who did not recognize the individual in a black clerical suit.

"What!" exclaimed the Bishop of Strasbourg (for it was he), "ya don't recognize Arthur?"

"Oh, Bishop Elchinger," said the Archbishop, who finally recognized his former fellow student from seminary, Léon-Arthur Elchinger.

"Arthur" asked: "Ya got quite a crowd here, from what I hear? At Strasbourg, things are not so hot. How d'ya do it?"[77]

How did he do it? But more to the point, how could he be stopped? Such was the question that troubled France, Fribourg, Sion, and Rome.

The storm broke suddenly on November 11, 1974: after breakfast the Archbishop gathered together the Ecône community to announce that they would that very day receive two apostolic visitors who were coming to conduct an inquiry on behalf of the three Roman Congregations, following orders from Paul VI himself.[78] In the corridor of the cloister while waiting for the visitors, Archbishop Lefebvre confided to Fr. Aulagnier: "I well suspected that our refusal to accept the New Mass would sooner or later be a stumbling block, but I would have preferred to die rather than have to confront Rome and the Pope!"

Msgr. Albert Descamps, secretary of the Biblical Commission, and Msgr. Guillaume Onclin, under-secretary of the Commission for the Revision of the Code of Canon Law, arrived at nine o'clock in the morning. For three days the two Belgians would question the priests and seminarians, and make theologically questionable remarks to them. They thought the ordination of married men was normal and inevitable, they did not

---

[75] *Spiritual Conferences at Ecône*, May 23, 1974.
[76] And twenty-five Frenchmen had just entered Ecône.
[77] Diary of Ecône, summer 1974, 148.
[78] On June 23, 1974, the commission formed by the heads of the three dicasteries decided on the canonical visit; a letter from the three cardinals dated November 5 notified Archbishop Lefebvre.

admit that truth is immutable, and they expressed doubts concerning the physical reality of Christ's Resurrection. They never went to chapel, and when they left offered no report of their visit for Archbishop Lefebvre to sign. However, they said to Fr. Gottlieb: "The seminary is 99% fine." And the priest said to himself: "99%? That only leaves 1% for the Mass, it's not much!"

A lady from the diocese came to see Bishop Adam on November 11 and told him: "Now I only want the Mass of St. Pius V. I'm going to Ecône."

The Bishop replied coldly: "I wouldn't bother; in any case, the unity of the Church will soon be sorted out."

Archbishop Lefebvre left for Rome on November 16. On November 21 while he was visiting one of the Congregations, a Swiss Guard who until that moment had been like a statue spoke to him suddenly: "Your Grace, you don't expect anything from those people, do you?"

Amazed, the Archbishop said nothing but he remembered the canonical visit and understood that he could expect nothing more from the Congregations. When he returned to Albano, "in a moment of indignation" as he would later say,[79] he wrote in one go and without correction an admirable statement of his principles. This he presented to the community at Ecône on December 2: "This has been the position of the seminary and the Society since the beginning, but it [the declaration] puts it in clearer and more definitive terms because the crisis has grown more serious."[80]

THE DECLARATION OF NOVEMBER 21, 1974

The entire reform "is consistent," explained the Archbishop, with the New Mass, new catechisms, and new seminaries. All these things come from the strains of liberalism, Protestantism, and modernism that emerged at the Council and that are now leading the Church to her ruin. Our backs are against the wall and we have to make a choice. Without rebelling, we choose the beliefs and practices of the Church of all time. Consequently:

> We adhere with our whole heart, and with our whole soul to Catholic Rome, the Guardian of the Catholic Faith and of those traditions necessary for the maintenance of that Faith, to eternal Rome, Mistress of Wisdom and Truth.

> Because of this adherence we refuse and have always refused to follow the Rome of neo-Modernist and neo-Protestant tendencies, such as were

---

[79] To Cardinal Garrone, on March 3, 1975: "Doubtless I was too indignant," he would say, although his admitting to exaggerated indignation does not seem fair.

[80] Diary of Ecône; *Spiritual Conferences at Ecône*, 12 A, Dec. 2, 1974.

clearly manifested during the Second Vatican Council, and after the Council in all the resulting reforms.

Archbishop Lefebvre had not even finished reading his declaration when the seminarians, aware of the importance of the moment, began to applaud. Scorning all human prudence and drawing on a vision of faith, the Archbishop had openly declared war on all the post-conciliar reforms.

On November 27, he confided in his professors: "Whatever sanctions are imposed upon us, there is no longer any question of obedience under these conditions. It is a matter of keeping the Faith. If ten, twenty, or even forty leave, I am staying!" However, by December 2, no one had left. Some seminarians had rushed to the telephone to tell their parents how happy they were to have been strengthened by this declaration.

When Fr. Barbara visited Ecône, the Archbishop gave him the text, and he hurried to publish it in *Forts dans la Foi* along with a sermon of St. Athanasius against the Arians: "They have the churches but we have the Faith." Soon the declaration was reprinted in *Itinéraires* and in other magazines.

On January 21, 1975, the two visitors submitted their reports to the three cardinals in the presence of Bishop Mamie. Cardinal Garrone brandished the declaration of Archbishop Lefebvre, saying: "See!" From then on, things moved quickly: on the 24th, Bishop Mamie asked Cardinal Tabera to authorize him to withdraw his predecessor's approval for the Society. The three cardinals considered that a warning should precede this measure, and on the 25th they summoned Archbishop Lefebvre in order to speak to him "concerning points that leave us somewhat perplexed" after the canonical visit.

The Archbishop met the three cardinals on February 13.

"The visitors' report is very favorable," said Garrone, "but they caught a whiff of opposition to the Council and the Pope. Look here," he said pointing at *Itinéraires* which was on his desk, "your declaration confirms this suspicion: you are against the Pope and the Council!"

Archbishop Lefebvre went on the counter-attack: "What about the new heterodox catechisms? And the New Mass which is none other than the Mass of Luther? And openness to Communism? And the Freemasons who are not excommunicated? And religious liberty that puts all religions on the same footing?"

A second meeting took place on March 3. Tabera explained: "You let yourself be called Athanasius!" Garrone shouted: "You are obsessed with liberalism!" And he added: "You are mad!" and claimed that "the Church is on a path of discovery." From these beginnings they came to the essence of their exchange: "Your manifesto is unacceptable. It teaches your seminarians to depend on their personal judgment and on Tradition such as they understand it. This is freethinking, the worst of all liberal doctrines!"

"That is false," replied the Archbishop, "the basis for our judgments is the Magisterium of the Church of all time."

"You recognize yesterday's Magisterium but not today's. But the Council belongs to the Magisterium, as the Pope wrote to Cardinal Pizzardo in 1966."

"The Church keeps her Tradition and cannot break with it. It is impossible. That is how the Church is."[81]

Certainly, as Garrone said, the living Magisterium of today is the rule of Faith; however, as Archbishop Lefebvre replied, it is only the rule in so far as it is itself ruled by yesterday's Magisterium, by Tradition. When the Magisterium malfunctions, it is Tradition that judges.

THE SOCIETY IS SUPPRESSED

However, Garrone ruled out any malfunctioning of the Magisterium: it was an absolute rule of Faith. As for the Council, he admitted that it had been followed by a crisis in the Church, but it was not the cause of that crisis. Before this wall of sententious incomprehension, Archbishop Lefebvre observed: "I was invited for a meeting and in fact I had to face a court that had decided to condemn me."[82]

As for his declaration, he said to the three cardinals: "I could put it differently, but I could not write anything different."

Back in Ecône at this time, the teaching staff took it into their heads to correct the manifesto and met together to draw up a "moderate declaration."

"Your Grace," they asked him, "withdraw your first text and sign this one."[83]

But the Archbishop would no more give in to Ecône than to Rome. He did not retract his declaration.[84] Consequently, he was certain to lose his case at the Vatican.

In fact on April 25, Cardinal Tabera assured Bishop Mamie that he "possessed all the necessary authority to withdraw the acts and concessions" of his predecessor. Unfortunately, this was correct! The Society had not even received Rome's *nihil obstat* and had not become a Society of diocesan right, but remained at the preliminary stage of *pia unio*. The Bish-

---

[81] Roland Gaucher, *Monseigneur Lefebvre, combat pour l'Eglise* (Albatros, 1976), 228-247; Yves Montagne, *L'évêque suspens* (Rome: Catholic Laymen's League, 1977), 52-75.

[82] Archbishop Lefebvre, *Relation sur la manière dont la commission des trois cardinaux a procédé* (Report of the manner in which the commission of three cardinals acted), *etc.*, Rome, May 30, 1975 (addressed to Paul VI).

[83] Aulagnier, *La Tradition sans peur*, 97.

[84] On May 5, 1974, on the Feast of St. Pius V and the day of Fr. Calmel's funeral, he even took the resolution to defend the traditional Mass, cost what it may. Letter to Friends and Benefactors, no. 16, March 19, 1979.

op therefore was able to dissolve it (cf. Canon 492, §§ 1-2, and 493) if he had a serious reason. In the view of those responsible, the "declaration" was a serious reason, even if it was not so before God.

On May 6, Bishop Mamie, therefore, informed Archbishop Lefebvre that he was withdrawing the approval given by his predecessor, and the same day the three cardinals upheld this decision with the approval of Paul VI. They added: once the Society is "suppressed," its seminary and all its activities lose the right to exist.

Archbishop Lefebvre replied in three ways: at Pentecost of that Holy Year, the Archbishop and his seminarians joined in the magnificent pilgrimage of the *Credo* association to show with the faithful their attachment to the Rome of all time; then, from Albano on May 31, he wrote a letter of submission to the successor of Peter containing a request for a review of his "trial"; finally, on June 5, he lodged an appeal with the court of the Apostolic Signatura against Bishop Mamie's decision. It was not the Bishop of Fribourg, he wrote, but the Holy See that had the power to suppress the Society (this first point is debatable); next, he has been judged on doctrine and only the Sacred Congregation for the Doctrine of the Faith is competent in this matter; finally, if his declaration deserves to be condemned, the condemnation should concern him and not his work.[85]

The appeal was rejected on June 10: the steps taken by Bishop Mamie had been carried out according to the decision of the cardinals' commission, itself approved *in forma specifica* by the Pope. Another appeal launched on June 14 asked for proof of this specific approbation; there was no reply because Cardinal Villot, Secretary of State, had written to Cardinal Staffa forbidding him to consider the appeal.[86]

On June 29, 1975, Archbishop Lefebvre ordained three priests and thirteen subdeacons at Ecône. The same day, Paul VI wrote him a letter demanding his submission, an act that "necessarily implied" accepting the suppression of the Society with all the practical consequences, and accepting the Council "which has no less authority than the Council of Nicea and in some ways is more important than it."

IV. ECÔNE CONTINUES

NOT COLLABORATING IN THE AUTO-DEMOLITION OF THE CHURCH

Jean Madiran highlighted this extraordinary claim that put Vatican II over Nicea. They said and repeated that this Council was a pastoral council and not dogmatic, and now they want to turn it into dogma![87]

---

[85] Letter to Cardinal Dino Staffa, Prefect of the Apostolic Signatura, May 21, and appeal submitted on June 5.

[86] Cardinal Staffa showed this letter to Archbishop Lefebvre's lawyer.

At Ecône, the question of survival was much closer to hand. Four professors left the seminary (not counting the two eminent Dominicans who would never come back), and during their final classes some even went as far as to explain to the seminarians why they were leaving. Others suggested to the Archbishop that he break the seminary up into small groups and continue clandestinely. Canon Berthod reacted: "Your Grace, that would be the death of the seminary. Either we continue, or we do not continue! We cannot continue if we are spread out: studies, perseverance, and recruitment would become difficult. Ecône must continue. Ecône is Ecône!"[88]

Besides, the seminarians were perfectly at peace. The Archbishop kept them continually informed of developments in great detail. His perspective on the situation was admirable, and he never attacked individuals, especially not the Pope. Thus, they had complete trust in the Archbishop who had promised them: "I will not abandon you!"[89]

Then Archbishop Lefebvre decided very simply: "The new school year starts on September 14. *The seminary goes on.* We want to do what the Church has always done. So, we are going to continue to develop and open a German-speaking seminary at Weissbad near Appenzell."[90]

The Archbishop's answer to the suppression was to march on. On November 21, 1975, the anniversary of his "declaration" and two months into a school year that saw 127 seminarians in the three seminaries of Ecône, Armada, and Weissbad, Archbishop Lefebvre clarified the basis of his rejection of "the cardinals'" orders (he was still avoiding calling Paul VI into question): "The Society still exists. Its suppression was illegal and in any case unjust. One day, Providence will allow its official rehabilitation. But it still exists before God and the Church....Law is meant to serve life. Now, at the moment they are using law to serve death and to go against the life of the Church. Human authority participates in the authority of God, the author of life. However, the laws of the Church since the Council are laws of death and spiritual abortion. These laws are invalid."[91]

On October 27, Cardinal Villot wrote to all the episcopal conferences telling them "solemnly" to refuse incardination to the members of the Society. Archbishop Lefebvre would not be stopped by this last policy of death: "If incardination is difficult, I will not hesitate to think about incardinating you in the Society."[92] He based his view on the letter of praise

---

[87] *Itinéraires*, no. 197 (Nov. 1975), editorial.

[88] *Spiritual Conferences at Ecône*, 47 B, Oct. 11, 1977.

[89] Handwritten letter to benefactors, June 17, 1975; Aulagnier, *La Tradition sans peur*, 101-103.

[90] *Spiritual Conferences at Ecône*, 20 B, June 28, 1975, eve of the ordinations.

[91] *Ibid.*, 23 A, Nov. 21, 1975; cf. 22 A, Sept. 29, 1975.

[92] *Ibid.*

from Cardinal Wright which was similar to a "decree of praise." He also founded it on the permission that the Sacred Congregation for Religious gave to three religious to enter the Society without asking explicitly to be incardinated in a diocese.[93] Finally he used the opinion of Bishop Adam who had told him: "Since your Society is spread throughout several dioceses, it certainly has the power to incardinate within its own ranks." All these arguments were probable ("colored" to use the canonical term).

At the end of August the Archbishop twice met the Bishop of Sion (not at the bishop's residence), who told him he had received a personal visit from Cardinal Villot. Thus, Archbishop Lefebvre was convinced that Jean Villot wanted to satisfy the demands of the French bishops and was responsible for the campaign against the Society from beginning to end. However, Nestor Adam advised him: "Ecône must continue! Put a bit of Paul VI in your Pius V Mass, and carry on."[94]

The Archbishop left the trickery to one side and merely accepted the encouragement: "Carry on." Paul VI wrote to him on September 8 and threatened to punish him for refusing to obey. Archbishop Lefebvre replied on September 24, professing his "devotion towards the successor of Peter, 'master of truth' for the whole Church," but he would not comply. There was far more at stake than the suppression of a new society and seminary. He explained his thinking to the seminarians: "Asking us to close the seminary at Ecône means asking us to take part in the destruction of the Church. When the good Lord calls me, I don't want to say in my conscience: 'Well, I have destroyed something that the good Lord allowed me to do through His Providence and which besides had canonical permission and was practically approved by the Roman visitors.' I am asked to destroy all that because it does not follow the post-conciliar tendencies that are destroying the Church. Well, no!"[95]

THE "SUSPENSION A DIVINIS"

However, Archbishop Lefebvre tried hard to meet the Holy Father. Cardinal Thiandoum, who acted as a go-between, saw Paul VI, and said to him: "Most Holy Father, you must know how upset people would be in Dakar if Archbishop Lefebvre were to be condemned. Please let him see you."

"Eminence, go and talk to Cardinal Villot."

---

[93] For example, the indult granted to Fr. Urban Snyder, a reformed Cistercian, on Oct. 16, 1972.

[94] *Spiritual Conferences at Ecône*, 21 A, Sep. 14, 1975; Archbishop Lefebvre, letter to Dom Jean Roy, Sept. 27, 1975.

[95] *Spiritual Conferences at Ecône*, Dec. 1, 1975; *Spiritual Conferences at Ecône*, 13 A, 2 part, Feb. 2, 1976.

At the Secretariat of State, Villot said to Thiandoum: "Archbishop Lefebvre's meeting the Holy Father is out of the question! The Pope might change his mind and that would cause confusion." The Archbishop concluded: "A barrier has been placed between the Sovereign Pontiff and me."[96]

Unhappy, Jean Villot got Paul VI to clarify the matter. The Pope wrote: "It is not true. We consider that before being received in audience, Archbishop Lefebvre ought to change his views, which are unacceptable."[97]

Then Archbishop Lefebvre met the Deputy Secretary of State, Archbishop Giovanni Benelli, who on April 21 demanded that he accept Vatican II and all its documents, show total attachment to Paul and to all his teachings, and adopt the new missal as concrete proof of his submission.

As nothing of the sort happened, Paul made an allocution during the Consistory on May 24, 1976, which was mostly concerned with Archbishop Lefebvre. He reproached him for refusing today's authority in the name of yesterday's, for leading people into disobedience "on the pretext of keeping his faith intact," and for refusing the New Mass because of a "sentimental attachment" to the old. Paul confirmed that "the new *Ordo* had been promulgated to replace the old." "This is nothing less than what our predecessor Pius V did when after the Council of Trent he made obligatory the missal that was reformed under his authority."

Archbishop Lefebvre was indignant at this misrepresentation of his fight for the Faith and still more indignant at the fallacious comparison that Paul VI had dared to make between his own reform and the reform of St. Pius V.[98] However, as the priestly ordinations approached, Rome was gripped in a fever: would the Archbishop dare to ordain priests without incardination or dimissorial letters? On June 12 and 25, Archbishop Benelli forbade him to ordain *de mandato speciali Summi Pontificis* without prejudice to the censures foreseen in Canon 2373, 1. He added that if his seminarians were "seriously prepared for a priestly ministry in true loyalty to the *conciliar Church*," Rome would undertake to find a better solution for them.

The envoy who brought the letter of June 25, Fr. Edouard Dhanis, professor and former rector of the Gregorian University, arrived in haste at the Maison Lacordaire in Flavigny where Archbishop Lefebvre was preaching a retreat to the ordinands. It was about 9 P.M. on June 27, two days before the ordinations. The Archbishop was struck by how nervous his visitor was, but even more by Archbishop Benelli's expression "conciliar Church." Holding a missal of Paul VI, Fr. Dhanis pleaded with the Arch-

---

[96] Interview by Louis Salleron. *La France Catholique-Ecclesia*, Feb. 13, 1976.
[97] Handwritten letter of Paul VI to Villot, Feb. 21, 1976.
[98] Cf. Madiran, *Itinéraires*, no. 205: 10-11.

bishop: "Your Grace," he said, "if today you agree to say this Mass with me, everything will be fine with Rome!"

"I have already said Mass," replied the Archbishop laconically.

And the poor priest left in despair.[99]

At Ecône the following day they turned a large tent into a sanctuary on the field next to the seminary. The ordinands came back from Flavigny. About 5 P.M., there was a knock at Fr. Aulagnier's door. "Surprise! It's the Archbishop!" He sat down: "Should we do these ordinations tomorrow?" he said looking serious. He was worried and thoughtful but perfectly calm. "What should I say to this great bishop?" the priest thought to himself. But finally he stammered his opinion in favor.[100] The Archbishop left. His decision was taken.

June 29, 1976. The large tent flapped in the wind, the sun beat down, and already lines of cars had turned an adjoining field into a car park. Several thousand Catholics who had come from every corner of Switzerland, Europe, and from across the globe, were in their seats; it was difficult to control the floods of photographers and journalists. At 9 o'clock the procession got underway and came slowly down the slope of the field. The Archbishop in miter and gloves walked with crosier in hand. His face was a little tense but he looked determined. He was going to ordain thirteen priests and fourteen subdeacons. He had just had a short visit from Cardinal Thiandoum.[101] But Archbishop Lefebvre had not given in.

In his sermon he explained at length why he was resisting.

> It is clear, crystal clear, that *the problem of the Mass is at the heart of this conflict between Ecône and Rome*....The way Rome's envoys have insisted on asking us to change rites makes us think....This New Mass is a symbol, an expression of a new and modernist faith. Because, if throughout the centuries the Holy Church wanted to keep this precious treasure that she gives us in the rites of Holy Mass as canonized by St. Pius V, it is not without good reason. In this Mass is found all of our Faith,...faith in the divinity of our Lord Jesus Christ, faith in Redemption by our Lord Jesus Christ, faith in the Blood of our Lord Jesus Christ that was shed for the redemption of our sins.[102]

On that day, the Archbishop incurred canonically a suspension *a collatione ordinum* which from then on forbade him to ordain.[103] On July 6, Cardinal Sebastiano Baggio, Prefect of the Sacred Congregation for Bishops, sent him a solemn admonition stating that he should "ask pardon from the Holy Father." On July 17, Archbishop Lefebvre replied to Paul

---

[99] *Spiritual Conferences at Ecône*, 87A, Jan. 16, 1982.

[100] Aulagnier, *La Tradition sans peur*, 107-108.

[101] Diary of Ecône. *Paris-Match* showed Thiandoum looking sad in the plane on his return journey from Geneva.

[102] Complete text in *Itinéraires*, no. 206 (Sep.-Oct. 1976).

[103] Declaration of Archbishop Panciroli, press conference room at the Holy See.

VI: give to the liturgy "all its dogmatic value and hierarchical expression according to the Latin Roman rite consecrated by so many centuries of use" and "Your Holiness will restore the Catholic priesthood and the reign of our Lord Jesus Christ over individuals, families, and civil society"; abandon this "harmful venture of compromise with the ideas of modern man that comes from a secret agreement between high dignitaries in the Church and those in Masonic lodges before the Council."[104]

On July 22, the secretary of the Sacred Congregation for Bishops notified Archbishop Lefebvre that since he had not provided the signs of repentance as requested, the Holy Father imposed on him the punishment of suspension *a divinis* according to Canon 2279 § 2, 2, depriving him of the right to confect any of the sacraments.

THE "HOT SUMMER"

At first the Archbishop was greatly hurt, but he pulled himself together and published "A few thoughts regarding the suspension *a divinis*" on July 29: "When all is said and done, this suspension forbids me…to say the New Mass or to give the new sacraments. I am asked to obey the 'Conciliar Church,' as Archbishop Benelli calls it. But this Conciliar Church is schismatic because it breaks with the Catholic Church of all time. It has its new dogmas [the dignity of the person], its new priesthood, its new institutions, and its new liturgy which have already been condemned in so many official and definitive documents."

This polemical tone grew sharper in the interview that Archbishop Lefebvre granted to *The Figaro*[105] on August 4:

The Council turned its back on Tradition and broke with the Church of the past. It is a schismatic council….If we are certain that the Faith taught by the Church for twenty centuries can contain no error, we are much less certain that the Pope is truly Pope. Heresy, schism, excommunication *ipso facto*, or invalid election all are causes that can possibly mean the Pope was never Pope, or is no longer Pope….

Because ultimately, since the beginning of Paul VI's pontificate, the conscience and faith of all Catholics have been faced with a serious problem. How is it that a Pope, the true successor of Peter, who is assured of the help of the Holy Ghost, can officiate at the destruction of the Church—the most radical, rapid, and widespread in her history—something that no heresiarch has ever managed to achieve?

The question deserved to be asked, but the Archbishop did not answer it; he left that up to the Church. But he did not hesitate to point out the

---

[104] He was referring to the agreement made between Bea and the B'nai-B'rith in New York.
[105] Taken from *La Libre Belgique* of Aug. 5.

schismatic nature or tendencies of the Council and the new model of the Church that came from it.

In that hot summer of 1976, Archbishop Lefebvre's popularity rose with the temperature; media surveys[106] showed that 27% of French people "recognized their own views" in his ideas, 24% disapproved of him, 23% made no comments, and 25% said that they were indifferent to the Archbishop's actions.

Some writers, artists, and academics were greatly alarmed. Eight French personalities wrote to Paul VI that they felt they were "now watching the sack of Rome";[107] on December 1, thirty university teachers manifested "their wholehearted agreement with Archbishop Lefebvre" and paid tribute to "the brave bishop who has dared to rise up, break the conspiracy of silence, and ask the Pope for true justice for the faithful."

The right wing French government was also stirred into action: they had to avoid disappointing potential "Lefebvrist" voters. President Valéry Giscard d'Estaing asked René Brouillet, former ambassador to the Holy See, for a report. The Prime Minister, Jacques Chirac, met with Jean Guitton of the Académie Française,[108] who was a confident of Paul VI. However, Chirac, a former representative in La Corrèze, had not forgotten Archbishop Lefebvre's impact on the Church in that region during his brief time as Bishop of Tulle. On July 16 he wrote the Archbishop a letter of "respectful friendship and trust":

> Christian France, eldest daughter of the Church by immemorial privilege, has ever given constant proof of her attachment to the successor of Peter....I am confident that in your wisdom you will know how to speak the language of reconciliation. What an example you will give at a time when fidelity is so constantly scorned and when true love is so tragically corrupted. Your fight for the faith and the Church will thereby receive the striking seal of authenticity, the seal that is given by total purity of conduct and the acceptance of sacrifice.

Were it a matter of sacrificing his personal ideas, the Archbishop would willingly have made the offering. But since it was a fight for the Faith, the sacrifice which Jacques Chirac exhorted him to make had quite another dimension: it was in fact the sacrifice of his honor. Suspended, "rebel," schismatic: Marcel Lefebvre resolutely accepted these hurtful labels for the love of the Faith and the Church.

He wrote a short reply to the Prime Minister and carried on his visits throughout France unperturbed. He appeared before thousands of people

---

[106] Survey of IFOP for *Le Progrès* of Lyons, in *Valeurs Actuelles*, Aug. 23-29, 1976, 25.

[107] *Nouvelliste du Valais*, Aug. 11, 1976.

[108] [An official body first established by Cardinal Richelieu in 1635 with responsibility for defining French vocabulary and grammar. There are forty members known as *académiciens*. Trans.]

who came together to assist at the first solemn Masses of Fr. Roch in Geneva and Fr. Groche at Besançon. Gérard Saclier de La Batie, president of the union of "Traditional Associations," and a few of his friends asked Archbishop Lefebvre to perform a special ceremony where he would show himself publicly to be the defender of the Faith. Lille was chosen.

At first the Archbishop refused: "No, I cannot; at Rome they would see it as provocative." But the next morning, August 22, he said to the secretary, Sister Marguerite: "I've slept on it, and I will go to Lille after all. I suggest August 29."

The headlines in the newspapers read: "New step towards schism: Archbishop Lefebvre wants to create a global sensation with his Mass in Lille on Sunday."[109] "The time for defying Rome has passed. Now for the test of strength."[110] "Today Archbishop Lefebvre defies Paul VI with a forbidden Mass."[111]

Despite receiving a new letter from Paul dated August 15, the Archbishop celebrated a Solemn Mass at Lille on August 29. Seven thousand people crowded into Lille's exhibition center, which was converted into an immense chapel for the occasion. During the Angelus at Rome, Paul VI denounced "the attitude of defiance against the Keys that have been put in our hands by Christ." In his own sermon, the Archbishop protested: "No, dear faithful, this is not defiance but a demonstration of your Catholic faith." The reader will bear with our summarizing the homily:

> The Revolution made martyrs, but that is nothing to what Vatican II has done: priests have apostatized from the priesthood! This marriage between the Church and Revolution wished for by the liberal Catholics who triumph saying: "With Vatican II, our principles are accepted": this marriage is adulterous. And this adulterous union can only produce illegitimate children. The new rite of Mass is an illegitimate rite,[112] the sacraments are illegitimate sacraments, the priests who come from the seminaries are illegitimate priests: they no longer know that they are made to ascend to the altar to offer the sacrifice of Our Lord Jesus Christ.
>
> Our Lord Jesus Christ is the only person in the world who can say "I am God." Therefore, He is the only king of humanity. There will be no peace on earth except through the reign of our Lord Jesus Christ. His reign—the reign of God's Commandments—will bring about justice and

---

[109] *France-Antilles*, Aug. 24, 1976.
[110] *France-Soir*, Aug. 28, 1976.
[111] *La Stampa*, Aug. 29, 1976.
[112] [The French word that the Archbishop used here was *bâtard*. In English this has been frequently and lamentably translated as *bastard*, but the vulgar nuances in the English are not at all present in the French word or in the Archbishop's meaning. By using *bâtard* the Archbishop is merely drawing out his metaphor on an adulterous couple (the Church and the Revolution) whose children would not be legitimate. Trans.]

peace. One sees this well in Argentina since they have had a government with principles, and authority.[113]

Feverishly, the journalists scribbled down this "praise for dictatorship." The Archbishop continued:

This is why we also want the Mass of St. Pius V, because it proclaims the royalty of our Lord Jesus Christ who reigns from the cross: *Regnavit a ligno Deus.*

In all sincerity, peace, and serenity, I cannot contribute, I do not want to contribute, to the destruction of the Church by [submitting to] the suspensions that are laid on me, by closing my seminaries, and by refusing to give ordination. When I die and our Lord asks me, "What did you do with your episcopacy, what did you do with the grace of the episcopacy and the priesthood?" I do not want to hear our Lord say: "You have joined with the others in destroying the Church."

Some reporters have said me: "Your Grace, don't you feel isolated?" I say: "Not at all. I have twenty centuries of the Church with me." I am told: "You judge the Pope." Archbishop Benelli said to my face: "You are not the one who makes the truth!" Of course I am not the one who makes the truth, but neither is the Pope.

These words caused a ripple through the congregation, and some reporters were seen leaving to telephone the "words of rupture" to their editors. But the Archbishop continued:

Our Lord Jesus Christ is the truth; you must refer to what the whole Church has taught. It is not I who judge the Holy Father, it is Tradition. A child of five with his catechism can tell his bishop a thing or two. If the bishop professes an error, who is right? The catechism!

If only every bishop gave us, gave the Catholic faithful, a church...that is what I will ask the Holy Father if he wishes to receive me: "Most holy Father, let us carry out this experiment of Tradition."[114]

THE AUDIENCE WITH PAUL VI

"If he wishes to receive me..." Archbishop Lefebvre no longer believed he did when to his great surprise after the Mass at Besançon, he was approached by Don Domenico Labellarte[115] through the intermediary of Angeline, Countess Albertini de Buttafoco, who lived near Frasne. This Italian priest had been sent by the Archbishop of Chieti, a personal friend of the Pope, and he assured the Archbishop: "Something has changed. You

---

[113] *L'Express* of August 30 reported that "General Videla, who has been brought to power by a *coup d'état*, has managed in desperate circumstances to rescue the economic situation in the country" after "inflation hit 800% during the final year of Isabel Peron's presidency."

[114] Full text in *Itinéraires*, no. 207 (Nov. 1976).

[115] Spiritual son of Padre Pio and founder of a priestly society. Cf. Michel de Saint-Pierre, interview in *L'Homme Nouveau*, Oct. 3, 1976 ; *Itinéraires*, no. 208.

will be received; the Archbishop of Chieti will take you to see the Holy Father."

The Archbishop accepted, and after having visited Fanjeaux where he was expected by the Dominicans, he was driven to Albano by his chauffeur, Marcel Pedroni. The unexpected had happened. Marcel Lefebvre wrote a brief request for an audience: "I did not intend to act against the Church and still less to offend Your Holiness; I am sorry if Your Holiness has been hurt by anything I have said or written."

Paul VI was shaken and telephoned Cardinal Villot, the Secretary of State. He feared that Paul, who was impressionable, might let himself give in. In the end, the Cardinal insisted: "Your Holiness cannot receive him without a witness. You must have a witness. Take Benelli."[116]

On September 11 in a deserted Castel Gandolfo, Archbishop Lefebvre was received by Paul at 10:30 A.M. Archbishop Benelli was already in the Pope's office. He did not utter a word but merely watched...more Montini than Lefebvre.

"You condemn me," Paul VI began nervously, "I am a modernist, a Protestant. It's intolerable! You are doing wicked work."

The Archbishop said he sensed that the Holy Father felt personally attacked.

"So then," Paul VI finished up saying, "now. Talk."

"Most Holy Father, I am not the 'leader of the traditionalists,' but a bishop who like many faithful and priests is torn, wishing to keep the Faith and also to be submissive to you. Now, we see that the direction taken since the Council distances us from your predecessors. The nuns who dress in lay clothes are accepted, but the sisters that I saw two days ago are reduced to the lay state and the bishop has been five times to ask them to abandon their habits. Similarly, priests who are faithful to the catechism of all time and to the Mass of their ordination are kicked out onto the streets; and those who are no longer like priests are accepted."

"This is intolerable. You are refusing to do what the Council asked for."

"I'm carrying on what I have always done. For thirty years I worked to train priests and suddenly I'm suspended."

"Because you did not want to accept the changes, the Council."

"Exactly! Look at the fruits: empty seminaries, and with us thirty-five vocations, in spite of the difficulties."

"Why do you not accept the Council? You signed the decrees."

"There were two that I did not sign."

"Yes, two, religious liberty and *Gaudium et Spes*."[117]

---

[116] Hebblethwaite, *Pablo VI*, 553.
[117] Paul VI was only repeating what Archbishop Lefebvre had already said publicly on other occasions: that he did not sign these two conciliar documents. In fact the Archbishop signed all the acts of the Council.

(I thought at the time: "I signed the others out of respect for the Holy Father." He went on:)

"And why not religious liberty?"

"It contains passages that are word for word contrary to what was taught by Gregory XVI, and Pius IX."

"Let's leave that aside! We are not here to discuss theology."

(I though to myself: "This is unbelievable.")

"You have no right to oppose the Council; you are a scandal for the Church, you destroy the Church. It is horrible, you raise up Christians against the Pope and against the Council. Do you feel nothing in your conscience that condemns you?"

"Nothing at all."

"You are irresponsible."

"I know I am continuing the Church. I train good priests."

"That is not true, you make priests against the Pope. You make them sign an oath against the Pope."[118]

"I do what?"

(On hearing this incredible allegation, I put my head in my hands.) I can still see myself doing this and saying: "Most Holy Father, how can you say such a thing to me? I have them sign an oath against the Pope! Can you show me a copy of this 'oath'?"

(He was amazed. He was so convinced of the truth of what Cardinal Villot —probably—had told him. He continued:)

"You condemn the Pope! What orders will you give me? What must I do? Hand in my resignation and then you can take my place?"

"Ah! (I put my head in my hands) Most Holy Father, don't say things like that. No, no, no! Let me carry on. You have the solution in your hands. You only need say one thing to the bishops: 'Welcome with understanding these groups of faithful who hold to Tradition, the Mass, the sacraments, and the catechism of all time; give them places to worship.' These groups will be the Church, you will find vocations among them and they will be the best in the Church. The bishops will see it. Leave me my seminary. Let me carry out this experiment of Tradition. I truly want to have normal relations with the Holy See, through a commission that you could name which would come to the seminary. But obviously, we will keep on going: we want to continue this experiment of Tradition."

"Very well, I'll think about it, pray, and consult with the Congregation of the Consistory and the Curia. These are difficult problems. I will write to you. Let us pray together."

(We prayed a *Pater Noster*, *Veni Sancte Spiritus*, and *Ave Maria*. He led me to the adjoining room, walking with difficulty.)

"Dialogue is impossible," he concluded, and then he left me.[119]

---

[118] Neither this oath nor anything like it ever existed. Ever! So the Archbishop had been calumniated in the Pope's hearing, which would explain Paul VI's sense of being personally offended.

[119] *Spiritual Conferences at Ecône*, Sept. 12, 1976; *ibid.*, 34, Sept. 18, 1976, in *Itinéraires*, no. 208 (Dec. 1976), and *Fideliter*, no. 11 (Sept. 1979).

But what could the decision of Paul possibly be? Two days earlier Jean Guitton had suggested he allow the Mass of St. Pius V in France. Pope Paul had replied: "That? Never!...That Mass of St. Pius V like one sees at Ecône has become the symbol for the condemnation of the Council. I will in no wise accept the Council being condemned by a symbol. If an exception were made, the whole Council would be questioned, and consequently the Apostolic authority of the Council."[120]

In fact the decision of the sovereign pontiff dated October 11, 1976[121]—given in Latin and laid out in a letter of eighteen typed pages— was to refuse Archbishop Lefebvre's proposition. Paul VI reproached him for his "rebellion" and his "ecclesiology that was warped on essential points" since he refused "to recognize the authority of Vatican II and the Pope in their entirety." "You claim to be the judge of what concerns Tradition....The concept of Tradition to which you refer is inaccurate. Tradition is not fixed or dead, something static that freezes at any one time in history the life of the active organism that is the Church." It belongs to the Pope and to Councils "to discern in the traditions of the Church" that which is immutable and that which must be brought up to date.

One must, however, recognize that it is Paul's ecclesiology which is wrong. For divine Tradition, one of the two sources of Revelation, is immutable.[122] And with its channels—the Fathers of the Church, Councils, Popes, Doctors, liturgy—it is the rule of the Magisterium which must be nothing other than its faithful echo. From behind these reproaches of the Pope emerge the errors of evolving, living Tradition[123] and the absolute Magisterium which wishes to be its own rule: the Magisterium of the new Rome.

"Rome has blocked all solutions; there is no sign of openness. In Rome they are awaiting my reply. Well, I think that the only response is in action. We reply by the existence of the seminary. And I will continue to travel throughout Europe and across the world to enlighten people and give them valid sacraments. *Omnia instaurare in Christo*: To establish and restore all things in Christ."[124]

---

[120] Guitton, *Paul VI secret*, ch. XIII; Hebblethwaite, *Pablo VI*, 554.

[121] Full text in *Itinéraires*, no. 208.

[122] In this text Paul VI confuses divine Tradition which is immutable with ecclesiastical traditions. The latter accompany divine Tradition and often transmit it, but they are susceptible to change. Cf. J. Madiran, *La condamnation sauvage de Mgr. Lefebvre*, commentary on the Consistory address of May 24, 1976.

[123] "You refuse to adhere to the living Church," Paul VI warned; a new and ambiguous expression! Cf. Gustave Corção, *Itinéraires*, no. 207: 30ff.

[124] *Spiritual Conferences at Ecône*, 35 A, Oct. 18, 1976.

CHAPTER 18

STRONGHOLDS OF THE RECONQUEST

I. THE RISKS OF CONFLICT

ACCUSING THE COUNCIL?

Until 1975 Archbishop Lefebvre refrained from attacking the Council and the Pope. In a talk to seminarians on May 30, 1971, he declared: "Above all never say 'The Archbishop is against the Pope and the Council.' That is not the case!" He often said that he "did not know and did not want to know if these directives came from the Pope." For a long time, he wanted to avoid calling Paul VI into question although he did not resort to the over-simplifications of some Catholics who were influenced by dubious messages from the Blessed Virgin to the effect that "Paul VI is a good man but he is the prisoner of his entourage."

However, when Paul VI asked him in 1975 for "a public act of submission to Vatican II and the post-conciliar reforms and tendencies in which the Pope was involved," the Archbishop declared: "From now on I will be obliged to lay out my position on the Council and its consequences. As a result, I will necessarily have to touch upon the question of the Pope. I can no longer avoid it. I will try to do so with sensitivity but also as objectively as possible."[1] The Archbishop would follow this plan to the letter by publishing his Letter to Friends and Benefactors No. 9 on September 3, 1975; *I Accuse the Council* in September, 1976; and a compilation of his 1974 lectures on liberalism under the title *They Have Uncrowned Him: From Liberalism to Apostasy, the Post-conciliar Tragedy* in 1987.

LIBERALISM AND THE COUNCIL

In 1975 he wrote:

The Popes [John XXIII and Paul VI] so favored the ambiguities of *aggiornamento* that liberal ideas were widely brought into the Council. Liberalism claims to do three things:

---

[1] Letter to General Lecomte, Aug. 28, 1975.

- To free the mind from every imposed objective truth: one endlessly searches for and makes truth, and nobody can claim to have exclusive possession of it.

- To free the Faith from dogma: it is impossible to accept a revealed truth that is defined for all time.

- To free the will from law whose bonds are contrary to dignity and conscience.

We can thus see how opposed the liberal is to our Lord Jesus Christ and His Church!

Among the consequences of liberalism, one must mention: "The denial of the supernatural, and thus of original sin, justification by grace, the real reason for the Incarnation, the sacrifice of the cross, the Church, and the priesthood!"

The Mass was no longer meant to apply the Redemption to each and every soul. "The entire liturgical reform shows the effect of that tendency." Liberalism also explains religious liberty, ecumenism, theological research, and the revision of Canon Law, all of which lessen "the triumphalism of a Church that claims to be the only ark of salvation."[2]

THE LIBERAL PLOT AND THE COUNCIL

Archbishop Lefebvre asked for what was done at the Council to be unveiled and denounced. There was to be found the starting point for the subversion of the Church: "There was a plot at the Council that was prepared in advance. They knew what they had to do and how they were going to do it. They knew who would start things off. Everything was prepared down to the last detail. Now we are dying because of the success of that plot. I was saying to Fr. Laurentin who was here on Sunday: 'You well know that for two and a half centuries, there have been two mentalities in the Church battling violently against one another: the conservatives and the liberals.'"[3]

Dom Delatte has defined these two groups: the "complete Catholics" whose "first concern was the Church's liberty of action and the defense of her rights in a society that was still Christian"; and the so-called "liberal" Catholics "who firstly tried to determine what degree of Catholicism modern society could put up with before then asking the Church to come down to that level."[4]

Archbishop Lefebvre added:

---

[2] Letter to Friends and Benefactors, no. 9.
[3] *Spiritual Conferences at Ecône*, 38 B, Jan. 17, 1977, 194-195.
[4] Dom Paul Delatte, *Vie de Dom Guéranger*, II, 11; *Spiritual Conferences at Ecône*, 3 A, Dec. 20, 1973.

For one and a half centuries, the Popes condemned the liberals, but I have to recognize that they [the liberals] triumphed at the Council....By taking advantage of a weak Pope [John XXIII] and of a Pope who was won over to radical change [Paul VI], the liberals have taken the levers of power,...to be sure of bringing about the ecumenical revolution that the enemies of the Church so wish for. In this pastoral Council, the spirit of error and lies could circulate at its ease, planting time bombs everywhere which would rip apart the Church's institutions when the moment came.[5]

THE CONCILIAR "TRILOGY"

"The Council itself transformed these ideas of the modern world—liberty, equality, brotherhood—into its doctrines of religious liberty, collegiality, and ecumenism";[6] "and these are the three principles of liberalism that came from the philosophers of the eighteenth century and which led to the French Revolution."[7]

The liberals asked: "What freedom from constraint in the social order is man entitled to by virtue of his nature, and can that freedom perhaps be defined as a right?" But Archbishop Lefebvre replied by rejecting the question as fallacious: absence of constraint is a poor definition for liberty. What constraint is more terrifying than the threat of hell? And it is God who brandishes it! True liberty cannot make do without such beneficial constraints because of error and sin.[8]

It is said: "Constraints must not be placed on individuals as long as they [those individuals] do not disrupt public order."

"This simply does away with civil society's ability to give guidance on religion and morality or to intervene in even the smallest way with individuals" who distance themselves publicly from Catholic worship and morality. "They even go as far as to say that the state is not competent in religious matters and that it cannot decide which is the true religion."

Cardinal Colombo declared: "*Lo stato non può essere che laico.*"[9] From this position the Church came to bless the lay State and the secularization of civil society. The Archbishop said: "This is what the Freemasons and likewise all the liberals have always wanted." "Doubtless they do not reject the idea of a society which favors Catholicism as long as the Catholics are in the majority. But the same goes for Islam where Muslims are in the majority. But favoring the Catholic religion because it is the only true religion: that is what they do not want!"

---

[5] *Principes et directives*, 6 pages typed, 1977.
[6] *Le coup de maître de Satan* (The Masterstroke of Satan), Oct. 13, 1974.
[7] *La messe de Luther*, Feb. 15, 1975.
[8] Lefebvre, *Ils L'ont découronné*, ch. 5.
[9] "The State can only be secular." Archbishop Lefebvre gave his reaction in a talk given at the home of Princess Palaviccini in Rome; the Cardinal replied in *Avvenire*, June 19, 1977.

The goal of the laicization of the State is also "the aim of the devil who is behind Freemasonry: [it aims for] the destruction of the Catholic Church by allowing freedom to all false religions and by forbidding the State to work for the Social Reign of our Lord Jesus Christ."[10] "How many Catholics are still able to accept that the work of our Lord's Redemption should also be brought about through civil societies?" That, however, is the truth because "everything has been created for our Lord Jesus Christ."[11]

RELIGIOUS LIBERTY: THE STENCH OF HELL

In implementing the Council, the Holy See had its Nuncios ask Catholic countries to give up on the principle of only recognizing the Catholic religion; in Colombia as in Spain, the constitution was changed in this way,[12] in spite of the heads of states publicly expressing their disgust at such a measure. In Valais, Bishop Adam wrote to the Catholics in his diocese asking them to approve the suppression of the article in the Valaisan Constitution recognizing the Catholic religion.[13]

Archbishop Lefebvre recalled:

I went off to see the Nuncio at Berne to ask him some questions: "Do you know what Bishop Adam is doing in Valais?"

"Yes," Archbishop Ambrogio Marchioni replied, "I asked him to do it."

"What? To say that our Lord Jesus Christ must no longer reign in Valais?"

"Ah, but now it is no longer possible."

"And what do you say about the encyclical *Quas Primas* of Pope Pius IX?"

"Well, the Pope would not write that these days."[14]

Thus in the name of the Council, the Holy See supported the death of Catholic States.

"This has led to Latin America being invaded by North American sects that have lots of money; until now the States forbade these sects in order to protect the Faith of their citizens. It is estimated that forty to sixty

---

10 Interview with the three cardinals, 1975.
11 *Spiritual Conferences at Ecône*, 46 B, Sept. 23, 1977.
12 Archbishop Lefebvre, talk in Barcelona, Dec. 29, 1975.
13 The vote on March 17, 1974, ratified the suppression of this article. *Spiritual Conferences at Ecône*, March 21, 1974.
14 Audience of March 31, 1976. Cf. *Spiritual Conferences at Ecône*, April 1, 1976; talk in Angers, Nov. 23, 1980; *Mes doutes sur la liberté religieuse* (My doubts concerning religious liberty; English version title: *Religious Liberty Questioned*), 185-186; talk in Sierre, Nov. 27, 1988.

million Catholics have apostatized."[15] "Our Lord asked His apostles to preach the Gospel to all nations," not to preach liberty!

Already in his "Message to Governments" at the end of the Council, Paul VI asked the question, "What does the Church ask of you?" and he replied: "She only asks you for liberty." It is frightening! I find this appalling because it smacks of hell; liberty exists to facilitate obedience to God: it depends on the truth, it depends on good, and it depends on God. But no, they want to make liberty into an absolute without reference to anything. And that is what religious liberty is. Bishop Pietro Rossano, quoting Bishop Pietro Pavin, has said it himself: "Yes, we have changed the criterion: it is no longer the truth, but the person."[16] This avowal is crucial, it contains the conciliar revolution.[17]

The Archbishop showed that this principle ruins all authority in families, the Church, and in religious organizations. "It is truly the interior revolution, *non serviam*! It is the cry of Satan: 'I will not serve!' I do not want to serve! Leave me alone, let me live! Freedom!"[18]

LIBERAL ECUMENISM

Ecumenism plans to bring the Churches together and unite them, a venture condemned by all Tradition and by Pius XI in *Mortalium Animos*, which taught that heretics should return to Catholic unity.[19] Archbishop Lefebvre, therefore, denounced ecumenism. He often spoke of "false ecumenism," but he knew of no true ecumenism other than the missionary agenda of converting dissidents as followed by Saints Fidelis of Sigmaringen and Francis de Sales. "Ecumenism is not the mission of the Church; the Church is not ecumenical, she is missionary. The missionary Church aims to convert. The ecumenical Church aims to find what is true in error and remain at that level. That is to deny the truth of the Church. Because of this ecumenism, there are no more enemies. Those who are in error are our brothers. So, there is no longer any need to fight. Let us cease hostilities!"[20]

This was why the Archbishop condemned the ecumenical acts of Paul VI, who had the Anglican primate Ramsay, "a layman, a Mason, and a

---

[15] Talk in Sierre.

[16] Congress held in Venice, May 1, 1988. *Il Regno-documenti* 9/88, 286-288: "going from the rights of truth to the rights of the person...essential differences, substantial developments." Cf. *Retreats at Ecône*, Sept. 9, 1988; *Fideliter*, no. 66: 29; *Spiritual Conferences at Ecône*, 133 A, March 3, 1989.

[17] Talk in Sierre, March 27, 1988.

[18] Interview with Fr. Marziac, 11.

[19] Jan. 6, 1928, *Enseignements pontificaux de Solesmes, The Church*, no. 872.

[20] *Spiritual Conferences at Ecône*, 58 A, April 14, 1978; cf. talk in Essen, April 9, 1978, in Ferdinand Steinhart, ed., *S. E. Erzbischof Marcel Lefebvre, Missionar und Zeuge in der nachkonziliaren Christenheit, 1974-1994* (Stuttgart: SSPX, 1994), 119.

heretic," bless the cardinals and bishops assembled at St. Paul Outside the Walls. The Archbishop rejected Paul VI's idea of "sister churches" which presupposed "a Church divided in herself."[21]

But soon, "liberal ecumenism" reached out to all religions. The Archbishop had to react; the Church traditionally recognizes baptism by desire which can lead souls to salvation and which consists in a supernatural disposition to follow the will of God. But it is wrong to think that Muslims or Buddhists are saved by their religion. "*In* their religion, perhaps, but not *by* their religion," because error is an obstacle to the Holy Ghost. If one can find salvation in any religion, why did our Lord say to the Apostles: 'Teach all nations?'"

"There is an implacable logic in believing in the divinity of our Lord Jesus Christ. For if one believes in His divinity, one must believe that He is our God incarnate. We are, therefore, obliged to believe that only His religion is true because He is God, and only His Church is the true religion. Consequently, [we believe] that the other religions are not true religions. They are false religions. They have been a means for the devil to lead millions of souls away from the true religion and to enslave them in error."[22]

ACCEPTING OR REJECTING THE COUNCIL?

The history of the Church had taught us to see ecumenical councils as infallible in authority. However, if Vatican II was a conduit for liberal and modernist error, this raises a theological problem: was it a true council? Was it not rather "a discussion group"? However, Pope Paul VI promulgated all its decrees with the support of the vast majority of the bishops.

This was true, as Archbishop Lefebvre conceded, but along with many observers he emphasized the atypical character of this ecumenical council that not only "avoided proclaiming dogmas bearing the note of infallibility," as Paul VI admitted, but had wanted to be more "pastoral" than doctrinal (even though doctrine was present throughout its documents). The Archbishop often referred to a memo issued to the Council on November 15, 1964, by the Secretary General: because of the Council's pastoral aims, it only defined doctrines of the Faith when it specifically said it was doing so [in fact never], and the authority of its documents would depend on the category into which each fell.

Archbishop Lefebvre commented: "Deliberately and by the grace of the Holy Ghost, the Council only wanted to be pastoral."[23] "The Council is a non-infallible act of the Magisterium and, therefore, it is open to being

---

[21] Cf. Open Letter to John Paul II, Nov. 21, 1983.
[22] Cf. Lefebvre, *Lettre ouverte aux catholiques perplexes*, 101-102; *Spiritual Conferences at Ecône*, 59 B, June 8, 1978.
[23] *Le coup de maître* (The Masterstroke of Satan); see our Chapter XII, 2.

influenced by a bad spirit." It was right, therefore, to exercise some discernment, and the Archbishop suggested using the criterion of Tradition; then, he said, it would be possible "to accept the Council in the light of Tradition," which meant "correcting the Council according to the eternal principles of Tradition."

"Besides, this is what Pope Paul started to do with the acts of the Council by putting the *Nota explicativa* in the document *Lumen Gentium*; we have to admit that such a thing is unheard of in a Council....Therefore, we need to apply the criterion of Tradition to the various Council documents in order to see what we can keep, what needs clarifying, and what should be rejected."[24]

However, some theologian friends such as Fr. Joseph de Sainte Marie[25] tried "to distinguish the Council from its wrongful interpretation." Following the canonist Don Composta, the Archbishop showed on the contrary that all the reforms—liturgy, sacraments, seminaries, religious congregations, *etc.*—had been carried out in the name of the Council and not in spite of it. "The same people wrote the acts of the Council and implemented them. They knew very well what they were doing. Consequently, these reforms are the authentic interpretation of the Council. And since these reforms have caused considerable turmoil in the Church, we can say that the origin of the destruction in the Church is to be found not only in the reforms but also in the Council."[26]

"This is why," concluded the Archbishop, "we reject the views of those who say to us: 'Such things are abuses, excesses, and misinterpretations of the Council. Help us to limit the damage and to rediscover and implement the "true" Council.' Insofar as it is opposed to Tradition, we reject the Council."[27]

Paul VI, a Liberal Pope

The same understanding applies to the Pope: "We applaud the Pope when he echoes Tradition and is true to his role of handing down the Faith, but we do not feel ourselves bound to conform to novelties that go against Tradition and threaten the Faith."[28]

But how is it possible for a Pope thus to favor novelty and disrupt the passing on of the deposit of the Faith? The Archbishop answered that it sufficed for Paul VI to be a child of his generation. Besides, this is what was predicted and planned for by Freemasonry a century before. The *Alta Ven-*

---

[24] *Principes et directives* (1977).
[25] *Le Courrier de Rome*, no. 188 (Jan. 1979).
[26] *Spiritual Conferences at Ecône*, 70 A, Feb. 22, 1979, 441-442.
[27] *Ibid.*, 38 B, Jan. 17, 1977, 195.
[28] Letter to Friends and Benefactors, no. 9, Sept. 3, 1975.

dita devised a plan that they called "the supreme attack." "That which we should seek and expect," wrote Volpe to Nubius, "is a Pope according to our wants"; and for that, "it is necessary to fashion for that Pope a generation worthy of the reign of which we dream." In a few years time it will be possible to elect as Pope a priest who is embued "in our doctrines." And their goal was "for the clergy to march under our banner in the belief always that they march under the banner of the Apostolic Keys....You will have fished up a revolution in Tiara and Cope, marching with Cross and banner." Thus we will bring about "the triumph of the revolution through a Pope."[29]

The Archbishop often quoted these texts in his talks and saw them realized in the person of Paul VI:

> I think that that is the truth as regards Pope Paul VI. His friend Cardinal Daniélou wrote as much in a posthumous book saying: "It is obvious that Paul VI is a liberal Pope." That is an historical truth: Paul is as it were the fruit of liberalism; he lived in liberalism, and his whole life was influenced by the liberals.[30] He did not hide it: at the Council, three of the four moderators he appointed were liberals. That showed where his sympathies lay. Louis Salleron has explained this well, describing Paul as being a "split personality": this is true in the psychological as well as the moral sense. Sometimes he spoke traditionally but then would do completely the opposite,[31] always lurching between contradictory positions and swinging regularly like a pendulum between Tradition and innovation.

"Such a Pope would provide the enemies of the Church with a great opportunity." This is why they encouraged him and supported him. On September 13, 1976, *Izvestia* denounced the suspended Archbishop as the bishop of fascists and of intolerance. "It's a little embarrassing to have friends like that."[32] In any case, for a Pope, "it suffices for him to be liberal to cause of all this chaos in the Church."[33]

A NEW MAGISTERIUM

Louis Salleron's article entitled "From the Ecône Affair to the Conciliar Church"[34] seemed "very important" to the Archbishop, who advised his seminarians to "read it attentively." What is the magisterium of this "Con-

[29] Permanent Instructions of the Alta Vendita, 1820 and 1824. Cf. Crétineau-Joly, *L'Eglise romaine et la révolution*, 2 vol. (1859; reprinted at Paris: Cercle de la Renaissance Française, 1976), 82-129. *Spiritual Conferences at Ecône*, 3 A, Dec. 20, 1973.

[30] Cf. Yves Chiron, *Paul VI, le pape écartelé*: Don Montini and the Fuci; Msgr. Montini and the Moral Rearmement; his secret relations with the Soviets, *etc.*

[31] Cf. "sacrifice" of Latin, Communion in the hand, *etc.*

[32] *Spiritual Conferences at Ecône*, 42 A, March 18, 1977, 229-230; Lefebvre, *Ils L'ont découronné*, 113.

[33] *Spiritual Conferences at Ecône*, 70 A, Feb. 22, 1979, 446.

[34] *Itinéraires*, no. 209 (Jan. 1977): 87.

ciliar Church" spoken of by Archbishop Benelli and referred to by Paul VI? The Archbishop explained:

> Since they cannot base themselves on Tradition—for what they ask of us is not in line with Tradition—they set up a new Magisterium, a modernist concept of the Magisterium, according to ideas condemned by St. Pius X in *Pascendi*. It is a living Church, *i.e.*, one that evolves and changes so that its religious statements remain adapted to the believer and his faith. Unquestionably, the Church is living, but nevertheless, the Magisterium cannot contradict what has been said previously. It must explain things and not change them. Now, this is what we have in the Church when Archbishop Benelli asks us to be faithful to the "Conciliar Church." "What does this fidelity consist of?" Salleron asks. "What is the meaning of this total innovation of a 'Conciliar Church' distinct from the 'Catholic Church'?...We see that an increasingly ill-defined Magisterium is making its own will the supreme rule of religious life."
>
> This is crucial. This sentence is of fundamental importance. This is what we are coming up against. "Obey, obey," they tell us, "if you are not obedient to the Pope, you do not have the true Faith!" But the Pope is the servant of the Faith. The Faith is not his servant. He cannot dictate to the Faith. He can define what is already in Tradition and make it explicit but he cannot dispose of it as he wishes. Otherwise he is "making his own will into the supreme rule of the religious life." That sums up the whole problem.[35]

Archbishop Lefebvre quoted Pius IX's insistence[36] on the doctrinal continuity that belongs to the true Magisterium. Then, following Salleron, he quoted former conciliar experts who recognize "with dubious innocence" the break between the Council and the previous Magisterium, justifying it in the name of the "historical conscience,"[37] or from the fact that "one cannot remain fixed at a moment in history."[38] The Archbishop concluded: "With such ideas there is no longer any truth possible. One could always say tomorrow that what one has said today no longer applies, since tomorrow we will be in a different social context. There is no longer any Faith possible, and no immutable deposit of revelation. There is nothing left."[39]

OSTPOLITIK AND THE REIGN OF CHRIST

The Council initiated the *Ostpolitik* of the Holy See: "The refusal of this pastoral Council to condemn Communism officially is alone suffi-

---

35 *Spiritual Conferences at Ecône* 37 B, Jan. 13, 1977.

36 Allocution of May 16, 1870, *Enseignements pontificaux de Solesmes, The Church*, no. 353.

37 John Courtney Murray; *Le Courrier de Rome*, no. 162: 14.

38 Yves Congar, *La crise de l'Eglise et Mgr. Lefebvre* (Cerf, 1977), 51-52.

39 *Spiritual Conferences at Ecône*, 38 A, Jan. 14, 1977, 188.

cient reason to make it ashamed before all of history, when one thinks of the millions of martyrs, the people scientifically depersonalized in psychiatric hospitals and used as guinea pigs for experiments."[40]

So, the Archbishop denounced the Vatican's philo-communist policy under John XXIII and Paul VI. Firstly, in Latin countries that were fighting Communism, they appointed Cardinal Archbishops such as Vincente Enrique y Trancón (Spain), Antonio Robeiro (Portugal), Juan Carlos Aramburu (Argentina), and Raúl Silva Henriquez (Chile) to implement this policy in opposition to the governments.[41] In Italy the reddest bishop, Bishop Luigi of the diocese of Ivrea, who was known to correspond with Enrico Berlinguer, head of the Italian Communist Party, was elected international president of Pax Christi.[42]

On the other hand, in Communist countries "bishops who in the past died in Soviet jails have been replaced by bishops who work with the Communists, persecuting faithful priests."[43] It was a betrayal: "They are removing from the Church her crown of martyrs."[44] They wanted to ignore clandestine bishops, and the activities of the underground Church; "Things must be regularized," and bishops named to vacant sees; but on what conditions? Archbishop Lefebvre quoted Fr. Floridi:

> It is known that the Czechoslovakian bishops whom Archbishop Casaroli consecrated work with the regime. Paul VI was happy at having been able to give a bishop to each Hungarian diocese, and paid tribute to János Kádar,[45]...but he did not say how high a price this "regularization" had cost: the appointment of "priests of peace" to important posts in the Church....In fact, Catholics were greatly surprised when they heard the successor of Cardinal Mindszenty, Cardinal Laszlo Lékai, promise "to further the dialogue between Catholics and Marxists."[46]

Archbishop Lefebvre remarked: "The Helsinki Accords were backed by the Church from start to finish;[47] the first address was given by Agostino Casaroli, consecrated Archbishop for the occasion."[48]

---

[40] Letter to Friends and Benefactors, no. 9, Sept. 3, 1975.
[41] *Spiritual Conferences at Ecône* 47 A, Oct. 10, 1977.
[42] *Ibid.*, 59 B, June 8, 1978.
[43] Preface of Fr. Marchal's book, Nov. 13, 1986.
[44] *Spiritual Conferences at Ecône* 102 B, Oct. 28, 1983.
[45] Involved in putting down the Hungarian uprising in 1956; he had himself struck Cardinal Mindszenty.
[46] Ulisse Floridi, *Moscou et le Vatican* (France-Empire, 1979), 368-369; A. Casaroli, *Il martirio della pazienza* (Turin: Einaudi, 2000), 158.
[47] Principle VII of final agreement, dated Aug. 1, 1975, proclaims "the individual's liberty to profess and practice alone or with others a religion or creed according to the dictates of his own conscience." This is *Dignitatis Humanæ*! "This principle has been very useful in our discussions with the Soviets," as John Paul II said to Archbishop Lefebvre, whose unheard reply was: only as an argument *ad hominem* and nothing more!

In 1988, John Paul II would send a message to the states that had signed up to the agreement: "Liberty of conscience and religion."[49] One year later, the Archbishop saw the pursuit and arrest of the leaders of Solidarity as ordered by the Polish government as the Soviet response to the papal demands for the rights of man in Communist states (December 13, 1981): "Would Moscow's slap in the face for the Vatican be enough to ruin this odious *Ostpolitik* and bring back the only attitude worthy of the Catholic Church, that of Popes Pius XI and XII?...You cannot talk with the devil, be he a Communist or a Mason. You exorcise him....The devil has no use for the rights of man, which he invented to put an end to the rights of our Lord Jesus Christ."[50]

Like his friend Dom Putti, the Archbishop thought: "One no longer feels a spirit of faith in what they say and do in Rome. It seems like a human government which acts and reacts in a purely human way" just like the world. [It is] inspired "by a system of thought, doctrine, and international organization, the UN, which is not yet a world government but which is getting there. All this is radically contrary to the reign of our Lord Jesus Christ."[51]

THE ERROR OF SEDEVACANTISM

"How could a successor of Peter have caused in so short a time more damage to the Church than the Revolution of 1789?...Do we really have a Pope or an intruder sitting on the chair of Peter? Happy are those who lived and died without having to ask themselves such questions!"

This was what Archbishop Lefebvre mused upon in *Cor Unum*, the Society's internal newsletter, on November 8, 1979. He was commenting on the late Pope Paul VI —as he had already done during the "hot summer" of 1976—but the same thing would soon apply to John Paul II. "Given the promises of help that our Lord Jesus Christ made to his Vicar, how can it be that this Vicar corrupts the faith of the faithful, either through his own actions or through others?"

Some people said: he speaks heresy, he promulgated religious liberty, and he signed Article 7 of the *NOM*; now, a heretic cannot be Pope, therefore, he is not Pope, and therefore, obedience is not owed to him. It was simple and comfortable logic based on a theological opinion that serious writers have upheld in the abstract. But in reality, can one hold that the Pope is in formal heresy? Who would have the authority to declare it? Who would give him the necessary warnings to make him aware of his situation?

---

[48] *Spiritual Conferences at Ecône*, Oct. 10, 1977.
[49] *Documentation Catholique*, 1798 (Dec. 1980): 1172-1175.
[50] "D'Helsinki à Varsovie," *Fideliter*, no. 25 (Jan. 1982).
[51] *Spiritual Conferences at Ecône*, 71 A May 1979.

Moreover, in the practical sphere, this reasoning "puts the Church into an inextricable situation. Who can say where the next Pope is going to come from? How can he be chosen since there are no more cardinals" (because the Pope is no longer Pope)? "This spirit is schismatic." Moreover, "the Church's visibility is too essential to its existence for God to let it be obscured for decades."

Rather than the "logical theories" of Fr. Guérard des Lauriers,[52] Archbishop Lefebvre preferred "a higher wisdom: the logic of charity and prudence."

> Perhaps one day, in thirty or forty years, a meeting of cardinals gathered together by a future Pope will study and judge the reign of Paul VI;[53] perhaps they will say that there were things that ought to have been clearly obvious to people at the time, statements of the Pope that were totally against Tradition.

> At the moment, I prefer to consider the man on the chair of Peter as the Pope; and if one day we discover for certain that the Pope was not the Pope, at least I will have done my duty.

> When he is not using his charism of infallibility, the Pope can err. So, why should we be scandalized and say, "So there is no Pope," like Arius, who was scandalized by our Lord being humiliated and saying in His passion, "My God, why have you abandoned me?" Arius reasoned, "Therefore he is not God!"

We do not know how far a Pope can lead the Church in losing the Faith when he is "influenced by who knows what spirit or training, under pressure, or acting negligently"; but "we can see the facts. I prefer to start from this principle: we have to defend our Faith; in that, there is no shadow of doubt concerning our duty."[54]

II. ENDLESS DIALOGUE

WHY I CARRY ON GOING TO ROME

Fr. de Nantes claimed: "A bishop, …a colleague of the bishop of Rome, …must break communion with him for as long as he gives no indication of faithfully carrying out the responsibilities of his supreme pontificate." Archbishop Lefebvre replied: "Let us be clear that if a bishop breaks with Rome, it will not be me!" Is breaking with the Pope not breaking with Rome? But Georges de Nantes continued his attacks in which he blamed

---

52   He held that Paul VI is the pope "materially but not formally."
53   The Third Council of Constantinople anathematized Honorius *post mortem* but did not declare that he had not been Pope.
54   *Ibid.*, 36 B, Dec. 2, 1976; 42 A, March 18, 1977; 60 B, Oct. 5, 1978; *Cor Unum*, no. 4 (Nov. 1979); *Spiritual Conferences at Ecône*, 74 A, Dec. 11, 1979; *Monde et Vie*, no. 324 (Feb. 1980); *Sermons at Ecône*, 25 B1, June 29, 1982.

Archbishop Lefebvre for trying to save the Church by founding a parallel Church, a "stand-in[55] Church.[56] Not so, explained Archbishop Lefebvre, rather, these were supplemental institutions "and I hope that one day all our seminarians can be placed back in the hands of the Holy Father. It is our deepest wish to enter into perfect communion with him, but in the unity of the Catholic Faith and not in a liberal ecumenism."

In the meanwhile, said the Archbishop, "I want to preserve an atmosphere that will make relations easy; I can never be accused of having been insolent towards the Holy Father.[57] How must we act with regard to the people in those positions? Should we carry on our resistance by locking ourselves away in an ivory tower? Or should we try to win over the Roman authorities? I have decided not to break off dialogue with Rome."

As in his Letter to Friends and Benefactors No. 16, the Archbishop observed: "Some pamphlets written against me are doing the rounds. I am a traitor and a Pilate because I discuss with Rome and say to the Pope: 'Let us follow Tradition.'" And to his seminarians, he retorted: "I do not think I have yet delivered you up; the only aim of my approaches to Rome is to attempt to break down this iron curtain which hems us in and to ensure that thousands of souls are saved through having the grace of the true Mass, the true sacraments, the true catechism, and the true Bible. That is why I go to Rome and why I do not hesitate to go every time they ask me." "If possible we must try to convert" the liberals. "If only we were tolerated, that would be progress; lots of priests would come back to the Mass, and lots of faithful would rejoin Tradition....This is why I cannot allow individuals in the Society to refuse to pray for the Holy Father or to refuse to recognize that there is a Pope: taking that road would lead to an impasse. I don't want to lead you into an impasse or put you in an impossible situation."[58]

FROM THE SUSPENSION TO THE INDULT

Paul VI launched an initiative of theological dialogue with Archbishop Lefebvre: on May 10 and 11, 1977, the Archbishop had doctrinal discussions with Frs. Edouard Dhanis, S.J., and Benedict Duroux, O.P., but without any outcome. Then, in June, a practical attempt at mediation by

---

55 [Fr. de Nantes's expression was "*Eglise de suppléance*," which seems to allude to the generalization of supplied jurisdiction granted in certain cases to ministers without faculties. Trans.]

56 *Contre-Réforme Catholique*, 89 (Feb. 1975); *Itinéraires*, 206 (Oct. 1976); Lefebvre, *Un évêque parle* (1976), 273. On April 10, 1973, Georges de Nantes handed in to the Holy See a *Libellum accusationis*: "To Paul VI, sovereign judge, case for heresy, schism, and scandal against Paul VI...." Archbishop Lefebvre was more realistic.

57 *Spiritual Conferences at Ecône*, 58 A, April 14, 1978; 43 A, March 27, 1977.

58 *Ibid.*, 76 B, May 3; 71 B, June 7; 74 A, Dec. 11, 1979.

Bishop Joseph Stimpfle of Augsburg, supported by Dr. Eric de Saventhem, failed. However, it brought about some conciliatory gestures: Archbishop Lefebvre postponed the ordinations and agreed to an interpretative commission's studying the obvious meaning of the Council. Rome also canceled the condemnation issued on June 14, 1977. It was suggested that every priest celebrating Mass in Latin could use the old Missal and that churches could be made available for this.[59] Paul VI refused.

The following year, Archbishop Lefebvre was brought before the Holy Office (CDF) and given a questionnaire on the Council, the New Mass, and the new rite of sacraments. He replied with twenty-four pages of doctrine based on the constant Magisterium.[60]

In June Cardinal Seper envisaged new "discussions" with the Archbishop, who ignored a renewed warning and ordained eighteen priests on June 29, 1978. In July the Pope told Bishop Mamie that he was "resolved to intervene more rigorously,"[61] without doubt by a threat of excommunication. However, on August 6, 1978, Paul died after having eliminated from the conclave all cardinals who were over the age of eighty—a policy against which Archbishop Lefebvre protested by questioning the validity of the following elections. After the brief reign of John Paul I, John Paul II was elected on October 16.

On November 18, through an initiative of Cardinal Siri,[62] the new Pope received the Archbishop, who said he was ready "to accept the Council in the light of Tradition," an expression used by Pope John Paul himself on November 6: "The Council must be understood in the light of all holy Tradition and on the basis of the constant Magisterium of the holy Church." The Pope said he was happy and saw the problem of celebrating the old Mass only as a disciplinary question. Then Cardinal Franjo Seper, whom the Pope had summoned, exclaimed: "Be careful, Holy Father, they make a banner out of this Mass!"

The Pope seemed disturbed; with other matters to attend to, he left it to the Cardinal "to arrange things which Archbishop Lefebvre" and said to

[59] Telex of June 16, 1977; Denis Marchal, *Monseigneur Lefebvre, vingt ans de combat pour le sacerdoce et la foi, 1967-1987* (NEL, 1988), 33; *Fideliter*, no. 141: 1.
[60] "Mgr. Lefebvre et le S.-Office" (Archbishop Lefebvre and the Holy Office), *Itinéraires*, no. 223 (May 1979): 27-109; Marchal, *Monseigneur Lefebvre, vingt ans de combat*, 35-37.
[61] Bishop Pierre Mamie, Interview with Fr. Savioz, March 16, 1994, Savioz, *La fondation de la Fraternité St. Pie X*, ann. 27, 3.
[62] Cf. Benny Lai, *Il Papa non eletto, Giuseppe Siri, cardinale di Santa Romana Chiesa* (Rome: Ed. Laterza, 1993), 283-285; Cavaterra, *Il prefetto del Sant'Offizio, Le opere ed i giorni del cardinale Ottaviani*, 166-167. The cardinal flattered himself with having brought Archbishop Lefebvre to "accept the whole Council," but the reservation expressed by the Archbishop was of capital importance.

the Archbishop as he left the room: "Stop, Excellency, stop!"[63] It was a surprising volte-face.

On January 11 and 12, 1979, instead of being heard personally by Seper, whom the Pope had made responsible for dealing with the Lefebvre affair, the Archbishop was again questioned at the Holy Office. At the meeting were Cardinal Seper, Bishop Mamie, Fr. Duroux, and two other experts. They accused the Archbishop of dividing the Church, and he replied: "We know from history that there has been a division in the Church between the Catholics and liberals for at least two centuries." The liberals were condemned by the Popes until Vatican II when "by an unfathomable mystery of Providence" they triumphed at the Council: "When I think that we are in the building of the Holy Office, the outstanding witness of Tradition and defender of the Catholic Faith, I cannot help thinking that I am on my own territory and that it is I whom you call 'the traditionalist' who should be judging you."[64]

Later Archbishop Lefebvre was concerned to see that, against the wishes of John Paul, he would be subject to the ordinary procedure of the Holy Office and consequently judged by a court composed of eleven cardinals, three of whom (Villot, Garrone, and Wright), in his opinion, had already condemned him. Consequently, he followed Don Putti's advice and broke off the process, sending the Pope a record of the discussions with two requests: to establish the Society as a prelature *nullius* with a bishop in charge, and to send a cardinal visitor.

At the end of 1980, a year before the death of Cardinal Seper and the arrival of his replacement at the CDF, Joseph Ratzinger, several cardinals offered help: Palazzini, Baum (Seminaries), Oddi (Clergy), Gonzalez-Martinez, Ratzinger, and Thiandoum. Archbishop Lefebvre would make a declaration about the Council, the Pope, and the new rites, and in return the Holy See would give every priest freedom to use the old Missal on one condition: that Society priests would undertake to celebrate the *Novus Ordo* when pastoral reasons made it necessary.[65] But the Archbishop had already replied to such a request during his jubilee: "How can they expect me to pronounce over my ordination chalice words other than those I pronounced fifty years ago over this same chalice?"

From then on, negotiations stagnated, and as is well known, an indult was granted on October 3, 1984, following Cardinal Knox's consultation of all the world's bishops: the bishops would grant permission for the old Missal to be used as long as the priests and faithful who asked for it public-

---

[63] Interview with André Cagnon.
[64] Marchal, *Monseigneur Lefebvre, vingt ans de combat*, 37.
[65] Conference for the Society, Sept. 8, 1980; *Spiritual Conferences at Ecône*, Dec. 15, 1980.

ly declared that "they had nothing to do—*nullam partem*—with those who question the legitimacy and doctrinal rectitude" of the New Missal.

"*Nullam partem*": this exclusion was made with respect to priests who were faithful to the traditional Mass for reasons of faith. Nevertheless, Archbishop Lefebvre considered that this indult "will perhaps change the climate of persecution completely."[66] Or even... The Society organized a petition to "free" the Mass of all time, collecting 129, 849 signatures, but to no avail; it had no visible effect.

III. MISSIONARY FORTRESSES

Fortunately, Archbishop Lefebvre had prepared himself for a long campaign. When Cardinal Ratzinger wrote to him using the expression of Urs von Balthasar that "razing the bastions is a pressing duty,"[67] the Archbishop replied in action: to keep the Faith and to propagate it, one must build strongholds of Christianity from which to launch one's attacks.

THE PRIORIES

"Priories are both strongholds of faith and beacons of Christianity from where spiritual sustenance is distributed to outlying posts."[68] In the priories, a group of priests together with a few brothers lead the common life according to the statutes. The Archbishop considered that this common life was most suited to such a scattered apostolate, and needed by the priests to preserve their priesthood. Sometimes priests would be sent to work on their own but only in emergency situations. The Archbishop often recalled the usefulness of the common life, which ensured that the priests led an orderly life and maintained their life of prayer.

However, the life of the community is not a cloistered life; the Society "is essentially apostolic because the Sacrifice of the Mass is apostolic" (Statutes, I, 2). Thus, the priests had to go out in all directions, providing Mass and catechism in nearby chapels or in distant "missions" visited weekly, monthly, or every two or three months ("like in the bush," said the Archbishop). In the latter case, the priests stayed for several days after which they returned to base to keep up their spiritual strength and prepare sermons, catechism lessons, and talks.

The "ideal priory"[69] in the Archbishop's opinion would not be downtown but rather on the outskirts near the countryside, to provide the priests with necessary peace and recollection, and protect them against

---

[66] Interview with the newspaper *Présent*, Oct. 17, 1984.
[67] *Les principes de la théol. cath.* (Téqui, 1985), 437.
[68] Framework for a talk at St. Nicolas du Chardonnet in Paris initially planned for May 5, 1988, but postponed until May 10.
[69] Talk at St. Nicolas du Chardonnet, May 10, 1988; *Cor Unum* June 30, 1988.

endless visits from the faithful. The chapels in towns, on the contrary, should be the epicenters of the apostolate. Priories could welcome children for days of recollection or accommodate adults for retreats. However, spiritual exercises were generally to be preached in special retreat centers where every year hundreds of retreatants could come and be encouraged to be "retreat apostles" operating through "former retreatants" associations. A small parish primary school might normally be situated near the priory but not at the priory itself. The prior would be in charge but classes could be given by sisters, oblates, or primary school teachers. Thus the "trinity" of priory, primary school, and downtown chapel was the model for a systematic apostolate suited to all needs.

SECONDARY SCHOOLS

By force of circumstances, the Society priests would take charge of boys' secondary schools and found new ones. When it was difficult to get things going, Archbishop Lefebvre would characteristically encourage his sons, saying: "You don't have the right to fail!"

Junior high schools such as those run for girls by the teaching Dominicans of Brignoles and Fanjeaux attracted families to move nearby; however, distances meant that boarding would be very common. Archbishop Lefebvre would have liked to see one large high school per district or country. However, it was preferable to set up many small high schools, the exception being St. Mary's, Kansas, with its hundreds of students and constantly growing parish.

Boarding required families to make considerable emotional and financial sacrifices, but as the Archbishop was wont to say, preserving the faith and morals of the children and giving them an entirely Catholic education across the school curriculum is more important than ease or well-being.

Archbishop Lefebvre approved the initiative of some university teachers to found the University Institute of St. Pius X in Paris in 1980. From a basis of Christian philosophy, it provided courses leading to the *Licence ès lettres*[70] in history or philosophy. St. Mary's would follow in its footsteps.

Today the schools of the Society succeed in educating Catholic characters, leaders of Christian families, and mothers who will raise many children. And they offer to God the raw material for solid religious and priestly vocations.

"YOUR CHURCHES ARE YOUR PARISHES"

The temporary Mass centers organized by laypeople and then taken over and firmly established by the Society were not, in spite of appearanc-

---

[70] [The French degree normally taken after three years of undergraduate studies. Trans.]

es, "parallel parishes": the priest responsible for souls did not have the jurisdiction of a parish priest. These foundations acted only in a substitute capacity. Nevertheless, Archbishop Lefebvre stated to the faithful: "Your chapels are your parishes,"[71] *i.e.,* do not go to your diocesan parishes but look to your priests and the places where you worship to find Holy Mass and the sacraments, as well as all desirable parish activities.

Some districts of the Society were able to buy existing churches or even construct new ones. In France, they would be seized out of necessity...On February 27, 1977, a crowd of Catholics summoned to the Maubert Mutualité Lecture Hall by Fr. Coache and Msgr. Ducaud-Bourget, processed into the nearby church of St. Nicolas du Chardonnet, sang a traditional Solemn High Mass...and stayed there. The same evening on *Antenne 2*, a priest in lay clothing questioned Fr. Coache: "Are you aware that Archbishop Lefebvre has disowned you?"

"I wouldn't know about that," the priest replied firmly.

He was right: the "disownment" only came from the rector of Ecône, the Swiss Canon René Berthod, who questioned the prudence of the combative priest's strong-arm tactics. Traveling in Germany, Archbishop Lefebvre refrained from disowning Fr. Coache, but he feared that the occupiers would be thrown out of the church. Returning to Ecône on March 3, he wrote to Msgr. Ducaud-Bourget expressing his support: "We are with you all the way. You have done everything to find a fair solution to an intolerable situation in which the most loyal Catholics are prevented from praying in churches. It is about time our Catholic 'assembly halls' became Catholic churches once more: that is justice. At last, in a Paris church, our Lord Jesus Christ will be honored as He deserves to be honored....May this courageous example encourage those in positions of responsibility to provide churches for the true faithful and true priests."[72]

And to his friend Renato Varani, the Archbishop confided: "We should seize a church in every diocese!"[73]

THE WORKS OF THE APOSTOLATE

In each district and across the whole Society, various projects were developed: the children's Eucharistic Crusade was reborn, archconfraternities for altar servers and prayer apostolate were resurrected, and the Catholic Scout movement continued. From 1976 onwards, the priests of the Society became the chaplains to the *Mouvement de la Jeunesse catholique de France* (MJCF—Movement of the Catholic Youth of France). Founded by some young people in 1970, the MJCF organized activity holidays aimed

---

[71] Sermon for tenth anniversary at Geneva, Oct. 27, 1985.
[72] In *Minute* of March 9-15, 1977.
[73] Ms. I, 31, 33.

1964: With Cardinal Michael Browne, sharing strategy during the dramatic Second Vatican Council.

In the Council aula.
The *Coetus* forged front-line friendships.

The "hard core" of the *Coetus*: Fr. Dulac, Msgr. Cabana, Msgr. Carreras, Fr. Marcos Frota, Msgr. Chaves, Fr. Pozo, Archbishops Griffin, Rocha, Morcillo, Tagle, del Campo, Gastón Lascano, Dom Proença Archirial,

1964: With the Irish president, Eamon de Valera.
"Do you really want to serve my Mass tomorrow?"

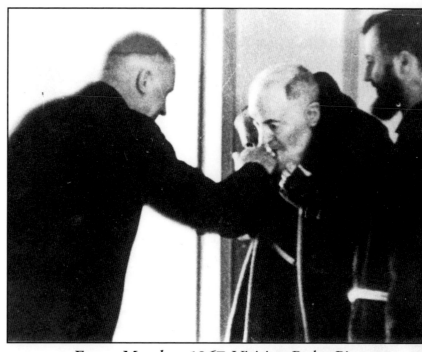

Easter Monday, 1967: Visiting Padre Pio,
the priest with the stigmata.

1971: Laying the first stone at Ecône.
Rebuilding at the age of 60, starting with nothing.

Bishop Adam of Sion visiting Ecône. He gave an ambiguous yes to the building of the seminary.

1975: After the Society's "suppression," the pilgrimage to Rome with Michel de Saint Pierre.

1976: The Mass at Lille, a "challenge" to Pope Paul VI.

1978: Support for Msgr. Ducaud-Bourget and the Catholic "occupiers" of St. Nicolas du Chardonnet.

The gentle, "pigheaded" bishop:
"I have two thousand years of Tradition with me."

On the Isle of Yeu, at Marshal Pétain's grave.

The tonsure: "Lord, you are
the portion of my inheritance."

The Sisters of the Society: handmaidens of the priesthood.

1983: With Bishop Antonio de Castro Mayer,
signing the open letter to Pope John Paul II.

May 5, 1988: Signing the "Protocol." Frs. Laroche and
Tissier de Mallerais (standing) were the Society's negotiators.

June 1988: Journalists record the announcement of "Operation Survival."

June 30, 1988: The Episcopal Consecrations. Assuring the continuation of the priesthood.

June 30, 1988: The bishops shake neo-modernist Rome.
At Archbishop Lefebvre's right, Bishop de Castro Mayer and Fr. Rifan.

Pontifical Mass at St. Nicolas du Chardonnet:
all the magnificence of Catholic liturgy.

The "Mystery of Faith":
The Precious Blood shed for our Redemption.

Preaching the Faith: when the Holy
Ghost took hold of him.

A sharp eye on the future of the priesthood.

April 2, 1991: The burial at Ecône. Mission accomplished: "I have handed on what I received."

at converting the young through the young and had as its base the doctrinal and apostolic training of the *"animateurs"* (group activity leaders); many baptisms and vocations were brought about through this work.

From the outset, Archbishop Lefebvre warned his priests about the mixing of the sexes in this movement; however, while he would not allow mixed secondary schools, he tolerated mixing in the MJCF because of circumstances and also because of their missionary objectives. He hoped that the priests would succeed in reducing the association of the sexes and asked that precautions be taken concerning the participation of priests in mixed camps.[74] In German-speaking countries, the *Katholische Jugendbewegung* (KJB) was founded by Fr. Schmidberger on the model of the MJCF, and similar youth movements were founded in many countries.

The apostolate of the press was encouraged by Archbishop Lefebvre. In 1973, he called for "the publication of a little review to refute error and give true doctrine."[75] In January 1978, when Fr. Aulagnier presented him with the first edition of the magazine *Fideliter* for the French district, the Archbishop, speaking to no one in particular in his lively, teasing way, said: "It's a bit of a 'pot-pourri,' your thing....Still, as long as it doesn't die the death!"

But it would last, as would *The Angelus* in the United States, *Mitteilungsblatt* in Germany, and many others, alongside publishing houses printing all sorts of books and leaflets: adventure stories, biographies, books on doctrine or the traditionalist movement, *etc.*

A CRUSADE TO REBUILD CHRISTIANITY

In the sermon for his priestly jubilee on September 3, 1979, before ten thousand faithful at the Porte de Versailles in Paris, Archbishop Lefebvre first gave an account of what one can call the "romance of the priesthood and the Mass," and then called upon the faithful to launch a "crusade based on the Mass," in order "to rebuild Christianity." It was to be a crusade for young people who would look for a true ideal, and choose a state in life or a spouse "by chastity, prayer, and reflection, not letting themselves be led away by their passions." It would also be a crusade for Christian families: homes consecrated to the Sacred Heart of Jesus, praying as a family, wishing to receive "the most beautiful gift of God: many children," and rejecting the "hateful slogans which destroy the family"; they should home school if possible, and go back to the land, "which is healthy, brings one closer to God, evens out temperaments, and encourages one to work."

There should also be a crusade for heads of families: "You have no right to let your country be invaded by socialism and Communism; you

---

[74] *Spiritual Conferences at Ecône*, 41 A, March 17, 1977.
[75] *Spiritual Conferences at Ecône*, Jan. 10, 1973.

must fight during elections to have Catholic mayors," according to the authentic politics of Christ the King which aim at converting heads of state by the grace of Holy Mass. The Archbishop said: "I saw that grace at work in Africa, and there is no reason why it should not be effective here." Finally there must be a crusade of priests to lead the other crusades: therefore there must be holy priests.

To all those present, priests and faithful, Archbishop Lefebvre made a solemn plea: "For the glory of the most Blessed Trinity, for the love of our Lord Jesus Christ, for devotion to the Most Blessed Virgin Mary, for the love of the Church, for the love of the Pope, for the love of the bishops, priests, and all the faithful, for the salvation of the world and for the salvation of souls: keep this testament of our Lord Jesus Christ! Keep the Sacrifice of our Lord Jesus Christ! Keep the Mass of all time!"[76]

Ten years later when he celebrated the twentieth anniversary of the Society at Friedrichshafen, the Archbishop would admire how young the congregation now appeared thirteen years after the Mass that he had celebrated at the end of the "hot summer," on October 24, 1976. His appeal for a crusade of large families had been widely answered.

At the end of the 1970's, there developed in France the "Henri and André Charlier Center" and the "Chrétienté Solidarité" group founded by Bernard Anthony (known as "Romain Marie"), from which originated Jean Madiran's review *Présent*. They enthusiastically supported the fight in Lebanon and Poland against the enemies of Christianity, but their hazy doctrine and the participation of these Catholic troops in the Chartres pilgrimage began to worry Archbishop Lefebvre. He was also unhappy about *Présent*'s over-dependence on Jean Marie Le Pen's National Front movement; he admired Le Pen's courage as a politician and recognized that his political efforts could be supported, but he saw his disregard for the social reign of Christ.[77]

Not long before his death, the Archbishop warned Fr. Aulagnier about the ambiguities of certain elements of Catholic Action in the ranks of Tradition.[78] As he recalled, we should distinguish on the one hand between "doctrinal teachings so important nowadays, and training in Christian virtues[79]—areas in which lay people are but helpers in the priests' apostolate"—and on the other hand the role of laypeople in families, professions, and civil society which is their specific apostolate and in which the clergy can only help them. Let us keep the distinctions so as to collaborate with-

---

[76] *Fideliter*, no. 12 (Nov. 1979): 13.
[77] Spiritual Conference at Flavigny, June 11, 1988.
[78] Letters of June 20, 21, and 23, 1990, to Fr. Aulagnier; Letter for the 20th anniversary of the MJCF, *Fideliter*, no. 79: 28-29.
[79] Quite a vague expression indicating some imprecise thinking. The Archbishop had been considerably clearer on this subject at the Council. Cf. Chapter XII, n. 1.

out getting things in a muddle! The Archbishop deplored Jean Ousset's own scuttling of his Cité Catholique.[80] Who would take up this torch but base his initiatives on a sounder footing? Moreover, the attempts of re-emerging Gnosticism[81] to infiltrate Traditionalist milieus, such as the neo-paganism of the "New Right,"[82] required vigilance: let us try, he warned, "to keep a watchful eye on these activities that are very dangerous for the battle we are waging."[83]

IV. THE ARCHBISHOP AND HIS TROOPS

FAITHFUL TROOPS AND INTERNAL CRISES

The faithfulness of most of his priests to his doctrinal line—"Neither heretics nor schismatics," neither liberals nor dogmatic pedants—delighted Archbishop Lefebvre. Unfortunately, the devil was working to sow cockle amongst his troops whom he sometimes exhorted in the most surprising ways: "If I am wrong, leave me! You can check. You have Tradition in your library, you can see for yourself."

Periodically the Society was shaken by the "fevers" of bitter zeal or infected with liberal "mange." Some seminarians aggressively labeled themselves "anti-liberals" and looked upon others as liberals, but the Archbishop reminded them: "Certainly, you must be informed about modern errors because preaching the truth involves preaching about distancing oneself from error; but do not make the negative, secondary aspect into the most important! Your first aim is not to fight against error but to know the truth. Your central concern should be study, your sanctification, silence, meditation, and the exercise of charity."

The Archbishop had to pick out some troublemakers who caused disputes at Ecône. Moreover, if he insisted on the need to fight errors and liberalism, he also recalled the true nature of this fight: "Ours is a supernatural fight against the spiritual powers of the devil and the fallen angels. It is a battle of giants, and not just a matter of discussions and intellectual jousts. By entering seminary, you enter the history of the Church and wage a battle that is not on the natural plain; otherwise you are way off the mark. Our battle is on the plain of divine grace. Be ready to argue with

---

[80] *Spiritual Conferences at Ecône*, 26 B and 27 A, Feb. 10 and 12, 1976.

[81] A theory that attributes salvation to the acquisition of knowledge rather than moral conversion. This doctrinal knowledge is more elevated than vulgar Christianity that it claims to contain within itself.

[82] [The Nouvelle Droite represented a tendency of the French Right inspired by the work of GRECE (Study and Research Group for European Civilization). It emphasized European identity and promoted Indo-European paganism at the expense of monotheism. It was strongly anti-communist but anti-capitalist and eugenicist in inclination. Its lead exponent was Alain de Benoist. Trans.]

[83] Letter of 1987, in *Lecture et Tradition*, no. 290 (April 2001).

people, but you will obtain the grace to conquer souls by prayer, sacrifice, mortification, and leading a holy life."[84]

Such was the anti-liberalism of Archbishop Lefebvre. Unfortunately, his words were not always listened to, and shoots that were once full of promise detached themselves from the tree and rejoined the Conciliar Church or sadly fell away. On the one hand, some seminarians who were frightened by the prospect of an imaginary schism into which they felt the Archbishop was leading them sought refuge in semi-clandestinity (1977), conciliar legality (1974, 1976, 1981, 1986), and ended up being duly "re-educated."[85] On the other hand, some priests and seminarians were attracted by sedevacantist theories that gave them reassurance in their extravagant or activist zeal, and broke away (1983, 1985, 1989), ending up sometimes as deluded "independent priests" divided among themselves. They were often driven by their own logic to receive orders, or even the episcopacy, at the hands of misguided or illegitimate bishops such as those consecrated by the former Archbishop of Hué, Archbishop Pierre Martin Ngô Dinh Thuc.

The most serious crises would affect first Ecône in 1977[86] when the rector and three professors left with a group of seminarians and tried to make a foundation in Brittany. Then it was the turn of the United States in spring 1983 when Archbishop Lefebvre had to go and see for himself the revolt of nine of his priests: "We can no longer work together," they told him before the definitive separation. The following year three young American priests would leave the Society on the day after their ordination entirely disregarding their sacred promises of loyalty to the Society and obedience to their bishop. Finally, in 1989 the seminary in Argentina would lose half of its students who followed the former rector into a failed venture. These were so many sorrows for the Archbishop who was deceived by some of his own sons!

One of his collaborators, Fr. Urban Snyder, reproached the Archbishop for too readily ordaining candidates of whom he was not absolutely sure. Sometimes the Archbishop would recognize the excessive trust he had in people, just as he had shown in Africa; but were not the needs of the faithful an imperative?

---

[84] *Spiritual Conferences at Ecône*, 27 B, 28 A, Feb. 13 and 23, 1976.

[85] *Spiritual Conferences at Ecône*, 54 A, Jan. 9, 1978. Archbishop Lefebvre gave news on the anti-Ecône Roman seminary: One of the seminarians who had been at Ecône and who was undergoing retraining admitted: "They made us go there to destroy our vocations."

[86] Aulagnier, *La Tradition sans peur*, 130-132.

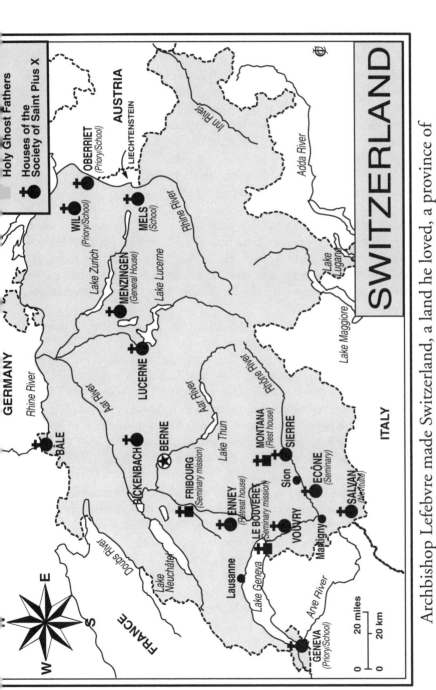

Holy Ghost Fathers

✚ ● **Houses of the Society of Saint Pius X**

SWITZERLAND

Archbishop Lefebvre made Switzerland, a land he loved, a province of the Holy Ghost Fathers, and then a district of the Society of Saint Pius X.

FRIENDSHIP WITH OTHER RELIGIOUS CONGREGATIONS

Fortunately, Archbishop Lefebvre's work would be complemented by other religious societies who were concerned about the fight for the Faith and faithfulness to the religious life. We have seen how generously the Dominicans of Pontcalec collaborated in getting Ecône off the ground; these religious would distance themselves little by little from the Archbishop through a poorly understood loyalty to Rome. The Archbishop showed great understanding towards the teaching Dominicans of Brignoles and Fanjeaux who were iniquitously sanctioned and driven out by their local bishops. Their educational work, which predated that of the Society, would provide much-needed schools for girls.

In 1973, Archbishop Lefebvre again saw his sister Christiane, a Carmelite in Parkes, Australia. Five years later a young Argentinean woman asked the Archbishop: "Is there a traditional Carmel in France?" From the boat on which he returned to France, August 3, 1977, the Archbishop wrote to Mother Marie Christiane: "I pray for all your intentions, particularly for a Carmelite foundation in France. There is no shortage of vocations..."

At the time, the Archbishop did not know[87] that his sister had decided to make this foundation. She was joined by another nun, Sister Marie Pierre, who like her had come to Australia from the Carmel in Tourcoing. Soon they moved provisionally to be near Fr. Paul Schoonbroodt in Belgium, and then they bought a convent at Quiévrain on the French border which became the Carmel of the Sacred Heart. Vocations flooded to them, and Mother Marie Christiane would later found five other Carmels: two in France, one in Germany, one in Switzerland, and one in the USA. Archbishop Lefebvre encouraged her in this: as at Sébikotane, he followed the motto "One seminary, one Carmel."

To found a Carmel in Europe, Mother Marie Christiane had obtained authorization from her ecclesiastical superiors. But when the Nuncio in Belgium learned of her links with the "suspended bishop," the tone changed. No matter, wrote the Archbishop: "Are they getting concerned? It proves how important maintaining Tradition is."[88]

He wrote to the prioress in America, summing up the role of the Carmelites: "[It is] to train souls in sanctity by example and prayer. The priests and the faithful need this example and these prayers to continue the good fight for the Faith against the assaults of hell."[89]

Finally, the Archbishop decided that after the death of his sister the Carmels of Tradition would form a federation under the authority of the

---

[87] *Spiritual Conferences at Ecône*, 46 A, Sep. 23, 1977.
[88] Letter to Mother M.-Christiane, Aug. 22, 1978.
[89] Letter to the Prioress of Spokane, Nov. 3, 1990.

prioress of Quiévrain and under the overall responsibility of one of the bishops: the prioress and bishop in question would supply "the real attachment of the Carmels to the Roman Catholic Church."[90]

Archbishop Lefebvre also supported Fr. Coache and his sister Mother Thérèse-Marie, who refounded the Little Sisters of St. Francis of Assisi at the Maison Lacordaire in Flavigny. This order had been originally founded in Angers in 1873 by Mother Josephine Renault. Similarly he encouraged Mother Marie de Magdala who, in the spirit of Fr. de La Chevasnerie, founded the Little Servants of St. John the Baptist in Le Rafflay near Nantes. Other communities were supported by the Archbishop: the work of L'Etoile for neglected children carried out by Fr. Maurice Raffali in Nîmes; Mother Gertrude de Maissin's Benedictine nuns of Our Lady of Confidence at Lamairé; the contemplative Dominicans at Avrillé; the Order of St. Clare at Morgon; Fr. Pedro de la Imaculada Muñoz's Sisters of the Oasis near Barcelona; the Disciples of the Cenacle founded by Don Francesco Putti at Velletri near Albano. Moreover, in German-speaking countries, the Sisters of Mary of the Precious Blood in German-speaking Switzerland and the nursing sisters of Mayence[91] both felt the benevolent influence of the Society.

TO GIVE REBIRTH TO THE RELIGIOUS LIFE

Archbishop Lefebvre was well aware of the aspirations of some of his seminarians to lead the religious life. However, he told them from experience, "it is difficult to follow a contemplative rule of life and devote oneself to the missionary life." He conceded that they could leave the Society "the day the Dominican, Franciscan, or Carmelite life is reborn," in order "to make a serious attempt at a common life, guided by a religious of the order to be re-established."[92]

Fr. Lecareux, parish priest of Mérigny, wanted to found a Society of the Transfiguration in the spirit of Msgr. Vladimir Ghika. The Archbishop approved of this wish: "If in normal times your Society would likely have obtained authorization from a bishop, I don't see why I should not accept it."[93] On the other hand, with characteristic discretion he disapproved of another religious foundation whose statutes he considered would not normally have been approved.

With the same breadth of vision and respect for the spirit of the Church, the Archbishop would encourage other religious foundations. While visiting a monastery of Benedictine nuns at Jouques on January 6,

---

[90] Letter to the Prioresses, Dec. 29, 1990.
[91] *Priestly and Religious Communities of the Catholic Tradition* (Dublin: SSPX, 1983).
[92] *Spiritual Conferences at Ecône*, 35 A2, Nov. 29, 1976.
[93] *Ibid.*, 46 A, Sept. 23, 1977.

1972, he met Dom Gérard Calvet, an Olivetan Benedictine monk from Tournay. Since 1970 the monk had lived at Bédoin near a charming Romanesque church in the Vaucluse, and he had also obtained the blessing of his Father Abbot to try to establish a foundation for the traditional Benedictine life. His commitment to the religious life and his attachment to the liturgy of all time persuaded Archbishop Lefebvre to provide ordination for Dom Gérard's candidates for the priesthood from 1974 onwards, although with the passage of time the ghosts of union with the Church and the Benedictine order would wear down the monastery's ability to resist the "Roman Sirens." The enthusiasm of benefactors for this project enabled the monks to build a beautiful Romanesque-style abbey in Le Barroux. A convent of Benedictine nuns founded at Uzès moved to be near the monks, and Le Barroux founded its daughter monastery of Santa Cruz in the Nova Friburgo mountains of Brazil.

A Capuchin priest, Romain Potez, whose name in religion was Fr. Eugène de Villeurbanne, had been a missionary in central Africa where he once met Archbishop Lefebvre. In 1971 he gave the Archbishop part of a legacy to contribute towards the building of Ecône. With the encouragement of Fr. Dulac—who advised him: "Delay no longer: the 'Romans' only wait for *infractions* to occur in order to legalize them"—Fr. Eugène moved to Verjon near Lyons in 1972 and informed the Archbishop of the rebirth of the canonically "wild" Capuchins.

The Archbishop replied: "May God bless the true renovators! May they be united as regards the true liturgy of the Holy Mass, the religious habit, and the Divine Office!"[94]

And as a true son of the third order of St. Francis, the Archbishop gladly ordained these enthusiasts of the Poverello's holy poverty and mortification.

Similarly in 1978 the Archbishop welcomed at Ecône the first members of a newly formed Dominican society who were formerly members of the MJCF. They received the habit of St. Dominic from the hands of Fr. Guérard des Lauriers, and were supported by Fr. Eugène and Dom Gérard. Between Ecône and Avrillé, the Dominican brothers began their training in theology and the religious life before in turn receiving ordination from the hands of Archbishop Lefebvre. The Archbishop was generous with his advice and encouraged them in founding their theological review, *Le Sel de la Terre*.

Finally, Michael Sim, a Redemptorist priest from New Zealand, came to see Archbishop Lefebvre at Ecône. In the same spirit of the Church, the Archbishop encouraged him to found a Redemptorist monastery in Great

---

[94] Letter to Fr. Eugène, Aug. 26, 1972. Cf. Yves Chiron, *Veilleur avant l'aube, le P. Eugène de Villeurbanne* (Clovis, 1997), 382-384.

Britain under the aegis of Tradition and in faithfulness to the program of St. Alphonsus de Liguori.

In Avrillé in 1981, the Archbishop received the perpetual profession of the first superior of the young Dominicans. He related his "satisfaction at witnessing and supporting the resurrection" of this religious order. Of course, he said, "I have not received permission from the Master General," but "if we do not follow the letter of the law, we at least follow the fundamental laws," among which is "the duty to preserve and renew" the religious state "which is proof of the principal mark of the Church: holiness." All these young people "who instead of attaching themselves to ephemeral things...consecrate themselves definitively to God" show forth the holiness of the Church, "the most convincing and attractive" mark of the Church![95]

Moreover, all these religious would be apostles; in their own way, they would complement the Society and help it carry out its apostolate.

AUXILIARY TROOPS

The troops of the Archbishop also included numerous priest friends, whether founders of societies, members of priestly associations (such as Fr. Michel André's Noël Pinot Association), or just operating independently. While doing confirmation tours in every continent, Archbishop Lefebvre enjoyed paying friendly visits to these priests, and loved even more preaching them retreats to maintain their holiness and priestly zeal. He willingly received them at Ecône and in his seminaries at ordination time where they took part in the greatly symbolic ceremony of imposing their own hands on the heads of the new priests.

Finally, the troops of the Archbishop also included the hordes of faithful who went to his chapels or elsewhere, even if the Archbishop rightly denied being the "leader of the traditionalists." Among these were the presidents of the St. Pius V and St. Pius X Associations who were proud to fight, and were also jealous of their authority. Sometimes the young priest fresh from Ecône seemed to be nothing more than their curate...The Archbishop encouraged his sons to be patient and to show great respect to these worthy laypeople.

V. "OCCUPYING THE GROUND"

Archbishop Lefebvre had the same motto as Bishop Kobès. Every year, his seminaries produced between ten and twenty-five priests. There was Ecône, Armada (which moved to Ridgefield, Connecticut, and then to Winona, Minnesota), and also Weissbad (which moved to Zaitzkofen,

---

[95] Sermon of April 27, 1981; letter from Avrillé, no. 18.

deep in Bavaria) which opened in 1978. The seminary in Buenos Aires opened in 1979 and there the Archbishop ordained his first two South American priests in 1980. It soon moved to La Reja where at first the only accommodation available was in a building with a corrugated iron roof. Other seminaries—Albano from 1979 to 1982, Flavigny from 1986 onwards, and Holy Cross in Australia—only provided the year of spirituality, or philosophy classes.

NEW RECRUITS AND MATERIAL MEANS

Fresh troops enabled the district superiors to spread out their resources across countries, founding new priories and chapels in the right places, according to the needs of the faithful. Before giving the green light for the purchase of a building, the Archbishop always wanted to visit the property, going from the basement to the attic together with an architect or one of his Swiss builder friends. Buying buildings sometimes required considerable cunning because of potential opposition...especially from the Church.

Similarly the Archbishop studied carefully the possible location for a district headquarters before coming to a decision: thus Fr. Aulagnier had to accept orders to leave his beloved Pointet and go up to Suresnes which was near Paris and obviously more central. The Archbishop saw to it that the buildings were adequately fitted out, as he had done in Africa. "I do not want luxury houses, but they need to have a minimum of facilities to enable the priests to carry out an effective apostolate."

Through his Bursar General, he watched over the financial and legal independence of foundations and works, a condition of their spiritual independence "which alone ensures that the truth can be affirmed in its entirety."[96] Legal advisers showed how gifts and legacies could be received.

As a realist, the Archbishop wrote two brief *Letters to Friends and Benefactors* every year giving details of how the various projects were progressing and containing selected photographs. He said to the seminarians: "This letter provides our daily bread. It reminds our friends that we exist and that we do not live only on fresh air and water. So, you have to put these letters into envelopes!"

Most donors were people of modest means who gave regular gifts of between twenty and fifty francs. Each month a poor woman from the USA sent a check for three dollars. The bursar asked the Archbishop: "Would it not be better to tell her to send one lump sum every six months? Each time I pay two dollars in commission."

"No," replied the Archbishop, "think about the widow in the Gospel."

---

[96] Aulagnier, *La Tradition sans peur*, 142.

The Archbishop recommended to his sons: "Be thrifty; St. Joseph helps us insofar as we do not waste what the benefactors deprive themselves of for us."[97] However, on the other hand, "Don't hoard your money; spend what is given to you."

"Above all, do not make our Lord into a liar: 'Seek ye first the kingdom of God and His justice, and all the rest will be given unto you.' Because if you seek money, money will flee from you. Be apostolic and St. Joseph will always be generous."[98]

EMERGENCY JURISDICTION AND APOSTOLATE

When the priests of the Society establish a new priory or assume jurisdiction over individuals in this time of crisis, the spiritual needs of the faithful always remain the supreme law and make their apostolate legitimate. In these exceptional circumstances, the jurisdiction of priests is neither delegated by the diocesan bishop, nor is it territorial. Rather, it is exercised over individuals who have need of it, case by case, according to the rules of supplied jurisdiction foreseen by Canon Law in specific laws (Can. 882, 1098, *etc.*) and more general rules (Can. 209), or in "the supreme law, the salvation of souls." It was in this sense that the Archbishop said to his priests: "The faithful give you authority." Obviously these words must be taken *cum grano salis*—with a pinch of salt. When he justified using "the Church's largesse" in supplying jurisdiction,[99]Archbishop Lefebvre readily referred to "the danger of the spiritual death of souls, asphyxiated by the lack of grace and finding themselves in exceptional circumstances."

On January 12, 1979, he was questioned by theologians of the Holy Office about the principle guiding his activities as a bishop in disobeying the letter of Canon Law, or even "going against the formal prohibition of the Pope." He replied: "No, I do not act starting from a principle....It was the facts—the circumstances in which I found myself —that constrained me to act."

However, as he explained to his seminarians, if he needed to have recourse to a principle, he would express it like this:

> Noting that across entire countries, the bishops no longer exercise their authority to ensure the faithful handing on of the Faith and grace, and seeing that even Rome seems tacitly to approve of them, a bishop has the duty to do all in his power so that faith and grace be given to the faithful who legitimately ask for them. He does this especially by training true and holy priests formed thoroughly according to the spirit of the Church, even if these priests only have a legally fictitious incardination.

---

[97] *Spiritual Conferences at Ecône*, Nov. 28, 1977.
[98] Abbé J.-Y. Cottard, ms. II, 20-21.
[99] *Spiritual Conferences at Ecône*, 43 A, March 27, 1977; *Cor Unum*, no. 16 (Oct. 1983).

In doing this a bishop would not act against the Pope but outside of the Pope, especially if he could have no contact with the Pope. Thus, he would act for the greater good of the Church and for the salvation of souls, following the example of other bishops like St. Athanasius or St. Eusebius at the time of the Arians (cf. Dom Gréa, *The Church and her Divine Constitution*, I, 209-232)."[100]

Without meaning to, Archbishop Lefebvre here sketched the principle which ten years later would enable him to consecrate bishops legitimately. History shows in what disastrous circumstances such "extraordinary episcopal action" has been undertaken "by bishops themselves fulfilling (as Dom Gréa, quoted by the Archbishop, says) the role of doctors to a flagging Church," and doing so when they are not able to have recourse to the Pope. Archbishop Lefebvre said:

> Now, this is our situation; Rome admits it cannot act. When I showed the Canadian Catechism to Cardinal Wright for him to see whether it was still Catholic, he said to me: "Oh! You know, we cannot go against the bishops' conferences." Cardinal Seper replied to me that "it is lay people who will save the Church because here in Rome we can no longer take care of everything." When Bishop Adam asked Rome to intervene in a particular case, he was rebuffed: "See the bishops' conferences." The episcopate is either paralyzed or no longer orthodox, and Rome says it cannot act. Are we going to let the faithful lose their souls? Must we abandon the future of the Church?[101]

VI. SO THAT THE CHURCH MAY GO ON

In order not to abandon this future of the Church before the progressive forces, Archbishop Lefebvre traveled all over the world and gave the Mass and priests to the faithful.

VISIT AND FOUNDATION IN LATIN AMERICA, 1977

In July, 1977, the Archbishop himself accompanied Fr. Jean-Michel Faure to his first post—a conquering outpost—in Buenos Aires. There he was joined by two priest friends: Frs. Antonio Mathet and Raúl Sanchez Abelenda. Fr. Julio Meinvielle and two eminent laymen (Andrès de Asboth and Roberto Gorostiaga) who were close to the Cité Catholique had established Catholic Action initiatives with the reviews *Verbo* and *Roma*. The

---

[100] *Spiritual Conferences at Ecône*, 70 A, Feb. 22, 1979, 443-445; *Cor Unum*, no. 3 (June 1979) ; "Mgr. L. et le S.-Office," *Itinéraires*, no. 233: 159-160; cf. Dom Grea, *The Church and Her Divine Constitution* (Éd. de Casterman, 1964), 235-238: emergency actions of the episcopate; case of necessity.
[101] *Spiritual Conferences at Ecône*, 70 A, 444-445.

apostolate was launched successfully, and Fr. Faure also went to Mexico to examine possibilities there.

On July 9, Archbishop Lefebvre went with Marcel Pedroni and his wife Mélanie to Texas where they met up with Fr. Faure. The Archbishop blessed the large parish that Fr. Hector Bolduc had acquired in Dickinson. However, the Archbishop was forbidden to enter Mexico because of pressure put on the government by the Nuncio.

In Caracas in a narrow street where the traffic was at a standstill, a taxi pulled up alongside the Archbishop's car. At the same time, a very well groomed priest in a Roman hat walked by along the sidewalk. Seeing the polished cleric, the taxi driver directed the Archbishop's attention to him saying: "Lefebvre!" And Archbishop Lefebvre said to himself: "That is the idea people have of Lefebvre."

In Bogota, Colombia, the Archbishop was surrounded by the press and by troops. A pack of journalists waited for him at the airport, and his car was accompanied everywhere by fifteen soldiers—military policemen and secret police. In the streets, the radio followed him and announced: "Archbishop Lefebvre is now on 45th Avenue, such and such a block." When he passed, the people shouted "*Viva Monseñor!*" and knelt to receive his blessing. At the airport as he was leaving to visit his sister, Mrs. Guy Toulemonde, in Pereira, a female journalist who saw that there was no driver in the car, opened the door, pushed her microphone in, and began asking the Archbishop questions. Marcel Pedroni then grabbed the impertinent young woman and removed her rapidly from the vehicle. The following day the newspaper spoke about "this ruffian Frenchman" to the great delight of the Swiss driver. In the plane going to Pereira, the captain invited the Archbishop into the cabin.

In Santiago in Chile on July 17, Archbishop Lefebvre could hear from the plane the shouts of the crowd: "*¡Lefebvre, sí! ¡Comunismo, no!*" The crowd stood there and it was impossible to clear a passage through them; escorted by two police vehicles, the Archbishop's car turned around and used the runways to leave the airport. The effort was wasted, for throughout the journey there were crowds with flags, all acclaiming the Archbishop. The headlines in the newspapers read: "Cardinal Silva Henriquez declares: 'Lefebvre is a Judas.'" The following day, they read: "Lefebvre replies: 'I am not a Judas, I did not kiss Fidel Castro.'" Eight hundred and fifty people attended a talk by the Archbishop, and six priests came to see him to assure him that half the clergy were with him.

Lastly, on his visit to Buenos Aires, the crowd and the journalists were there as always. However, the police forbade entry to the building where the Mass was to be held. No matter: it was celebrated outside instead, and attended by fifteen hundred people. The talk that Archbishop Lefebvre gave on July 21 narrowly avoided being disrupted by an attack: a bomb was discovered in a cubby-hole and defused just in time.

After these events, the Archbishop returned to Europe by boat. During a similar voyage on which he was accompanied by a friend and his wife, he made one evening this charitable reproach: "Oh! Madam, excuse me, I am embarrassed, but in light of the way you are dressed [too worldly], I don't think I can dine with you this evening." And the woman went and changed.

One August evening in 1977, Archbishop Lefebvre returned to Ecône to learn that the rector and several teachers were leaving (as we have already related): it was a very trying time, as the Archbishop would say.[102]

STARTING "ST. PIUS X" IN GABON, 1986

Among the Archbishop's other symbolic trips were his brief visits to Gabon in preparation for a foundation there. He made a sort of pilgrimage in January, 1985, raising hopes, and drawing out confidences such as the one made by an "old chap" of Donguila to Marcel Pedroni: "When Fr. Marcel left us, it was as if the Good Lord had left us." Even the retired Bishop of Oyem, Bishop François Ndong, the Archbishop's former pupil at Libreville, encouraged the Society of Saint Pius X to come to Gabon. He skilfully succeeded in arranging an audience for the Archbishop with the President of the Republic, Omar Bongo. The meeting was so positive that it was featured on the television news, and the President chartered a small jet plane so that Archbishop Lefebvre could go and visit his other former pupil, Bishop Makouaka, Bishop of Franceville.

The pioneering prior, Fr. Patrick Groche, made a last preparatory visit in August, 1985. He was greeted by the Bishop of Mouila, Cyriaque Obamba, a former student of Fr. Marcel: "Yes, come, but you would be better at Libreville!" Arriving in the capital on January 14, 1986, Fr. Groche announced to Bishop Ndong: "We are moving in." With his African wisdom, the prudent bishop advised that Archbishop Lefebvre should make another visit "to speak to the President," without whose agreement work permits would not be granted. Fr. Groche was in limbo with his right hand man, the deacon Karl Stehlin, who arrived on January 6. Their cases lay on the floor of the house that they had rented but they did not know if it was worth opening them.

Finally, at the end of February, Archbishop Lefebvre arrived. "His presence alone inspired us with peace, serenity, and courage," Reverend Stehlin noted. However, the President was away; in the interim, the Archbishop visited his old friends Frs. Heidet and Jules Pandjo. At last the deci-

---

[102] Notes from the Road, Marcel Pedroni; *Spiritual Conferences at Ecône*, 48 B, Oct. 18, 1977.

sive meeting took place on March 4, 1986. Delicately, Bongo confided: "Your Grace, I have never been told that you are *persona non grata.*" It was done! On his return, the Archbishop was able to say to his troops: "I think that now you can unpack your trunks."[103] The "St. Pius X Mission" of Peyrie was founded. Soon hundreds, then thousands, of faithful would crowd into the mission church which had to be extended several times. Priestly and religious vocations were raised up by the Mass of all time and the perennial religious life, all thanks to the Archbishop.

CARRYING ON THE CHURCH

Year by year, the foundations grew more numerous, and districts and autonomous houses were added: USA (summer, 1973), France (February, 1974), Italy (1974), Germany (1976), Switzerland (1977), Canada (March, 1977), Argentina (November 27, 1977), Spain (September 10, 1978), Belgium (September, 1979), Austria (September, 1981), Australia (August 1982), Ireland (summer, 1983), the Low Countries (August, 1984), Mexico (September, 1984), Southern Africa (September, 1984), Portugal (September, 1984), Gabon (1986), and India (September 3, 1986).

At the Archbishop's request, the General Chapter gathered at Ecône in July, 1982 (at the end of the first twelve years of the Society, or the duration of a Superior General's mandate according to the Statutes). They elected a "Vicar General" for the Archbishop in the person of Fr. Franz Schmidberger, whose initiative and powers of organization had been noted by the founder. At the 1983 ordinations, the Archbishop announced to the faithful that he was passing on to Fr. Schmidberger the responsibilities of Superior General, while keeping for himself responsibility for relations with Rome.

At that time the Society numbered 205 seminarians (of whom 174 were already members of the Society) in four seminaries, and 119 priests working in forty-eight houses or secondary schools situated in twelve countries. The Archbishop explained to his seminarians the spirit of this modest reconquest: "For my part, I try, I assure you, to have the true spirit of the Church. If I had serious doubts about the legitimacy of the fight that I am waging and which I have led you—I would say—into waging with me, I would stop right now. I am convinced that the good of the Church and her continuance make it necessary for us to be ever-strong in the Faith and to keep on training priests. And so I carry on without hesitating in spite of the opposition which comes to us even from the very highest authorities in the Church."[104]

---

[103] *Cor Unum*, no. 23 (March 1986); Oct. 25, 1986.
[104] *Spiritual Conferences at Ecône*, 85 B, June 23, 1981.

CHAPTER 19

OPERATION SURVIVAL

I. SCANDALS IN HIGH PLACES

UNIVERSAL REDEMPTION AND ECUMENISM

At first Archbishop Lefebvre was well disposed towards John Paul II, a Polish Pope who (he thought) would probably be against Communism, and preach Catholicism robustly to the world. However, he became disenchanted when he read the Pope's inaugural encyclical *Redemptor Hominis*, issued on March 4, 1979. A note in his thin handwriting found in the margin of a copy of the encyclical reads: "No. 11 presents a wholly new conception of Christianity. It is Teilhardian humanism." In the margin next to No. 13 in which John Paul II speaks of "man in all the fullness of the mystery in which he has become a sharer in Jesus Christ, the mystery in which each one…has become a sharer from the moment he is conceived beneath the heart of his mother," the Archbishop put a large exclamation mark and noted lower down: "Where does he speak of incorporation in Christ through baptism?"

From among the rising flood of texts flowing from the pen of the new Pope, we do not know if the Archbishop read the "Message to the People of Asia" given two years later in Manila on February 21, 1981. The Pope here claims that "in the Holy Spirit, and by the cross and Resurrection of Christ, each person and each nation have become children of God, participants in the divine nature, and heirs of eternal life."[1]

Whether or not he had read this, the fact remains that one month later Archbishop Lefebvre wrote to a friend: "Reading these pages in this modern and unintelligible style leaves me feeling overwhelmed. It is sickening! They are not simple, enlightening, and supernatural in the style of the faith of the Church."[2]

THE NEW CODE OF CANON LAW—OPEN LETTER TO THE POPE

On January 25, 1983, John Paul published the Apostolic constitution promulgating the new Code of Canon Law which officially recognized "the double subject of the supreme power of the Church"[3] (Canon 336),

---

[1] On Radio Veritas, *Documentation Catholique*, 1894 (March 15, 1981): 281.
[2] Letter to Professor G. Salet, April 22, 1981.

allows heretics to receive Holy Communion from the hands of a Catholic priest (Canon 844, § 4), and reverses the two ends of marriage (Canon 1055). Archbishop Lefebvre was stupefied when John Paul dared to speak of "the new aspect" which is found in the new Code; he wrote about it to his friends and benefactors.

Firstly he quoted the Pope explaining that "this new Code can be thought of as a serious attempt to translate into canonical language the conciliar ecclesiological doctrine." The Pope listed five principal areas: "The Church as the People of God; ecclesiastical authority as service; the Church as communion; the members of the people of God each participating in his own way in Christ's triple power: priestly, prophetic, and royal; and finally, the task of ecumenism." The Archbishop wrote:

> Here we have so many ambiguous notions which henceforth will enable modern and Protestant errors to inspire the legislation of the Church. But the authority of the Pope and the bishops will suffer for it; the distinction between the clergy and lay people is also whittled away. The necessary and absolute character of the Catholic Faith is watered-down in favor of heresy and schism, and the fundamental realities of sin and grace are blurred. These [ambiguities] represent a dangerous attack on the Church's doctrine and the salvation of souls.[4]

> In his *Normae Generales*, Professor Michiels writes that "the foundation of the supernatural life given to the Church is the Faith. Consequently, the duty of law is to determine whatever regards Faith: how it is preached, explained, outwardly confessed, received, and defended." All these things are put in danger by the new Code. Therefore, it is impossible to accept it in its entirety; on essential points, it favors heresy.[5]

In a certain sense, this new Code is more serious than the Council because it boils down the Council's deviations into laws.

The decisive change that now occurred in the Archbishop's attitude cannot be emphasized enough. From this point onwards, he seriously thought about performing episcopal consecrations. He also began publicly protesting against the scandals perpetrated by holders of the highest offices in the Church.

Archbishop Lefebvre finally considered that "enough was enough" when, just before the new Code inevitably became law, the mixed Catholic-Lutheran commission issued a declaration concerning seven important

---

3   The Pope on the one hand and the Pope with the bishops on the other. The *nota praevia* that corrected the interpretation of *Lumen Gentium* is not repeated in the 1983 Code. So the bishops could demand to take part in governing the Universal Church at any time! [The English translation reads: "The College of Bishops…is, in union with its head and never without this head, also the subject of supreme and full power over the universal Church." Canon 336 in *The Code of Canon Law* (London: Collins, 1983), 58. Trans.]

4   Letter to Friends and Benefactors, no. 24, March 7, 1983.

5   *Spiritual Conferences at Ecône*, 100 A, March 15, 1983.

points "among the ideas of the Second Vatican Council in which one can see Luther's demands being welcomed."[6] Together with Bishop de Castro Mayer, who had been forced to resign from Campos in September 1981, he addressed to the Pope an open letter that was made public at the same time in several of the world's major capitals.[7]

Considering that the "Church seems like an occupied city," that the auto-demolition was continuing and that the steps they had taken privately for fifteen years had been in vain, they saw themselves obliged to address the Pope publicly with the same sentiments as St. Paul with regard to St. Peter when he reproached him for not walking according to the truth of the Gospel (Gal. 2:11-14). They denounced six errors or deviations which were explained in detail in an annex to the letter.

- A latitudinarian[8] and ecumenical idea of the Church with no unity of faith, as condemned especially by the *Syllabus*, proposition 28, DS 2918 (*Lumen Gentium, Unitatis Redintegratio* of Vatican II, and *Catechesi Tradendæ* of John Paul II).

- Collegial government and the new democratic tendencies of the Church, particularly condemned by Vatican I, DS 3055 (*Lumen Gentium* of Vatican II and the new Code of Canon Law).

- A false concept of the natural rights of Man which clearly appears in the document on Religious Liberty and was particularly condemned by *Quanta Cura* (Pius IX) and *Libertas Præstantissimum* (Leo XIII). (*Gaudium et Spes* and *Dignitatis Humanæ* of Vatican II, *Redemptor Hominis* of John Paul II).

- A mistaken idea of papal authority considering it as absolute whereas it is subject to divine authority as expressed in Tradition, Holy Scripture, and the definitions already promulgated by the Magisterium of the Church (DS 3116).

- A Protestant notion of the sacrifice of the Mass and the sacraments as condemned by the Council of Trent (Sess. XXII).

- Finally, speaking generally, the freedom given to heresy, characterized by the suppression of the Holy Office.[9]

The Archbishop presented this episcopal manifesto to the press at Roissy airport on December 9. He concluded: "In history, they will say

---

[6]   *Documentation Catholique*, 1855 (July 3, 1983): 696. John Paul II for his part praised "Luther's profound religiosity."
[7]   The first idea for a public letter came from Archbishop Graber. The Cardinal Archbishop of Toledo and Bishop Nestor Adam were going to sign it. However, Graber saw Ratzinger, who advised against this step and had him named assistant at the Pontifical Throne. *Spiritual Conferences at Ecône*, 105 A, Dec. 15, 1983.
[8]   The idea of a broad Church encompassing all the other Christian churches and even the healthy elements of non-Christian religions.
[9]   *Fideliter*, no. 36 (Nov.-Dec. 1983).

that at that moment in the Church when all seemed lost and destroyed, there were two bishops who raised their voices and gave a cry of alarm."[10]

NEW SCANDALOUS ACTS AND DECLARATIONS

Two days after the bishops' cry of alarm, John Paul II went to preach in a Lutheran church in Rome on December 11. At the beginning of 1984, he met the Orthodox Metropolitan of Myre in Bari. On this occasion he said: "Unity is neither absorption nor even fusion"; it is "a symphonic unity" between "two sisters Churches."[11]

On February 18, an agreement was reached on the reform of the concordat between the Holy See and Italy. The concordat under Pius XI contained the principle that "the Roman and Apostolic Catholic religion is the only religion of the State." This principle was now abolished.

Cardinal Casaroli personally congratulated himself for this: the Church, he said, will ask for no more "privileges" over "citizens of other religious faiths." Archbishop Lefebvre wondered: "Privileges for whom? For what? Is the social royalty of our Lord Jesus Christ a privilege? In a Catholic State, it is His strict right to be King of society. It is not a privilege."[12]

In spring 1984, the liberal ecumenism of John Paul II reached out to Buddhists. In Korea on May 6, the Pope sent "particular greetings to the members of the Buddhist tradition who are preparing to celebrate the feast of the coming of the Lord Buddha."[13] On May 10, he visited a Buddhist temple in Thailand, took his shoes off, and sat at the feet of the bonze who was seated with his back to an altar on which stood a large statue of Buddha. In Geneva during his visit to the headquarters of the Ecumenical Council of Churches, the Pope took part in a "liturgy of the word" in the ECC's chapel and there reaffirmed that "the Catholic Church's involvement in the ecumenical movement is irreversible."[14]

REJECTING THE TEMPTATION TO *"RALLIEMENT"*[15]

Archbishop Lefebvre reacted to the publication of the indult on October 3, 1984 (granting freedom to the Traditional Mass on condition[16] that one accept the New Mass), and also to an interview of Cardinal Ratzinger, "Why the Faith Is in Crisis," in the November edition of the Italian monthly magazine *Jesus*. "Let our troops not weary of the fight!" he said.

---

[10]   *Fideliter,* no. 37 (Jan.-Feb. 1984): 10.

[11]   *L'Osservatore Romano* translated from French edition; *Documentation Catholique,* 1872: 414 (expurgated text).

[12]   *Spiritual Conferences at Ecône,* 109 A, March 15, 1984; talk in Turin, March 24.

[13]   *L'Osservatore Romano,* May 7-8, 1984; *Documentation Catholique,* 1876: 619, no. 4.

[14]   June 12, 1984, *Documentation Catholique,* 1878: 704.

Some traditionalists happily noted that the Mass was being made available and that the Cardinal recognized and gave a detailed analysis of the crisis in the Church—due in his view to an "anti-spirit of the Council" which made him call for "a return to the true Council." "What more can we ask for?" thought some of the faithful. "Let us accept the indult and enter again within the confines of the visible Church; once we are within, we will be able to shake things up, and sort them out."

This reasoning was absolutely false, according to Archbishop Lefebvre.

> We cannot enter into a system under superiors who are in a position to stamp us out. "Once we are recognized," you say, "we will be able to act from within the Church." This is completely wrong; it is to totally misunderstand the minds of those in the present hierarchy. To realize this, one only need read that much talked about remark of Cardinal Ratzinger in his interview.
>
> The *porporato* said that the challenge of the 1960's was to take on board the best values from two centuries of liberal culture. Even if these values were not born in the Church, once they are purified and corrected, they can find their place in the vision that the Church has of the world.[17] This is what was done. It is true that the results have disappointed some hopes that were perhaps naive. This is why there is a need to find a new balance.

The Archbishop's commentary was ruthless: so, the Cardinal recognizes that the crisis in the Church is due to the Council's attempts to marry the Church and the Revolution, and bring together Catholic principles and liberal "values": ecumenism, the Declaration of the Rights of Man, and religious liberty. In a word, the Cardinal admits that these attempts have caused the crisis; this is why he wants to find a "new balance," which is an impossible balance: "This is terribly serious. It condemns everything he says in his interview. It is at the heart of his ideas, and it is this that we do not want."

---

[15] [The French word "Ralliement" (rallying) has a particular connotation in French traditional circles, recalling as it does the Church's appeal to French monarchists in 1890 to take part in the democratic processes of the French Republic. "Ralliement" meant the royalists giving up trying to re-establish the monarchy, and banding together with moderate Republicans to defeat the influence of the anti-clerical Radicals and Socialists in the French parliament. However, this involved putting aside monarchist objections to the Republic which saw it as the embodiment of the anti-Christian Revolution. To traditional French circles, "Ralliement" has, therefore, always represented political opportunism and coalition at the expense of principles. Trans.]

[16] Letter of the SCCD signed by the pro-prefect Augustin Mayer and the secretary Virgilio Noé: *Quattuor Abhinc Annos, L'Osservatore Romano*, Oct. 17, 1984; *Itinéraires*, no. 288 (Dec. 1984) with the commentary of Jean Madiran, cf. p.40.

[17] Cf. Yves Congar, *Vraie et fausse réforme dans l'Église* (Paris: Cerf, 1950), 345-46; Roger Aubert, in *Tolérance et communauté humaine* (Casterman, 1951), 81-82.

He concluded: "We cannot place ourselves under an authority whose ideas are liberal and who little by little would condemn us, by the logic of the thing, to accept these ideas and their consequences, and firstly the New Mass." As for the indult, "it has not been created for us" because it gives the traditional Mass to those who accept the New Mass. "Mr. Madiran, who always sums things up so well, has written: 'In short, the Roman circular [indult] enables those who wanted to suppress the traditional Mass to permit its celebration by those who show that they have no reason to want it.'"

THE PASSION OF THE CHURCH

That year, 1984, Archbishop Lefebvre read the "engrossing pages" on the Church that Fr. Emmanuel had written just one century earlier. The priest had described in particular what dramatic times the Church would pass through at the end of the world: "Since the Church must be like our Lord in everything, before the end of the world she will suffer trials that will be a true passion." The Archbishop recounted the impression that these pages made on him: "One can feel in them the breath of the Holy Ghost. Some of them are even prophetic when they describe the Passion of the Church."[18]

He wrote to the friends who had suggested this reading to him: "One has had to live from 1960 to the present moment to discover that Popes can lead the Church to her ruin. Such a thing seemed impossible to us, given the promises of the Holy Ghost's assistance. *Contra factum non fit argumentum*. Against the facts, there is no argument. The facts are there before our eyes. So, we have to conclude that when our Lord spoke of help until the end of time, he did not exclude periods of darkness and a time of Passion for His mystical Spouse."[19]

FROM THE SYNOD TO THE ASSISI ANNOUNCEMENT

On January 25, 1985, at St. Paul Outside the Walls, John Paul II announced the meeting of an extraordinary Synod of bishops for the twentieth anniversary of the closing of Vatican II. It would examine how the Council was being applied, and "promote its constant implementation in the life of the Church."[20] Reacting to this, Archbishop Lefebvre and Bishop de Castro Mayer wrote to the Sovereign Pontiff to warn him solemnly. They denounced religious liberty and its consequences: the predominant religious indifferentism, ecumenism as practiced by John Paul II, and indulgence towards all the enemies of the Church. "If the Synod does not

---

[18] Archbishop Lefebvre, preface to *L'Eglise*, by Fr. Emmanuel, *Itinéraires*, no. 289: 79-80.
[19] Letter to Mrs. Jean-Marc Le Panse, Ecône, Jan. 29, 1984.
[20] *Documentation Catholique*, 1891 (March 3, 1985): 283.

step back from such errors," the two bishops would be led to conclude that "the members of the Synod no longer profess the Catholic Faith" and John Paul II "is no longer the good shepherd."[21]

However, the Synod which ended on December 8, 1985, decided "unanimously to continue along the road that the Council pointed out to us." An anecdote: when John Paul II met Bishop Schwery, Bishop of Sion, in the corridor during the Synod, he gave him a wink and said: "Watch out! Now I am no longer the good Shepherd."[22]

Archbishop Lefebvre returned full of hope from a trip to his Argentinean seminary of La Reja where he had ordained eight priests on December 1. He was also there to see his friend Dom Antonio de Castro Mayer confer minor orders. He said how upset he was by such stubbornness in error (at the synod).

During the closing ceremony for the Week of Christian Unity on January 25, 1986, the Pope announced "a special prayer meeting for peace in the town of Assisi," "with representatives not only from the various Christian churches and communions but also from other religions across the world."[23] No one in the Roman Curia had expected such an announcement. However, Archbishop Lefebvre had said to his close associates in 1985: "I am sure that the Pope has it in mind to organize a congress for all religions."

When it was announced, the Archbishop reminded the seminarians of Ecône of the famous "motley congress" of religions[24] held in Chicago in 1895 which Leo XIII had condemned. The same thing was going to be seen again but this time organized by the Pope. Archbishop Lefebvre said: "It is demonic. It is an insult to our Lord Jesus Christ. Who will they pray to? What god will they pray to for peace? What peace can they ask for if they are not praying to the only true God? They will not be praying to our Lord Jesus Christ. The Jews do not want him, the Muslims and the Buddhists do not want Him either. Lots of Protestants do not believe in the divinity of Jesus Christ. What god will they pray to? God was made flesh and came and lived amongst us to save us. We have no right to pray to anyone else. If we put Jesus Christ aside, we are not praying to the true God. It is an indescribably impious act against our Lord Jesus Christ."[25]

John Paul II took part in several animist ceremonies during August 1985 in Togo. He went to India the following year and on February 5, 1986, in Madras he received the sacred ashes of the Hindu religion; he

---

21 Aug. 31, 1985, *Fideliter*, no. 49: 4-6.
22 *Nouvelliste du Valais*, Dec. 9, 1985, 1
23 *Documentation Catholique*, 1913 (March 2, 1986): 235.
24 Jacques Ploncard d'Assac, *L'Eglise occupée* (DPF), 191; Fr. Emmanuel Barbier, *Histoire du catholicisme libéral*, III, 226; *Spiritual Conferences at Ecône*, 121 B, Jan. 16, 1987.
25 *Spiritual Conferences at Ecône*, 117 B, Jan. 28, 1986, 126-127.

preached mutual understanding of religions in order to promote universal brotherhood.[26] Archbishop Lefebvre denounced such scandals as *communicatio in sacris*, *i.e.*, participation in non-Catholic rites. These things were forbidden by traditional canon law (Canon 1258) and made the person "suspect of heresy" (Canon 2316) because they imply profession of a false religion and consequently the denial of the Catholic Faith.[27]

Thus, in his sermon on Easter Sunday 1986 at Ecône, the Archbishop exclaimed:

> This is the situation in which we find ourselves. I have not created it. I would die to make it go away! We are faced with a serious dilemma which, I believe, has never existed in the Church: the one seated on the chair of Peter takes part in the worship of false gods. What conclusions will we have to draw, perhaps in a few months' time, faced with these repeated acts of taking part in the worship of false religions, I do not know. But I do wonder. It is possible that we might be forced to believe that the Pope is not the Pope. Because it seems to me initially—I do not yet want to say it solemnly and publicly—that it is impossible for a Pope to be publicly and formally a heretic.[28]

THE SIN OF SCANDAL AGAINST THE FAITH: ASSISI

For the second time since 1976, the sedevacantist temptation haunted Archbishop Lefebvre; but he did not succumb to it. He knew that the faithful's instinct for the Faith would not follow him down such a path, and that what God asked of him was to fight for the Faith and denounce scandal: "A major scandal in the true sense of the word *scandal*: to encourage someone to sin. Through ecumenism and taking part in the worship of false religions, the Catholics are losing the Faith: there is the scandal. They no longer believe that there is one true religion or only one God, the Holy Trinity and our Lord Jesus Christ."

The scandal was repeated on April 13 when John Paul was received in the synagogue of Rome by a leading rabbi and those whom the Pope called "our elder brothers in the Faith." The Archbishop commented: "With satellite broadcasting, across the world, perhaps one billion people saw the Pope at the synagogue. Did they realize the seriousness of these actions? And if not, it is because they no longer believe in our Lord Jesus Christ. They have lost their faith in the unique Savior of the world who is our Lord Jesus Christ."[29]

On August 27, 1986, Archbishop Lefebvre wrote to eight cardinals in view of the Assisi meeting. He asked of them to protest against the actions

---

[26] *Ibid.*
[27] Cf. Raoul Naz, *Dictionnaire de droit canonique.*
[28] *Sermons at Ecône*, 35 B1, March 30, 1986.
[29] *Spiritual Conferences at Ecône*, 118 A, April 15, 1986.

of John Paul II, in particular "the planned procession of religions in the streets of the town of St. Francis": "He who now sits upon the Throne of Peter mocks publicly the first article of the Creed and the first Commandment of the Decalogue. The scandal given to Catholic souls cannot be measured. The Church is shaken to its very foundations."

In a press conference, Cardinal Etchegaray said: "You must not expect us to pray together, but we will be together to pray."[30] Therefore, there would be no *communicatio in sacris*; however, the Pope would nevertheless lead this day of successive public demonstrations of each cult, from the chant of the Dalaï Lama to the address of the great Rabbi Elio Toaff, via the peace pipe of John Pretty-on-Top, and the speech of the Shintoist representative. One month to the day before this meeting, Archbishop Lefebvre sent the Pope two small cartoons that were "a little catechism in pictures."[31] One showed John Paul II refusing to let our Lord Jesus Christ and His most holy Mother into the meeting at Assisi: "You are not ecumenical." The other showed our Lord refusing to let John Paul II into heaven, reminding him that He alone is the door of salvation.

On October 28, the colorful congress took place, and on December 2, Archbishop Lefebvre and Bishop de Castro Mayer publicly protested: "Public sin against the unicity of God, the Word Incarnate, and His Church makes one shudder with horror: John Paul has encouraged false religions to pray to their false gods: it is an unprecedented and immeasurable scandal,...an inconceivably impious and intolerable humiliation to those who remain Catholic, loyally professing the same Faith for twenty centuries."[32]

On December 22 in his allocution to the cardinals and Curia, John Paul II attempted to exonerate himself. He referred to the "right key: the teaching of Vatican II," to the Church as "sacrament of the unity of humankind" (*Lumen Gentium*, 1, 9; *Gaudium et Spes*, 42), and to the "seeds of the Word that lie hidden among all religions" (*Ad Gentes*, 11).[33]

Universal unity based on Creation and Redemption cannot but leave a mark in the real life of men, even if they belong to different religions.[34] God's universal will to save man, and the redemptive work of Christ must necessarily be a reality in the heart of every man and in the worship of every religion.[35] Is not this rereading and development of the Council that

---

[30] *Documentation Catholique*, 1924 (Sept. 7-21, 1986): 799.

[31] *Fideliter*, no. 54 (Nov.-Dec. 1986): 17-20.

[32] *Fideliter*, no. 55 (Jan.-Feb. 1987): declaration signed in Buenos Aires.

[33] Cf. Jean Paul II, encyclical *Redemptor Hominis*, no. 11. Cf. Commentary in *Le Sel de la Terre*, no. 38: 1-4.

[34] *Documentation Catholique*, 1963 (Feb. 1, 1987), 133-136.

[35] Cf. "Le christianisme et les religions" (Christianity and other religions), document of the International Theological Commission (Cardinal Ratzinger, chairman), Oct. 1996, no. 85; cf. *Courrier de Rome*, *Sí Sí No No* 383, no. 193 (Sept. 1997).

the Pope, a former Council Father, makes in the light of Assisi, the most authentic interpretation of Vatican II? It would lead John Paul to teach that "Christ is thus the fulfilment of the yearning of all the world's religions and, as such, he is their sole and definitive completion."[36]

Archbishop Lefebvre did not need to hear this sophism. His missionary experience confirmed this point of the catechism for him: no false religions lead to Christ, because they deny Him and keep souls far from Him in the chains of their errors.

From then on, the Archbishop tried hard to make those around him understand that the problem was no longer "Archbishop Lefebvre"—of course—nor even the Church (a city occupied by the enemy), but the Pope, as it were invaded and occupied by an ideology that was contrary to the Catholic Faith. Beyond the painful questions that this fact raised, serious practical decisions were becoming more and more legitimate and indeed necessary.

II. THE CRUCIAL DECISION OF THE EPISCOPAL CONSECRATIONS

In 1974, Fr. Roger-Thomas Calmel, O.P., wrote to Archbishop Lefebvre[37] to tell him that a day would come when he would have to consecrate a bishop to take his place. Did the Archbishop reply with the words Marc Dem still attributed to him in 1984? "I know that throughout the world there will be enough bishops to ordain my seminarians."[38] It is possible. However, from February 1981, when he was hospitalized in Sierre, the question of performing episcopal consecrations occupied his thoughts. His health was not good, and as things stood, he had to recognize that no bishop would agree to ordain his seminarians, not even Bishop Pintonello. Certainly there was a promise from Rome of a document granting freedom to the Traditional Mass and a proposal for sending a Cardinal Visitor to Ecône. But what if things went badly?

The Archbishop answered this question in an interview with André Figueras in the French magazine *Monde et Vie*: "If the situation in the Church were to get worse, and if Providence showed me clearly that I had to do it, doubtless I would resign myself to consecrating a bishop since I can do so validly. But in that act I would be breaking with Rome—the possibility of which scares them—and I would do everything to avoid it."[39]

---

[36] Apostolic letter *Tertio Millennio Adveniente*, Nov. 10, 1994, no. 6.
[37] Fr. Aulagnier said that he read this letter.
[38] Lefebvre, *Lettre ouverte aux catholiques perplexes*, 216.
[39] *Monde et Vie*, June 12, 1981, 12-13.

What did "breaking with Rome" mean? Archbishop Lefebvre did not think that such a consecration would be breaking with the Catholic Church or with eternal Rome. However, it would be a *de facto* break with present-day Rome. During a retreat that he preached in the autumn, he exhorted his priests to love the Church of Rome: "It really is a Catholic thing to love Rome. Since we are so painfully struck and tormented by the hardening of thinking in the Roman Church, ought we to separate ourselves from her? And 'attach ourselves directly' to our Lord Jesus Christ? That is a dangerous error! Our duty is to think the question through so as not to be confused, and to avoid following feelings and tendencies that will well and truly lead us out of the Church."[40]

Schismatic tendencies? Yes, those that could lead traditionalists to disregard utterly the Roman authorities, act as they please, and found "another Church"—all things that the Archbishop held in horror. However, for the time being he wanted still to trust:

"A young Australian said to me: 'I would like to enter your seminary but in six years you'll be dead. It's not worth it.' And when I cough, the seminarians tremble: 'At least let the Archbishop last until my ordination!' Well, let's trust in Providence and wait and see what it is the good Lord wants to bring about."[41]

THEOLOGICAL CONSULTATION CONCERNING A CONSECRATION

However, Archbishop Lefebvre decided to consult his entourage about the legitimacy of an episcopal consecration without a mandate from the Pope. One of his professors at the seminary of Albano, Fr. Philippe Le Pivain, who taught the treatise on the Church, wrote a brief study saying that such an act would usurp the prerogative of the Supreme Pastor who alone can assign subordinate pastors to particular flocks; consequently, there would be a break in apostolicity. After reading this, the Archbishop, said: "It is the doctrine of the Church." This was the general opinion of his collaborators; but he thought: "This doctrine presupposes a Catholic Pope that we can have access to."

When Archbishop Lefebvre visited Rio, Dom Antonio said to him that there was "open persecution" in Campos, where Bishop Alberto Navarro had replaced him. The new bishop had closed the seminary, thrown out the professors and seminarians, and was driving priests loyal to the Mass of all time out of their parishes, in spite of the people who gathered before the churches carrying banners saying: "Leave us our priests!" The Nuncio, the Brazilian episcopate, the Sacred Congregation for Worship—everyone—was ganging up on them. The Archbishop advised them:

---

[40] *Retreats and Instructions preached at Ecône*, Sept. 7, 1981.
[41] *Spiritual Conferences at Ecône*, 88 B, Jan. 19, 1982.

"Form emergency parishes now without waiting to be kicked out by the police." A leaflet explaining the reasons for their faithfulness to the old Mass went unanswered by the Roman Congregations: all recourse to Rome was useless.[42]

The same went for the Society: in Rome, they had reached an impasse, in spite of Cardinal Ratzinger's attempts to understand the situation. For while the Archbishop considered that the New Mass was "dangerous for the Faith," Rome wanted him to recognize its legitimacy and not to turn the faithful against it. On this condition (unacceptable for him), Rome would agree to send Ecône an Apostolic Visitor,[43] as the Archbishop wanted.

Nineteen eighty-three brought the first ecumenical scandals and the unveiling of a new code of law for the Church. Again the Archbishop consulted with his collaborators, as did Fr. Schmidberger, his successor in charge of the Society. Meetings were held at the motherhouse in Rickenbach.[44] Fr. Josef Bisig, the second assistant, explained his objections, which were exactly those of Fr. Le Pivain: it would be "practically to deny the primacy of jurisdiction" that belongs to the Pope by divine right.

Yes, that is the Catholic doctrine, as Frs. Tissier and Williamson recognized. However, it presupposes a Pope who is morally accessible and not "occupied" by errors. "Who is the judge of that?" asked Fr. Bisig; the explicit desire of the Pope which concerns the visible Church has more authority than an habitual and implicit desire. However, as Frs. Tissier and Alain Lorans insisted, the crisis in the Church and the situation of the Pope must enter into the argument because they would be the only reason for the consecration.

This was indeed the opinion of Archbishop Lefebvre, who commented on the written remarks of Fr. Bisig: "The situation for the papacy since John XXIII and under his successor poses problems that are getting more and more serious....They are founding a new Conciliar Church, with a new ecclesiology. Instead of being apostles for Christian social order through the Social Reign of our Lord, these Popes are becoming partisans of socialism or Communism with a tinge of Christianity.[45]...Is this Church still Apostolic or Catholic? Must we still consider the Pope to be Catholic?"

---

[42] *Ibid.*, 94 A, Dec. 3, 1982.
[43] Letter of Cardinal Ratzinger, Dec. 23, 1982.
[44] On Dec. 3, 1983, Feb. 4 and March 5, 1984.
[45] "Since the Council the Church has assumed and gone beyond the French Revolution. She is now assuming and going beyond Communism thanks to taking on board post-Marxist socialism which is democratic, rooted in Christianity, respectful of self-determination and non-totalitarian." Summary of the encyclical *Laborem Exercens* of Sept. 14, 1981, by Archbishop Lefebvre, matching the commentary of Professor Marcel De Corte, *Courrier de Rome* 211, no. 21 (Dec. 1981): 1-5.

ARCHBISHOP LEFEBVRE'S LINE OF ARGUMENT

The Archbishop avoided basing his arguments on sedevacantism, and reasoned as follows: "The problem of the situation of the faithful and the present papacy renders obsolete the difficulties of jurisdiction, disobedience, and apostolicity. These notions presuppose a Pope who is Catholic in his faith and in his government [of the Church]."[46]

The argument from history would later come to complete this radical reasoning. The example of St. Eusebius, Bishop of Samosate (†380), spoke for itself. At the time of the Arian crisis, when he returned from exile, he learned that numerous local Churches were in need of pastors. So he began to go throughout Syria, Phoenicia, and Palestine, ordaining priests and deacons and consecrating solidly orthodox bishops, even though he had no jurisdiction over these Churches.[47] Archbishop Lefebvre read and approved Dom Gréa's commentary:

> So if history shows us bishops who took it on themselves to perform this office of "doctor" to failing churches (Roman Breviary, December 16, Feast of St. Eusebius of Verceil), it shows us at the same time what pressing circumstances dictated this conduct. To make it legitimate, the need had to be such as to concern the very existence of religion —a situation in which the ministry of particular pastors was entirely destroyed or made ineffectual, and wherein no possible recourse to the Holy See could be hoped for.[48]

Such was indeed the situation now. While it was still physically possible, recourse to Rome was rendered morally impossible by the mentality of the Holy Father: "communion with false religions," an "adulterous mood dominating the Church," "this spirit is not Catholic." "For twenty years we have tried patiently and firmly to make the Roman authorities understand that they need to return to sound doctrine and Tradition for the renewal of the Church, the salvation of souls, and the glory of God. But they remain deaf to our pleas, and what is more, they ask us to recognize that the Council and the reforms ruining the Church are well founded."[49]

The three conditions mentioned by Dom Gréa were thus fulfilled.

---

[46] Handwritten notes of Archbishop Lefebvre on Fr. Bisig's study, Nov. 1983; *Fideliter*, no. 123: 29.

[47] Cf. Théodoret de Cyr, *Histoire ecclésiastique*, bk. IV, ch. 12, p. 82, 1147, and bk. V, ch. 4, p. 2, 1203, partially quoted by Dom Adrien Gréa, *L'Eglise et sa divine constitution*, chapter 21, "L'action extraordinaire de l'épiscopat" (The actions of the bishops in emergency situations).

[48] Dom Gréa, *op. cit.* (edition of 1965), 236-237. This refers to episcopal power. We have abridged the author's text while remaining faithful to it.

[49] Note from Albano, Oct. 19, 1983, which became the "public declaration" of June 1988.

THE MEDIA BISHOP

Moreover, the intervention of the Holy See in the institution of a bishop is not required by divine law. The history of the first centuries of the Latin Church shows this.

"Everything was implicit and bound up in the simple desire for *communio cum Sede Apostolica*. As long as they were not acting against the Holy See, it was recognized, and by the Holy See itself, that they were acting in accord with it."[50] "Therefore I will not be acting against the Holy See," thought the Archbishop, "because I will be acting to save the Catholic priesthood."[51]

Moreover, as it was pointed out to him, although the supreme jurisdiction of the Pope is of divine right, it is only a jurisdiction, *i.e.*, a power ordained to the common good of the Church, and not a dominating or discretionary power. Therefore, there is no failure of that authority endangering the common good that the Church cannot herself supply for—for example, by an extraordinary act of a member of the episcopal body.

The more the Archbishop's scruples faded, the more Rome grew alarmed. On July 20, 1983, Cardinal Ratzinger considered it appropriate to write to him: "The Holy Father…knows that you will not allow yourself to do what would really be the start of a schism, namely consecrate a bishop."

The Cardinal got his answer through the media: when speaking to the journalists present at Roissy on December 9, 1983, the media-conscious Archbishop took advantage of the opportunity provided by his "episcopal manifesto" and was delighted to reply to Rome by testing the waters: "You all came thinking I would announce that I am going to create bishops" (laughter).

"Your Grace," said a reporter, "why don't you create bishops?"

"Because I still think that it would apparently be a break with Rome, and that would be serious. I say again 'apparently,' because I think that before God it is possible for my action to be necessary for the history of the Church, for the continuation of the Church…and the Catholic priesthood. So I do not say that one day I will not do it, but the circumstances would have to be rather more tragic."[52]

Two years later on the eve of the synod, Archbishop Lefebvre and Bishop de Castro Mayer wrote to the Pope and confirmed for him that they might be led "to take all necessary decisions for the Church to maintain a clergy that is loyal to the Catholic Faith."[53]

---

[50] Fr. V.-A. Berto, Letter of Feb. 7, 1974, to Archbishop Lefebvre, in *Sainte Église romaine*, 302.
[51] Note from Albano, Oct. 19, 1983.
[52] *Fideliter*, no. 37: 15-17; *Le Figaro*, Dec. 10-11, 1983.

Naturally, Cardinal Ratzinger informed the determined Archbishop that the Pope asked him "not to do something that would constitute a definitive break with the communion of the Church."[54] Five days later with the announcement concerning Assisi, Archbishop Lefebvre considered that he had received from Providence[55] the first sign that he was waiting for.

FLURRY OF OPINIONS

"If we must act, Providence will direct circumstances such that our decision will be clear, and conformed to the faithfuls' *sensus fidei*, the sense of the Faith."[56] This was why in 1985 the Archbishop discreetly spoke to some lay friends who shared with him their opinions accompanied by doctrinal or pastoral arguments. On February 22, he wrote to his friend Jacques Chevry, Secretary General of *Credo*: "The consecration question is terribly difficult and opinion is much divided. I am grateful to you for having sent me the well-crafted study[57] by Fr. Quénard, whom I know well. Before our eyes Providence is unfolding the deeds, actions, and words of the Pope, and I must say that we are more and more dumbfounded to such an extent that one can really wonder who this man is."

The months went by and the Archbishop received much advice: like the "high councillors" of old, Fr. J. Reynaud suggested to Archbishop Lefebvre that he consecrate "entirely in secret." The Archbishop replied that he would act publicly since such an ecclesial action could not be subject to the least ambiguity.

In his newsletter *De Rome et d'Ailleurs*, Michel Martin wrote a leader entitled: "Traditionalism must not commit suicide by ill thought through reactions." He wrote: "Unquestionably, if they had to choose between the normal Church, John Paul II's Church, and a dissident Church, the vast majority of traditionalists would disassociate themselves from Archbishop Lefebvre."[58] "If there is a break, what will become of your priests?" wrote Jean Guitton to the Archbishop. "What terrible questions of conscience will they have to face while divided and confused?"[59]

---

[53] "Solennelle mise en garde" (Solemn Warning), Aug. 31, 1985.
[54] Letter of Jan. 20, 1986.
[55] *Retreats at Ecône*, Sept. 6, 1985; *Spiritual Conferences at Ecône*, 115 B2, Oct. 28, 1985.
[56] *Retreats at Ecône*, Sept. 6, 1985, 3 P.M.
[57] This study referred to the virtue of equity, according to St. Thomas, which enables a subject to correct a law in the spirit of the legislator when the latter has not foreseen such and such a case. But how can equity and its act be admitted when the legislator is God, unless God has provided the Church with more general rules to be applied in certain cases?
[58] No. 69 (May 1986): 13.
[59] Letter of July 3, 1986.

Dom Gérard was reticent and on August 22, 1986, the feast of the Immaculate Heart, he prayed to the Holy Virgin "that the menacing waves of schism (and heresy) might break against our ramparts without ever getting through."[60]

Just as numerous were the requests urging the Archbishop to perform an episcopal consecration in the face of the apostasy and scandals in high places. "One of the original traditionalists from St. Nicolas [Paris]" begged for "strong and timely action from an ever-faithful and ever-renewed episcopate." He wrote: "Your Grace, who can give us this episcopate without breaking the chain that unites us to St. Peter, if not you?[61] This common sense consideration was full of a magnificent *sensus fidei*: the apostolicity of the doctrine was central.

Finally, Dr. Joseph Knittel was perhaps the wisest of all: "Whatever you decide to do in this dreadful business, you can count on my unshakable loyalty to you and to the Church."[62]

BISHOPS WITHOUT JURISDICTION

Within the Society, most of the troops trusted the Archbishop; nevertheless there were doubts and wariness amongst the priests at the Bavarian seminary, while at Ecône six seminarians who were spreading dissent had to be expelled. In France, the District Superior, Fr. Paul Aulagnier, had a study prepared on the action of the episcopate in extraordinary circumstances,[63] while Fr. François Pivert wrote a text[64] justifying the consecrations without Pontifical mandate: this he could do with the supplied jurisdiction of the Church no different from that which already allowed Archbishop Lefebvre to preach and to confirm in dioceses without the permission of the Ordinaries.

During a priestly retreat at Ecône in September 1986, Archbishop Lefebvre already defined the limited role of the bishops that he would create and which would avoid any connotations of schism:

> They would be my auxiliaries but have no jurisdiction. They would only be there to give confirmation and ordination, and they could still have some other post within the Society. But in the eyes of the Church it is the Superior General who will count; the bishops will be at the service of the Society. It is the Society that belongs to the Church and that received the approval of the Church.

---

[60] *Livre blanc, reconn. canonique du monastère* (du Barroux) (White Book: Canonical Recognition of Le Barroux Monastery), (St. Madeleine Abbey).

[61] Letter of March 5, 1986; *Le Chardonnet*, no. 37 (June 1988).

[62] Letter of June 27, 1987.

[63] *Bulletin Officiel* of the district, Jan. 1987.

[64] François Pivert, *Des sacres par Mgr. Lefebvre, un schisme?* (Consecrations by Archbishop Lefebvre: A schism?) (Paris: Éd. Fideliter, 1988).

This has nothing to do with setting up a "parallel Church." The aim is simply to continue the Society so that it does not die the death because there is no one to ordain its priests.

And the day the truth of the Church of all time comes back to Rome, these bishops will put their episcopal dignity into the hands of the Pope and say to him: "Here we are. What will you do with us? If you wish, we will live now as simple priests; if you want to make use of us, you can do so."

But what remains is the Society. That is the work of God, willed by God.[65]

At the seminary in Zaitzkofen, the Archbishop asked the key question: "If Rome refused permission for the consecrations, would it be because such an act would be wrong? No, but because it would be against the present liberal, modernist tendencies of Rome." He concluded: "I do not think God wants the Society to disappear when He has given it so many graces. I do not think the good Lord would have said until now: 'Go, go, go!' only now suddenly to say: 'Stop!' When what we do is good, He wants it to continue."[66]

The consecrations, therefore, would only be a humble, provisional measure of self-preservation for the survival of a work that God wills for the good of His Church. Its historical importance, however, would match that of the crisis shaking the Church.

ROME'S REPLY TO THE *DUBIA*—DECISION

The Archbishop saw a "second providential sign" in the reply Rome gave to the *Dubia*[67] on March 9, 1987. In October 1985, he had submitted to the Congregation for the Doctrine of the Faith thirty-nine doubts concerning the discrepancies between the doctrine on religious liberty and the previous teaching of the Church. It may be remembered that this traditional teaching, summed up by Pius IX in his encyclical *Quanta Cura*, recognized the civil authority's "power to use the law to deal with those who violate the Catholic religion" in order to protect the one true religion. Now, the conciliar declaration on religious liberty desired that no human authority should have the power to stop whomsoever publicly exercising an erroneous religious cult merely on the grounds that it is false (*DH* 3).

Rome's reply to the *Dubia* was written in French by a "particularly qualified and trusted theologian"[68]; it was fifty pages long. It considered none of the doubts in particular; whilst it admitted that the doctrine on

---

[65] *Retreats at Ecône*, 77 A, Sept. 8, 1986, *Fideliter*, no. 57: 12; cf. *Letter to priests*, April 27, 1987, in Pivert, *Des sacres par Mgr. Lefebvre*, 57-58.

[66] *Fideliter*, no. 57: 15, 16, 18.

[67] *Mes doutes sur la liberté religieuse*.

[68] Letter of Cardinal Ratzinger, March 9, 1987.

religious liberty was "incontestably a novelty," it claimed that it was the outcome of "doctrinal development in continuity."

With his customary intuition, Marcel Lefebvre immediately got to the heart of the CDF theologian's argument: it was the so-called "social space of autonomous activity" where because of his dignity the person can act publicly in religious matters without the State intervening. "No!" replied Archbishop Lefebvre to Cardinal Ratzinger on July 8, 1987, "There is no domain where the State cannot intervene regarding public, human [moral] acts of individuals in society. Since these acts are public and human, they express a morality that can edify or cause scandal. Insofar as the State believes it has to accept scandal, it acts according to tolerance as spoken of in all Tradition."[69]

The Archbishop wrote to one of his priests, and put the matter succinctly: "Those who hold to this new notion of religious liberty want at any price to make the human person escape in some way from the providential order established by God: *i.e.*, from the societies He has founded and the laws that He has given them to rule over individuals."[70]

When all is said and done, the space of social autonomy is withdrawn from the generous outpouring of the charity of God.[71]

In June 1987, the Archbishop published his book on the destruction of the social reign of our Lord Jesus Christ: *Ils L'ont découronné* (*They Have Uncrowned Him*). It called into question Pope Paul VI, the Council, and "the present day Roman authorities." Then, his sermon on June 29 broke like a crack of thunder. The Archbishop threatened to consecrate bishops. He said Rome's reply to the *Dubia* was the "sign that I was waiting for, a more serious sign than Assisi. For it is one thing to perform a serious and scandalous act, but quite another thing to affirm false principles that in practice have disastrous conclusions," namely, the uncrowning of our Lord Jesus Christ and "the pantheon of all religions."

Witnessing these things had forced him to think about the consequences of this apostasy for the Society ("this work that God has placed in our hands") and for the Church that he did not wish to abandon in the "Passion through which she is living." "There is an obvious necessity. That is why it is likely I will give myself successors to continue this work, for Rome is in darkness."[72] And *in petto* (in secret), he fixed the date for the feast of Christ the King.

The little universe of tradition was shaken by this shot across the bows. Rome was nervous. The Archbishop took advantage of the shock he had caused to move from a threat to a plea. He wrote to Cardinal Ratzing-

[69] Annex to the letter of Archbishop Lefebvre of July 8, 1987.
[70] Letter to Fr. Tissier de Mallerais, May 13, 1987.
[71] Cf. *Spiritual Conferences at Ecône*, 133, March 3 and 6, 1989.
[72] *Fideliter*, no. 58: 2-3, 5-6.

er on July 8: "Through you, we beg the Holy Father to grant freedom to Tradition" and to allow "His Excellency Bishop de Castro Mayer and myself to provide ourselves with auxiliaries of our own choosing."

However, the following words were far from a *captatio benevolentiae*: "A new Magisterium without roots in the past and thereby contrary to the Magisterium of all time can only be schismatic if not heretical. The continued desire to destroy Tradition is suicidal, and in itself justifies true and faithful Catholics taking all the measures necessary to our survival and to the salvation of souls."

III. NEGOTIATIONS

UNEXPECTED OPENNESS FROM ROME[73]

Under pressure, Rome gave in. On July 14, Cardinal Ratzinger received Archbishop Lefebvre at the Holy Office. At first the Cardinal persisted in arguing that "the State is incompetent in religious matters."

"But the State has an ultimate and eternal end," replied the Archbishop.

"Your Grace, that is the case for the Church, not the State. By itself the State does not know."

Archbishop Lefebvre was distraught: a Cardinal and Prefect of the Holy Office wanted to show him that the State can have no religion and cannot prevent the spread of error. However, before talking about concessions, the Cardinal made a threat: the consequence of an illicit episcopal consecration would be "schism and excommunication."

"Schism?" retorted the Archbishop. "If there is a schism, it is because of what the Vatican did at Assisi and how you replied to our *Dubia*: the Church is breaking with the traditional Magisterium. But the Church against her past and her Tradition is not the Catholic Church; this is why being excommunicated by a liberal, ecumenical, and revolutionary Church is a matter of indifference to us."

As this tirade ended, Joseph Ratzinger gave in: "Let us find a practical solution. Make a moderate declaration on the Council and the new missal a bit like the one that Jean Guitton has suggested to you. Then, we would give you a bishop for ordinations, we could work out an arrangement with the diocesan bishops, and you could continue as you are doing. Ask for a Cardinal Protector, make your suggestions."

How did Marcel Lefebvre not jump for joy? Rome was giving in! But his penetrating faith went to the very heart of the Cardinal's rejection of

---

[73] Archbishop Lefebvre, notes from the interview; Fr. Tissier de Mallerais, notes on the meeting of July 22 in St.-Michel-en-Brenne; *Retreats at Ecône*, Sept. 4, 1987; *Le Sel de la Terre*, no. 31.

doctrine. He said to himself: "So, must Jesus no longer reign? Is Jesus no longer God? Rome has lost the Faith. Rome is in apostasy. We can no longer trust this lot!" To the Cardinal, he said:

> Eminence, even if you give us everything—a bishop, some autonomy from the bishops, the 1962 liturgy, allow us to continue our seminaries—we cannot work together because we are going in different directions. You are working to dechristianize society and the Church, and we are working to Christianize them.
>
> For us, our Lord Jesus Christ is everything, He is our life. The Church is our Lord Jesus Christ; the priest is another Christ; the Mass is the triumph of Jesus Christ on the cross; in our seminaries everything tends towards the reign of our Lord Jesus Christ. But you! You are doing the opposite: you have just wanted to prove to me that our Lord Jesus Christ cannot, and must not, reign over society.

Recounting this incident, the Archbishop described the Cardinal's attitude: "Motionless, he looked at me, his eyes expressionless, as if I had just suggested something incomprehensible or unheard of." Then Ratzinger tried to argue that "the Church can still say whatever she wants to the State," while Lefebvre, the intuitive master of Catholic metaphysics, did not lose sight of the true end of human societies: the Reign of Christ. Fr. de Tinguy hit the nail on the head when he said of Marcel Lefebvre: "His faith defies those who love theological quibbles."

"WE CANNOT WORK TOGETHER"

Throughout the summer, the realism of the Archbishop's deep faith—not pessimism, which was not in his character—made him say to himself: "We cannot work together with these enemies of our Lord's reign." However, the letter the Cardinal wrote him on July 28 was encouraging. Starting from a negative premise, it proved to be a prelude to the unprecedented concession of "auxiliaries": "The Holy See cannot grant the Society of Saint Pius X auxiliaries without the Society being given an adequate juridical structure." The letter spoke of granting the Society "its proper autonomy" and confirmed that the seminaries, ordinations, and use of the 1962 missal could continue. It announced the "immediate and unconditional" appointment of a Cardinal Visitor who, it was true, would have to guarantee "the orthodoxy of the teaching" in the seminaries and "the ecclesial spirit," and who would determine who was to receive orders.

On August 22, 1987, in Fatima where the Archbishop went—in the absence of the Pope who was procrastinating—to consecrate Russia to the Immaculate Heart of Mary according to the request of the Blessed Virgin,[74] the Archbishop called a meeting of his closest collaborators: the Superior General, Fr. Schmidberger; the two assistants, Frs. Aulagnier and Bisig; and Frs. Tissier de Mallerais, Williamson, de Galarreta, and Fellay.

He had already chosen some of these to become his "auxiliaries." He underlined the excessive powers that the Cardinal Visitor would have: "It risks dividing us and driving away our seminarians."

"We cannot follow these people. They're in apostasy, they do not believe in the divinity of our Lord Jesus Christ who must reign. What is the use in waiting? Let's do the consecration! I suggest the date of the feast of Christ the King, October 25."

But the general opinion of the collaborators was not to rush into things: "Let us rather wait and see where the Rome opening leads. Let us work out an appropriate canonical structure and obtain permission for the consecration. In this way we will have nothing to reproach ourselves with, we will have tried everything."

The Archbishop seemed to agree with this opinion. However, when he returned to France to stay at Gigondas with his friends Mr. and Mrs. Laurent Meunier, the peace he found there enabled him to get down on paper a letter addressed to the future bishops. It was dated August 29 and was doubtless conceived the evening before (whence the allusion to St. Augustine at the end of the letter) although he did not send it:

My dear Friends:

The See of Peter and the posts of authority in Rome being occupied by anti-Christs, the destruction of the Kingdom of our Lord is being rapidly carried out...especially through the corruption of the Holy Mass which is both the splendid expression of the triumph of our Lord on the Cross—*Regnavit a ligno Deus*—and the source of the extension of His kingdom over souls and over societies....I find myself constrained by Divine Providence to pass on the grace of the Catholic episcopacy which I received, in order that the Church and the Catholic priesthood continue to subsist....I will bestow this grace upon you, confident that without too long a delay the See of Peter will be occupied by a successor of Peter who is perfectly Catholic, and into whose hands you will be able to put back the grace of your episcopacy so that he may confirm it.

Including Christ in the Assisi pantheon and rejecting His reign over society: were these things not a rejection of His divinity, "dissolving Christ" and being, as St. John the Apostle says, an "anti-Christ" (I Jn. 2:22; 4:3)?

Since the venue at Martigny where he had planned to hold the consecration was not available on October 25, he secretly put the date back to December 27, the feast of the Apostle St. John.

---

[74] "Autant qu'il est en Notre pouvoir [As much as it is in our power]," said he. *Fideliter*, no. 59: 136-137.

APOSTOLIC VISIT OF CARDINAL GAGNON

Yet, clearly, Marcel Lefebvre was not a man to be second-guessed. Again he considered and reconsidered Rome's proposals of July 28. "I am no longer asked to make a declaration. They are granting me the Mass, a bishop, a juridical structure of relative autonomy,[75] and they propose a visitor. For such a long time I have asked for this visit so Rome might know us better." Moreover, in August Jean Guitton, the *académicien* who had come to like Marcel Lefebvre, approached Cardinal Ratzinger and requested that the Cardinal Visitor go only on a fact-finding mission and not have any power over the Society. Cardinal Oddi supported this request and Ratzinger agreed, sending a short note to Archbishop Lefebvre via Eric de Saventhem.

Imponderable matters tip the balance of destiny.[76] On October 3 the Archbishop made a public u-turn. Four thousand faithful were gathered at Ecône to give thanks with him for his fortieth episcopal jubilee. All the seminarians were there from Ecône, Zaitzkofen, and Flavigny, and there were numerous priests and religious allies amongst whom was Dom Gérard. To this assembly, the Archbishop said he had been "offered seemingly extraordinary solutions." "There is a glimmer of hope," he said prudently. However: "If Rome really wants to give us true autonomy, like we have now but with our submission—we would like to be submitted to the Holy Father, and we have always wished for it—...if Rome agrees to let us try this experiment of Tradition, there will no longer be any problem."[77]

While the media reported this *coup de théâtre* and spread the news of the "renewal of dialogue," the traditionalist world shook with intense emotion: some with "unspeakable joy," most with "relief," and others with "prudent hope." Meanwhile, Fr. Schmidberger asked for prayers to the Blessed Virgin "to preserve us from all false solutions."[78]

Finally, Cardinal Edouard Gagnon, the Canadian chairman of the Pontifical Council for the Family, arrived in Ecône on November 11. He was the ideal visitor: smiling, kind, patient, and discreet. He never hid his sympathy for the Archbishop's work, and as a priest of St. Sulpice, the issue of priestly training was close to his heart. Mostly accompanied by his gray eminence, the Luxembourgeois Msgr. Camille Perl, he visited the most important houses of the Society and its allies in France, Switzerland, and

---

[75] Handwritten plan for conference to seminarians on Oct. 22, 1987. Letter of Archbishop Lefebvre to Ratzinger, Oct. 1; press conference of Archbishop Lefebvre, Oct. 2; *Spiritual Conferences at Ecône*, 122, Oct. 22, 1987.

[76] Letter of Guitton to Ratzinger, Aug. 4; Letter of Guitton to Archbishop Lefebvre, Aug. 6.

[77] *Fideliter*, no. 60 (Nov.-Dec. 1987): 18-19.

[78] *Nouvelliste du Valais*, Oct. 5; circular letter to superiors, Oct. 1987.

Germany: priories and schools, convents and seminaries, youth groups and novitiates.

Everywhere he went, he was satisfied. Thus, he was anxious to carry back to Rome not only a satisfactory report but also a draft solution. He asked the priests he met: "What sort of solution do you see?" The constant reply was that "a priest of the Society should be consecrated bishop." But then the visitor's face clouded over.

The visit ended on December 8 at Ecône where the Cardinal did not hesitate to assist publicly at a Pontifical Mass of the suspended archbishop and witness young men making their engagement in a suppressed Society. In the seminary's visitors' book, he wrote: "May the Immaculate Virgin hear our fervent prayers that the work of priestly training so marvelously carried out in this place might spread its influence widely for the life of the Church."

NEW ULTIMATUM

By January 5, 1988, his Eminence's report was on the desk of the Pope, who read it immediately. Theoretically very favorable, the document—if we are to believe *30 Giorni*[79]—contained some strange statistics: "Eighty percent of traditionalists desire peace and communion with Rome, more than half are above all scandalized by liturgical abuses, and only fifteen percent come from political or intellectual milieus associated with *Action Française*. Most of the supporters and benefactors of the Archbishop are humble people, but he could be overrun by the 'hardliners' in his movement."[80]

So much for the questionable statistics of Msgr. Perl! The only hardliner was Lefebvre himself, who was unceremoniously shaking Rome with his calm independence. He had already indicated to Cardinal Gagnon his three "demands": to guarantee independence from the diocesan bishops, the Society should have the Superior General as its Ordinary; there should be a Roman commission chaired by a Cardinal but all its members, including the Archbishop-Secretary General, must be nominated by the Superior General; finally, there should be three bishops including the Superior General himself.[81]

The Archbishop had his candidates in mind and also a date which he shared with his closest associates: April 17, Good Shepherd Sunday. In other words, with or without an agreement I will consecrate! However, as

---

[79] [An Italian Catholic magazine published in English as *30 Days*. Trans.]

[80] *30 Giorni*, Feb. 1988; *ABC* and *Nouvelliste du Valais*, Jan. 30-31.

[81] *Proposition de règlement* (Proposal for regularization), annex to a letter to Cardinal Gagnon, Nov. 21, 1987. Archbishop Lefebvre mooted a jurisdictional model similar to the one used for armies as defined in the apostolic constitution *Spirituali Militiæ* of April 21, 1986, *Documentation Catholique*, 1920: 613.

time passed by, nothing came from Rome. April now seemed too soon, and it would be cold: the ceremony was put off to June 30. But then— Who knows how? Through someone's indiscretion?—*Agence France Presse* got hold of a rumor and it spread throughout the media: "New ultimatum from Archbishop Lefebvre: agreement with Vatican on April 17 or schism!"[82] The frightened traditionalists began to tremble; Jean Madiran published the story and then withdrew it.[83]

On February 2 Archbishop Lefebvre confirmed the news: "I am resolved to consecrate at least three bishops on June 30, and I hope to have the approval of John Paul II. But if he were not to give it to me, I would do without it for the good of the Church and for the continuance of Tradition."

He explained the practical side of his decision to Michèle Riboul, an associate of Guitton and writer for *Le Figaro*: "You see, June 30 is the day after the ordinations. The faithful can stay around, and the tent for the priestly ordinations will do for the consecrations."[84]

Alarmed, Gagnon wrote to him: "Your Grace, please! Have some patience and discretion!" Guitton, who was more realistic, simply wrote: "I see your serenity based on the Faith," but keep to your decision and do it in October,[85] *i.e.*, seek for an agreement! However, Lefebvre was not seeking an agreement at any price. He tried his luck but he knew when to stop, or rather he knew exactly what he wanted: the minimum to avoid being contaminated, divided, or absorbed later on, and the "three necessary points" which were always the same and which he again repeated, this time to the Pope in a letter of February 20 in which he added that the "consecration of bishops to succeed me" must be resolved "before June 30."

John Paul met with several cardinals: "What are we going to do?" One of the cardinals made a suggestion: "Someone must write to him and propose something, but it should not be the Holy Father." Casaroli said: "Yes, but I cannot write either; for Archbishop Lefebvre I am the devil!"[86]

Finally, on March 18, Cardinal Ratzinger, who was put in charge of the "regularization," wrote to the Archbishop suggesting that he choose two experts, a canonist and a theologian, to "exchange views concerning concrete proposals" with experts from the Holy See. The Archbishop chose Frs. Patrice Laroche and Bernard Tissier de Mallerais to face Frs. Tarcisio Bertone (future bishop of Verceil) and Fernando Ocariz (of *Opus Dei*), consulters to the CDF, with Fr. Benoît Duroux, O.P., as moderator and Cardinal Ratzinger as chairman.

---

[82] *Le Méridional; Nouvelliste du Valais*, Jan. 30-31. *Le Figaro*, Feb. 1.
[83] *Présent*, Feb. 1, 3, 4, and 5.
[84] *Le Figaro*, Feb. 4, 1988.
[85] Cardinal Gagnon, Feb. 15; J. Guitton, March 14, 1988.
[86] Related by Fr. du Chalard, *Relations between Rome and Ecône*, 1926.

The meetings, held on April 12 and 13 near the Holy Office, led to a declaration in five points. After adding a few corrections on May 4, Archbishop Lefebvre would decide that he could sign it since it allowed him to speak about "certain points of the Council and the reform of the liturgy and Canon Law that seem to him difficult to reconcile with Tradition."

On the other hand, would Rome grant him his three demands? That was where things got a little uncomfortable! Disagreement was open and entire. The commission "working for the Holy Father would be made up of individuals from the Roman congregations": that was all. And the bishops? "You don't need any," said Fr. Duroux, "once you are approved 'by pontifical right,' you will have all the world's bishops to do ordinations." But in the end Fr. Bertone conceded: "For practical and psychological reasons, one could foresee the usefulness of consecrating a bishop from within the Society."

Concerning autonomy from the diocesan bishops, "confirmations by the Ordinaries in their jurisdiction must be recognized; we must not officially approve a state of division." As regards the present liturgy, Ratzinger considered that "the rites must be mutually accepted." And as for the communities linked with the Society, Duroux nodded his agreement that "they should be reincorporated in their respective orders" with, however, "a particular statute."

THE SIGNATURE OF MAY 5

The outlook was gloomy. In search of some light, the Archbishop tried to dislodge the cardinal out of his entrenched positions: regarding as a given what had only been envisaged, he said he was "delighted to have a successor in the episcopate," and in the same breath asked for a "second within six months." As for the Commission, he said "I would want to give it my assistance."[87] This really meant: I will be on it!

Ratzinger responded to this impetuous harassment by stalling for time. Concerning "the problem of appointing a bishop, the Holy Father is inclined to consider your proposal," but such an appointment cannot take place immediately "because of the time necessary to examine the candidates profiles." No matter! On May 3, Archbishop Lefebvre sent the names of four episcopal candidates, and said he would soon submit their files.

On May 3, in a discreet convent on the Via Aurelia, the decisive meeting took place between the Archbishop and the Cardinal with their respective experts. A declaration was drawn up without a hitch, and the process of normalization posed no difficulties. Then Ratzinger ventured: "I think

---

[87] Letter of April 15, 1988, to Cardinal Ratzinger.

that in addition to the Masses of the Society, St. Nicolas du Chardonnet should have a parish mass; the Church is one."

Straightaway Marcel Lefebvre was wary and opened his eyes: "So," he said to himself, "they want the rites to cohabit within the Conciliar Church." And when the Cardinal went through the make-up of the Roman Commission—"a cardinal as chairman, a vice-chairman or Roman secretary, five members with two from the Society, one of whom would work in its main office"—the Archbishop went quiet: "Understood!"

Then his Eminence confirmed that it would be "suggested" to the Holy Father "to appoint a bishop chosen from within the Society, nominated by Archbishop Lefebvre." The Archbishop remained silent.

"There remains the question of the date for the consecrations," observed shrewdly the hard-nosed Fr. Patrice Laroche. The moment of truth had come when all would be revealed. The Cardinal now fell silent. So, Fr. Laroche suggested: "Before the end of the Marian Year? Before the 15th of August?"

"All departments are closed then," replied the Cardinal.

The Archbishop asked, "What about All Saints?" and added, "Our colleagues were expecting June 30."

The Cardinal avoided the question: "Let Archbishop Lefebvre say that everything is being seen to."

They ate lunch together but the gathering was unusually silent. Afterwards, the Archbishop said forcefully to his two assistants: "Let's stop now. I do not want to continue! Did you hear the Cardinal? Cohabitation, a minority on the Commission, and no date for the consecration!"

Nevertheless, the meeting continued: "As soon as Your Grace has signed the protocol, a press communiqué will relay the progress made in the reconciliation," said the Cardinal.

"I have a bishop," thought Archbishop Lefebvre, "but for what kind of reconciliation?"

It was with these mixed feelings that on May 5, the Feast of St. Pius V (which seemed to the Archbishop a good sign), he put his signature on the declaration and wrote an accompanying letter to the Pope in which he expressed his desire to see the protocol's measures fully realized. He did not speak explicitly of the consecration. Finally, he signed the protocol which was brought to him at Albano at 4:30 P.M. by Fr. Josef Clemens, the Cardinal's secretary. The photo taken at the time shows the Archbishop half smiling, half frowning, leaning over the text that he is rereading carefully. His face perfectly expresses the mixed feelings which gripped him: "real satisfaction," as he would write to Ratzinger, and silent mistrust which he spoke of to the sisters in the *Cenacolo* convent at 3 P.M.: "If Don Putti were here, what would he say? 'Your Grace, where are you going? What are you doing?'"

"RISK IT ON ONE TURN OF PITCH AND TOSS"

"Marcel, what's going to become of you?" The Archbishop prayed with his head in his hands throughout the rosary and Benediction in the chapel, sometimes sighing. Then without saying anything, he retired to his room. He did not sleep that night. He was thinking: "They do not want to give us a date because they do not want to give us a bishop." He was seized by doubts and said to himself: "I must absolutely know what will happen with the appointment of a bishop." Later he shared all this with his driver and confidant, Jacques Lagneau: "If only you knew what a night I passed after signing that infamous agreement! Oh! How I wanted morning to come so that I could give Fr. du Chalard my letter of retraction which I had written during the night."[88]

The following day after Mass and Prime, he finished off his letter and put it in an envelope which he showed to Fr. du Chalard at breakfast: "Father, before leaving, it is essential that this letter be taken to Cardinal Ratzinger. It's a little bomb."[89]

It was a new ultimatum:

> The date of June 30 was clearly given as a deadline in one of my previous letters. I have given you a file concerning the candidates. There are still nearly two months to prepare the mandate....The Holy Father can easily shorten the process so that the mandate can be sent by mid-June.
>
> Were the reply to be in the negative, I would see myself obliged in conscience to go ahead with the consecration, basing my actions on the Holy See's agreement in the protocol for the consecration of a bishop from within the Society.
>
> The obvious reticence in your letters and our discussions with regard to the episcopal consecration of a member of the Society gives me legitimate cause for concern.

For Archbishop Lefebvre, fixing a date was the test of Rome's sincerity, the proof that he was not being hoodwinked and that Rome would not simply wait for him to die: "*Muerto el perro, se acabó la rabia*" as the Spanish proverb goes. In English, "The rabies dies with the rabid dog."

Unfortunately, Ratzinger did not seem to understand; he simply canceled the press communiqué. On May 6 in the evening, he saw the Holy Father and gave him the letter the Archbishop had written for him on May 5, but said nothing about the ultimatum. He thought he could not disturb the Pope, and that he had to follow the plan he had drawn up: firstly, lift the suspension after the Archbishop's request for pardon (without doubt for the "little cartoons" that had shocked John Paul II), then establish the Roman Commission, then regularization... But all that would take time.

88 Jacques Lagneau, *Souvenirs d'un chauffeur* (n.p.: April 21, 1997), 16.
89 Related by Fr. Anthony Esposito, *Relations between Rome and Ecône*, 1909; talk at St. Nicolas du Chardonnet, May 10, 1988.

Without even waiting for his meeting with the Pope, he wrote to the Archbishop and asked him "to reconsider his position."

The Archbishop returned to Ecône; his chauffeur noticed he was "unusually sad and quiet." On May 10, he explained the situation in detail to his priests at St. Nicolas du Chardonnet: "The ball is in their court and I am waiting for them to reply. June 30 is the deadline. I feel I am coming to the end of my life, my strength is failing; I find it difficult to travel by car. I cannot put it off any longer; I would be endangering the future of the Society and our seminaries. As I said on the television in Germany: on June 30 there will be episcopal consecrations, with or without Rome's agreement."[90]

On May 17 Ratzinger wrote to Lefebvre: a letter to the Holy Father "humbly requesting" reconciliation and forgiveness would be welcome; the request for a bishop from the Society could be raised "without demanding any date." Had Archbishop Lefebvre already received this letter when on May 20 he decided to write directly to the Pope? Not only did he underline that June 30 was for him the deadline to assure "his succession," but he also considered it necessary to have several bishops.

On May 23, he left for Rome: "This meeting is the last chance," he said to his driver Marcel Pedroni, who noticed he looked tired and sad on the morning of the 24th.

"Are you not well, Your Grace?"

"I did not sleep. I have barely slept for months."

In Rome on May 24, the Archbishop gave the Cardinal his final request: "Before June 1, let me know the Holy See's intentions as regards the consecration of three bishops planned for June 30, and concerning the majority of traditionalists on the commission. As I wrote to the Pope, one bishop alone will not be enough for all of the apostolate."[91]

Ratzinger was "a little taken aback" but he passed on the request.

John Paul II replied through the Cardinal on May 30; the request concerning the Society's majority on the commission was rejected because it would not be necessary; as for the bishops, "the Holy Father is ready to appoint a bishop from the Society…such that the consecration could take place before August 15."[92] To this end, the Archbishop had to send a larger number of files so the Holy Father could freely choose a candidate with "a profile as foreseen by the agreements." The Archbishop had to "have trust in the Holy Father and the Lord."

The invitation "to have trust" could not have been more misplaced. The Archbishop was above all concerned to "preserve the traditional fami-

---

[90] *Relations between Rome and Ecône*, 1947, 1956.
[91] Archbishop Lefebvre then gave the Cardinal his letter to the Pope of May 20 and one for Ratzinger himself, dated that day, May 24.
[92] John Paul II himself said: "*intro l'anno mariano*" (within the Marian Year).

ly" from division, contamination by modern errors, or compromise with post-conciliar reform. So, he wrote a note: "The mood of the meetings and the thinking expressed by various individuals in conversation clearly show that the Holy See wants to bring us into line with the Council and its reforms, and to bring us back within the bosom of the Conciliar Church.[93] Consequently, do we really need to consider the 'advantages' of the 'canonical normalization' of our work, the guarantee for the 'liturgy and the training of our members, easier missionary contacts to convert priests and faithful to Tradition, and finally a bishop consecrated with the agreement of the Holy See'?"

MEETING AT LE POINTET—DISCUSSIONS BROKEN OFF

For years the Archbishop had prayed to the Holy Ghost to enlighten him, and to the Blessed Virgin to guide him. Every night in March 1987, when he could not sleep, he got up to pray. He often exclaimed: "Oh! If only the Blessed Virgin could appear to me to tell me what I must do." But he had to fall back on his own reason enlightened by faith.

Lately he had readily questioned his drivers, to whom he was close. "What would you do in my position?" "What should I say?" Marcel Pedroni asked himself. "He does not need my advice."[94] "What does Divine Providence want?" was his favorite question. On May 25, 1988, at Albano, he asked his priests: "What must I do?" Then he added: "I am not the Superior General, I must refer the matter to Father Schmidberger." The Superior General, who was contacted by telephone in America, canceled his trip to Canada, and came quickly to Rome.[95]

In 1984, the Archbishop had consulted "the leaders" of Traditionalist resistance on the subject of the "indult Mass": Msgr. Ducaud-Bourget, Frs. André, Coache, Vinson, Dom Guillou, *etc.* Similarly, he now decided to call a meeting on May 30, 1988, at the priory of Our Lady of Le Pointet to gather together the great priest defenders of the Faith and the superiors of the allied religious communities, both monks and nuns.

"I am inclined to consecrate four bishops anyway on June 30. My age and my failing health urge me, before the good Lord calls me to Him, to assure the safeguarding, not of 'my work,' but of this modest venture to restore the priesthood and preserve the Catholic Faith. This I can do by giving the episcopacy to 'bishops who are free to make the Faith live,' 'in a

---

[93] "Exposé de la situation concernant ce que Rome appelle la 'réconciliation'" (*Exposé* concerning the situation that Rome calls the "reconciliation"), notes drawn up for the meeting of May 30.

[94] M. Pedroni, notes from the road and memoirs.

[95] Related by Frs. Esposito and du Chalard, *Relations between Rome and Ecône*, 1912, 1918.

setting that is entirely cut off from modern errors,' as I wrote to John Paul II on May 20. I want to know what you think."

Everyone was touched by the Archbishop's attentiveness, his concern to keep them informed, and his desire to find a consensus among the veterans as well as among the younger religious superiors. Everyone understood the importance of the meeting, which would ensure that when sanctions and calumny began raining down after the consecrations, Tradition would stand together united.[96]

By telephone, Fr. du Chalard related the contents of Cardinal Ratzinger's letter dated the same day: the candidates nominated by Archbishop Lefebvre were not satisfactory. They did not have the right "profile." Would Rome find in the Society an episcopal candidate with the right profile, *i.e.*, accommodating, weak, and completely liberal? It was not an idle threat; Msgr. Perl had carefully studied the possibilities during the Apostolic visit.

Then, each member of this little Council of Tradition gave his opinion frankly. Fr. Lecareux, the Capuchins, and Fathers Coache and Tissier de Mallerais were in favor of the agreements. So was Dom Gérard: "If a break happens we will become sociologically a sect like the 'little churches' who never come back to the larger Church." As for the dangers mentioned by the Archbishop: "It is up to us to defend ourselves! Let us not underestimate our strength which is in our doctrine; let us draw up a common charter of charity, a Catholic pact to do nothing to harm our united front or create discord amongst our brothers."

Fr. André said quite the opposite: "Let us press our demands. Otherwise let us keep our liberty and put up with the accusations and label of excommunication."

Fr. Aulagnier talked the language of prudence: "In Rome there is a theological and philosophical system of thought that opposes the thinking of the Church. I'm afraid of this agreement; I am afraid it is a trick of the devil, our enemy. I do not see myself discussing with Lustiger, Decourtray, and the Pope of Assisi. The consecrated bishop would have no moral authority. I fear Roman bureaucracy. 'I adhere to Catholic Rome and reject Modernist Rome,' which could prove to be the Leviathan that devours us."

The Sisters were almost all categorical: "We cannot deal with bishops who have lost the Faith," said the Dominicans of Fanjeaux. The Sisters of Brignoles considered that depending on Rome would force them into having "contacts with their former congregations that are now modernist," and "that is impossible." The Society Sisters mentioned "the risk for the

---

[96] Aulagnier, *La Tradition sans peur*, 182-184.

Faith and cohesion of Tradition." Finally, the Carmelites said that it was "a Trojan horse within Tradition."

Archbishop Lefebvre, who had objectively set out the advantages and disadvantages of the agreement, indicated finally which way the balance was now tilting. The principle he invoked is enlightening: "The official link with modernist Rome is nothing against the preservation of the Faith!"[97]

As the meeting closed, everyone promised: "We will go along with the decision of the Archbishop."

Then, however, Dom Gérard took the Archbishop aside: "The monastery's circumstances are particular, and attempting to have normalization is not as dangerous for us as for the Society."

The Archbishop conceded the point: "For you, it is not the same thing. You have your monks around you whereas I have eighty priories and five hundred chapels. It would be division."[98]

But the division the Archbishop was implying was between Le Barroux and the Society. Dom Gérard did not understand. Forgetting his idea of a pact and a united front, he would negotiate a separate agreement with the Roman authorities.

IV. THE CONSECRATIONS

ALONE ABLE TO MAKE THE DECISION

Having asked for advice, Archbishop Lefebvre now had to decide. Such is the virtue of prudence: slow to think things through and prompt in deciding. He would make this decision alone. The Vatican believed him to be the "prisoner of his entourage," and on the eve of the consecrations expressly sent a large Mercedes to Ecône to rescue him from his supposed jailers. He later said: "It is surprising that they always talk about my entourage, while it is I who have led my entourage to the consecrations."[99]

It was true: neither the tenacious Schmidberger nor the effervescent Aulagnier had driven him to it. Archbishop Lefebvre was the only one able to make the decision to consecrate. Filled with a sense of the Church since his seminary studies in Rome, then in Africa as Delegate and confidant of Pius XII, and as herald of the Faith during the Council, who better than he to judge Authority's betrayal of the truth of the Church? As a Catholic bishop and a successor of the Apostles for forty years, he felt deeply the terrible responsibility on his shoulders. He felt that he alone was in a posi-

---

[97] According to the author's notes and the Archbishop's *exposé* given out to those in attendance.

[98] *Livre Blanc, reconn. canon. du monastère, 1970-1990.*

[99] Aulagnier, *La Tradition sans peur*, 183.

tion to judge that the exceptional measures he envisaged for the common good were legitimate, Catholic, and far from being illicit. He also considered that rather than being sinful his actions were good and virtuous. He said after the consecrations: "If I had thought in my conscience I was committing a sin, I would not have done it."[100]

Thus on the feast of Corpus Christi, June 2, 1988, he sent his decision in writing to the Pope:

> Given the refusal to consider our requests, and it being evident that the purpose of this reconciliation is not at all the same in the eyes of the Holy See as it is in our eyes, we believe it preferable to wait for times more propitious for the return of Rome to Tradition.
>
> That is why we shall give ourselves the means to carry on the work which Providence has entrusted to us, being assured by His Eminence Cardinal Ratzinger's letter of May 30, that the episcopal consecration is not contrary to the will of the Holy See, since it was granted for August 15.
>
> We shall continue to pray for modern Rome, infested with Modernism, to become once more Catholic Rome and to rediscover its two thousand year old tradition. Then the problem of our reconciliation will have no further reason to exist and the Church will experience a new youth.[101]

HOW DOES ONE GO ABOUT AN HISTORICAL ACTION?

The letter John Paul II wrote him on June 9 calling his plans "a schismatic act" could not stop Archbishop Lefebvre. Faced with his firmness, Rome backed off again, and Fr. Duroux suggested reconsidering the make-up of the Commission. Cardinal Ratzinger's secretary had a long meeting with the Archbishop in Ecône on June 10: but there was no outcome. Dom Gérard, who came to plead the cause of his monastery's independence on June 3, returned to Le Barroux empty-handed.

The Archbishop secured the agreement of the four priests on whom his choice had gradually settled. Sometimes he questioned whichever driver was with him: "Who would you have?" And he wanted names![102] The seminarians were making forecasts with wild abandon. It was only on June 13 that the four candidates appeared together at Ecône: the Englishman Richard Williamson, rector of the North American seminary; the Spaniard Alfonso de Galarreta, the District Superior in South America; the young Swiss Bernard Fellay, the General Bursar, who had spent his youth close to Ecône; and the Frenchman Bernard Tissier de Mallerais, the Secretary General. These last two candidates were resident at Rickenbach along with

---

[100] *Retreats at Ecône*, 89 (3 A), Sept. 19, 1988; cf. *Fideliter*, no. 123: 28-29.
[101] *Fideliter* special edition, June 29-30, 1988.
[102] Ms. III, 34.

the Superior General Fr. Schmidberger, who teased them: "Excellency..."
"There is no Excellency here!" was the usual reply.

Far from it, they would be "auxiliary prelates of the Church," condemned to excommunication, or what would pass for it. But they trusted the Archbishop and cheerfully did their duty: "The Archbishop has the graces to decide, and we have the grace to follow him."[103]

Archbishop Lefebvre prepared the ceremony carefully: the tent for the consecrations, the large book of ceremonies, and the four little barrels of wine which the future bishops would offer him. He went to Rome to buy pectoral crosses, and he had pastoral rings made and violet cassocks tailored. He took the time to explain his actions to the seminarians in Ecône and Flavigny, and approved articles and pamphlets explaining matters to the faithful. He knew perfectly well how to use the media whom he invited to Ecône for a press conference on June 15: it started just after he had arrived by car from another trip.

The handouts for the press prepared by the rector, Fr. Alain Lorans, included a public declaration by the Archbishop which had remained amongst his papers since it was written on October 19...1983. It reads: "The Church holds all communion with false religions and heresy...in horror. The only unity she recognizes is within her bosom....To safeguard the Catholic priesthood which perpetuates the Church and not an adulterous Church [sic], there must be Catholic bishops."

He always wrote in the same style—concise, incisive, forceful, and true. The declaration was accompanied by a long text written by the Archbishop on March 29, 1988. There was also a study by a professor of Canon Law from Mayence, Georg May, on the law of necessity in the Church, "the group of juridical rules which apply when the continuance or activity of the Church is under threat."[104]

When the Archbishop had finished his *exposé*, the questions came thick and fast from the hundred journalists who were crammed into a large classroom:

"The schism will drive numerous faithful away from you..."

"Well, we will see. Even if it lasts ten or twenty years."

Archbishop Lefebvre calmly answered all the questions with a kindness that amazed all the reporters. This did not stop one of them openly confessing to a seminarian as he left: "I'm going to bring your boss down in flames!"[105] Indeed, the following day the headlines in the press all crowed in chorus: "Archbishop Lefebvre: the schism announced" (Jean Bourdarias, *Le Figaro*, June 16); "Archbishop Lefebvre at the gates of hell" (*Le Quotidien*); "He is defying John Paul II" (*Tribune de Genève*). There

---

[103] *Fideliter*, no. 123 (May-June 1988): 29.
[104] *Notwehr, Widerstand, Notstand* (Legitimate defense, resistance, necessity), 1984.
[105] Diary of Ecône, June 15, 1988.

were other more fanciful headlines: "The Holy War" or: "Miter Wars." And the more conventional: "Schism Scheduled" or "The Rift."

André Frossard, who is occasionally inspired, went at the story in a light-hearted manner that did not conceal his article's overall weaknesses: "What is most saddening is the determination of the prelate from Ecône to show no appreciation for the generosity of a Pope who would have gone far, indeed very far, to stop him going down the road to schism. He is the prisoner of terribly rigid ideas that leave his intelligence but little room for flexibility. He is the prisoner of his organization. Perhaps from the logic of his disobedience, he could only carry on to a rift. Nevertheless he did not have to take things to the absurd."[106]

Jean Guitton, his liberal friend, wrote to the Archbishop on June 21. It was a final letter written in blood red ink: "I have always defended you. I said you were a 'mutineer' and not a 'mutant' and that you were fighting for the Truth which cannot change in its essence....In my life June 30 will be a date which will wound me more deeply than anything else....I ask you to receive me alone before June 30...so that like a son to his father I can say to you that word so full of hope and of mystery that one says at final partings...A-DIEU!"[107]

VICTORY

The Archbishop rose above the insults and pleas, and calmly ignored Cardinal Gantin's monition.[108] Smiling and relaxed, he was delighted to give a solemn welcome at Ecône on June 25 to his friend Bishop Antonio de Castro Mayer, Bishop Emeritus of Campos, who had come with several of his priests. Then on the 29th, he proceeded to ordain fifteen priests. In the afternoon he received his friend Guitton and listened to him, as friendly as ever but unbending.

"I admire your calm," said Guitton.

"The thing that makes me calm," replied the Archbishop, "is that I feel I am doing the will of God. That is more important than anything. And then, what will be, will be. Since I intend to do the will of God and not to separate myself from the Church of Peter, I am at peace."[109]

---

[106] *Le Figaro*, June 16, 1988.

[107] [The English "Goodbye," like the French word "Adieu," comes from a blessing: "God be with you." But "Adieu" is used when one will not see one's interlocutor for a long time, or never again. Since Guitton was a member of the Académie Française, he probably did not choose this particular word at random either in his letter or in his final farewell to the Archbishop. Trans.]

[108] Prefect of the Sacred Congregation for Bishops, monition of June 17, 1988, enjoining the Archbishop not to follow through on his plans under pain of excommunication *ipso facto* as foreseen in Canon 1382 of the Code of Canon Law.

[109] Jean Guitton, *Un siècle, une vie* (Paris: Robert Laffont).

And they said "Adieu."

In the evening, a messenger from the nunciature brought a telegram from Cardinal Ratzinger: "The Holy Father asks you paternally but firmly to leave today for Rome without further ado, *etc.*"

The Archbishop confided in Fr. Cottard: "If today they brought me the pontifical mandate duly signed, I would put the consecrations back to August 15 and make an announcement about it tomorrow."

But he had not to think about it any more.

The following day, June 30, 1988, in the morning, the field of Ecône filled up with ten thousand faithful who had come from all over the world. Journalists flooded in and were seated on a special platform from where they had a sweeping view of the sanctuary. The procession set off: seminarians from several of the Society's six seminaries, hundreds of priests and religious (amongst whom was Dom Gérard), the masters of ceremonies, the *consecrandi*, the sacred ministers, and the two consecrating bishops. A helicopter that had been circling suddenly dove towards the procession but it was only to get a better camera shot.

The ceremony began with the reading of the pontifical mandate: "Do you have the Apostolic mandate?"

"We have it."

"Let it be read!"

"We have the mandate of the Roman Church ever-faithful to the holy traditions received from the Apostles..."

Then in a simple and lively style, Archbishop Lefebvre presented a beautiful explanation of the case of necessity in which he found himself, and of his duty to pass on the episcopacy:

> ...I am simply a bishop of the Catholic Church who is continuing to transmit Catholic doctrine. I think, and this will certainly not be too far off, that you will be able to engrave on my tombstone these words of St. Paul: "*Tradidi quod et accepi*—I have transmitted to you what I have received," nothing else....
>
> It seems to me, my dear brethren, that I hear the voices of all these Popes—Gregory XVI, Pius IX, Leo XIII, St. Pius X, Benedict XV, Pius XI, Pius XII—telling us: "Please, we beseech you, what are you going to do with our teachings, with our preaching, with the Catholic Faith? Are you going to abandon it? Are you going to let it disappear from this earth? Please, please, continue to keep this treasure which we have given you. Do not abandon the faithful, do not abandon the Church. Continue the Church! Indeed, since the Council, what we formerly condemned the present Roman authorities have embraced and are professing."

Now, to pass on the Faith intact, there must be priests, and "there cannot be priests without bishops." From whom will these seminarians receive the sacrament of orders? From Modernist bishops? I cannot leave them orphans "dying without having done anything for the future. This would go against my duty."

The Archbishop, therefore, would respond to the silent pleas of all the Popes, and together with Bishop de Castro Mayer pass on the episcopacy that he had received. Thus would they perform "Operation Survival" for Catholic Tradition. When this Tradition has recovered its rightful place in Rome "we will be embraced by the Roman Authorities and they will thank us for having kept the Faith."[110]

In passing and with a mischievous smile, he teased the media who "will no doubt flash up headlines like: 'Schism and Excommunication!' But we are convinced that all these accusations and penalties to which we are subject are completely invalid."

The Archbishop sat down, and then it was the turn of Bishop de Castro Mayer to speak with the same concise pastoral and theological forcefulness:

> We live in an unprecedented crisis in the Church, a crisis which touches it in its essence, in its substance even, which is the Holy Sacrifice of the Mass and the Catholic Priesthood, the two mysteries essentially united, because without the holy Priesthood there is no Holy Sacrifice of the Mass, and, consequently, no form of public worship whatsoever. Equally, it is on this basis that one constructs the social reign of our Lord Jesus Christ....
> . I am here to accomplish my duty: to make a public Profession of Faith....I wish to manifest here my sincere and profound adherence to the position of His Excellency Archbishop Marcel Lefebvre, which is dictated by his fidelity to the Church of all centuries. The two of us have drunk at the same source, which is that of the Holy, Catholic, Apostolic, and Roman Church.[111]

When he heard these words of unity from his friend and fellow bishop, the Archbishop's face relaxed and lit up, and his heart grew light. True, he was not alone. The Church was there that morning. It was she who motivated him, carried him, and supported him in all his deeds. For ten days, he had been saying: "My head is banging day and night." In the sacristy at the end of the ceremony, he said to his assistants: "I thought I wasn't going to last out till the end." But when a little before he had placed the miters on the heads of his sons, all those present noticed the Archbishop's radiant joy as his face lit up with a triumphant smile. A profound joy followed on the calm firmness of the evening before, and it carried his exhausted body through the day. The Archbishop had not gone about the consecrations ill at ease and worried. With the rules for the discernment of spirits, we can discern behind this calm happiness the peace of a good con-

---

[110] *Fideliter*, no. 64 (July.-August 1988): 4-8.
[111] *Ibid.*, 9.

science. We can even judge indirectly the moral goodness of the act performed.

Archbishop Lefebvre could now sing his *Nunc Dimittis*: "Let now, Lord, Thy servant depart in peace..." He had truly passed on what he had to pass on at the moment selected by Providence; he acted neither too soon nor too late and in full possession of his faculties. And during the three years that God would leave him from 1988 to his death on March 25, 1991, he would accompany in spirit his four young auxiliaries and initiate his heirs in their responsibilities. From then on he allowed them to perform ordinations ceremonies which he would quietly attend following with his keen eyes the actions of his sons as they in turn passed on the priesthood.

Above the greatness of soul residing in this attitude of humility, there was a deep desire to assume responsibility for his decisions and to follow those decisions through.[112] And in that sad gaze lit up by the flame of an inextinguishable faith, what a profound understanding he showed of the importance of those decisions for the future!

---

[112] Cf. Aulagnier, *La Tradition sans peur*, 184.

CHAPTER 20

I HAVE HANDED ON
WHAT I RECEIVED

I. THE MOST MAGNANIMOUS ACT

Faced with a disastrous situation in which the salvation of souls, the purity of the priesthood, and the Faith were in decline, Archbishop Lefebvre showed great discernment and a capacity for mature, prudent decision-making. Alone able to provide a solution to this "need for wholly Catholic bishops to continue the Catholic Church,"[1] and moreover, given Rome's paralysis and "spiritual AIDS," he deliberated, decided, and acted with a sense of the love of the Church. The solution provided by the consecrations constituted, as Fr. Philippe Laguérie wrote, "Archbishop Lefebvre's most magnanimous act: when it came to the honor of Jesus Christ, the whole world could not make him cower."[2]

HUNGER AND THIRST FOR JUSTICE

The Church must one day judge whether this act was heroic. To deny it was thus would be easy: did not Archbishop Lefebvre go in the direction he was tending? His "obstinate" character, his complete trust in *his* principles, his self-confident judgment, and, finally, his allergy to liberalism: would all these things not inevitably have inclined him to assume the role of the "lone knight"? Readers who have come this far will know how to correct these clichés, and think of the Archbishop as a man of the Church who was respectful towards authority, long-suffering obedient, loyal to his superiors, an enemy of any conspicuous or scandalous opposition, and a man of prayer and wisdom whose only desire was to follow Providence. At least the reader should be able to ask himself: is not the Archbishop's conduct to be explained by a special grace attached to his particular mission? This grace enabled him to meet all the demands of a mission which

---

[1] Lefebvre, *Itinéraire spirituel*, prologue.
[2] Quoted by Joseph Lagneau. We make use here of his *Points de vue autour des sacres* (Opinions concerning the Consecrations), a text sent to Archbishop Lefebvre "by a witness," on Nov. 19, 1989.

he clearly foresaw, but which he carried out day by day, cost what it may, according to the indications of Providence.

He always wanted to "follow" Providence. However, confidence is not nonchalance. His friend Fr. Calmel was well aware of this: "Leaving things up to the grace of God is not to do nothing! It is to do everything in our power, while continuing in love." Holy abandonment is found "not in resignation and laziness but at the heart of action and initiative."[3] It would be dishonest to pray to God for victory without actually fighting for it.[4] Here we find magnanimity: responding generously to divine grace. Magnanimity asks us to give something beyond prayer that one must pay for with one's own person: "The things I pray for," St. Thomas More prayed magnanimously, "dear Lord, give me the grace to work for."

For those readers who would accuse us of not having the necessary critical distance, or of resorting lazily to panegyric, we will leave it to another St. Thomas, the Angelic Doctor, to paint a picture of the magnanimous man.

Magnanimity means conceiving of and doing great things for some vast and glorious end; it is an integral part of the virtue of Fortitude and helps man not to falter before the dangers involved in carrying out some undertaking. By "great things," we must understand those things that are worthy of great honor. If doing them incurs some undeserved dishonor, the magnanimous man is not discouraged, but scorns such fate. Thus to do what is truly great he confronts danger, not through love of risk like the foolhardy but as a man who is unperturbed, the opposite of the timorous soul who only becomes timid through some blameworthy action. The strong man is as determined to persevere in difficult undertakings as he is to bear with painful set-backs.

If he thinks himself worthy to do great things, it is because of the gifts that God has given him, for as a humble man, he is aware of his faults, and sees himself as nothing. Thus, magnanimity combined with humility becomes Christian virtue.

Of course, it belongs to the virtue of Fortitude not to falter in doing good in spite of contradiction. But as for fully accomplishing some good work and coming thereby to eternal life—the ultimate end of all good works—that is a gift of the Holy Ghost, who alone infuses into the soul the confidence that drives out any contrary fear.

Does not our Lord promise beatitude to the magnanimous? Since they aspire to, and labor for, the great works of justice, they are assured of seeing their desires fulfilled both in this world and in the next: "Blessed are they that hunger and thirst after justice, for they shall have their fill" (Mt. 5:6).[5]

---

3   Article in *Itinéraires*: "De véritable abandon" (True Abandonment).
4   *Itinéraires*, no. 325-326 (July-Aug. 1988), Jean Madiran, quoting Charles Péguy.

THOSE WHO NEITHER HUNGER NOR THIRST

Sitting to one side at the top of the slope that led down to the consecration tent, Dom Gérard distanced himself from the proceedings. On the afternoon of June 30, 1988, he left his friend Laurent Meunier aghast by saying: "This nonsense has lasted long enough, this meeting, all this applause. We can do nothing more here, let's go home!" On July 26 at Gigondas, he met Archbishop Lefebvre for the last time. At the end of a meeting lasting four hours, the monk assured the Archbishop: "We will do nothing with Rome without consulting you."[6] However, the agreement had already virtually been ready since June 16. Dom Gérard had even written to the Pope on June 8: "We object to any idea of separating ourselves from the Church by approving of an episcopal consecration conferred without apostolic mandate."[7] And on July 29, the monastery of Le Barroux was integrated within "the visible perimeters of the Church," as Dom Gérard said. Archbishop Lefebvre lamented the defection of one for whom he had done so much.

He was almost more moved by the loss to the Society of fifteen priests and fifteen seminarians following the decree of his excommunication and John Paul II's *motu proprio Ecclesia Dei Adflicta* (The Church of God afflicted). In Rome on July 5 and 6, the Pope received Fr. Josef Bisig along with seven other priests, and welcomed their plan to found a new priestly society. This was done on July 8 at the Cistercian abbey of Hauterive near Fribourg. According to their press release, the founding members canonically elected Fr. Bisig as Superior General, and Frs. Denis Coiffet (a Frenchman) and Gabriel Baumann (a Swiss) as his assistants. All were former members of the Society of Saint Pius X.

Like Le Barroux and other priestly and religious organizations of the same ilk, the Priestly Society of Saint Peter depends on the pontifical commission *Ecclesia Dei* as foreseen in the *motu proprio* "to provide for the full ecclesial communion of priests *etc.* who wish to remain united to the successor of Peter in the Catholic Church while preserving their spiritual and liturgical traditions."[8] So, it is a question of taste and preference rather than of a fight for the Faith.

In favor "of all those who feel themselves bound to the Latin liturgical tradition," John Paul II recommended to the bishops "a wide and generous application" of the indult of October 3, 1984. The regime of the indult

---

[5] *Summa Theologica*, II II, q. 128, a. 1; a. 2, c. and ad 3; a. 3, ad 4; a. 5, ad 2 and 3; q. 139, a. 1 and 2.

[6] Interview with Laurent Meunier, May 31, 1997, pp. 2, 11.

[7] *Fideliter*, no. 67 (Jan.-Feb. 1989): 10. The monk's remark was convoluted.

[8] Motu proprio *Ecclesia Dei Adflicta*, July 2, 1988, *Documentation Catholique* 1967 (Aug. 7, 1988): 789, (no. 6); *Fideliter*, no. 65: 13-14.

Mass was thus established within the unpredictable limits of the bishops' generosity towards a particular religious sensibility.

THE PSYCHOLOGY OF "ECCLESIA DEI"

The "Ecclesia Dei" Catholics are driven by various things. Fr. Bisig is the noblest with his faith in Rome; but his is an ill-informed faith that wishes to forget that Rome is occupied. He deals with a Rome that is happy to snatch a few followers from the "excommunicated" Archbishop and bring them back very gently to Vatican II. Archbishop Lefebvre commented: "It is obvious that by putting themselves in the hands of the present conciliar authorities, they implicitly accept the Council and the reforms that came from it, even if they receive privileges which remain exceptional and provisional. Their acceptance stops them saying anything. The bishops are watching them."[9]

Occupied Rome is also happy to prove that the situation of necessity asserted by the Archbishop does not exist. You see, they say, we give you everything that we offered to Archbishop Lefebvre on May 5: the Mass, the seminaries, continuation of ordinations according to the 1962 rite, pontifical right. Everything...except for a bishop!

"Precisely," as Archbishop Lefebvre emphasized, "what sort of bishop would it be if ever Rome granted one to 'Ecclesia Dei'"?

"What bishop? A bishop who suits the Vatican. In this case they would have a bishop who would lead them very gently back to the Council. It is obvious. They will never have a bishop who is fully traditional and opposed to the errors of the Council and the post-conciliar reforms. That is why they did not sign the same protocol as ours because they do not have a bishop."[10]

The last thing occupied Rome wants is a fully traditional bishop.

Other "Ecclesia Dei" Catholics consider that ecclesial unity is as important as the unity of faith. This is a truth for times of peace but not for an epoch of heresy and schism from Tradition. Moreover, as Archbishop Lefebvre said, the unity of the Church is not merely horizontal in space but also vertical in time.

Dom Gérard, along with Jean Madiran, considered it "prejudicial to the very Tradition of the Church" to be "relegated outside of the official visible limits of the Church."[11] The Archbishop replied: "This business of the visible Church according to Dom Gérard and Mr. Madiran is childish. It is unbelievable that they can speak of the Conciliar Church as the visible

[9] Letter to Fr. Daniel Couture, March 18, 1989.
[10] Interview "One Year after the Consecrations," *Fideliter*, no. 70 (July-August 1989): 5. Equally the "ralliés" [those who have taken part in the *Ecclesia Dei* "Ralliement": see Chapter 19, n. 15. Trans.] have no voice on the *Ecclesia Dei* commission.
[11] Declaration of Dom Gérard, *Présent*, Aug. 18, 1988; *Fideliter*, no. 65: 18, 20.

Church in opposition to the Catholic Church which we are trying to represent and continue. Mr. Madiran, who knows the situation very well, says that we are not in the visible Church and that we are leaving the visible Church which has infallibility; these words do not express the reality of the situation."[12]

"*Ecclesia Dei*" Catholics in general think they work more effectively "from inside the Church" than Archbishop Lefebvre who, they say, has placed himself "on the outside." The Archbishop replied energetically to this objection:

> What Church are we talking about? If it is the Conciliar Church it would supposedly have been necessary for us (who fought against her for twenty years and who want the Catholic Church) to re-enter the Conciliar Church to make it, as it were, Catholic. This is a complete illusion. Subjects do not make the superiors; it is the superiors who make the subjects. With all the Roman Curia and in the midst of all the bishops of the world who are progressives, my voice would have been completely drowned out. I would have been incapable of doing anything to protect the faithful and the seminarians. They would have said to us: "Well, we are going to give you this bishop to do the ordinations; your seminarians will have to accept these professors from such and such a diocese." It is impossible! In the Society of St. Peter they have professors from the diocese of Augsburg. Who are these professors? What do they teach?[13]

Finally, other "*Ecclesia Dei*" Catholics are worried about the practical side of avoiding the harm inevitably caused to the development of the apostolate by the label of "excommunication,"[14] especially in the middle classes, or "the smart set." The priests who remained faithful to Archbishop Lefebvre's fight—the immense majority—chose this risk rather than having to silence or diminish the truth. Above all they refused to see the traditional missal reduced to an "old-fashioned sensibility," sidelined by conciliar pluralism, or ill-protected by a precarious indult.

Mr. Madiran, too, was of this opinion. Why did he not follow Archbishop Lefebvre? He is not a follower, and he has only ever understood the Society and the Archbishop as "priests for the catacombs and our Noah's arks."[15] Organizing stable institutions based on supplied jurisdiction seems to him strange or optional. The consecrations of June 30 were for him a question to be freely discussed, and his friendship for Romain Marie[16] and Dom Gérard made him at first refrain from taking sides. The

---

[12] *Fideliter*, no. 70: 6-8.

[13] *Ibid.*

[14] Cf. This topic is mentioned in the declaration of Dom Gérard quoted above.

[15] Letter to Archbishop Lefebvre, Nov. 10, 1987.

[16] Criticized for the ill-defined doctrine of his "H. et A. Charlier Center" in a conference of the Archbishop to seminarians in Flavigny on June 11, he distanced himself from the Archbishop on June 23, 1988, (*National Hebdo*).

Archbishop was concerned, and on August 19, 1988, he asked the journalist to choose: "During our twenty year fight your opinion and judgment have been of immense importance in sustaining and guiding the troops; this time once again, make the right choice." But it was too late. Jean Madiran did not understand that once the consecrations were done, the nature of the question changed; while the consecrations were once a matter for free discussion, on June 30 they became the result of a leader's prudent decision, requiring genuine agreement and confident, loyal support. As a victim of his scientific mind (in the sense of science as the intellectual virtue of proving an argument), Madiran wanted to prove a point where it was necessary to give loyal support.[17] Unable to prove anything, he doubted, and in his doubt he distanced and separated himself from the Archbishop.

Archbishop Lefebvre did not pour sarcasm or injury on those who did not come along with him; he recommended this noble attitude: "I think that we must perhaps be careful to avoid over-harsh language that could show our disapproval of those who have left us; we should not saddle them with names that they might take as insults. Personally, I have always had this attitude towards those who have left us....I've always taken as my principle: 'When relations are done with, it's all over.'"[18] This rule is justice and not at all contrary to charity; these two virtues complemented each other in the spiritual and practical Archbishop Lefebvre.

Before recounting the end of his earthly life, we must now attempt to sketch a brief spiritual, psychological, and moral portrait of Marcel Lefebvre.

II. A CONTEMPLATIVE AND ACTIVE MAN

Archbishop Lefebvre admitted in 1974: "I have had no special revelation and unfortunately I am not a mystic. I have been moved to act through circumstances."[19] Although pragmatic, the Archbishop was in reality, without wanting to say it, above all a man of faith. He was guided by a faith that was both active and contemplative, the fruit of the Gift of Intelligence which perfected in him a deep mind that was reflective and intuitive. Visiting one day the Carmel at Tourcoing together with Bishop Graffin, he was pestered with questions by the sisters. Bishop Graffin's replies came straight back like arrows. But, said his sister Christiane: "Marcel

---

[17] Joseph Lagneau, *op. cit.* J. Madiran tried to justify his position in *Itinéraires*, no. 325-326: "My loyalty [to the Archbishop] was general, thought-out, fervent, long-standing, well-known, open and accompanied by deep and filial gratitude...until June 11, 1988."

[18] *Fideliter*, no. 66 (Nov.-Dec. 1988): 31.

[19] *Spiritual Conferences at Ecône*, 1 A, May 30, 1974.

on the contrary took his time and thought carefully. But his replies were so weighty that it was worth having a bit of patience."[20]

What did Marcel Lefebvre think of during his prayers? Quite simply, God; this was at least the case towards the end of his life. It was also the theme of some retreats that he preached, as he revealed to one of his drivers: "Do you know what I am going to preach about?"

"No, Your Grace."

"About God (he pronounced this word very slowly). What an immense topic...Deep down everything is there...God, the Holy Trinity!"[21]

The pages of Fr. Emmanuel on "the good Lord" deserved in his opinion to be reprinted in *Fideliter*.[22] He wrote: "The writings of Fr. Emmanuel fill me with spiritual joy. With what doctrinal clarity and simplicity he speaks of the most important matters in our Faith!"[23]

To a young priest who asked him for a motto in his apostolate, the Archbishop penned these few revealing lines: "In the apostolate, have but one goal: that of our holy patron, St. Pius X: '*Omnia instaurare in Christo*' (To restore all things in Christ). And in the midst of your apostolate, keep secure in the depths of your heart the same desire for contemplation, prayer, and union through Jesus and Mary to the infinitely Blessed Trinity."[24]

Archbishop Lefebvre was filled with a "basic conviction" and "disposition that went to the roots of his soul": "Recognizing our nothingness before God and our continual dependence on God for existence and in all we do."[25] This thought which also includes the thought of the presence of God in us "must bring us to an habitual state of adoration; and this adoration brings us to do the will of God,...it compels us, therefore, to have a true and simple spirituality."[26]

THE SPIRITUAL JOURNEY

Since he had never had the leisure necessary to write the spiritual and pastoral directory that he dreamed of giving to his sons,[27] he contented himself in the evening of his life with giving them the *Spiritual Journey according to St. Thomas of Aquinas in his Summa Theologica*. Only the *Summa*, with its unifying plan and gem-like aphorisms, seemed to him capable of "saving the heritage of the priesthood of our Lord Jesus Christ."

---

[20] Mother Marie-Christiane, *Mon frère, Monseigneur Marcel*, 2-3.
[21] Jacques Lagneau, *Souvenirs de route*.
[22] *Fideliter*, no. 52 to 66, July, 1986-Dec. 1988.
[23] Letter to Mrs. Jean-Marc Le Panse, Nov. 11, 1986.
[24] Letter to Fr. Bertrand Labouche, Nov. 29, 1989.
[25] Talk at St. Nicolas du Chardonnet, Dec. 13, 1984, *Cor Unum*, 99-100.
[26] *Retreats at Ecône*, March 24, 1975; *Spiritual Conferences at Ecône*, 25 B, Dec. 2, 1975.
[27] *Spiritual Conferences at Ecône*, 25 A, Nov. 28, 1975, 6:30 P.M.

St. Thomas...but also two recent theologians that the Archbishop appreciated: Fr. Emmanuel and Fr. Calmel: "They are the two great spiritual authors of our time. They are profoundly Thomistic, and that gives a solid base to their spirituality, unlike other authors influenced by St. Sulpice, such as Libermann. With them, one risks falling into sentimentalism, voluntarism, or pacifism. Because of that the clergy was ready to fall when the moment of crisis came; they lacked a strong spirituality."[28]

From St. Thomas he acquired this "principle and foundation": man is *a Deo ad Deum*: man is from God going to God.[29] He must return to his beginning which is also his end. He is governed "by an order that is not static but dynamic,"[30] because every order involves a finality: "It belongs to Supreme Intelligence to put order in things and to give them a finality: some things are meant for others. Man is meant for God. He must *tendere in Deum*, tend towards God. Let us give our people a strong spirituality based on the fundamental truths."[31]

From this perspective the conciliar doctrine of *Gaudium et Spes* seemed monstrous; it made man and not God the center and summit of all the earth (*GS* 12,§1) "the principle and end of all his institutions" (*GS*25, §1). Quite the contrary, as the Archbishop stated, "the principle of finalization [towards God] bringing about the spreading of charity will be what drives all our activities." Whence the fundamental error of liberalism in spirituality as in public order: "It tends to ignore the purpose and end of liberty to the detriment of the divine law" and the "reign of God's love."[32]

But "the return of the rational creature to God" in which consists the Christian life both for individuals and society is not merely a matter of obedience to the commandments of God. Grace is also necessary. There is a more real and inspiring approach to the moral life than merely following the precepts: the morality of the supernatural virtues and gifts of the Holy Ghost. This is the life of spiritual combat opposed to which the error most to be feared is naturalism—the naturalism of Paul VI, for example.

Had the Pope not once proclaimed "the autonomy of the temporal order" and considered that "the world [was] to some degree self-sufficient"? Archbishop Lefebvre had immediately reacted and sent a letter to Cardinal Seper protesting against this "inaccurate and incomplete description of the world" which forgets that the supernatural order is not a matter of choice, and leaves to one side the fall of human nature. In reply Cardinal Villot sent a message by telephone to the Archbishop ordering him to

---

[28] Remarks compiled by Fr. Philippe François.
[29] *Retreats at Ecône*, Sept. 4, 1986, 9 A.M.
[30] Spiritual Conference, Fribourg, Nov. 29, 1970.
[31] *Retreats at Ecône*, 4 Sep. 1986 ; cf. *Retreats at Ecône*, March 24, 1975, 9 A.M.
[32] Lefebvre, *Itinéraire spirituel*, 27-28.

leave Rome and never to return. The Archbishop replied: "Let them send a battalion of Swiss guards to make me!"[33]

Such was the extent of the virile principles that led the Archbishop into spiritual combat. However, this combat is impossible without Christ who is, as St. Thomas says, "the path that we must take to go to God."

JESUS CHRIST OUR WISDOM IN GOD

Archbishop Lefebvre was captivated by the mystery that had seized him in seminary: the mystery of "Jesus Christ and of Jesus Christ crucified" (I Cor. 2:2) in which he found with St. Paul and St. Louis-Marie Grignion de Monfort[34] the Incarnate Wisdom of God. "Our theology is not purely intellectual. It sets out to study a Person: Our Lord Jesus Christ who is God. It is a living and incarnate theology. It is the wisdom that is taught by Revelation. We could meditate on this for four or five years or throughout our whole life and we would never exhaust the mystery of our Lord Jesus Christ. [It is] the great mystery of His divine Person and also of His human reality,...the immensity of His knowledge and His charity. That is what we will have to preach."[35]

He asked his seminarians to bring back all their studies to our Lord Jesus Christ. May we consider everything "as our Lord saw it in His human intelligence"!

The personal prayer of the Archbishop was no longer vocal prayer, and it was hardly even mental prayer. It was a "prayer of the heart." To one of his priests he wrote: "The older I get, the more I think that it is the 'prayer of the heart' which transforms the soul and puts it in a state of continual offering. All our vocal and mental prayer must lead to this end."[36] "If contemplation is a look of love on Jesus Christ crucified and glorified, it puts the soul in the hands of God" to accomplish "His holy will."[37]

"No one is more active than a great contemplative," said Donoso Cortes; this rule was realized in Marcel Lefebvre. Instinctively his systematic faith derived from its contemplation a clear line of conduct and reasons to

---

33 *L'Osservatore Romano*, April 24, 1969 (allocution to a general audience, April 23); Letter of Archbishop Lefebvre dated April 24. Note adjoined to the declaration of Oct. 19, 1983, *Fideliter*, June 29-30, 1988; *Spiritual Conferences at Ecône*, 124 B, March 22, 1988. Fr. Lécuyer received the order from Villot and passed it on to Archbishop Lefebvre.

34 *The Love of Eternal Wisdom* was a book the Archbishop recommended. Apparently it was a compilation of talks given to the community of Poullart des Places. "What a fortunate link!" as the Archbishop noted.

35 *Spiritual Conferences at Ecône*, 39 B, Jan. 10, 1977. Cf. Dom Columba Marmion, an author very much appreciated by the Archbishop for his *Christ the Ideal of the Priest*, Chapter 4, "Priestly Faith."

36 Letter to Fr. Giulio-Maria Tam, April 11, 1990.

37 "*L'esprit de la Fraternité*" (The Spirit of the Society), June 26, 1982, *Cor Unum*, 64-65.

act. When one has contemplated the mystery of God, the weight of sin and grace, and the mystery of Jesus Christ, one finds that "all these things transform life," said Marcel Lefebvre. Such truths are at the very root of action.

III. A LEADER'S CHARISMA

Archbishop Lefebvre served one great principle: "to bring everything back to Christ." He was, therefore, a great leader. Moreover "he was imposing, had a confident bearing, and his face shone with interest and goodness. When he spoke he made an immediate and deep impression. He had a particular magnetic quality: something more than charm. He always retained this aura of distinction, this irresistible personal power."[38]

Instinctively his mind identified principles, and he was unequaled in his ability to get to the heart of a question, draw out an idea or the fundamental error of a text that he would then expound in surprisingly clear language. He was an excellent judge of things, places, and events, but only a mediocre prophet of the future. As a sharp psychologist, he understood individuals quite well, although he was sometimes mistaken about a collaborator's supposed faults or hidden qualities.

He kept himself up-to-date with everything: general politics, the religious situation, the good management of his houses. "He kept his eye on things." With that, his head was full of new and abundant ideas that were even occasionally contradictory. Sometimes daringly original, he was, according to Fr. Emmanuel Barras, "very open-minded and in some ways avant-garde."[39]

Age seemed to multiply his energy tenfold. In Dakar they noticed: "He does not have five minutes free," and the Vicar General wondered: "He runs like a good motor! How does he do it?" He was inclined to things practical, and "on material questions he was extraordinary," but this was always at the service of things spiritual: it was a matter of improving resources and putting things in order so as to facilitate the free reign of the soul. The "foster father" of Mortain thus passed on doctrine and the spiritual life. He was, as Fr. Gravrand said, "both a spiritual man and a factory manager."[40]

---

[38] Koren, *Les Spiritains*, 545; Fr. Michael O'Carroll, in *Mission Outlook*, Nov.-Dec. 1976; *A Priest in Changing Times*, 95; Michel Lefebvre, ms. II, 5, 52-69; 6, 1-10.

[39] Michel Lefebvre, ms. II, 6, 42-44; ms. II, 20, 29-50; Marziac, *Monseigneur Lefebvre, soleil levant*, 91; ms. I, 51, 10-11; III, 5, 54-55.

[40] Ms. I, 10, 38-42; 14, 20; 18, 57; 37, 26; 57, 25; II, 24, 48—I, 10, 14-15; 65, 24-41; 67, 28-48; II, 27, 50 —I, 25, 39-55; 49, 40-46; 50, 28-30; 52, 20-21; 61, 46-52; II, 71, 49-50.

A "brilliant organizer," he had a sense of the goals to aim for and the order in which things should be done. He had a feeling for "investing well so as to get the best return from the available means without neglecting anything essential."[41] Everywhere he brought order, insisting on the chapters of religious, the cloistering of sisters, clarifying the pastoral faculties enjoyed by his priests, insisting on regularity in community prayers, preserving the common life, and ensuring good order in confirmation ceremonies. One day in Chile, he refused to confirm "until things were properly organized," and he showed them what do.[42]

He had an extraordinary influence on people and on things: "I follow my priests closely," he said in Dakar, which meant even when he was away in Madagascar. He was closely informed of their apostolate and knew how to call for fresh troops from Fr. Griffin, the Superior General: "We are making a breakthrough, we need reinforcements!"

On principle, he trusted his subordinates, district superiors, and seminary professors. Apart from what he prescribed in the Society statutes, he was not dogmatic in matters of organization. One had to know how to ask him for advice: then, he would answer clearly and concisely. When visiting, he would observe but ask no questions, with that excessive delicacy he had inherited from his father. He thought anything else would show a lack of trust. He did not like to show curiosity. One day while visiting San Damiano, he was asked to go and say hello to the seer. He stayed with her for twenty minutes. What happened? Had there been a message from heaven for him? When he came back, he said: "She seems very kind and simple; we prayed a rosary together and that's all. I did not want to ask any questions."[43]

But Archbishop Lefebvre did not hesitate to make his disagreement felt, like the day he arrived at the École St. Michel where the principal, a priest with a deep "Moorish" complexion, had taken the initiative of having all the trees cut down. Saddened by what he saw, he exclaimed: "You really are a Moor, and you behave more and more like one; when you have finished there'll be nothing but desert."[44]

Generally he corrected others with a little teasing. To his successor in charge of the Society, who was even more expansionist than the Archbishop, he fired across the table at Ecône: "You! You'd found a priory on the moon!" When dealing with more personal faults, he would say something

[41] Ms. I, 8, 33 ; 11, 1-4 ; 25, 51 ; 67, 6-9 ; II, 71, 38 et 50 ; 73, 44.
[42] Michel Lefebvre, ms. II, 7, 14-30.
[43] Fr. Bussard, ms. I, 11, 18-21; Fr. Gravrand, ms. II, 74, 2-5; 76, 27-30; III, 14, 5-7; Fr. F.-O. Dubuis, in Savioz, *Essai historique sur la fondation de la Fraternité Saint-Pie X,* annex. 2.1, 4; Interview, Rémy Borgeat, ms. III, 33, 31-37; Fr. Thibault, ms II, 46, 37-38 and 44.
[44] Interview with Fr. Laurençon, Nov. 15, 2001.

in private. He would give a little embarrassed chuckle with the tip of his tongue between his lips, and the telling off would carry home all the better for being more delicately done.

The Archbishop rightly knew how to sort out a problem by taking the necessary decisions quickly. He did not let a painful situation "fester." Occasionally he would act forcefully and use his authority as a prelate.[45] However, mostly he unveiled his perfectly thought out and settled decisions with great sensitivity, or, one could even say, a hint of timidity. He was not a "heavy-handed" bishop, but he was full of authority. "Everyone obeyed him, and no one ever refused," said Fr. Bussard. "I always agreed with what he said," said Fr. Gravrand, "because I liked him a lot and when you like someone you want to do what he does." He was called "the iron fist in the velvet glove." And this made him "very effective."[46]

IV. "GENTLY PIGHEADED"

With his great intelligence and solid judgment, Marcel Lefebvre was very sure of himself. His "iron will," "enormous energy," and constant calm[47] gave him the physiognomy of a strong individual who did not lack delicacy of heart, lending a fine balance to his abilities. Nevertheless, his personality had its little failings that deserve to be looked at.

THE BONHOMIE OF A TENACIOUS MAN

Gentleness goes hand in hand with strength. The gentleness of Marcel Lefebvre was proverbial: a humble gentleness with a touch of shyness. His "little voice" was deceiving; at Mortain or Lambaréné, he was taken to be a brother. In Dakar he would assert himself: "He could have been a shrinking violet who did nothing," but he was the opposite, said Fr. Bussard. When visiting him in Senegal, his brother Michel noted that he was "at ease with the governors" and later also "with the aristocrats whose manners he knows and makes fun of"; he is at his best with the latter, putting himself on their level, listening to them, and never feeling embarrassed.[48]

At table at Ecône Fr. Dubuis noticed that he "was exactly the same with an archduke as with an ironmonger, just as friendly and just as open. I saw that, and it really struck me. I greatly admired it; he was the same, it

---

[45] Personal memories; Fr. Bussard, ms. I, 10, 11-14; Interview with André Cagnon, Feb. 21, 1997; nomination of Bishop Baud.

[46] Fr. Bussard, ms. I, 11, 28-35 ; 13, 29; P. Carron, ms. I, 58, 38-55; 61, 3; P. Gravrand, ms. II, 77, 64-65; Fr. Christian Winckler, ms. I, 67, 11-18 and 33; Fr. Berclaz, ms. I, 52, 15-16.

[47] Fr. Christian Winckler, ms. I, 67, 16-17.

[48] Ms. I, 18, 36-37; 35, 40; 67, 9-14; II, 8, 22-28 and 67; 71, 11-17 (Frs. Fourmond, Gravrand, Bussard, Fr. Christian, Michel Lefebvre).

was not forced. He was very pastoral." He had no equal in making a witty or humoristic toast at the end of an ordination banquet. Everywhere Marcel Lefebvre showed remarkable "human warmth and ability to speak with people." He was so open that one could say anything to him. Eight years after Mortain, Fr. Barras met him again on the Niger: "How you have aged, Your Grace!" he blurted out. And the Archbishop smiled.[49]

This gentleness and bonhomie hid a strong will: what he had decided and organized had to be carried out as he intended, and he would keep his eye on how things were done. When discussing ideas with friends or his sons in the Society, he said what he thought with surprising openness, as Fr. O'Carroll noted. If one attacked a principle, as for example suggesting that over-population in Colombia could be solved by family-planning, he would react: "Oh no! Out of the question! One must not abandon principles to solve a problem." He expressed his views "energetically and with conviction," said his brother Michel. However, added Fr. Berclaz, C.S.Sp., "even with his fixed ideas, the way he spoke was very gentle, and his tone of voice was never hurtful." With families, he would pass a quiet remark: "You have the Society schools." His advice was positive and he did not set out to tell people off. He sent information and held meetings with families to explain his positions.[50]

In spite of everything, Marcel Lefebvre knew how not to force his ideas on others. He was an extraordinary listener and faithfully sought to understand his neighbor. He was ready to take on board the views of others and concede whatever he could if it meant he could to lead others to the truth. He advised the seminarians: "When you discuss matters with the faithful, remain charitable, and do not show any useless intolerance. We are not obliged to make the truth disagreeable! Firstly let us know how to listen, and then express our reservations."[51]

Thus, when Bishop Schwery of Sion was once visiting Ecône, he managed to get the Archbishop to admit that one "must practice ecumenism because there is not one Christian who is not concerned with unity." No doubt, the Archbishop retorted that there is ecumenism and ecumenism!

In behavior he was equally accommodating. One day he celebrated Mass at Ecône after Fr. Merle, who had left out the Last Gospel. So he himself left out the Last Gospel. Yes, as the priest commented: "He had a

---

[49] Interview Oct. 31, 1992, Savioz, *Essai historique sur la fondation de la Fraternité de Saint-Pie X*, annex, 2.1, 1 (Rudolph of Austria and Marcel Pedroni); Fr. Fourmond, ms. I, 24, 7-8; Fr. Barras, ms. I, 51, 45-48.

[50] Fr. Gravrand, ms. II, 74, 18-27; Fr. Bourdelet, ms. II, 55, 45-58; Fr. O'Carroll, Interview Nov. 26, 1997; Michel Lefebvre, ms. II, 11, 30-36 and 45-48; Fr. Berclaz, ms. I, 50, 5-7.

[51] Michel Lefebvre, ms. II, 11, 42 and 47; *Spiritual Conferences at Ecône*, June 26, 1973; Fr. Dubuis, in Savioz, *Essai historique sur la foundation de la Fraternité de Saint-Pie X*, annex 2.1, 1.

very human kindness and wished to avoid making trouble, even if he remained adamant."

On another occasion, he had just heard about the death of his sister-in-law Monique whilst he was with her brother Fr. Xavier Lefebvre, a Jesuit and a charismatic. Fr. Lefebvre, who was very demonstrative, suggested: "Let us kneel and pray to the Lord; wherever we are gathered together, God is there!" According to the Archbishop's brother Michel, all this was done in a very impassioned manner that Marcel did not like at all. But that did not stop him from agreeing to pray, even if it was done too ostentatiously for his tastes.

But when a principle was at stake, Archbishop Lefebvre gave no quarter. In conversation with the Archbishop at table at Ecône, a Dominican theologian ventured: "At the moment there is so much talk of pluralism, but those who talk about it reject the legitimacy of a more traditional way of seeing the problem."

"That is a very poor line of argument you are making, dear Father!" replied the Archbishop who was a polished metaphysician.

"But why is that?"

"One must never say that because the truth is one."[52]

And the Dominican theologian was silenced by this hammer blow of philosophical truth. But, added the priest, "he said that to me very gently."[53]

THE TWO SIDES TO MARCEL LEFEBVRE

But there were times when the man of dialogue became really stubborn. Faced with strong-minded people, he was "a reactionary."[54] One could then be exposed to some sharp words from a man who clung grimly to his opinion, sometimes to the extent of denying the obvious in his exasperation, or in his embarrassment at having to explain himself: he then showed the downside of his character, or rather the excess of his tenacity.[55]

This was a rare occurrence because usually he was very calm. He was able to put up for six years with an assistant in the Holy Ghost Fathers who was an innovator. Without turning a hair he could listen to the tirade of an adviser or religious who attacked him verbally. Sometimes, said Fr. Bussard, he had "to hide things—reproaches, criticism—because he was bound to keep something secret." Nevertheless, one day when a layman

[52] A familiar saying of the Archbishop. Cf. de Stephano, *op.cit.*, 134.

[53] Msgr. Schwery, Interview on June 15, 1993, Savioz, *La foundation de la Fraternité de Saint-Pie X*, annex 2.2, 6-7; Fr. Mehrle, in *ibid.*, annex 2.6, p. 3; Michel Lefebvre, ms. II, 11, 69-12, 15; Fr. Mehrle, *ibid.*, p. 2, 6, 7 and 8.

[54] Ms. I, 74, 45-48; II, 31, 11-12; III, 12, 4-6 (Frs. Béguerie, Carron, Gravrand).

[55] Robert Serrou, *Paris-Match*, Sept. 1976; Michel Lefebvre, ms. II, 11, 59-67; Fr. Carron, ms. I, 57, 32-39; Fr. Lucien Deiss, ms. II, 32, 33-35.

had been explaining to him for a quarter of an hour how he should train his priests, the Archbishop finally grew furious and interrupted him: "Listen, Sir, I know what I have to do, so mind your own business. And now, Sir, I'm going to ask you to leave!"[56]

Faced with wrongheaded people, he preferred to be silent rather than to argue, especially when his interlocutor was a superior or knew more than he did. During a meeting of "Fr. Deco's Old Boys," he put up with Bishop Georges Leclercq attacking him virulently and did not answer back. He later told his brother Michel: "It's appalling what can be said. Truly, it's frightening." But he had not tried to discuss things. He had been as it were paralyzed.

He felt all too keenly how useless it was to discuss matters when first principles were denied. Besides, he found it inconceivable that a scholar or a prelate should contradict doctrine. Overall, he had deep respect for those in authority, a great respect for individuals, and too much respect for his neighbor: all this came from a great charity which was the opposite of scorn for others.

Marcel Lefebvre was careful not to humiliate other people and not to hurt his subordinates. Thus, he suffered when he had to point out to them their failings or move them from one post to another. In one such case, he said: "I did not sleep for nights. It was as if the sword of Damocles were hanging over my head before I took the decision to move him away."[57]

This excessive delicacy was of a particular kind since it did not affect him in public, but only in personal relations. He had some difficultly in communicating when what he said would show a loss of respect for his neighbor. But this was the strength of the way he governed others, and of his perseverance in negotiating with the authorities of the Conciliar Church.

What is admirable in Marcel Lefebvre is this contrast, or better still, this balance between the greatest self-confidence and the most delicate attentiveness to others; it made him a very human and attractive personality who inspired trust and friendship. Numerous Holy Ghost Fathers who did not agree with his traditionalism, such as Fr. O'Carroll, said to us: "Oh! How I was attached to that man! I still am."[58]

None managed to reconcile the two sides of Archbishop Lefebvre. "Your gentleness is hard," Jean Guitton said to him before the consecra-

---

[56] Fr. Berclaz, ms. I, 49, 29-35; Fr. Bussard, ms. I, 13, 29-30; 67, 18-26; Rémy Borgeat, ms. III, 36, 55-68.

[57] Bishop Milleville, ms. I, 40, 50-55; II, 41, 1-2; Michel Lefebvre, ms. II, 11, 49-57; Fr. du Chalard, Interview June 8, 1998, p. 2; Fr. Bussard, ms. I, 14, 28-29; Fr. Buttet, ms. I, 28, 26.

[58] Cf. Chapter on "Mortain"; Fr. O'Carroll, Interview Nov. 26, 1997; Fr. Barras, ms. I, 51, 20 ; 53, 12-13 and 46-47.

tions. Others said: "He is over-proud!" "No," replied Fr. Louis Carron, "personally he is humble. It is his doctrine that is proud. It is a formula..." Yes, it was well and truly a formula, dear Fr. Carron. Your bishop was not liberal and, nonetheless, he was completely charitable *in re* and *in modo*: in what he said and did, and in the way he said and did it. In him, as the Psalmist says: "Mercy and truth have met each other: justice and peace have kissed" (Ps. 84:11).

"No man was ever gentler than Moses, and yet it was he who broke the tables of the Law in a fit of holy anger. When a gentle person starts getting tough, he can go very far."[59] This reflection of Fr. Mehrle concerning Archbishop Lefebvre is very astute. However, the strength of Archbishop Lefebvre goes back even further to the lively enthusiasm of his youth when, aged twenty, he received at Santa Chiara the torch whose flame consumed him, and which he was bound to pass on.

Thus, this "gentle, pigheaded man" with modest reserve attained the stature of a magnanimous giant. The prudent zeal of the religious missionary provided the raw material for the sort of bishop needed by the Church.

V. THE LEVELHEADEDNESS OF A MODEL PRIEST

THE VIRTUE OF DISCRETION

Although both prudent and strong, this leader was also a priest who was possessed of a fine and delicate pastoral zeal which was wholly supernatural in its effectiveness. One day one of his seminarians told him about the difficult situation of his grandfather. The man was a friend and benefactor of Ecône, but he had formerly lost the Faith and, wanting to be consistent, he no longer practiced. Now, however, he was seriously ill, and the family were concerned about his salvation.

At the request of the young cleric, the Archbishop made a detour during a round of confirmations to visit the old man. On his return to Ecône, the Archbishop declared: "But he is well disposed, your grandfather!"

"Your Grace, did you not speak to him of converting? Of making his confession?"

"Oh, no."

"...or the four last things?"

"Oh no, no, no."

"And he spoke adamantly, meaning: "Especially not!"

The Archbishop explained: "You see, it's not worth it. The one thing you risk is provoking him to refuse. And if unfortunately he were to be

---

[59] Michel Lefebvre, ms. II, 11, 24-42; Fr. Fourmond, ms. I, 35, 47-51; Guitton, *Un siècle, une vie, passim*; Fr. Carron, ms. I, 57, 41-52; Fr. Mehrle, in Savioz, *La foundation de la Fraternité de Saint-Pie X*, annex. 2.6, 8; cf. our Chapter III.

damned, you would only have made his case worse. You would risk a blasphemy, and a positive refusal; and you must avoid that above all!"

The seminarian was hardly reassured, and went to speak to his spiritual director Fr. Le Boulc'h who comforted him: "Obviously, the Archbishop has prayed for him; no doubt your grandfather will be saved."

It was known that through his own natural honesty the old man had long since put right any wrong he had done to others. But his Faith did not return. They prayed, and they waited. Finally, not long before he fell into a coma, a priest friend said: "I am going to see him and I will offer him my blessing but I will give him sacramental absolution."

This was not, theologically speaking, quite right... He went, and in the end said to the patient: "Sir, I am going to give you my blessing."

Then thinking better of it, he decided to lay his cards on the table: "No, rather I am going to give you absolution!"

And he gave him absolution. Then, the grandfather kissed his hands and said: "I have confidence in what these hands have done."

That was all. God had given the sign. The prayers and pastoral prudence of Archbishop Lefebvre had succeeded where a less discreet zeal would no doubt have failed.

He was the kind of fair and level-headed priest that the Church always looks for, a minister of God who brings order into souls and keeps his own soul and body in order. As a youth, a young cleric, a missionary, or as a bishop, Marcel Lefebvre brought peace to people by helping them bring order back into their lives. His very first spiritual conference on October 15, 1969, to the young men he had gathered together in Fribourg made this ideal very clear. "What ought to be one's dispositions upon entering the seminary?" he asked: "I come here to put in order those things in me that are disorderly because of original sin and the spirit of the world. I come to divest my mind of every error and to learn that I am nothing and that God is everything; I come to make myself dependent on God and our Lord Jesus Christ. I have also come so that later on I can bring back souls to order. Justice, the source of order, is firstly giving God what is due to Him. And secondly it is love of neighbor: loving in him what is from God and loving him to bring him to God."

In his diocese and Delegation, as in the Holy Ghost Fathers or the Society, the order that Marcel Lefebvre brought came through guidance rather than over-discipline. All order comes from arranging things with a view to some goal; such was the order the Archbishop established. He was ordered towards God.

Archbishop Lefebvre also embodied the portrait of the perfect priest, as drawn by Fr. Spicq: "[He is] a profoundly religious man who lives in the adoration of God and respect for holy things. [He] is distinguished as much by his interior uprightness and honesty as by his exterior decency."[60]

Always and everywhere in matters relating to manners—which reflect the soul and are reflected in the soul—he was a perfectly modest man because he was full of reverence and piety towards God. Justice and temperance went hand in hand in Marcel Lefebvre. With its central role as a cardinal virtue this temperance gives a sense of the right measure in all things. St. Paul, and later the Council of Trent,[61] speak of this virtue as being the characteristic virtue of a priest. Fr. Spicq again states: "It [temperance] is made up of moderation, modesty, reserve, and simplicity; so much so that one of the most essential priestly virtues is levelheadedness, *i.e.*, measured judgment and clear thinking, allied to moderation in behavior and to temperance, whence the 'egkrateia' (Tit. 1:8) which is the moderation of a man who has perfectly mastered himself, controlling his desires and impulses thanks to the Gift of the Holy Ghost (Gal. 5:23)."[62]

THE QUIET ASCETIC

Let us recall Fr. Bussard's admiration for the Archbishop of Dakar's self-mastery and quiet asceticism, or Fr. Berthet's esteem for the exemplary seminarian in Rome. The Archbishop walked the corridors of Ecône with a quick and quiet pace, his eyes modestly cast down. In the lecture room, he sat upright without leaning against the back of the chair, his feet together, hands joined and placed on the table, eyes down. His deportment was not rigid but characterized by a natural simplicity that radiated goodness.

His office where he welcomed his visitors with a smile was no different from those of the seminary professors. The same shelves made of chipboard bore neatly arranged books; the only difference was in the very small number of volumes, their modest binding or lack of it denoting detachment. The Archbishop kept to hand the *Summa* of St. Thomas, the acts of the Popes, a dictionary, a world atlas, and a language teach-yourself book, *L'anglais sans peine.*[63] On other shelves were found works on law and theology, alongside a number of counter-revolutionary and anti-liberal books.

In the cupboard were filed the schemas and documents of Vatican II, as well as the Archbishop's archives properly classed in labeled sleeves: notes from seminary and the novitiate, notes from Africa, Tulle, Rome, and the Council, and plans for lectures and retreats. There is plenty there to satisfy the apprentice historians of tomorrow! "They'll find all that after my death," he explained to André Cagnon and to other close friends.

---

[60] C. Spicq, O.P., *Spiritualité sacerdotale d'après saint Paul* (Paris: Cerf, 1949), 146.

[61] Council of Trent, Session. 22, De ref., c. 1; St. Paul, 1 Tim. 3:2-3; 2 Tim. 2:24-25; Tit. 1:8-9.

[62] Spicq, *op. cit.*, 148.

[63] [This was the Assimil book *English Without Toil.* Trans.]

In this cramped room, there was only an ivory crucifix (upon which he often looked)[64] and a wretched painting of St. Francis de Sales, along with an icon of the Virgin Mary that cheered the room up a little.

The adjoining bedroom was frankly ascetic: the narrow bed with its hard mattress was flanked by bare, undecorated walls. There was just a poor copy of a painting of the Immaculate Conception on which were fixed a few cherished photos of deceased friends, and also an artless crucifix. In the corner there was a tiny bedside table. There reigned the Spartan poverty of the faithful religious and seasoned missionary. All the presents and souvenirs that he received in Africa and from all over the world were passed on to his friends and his family, or to the sacristy and library in the seminary. In Caserta, his friend Archbishop Vito Roberti, the former Nuncio, had some treasures he had received in Africa. But Archbishop Lefebvre observed: "It's true, one was given many things, but I always passed them on. It is no use keeping anything: we take nothing with us to heaven!"[65]

He kept nothing; moreover, none of his books were marked with his name: quite simply he possessed nothing.

His religious and priestly detachment was also apparent in his dress, but it was allied to a careful cleanliness as shown by his ever impeccably polished shoes.

The Archbishop recommended the same sobriety to his sons: "The cassock hides the form of the body letting nothing appear but the face. Let not this penitential habit that marks our effacement and separation from the world be influenced by the spirit of the world."[66]

Archbishop Lefebvre also practiced renouncement at the altar, and demanded it of his priests: "The rite of Mass...must be *perfect* in its *details*. Consequently it is not a matter of getting it more or less correct! It is very important to leave nothing to individual initiative. Mass is above all a *public* act and not an act of private devotion. One is not free to choose the way in which the gestures are to be done. One should avoid both negligence and ostentation."[67]

---

[64] Cf. *Fideliter*, no. 59: 4.
[65] Interview with Rémy Borgeat, ms. III, 37, 1-22.
[66] *Spiritual Conferences at Ecône*, Dec. 3, 1973.
[67] *Ibid.*, 64 B, 28 Oct. 1978, to future deacons.

VI. LECTURER AND PREACHER

MIND-NUMBING AND CAPTIVATING BY TURNS

Archbishop Lefebvre's spiritual conferences were rarefied and *sui generis*. When he explained the four types of knowledge in Christ or the hypostatic union, superficial minds thought to themselves: "But I learned all that in theology!" They did not immediately see the concrete applications that the Archbishop saw. Talks with Fr. Barrielle based on examples from the Saints seemed lively and appealing. Marcel Lefebvre belonged to a special genre of speaker that was more arid. His style was not abstract and not at all difficult, but less striking and less attractive. He appealed little to the emotions and entirely to faith. Consequently, his talks went to the essence of things and were all the deeper and more contemplative for it!

For the minds of those students who were strict logicians or desperately sentimental, the meditations of the Archbishop countered their natural tendencies, raising the debate, and refocusing their sights on higher things like the mystery of God and our Lord Jesus Christ. This simplicity was puzzling but it was much more effective.

His style as an orator did him no favors. One's attention was not helped by the lack of any gestures or by his quiet voice that had little projection. He knew all this himself: "I know very well I have the reputation of being mind-numbing," he said. The seminarians were amused by this comment, for it was more or less the reality of the situation.[68]

However, to numerous students Archbishop Lefebvre was never boring. In all simplicity, he made them contemplate what he himself usually contemplated. Without saying as much, it was his soul and his prayer life that he passed on to his listeners, bringing them to the simple contemplation of the Faith and inviting them to draw all the practical consequences from the Christian mysteries: "'Every spirit which confesses that Jesus Christ is come in the flesh is of God' (I Jn. 4:2). The consequences of this are immense: everything among men is decided with respect to Jesus and His divinity. St. Paul to the Hebrews and Colossians makes no distinction between Jesus and the Word: there precisely is the mystery! So, how can this Being not be Prophet, Priest, and King? How can we think it is a matter of indifference to any creature that we have the presence of the Word of God among us?"[69]

A few months later the Archbishop came back to the same subject and answered an implicit objection:

> It is said my conferences are a little abstract! But if our Lord Jesus Christ is God, there are all sorts of consequences for societies, individuals,

---

[68] Fr. Buttet, ms. I, 30, 52.
[69] *Spiritual Conferences at Ecône*, 52 A and B, Dec. 5 and 6, 1977.

and for everything. The conferences I gave in Madrid were not at all abstract: five thousand people were in the streets even before I started my talk already expressing their convictions: "Long live Christ the King!" And all the time in the streets nearby they never stopped shouting: "Arriba Cristo Rey!" If Christ is not King, the devil will reign in Spain by pushing socialism and ruining families. The Spaniards feel that our Lord is no longer King of Spain and these people have the tradition of the Royalty of our Lord Jesus Christ.

And we, if we are not convinced of that, we will not have the strength to maintain and affirm what people expect. And there would be serious consequences for [the impact of] this truth on the morality of States, families, and individuals.[70]

As we can see, the public talks of the Archbishop were not at all dull. Neither were his conferences at the seminary boring, for the Archbishop would apply principles to questions of current affairs. Political and religious events provided very lively matter for the highest truths of the Faith (that are also perhaps the least understood). In public, his style as a speaker became livelier: his expressions were colorful, sometimes mocking or even ironic. He could be sharply ironic when in good form and facing members of the media whom he knew how to alienate by his political stances, or to win over by cutting the puzzling and attractive figure of a resistance fighter.

His language was often innovative, as in this unusual description of the Blessed Virgin: "[She is] neither liberal nor modernist nor ecumenical; [she is] allergic to all error and therefore much more to heresy and apostasy."[71] On another occasion he said: "Would a mother deprive its child of her milk until he decides whether he wants to live or die?" He hurled this mocking retort at priests who put off baptism until "the individual is able to decide for himself."

At Essen in Germany in the *Grubahalle*, before an audience of six thousand, he explored an extended metaphor to lampoon liberal ecumenism which "considers error with the same respect as the truth": "[There are] no more enemies now, only brothers! No more need to fight! An end to hostilities!" In his view, that is exactly what Vatican II did:

> Imagine a world congress of 2,500 doctors who, having studied their reports, came to the conclusion: It really is unacceptable to be always fighting illness. We must have done with illness once and for all. We have now been fighting it for centuries. Let's decide that from now on illness is health! Let's say that patients are in fact healthy individuals. There will be no need for medical schools, the doctors can go home. There will be no need for hospitals: illness will be health![72]

---

[70] *Spiritual Conferences at Ecône*, 57 A, March 13, 1978.
[71] Lefebvre, *Itinéraires spirituel*, ch. IX.
[72] Talk at Essen, April 9, 1978, cf. *Spiritual Conferences at Ecône*, 58 A, April 14, 1978.

His listeners were at first flabbergasted and then they raised the roof with their applause. Is it surprising that media and newspaper surveys said Archbishop Lefebvre was "rather likeable"? Journalists themselves did not always do their job, forgetting under the spell of his charm to "bring him down in flames." André Frossard called him a "lone knight" in *Le Figaro* but did not hide his admiration for this solitary anticonformist.

MODESTY AND BOLDNESS AS A PREACHER

After the Mass at Lille, Robert Serrou, another journalist and a writer for *Paris-Match*, sketched the style of the Archbishop's sermons in a few lines: "Although the tone is gentle, the words are impassioned, and the remarks hard-hitting. At one and the same time, he is shy and bold, modest and full of assurance."

In times of tension Archbishop Lefebvre often made hard-hitting remarks such as "In Argentina at least there is order" or "the Pope does not make the truth." However, generally he spoke as a fatherly priest or a bishop who knew how to teach. His confirmation sermons could be quite informal in this respect. In contrast, his sermons for feasts: Christ the King, All Saints...set out the teaching of a doctor of the Faith.

The Archbishop always expounded on *doctrine—the only doctrine possible*—without moralizing. For him, the moral applications naturally unfolded from his presentation of dogma:

> Souls need to be enlightened by the truth, and by teachings concerning our Lord and God. Often, we speak relatively little of God Himself and more about what God does. We could make an effort to speak about the divine perfections, the Holy Trinity, and our Lord who is God, because the more souls grow close to God, the more they want to serve Him and the more they hate offending Him. If a soul makes just a little progress in getting to know God, it is wonder-struck, and at the same time frightened and trembling. The closer we are to God the more we tremble. 'The angels tremble, the archangels are in awe' says the Preface of the Mass. The more a soul is taught about the grandeur and perfection of God, the more that soul desires to love and serve God, and is afraid: it realizes more and more what a terrible thing it is to go against God's will.[73]

Here again the Archbishop revealed his prayer life: the adoration of faith. Thus, his preaching aimed at presenting the foundations of the Faith. He pointed out to his future priests the danger of basing sermons on more or less unlikely private revelations:

"That is dangerous! Certainly the devil takes advantage of that to turn souls away from the foundations of the Faith and draw them towards sentimentalism or a piety that is not based truly on faith and on our Lord.

---

[73] *Retraite d'ordinations* [Ordination retreat], Montalenghe, 1989, on preaching.

Personally I have tried very hard at the seminary—at Ecône—to give at all times the principal foundations of the Faith."[74]

And he added that when expounding the Faith: "Do not prove it, proclaim it."[75] Too often we seek to give proofs or to get into apologetics, but that is not the Faith. The Faith means adhering to God who reveals His mystery.

And what mystery should be preached above all if not the mystery of our Lord Jesus Christ? "A sermon where our Lord Jesus Christ is not mentioned is useless; the goal and the means are missing."[76] "We do not preach ourselves, declares St. Paul, but Jesus Christ our Savior (II Cor. 4:5)." "Jesus Christ must always come into our sermons because everything goes back to Him. He is the Truth, the Way and the Life [sic]. So, asking the faithful to become more perfect and to convert but without talking about our Lord is to deceive them and to withhold from them the means by which they can attain to such things: 'We preach Jesus Christ crucified' (I Cor. 1:23)."[77]

As for the moral teachings preached by Archbishop Lefebvre, they were not concerned only with natural ethics but also with the Christian morality of supernatural virtues that are perfected with the help of grace.

> One fault of modern preaching is that we no longer believe in grace or in the words of our Lord: "Without me you can do nothing."

> Sometimes, we do not show enough trust in souls and in the possibility of growing in virtue and the grace of our Lord, obviously. Sometimes the faithful are captivated when we speak to them about the Gifts of the Holy Ghost, the Beatitudes, and the fruits of the Holy Ghost which are part of the spiritual organism in every soul as soon as it receives grace in baptism. When we preach these things, how many of the faithful are filled with wonder and say: "But no one ever spoke to us about that! We did not know that the Holy Ghost acted like that in us."[78]

Archbishop Lefebvre recalled that his mother had felt this same joyous surprise when she read a book that he had left behind at the house after a holiday from seminary in Rome: *The Indwelling of the Holy Ghost in the Souls of the Just.* "How can they not tell us about such things?" she had written to Marcel.[79]

---

[74] *Ibid.*; *Retreats at Ecône*, March 25, 1975, 3 P.M.
[75] Aulagnier, *La Tradition sans peur*, 297.
[76] Instructions to the futures bishops, Sierre, June 24, 1988.
[77] *Retr. d'ordin.*[Ordination retreat], Montalenghe, 1989, 99, 2 A.
[78] *Ibid.*
[79] *Retreats at Ecône*, March 23, 1975, 6 P.M. The book is by Fr. Froget, O.P.

When the Holy Ghost Took Hold of Him

But the content of a sermon is not everything: there is also the form. Archbishop Lefebvre spoke so as to be heard and understood. Since his voice was not strong, he was happy to use a microphone. He preached without any oratorical polish saying what he had to say calmly and simply. His voice was not monotonous although he did not have the inflections of an orator. His preaching did not appeal to the heart and was not sentimental, but rather it fed the mind and called the will into action.

However, without meaning to, he sometimes became an orator when the Holy Ghost seemed to fall upon him, take hold of him, and inspire him. Wearing his miter during ordination sermons, he felt a pressing need to communicate with the congregation: the style grew livelier, the voice occasionally grew stronger, he pointed with his finger and, aiming at the enemies of the Church or the priesthood, he hurled imperious truths and the reasons for his fight.

This shy man then became bold, and his modesty turned to self-assurance. He even seemed stronger from afar than from near. He appeared more vehement and audacious when he preached than when he was in discussion with an unbelieving cardinal. Quite simply, when discussing things one-to-one, respect held him back. But when speaking in public he felt free and became a lion.

Archbishop Lefebvre always prepared his sermons carefully. Did he write them down? Apparently not. Moreover, no framework is to be found beneath them; he read the liturgical texts of the day from the missal or from the Pontifical, flicked through the Gospel, gathered this or that favorite quote from St. John or St. Paul, and put his ideas in order. Then on the day he presented them calmly, orderly, and, it seemed, effortlessly. One day, however, the missionary Archbishop was preaching in a city. With the fatigue of the journey, his memory failed him and he drew a complete blank. He stopped speaking, was seized with anxiety, and beads of sweat appeared on his forehead. However, suddenly a short-circuit plunged the church into darkness. By the time the fuse was sorted out, he had remembered the thread of his sermon, and he finished it as if nothing had happened.

As Fr. Bourdelet recalled, "He expounded the truths of Faith with remarkable clarity." The jurist Yves Pivert even considered Archbishop Lefebvre to be an orator "in the sense that he convinces [his listener]": "It was a gift he had: the gift of making things appear obvious. It is like a finely wrought plea in court: you cannot be of any other opinion. Everything lay in the quality of his reasoning."[80]

When inspired, the Archbishop could be inimitable. For example: "Our Lord is the only man who is God. Therefore, He is king, and therefore, He must reign. Consequently He is entitled to His say about everything."

Such expressions resemble the "words of truth" of St. Paul speaking *in verbo veritatis* : "There are no Buddhists or Muslims in heaven. And if there are any, they have converted."[81] Or: "Reaffirming our Lord Jesus Christ's divinity is the ruining of ecumenism."[82]

These are like the "words of Faith" that grace the writings of the Apostle. Brief and concise, they break through the mists of ambiguity and shed light from on high. Such words of "wisdom and knowledge" are considered by St. Paul and St. Thomas to be a charism by which "someone communicates his Faith to others, sharing it with pious men and defending it against the impious."[83]

So Archbishop Lefebvre can be numbered among the authentic charismatics, although we must add that his was the charism of the confessor and doctor of the Faith.

Yes, this prelate who was completely given over to his work of restoration was, almost without meaning to be, a true doctor: a doctor of the priesthood.

VII. Doctor of the Priesthood

Archbishop Lefebvre contemplated the priesthood through its principle which is the Person of the Word Incarnate. He loved "St. Paul's marvelous description" of the Son of God made man: "The image of the invisible God, the firstborn of every creature," by whom, in whom, and for whom everything was made, and in whom everything subsists (Col. 1:15-17). "This presence of God Incarnate in the history of humanity can only be the center of that history, as the sun towards which everything goes or from which everything comes."

He meditated on the hypostatic union: the assumption of a human nature in the Divine Person of the Word. "When God took charge of this soul and this body He gave this man attributes, rights, unique privileges,...and unique titles: Mediator, Savior, Priest, and King. All mediation, priesthood, and royalty among creatures can only be a participation in these jewels that belong to our Lord Jesus Christ."[84]

---

[80] Fr. Mehrle, Interview Nov. 16, 1993, Savioz, *Essai historique sur la fondation de la Fraternité Saint-Pie X*, annex 2.6, 4; Fr. du Chalard, Interview on June 28, 1998, 1; Fr. Jules Bourdelet and Y. Pivert, Interview in Vieux-Rouen, May 28, 1999, ms. II, 65-66.

[81] Talk in Sierre, Nov. 27, 1988.

[82] Lefebvre, *Lettre ouverte aux catholiques perplexes*, 101-102; *Spiritual Conferences at Ecône*, 59 B, June 8, 1978.

[83] *Summa Theologica*, II II, q. 177, a. 1, ad 4; cf. St. Aug. *De Trin.*, L. XIV.

Following St. Paul (Heb. 10:5), the Archbishop taught that our Lord was made Priest by his very Incarnation; the Divinity was like the oil of consecration that anointed His humanity from the first instant of its conception by the Virgin Mary. As the venerable Fr. Le Rohellec taught: "Mary is, therefore, a blessed sanctuary where the first priestly ordination was performed...and she brought forth Jesus in His very capacity as Priest."[85] Whence it follows that the Holy Virgin is also the Mother of those who by the character of the sacrament of order—the "participation in his grace of union that belonged to our Lord"[86]—are configured with Christ the Priest.

Our Lord Jesus Christ whose blessed soul was assumed by the Word was from the beginning adorned with the fullness of sanctifying grace and charity, and flooded with the splendors of the beatific vision. Plunged in adoration before His Father and moved by obedience to love, He offered Himself in sacrifice to God His Father to make satisfaction for the sins of men (Heb. 10:5-10).

THE VERITABLE "MYSTERY OF THE FAITH"

Through the priestly character the priest receives the power to renew *in persona Christi* the sacrifice of obedience and charity accomplished on the cross; he offers it in an unbloody way on the altar at each Mass he celebrates. This doctrine belongs to Tradition and is found in St. Thomas, the Council of Trent, and Pius XII. The priest essentially is made for the Holy Sacrifice of the Mass, for the sacrifice, for *sacrum facere*, "to do sacred things"; he is defined by the Mass.

According to Archbishop Lefebvre, after Bérenger and the Protestants had denied the real presence of Christ in the Eucharist, catechisms and piety then insisted too exclusively on the real presence and adoration of the Blessed Sacrament, and blurred devotion towards the Mass itself:

> And that is very serious because it changes the perspective on the Holy Eucharist itself, which becomes only food or a spiritual restorative; this new perspective does not focus as much upon immolation and our Lord Jesus Christ the Victim who offers Himself as a sacrifice of propitiation for our sins. This is why it was so easy to go over to the idea of a meal-mass similar to the Protestants...who hate this veritable, propitiatory sacrifice. Now, this sacrifice is the essential work of the Church; when the Church gives out Communion, she unites the faithful to the Victim who contin-

---

84 Lefebvre, *Itinéraire spirituel*, ch. 6.
85 P. J. Le Rohellec, *Marie et le sacerdoce* (ex typis "Cor Unum," n.d.).
86 Lefebvre, *Itinéraire spirituel*, ch. 6; *Retreats at Ecône*, 92, 6 A, New School Year, Sept. 21, 1988. The vocabulary of "participation" is quite flexible and allows such a theologically bold claim; however, strictly speaking, the hypostatic union is a grace that cannot be participated in.

ues to offer Himself to God the Father. We therefore have a participation in this state of victimhood....If we do not insist on this aspect, we will end up no longer having a truly Catholic spirit....The spirit of Christianity consists in making us into victims united to our Lord Jesus Christ: suffering and offering are the most beautiful, profound, and real treasures in the Catholic religion.[87]

One must then be careful not to separate the sacrament from the sacrifice, just as one must not separate the sacrifice of the Mass from the sacrifice of Calvary. St. Thomas sums up these two indissoluble unions in one sentence: "In the celebration of this sacrament—of the Eucharist—Christ is immolated (III, q. 83, a. 1).

Archbishop Lefebvre said that the Mass is the "reactualization of the sacrifice of Calvary (which is the reason for the Incarnation), the bringing about of Redemption, and the act that infinitely glorifies God and opens the gates of heaven to sinful humanity."[88]

"The more we study the Holy Sacrifice of the Mass, the more we realize that it truly is an extraordinary mystery. The priest is like someone who is outside of time and who passes almost into eternity because all his words have an eternal value....[The Mass] is not a simple rite carried out today, but an eternal reality that exceeds time and which has eternal consequences for the glory of God; it saves souls from purgatory, and sanctifies us. Each Mass truly has the weight of eternity in it."[89]

In view of this, the Archbishop stated that the Mass, and not only the cross, is the source of the graces of all the other Sacraments.[90] "The Church is organized around the sacrifice of the Mass, and the priesthood lives out this sacrifice to build up the Mystical Body"[91] through preaching, baptism, and the other Sacraments.

THE INTEGRITY OF THE PRIESTHOOD AND MISSIONARY ZEAL

"This marvelous plan designed by the Eternal Wisdom of God could not have been realized without the priesthood....The influence of priestly grace is the influence of the cross. The priest is thus at the heart of the renewal merited by our Lord. His influence is decisive on souls and on society. A priest enlightened by his faith and filled with the virtues and the Gifts of the Holy Ghost can convert numerous souls to Jesus Christ, raise vocations, and transform pagan society into Christian society."[92]

---

[87] *Retr. d'ordin.*[Ordination retreat], Montalenghe, 1989, 99 2 B, 4th Instruction.
[88] Lefebvre, *Itinéraire spirituel*, ch. 7, 59-61.
[89] *Spiritual Conferences at Ecône*, 85 A, March 23, 1981.
[90] *Retreats at Ecône*, 92, 6 A, New School Year Retreat, Sept. 21, 1988.
[91] Lefebvre, *Itinéraire spirituel*, ch. 7, 59-61.
[92] *Ibid.*, ch. 7. Cf. Reflexions on the Priesthood, in *Le Courrier de Rome* 201, no. 11 (Jan. 1981).

In this sense, the priest is also one who creates civilization. He is the pioneer of the social reign of our Lord Jesus Christ. Archbishop Lefebvre considered that a Church without priests was thus inconceivable. "The Church is truly priestly. Our Lord is essentially a priest, and the priesthood is there essentially to realize and continue the work of Calvary, carrying it on by the Holy Sacrifice of the Mass. It cannot but be the most essential aspect of our holy religion and of the life of the Church."[93]

"Our Lord came to teach us to be religious,[94] and to rediscover our condition as religious. He came to restore not only natural religion but supernatural religion. He teaches us to pray by His own prayer, the Holy Sacrifice of the Mass, the great prayer of our Lord which is henceforth the most perfect act of religion."[95]

What is true for the simple faithful is even truer for the priest, and like Monsieur Olier,[96] Archbishop Lefebvre said that the priest was the veritable "religious of God." However, the Archbishop balanced the French school of spirituality by a Thomistic synthesis: religion is not the only "key virtue" of the priest; that role must also go to charity and prudence. As for the Mass, insofar as it continues Calvary, it is the source of the grace of the seven sacraments and of the whole life of the Church. Cardinal Journet quite misunderstood the work of Archbishop Lefebvre when he gave an account of the Archbishop's visit to him at the end of 1970: "I listened to him talk about his ideal of doing again today what Condren and Bérulle[97] did in the seventeenth century."[98]

His incomprehension would become complete when after the "suppression" of the Society, he wrote to a nun: "Ecône is the continuation of Port Royal[99] but without the brains."[100]

On the contrary, along with the integrity of the priesthood, Archbishop Lefebvre inevitably passed on the ideals of the sanctity of the priest and

---

93 *Retr. d'ordin.*[Ordination Retreat], Montalenghe 1989, 99 2 B, 4th Instruction.
94 [The Archbishop is using the word *religious* here in a general sense to describe the quality connected with our position as rational creatures who thereby owe worship to God through the virtue of religion. Trans.]
95 *Spiritual Conferences at Ecône*, 25 B, Dec. 2, 1975.
96 Jean-Jacques Olier (1608-1657) was the founder of the seminary and the Society of St. Sulpice which tried to carry on the work of the Oratorian Fr. de Condren in training priests in accord with the rulings of the Council of Trent. He also did great work in reforming the parish of St. Sulpice in the Faubourg Saint Germain of Paris and in helping the poor. St. Vincent de Paul regarded him as a saint.
97 [Cardinal Pierre Bérulle (1575-1629) was the founder of the French Oratory whose work was continued by Fr. de Condren. The Oratorian congregation was instrumental in helping to reform the French clergy at the time. Bérulle also wrote extensively and Urban VIII called him the "Apostle of the Word Incarnate." Trans.]
98 Letter to Bishop Mamie, Jan. 10, 1973, Savioz, *Essai historique sur la fondation de la Fraternité Saint-Pie X*, annex. 1. 78; Diocesan Archives of Lausanne, Geneva, and Fribourg, classer I, document 22.

his apostolic zeal. He simply said to the seminarians: "It is my vocation! A bishop is made to make priests. A bishop makes the Church grow and in this way he is a missionary. It is a torment to me to have this continual worry, so much do I desire to send good priests to the District Superiors and faithful....Where are priests made? In the seminary!"[101]

The priest and the future priest must find in his priesthood all his religious and apostolic virtues, and firstly the virtue of religion; hence he will respect "the primacy of God's love, divine praise, adoration, and prayer."[102]

Archbishop Lefebvre often warned his priests against disorganized outward activities: activism. "How many priests have lost all sense of their priesthood, and all interest in contemplation or prayer through activism supposedly related to the apostolate!"[103]

Thus when he summed up the spirit of the Society, he could say: "It is both contemplative and missionary." And he explained:

> There is no apostolate without contemplation. Contemplation is not necessarily for the cloister. It is the Christian life: a life of Faith and the realities of our Faith. The great reality to contemplate is the Holy Mass. This is what must characterize the members of the Society: contemplating our Lord on the cross and seeing there the summit of God's love, a love even unto supreme sacrifice. That is what our Lord is! This is what the Church contemplates primarily....
>
> And by this we will be missionaries: by the desire to pour out the blood of our Lord on souls. This is the *Mysterium fidei* to contemplate and to work for, the priestly mission *par excellence*. And the faithful gather around us because of the Holy Sacrifice of the Mass and for nothing else. One cannot be attached to the cross of our Lord without being a missionary....
>
> We must have total trust in the position we have taken because it is the Church's attitude. It is not mine, it is not "that of Archbishop Lefebvre," it is that of the Church. One day or another, all the rest will collapse.[104]

The Archbishop's faith in a future complete restoration was total. His sons shared it as did those he allowed into his inner circle. Let us study their testimonies to see what Archbishop Lefebvre was like in private.

---

[99] [Port Royal was the famous abbey on the Rue Saint Jacques in Paris which was notorious as the headquarters of the Jansenists. With its theorists and the patronage of writers such as Racine and Pascal, it was reputed as an intellectual center: hence Cardinal Journet's remark. Trans.]

[100] Savioz, *Essai historique sur la fondation de la Fraternité Saint-Pie X,* annex. 2.7, 4.

[101] *Spiritual Conferences at Ecône,* 96 A, Feb. 11, 1983.

[102] Letter to the members of the SSPX, Christmas 1976, *Cor Unum,* 18-19.

[103] Letter to members of the SSPX, Nov. 18, 1978, *Cor Unum,* 39.

[104] *Spiritual Conferences at Ecône,* 94 B, Dec. 3, 1982.

VIII. THE FRIEND

AS HIS DRIVERS SAW HIM

Archbishop Lefebvre's friends were found especially among his able and faithful drivers, whether from Valais or elsewhere. Some of them were builders and helped restore his priories. He used their talents during his ceaseless and sometimes extended travels: in spite of everything he remained a missionary (one could call him "perpetual motion"). He drew up a plan every quarter, and Marcel Pedroni would give out the tasks to the various members of the drivers' "company," issuing his orders—clear, brief, with no room for discussion, although he was always fraternal and friendly—a fortnight before the trip. One of them who was an insurance underwriter was concerned about the harm that his business might suffer because of the very frequent trips with the Archbishop. He then had the idea of "making a contract with St. Joseph," and later noted: "The more I go away with the Archbishop, the better business is."

The Archbishop would himself prepare the routes; often he chose to take the "good old roads" in preference to the motorways. In the car he followed their progress on the map. He had an innate sense of direction and a talent for map reading, and indicated shortcuts to his driver to avoid built-up areas.

"Here for a kilometer you can hit the gas, it's straight ahead. Then there is a road on your right. Then we go down a gentle incline, and when the road follows the edge of a forest, you can put your foot down again."

Once it was like a rally, a race against time, to go from Paris to Blois via Dinan leaving at 6 o'clock in the morning and arriving at 2 P.M. The drivers had to avoid going slowly and the Archbishop would make a discreet remark about time to make the driver understand that he had to go faster to cover the next stage of the journey on schedule. When the media made him a well-known figure, the inevitable speeding was quickly forgiven by indulgent traffic police. His violet skullcap carelessly thrown on the rear window shelf of the car would confirm that the driver was telling the truth: "Do you know whom you have stopped? Archbishop Lefebvre!"

"Oh! That's okay then. And in that case we will ride with you."

And the Archbishop's car would race along at 160 kmp[105] on a simple highway, escorted by two enthusiastic and delighted motorcycle cops, one in front and one behind.

When it was time for the news, he turned on the radio. And after five or ten minutes, he would say: "Good, come on, let's say the rosary." After the rosary he would stop to pray for a while and then say a second rosary. Later a third would be recited and thus all fifteen decades could be said.

---

[105] [Approximately 100 mph. Trans.]

However, in his final years his deafness induced him to pray his rosary in silence.[106]

In the back seat with his breviary, the Archbishop prayed his office, meditated, and thought about his plans and sermons: he did not lose a minute. In conversation, his drivers admired his great culture concerning the movement of ideas, his practical knowledge of building, and his contemplation of the marvels of creation (rather than in questions of literature). He thought and spoke about the earth's wonders: "What explains that?" He said surprising things about the work of the angels. He also knew animals, plants, regional specialities, and cooking.[107]

When traveling as a Holy Ghost Father, the Archbishop would make do with buying a couple of sandwiches and some mineral water for himself and his driver,[108] but later he really looked after his driver friends. He knew of suitable restaurants everywhere, and even of ones that were open to him on days when they were otherwise closed to the public. He advised his drivers on what to choose and did not fail to thank the manager, congratulating him when signing the visitors' book "on good Champagne cooking and true French service" which he knew how to appreciate. If he saw that in the afternoon his driver was getting tired, he would tactfully say to him, especially if the driver's wife was with them: "Near here I know of a good inn: let's stop and have a drink. I'm sure your wife would like a nice cup of tea."

He readily spent the night in a hotel so as not to disturb a priory at a late hour or else to accommodate those traveling with him. And he did not go to bed before inspecting his driver's room and swapping with him if necessary: "You are the driver and you need a quiet room; besides I am deaf."

He thought firstly of others. One day when coming back from Corrèze to Clermont-Ferrand, his leg was very painful but he refused to stop: "No," he said, "we must continue. Fr. Bourdon is waiting for us in his new priory."

ACTIVE CHARITY

During confirmation rounds or lecture tours, he showed himself to be "charming, suaveness itself,"[109] ready to speak to all, and never offended by the forgetfulness or over-familiarity of the faithful towards him. He encouraged others to chat and always found the right thing to say to people,

---

[106] Interview with Jacques Lagneau, April 21, 1997; Rémy Borgeat, ms. III, 37-38; Marcel Pedroni, notes from the road (June 16, 1998); Interview, May 17, 2001.
[107] Interview with Rémy Borgeat, ms. III, 33, 52-63.
[108] Fr. Berclaz, ms. I, 49, 28.
[109] Fr. O'Carroll, Interview, Nov. 26, 1997.

adapting himself to every situation. He was more casual with the simplest people, and more delicate with the most refined: all things to all men. After a ceremony he would mingle with the crowd and say hello to anyone. If he saw a face he knew, he would raise his arms in joyful greeting.

While traveling he remained a priest and apostle. At Fribourg-en-Brisgau, he realized: "There is a benefactor in Strasbourg who would like to meet me but I do not have her address." The driver called Ecône, the address was obtained, and they made a detour to Strasbourg.[110] On another occasion the Archbishop made the driver take a detour via Paray-le-Monial: "A seminarian wrote to me, he is asking himself questions. Here is his name." And the driver went and found the young man who was able to speak with the Archbishop in Rue de la Visitation. One day, accompanied by a priest, he visited an old lady; when he returned to the car he said: "I have just reconciled an old lady with the Church. She had not been practicing since the condemnation of Action Française."[111]

In addition to being zealous, Archbishop Lefebvre liked to give pleasure to others. Traveling near Voiteur, he thought: "But we are very near Cressia! Let's make a detour. The Dominican sisters would be very happy." He also knew how to take advantage of the hospitality available in restful spots. At Berberino near Florence he would visit his friend Mrs. Bonomi, and then Marcel Pedroni would always go with him. He even knew how to invite himself to the homes of the faithful: "What would you say if Archbishop Lefebvre came and knocked on your door after visiting St-Michel-en-Brenne? I could use a friendly stopover on the way to Vannes. Either we'll come over to your house or else you can come with us to a restaurant."[112]

At other times, in contrast, he was sensitive enough not to want to put people out:

"We are passing by St. Michel, let us stop at the Sisters," the driver suggested.

"No," replied the Archbishop. "Of course they will say 'What an honor,' but you can't imagine what chaos it causes in a community where everything is timed to the minute."

On his return to Ecône, he would drop off his small suitcase and briefcase in his office and go straightaway to the chapel if rosary was being said. "Community prayer comes first!" he explained to the driver, even though he had already prayed his rosary during the journey. Then after supper he would attack the pile of mail that was waiting for him; on his always clear

---

[110] Marcel Pedroni, notes from the road, on Nov. 16, 1973.

[111] [Action Française was under siege throughout the latter part of 1926 until Pope Pius XI's official condemnation in December of that year. Ecclesiastical sanctions were not imposed until early the following year. Trans.]

[112] Archbishop Lefebvre, Letter from Ecône, July 11, 1989, to Commandant Pupin.

desk, he would methodically pen a dozen or so notes in his fine, neat, sloping handwriting, and put them in envelopes. Thus each of his correspondents would have a brief hand-written reply that was concise and answered his concerns. To finish off his letters, he always came up with a carefully polished sentence specifically for the addressee. To a young girl he wrote: "Thank you for your encouragement, loyalty, and prayers, and let me assure you of my respect and gratitude in Jesus and Mary."

To one of his drivers, he wrote: "Please remember me to Mrs. X—wife of the driver—and be assured of my friendship and prayers."

To one of his priests: "May God help you in your great ministry. Keep the traditions of the Church. Yours truly *in Xto et Maria*."

He also used a dictaphone and the wife of one of his drivers typed his mail at home. She noticed how Archbishop Lefebvre was entirely unyielding towards those who attacked the Faith; he replied even to insulting letters without however answering their attacks but rather speaking with "immense charity" about the Faith or the personal problems of his correspondent. Little by little this charity would convert her to the traditions of the Church, especially when Archbishop Lefebvre came in person to their home: he was kindness itself towards the children.[113]

He was very "family orientated" with regard to his brothers, sisters, and cousins. He kept up-to-date with births, marriages, and deaths, and never failed to send a birthday present to his goddaughter. When she was about thirteen or fourteen, he gave her a box of make-up: everything she needed to do her nails and "smell nice." "Well!" he said, "now you are a young lady, you must certainly need all those things." The presents he was given were showered on all his drivers. On the Ile d'Yeu, he was given an earthenware plate with the face of Marshal Pétain on it. "What am I supposed to do with this? Take it and make someone happy at home."[114]

The Archbishop's charity also made him helpful: in stairwells he always left the banister to others; at table when there were only two, he would get up to fetch whatever was missing; in the refectory he made sure that others were served, looked to see what they were in need of, and had the dishes passed around; he did all this naturally and discreetly. On December 26 at Ecône after breakfast, the seminarians were in a hurry to catch the train for holidays, but there were the dishes to do. "Leave those," said the Archbishop, "I will clear everything away," and he washed the bowls and spoons. At Suresnes, the young altar boy who served his Mass had to eat breakfast in a dreadful hurry "to be on time at school." So the Archbishop spread butter on bread for him: "Then you'll have the time to eat."[115]

---

[113] Rémy Borgeat, ms. III, 38-55.
[114] Michel Lefebvre, ms. II, 7, 47-58; 12, 45.

During meals, he was a "joyful guest," excellent at telling "screamingly funny" stories from Africa according to those who ate with him and remember some happy times. He was good at teasing nuns or "winding them up," and when they no longer knew how to react, he laughed heartily. He gently tormented his priests as well, sometimes over serious matters. He arrived one evening at St-Michel-en-Brenne with Fr. Le Boulc'h to whom he said: "Father, I really feel tired, you will have to preach the retreat instead of me." At breakfast the next day, however, he said to the priest: "I'm feeling better... Ah! I had thought they would bury me here near my sister. But before I died I would have had to consecrate four bishops [This was in April 1988 in the middle of negotiations with Rome]. Now, there are three of you here. We would have had to fetch Fr. Moulin to be the fourth. Oh, Father, it's a shame, you would have been a bishop!"

He thus knew how to create a relaxed atmosphere and to have fun himself. His brother Michel said: "He always seemed calm and joyful, and one never found any sadness in him."[116]

IX. AGE DID NOT SLOW HIM DOWN

HONORING ARCHBISHOP LEFEBVRE

Age has not slowed him down. Neither is he hurried because of the little time that remains for him to accomplish the great work that he has to do. Archbishop Lefebvre goes forth with the serenity of a man who is being led.

What is striking in this individual is his goodness. I mean he radiates goodness. One feels it like the warmth of a hand. It touches you. Immediately it makes one want to be better, to be less indulgent towards oneself, one's failings and faults and to be more worthy of the respect one is shown.

Only one other man inspired me with the same feeling: Marshal Pétain. He and Archbishop Lefebvre share the same natural dignity, the same good-humored authority and the same the simplicity.

They are the type of men whose intelligence is not intellectual. There is no posturing in their seriousness. They are mischievous without being malicious. Spontaneously they inspire loyalty even unto sacrifice, because one knows instinctively and with a sudden and deep conviction that from the outset they have totally sacrificed themselves to their duty.

They do not deceive nor do they cheat. They do not go off at a tangent or give twisted explanations. Their yes is yes and their no is no. Trials

---

[115] Borgeat, ms. III, 42, 1-38; Marziac, *Monseigneur Lefebvre, soleil levant*, 64; Fr. Cottard, ms II, 52, 25-30.

[116] Michel Lefebvre, ms. II, 8, 4-20, 66; Fr. Cottard, ms. II, 52, 8-10; Jacques Lagneau, Interview April 21, 1997.

do not change the way they behave. One served France. The other serves God. With the same calm courage and the same confidence, they followed out the terms of their commitment to the very end without swaggering and without weakness.

Before judging them, one must first acknowledge their destiny with a heart full of gratitude and love for the lesson of grandeur they gave.[117]

We were anxious to cite in its entirety this passage of François Brigneau written in June 1988 just before the consecrations. It is one of the most beautiful tributes to the person and work of Archbishop Lefebvre, who continued leading his life of prayer and active charity with the pace of an ordered soul that quickened the nearer it came to the end of its time on earth.

ADVICE FOR THE FUTURE

Relieved by his auxiliaries of responsibility for confirmations and ordinations, the Archbishop gave himself more than ever to preaching retreats and days of recollection where his meditative and apostolic soul opened itself more intimately to his future priests; and he gave to his priests his *novissima verba*, his last thoughts. On the topic of the necessary priestly attitude to the apostolate, never had he spoken to them with so much clarity, so many detailed examples drawn from his rich experience, or even with so much emotional intensity. He recommended the virtues of prudence, caution, and organization: reconciling outward activities and the life of prayer, not allowing themselves to be thrust into secondary activities while neglecting the essential, and keeping proportion between their efforts and their available strength.[118] Above all, he recommended the virtue of discretion—a blend of sweetness and levelheadedness.

He called on his priests to be gentle towards sometimes critical layfolk. To one of his sons he wrote: "If you had asked me, I would have advised you to keep your silence and not to make those remarks." "Continue your apostolate without worrying about criticism or praise. May serving our Lord and being united to Him be your only recompense."[119]

Was this not what the Archbishop himself practiced and lived? He also warned his future priests to avoid having a domineering attitude towards souls, or telling them any misplaced secrets which would allow people, even if they were pious, to have some power over them. He wished to insure both their purity of intention and their freedom of action as priests.[120]

---

[117] François Brigneau, *Pour saluer Mgr. Lefebvre,* "Mes derniers cahiers," no. 1 (1991): 3.
[118] Letter to Fr. A. de Galarreta, Sept. 10, 1985; to Fr. G. Tam, Feb. 22, 1988; to Fr. Jesús Mestre, Nov. 21, 1990; Ordination Retreat, Montalenghe, 1989, 8th Inst., 101 4 B.
[119] Letter to a priest, March 17, 1982.
[120] Ordination Retreat, Montalenghe, June 24, 1989, 101 B 4.

In order to help priests in their ministry or nuns with difficult cases to resolve (problems normally dependent on episcopal authority or even on Rome), he foresaw the setting up of a canonical commission chaired by one of his auxiliary bishops. The decisions or judgments of this body would make up for the deficiencies of Roman courts or dicasteries influenced, like the new Code of Canon Law, "by false principles of ecumenism and modernism."[121]

In the same spirit of broadly applying the supplied jurisdiction that the Church grants in case of necessity to those with the supreme power of orders—the bishop—he suggested to his friend Bishop de Castro Mayer, whose health was failing, "a possible episcopal consecration of someone to succeed him—in Campos—to transmit the Catholic Faith and confer the sacraments reserved to the bishops." The priests of Campos could choose a successor who would be consecrated by the auxiliary bishops of the Society in their capacity as Catholic bishops.[122] The jurisdiction of the new bishop would "not be territorial but personal" and come to him "from the priests and faithful who appeal to him to take care of their souls." In light of this and given that his authority as a bishop would not be by Rome's appointment but from the need to save souls, "he will have to exercise his authority with particular care, and take more notice of his priestly council" of whom he would be president for life.[123]

Dom Antonio would die after the Archbishop one month later to the day, on April 25, 1991. His successor in supplied jurisdiction, Dom Licinio Rangel, was elected by his peers as Superior of the St. Jean-Marie Vianney Association and consecrated at São Fidelis in Brazil by three of the auxiliary bishops of the Society of Saint Pius X on July 28, 1991.

THE NEW WORLD ORDER AND ISLAM

The Archbishop never limited his fight to presbyteries and sacristies. For him, Christ King and Priest was the light that illuminates the life of the Church as much as the life of civil society. He wished that like himself his priests should not remain ignorant of politics at home and abroad, and he remained up-to-date on current affairs in order to be able to give Catholic guidance on this topic to the faithful. Thus he suggested to his sons in the priesthood to support "by apostolic action"—*i.e.,* by recalling the usefulness of the civil authorities (that are neither secular nor atheist but Catholic) in the salvation of souls —"the election of candidates with polit-

---

[121] Letter to Fr. Franz Schmidberger, Jan. 15, 1991.
[122] Letter to Bishop de Castro Mayer, Dec. 4, 1990; *Fideliter,* no. 82: 13-14.
[123] *Note au sujet du nouvel évêque succédant à S. Exc. Mgr. de Castro Mayer* (Note concerning a new bishop to succeed His Excellency Bishop de Castro Mayer), sent on Feb. 20, 1991, to Fr. Fernando Arêas Rifan in Campos.

ical agendas that favor the social reign of Christ, even if they have a few faults."[124]

Considering Christ the King led him to make reflections on Judaism, the One World movement, and Islam.

He collaborated with Fr. Marziac[125] in writing the *Précis de la doctrine sociale* (The Summary of Social Doctrine) and suggested adding a few extra lines on the chapter concerning the mystery of Israel:

> Since Israel refused the true Messiah, it would give itself another messianism that is temporal and earthbound, dominating the world by money, Freemasonry, Revolution, and social democracy. We must not, however, forget that those Jews who were disciples of the true Messiah founded the true Israel, the spiritual Kingdom, which prepares the heavenly Kingdom. The worldwide designs of the Jews are being brought about in our time, but they started with the foundation of Masonry and the Revolution which has decapitated the Church and set up worldwide socialist democracy.[126]

In Bourget on November 19, 1989, the Archbishop recalled "the predictions made by Masonic sects and published at the request of Pius IX by Jacques Crétineau-Joly: they make allusion to world government and the subjection of Rome to Masonic ideals." [127]

On another occasion he explained that the Apocalypse of St. John predicts in the vision of the two beasts in Chapter 13 how the leaders of the Church commit sacrilegious profanation and put their spiritual power at the service of the Anti-Christ's synarchy. It is a penetrating vision. Fr. Du Chalard noted: "Neither age nor illness altered his mind and he was still curious and informed about everything. During the [first] Gulf War (1990-1991) he followed the unfolding of military operations almost hour by hour. He passed comment. He explained. He predicted what would happen. It was fascinating."[128]

However, the establishment of a New World Order clashed with another view of the world that was theistic in its preaching, globally encompassing in its vision of society, and militant in its expansionism. Islam was gradually undertaking a "gentle conquest" of what was left of Christianity.

---

[124] *Spiritual Conferences at Ecône*, 22 B, Sept. 30, 1975, 71-74.

[125] *Précis de la doc. sociale de l'Eglise à l'usage des chefs d'Etats* (Summary of the Church's Social Doctrine for use by Heads of State), by Fr. Marziac, former missionary, with the help of several contributors (Caussade, 1991), 164 pages.

[126] Keren Hayessod, the "Appel unifié pour Israël (Unified Appeal for Israel)" in his magazine "*Contact*" (October 1976), noted that Archbishop Lefebvre "has said nothing about the Jews...because he is too clever to talk about us directly..." while perceiving that "under the labels of Freemasonry and the Communist movement, Archbishop Lefebvre is including the Jews when he speaks of Vatican II's mistaken openness."

[127] *Fideliter*, no. 73: 14-15.

[128] Cf. F. Brigneau, *Pour saluer Mgr. Lefebvre*, 49.

The Archbishop wondered about this in an interview with François Brigneau for Radio Courtoisie: "How should we interpret...this invasion of Europe by Islam? While Christian Europe always defended itself against this invasion, now suddenly they have the protection of governments and even the Church, and we are invaded by a religion that is essentially anti-Christian, I repeat, essentially anti-Christian; it is very militant and, therefore, very dangerous for our Christian civilization."[129]

And the Archbishop warned bishops about providing accommodation for mosques. This would be to organize Islam religiously and, therefore, also politically, because for Islam, "there is no difference between religion and politics." Again he explained that while Muslims are a minority in a Christian country they accept its laws, but "when they are numerous and organized, they become aggressive and want to impose their laws."

On this question of where religion becomes politics, the Archbishop had also expressed his views a few days before on November 14, 1989, during a press conference at the Hôtel Crillon to mark his jubilee. At the time the Islamic foulard was creating a stir in French public opinion.[130] Answering a journalist's question, he made some remarks that, at the request of LICRA (International League Against Racism and Anti-Semitism) caused him to be brought before the 17th Magistrate's Court. Brilliantly defended by his lawyers Georges Paul Wagner and Dominique Remy, the Archbishop, whose case went to appeal on March 21, 1991, was nevertheless found guilty before the 11th chamber of the appeal court of "public defamation of a group of individuals because of ...their membership...of a religion."[131] Even on his deathbed the judgment of men pursued the "suspended and excommunicated" Archbishop in the civil domain: his honor but lacked this last decoration. However, the fine witness statement of his friend Cardinal Hyacinthe Thiandoum was enough to exonerate him from the accusation of racism.[132]

---

[129] Interview broadcast by Radio-Courtoisie on Nov. 22, 1989 (recorded at Suresnes on Nov. 18), cf. Brigneau, *Pour saluer Mgr. Lefebvre*, 27.

[130] [The controversy over the "foulard" (scarf worn by Muslim women to cover the head) resulted from the fact that the French education system (which prides itself on being "free," "obligatory," and "secular") does not in principle allow religious symbols to be worn conspicuously in school since this militates against the secular character of education. However, with the increasing number of Muslim children in French schools who wished to wear the "oulard," it had become a serious problem. Trans.]

[131] Cf. Law of July 29, 1981, art. 29, 1 and 32, 2. After the death of Archbishop Lefebvre, the Society appealed to the Court of Cassation (Higher Appeal Court) which declared the public prosecution to be exhausted.

[132] G.-P. Wagner and D. Remy, *La condamnation* (Ulysse, 1992), 45. One can also read in this work (139) the statement of the Muslim Ababacar Sadikhe Thiam, from Dakar. Cf. see Appendices.

FINAL JUBILEES

The former Archbishop of Dakar had never wanted to be anything else but the Herald of the Reign of Christ and His Cross. This was the beautiful priestly and episcopal agenda that he evoked at Bourget before 23,000 people on November 19, 1989, when he celebrated his 60th Jubilee as a priest. On April 29, 1990, at Friedrichshafen, he gave the same message to ten thousand German-speaking faithful and explained how through the New Mass "the spirit of the Catholic Church essentially based on the Cross and on the spirit of sacrifice"[133] had disappeared.

He developed this same theme magnificently in the more private celebration of the Tenth Priestly Jubilee of one of his priests, Fr. François Pivert, at Rouen on May 1, 1990:

Since the Mass is a sacrifice, the whole Catholic religion is marked by sacrifice and by the cross of Jesus Christ. This is why we must have the cross of Jesus Christ everywhere, in our bedrooms, houses, and at crossroads: to remind us of what our Lord Jesus Christ, God crucified, is, and of the lesson of sacrifice that He gives us.

We do not have the choice: those who do not go by the cross of our Lord will not pass through the gate of the true flock that is our Lord Jesus Christ.

Why sacrifice oneself? Why love but for charity's sake! And, you understand this well: what do a father and a mother of a family do if not sacrifice themselves for their family and for one another? You must sacrifice yourselves, otherwise there is no love!

Is not Marcel Lefebvre's entire life summed up in these nine small words?

ILLNESS—SHORT HOLIDAYS—BIRTHDAY

For the last twelve years his life had been touched by the trial of physical illness. The Archbishop suffered from intestinal troubles: he wondered, "Might I have cancer?"[134] Had not his mother died this way? They had discreetly spoken of an intestinal obstruction.

In the evening the Archbishop could no longer eat anything. Invariably he was happy just to take a cup of herbal tea in spite of the protests from his hosts. The restaurant owner of the *Faisan doré* in Fontenai-sur-Orne became offended: "But, Your Grace, you are going to go into the dining room." "But, Your Grace, we're going to prepare for you an excellent meal!" However, nothing could be done, and although he ordered two beers, one for himself and one for his driver, he then retired. In priories or

[133] Le Bourget: *Fideliter*, no. 72: 1-3; no. 73: 14-15; Friedrichshafen: *Fideliter*, no. 76: 10.
[134] Fr. Pierre Verrier, ms. II, 53, 43-49.

with friends, he made his drink last so as to remain a while with his hosts or honor his priests, and then he asked to be excused.[135]

Sitting down for a long time in a car or on a plane bothered him. His heart was "none too good" either. He also suffered from insomnia. He simply said: "At night I don't need much sleep; on the stroke of midnight I get up, say Matins,[136] deal with some mail, think a little, and then go back to bed."[137]

He had to reduce the number of his trips; even before the consecrations he announced that soon he would no longer cross the oceans "to make the priests and faithful," as he said, "more aware of the situation of necessity."

Thus families hurried to where he was doing confirmations to present him with children, even "those as young as five," as he himself suggested; and each time he confirmed hundreds of them. Often he alluded to his death "which cannot be long off."

At Ecône he showed the funeral crypt to friends who were visiting. He had had it built for those who died in the community: "That is where they are going to bury me," he said.[138]

Returning from the jubilee celebrations at Bourget, he admitted to bouts of feeling ill and dizzy and stated that he wanted take some rest. He had not taken a real holiday since 1947 except for three or four days here and there with his brother Joseph.[139] He decided to go for three months to Italy, Spain, and France and stay in a few quiet spots where he could write "a little book" which would be his *Spiritual Journey*. On December 24, 1989, he wrote to Fr. Simoulin from Albinia where he was staying with Marcel Pedroni and his wife:[140] "My work is going slowly and it will take me a good month to do anything useful....I am spending more time praying than working. It's not too soon!"

Nevertheless in 1990, the Archbishop began making more trips. At Friedrichshafen on April 29 he remained standing for over an hour during his sermon and its translation. On June 7, he took a plane for Gabon to make a final pilgrimage back to his roots—his last intercontinental flight—together with four of his drivers and faithful bodyguards. He went to bless the chapel of the Mission of St. Pius X and to give confirmation.[141] As he was leaving Ecône, he opened up his quilted jacket with a mischie-

---

[135] Jacques Lagneau, *Souvenirs de voyages* (April 21, 1997).

[136] Fr. Simoulin had a little private chapel set up next to Archbishop Lefebvre's office at Ecône where he celebrated Mass and could pray in front of the Blessed Sacrament.

[137] Fr. Pierre Epiney, Interview Jan. 6, 2001, ms. III, 18, 43-50; Archbishop Lefebvre, letter to Fr. Simoulin, Feb. 8, 1990.

[138] Fr. Michael O'Carroll, Interview Nov. 26, 1997.

[139] *Fideliter*, no. 59: 5; ms. I, 48, 30-40.

[140] Marcel Pedroni, *Notes from the Road*.

[141] *Ibid.*, and André Cagnon, *Fideliter*, no. 76: 29-33.

vous wink of youthful triumph to reveal a white cassock with violet buttons clasped in an equally violet cord cincture: "It's the Dakar one!" he said, before giving a fresh, happy laugh and setting off on his journey.[142]

Finally, on September 6 during a priests' retreat at Ecône, Archbishop Lefebvre unveiled his *Spiritual Journey*. It was the spiritual message that he considered he had not yet passed on to his sons, at least not in this form condensed into eighty pages. "With this I have given everything I could; I cannot see what more I can give...I ask you to pray so that I may make a good and holy death because that is the only thing I have left to do."

In mid-October, Maître Le Panse was his driver as he traveled throughout France. On one occasion when he passed through Mesnil-Saint-Loup where the lawyer and his family lived, Archbishop Lefebvre said at table under his breath to Mrs. Le Panse: "We are nothing, absolutely nothing!" And fearing that he was not understood, he insisted in the same tone of voice: "Do you understand me? Nothing...nothing at all!"[143]

To thank his drivers for their work, he went with them and their wives for ten days to a remote part of the Spanish coast between Gibraltar and Cadiz. It was to be a relaxing break which, as he wished, "would also have a spiritual and religious side to it." A room of the small hotel was transformed into a chapel and from November 6 to 14, a whole "tribe of drivers" and their wives followed an almost monastic program: Mass, breakfast, spiritual talk ("a little *fervorino*" said the Archbishop), tourism, bathing for those who desired, rosary together, supper (herbal tea for the Archbishop), and a sing-along in which the Archbishop joined enthusiastically "to the great astonishment of the hostess who had never seen guests so happy and joyous; and that, added Rémy Bourgeat with tongue in cheek, in spite of the life of prayer that we were leading."[144]

On November 29 after saying goodbye to Corrèze and Quiévrain, the Archbishop celebrated his eighty-fifth birthday at Ecône. He said to the faithful who came to assist at his Mass: "At the age that God has allowed me to reach, it is quite normal to think about the end of one's life. One has to think about it throughout one's life but particularly when the time grows near. So, I would be grateful if you would pray for me so that, if it please God, this year He will grant me a holy death. Finishing well is everything."

On February 11, 1991, he gave his last conference to the seminarians and concluded: the situation in the Church is more serious than if it were

---

[142] Fr. Michel Simoulin, *In Memoriam*, Letter to Former Seminarians, no. 14, June 29, 1991.

[143] Letter of Mrs. Jean-Marc Le Panse, June 13, 1996.

[144] Letter of Archbishop Lefebvre to his drivers, July 30, 1990; Marcel Pedroni, ms. III, 20-21; Rémy Borgeat, ms. III, 35-36.

just a question of a loss of faith. *We are seeing another religion established,* with other principles that are not Catholic.

In spite of his heart, "which was playing up," Archbishop Lefebvre left on February 13 to make a last trip, firstly to Gigondas and then on to Fanjeaux and Brignoles. When one of the Sisters' superiors mentioned plans for the near future, the Archbishop replied: "I won't be there any more...I would have done it willingly but I will be gone."

And as he left the community who had invited him to return, he said: "Mother, I have worked for a long time. Everything is in place and you have bishops. Now, for me, *requiem aeternam!*"

And as he was getting into the car: "I have finished my job...now, rest!"[145]

In Nice he saw Dom Guillou for the last time. The Archbishop and his driver had just reached Italy when he spoke of a letter that he had received from "those islands down there" sent by three benefactors, the Monzita sisters; he wanted to thank them. And so he took the boat from Civitavecchia to Sardinia to visit the three old ladies who could not believe their eyes when they saw him. Until the end, his charity made him want to give pleasure to others.

X. PASSIONTIDE

Having learnt of the death of his older sister Jeanne, Archbishop Lefebvre decided not to go to the funeral: "I pray every day that I might die before losing my mind. I would like to go because if I contradicted myself, they would say: 'There it is; he said he got it wrong!' And they would take advantage of that."

Many times the Archbishop mentioned the gentle death of his elder sister who was called home to God when she had just gone off for a doze; he would have liked to die like that although with extreme unction. But God would ask the priest and bishop who was Marcel Lefebvre to take part fully in His redemptive suffering.

On March 7, 1991, the feast of St. Thomas Aquinas, the Archbishop gave friends and benefactors from Valais the traditional lecture. Full of faith and eloquence, he concluded with these words: "We will have them!" And the following day at 11 A.M. he celebrated what would be his final Mass on earth. But such were his stomach pains and fatigue that he really thought he would not be able to finish it. Nevertheless he set off by car for Paris to attend the meeting of religious founders in the "Circles of Tradition": "It is too important a thing," he said, "and it is very close to my heart."

---

[145] *In Memoriam.* Most of the facts in the following pages are gleaned from this compilation.

HOSPITALIZATION, OPERATION

He did not get beyond Bourg-en-Bresse; about 4 A.M., he woke up his driver, Rémy Bourgeat: "I'm not well," he said, "let's go back to Switzerland." And at his request he was taken into hospital as an emergency on March 9 in the morning. The director of the hospital in Martigny, Mr. Jo Grenon, was a friend of Ecône. The Archbishop was admitted to the surgical wing in Room 213. Behind the mountains surrounding the town were Forclaz, and France, and not too far away, the Great Saint Bernard Pass, Italy, and Rome.

The Archbishop was confident but he was suffering: "It is like a fire burning my stomach and it comes up towards my chest."

Fr. Simoulin brought him Holy Communion, which he would receive until his operation. He thanked him: "I have made you miss Vespers...but you have done a work of charity. You have brought me the best Doctor. None of them can give me more than what you have given me."

He admired the crucifix that had been brought for the temporary altar in his room:

"That helps one bear one's sufferings."

Painkillers helped lessen his suffering and he was fed intravenously. He joked, saying to the nurses: "You have got a good deal out of me: I am paying full price and you are not even feeding me!"

He was moreover very patient and the doctors had to tell him off so that he would speak about his pains. The nurses found him very gentle and exceptionally discreet: he never used the bell to call for attention. He did not want to disturb others. He was a little concerned about the consequences of an operation, but at the same time he was resigned and trusting. Several times, he said: "I have finished my work and I can do no more. Nothing remains for me to do but pray and suffer."

On Monday, March 11, he felt a cold sensation rising up his legs and he asked for extreme unction, which he received with great recollection and simplicity, keeping his eyes closed and answering the priest very clearly. Next he asked for the apostolic benediction *in articulo mortis* (at the time of death), and then he opened his calm eyes, smiled, offered his thanks to the priest and added: "As for the prayers for the dying, we can wait yet a while."

He was a little better but he had not yet started saying his breviary again. "So I say some simple prayers. I'm good for nothing else. It's no bad thing."

He had already undergone numerous examinations when on Thursday, March 14, the doctors decided to give him a meal which he would enjoy and which would give him some strength. But he did not eat it so that he could receive Holy Communion...the priest was running late. On the same day one of the doctors said to Fr. Denis Puga: "Father, I must tell you something. I have spent the day with the Archbishop because of the examinations. He is an extraordinary man, and it is truly a pleasure to be with him. What goodness! One can see the divine goodness in his face. You are really privileged to be so close to him. People don't realize when they see him in the newspapers. I asked the Archbishop to pray for me."

This doctor was not Catholic. On Friday, March 15, Archbishop Lefebvre was taken to Monthey to be examined by scanner. He returned to the hospital where his priests found him in some difficulty because of the IV's, which were causing swelling:

"Your veins are too hard," Fr. Simoulin said to him.

"No, quite the contrary, it seems that they are too fine and small. How about that...in an iron bishop!"

On Saturday the 16th, *Sitientes*, the ordinations to the subdiaconate took place at Ecône. "I was united in prayer with the ordination," said the Archbishop to Fr. Puga.

"It's the first ordination that could not have taken place if you had not given us bishops."

"Yes, really that year 1988 was a great grace, a blessing from the good Lord, a real miracle. This is the first time when I have been seriously ill that I have also been perfectly at peace. I must admit...I'm sorry...but before when I was ill, I was always worried that the Society still needed me and that no one could take on my work. Now I am at peace, everything is ready, and everything is working nicely."

On Sunday the 17th, Passion Sunday, after having received Holy Communion, he explained that he would be operated on the following day and remarked: "Let the good Lord take me if he wants."

So, the operation took place on Monday of Passion Week: "When the doctor told me to count up to ten as I was falling asleep, I made a large sign of the cross...then...there was nothing. Then I woke up and asked: 'Is the operation not going ahead then?'"

"But Mr. Lefebvre [*sic*], it's done," they answered.

Such was the account that the Archbishop gave of his operation. The surgeon removed a large tumor about the size of three grapefruits. It turned out to be cancerous, but nothing was said to the patient. He was exhausted by the operation but smiled from behind his oxygen mask and stomach tube. On Wednesday evening he became anxious; his limbs were terribly swollen and he had pains in his back and head. He said: "It is the end, I've a terrible headache. The good Lord must come and fetch me. I truly want to die with a few of my priests around me to say the prayers for the dying. They cannot refuse me that."

He thought that his priests were being stopped from coming to see him, and Fr. Puga's arrival on Thursday morning calmed him down. He became optimistic again and much more upbeat. On Saturday of Passion

Week Archbishop Lefebvre spoke about the humiliating and painful procedures that he had to undergo, and said that the least effort left him exhausted. His hands were swollen.

"We are in Passiontide," said Fr. Simoulin.

The Archbishop closed his eyes and repeated: "Yes, it is the passion!" He could not yet receive Communion: "I miss it...I need it...it gives me strength," he said sadly.

The evening of the same day, Fr. Puga told him about some remarks of Cardinal Gagnon in *30 Giorni* to the effect that he had found no doctrinal error at Ecône. The Archbishop shrugged his shoulders: "One day the truth will out. I don't know when, the good Lord knows. But it will out."

PAINFUL DEATH

Right to the end, the Archbishop had not the slightest doubt that he had done the right thing. And as we shall see, his end was, like his life, centered on and strengthened by a faith that was simple, discreet, and modest. It seems there were no spiritual messages or *novissima verba*—"last words." He made a few remarks that were apparently commonplace or "even mischievous though not malicious," the importance of which would only be apparent afterwards, especially with regard to those who knew Archbishop Lefebvre little or not at all, and who could not imagine how he died since they had not seen him live.[146]

On Sunday, March 24, the first day of Holy Week, the patient's condition suddenly got worse. On Friday he had asked for his watch and hearing aid (proof that the patient was feeling better) and on Saturday they had thought about moving him back to his room the following day. But on Sunday, hope gave way to concern: the Archbishop had a very high temperature and the cardiologist decided to keep him in the intensive care unit. He was agitated and in pain, and he talked incessantly but because of the oxygen mask it was difficult to understand him. However, Jo Grenon made out: "We are all His little children." When Grenon left him, the Archbishop smiled at him and extended his hand to say farewell.[147]

When Fr. Simoulin told him that his brother Michel Lefebvre had come, he smiled as much as he could and joy shone in his face. Around 7 P.M. the rector of Ecône returned to the hospital but as soon as he entered intensive care, he heard the terrifying sound of forceful groaning which could be heard above the noises coming from the equipment nearby; it was amplified more by the oxygen mask. The Archbishop was utterly exhausted and could not speak, but he understood everything that the priest said

---

[146] *In Memoriam*, preface.

[147] Interview with Jo Grenon, *Les 17 derniers jours de Mgr. Lefebvre* (The Last Seventeen Days of Archbishop Lefebvre), in *Controverses*, no. 30 (April 1991): 3.

to him: "Your Grace, the retreat that you were to have preached to us…you are now preaching it in a way we had not foreseen!" The Archbishop smiled. "Some of the faithful from Valais including the drivers are following the retreat with us." And the Archbishop smiled again.

Then the priest noticed the crucifix of the cubicle and made a remark in praise of the hospital and its good director who placed every patient under the watch of the Redeemer. Very slowly the Archbishop turned his head to look where the priest was pointing towards his left, then he gently closed his eyes.

A smile…a look upon the Crucified…these where the last words of Archbishop Lefebvre. A smile…to say thank you, to reassure, to encourage others to have the same serenity, a smile of charity and attentiveness to others in self-forgetfulness. A look towards the crucifix, the last conscious gesture that his sons saw him make: the look of the adoring worshiper and priest.[148]

About 11:30 P.M. the hospital called Ecône: Archbishop Lefebvre had just had a cardiac arrest and was in resuscitation. Frs. Simoulin and Laroche found the Archbishop breathing with great difficulty: his eyes were fixed and glazed. He had been given a cardiac massage and must have suffered a pulmonary embolism.

While Fr. Laroche returned to the seminary to wake up the community and bring them to the chapel to pray, Fr. Simoulin stayed with the Archbishop, who was making painful attempts to breathe; it was like the agony of the Crucified. As the time passed his face became more and more lined with pain while the readings on the monitors went down little by little.

About 2:30 A.M., his decline accelerated and his breathing slowed while pain still drew a line across his brow. Little by little everything subsided. About 3:15 A.M. the priest said to the nurse, "His soul is only waiting for one thing: to leave this body that is suffering and be with God."

"I think the soul is leaving now," said the nurse who then withdrew.

Fr. Simoulin began the prayers for the dying. "At the very moment that I finished," he said, "it was almost 3:20 A.M. and the Superior General, Fr. Schmidberger, entered intensive care. The pulse reading had fallen to '00' but a breath could still be heard: was it the Archbishop or the machine? I offered the Ritual to Fr. Schmidberger, who began again the prayers *in expiratione*."

A few last surges of pain flashed across the Archbishop's face and then about 3:25 A.M. the suffering ceased altogether and he became peaceful again. The Superior General then closed the eyes of the beloved father.

It was Monday of Holy Week, March 25, Feast of the Annunciation of the Most Blessed Virgin Mary, the day that Heaven smiled at Earth and

---

[148] Cf. Fr. M. Simoulin, *Controverses*, no. 30: 10.

when hope was reborn in souls: the day of the Incarnation of the Son of God and the priestly ordination of Jesus Christ as Sovereign Priest. On this day the soul of Marcel Lefebvre was judged...

At Lille fifteen years before he had said: "When I am before my Judge, I do not want Him to be able to say to me: 'You as well, you let the Church be destroyed.'"

So on that March 25, 1991, when God asked him what he had done with the grace of his priesthood and episcopacy, what indeed might he have replied, this old soldier for the Faith, this bishop who had restored the Catholic priesthood?

"Lord, look, I have handed on everything that I could hand on: the Catholic Faith, the Catholic priesthood, and also the Catholic episcopacy; You gave me all of that, and all of that I handed on so that the Church might continue.

"Your great Apostle said, *'Tradidi quod et accepi'* and like him I wanted to say: *'Tradidi quod et accepi,'* I have handed on what I received. Everything that I received I have handed on."

XI. GREATER LOVE HATH NO MAN

The remains of the faithful warrior were solemnly brought back to Ecône. Dressed in pontifical vestments, they lay in state in the chapel of Notre Dame des Champs. The crowd filed by throughout the week; the Nuncio and Bishop Schwery of Sion even came and blessed the body of one the Pope had declared excommunicated. The body was watched day and night from Monday to Easter Tuesday. The Archbishop received a final blessing on that morning of April 2, and then the coffin was closed. A plaque was fixed upon it bearing the arms of the Archbishop and these words that he had asked be engraved: *Tradidi quod et accepi.*

Slowly the Archbishop was borne on the shoulders of his priests and passed through the crowd of twenty thousand faithful who had gathered together for the funeral. He was carried down the field in front of Ecône down which he had often processed to hand on the grace of the priesthood. Then he arrived at the "canvas basilica" at the bottom of the field where the Mass and Pontifical Absolutions would take place. The weather was cold and gray; the sun only shone on the opposite side of the valley. Suddenly in the middle of the ceremony, it shed its light on the immense crowd of friends of the Society of Saint Pius X. The warmth spread. Then when the body was carried back up the field towards the blue sky and to its last resting place at Ecône, twenty thousand souls felt in their hearts that here was life passing and continuing. This too was the feeling in the hearts of his sons in the priesthood, each holding a small, lit candle in the dazzling light reflected off the cliffs behind Ecône. Tradition was alive.

In a book of condolence, one of the "rank and file Catholics" who followed the Tradition of the Church thanks to Archbishop Lefebvre, wrote these few brief lines: "Thank you for having stepped in, for having saved the priesthood, for having been our standard bearer, and for having offered yourself as a holocaust to save your people."

Yes, he loved the Church with his whole heart even to love's very limits: *in finem dilexit*. Did he not show the greatest love possible? He loved more than many, this man who to the very end "believed in the charity that God has for us."

APPENDICES

I

INSCRIPTION IN THE VISITORS' BOOK AT THE BOURGUILLON HOSPICE (AUGUST 7, 1952)

The Missionary often feels weak and powerless faced with the enormity of the task he has to accomplish. The One who has sent him to preach the Gospel to the poor has not promised him an easy victory. So the Missionary seeks everywhere for help to enlighten souls and enflame them with charity, while they in their millions dwell insensibly in the darkness of error and the slavery of sin. On the contrary those who are sick hold in their hands an unfathomable and mysterious treasure, but sometimes they are greatly pained to think that they suffer in vain; firstly as regards their own perfection (because they are not always resigned to their pain), and secondly as regards others (for the Good Lord does not yet allow them to grasp all the marvels that are worked by their sufferings when they are joined to those of Jesus Crucified).

Thus has Our Lord in His infinite wisdom willed that each one of us carry his cross in union with Him. Like the union between the Missionary and the Contemplative, does there not exist between the Missionary and those who are sick—between these chosen ones of the Lord—a mystical union in Jesus the Apostle and Jesus Crucified? Yes! Blessed be this Hospice of Our Lady of Bourguillon which brings about in our Lord and through the Virgin Apostle and the Mother of Sorrows this real and effective union of the Missionary and those who are sick.

To the many other requests herein, I add those of the Vicar Apostolic of Senegal for all his vicariate, and especially for his mission among the Sérères who are coming in large numbers to ask for Baptism. I will ask all the priests who are laboring in this region and all those in my vicariate to pray in turn for the sick who offer up their sufferings with the particular intention of praying for the Vicariate of Dakar.

Since I am convinced of the enormous benefits that the offerings of the beloved sick can bring about for all the Missionaries, I recommend the fifty vicariates and apostolic prefectures of the Apostolic Delegation of Dakar to your pious intentions, and I thank you most sincerely as well as those who work devotedly for the Hospice of Our Lady of Bourguillon.

May Our Lord and the Virgin Mary deign to heap many blessings on our beloved spiritual benefactors.

†Marcel Lefebvre
Delegate and Vicar Apostolic of Dakar
Fribourg, August 7, 1952

II

MEMBERS OF THE CŒTUS INTERNATIONALIS PATRUM (1963-65)

Reliable list of a small number of the members of the Cœtus, those whom Archbishop Lefebvre called "the most solid, the most militant":

Geraldo de Proença Sigaud, Arch. of Diamantina, Brazil
Marcel Lefebvre, Superior General of the Holy Ghost Fathers
Antonio de Castro Mayer, Bp. of Campos, Brazil
Luigi Carli, Bp. of Segni, Italy
Dom Jean Prou, O.S.B., Abbot of Solesmes, France
Georges Cabana, Arch. of Sherbrooke, Canada
Xavier Morilleau, Bp. of La Rochelle (former Spiritain novice)
Alfredo Silva Santiago, Rector of the Univ. of Santiago, Chile
Secondino Lacchio, O.F.M., Arch. of Changsha, China
Joseph Corofiro, Arch. of Karachi, Pakistan
R.P. Luciano Rubio, Sup. Gen. of Augustinians
Pierre de La Chanonie, Bp. of Clermont-Ferrand, France
Julien Le Couédic, Bp. of Troyes, France
Luiz Gonzaga da Cunha Marelim, Bp. of Caxias of Maranhão, Brazil
João Pereira Venancio, Bp. of Leiria, Portugal
José Luis Castro, Bp. of San Felipe, Chile
Carlo Saboia Bandeira de Mello, O.F.M., Bp. of Palmas, Brazil
José Nepote Fus, Prelate nullius of Rio Branco, Brazil
Giocondo Grotti, O.S.M., Prelate nullius d'Acre and Purús, Brazil
Auguste Grimault, C.S.Sp., former Vic. Ap. of Dakar

René Graffin, C.S.Sp., former Arch. of Yaoundé, Cameroun
Alfred Marie, C.S.Sp., Bp. of Cayenne, French Guiana
John Charles McQuaid, C.S.Sp., Arch. of Dublin, Ireland
Richard Ackerman, C.S.Sp., Bp. of Covington, Kentucky, USA
Michael Moloney C.S.Sp., Bp. of Bathurst, Gambia
Laureano Castán Lacoma, Bp. of Sigüenza-Guadalajara, Spain
Jean Rupp, Bp. of Monaco
Dino Staffa (Curia)
Casimiro Morcillo, Bp. of Saragossa, then Arch. of Madrid
José Martínez Vargas, Bp. of Armeria, Colombia
Anibal Muñoz Duque, Arch. of Nueva Pamplona, Colombia
José Pimiento Rodriguez, Bp. of Garzón-Neiva, Colombia
Dom Ildefonse Rea, O.S.B., Abbot of Monte Cassino,Italy
Dom Aelred Sillem, O.S.B., Abbot of Quarr, England
Abilio del Campo, Bp. of Calahorra, Spain
Cesario d'Amato, O.S.B., Abbot of Saint Paul Outside the Walls, Italy
Jorge Carreras, Aux. Bp.. of Buenos Aires then Bp. of San Justo
  (1965), Argentina
Georges Pelletier, Bp. of Trois-Rivières, Canada
João Batista Przyklenk, M.S.F., Bp. of Januaria, Brazil
Manoel da Cunha Cintra, Bp. of Petropolis, Brazil
Enrique Barbosa Chaves, Arch. of Cuiaba, Brazil
Carlo Quintero Arce, Bp. of Ciudad Valles, Mexico
Alfonso Espino y Silva, Arch. of Monterrey, Mexico
Angel Temiño Saiz, Bp. of Orense, Spain
Francisco Rendeiro, O.P., Bp. of Faro, Portugal, then Coadj. of
  Coïmbra (1965)
Manoel dos Santos Rocha, Bp. of Beja, Portugal
Mario Di Lieto, Bp. of Ascoli Satriano, Italy
Felice Leonardo, Bp. of Telese, Italy
Giovanni Leonetti, Arch. of Capua, Italy
Giuseppe Bonfiglioli, Coadj. of Syracuse, Italy
Artemio Prati, Bp. of Carpi, Italy
Arrigo Pintonello, Military Ordinary of Italy
Rudolf Graber, Bp. of Ratisbonne, Germany
Richard Guilly, S.J., Bp. of Georgetown, Br. Guiana
Santos Moro Briz, Bp. d'Avila, Spain
Demetrio Mansilla Reoyo, Aux. Bp. of Burgos, then Bp. of Ciudad
  Rodrigo (1964), Spain
Elias McHonde, Bp. of Mahenge, Tanzania (1964)
Edgard Marantá, O. F. M. Cap., Arch. of Dar-es-Salaam, Tanzania
Charles Lemaire, Sup. Gen. of Foreign Missions of Paris
Antonio Lanucci, Bp. of Pescara, Italy

Vito Roberti, Apost. Delegate to the Congo (1962)
Pacifico M. Luigi Perantoni, O.F.M., Bp. of Gerace-Locri, Italy (also,
    Secretary of the Bishops' Secretariat at the Council)
Giovanni Proni, Bp. of Termoli, Italy
Bertrand Lacaste, Bp. of Oran, Algeria
Henry Pinault, Bp. of Changtu, China (expelled)
Moises Alves de Pinho, C.S.Sp., Arch. of Luanda, Angola
Dino Romoli, O.P., Bp. of Pescia, Italy
Adolfo Tortolo, Arch. of Paraná, Argentina
Emilio Tagle Covarrubias, Aux. Bp. of Santiago, then Bp. of Valparaiso, Chile

III

ERECTION OF THE PRIESTLY SOCIETY OF SAINT PIUS X (NOVEMBER 1, 1970)

Chancery of Lausanne,
Geneva, and Fribourg
                    Decree of Erection of the
            "International Priestly Society of Saint Pius X"[1]

Given the encouragements expressed by Vatican Council II, in the decree *Optatam totius,* concerning international seminaries and the distribution of the clergy;

Given the urgent necessity for the formation of zealous and generous priests conforming to the directives of the cited decree;

Confirming that the Statutes of the Priestly Society correspond to its goals:

We, François Charrière, Bishop of Lausanne, Geneva, and Fribourg, the Holy Name of God invoked and all canonical prescriptions observed, decree what follows:

1. The "International Priestly Society of St. Pius X" is erected in
    our diocese as a "*Pia Unio*" (Pious Union).

---

[1] Translation taken from: Michael Davies, *Apologia pro Marcel Lefebvre* (Angelus Press, 1979), I, 443-4.

2. The seat of the Society is fixed as the Maison Saint Pie X (St. Pius X House), 50, rue de la Vignettaz, in our episcopal city of Fribourg.

3. We approve and confirm the Statutes, here joined, of the Society for a period of six years *ad experimentum,* which will be able to be renewed for a similar period by tacit approval; after which, the Society can be erected definitely in our diocese by the competent Roman Congregation.

We implore divine blessings on this Priestly Society, that it may attain its principal goal which is the formation of holy priests.

Done at Fribourg, in our palace.
1st November 1970, on the Feast of All Saints,

†François Charrière
Bishop of Lausanne, Geneva, and Fribourg

IV

LETTER OF ENCOURAGEMENT FROM CARDINAL WRIGHT (FEBRUARY 18 1971)

(Translated from the Latin)[2]

Sacred Congregation
for the Clergy

Prot. n. 133515/1

Rome, 18 February 1971

With great joy I received your letter, in which your Excellency informs me of your news and especially of the Statutes of the Priestly Society.

As Your Excellency explains, this Association, which by your action, received on 1 November 1970, the approbation of His Excellency François Charrière, Bishop of Fribourg, has already exceeded the frontiers of Switzerland, and several Ordinaries in different parts of the world praise and

---

[2] Translation taken from Davies, *ibid.*, 445.

approve it. All of this and especially the wisdom of the norms which direct and govern this Association give much reason to hope for its success.

As for this Sacred Congregation, the Priestly Society will certainly be able to conform to the end proposed by the Council, for the distribution of the clergy in the world.

I am respectfully, Your Excellency,

Yours in the Lord,

J. Card. Wright, Prefect.

P. Palazzini
Secretary

To the Most Excellent and Reverend
Lord Marcel Lefebvre
Titular Archbishop of Synnada in Phrygia
Via Casalmonferrato, n. 33
Rome

V

THE DECLARATION OF NOVEMBER 21, 1974

We adhere with our whole heart, and with our whole soul to Catholic Rome, the Guardian of the Catholic Faith and of those traditions necessary for the maintenance of that Faith, to eternal Rome, Mistress of Wisdom and Truth.

Because of this adherence we refuse and have always refused to follow the Rome of neo-Modernist and neo-Protestant tendencies, such as were clearly manifested during the Second Vatican Council, and after the Council in all the resulting reforms.

All these reforms have, indeed, contributed and still contribute to the demolition of the Church, to the ruin of the priesthood, to the destruction of the Holy Sacrifice and the Sacraments, to the disappearance of religious life, and to naturalistic and Teilhardian teaching in universities, seminaries, and catechetics, a teaching born of Liberalism and Protestantism many times condemned by the solemn magisterium of the Church. No authority, even the very highest in the hierarchy, can constrain us to abandon or to diminish our Catholic Faith, such as it has been clearly expressed and professed by the Church's magisterium for nineteen centuries.

"But though we, or an angel from heaven, preach a gospel to you besides that which we have preached to you, let him be anathema" (Gal. 1:8). Is this not what the Holy Father is repeating to us today? And if a certain contradiction is apparent in his words and actions, as well as in the acts of various Roman Congregations, then we choose what has always been taught, and we turn a deaf ear to the innovations which are destroying the Church.

The *lex orandi* (law of prayer) cannot be profoundly changed without changing the *lex credendi* (law of belief). The New Mass is in line with the new catechism, the new priesthood, new seminaries, new universities, and the charismatic or Pentecostal church, all of which are in opposition to orthodoxy and to the age-old magisterium.

This reform, since it has issued from Liberalism and from Modernism, is entirely corrupt. It comes from heresy and results in heresy, even if all its acts are not formally heretical. It is thus impossible for any faithful Catholic who is aware of these things to adopt this reform, or to submit to it in any way at all. To ensure our salvation, the only attitude of fidelity to the Church and to Catholic doctrine is a categorical refusal to accept the reform.

It is for this reason that, without any rebellion, bitterness, or resentment, we pursue our work of the formation of priests under the star of the age-old magisterium, in the conviction that we can thus do no greater service to the holy Catholic Church, to the Sovereign Pontiff, and to future generations.

For this reason we hold firmly to all that has been believed and practiced by the Church of all time, in her faith, morals, worship, catechetical instruction, priestly formation and her institutions, and codified in the books which appeared before the Modernist influence of the late Council. Meanwhile, we wait for the true Light of Tradition to dispel the darkness which obscures the sky of Eternal Rome.

By acting thus we are sure, with the grace of God, and the help of the Blessed Virgin Mary, St. Joseph, and St. Pius X, of remaining faithful to the Catholic and Roman Church, to all the successors of St. Peter, and of being *fideles dispensatores mysteriorum Domini nostri Jesu Christi in Spiritu Sancto.*

† Marcel Lefebvre
Rome on the Feast of the Presentation
of the Blessed Virgin Mary[3]

VI

LETTER OF ARCHBISHOP LEFEBVRE TO POPE PAUL VI (17 JULY 1976)

In reply to the letter of Cardinal Baggio, Prefect of the Sacred Congregation of Bishops, received on 10 July 1976 intimating that he manifest to the Holy Father his regret for the ordinations conferred on 29 June. He was given ten days' grace. Paul VI's response was the suspension *a divinis* inflicted on 22 July.

Most Holy Father,
All access permitting me to reach Your Holiness being forbidden me, may God grant that this letter reach you to express to you my feelings of profound veneration, and at the same time to state to you, with an urgent prayer, the object of our most ardent desires, which seem, alas!, to be a subject of dispute between the Holy See and numerous faithful Catholics.

Most Holy Father, deign to manifest your will to see the Kingdom of Our Lord Jesus Christ extended in this world,

by restoring the Public Law of the Church,

by giving the liturgy all its dogmatic value and its hierarchical expression according to the Latin Roman rite consecrated by so many centuries of use,

by restoring the Vulgate to honor,

by giving back to catechisms their true model, that of the Council of Trent.

By taking these steps Your Holiness will restore the Catholic priesthood and the Reign of Our Lord Jesus Christ over persons, families, and civil societies.

You will give back their correct concept to falsified ideas which have become the idols of modern man: liberty, equality, fraternity and democracy—like your Predecessors.

Let Your Holiness abandon that ill-omened undertaking of compromise with the ideas of modern man, an undertaking which originates in a secret understanding between high dignitaries in the Church and those of Masonic lodges, since before the Council.

---

[3]   English version taken from: Rev. Fr. François Laisney, *Archbishop Lefebvre and the Vatican*, 2nd ed. (Kansas City: Angelus Press, 1999), 8.

To persevere in that direction is to pursue the destruction of the Church. Your Holiness will easily understand that we cannot collaborate in so calamitous a purpose, which we should do were we to close our seminaries.

May the Holy Ghost deign to give Your Holiness the grace of the gift of fortitude, so that you may show in unequivocal acts that you are truly and authentically the Successor of Peter, proclaiming that there is no salvation except in Jesus Christ and in His Mystical Spouse, the Holy Church, Catholic and Roman.

† Marcel Lefebvre
Former Archbishop-Bishop of Tulle[4]

VII

LETTER TO EIGHT CARDINALS ABOUT THE ASSISI EVENT (AUGUST 27, 1986)

Your Eminence,

Confronted with events taking place in the Church that have John Paul II as their author and faced with those he intends carrying out at Taizé and Assisi in October, I cannot refrain from addressing you and begging you in the name of numerous priests and faithful to save the honor of the Church never before humiliated to such an extent in the course of her history.

The speeches and actions of John Paul II in Togo, Morocco, and the Indies cause a righteous indignation to rise up in our heart. What do the Saints and the holy men and women of the Old and New Testaments make of this? What would the Holy Inquisition do if it were still in existence?

He who now sits upon the Throne of Peter mocks publicly the first article of the Creed and the first Commandment of the Decalogue. The scandal given to Catholic souls cannot be measured. The Church is shaken to its very foundations. If faith in the Church, the only ark of salvation, disappears, then the Church itself disappears.

---

[4] Translation of the letter taken from Davies, *Apologia pro Marcel Lefebvre*, I, 234-5.

Is John Paul II to continue ruining the Church, in particular at Assisi, with the planned procession of religions in the streets of the town of St. Francis and the sharing out of religions in the chapels of the basilica with a view to practicing their worship in favor of peace as conceived by the United Nations? It is what Cardinal Etchegaray, in charge of this abominable congress, has announced.

Is it conceivable that no authoritative voice has been raised in the Church to condemn these public sins? Where are the Machabees?

Eminence, for the honor of the one true God and of Our Lord Jesus Christ, make a public protest, come to the help of the still faithful bishops, priests, and Catholics.

Eminence, if I took the step of contacting you it is because I do not doubt your sentiments in this matter.

I am also addressing this appeal to those Cardinals named below so that eventually you may be able to work together.

May the Holy Ghost come to your aid, and please accept, Eminence, my devoted and fraternal greetings in Christ and Mary.

†Marcel Lefebvre
Emeritus Archbishop-Bishop of Tulle[5]

His Eminence Cardinal Giuseppe Siri, Archbishop of Genoa
His Eminence Cardinal Paul Zoungrana, Archbishop of Ouagadougou
His Eminence Cardinal Silvio Oddi, in residence at Rome
His Eminence Cardinal Marcelo Martin Gonzalez, Archbishop of Toledo
His Eminence Cardinal Pietro Palazzini, in residence at Rome
His Eminence Cardinal Hyacinthe Thiandoum, Archbishop of Dakar
His Eminence Cardinal Alfons Stickler, Librarian S.R.E. at Rome
His Eminence Cardinal Edouard Gagnon, in residence at Rome

---

[5] Translation taken from *The Angelus*, February 2002.

VIII

LETTER TO THE FUTURE BISHOPS (AUGUST 29, 1987)

On the Feast of St. Augustine,
August 29, 1987
Adveniat Regnum Tuum

My dear friends,

The See of Peter and the posts of authority in Rome being occupied by anti-Christs, the destruction of the Kingdom of Our Lord is being rapidly carried out even within His Mystical Body here below, especially through the corruption of the Holy Mass which is both the splendid expression of the triumph of Our Lord on the Cross—*Regnavit a Ligno Deus*—and the source of the extension of His kingdom over souls and over societies. Hence the absolute need appears obvious of ensuring the permanency and continuation of the adorable Sacrifice of Our Lord in order that "His Kingdom come." The corruption of the Holy Mass has brought the corruption of the priesthood and the universal decadence of Faith in the divinity of Our Lord Jesus Christ.

God raised up the Priestly Society of Saint Pius X for the maintenance and perpetuity of His glorious and expiatory Sacrifice within the Church. He chose Himself some true priests instructed in and convinced of these divine mysteries. God bestowed upon me the grace to prepare these Levites and to confer upon them the grace of the priesthood for the continuation of the true Sacrifice according to the definition of the Council of Trent.

This is what has brought down upon our heads persecution by the Rome of the anti-Christs. Since this Rome, Modernist and Liberal, is carrying on its work of destruction of the Kingdom of Our Lord, as Assisi and the confirmation of the Liberal theses of Vatican II on Religious Liberty prove, I find myself constrained by Divine Providence to pass on the grace of the Catholic episcopacy which I received, in order that the Church and the Catholic priesthood continue to subsist for the glory of God and for the salvation of souls.

That is why, convinced that I am only carrying out the holy will of Our Lord, I am writing this letter to ask you to agree to receive the grace of the Catholic episcopacy, just as I have already conferred it on other priests in other circumstances. I will bestow this grace upon you, confident that without too long a delay the See of Peter will be occupied by a successor of Peter who is perfectly Catholic, and into whose hands you will be able to put back the grace of your episcopacy so that he may confirm it.

The main purpose of my passing on the episcopacy is that the grace of priestly orders be continued, for the true Sacrifice of the Mass to be continued, and that the grace of the Sacrament of Confirmation be bestowed upon children and upon the faithful who will ask you for it.

I beseech you to remain attached to the See of Peter, to the Roman Church, Mother and Mistress of all Churches, in the integral Catholic Faith, expressed in the various creeds of our Catholic Faith, in the Catechism of the Council of Trent, in conformity with what you were taught in your seminary. Remain faithful in the handing down of this Faith so that the Kingdom of Our Lord may come.

Finally, I beseech you to remain attached to the Priestly Society of Saint Pius X, to remain profoundly united amongst yourselves, in submission to the Society's Superior General, in the Catholic Faith of all time, remembering the words of St. Paul to the Galatians (1: 8-9): "But even if we or an angel from heaven were to teach you a different gospel from the one we have taught you, let him be anathema. As we have said before, now again I say: if anyone teaches you a different gospel from what you have received, let him be anathema." My dear friends, be my consolation in Christ Jesus; remain strong in the Faith, faithful to the true Sacrifice of the Mass, to the true and holy priesthood of Our Lord for the triumph and glory of Jesus in heaven and upon earth, for the salvation of souls, for the salvation of my own soul.

In the hearts of Jesus and Mary I embrace you and bless you.

Your father in Christ Jesus,
†Marcel Lefebvre[6]

---

[6]   Translation taken from *The Angelus*, July 1988, 38.

IX

LETTER OF ARCHBISHOP LEFEBVRE TO POPE JOHN PAUL II (FEBRUARY 20, 1988)

Most Holy Father,

His Eminence Cardinal Gagnon has just sent me a letter in which he informs me of an audience he had with you, after he gave you the report of his visit.

In this regard, permit me to express the profound satisfaction this Visit caused for everybody who was the object of it, and to inform you of our profound gratitude.

It would be regrettable if the hopes raised by this Visit turned into disappointment, observing the continual delays in the application of even a temporary solution.

May I permit myself to propose some suggestions on the subject of this solution:

In the first place, to take up again the doctrinal problems right away seems to be excluded, since this would be returning to the point of departure, and would renew the difficulties which have endured for fifteen years. The idea of a Commission intervening after the juridical arrangement appears the most suitable one if we really want to find a practical solution.

Since the Priestly Society of Saint Pius X had been recognized for five years by the diocese of Fribourg and by the Sacred Congregation for the Clergy from 1970 to 1975, there should be no difficulty in recognizing it once again; it would then be recognized as being "of pontifical right."

Three particular points seem necessary for a happy solution:

1. To establish at Rome an Office, a Commission—the term is not very important—which would have the same role *vis-à-vis* all the initiatives of Tradition, as the Congregation for the Missions has. This commission would be headed by a Cardinal, if at all possible Cardinal Gagnon, aided by a secretary general and one or two collaborators, all chosen from Tradition. This office would be charged with regulating all the canonical problems of Tradition, and would conduct relations with the Holy See, the dicasteries,[7] and the bishops.

---

[7] A *dicastery* is an organ of the Roman Curia, such as the Congregation for the Doctrine of the Faith.

The bishops exercising their ministry within Tradition would depend on this organism for their ministry.

It does not seem that the erection of this Roman organism would offer difficulties.

2. The consecration of bishops succeeding me in my apostolate appears indispensable and urgent.

For the first designation, and while waiting for the Roman office to assume its functions, it seems to me that you can entrust it to me, as is done with the Eastern patriarchs.

If this is agreed to in principle, I will present the names to Cardinal Gagnon.

This second point is the most urgent one to be resolved, given my age and my fatigue. It is now two years that I have not done any ordinations at the seminary in the United States. The seminarians ardently aspire to be ordained, but I no longer have the health to be crossing oceans.

This is why I entreat Your Holiness to resolve this point before June 30 of this year.

These bishops would be in the same situation *vis-à-vis* Rome and *vis-à-vis* their Society that the missionary bishops were *vis-à-vis* the Congregation for the Propagation of the Faith and their own Society. Instead of a territorial jurisdiction, they would have a jurisdiction over individuals.

It goes without saying that the bishops would always be chosen from among the priests of Tradition.

3. The exemption *vis-à-vis* the local Ordinaries.

The works and initiatives of Tradition would be exempt from the jurisdiction of the local Ordinaries.

For the resumption of good relations, however, the superiors of traditional works would make a report on the houses existing in the dioceses and communicate it to the local Ordinaries; similarly, before founding a new center, they will submit a report to the Ordinary, but are not required to ask for authorization.

After examining these diverse points, I think that Your Holiness will recognize that the problem of Tradition can find a rapid and satisfactory solution.

We would be happy to renew normal relations with the Holy See, but without changing in any way what we are; for it is in this way that we are assured of remaining children of God and the Roman Church.

Deign to accept, Most Holy Father, the expression of my most respectful and filial devotion in Jesus and Mary.

† Marcel Lefebvre
Ecône
February 20, 1988[8]

X

THE PROTOCOL OF ACCORD
(MAY 5, 1988)

This is the first part of the protocol of accord established during the meeting held at Rome on May 4, 1988, between His Eminence Cardinal Joseph Ratzinger and His Excellency Archbishop Lefebvre, signed May 5 by the Archbishop.

I, Marcel Lefebvre, Archbishop-Bishop Emeritus of Tulle, as well as the members of the Priestly Society of Saint Pius X founded by me:

a) Promise to be always faithful to the Catholic Church and the Roman Pontiff, its Supreme Pastor, Vicar of Christ, Successor of Blessed Peter in his primacy as head of the body of bishops.

b) We declare our acceptance of the doctrine contained in §25 of the dogmatic Constitution *Lumen Gentium* of Vatican Council II on the ecclesiastical magisterium and the adherence which is due to it.

c) Regarding certain points taught by Vatican Council II or concerning later reforms of the liturgy and law, and which do not appear to us easily reconcilable with Tradition, we pledge that we will have a positive attitude of study and communication with the Apostolic See, avoiding all polemics.

d) Moreover, we declare that we recognize the validity of the Sacrifice of the Mass and the Sacraments celebrated with the intention of doing what the Church does, and according to the rites indicated in the typical editions of the Roman Missal and the Rituals of the Sacraments promulgated by Popes Paul VI and John Paul II.

e) Finally, we promise to respect the common discipline of the Church and the ecclesiastical laws, especially those contained in the Code of Canon Law promulgated by Pope John Paul II, without prejudice to the special discipline granted to the Society by particular law.[9]

---

[8] English version taken from Laisney, *Archbishop Lefebvre and the Vatican*, 42.
[9] *Ibid.*, 73-4.

XI

LETTER OF ARCHBISHOP LEFEBVRE TO POPE JOHN PAUL II (JUNE 2, 1988)

Most Holy Father,

The conversations and meetings with Cardinal Ratzinger and his collaborators, although they took place in an atmosphere of courtesy and charity, persuaded us that the moment for a frank and efficacious collaboration between us has not yet arrived.

For indeed, if the ordinary Christian is authorized to ask the competent Church authorities to preserve for him the Faith of his Baptism, how much more true is that for priests, religious, and nuns?

It is to keep the Faith of our Baptism intact that we have had to resist the spirit of Vatican II and the reforms inspired by it.

The false ecumenism which is at the origin of all the Council's innovations in the liturgy, in the new relationship between the Church and the world, in the conception of the Church itself, is leading the Church to its ruin and Catholics to apostasy.

Being radically opposed to this destruction of our Faith and determined to remain with the traditional doctrine and discipline of the Church, especially as far as the formation of priests and the religious life is concerned, we find ourselves in the absolute necessity of having ecclesiastical authorities who embrace our concerns and will help us to protect ourselves against the spirit of Vatican II and the spirit of Assisi.

That is why we are asking for several bishops chosen from within Catholic Tradition, and for a majority of the members on the projected Roman Commission for Tradition, in order to protect ourselves against all compromise.

Given the refusal to consider our requests, and it being evident that the purpose of this reconciliation is not at all the same in the eyes of the Holy See as it is in our eyes, we believe it preferable to wait for times more propitious for the return of Rome to Tradition.

That is why we shall give ourselves the means to carry on the work which Providence has entrusted to us, being assured by His Eminence Cardinal Ratzinger's letter of May 30, that the episcopal consecration is not contrary to the will of the Holy See, since it was granted for August 15.

We shall continue to pray for modern Rome, infested with Modernism, to become once more Catholic Rome and to rediscover its 2,000 year-old tradition. Then the problem of our reconciliation will have no further reason to exist and the Church will experience a new youth.

Be so good, Most Holy Father, as to accept the expression of my most respectful and filially devoted sentiments in Jesus and Mary.

† Marcel Lefebvre[10]

XII

LETTER OF POPE JOHN PAUL II TO ARCHBISHOP LEFEBVRE (JUNE 9, 1988)

Excellency,

It is with intense and profound affliction that I have read your letter dated June 2.

Guided solely by concern for the unity of the Church in fidelity to the revealed Truth—an imperative duty imposed on the Successor of the Apostle Peter—I had arranged last year an Apostolic Visitation of the Saint Pius X Society and its work, which was carried out by Edward Cardinal Gagnon. Conversations followed, first with experts of the Congregation for the Doctrine of the Faith, then between yourself and Cardinal Ratzinger. In the course of these meetings solutions had been drawn up, accepted, and signed by you on May 5, 1988. They permitted the Saint Pius X Society to exist and work in the Church in full communion with the Sovereign Pontiff, the guardian of unity in the Truth. For its part, the Apostolic See pursued only one end in these conversations with you: to promote and safeguard this unity in obedience to divine Revelation, translated and interpreted by the Church's magisterium, notably in the twenty-one Ecumenical Councils from Nicæa to Vatican II.

In the letter you sent me you appear to reject all that was agreed on in the previous conversations, since you clearly manifest your intention to "provide the means yourself to continue your work," particularly by pro-

---

[10]   *Ibid.*, 108-9.

ceeding shortly and without apostolic mandate to one or several episcopal ordinations, and this in flagrant contradiction not only with the norms of Canon Law, but also with the Protocol signed on May 5 and the directions relevant to this problem contained in the letter which Cardinal Ratzinger wrote to you on my instructions on May 30.

With a paternal heart, but with all the gravity required by the present circumstances, I exhort you, Reverend Brother, not to embark upon a course which, if persisted in, cannot but appear as a schismatical act whose inevitable theological and canonical consequences are known to you. I earnestly invite you to return, in humility, to full obedience to Christ's Vicar.

Not only do I invite you to do so, but I ask it of you through the wounds of Christ our Redeemer, in the name of Christ who, on the eve of His Passion, prayed for His disciples "that they may all be one" (Jn. 17:20).

To this request and to this invitation I unite my daily prayer to Mary, Mother of Christ.

Dear Brother, do not permit that the year dedicated in a very special way to the Mother of God should bring another wound to her Mother's Heart!

Joannes Paulus PP. II
From the Vatican, June 9, 1988[11]

---

[11] *Ibid.*, 110-11.

XIII

THE "MANDATUM" (JUNE 30, 1988)

At the beginning of the rite of consecration the following dialogue takes place between the consecrating bishops and the Archpriest who presents the bishops-elect for consecration:

–Do you have the Apostolic Mandate?
–We have it!
–Let it be read.

We have this Mandate from the Roman Church, always faithful to the Holy Tradition, which She has received from the Holy Apostles. This Holy Tradition is the Deposit of Faith which the Church orders us to faithfully transmit to all men for the salvation of their souls.

Since the Second Vatican Council until this day, the authorities of the Roman Church are animated by the spirit of modernism. They have acted contrary to the Holy Tradition, "they cannot bear sound doctrine, they turned their ears from the Truth and followed fables," as says St. Paul in his second Epistle to Timothy (4:3-5). This is why we reckon of no value all the penalties and all the censures inflicted by these authorities.

As for me, "I am offered up in sacrifice and the moment for my departure is arrived" (II Tim 4:6). I had the call of souls who ask for the Bread of Life, Who is Christ, to be broken for them. "I have pity upon the crowd" (Mk. 8:2). It is for me therefore a grave obligation to transmit the grace of my episcopacy to these dear priests here present, in order that in turn they may confer the grace of the priesthood on other numerous and holy clerics, instructed in the Holy Traditions of the Catholic Church.

It is by this Mandate of the Holy Roman Catholic Church, *semper fidelis* (always faithful), then that we elect to the rank of Bishop in the Holy Roman Church the priests here present as auxiliaries of the Priestly Society of Saint Pius X:

The Reverend Bernard Tissier de Mallerais,
The Reverend Richard Williamson,
The Reverend Alfonso de Galarreta,
The Reverend Bernard Fellay.[12]

---

[12] *Ibid.*, 123.

XIV

LETTER OF ARCHBISHOP LEFEBVRE TO BISHOP DE CASTRO MAYER (DECEMBER 4, 1990)

Very dear Msgr. Antonio de Castro Mayer,

Rumors reach me from Brazil concerning your health which they say is declining! Is the call of God drawing nigh? The mere thought fills me with deep grief. How lonely I shall be without my elder brother in the episcopate, without the model fighter for the honor of Jesus Christ, without my one faithful friend in the appalling wasteland of the Conciliar Church!

On the other hand, there rings in my ears all the chant of the traditional liturgy of the Office of Confessor Pontiffs... Heaven's welcome for the good and faithful servant! if such be the good Lord's will.

Under these circumstances, I am more than ever by your bedside, close to you, and my prayers mount unceasingly towards God for your intentions, entrusting you to Mary and Joseph.

I would like to make use of this opportunity to put in writing, for you and for your dear priests, my opinion—for it is only an opinion—concerning the eventual consecration of a bishop to succeed you in the handing down of the Catholic Faith and in the conferring of the sacraments reserved to bishops.

Why envisage such a successor outside of the usual norms of Canon Law?

Firstly, because priests and faithful have a strict right to have shepherds who profess the Catholic Faith in its entirety, essential for the salvation of their souls, and to have priests who are true Catholic priests.

Secondly, because the Conciliar Church, having now reached everywhere, is spreading errors contrary to the Catholic Faith and, as a result of these errors, it has corrupted the sources of grace which are the Holy Sacrifice of the Mass and the Sacraments. This false Church is in an ever deeper state of rupture with the Catholic Church. Resulting from these principles and facts is the absolute need to continue the Catholic episcopacy in order to continue the Catholic Church.

The case of the Priestly Society of Saint Pius X presents itself differently from the case of the Diocese of Campos. It seems to me that the case of the Diocese of Campos is simpler, more classical, because what we have here is the majority of the diocesan priests and faithful, on the advice of their former bishop, designating his successor and asking Catholic bishops to consecrate him. This is how the succession of bishops came about in the early centuries of the Church, in union with Rome, as we are too in union with Catholic Rome and not Modernist Rome.

That is why, as I see it, the case of Campos should not be tied to the Society of Saint Pius X. Resort would be had to the Society's bishops for an eventual consecration, not in their role as bishops of the Society but as Catholic bishops.

The two cases should be kept clearly separated. This is not without its importance for public opinion and for present-day Rome. The Society must not be involved as such, and it turns over the entire responsibility—altogether legitimate—to the priests and faithful of Campos.

In order for this distinction to be quite clear, it would be altogether preferable for the ceremony to take place at Campos, at least outside the diocese. It is the clergy and the Catholic people of Campos who are taking to themselves a Successor of the Apostles, a Roman Catholic bishop such as they can no longer obtain through Modernist Rome.

That is my opinion. I think it rests upon fundamental principles of Church Law and upon Tradition.

Very dear Monsignor, I submit my thinking to you in all simplicity, but it is you who are the judge and I bow to your judgment. May God vouchsafe to grant you strong enough health to perform this episcopal consecration!

Kindly believe, most dear Monsignor, in my profound and respectful friendship in Jesus and Mary.[13]

† Marcel Lefebvre

---

[13] *Angelus*, August 1991, 4.

XV

A MUSLIM'S CONDOLENCES (MAY 26, 1991)[14]

Mr. Ababacar Sadikhe THIAM
Sicap Amitié I, Villa 3038
Avenue Bourguiba
DAKAR
Senegalese Trade Unionist

To His Excellency
Yacinthe THIANDOUM
Bishop of Dakar
DAKAR

Dear Cardinal and Bishop,

It is a great honor for me most respectfully to offer you, and through you the whole Catholic community of Senegal, my condolences on the death of Arch Bishop Marcel LEFEVRE who has been called to God.

Arch Bishop LEFEVRE was more than a friend. He was a brother and my true spiritual guide, devoid of all materialism, he was a man I worshipped.

I must tell you I went faithfully as a pilgrim to Ecône where he often spoke to me about you during my trips to Switzerland, one of the reasons why I send you a New Year's card every year.

He has gone, His Excellency, the Bishop, the Dakarian, the Senegalese, the greatest builder, the man of God.

I will never again eat with him at Ecône, surrounded by his parishioners of every nationality.

He blessed me and prayed for me before all these people who had come from every corner of the world, and he loved to introduce me as a Senegalese Muslim, which made me proud and happy. A wonderful man with a lively intelligence who only loved God and Jesus.

I beg you to grant me an audience so I might present my condolences to you in person, and I will be at the Requiem Mass that you are planning for the repose of his soul.

---

14 [In the French edition the original punctuation and spelling of this letter written in Senegalese French were conserved. This translation attempts to a give a flavor of the original's idiosyncrasies. Trans.]

I have enclosed a photocopy of a greetings card and a prayer that he sent me every year. May Almighty God welcome him into His Eternal Paradise.

Dear Cardinal and Bishop of Dakar, please accept my request to pray for your people and all men on earth.

My best wishes,

A.S. THIAM.

P.S. My bedside book is *Fideliter – Mgr. Lefebvre, mes quarante ans d'Episcopat* (*Archbishop Lefebvre: My Forty Years as a Bishop*) which he gave to me.

CHRONOLOGICAL OVERVIEW

1905: *November 29*: born in Tourcoing. *November 30*: baptized at Tourcoing.

1910: *December 25*: First Holy Communion, writes to St. Pius X.

1923: *October 25*: enters the French Seminary in Rome then under the direction of Fr. Le Floch.

1926-27: Condemnation of Action Française. Military service at Valenciennes.

1929: *September 21*: ordained priest in Lille by Cardinal Liénart.

1930-31: Curate at Lomme, working class area of Lille.

1931: *September 1*: enters novitiate of the Holy Ghost Fathers at Orly.

1932: *September 8*: religious profession. *November 12*: sails from Bordeaux for Gabon as a missionary.

1935: *September 25*: perpetual vows in religion.

1945: *October 16*: appointed superior of the scholasticate at Mortain in Normandy.

1947: *June 12*: appointed Vicar Apostolic of Dakar.

September 18: consecrated bishop at Tourcoing by Cardinal Liénart.

1948: *September 22*: appointed Apostolic Delegate for French Black Africa and Madagascar, with the rank of archbishop.

1955: *September 14*: made first Archbishop of Dakar.

1958: *June 12*: receives the pallium.

1959: *July 22*: relieved of duties as Apostolic Delegate but remains Archbishop of Dakar.

1960: *November 15*: appointed Assistant to the Pontifical Throne.

1962: *January 23*: reassigned to diocese of Tulle with the title of Archbishop-Bishop.*March 13*: appointed consulter to the Sacred Congregation *de Propaganda Fide.July 26*: elected (recommended) Superior General of the Holy Ghost Fathers.

1962-65: Council Father and resistance leader during the Second Vatican Council.

1968: *October 28*: leaves his post of Superior General during the General

Chapter for the "renovation" of his congregation.

1969: *October 13*: opens "International House of St. Pius X" in Fribourg with encouragement of local bishop.

1970: *October 1*: with permission from bishop of Sion, opens a "year of spirituality" at Ecône in Valais, Switzerland, as a prelude to seminary studies. *November 1*: receives from Bishop Charrière of Fribourg official approval for the Priestly Society of Saint Pius X for six years *ad experimentum.*

1974: *November 11-13*: Apostolic visit of seminary at Ecône.

November 21: Archbishop Lefebvre's "declaration."

1975: *May 6*: Approval for the Priestly Society of Saint Pius X is withdrawn by His Excellency Bishop Pierre Mamie, successor of Bishop Charrière.

1976: *July 1*: *suspens a divinis* by Pope Paul VI. *August 29*: celebrates the "forbidden Mass" at Lille, which makes his fight known to the world.

1978: *August 6*: death of Paul VI. *September 29*: death of John Paul I.

October 16: election of John Paul II. *November 18*: audience with John Paul II.

1983: *November 21*: with Bishop de Castro Mayer sends open letter to the Pope.

1986: *August 27, September 28, December 2*: protests against the "scandal" of the interreligious meeting chaired by John Paul II at Assisi.

1988: *June 30*: consecrates four bishops at Ecône with the pontifical mandate "of the Church of all time."

1991: *March 25*: death in Martigny, Valais, Switzerland.

His Excellency Archbishop Lefebvre graduated as:
- doctor in theology and philosophy from the Gregorian Pontifical University,
- doctor *honoris causa* from the University of Pittsburgh, Pennsylvania.

He received the following awards:
- Officer of the Legion of Honor, France;
- Commander of the Order of Christ, Portugal;
- Grand Officer of the Order of the Nation, Senegal;
- Officer of the Equatorial Star, Gabon.

SOURCES

ARCHIVES

We have consulted Archbishop Lefebvre's archives at Ecône; the archives of the motherhouse of the Priestly Society of Saint Pius X, which contain some of the Archbishop's correspondence; the archives of *Le Courrier de Rome* and *Fortes in Fide* and the Papal Missionary Works (Lyons). Unfortunately, we were not allowed access to the archives of the Holy Ghost Fathers, nor to those of the diocese of Lille, the archdiocese of Dakar, the Apostolic Delegation of Dakar, and the Holy See.

MANUSCRIPTS

We have referred to our own notebooks (Ms. I, II, III) in which we gathered statements from around thirty friends and colleagues of the Archbishop, especially in the Holy Ghost Fathers. The interviews were mostly recorded and then transcribed. To these statements were added correspondence from various relatives and former colleagues of the Archbishop. These were compiled by Fr. Jean Marc Ledermann who deserves our thanks. Finally, the thesis of Fr. Jean Marie Savioz (see bibliography) on the foundation of the seminary with its many letters and transcripts of interviews is a mine of information on the psychology of the Archbishop and his practical know-how.

Family correspondence from 1900 to 1948 is especially valuable but Marcel Lefebvre's letters before 1944 are almost all missing.

DOCUMENTARY AND AURAL SOURCES

As a key primary source, we have used throughout the recordings of spiritual talks given by Archbishop Lefebvre at Ecône as well as his sermons (which were carefully and devotedly transcribed by Mr. and Mrs. André Cagnon). We have also used his retreats preached at Ecône.

Much information was gleaned from transcripts of interviews with various individuals in Gabon and Senegal, and from conversations with Frs. Groche, Aulagnier, and Marziac, and the Archbishop's drivers. We also used an interview the Archbishop gave to André Cagnon published in *Fideliter* No. 59.

The documents compiled and typed by André Cagnon with commentaries from the Archbishop will be useful to all researchers.

PERIODICALS

The *General Bulletin* of the Holy Ghost Fathers, the *Échos de Santa Chiara*, the *Courrier de Rome*, the SSPX's French magazine *Fideliter*, the Letters to Friends and Benefactors, and the SSPX's internal newsletter *Cor Unum* are all essential sources. Some special editions of *Controverses, La Cloche d'Ecône*, and *Lettre aux Anciens d'Ecône* are informative. Finally, the magazine *Itinéraires* contains many official articles and letters of the Archbishop from 1964 to 1987.

Selected Bibliography

Acts of the Magisterium

Acta Apostolicæ Sedis [*A.A.S.*].

Acta Sanctæ Sedis [*A.S.S.*].

Acta et documenta de concilio Vaticano II apparando; Polygl. Vat. [*A. Doc.*]

Acta Synodalia Concilii Vat. II [*A. Syn.*]

Acts of Popes Léon XIII, Pie X, Pie XI. Éd. de la Bonne Presse.

Les enseignements pontificaux, ed. by the Monks of Solesmes. Desclée. Particular volumes:
— *La Paix intérieure des nations* [*PIN*]. 1962.
— *L'Eglise* (The Church).
— *Le Laïcat* (The Laity).

Documents pontificaux de S.S. Pie XII. St.-Maurice, Switzerland: Éd. S. Augustin. 20 vol. (1961) and 1 of tables (1984).

Works by Archbishop Lefebvre

En cette crise de l'Eglise, gardons la foi, conf. at Brest, Jan. 17, 1973. Martigny, Switzerland: Éd. S. Gabriel, 1973.

Un évêque parle, conférences et allocutions. DMM, 1974; expanded in 1975 and 1976. [English version: *A Bishop Speaks: Writings and Addresses, 1963-1975*. Tr. V.S.M. Fraser. Scottish Una Voce, n.d.]

La messe de Luther. Éd. S. Gabriel, 1975. (Two talks from 1975.)

Homélies "été chaud 1976". Lille, Geneva, Besançon, Ecône: Éd. S. Gabriel, 1976.

J'accuse le concile. Martigny: Éd. S. Gabriel, 1976. (Interventions of Msgr. Lefebvre at the Council.) [English version. *I Accuse the Council*. Angelus Press, 1982.]

Le coup de maître de Satan: Ecône face à la persécution. Martigny: Éd. S. Gabriel, Martigny, 1977. (Notes and conferences, 1974-1977).

Lettre ouverte aux catholiques perplexes (in collab. with Marc Dem). Albin Michel, 1985. [English version: *Open Letter to Confused Catholics*. Tr. Rev. Michael Crowdy. Angelus Press, 1986.]

Ils L'ont découronné (in collab.). Fideliter, 1987. (Conferences on liberalism.) [English verson: *They Have Uncrowned Him*. Angelus Press, 1988.]

Mes doutes sur la liberté religieuse (in collab.), foreword by Archbishop Lefebvre. 1987; re-ed. Clovis, 2000. [Known familiarly as "The Dubia"; English version: *Religious Liberty Questioned*. Tr. Rev. Jaime Pazat de Lys. Angelus Press, 2002.]

Lettres pastorales et écrits. Fideliter, 1989. (Bishop at Dakar, Superior General, 1948-1968.) [English version (incomplete, includes letters for 1948-1961): *Pastoral Letters*. Angelus Press, 1992.]

Cor Unum, Lettres et avis aux membres de la FSSPX, 1970-1989. Ecône, 1989.

Itinéraire spirituel, à la suite de saint Thomas d'Aquin dans sa Somme théologique. Ecône, 1990; re-ed. Bulle: Tradiffusion, 1991. [English version: *Spiritual Journey.* Angelus Press, 1991.]

Petite histoire de ma longue histoire (The Autobiography of Archbishop Lefebvre told to the Society Sisters). *Courrier de Rome,* 1999. [English version: *The Little Story of My Long Life.* Browerville, Minnesota: Sisters of the Society of Saint Pius X, 2002.]

Damit die Kirche fortbestehe, S.E. Erzbischof Marcel Lefebvre, der Verteidiger des Glaubens, der Kirche und des Papsttums. Stuttgart: Society of Saint Pius X, 1992. (Compilation of writings and allocutions of Msgr. Lefebvre, 1966-1991, with explanatory notes, by Dr. Ferdinand Steinhart.)

S.E. Erzbischof Marcel Lefebvre, Missionar und Zeuge in der nachkonziliaren Christenheit. Stuttgart: Society of Saint Pius X, 1994. (Compilation of conferences and circular letters, 1974-1994.)

C'est moi l'accusé qui devrais vous juger. Etampes, France: Fideliter, 1994. (Course on the Acts of the Magisterium.) [English version: *Against the Heresies.* Angelus Press, 1997.]

Le mystère de Jésus. Etampes: Clovis, 1995. (Spiritual conferences on the person of our Lord Jesus Christ.) [English version: *The Mystery of Jesus.* Angelus Press, 2000.]

Notre croisade. Lyons, France: Éd. du Lion, 1997. (Homilies given at Lille, 1976, and for the jubilee, 1979.)

Sermons historiques, Les classiques retrouvés. Éd. Servir, 2001.

WORKS ABOUT ARCHBISHOP LEFEBVRE

Gaucher, Roland. *Monseigneur Lefebvre, combat pour l'Eglise.* Albatros, 1976.

Hanu, José. *Non, Entretiens de José Hanu avec Mgr. Lefebvre.* Stock, 1977. [English version: *Vatican Encounter: Conversations with Archbishop Marcel Lefebvre.* Kansas City, Mo.: Sheed Andrews and McNeel, 1978.]

Marziac, Rev. Jean-Jacques. *Monseigneur Lefebvre, soleil levant ou couchant?.* Paris: NEL, 1979.

Marziac, Rev. Jean-Jacques. *Des évêques français contre Mgr. Lefebvre.* Fideliter, 1989.

Muzzio, Nelly C. *Por razón de fe, Vida de Monseñor Marcel Lefebvre,* 2nd ed. Buenos Aires, 2000.

THE FIGHT FOR THE FAITH, 19TH- 20TH CENTURIES

Amerio, Romano. *Iota Unum, Étude des variations de l'Eglise catholique au XXème siècle.* Paris: NEL, 1987.

Berto, Abbé Victor-Alain. *Notre-Dame de Joie.* Paris: NEL, 1974.

Calmel, R.-T., O.P. *Brève apologie pour l'Eglise de toujours.* Maule: Éd. Difralivre, 1987.

Castro Mayer, Antonio de, Bishop of Campos. *Por um Cristianismo antêntico* São Paulo: Éd. Vera Cruz, 1971. (Pastoral letters and writings).

Coache, Abbé Louis, *Les batailles du Combat de la Foi.* Chiré, 1993.

Marteaux, Jacques. *L'Eglise de France devant la révolution marxiste,* 2 vol.: *Les catholiques dans l'inquiétude, 1936-1944; Les catholiques dans la tourmente, 1944-1958.* LTR, 1958 and 1959.

Vatré, Eric, *La droite du Père, enquête sur la tradition catholique aujourd'hui* (in collab.), Guy Trédaniel. Éd. de la Maisnie, 1994.

White, Dr. David Allen. *The Mouth of the Lion: Bishop de Castro Mayer, the Diocese of Campos, Brazil.* Kansas City, Mo.: Angelus Press, 1993.

FAMILY, VOCATION, SEMINARIAN, VICAR

Berto, Abbé V.-A. *Notre-Dame de Joie, correspondance de l'abbé V.-A. Berto, prêtre 1900-1968.* Paris: NEL, 1974.

Delsalle, Paul. *Lille, Roubaix Tourcoing, histoire et traditions.* Éd. Charles Corlet, 1991.

Hache, Victor. *Généalogies des familles de Roubaix-Tourcoing et environs.* Roubaix, 1950.

Le Crom, Rev. Louis, *et alii. Un père et une mère, brève biographie de M. et Mme Lefebvre, parents de S. Exc. Mgr. Marcel Lefebvre.* Bulle, Switzerland: Controverses, 1993.

Le Floch, Rev. Henri. *Les événements du Séminaire français de mars à juillet 1927.* Typescript.

Le Floch, Rev. Henri, *Cinquante ans de sacerdoce.* Aix-en-Provence: imp. E. Fourcine, 1937.

Michel, Joseph. *Claude-François Poullart des Places.* Paris: Éd. S. Paul, 1962.

Michel, Joseph. *L'influence de l'AA (association secrète de piété) sur Cl.-F. Poullart des Places.* Beauchesne, 1992.

Minier, Marc. *L'épiscopat français du ralliement à Vatican II.* Padua: Éd. Dott. Ant. Milan, 1982.

Pierrard, Pierre, ed. *Histoire des diocèses de Cambrai et de Lille.* Beauchesne, 1978.

Pouchain, Pierre. *Les maîtres du Nord du XIXᵉ siècle à nos jours.* Perrin, 1998.

Prévost, Philippe. *La "condamnation" de l'Action française vue à travers les archives du ministère des Affaires étrangères.* Paris: La Librairie Canadienne, 1996.

Prévost, Abbé Robert. *Dieu n'échoue pas, 1895-1980,* 3 vol. Téqui, 1983. Vol. I: *Un témoin se lève* (autobiography).

Prévotat, Jacques. *Les catholiques et l'Action française, histoire d'une condamnation,* 1899-1939. Fayard, 2001.

Valynseele, Joseph and Denis Grando. *A la recherche de leurs racines, Généalogies de 85 célébrités.* First series, *L'intermédiaire des chercheurs et des curieux.* Paris, 1988.

SPIRITAN AND AFRICAN: GABON, DAKAR

Le cardinal Liénart et la mission universelle (in collab.). Lille: MSR, Vol. 54, 1997, no. 3.

Biarnès, Pierre. *Les Français en Afrique Noire de Richelieu à Mitterrand.* Armand Colin, 1987.

Bouchaud, P. Joseph. *Mgr. Pierre Bonneau, év. de Douala.* Yaoundé: Éd. de l'Effort Camerounais, 1959.

Chort-Rouergue, Gabrielle. *Mémoires d'Outre-Mer.* N. p.: Éd. Alma, n.d.

Criaud, Jean. *La geste des spiritains, histoire de l'Eglise au Cameroun, 1916-1990.* Mvolyé-Yaoundé: Publications du Centenaire, 1990.

Dedet, Christian. *La mémoire du fleuve, l'Afrique aventureuse de Jean Michonnet.* Paris: Éd. Phébus, 1984.

Delcourt, P. Jean. *Histoire religieuse du Sénégal.* Dakar: Éd. Clairafrique, 1976.

Dugon, Robert. "Dakar et ses premiers missionnaires." *L'Église catholique en Afrique, AOF Magazine,* no. 15, August, 1956.

Gravrand, Henri. *Visage africain de l'Église.* Coll. Lumière des nations. Paris: Orante, 1961. (The mission in Senegal.)

Koren, H., C.S.Sp. *Les Spiritains, trois siècles d'histoire religieuse et missionnaire.* Paris: Beauchesne, 1982.

Lenoble-Bart, Annie. *Afrique Nouvelle, un hebdomadaire cath. dans l'histoire, 1947-1987.* Toulouse: Éd. de la Maison des Sciences de l'Homme d'Aquitaine, 1996.

Liagre, Louis, C.S.Sp. *Retraite avec sainte Thérèse de l'Enfant Jésus.* Éd. Office Central Lisieux, 1991.

Messmer, Pierre. *Après tant de batailles.* Albin Michel, 1992.

Nyonda, Vincent de Paul. *Autobiographie d'un Gabonais, du villageois au ministre.* L'Harmattan, 1994.

Pannier, Guy. *L'Église de Pointe Noire.* Coll. Mémoire d'Église. Paris: Karthala, 1999.

Sorel, Jacqueline. *Léopold Sédar Senghor, la raison et l'émotion.* Éd. Sépia, 1995.

Vieira, Gérard, *Sous le signe du laïcat, l'Église catholique de Guinée.* Vol. II: *Le temps des prémices, 1925-1958.* N.p., n.d. (after 1992).

MORTAIN, TULLE, SUPERIOR GENERAL

Agulhon, Maurice, André Nouschi, and Ralph Schor. *La France de 1940 à nos jours.* Fac. histoire, Nathan, 1995.

Buisson, Gilles. *Mortain 44: objectif Avranches.* Coutances: Éd. OCEP, 1997.

Buttet, André. *Le bâton et le rocher.* Sion: Valprint, 1977. (Collection of parishioners' comments.)

Dickès, Jean-Pierre. *La blessure.* Etampes: Clovis, 1998. (The revolution in a seminary at the time of the Council.)

Madiran, Jean. *La Cité catholique aujourd'hui.* From *Itinéraires,* nos. 61, 62, 64, 65. Paris, 1962.

O'Carroll, Michael, C.S.Sp. *A Priest in Changing Times.* Dublin: The Columba Press, 1998.

Saint-Marc, Hélie de. *Mémoires, Les champs de braises.* Perrin, 1995.

Vinatier, Jean. *Histoire religieuse du Bas-Limousin et du diocèse de Tulle.* Lucien Souny, 1991.

VATICAN COUNCIL II

Eglise et contre-Eglise au Concile Vatican II. Acts of the Second Theological Congress of *Sì, Sì, No No,* Jan. 1996. Publications du *Courrier de Rome,* 1996. Anthology, articles by:

— Lovey, Abbé Philippe. "Les schémas préparatoires."

— Simoulin, Abbé Michel. "Les vota des évêques en réponse à la consultation préparatoire au concile."

— Fellay, Bishop Bernard. "Les interventions de Mgr. Lefebvre au concile."

Alberigo, Giuseppe. *Jean XXIII devant l'histoire.* Seuil, 1989.

Caprile, Giovanni, S.J. *Il concilio Vaticano II, Cronache del concilio Vaticano II.* Rome: Civilta Cattolica, vol. V, 1968.

Davies, Michael. *Pope John's Council. Liturgical Revolution* Vol. II. Chawleigh, Devon: Augustin Publishing Company, 1977.

Davies, Michael. *The Second Vatican Council and Religious Liberty.* Long Prairie, Minn.: The Neumann Press, 1992.

Dulac, Raymond. *La collégialité épiscopale au deuxième concile du Vatican.* Paris: Cèdre, 1979.

Fouilloux, Etienne. *Vatican II commence.* Louvain: Catholic Univ. of Louvain, 1993.

Guitton, Jean, *Paul VI secret.* Paris: Desclée de Brouwer, 1979.

Routhier, G. "Le cardinal Léger et la préparation de Vatican II." *Revue d'Histoire de l'Église de France,* no. 205, 1994.

Schmidt, Stjepan. *Augustin Bea, der Kardinal der Einheit.* Graz: Styria, 1989.

Wenger, Antoine. *Vatican II, chronique de la troisième session.* Paris: Centurion Press, 1965.

Wiltgen, Ralph. *Le Rhin se jette dans le Tibre.* Cèdre, 1975. [English version: *The Rhine Flows into the Tiber.* Devon: Augustine Publishing Co., 1978.]

ARCHBISHOP LEFEBVRE AT THE COUNCIL: THE CŒTUS

Alberigo, Giuseppe, ed. *Histoire du concile Vatican II, La formation de la conscience conciliaire.* Cerf, 1998.

Berto, Abbé V.-A., *Pour la sainte Eglise romaine: textes et documents de V.-A. Berto, prêtre, 1900-1968.* Paris: Cèdre, 1976.

Buonasorte, Nicla, Università cattolica del Sacro Cuore di Milano, Dottorato die Ricerca in Storia Sociale e religiosa, XI ciclo. *Percorsi e prospettive del tradinazionalismo cattolico italiano del Concilio Vaticano II al postconcilio,* an. 1997-1998.

Perrin, Luc. "Le *Cœtus internationalis Patrum* et la minorité à Vatican II." In *Catholica s.v.* "Histoire religieuse contemporaine."

POST COUNCIL

L'œcuménisme, Assise, solution ou dissolution ? (Articles published in *Sì Sì No No* and the *Courrier de Rome,* 1984-1989). Versailles: Publications du *Courrier de Rome,* 1990.

La tentation de l'œcuménisme, actes du IIIe congrès théologique de Sì Sì No No, avril *1998.* Versailles: Publications du *Courrier de Rome,* 1999.

La raison de notre combat, la messe catholique. Etampes: Clovis, 1999. (Doctrinal writings of Card. Ottaviani and Bacci, R.-Th. Calmel, O.P., Msgr. Lefebvre, Didier Bonneterre, Paul Aulagnier, Dom Edouard Guillou, Raymond Dulac.)

FSSPX. *Le problème de la réforme liturgique: La messe de Vatican II et de Paul VI, étude théologique et liturgique.* Etampes: Clovis, 2001.

Bonneterre, Abbé Didier. *Le mouvement liturgique.* Éd. Fideliter, 1980.

Bugnini, Annibale. *La Riforma liturgica.* Rome: CLV, 1997.

Coomaraswamy, Rama P. *Les problèmes de la nouvelle messe.* (Trans. from English.) Lausanne: Éd. Age d'Homme, 1995.

Da Silveira, Arnaldo Xavier. *La nouvelle messe de Paul VI, qu'en penser ?* (Trans. from Portuguese.) Chiré-en-Montreuil: DPF, 1975.

Davies Michael. *Pope Paul's New Mass. The Liturgical Revolution*, Vol. III. Dickinson, Tex.: Angelus Press, 1980.

Dörmann, Johannes. *La théologie de Jean-Paul II et l'esprit d'Assise*. (Trans. from German.) Versailles: Publications du *Courrier de Rome*, 1995. (Commentary of the encyclical *Redemptor Hominis* in light of the ecumenical meeting at Assisi in 1986).

Giampietro, Nicola, O.F.M. Cap. *Il Card. Ferdinando Antonelli e gli sviluppi della riforma liturgica del 1948 al 1970*. Rome: Studia Anselmiana, 1998.

Madiran, Jean. *L'hérésie du XXᵉ siècle*. Paris: NEL, 1968.

Missus Romanus in *Courrier de Rome, La Révolution permanente dans la liturgie*. Paris: Éd. du Cèdre, 1975.

Ottaviani, Card. Alfredo and Card. A. Bacci, *Bref examen critique du nouvel "Ordo missæ."* Foundation "Lumen Gentium." Lichtenstein: Vaduz, n.d. (1970). Reprinted in *La raison de notre combat*.

Salleron, Louis. *La nouvelle messe*. Collection Itinéraires. Paris: NEL, 1970.

ARCHBISHOP LEFEBVRE, THE FSSPX, AND ROME

Ecône portes ouvertes. Martigny: Éd. S. Gabriel, 1976.

La religion, spécial Ecône, no. 6 of Christmas, 1976 *Item, Revue d'opinion libre*. Paris: SPL, 1976. ("Examen": Ecône or the true religion; Opinions: 23 authors talk about Ecône and Tradition.)

La condamnation sauvage de Mgr. Lefebvre. Itinéraires, special issue (the documents, Nov. 1974 to March 1977, annotated by Jean Madiran).

Mgr. Lefebvre et le Saint-Office. Itinéraires, no. 233 (May, 1979). (The official texts, Jan. 1978 to Jan. 1979.)

Fideliter, no. 11, Sept. 1979; no. 59, Sept. 1987; no. 85, Jan. 1992.

Mgr. Marcel Lefebvre et le Vatican sous le pontificat de Jean-Paul III. Itinéraires, special issue, no. 265 bis. . (The documents from March 1979 to Oct. 1981).

La Fraternité Saint-Pie X, une œuvre d'Église, le miracle d'Ecône. Martigny: Éd. S. Gabriel, 1982.

La Tradition excommuniée. Versailles: Publications du *Courrier de Rome*, 1989. (Unpublished articles or published in *Sì Si No No* and *Courrier de Rome* about the episcopal consecrations of 1988).

Anzevui, Abbé Jean. *Le drame d'Ecône, analyse et dossier*. Sion: Valprint, 1976.

Aulagnier, Abbé Paul. *La Tradition sans peur*. Paris: Éd. Servir, 2000.

Cagnon, André. *Les relations de Rome avec Ecône*, typed compilation of documents annotated by Archbishop Lefebvre.

Chalet, Jeanne-Anne. *Monseigneur Lefebvre, dossier complet*. (The "Hot Summer" of 1976). Paris: Pygmalion, 1976.

Chiron, Yves. *Paul VI: Le pape écartelé*. Perrin, 1993.

Davies, Michael. *Apologia pro Marcel Lefebvre*, 3 vol. Kansas City, Mo.: Angelus Press, 1979, 1983, 1988.

Foucart, François. "Mgr. Lefebvre un an après." In *Les dossiers de France-inter: La vérité sur Mgr. Lefebvre*. Paris: Presses de la Cité, 1977. (The seismic shock of the summer of 1976 and its aftermath.)

Guitton, Jean. *Paul VI secret*. Paris: Desclée de Brower, 1979.

Krämer-Badoni, Rudolf. *Revolution in der Kirche, Lefebvre und Rom*. Munich: Herbig, 1980.

Laisney, Rev. François. *Archbishop Lefebvre and the Vatican: Documents and Commentary, 1987-1988*, 2nd. ed. Kansas City, Mo.: Angelus Press, 1999.

Le Roux, Daniel. *Pierre m'aimes-tu? Jean-Paul II: pape de tradition ou pape de la révolution?* Éd. Fideliter, 1988.

Madiran, Jean. *La condamnation sauvage de Mgr. Lefebvre.* Special edition of *Itinéraires*, no. 200 bis, Feb. 1976, enlarged Dec. 1976. (The official texts commented by J. Madiran.)

Marchal, Abbé Denis. *Monseigneur Lefebvre, vingt ans de combat pour le sacerdoce et la foi, 1967-1987.* Paris: NEL, 1988. (Résumé of all the documents of relations between Rome and Écône.)

Montagne, Yves, *L'évêque suspens.* Rome: Catholic Laymen's League, 1977.

Perol, Huguette. *Les Sans-papiers de l'Eglise.* Paris: F.-X. de Guibert, 1996.

Savioz, Abbé Jean-Marie. *Essai historique sur la fondation de la Fraternité sacerdotale Saint-Pie X par Mgr. Marcel Lefebvre et sur l'installation de son séminaire à Écône en Valais, 1969-1972* (master's thesis in theology). University of Fribourg, 1995.

Wagner, Georges-Paul, and Dominique Remy. *La condamnation.* Bordeaux: Ulysse, 1992. (The lawsuit by the LICRA: Statements about Islam.)

INDEX

A reference to a footnote is indicated by "*n*" after the page number.

and *Dubia* of Abp. Lefebvre, 545–547
fight against by *Coetus*, 306–311
origins of, 497–499
promulgation of by Paul VI, 311–313
schemas for Vatican Council II and, 281–286
Rémy, Fr. Charles, 99
Remy, Dominique, 604
republicanism, 145–146
resignation, of Abp. Lefebvre from Holy Ghost Fathers, 368–374
retreats, and goal of Society of Saint Pius X, 436
La Révolution française, à propos du centenaire de 1789 (Freppel), 145–146
Reynaud, Fr. J., 543
Riaud, Alexis, 49–50
La Riforma liturgica (Bugnini), 389
Rivière, Fr. Augustin, 198, 417
Robin, Marthe, 409
Romanity, 43, 63–65, 453
Rome-Moscow Agreement, 303–304
Roncalli, Angelo (later John XXIII), 233
Rossi, Abp. Carlo Raffaele, 65
Roubaix, France, 3–6, 27
Roul, Fr. Alphonse, 39, 45
Royalty of Christ. *See* social reign of Jesus Christ
Roy, Dom Jean (Abbot of Fontgombault), 410, 424, 450
Ruffini, Ernesto, Cardinal, 284
rule
common life and, 429
at Ecône seminary, 427–428
at Fribourg foundation, 413–415
Russia, and consecration of to Mary, 300

Russian Orthodox observers, at Vatican Council II, 303–304

S

Saclier de La Batie, Gérard, 489
Sacred Heart School (Tourcoing, France), 15–16
Sacred Scripture, and schema on Divine Revelation, 305–306
Sacrosanctum Concilium, 329–330, 389
Saint abandon (Lehodey), 87
Saint-Avid, Dom Albert de, 35
Sainte Marie, Fr. Joseph de, 501
Saint Pierre, Michel de, 387
Saint Pius X Association for Priestly Training, 410–420
Salleron, Louis, 502–503
Sanborn, Fr. Donald, 448
Sangnier, Marc, 27
Santa Chiara. *See* French Seminary
Saventhem, Dr. Eric de, 385, 420, 550
schemas, for Vatican Council II, 275–278, 281–286
Schillebeeckx, Fr. Edward, 298
schism, issue of and Abp. Lefebvre, 547
Schmidberger, Fr. Franz, 450, 513, 527, 540, 548–549, 612
Schmidt, Pastor Wilhelm, 323
schools
in Dakar, 163–165
goal of, 207
need for in Lambaréné, 124
and Society of Saint Pius X, 436, 511
in Tulle, 266
Schoonbroodt, Fr. Paul, 518
Schorer, Edgar, 420
Schuster, Dom Ildefonse, 53
Schweitzer, Albert, 125